Enterprise Information Systems for Business Integration in SMEs:

Technological, Organizational, and Social Dimensions

Maria Manuela Cruz-Cunha
Polytechnic Institute of Cavado and Ave, Portugal

A volume in the Advances in Business
Information Systems and Analytics
(ABISA) Book Series

Director of Editorial Content: Kristin Klinger
Senior Managing Editor: Jamie Snavely
Assistant Managing Editor: Michael Brehm
Publishing Assistant: Sean Woznicki
Typesetter: Kurt Smith, Sean Woznicki
Cover Design: Lisa Tosheff

Published in the United States of America by
    Business Science Reference (an imprint of IGI Global)
    701 E. Chocolate Avenue
    Hershey PA 17033
    Tel: 717-533-8845
    Fax: 717-533-8661
    E-mail: cust@igi-global.com
    Web site: http://www.igi-global.com

Library of Congress Cataloging-in-Publication Data

Enterprise information systems for business integration in SMEs : technological, organizational, and social dimensions /
Maria Manuela Cruz-Cunha, editor.
       p. cm.
   Includes bibliographical references and index.
   Summary: "This book is a compilation of contributions on the main issues, challenges, opportunities and developments
related to enterprise information systems from the social, managerial and organizational perspectives, offering current
achievements and practical solutions and applications"--Provided by publisher.

   ISBN 978-1-60566-892-5 (hbk.) -- ISBN 978-1-60566-893-2 (ebook) 1. Management information systems. 2. Information technology--Management. 3. Small business--Management. I. Cruz-Cunha, Maria Manuela, 1964- II. Title.

   HD30.213.E584 2010
   658.4'038011--dc22

                                           2009012051

This book is published in the IGI Global book series Advances in Business Information Systems and Analytics (ABISA)
Book Series (ISSN: 2327-3275; eISSN: 2327-3283)

British Cataloguing in Publication Data
A Cataloguing in Publication record for this book is available from the British Library.

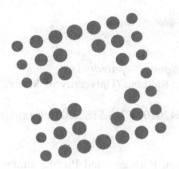

Advances in Business Information Systems and Analytics (ABISA) Book Series

Madjid Tavana
La Salle University, USA

ISSN: 2327-3275
EISSN: 2327-3283

MISSION

The successful development and management of information systems and business analytics is crucial to the success of an organization. New technological developments and methods for data analysis have allowed organizations to not only improve their processes and allow for greater productivity, but have also provided businesses with a venue through which to cut costs, plan for the future, and maintain competitive advantage in the information age.

The **Advances in Business Information Systems and Analytics (ABISA) Book Series** aims to present diverse and timely research in the development, deployment, and management of business information systems and business analytics for continued organizational development and improved business value.

COVERAGE

- Big Data
- Business Decision Making
- Business Information Security
- Business Process Management
- Business Systems Engineering
- Data Analytics
- Data Management
- Decision Support Systems
- Management Information Systems
- Performance Metrics

IGI Global is currently accepting manuscripts for publication within this series. To submit a proposal for a volume in this series, please contact our Acquisition Editors at Acquisitions@igi-global.com or visit: http://www.igi-global.com/publish/.

Titles in this Series

For a list of additional titles in this series, please visit: www.igi-global.com

Managing Enterprise Information Technology Acquisitions Assessing Organizational Preparedness
Harekrishna Misra (Institute of Rural Management Anand, India) and Hakikur Rahman (University of Minho, Portugal)
Business Science Reference • copyright 2013 • 345pp • H/C (ISBN: 9781466642010) • US $185.00 (our price)

Information Systems and Technology for Organizations in a Networked Society
Tomayess Issa (Curtin University, Australia) Pedro Isaías (Universidade Aberta, Portugal) and Piet Kommers (University of Twente, The Netherlands)
Business Science Reference • copyright 2013 • 432pp • H/C (ISBN: 9781466640627) • US $185.00 (our price)

Cases on Enterprise Information Systems and Implementation Stages Learning from the Gulf Region
Fayez Albadri (ADMO-OPCO, UAE)
Information Science Reference • copyright 2013 • 370pp • H/C (ISBN: 9781466622203) • US $185.00 (our price)

Business Intelligence and Agile Methodologies for Knowledge-Based Organizations Cross-Disciplinary Applications
Asim Abdel Rahman El Sheikh (The Arab Academy for Banking and Financial Sciences, Jordan) and Mouhib Alnoukari (Arab International University, Syria)
Business Science Reference • copyright 2012 • 370pp • H/C (ISBN: 9781613500507) • US $185.00 (our price)

Business Intelligence Applications and the Web Models, Systems and Technologies
Marta E. Zorrilla (University of Cantabria, Spain) Jose-Norberto Mazón (University of Alicante, Spain) Óscar Ferrández (University of Alicante, Spain) Irene Garrigós (University of Alicante, Spain) Florian Daniel (University of Trento, Italy) and Juan Trujillo (University of Alicante, Spain)
Business Science Reference • copyright 2012 • 374pp • H/C (ISBN: 9781613500385) • US $185.00 (our price)

Electronic Supply Network Coordination in Intelligent and Dynamic Environments Modeling and Implementation
Iraj Mahdavi (Mazandaran University of Science and Technology, Iran) Shima Mohebbi (University of Tehran, Iran) and Namjae Cho (Hanyang University, Korea)
Business Science Reference • copyright 2011 • 434pp • H/C (ISBN: 9781605668086) • US $180.00 (our price)

Enterprise Information Systems Design, Implementation and Management Organizational Applications
Maria Manuela Cruz-Cunha (Polytechnic Institute of Cavado and Ave, Portugal) and Joao Varajao (University of Tras-os-Montes e Alto Duoro, Portugal)
Information Science Reference • copyright 2011 • 622pp • H/C (ISBN: 9781616920203) • US $180.00 (our price)

www.igi-global.com

701 E. Chocolate Ave., Hershey, PA 17033
Order online at www.igi-global.com or call 717-533-8845 x100
To place a standing order for titles released in this series, contact: cust@igi-global.com
Mon-Fri 8:00 am - 5:00 pm (est) or fax 24 hours a day 717-533-8661

Table of Contents

Section 1
Models, Applications and Solutions

Section 2
Supporting Technologies and Tools

Section 3
Managerial and Organizational Issues

Section 4
Critical Success Factors and Case Studies

Detailed Table of Contents

Section 1
Models, Applications and Solutions

    Maria Argyropoulou, Brunel University, UK
    George Ioannou, Athens University of Economics and Business, Greece
    Dimitrios N. Koufopoulos, Brunel University, UK
    Jaideep Motwani, Grand Valley State University, USA

In the first chapter, "Measuring the Impact of an ERP Project at SMEs: A Framework and Empirical Investigation", Argyropoulou, Ioannou, Koufopoulos and Motwani analyze and test a novel framework for the evaluation of an ERP project. The framework incorporates specific performance measures, which are linked to a previously developed model, (the 'six-imperatives' framework) and are relevant to ERP implementation. Two case studies illustrate the use of the framework in two Greek companies aiming to measure, in practical terms, the impact of the ERP project on their operations. The main results indicate that the 'six-imperatives' provide a comprehensive methodology based on the profound exploration and understanding of specific business processes and objectives that should be met in order to assess an ERP project.

    Efrem G. Mallach, University of Massachusetts Dartmouth, USA

Information system conversion has been with us since users of punch-card tabulating systems first moved to vacuum-tube computers. However, it is often seen as an afterthought: once the "interesting" work of analysis, design and so on is done, it will somehow happen. Efrem Mallach, in the second chapter, "Information System Conversion in SMEs," attempts to view the process holistically, from both the technical and human viewpoints, reflecting the fact that information systems have both technical and human components. It shows how ignoring one side or the other can lead to problems, which can be avoided if all aspects are considered together. It proposes a systematic approach to considering these issues and points out benefits of using it.

Chapter 3

Nowadays, the implementation of business process management modern tools in companies becomes a matter of acceptation of an effective organization management. The first ultimate precondition for achieving this goal is a properly structured company. Vladimír Modrák in "Business Process Management as a Critical Success Factor in EIS Implementation" places the focus on business process reengineering due to preparing preconditions for smooth implementation of EIS. Since there are differences between tools of business processes redesign and information systems development, then a main focus was on overcoming existing semantic gaps. With the aim of solving this problem, the specific modeling method has been used that was clear for company's staff and usable for EIS designers.

Chapter 4

For Cheung and Schaefer in "Product Lifecycle Management: State-of-the-Art and Future Perspectives," while most SMEs in general are willing to invest into Product Lifecycle Management (PLM) systems, many are still apprehensive to the sometimes large initial investment to be made in terms of both software cost and the time needed to implement and integrate such system into their digital enterprise technology infrastructure. In light of this, it is crucial for their decision makers not only to understand the current PLM market, but also to become familiar with emerging trends and future developments in order to select a PLM solution that best fit the needs of their enterprise. In this chapter, the authors summarize a detailed analysis of the PLM market with the aim to provide educators, students, and decision makers in industry with an overview of the current PLM market as a whole. In addition, emerging trends and future developments are addressed.

Chapter 5

In chapter five, "ERP Systems Supporting Lean Manufacturing in SMEs," according to Halgeri, McHaney and Pei, the explosive growth of e-business methodologies and the resulting pressure to become nimble and embrace rapid change forced many SME to rethink their production approaches, particularly in regard to where they stand in relation to these two methodologies (ERP systems and Lean Manufacturing). Over time, ERP vendors recognized the power and advantages of Lean manufacturing and developed ways to incorporate Lean-related features into their software. The main objective of this chapter is to explore how ERP and Lean methodologies can coexist in SMEs. The chapter discusses misconceptions about the fit between ERP and Lean then summarizes differences and synergies between the two methodologies. It also emphasizes how linking ERP and Lean methods can lead to competitive advantage then explores key Lean toolsets available in leading ERP systems used by SMEs. Further focus is provided with additional insight on several leading ERP vendors offering Lean-enabled software modules.

Planning and management of Virtual Organisations (VOs) depends on accurate prognosis and forecasting of several organizational aspects. New and innovative business models such as the VO offer a variety of new options for SME to do business. In the sixth chapter, "A Forecasting Concept for Virtual Organisations Supporting SMEs," Eschenbacher and Duin present a system-oriented view to understand planning and forecasting needs in VOs. The strategic issues in planning will be elaborated by using the cross-impact analysis. For the medium-term planning the focus lies on investigations based on the so-called collaborative network analysis. An industrial case study is introduced to demonstrate the application of the concept.

In the seventh chapter, "Business Integration Model in Services Sector SMEs," Pantelic shows the importance of integration business processes and information systems for service sector SMEs and presents an opportunity of synchronous and simultaneous development of both business process integration (BPI) and enterprise information system (EIS) utilizing the introduced Business Integration Model (BIM). BIM approach is based on modeling core business processes, which are supported by modern IS. Process centric and customer centric modern organization relies on enterprise management standards like ISO 9000 family. The task is to achieve the business goal of the process measured by defined Key Performance Indicator (KPI) and to improve the processes continually. The presented "Autotransport" case describes BIM design and implementation for the core process "Transport services management." The critical factor of the success of implementation of Business Integration Model (BIM) is undoubtedly the readiness of employees to accept a process approach in the execution of their tasks.

Multi-project business operations in SMEs require adaptation of management processes and, consequently, revision of information systems. Present ERP solutions are not suitable in a multi-project environment. Chapter eight, "Conducting Multi-Project Business Operations in SMEs and IS Support" by Vrečko, Hauc, Čančer and Perko presents a newly designed IS model that supports strategic and commercial multiple project operations. The importance of connecting business goals with project performance and upgrading operational CRM into multi-partner management technology is considered. Significant added functions of IS in a multi-project environment should support project evaluation and management of project portfolios, intra- and inter-project communication, and mastering multi-task workflow. To reduce the need to spend limited SMEs' resources, technological development of the designed IS model must assure its simplicity for use and deployment.

Chapter 9

Fahd Alizai, Victoria University, Australia
Stephen Burgess, Victoria University, Australia

In chapter nine, "An ERP Adoption Model for Midsize Businesses," Alizai and Burgess theorize the development of a conceptual ERP adoption model, applicable to midsize businesses, identifying the general business factors associated with ERP implementation along with the corresponding organisational benefits. This chapter also highlights the constraints that confront midsize businesses whilst implementing sophisticated applications. The needs for ERP adoption can occur due to an attempt to be more competitive or due to an external pressure from large businesses to adopt an ERP application. The proposed conceptual model uses a strategic approach containing; ERP implementation processes, stages, factors & issues associated with ERP adoption in midsize businesses. This research also focuses on identification of strategies in the organisational, social and technical domains that could be influential for ERP adoption.

Chapter 10

Enterprise Information Systems for Business Integration in Global International
P. H. Osanna, Vienna University of Technology, Austria
N. M. Durakbasa, Vienna University of Technology, Austria
M. E. Yurci, YILDIZ Technical University, Turkey
J. M. Bauer, National University of Lomas Zamora, Argentina

The importance of SMEs today is far beyond any discussion in countries all over the world - in European countries as well as in Asia and in USA, in Africa as well as in Latin America. In chapter 10, "Enterprise Information Systems for Business Integration in Global International Cooperations of Collaborating Small and Medium Sized Organisations" and according to its authors, Osanna, Durakbasa, Yurci and Bauer, to meet market demands in present and future global industrial world, manufacturing enterprises of any kind and any size must be flexible and agile enough to respond quickly to product demand changes. With the support of artificial intelligence and modern information technology, it is possible to realise modern cost-effective customer-driven design and manufacturing taking into account the importance and basic role of quality management and metrology. This will be especially possible on the basis of the innovative concept and model for modern enterprises the so-called "Multi-Functions Integrated Factory - MFIF" that makes possible an agile and optimal industrial production in any kind of industry and especially in up-to-date SMEs.

Section 2
Supporting Technologies and Tools

SME have specific requirements on the software systems (SWS) they use, described by Král and Žemlička in "Software for Small-to-Medium Enterprises." The solution to this issue or overtaking of its consequences can be based on the variant of service-oriented architecture (SOA) discussed in the chapter. A proper use of modern software systems depends on the skills and knowledge of (end) users of the systems. The extent of a new software-oriented knowledge of the users needed to specify, install, and use the systems depends on the architecture of the system. Authors further show that a properly used SOA can substantially reduce the need to learn new knowledge at users' side. The kernel of the solution should be based on the SOA-based generalization of the concept of usability and on a technical turn enabling agility of business processes. The solution can simplify the development of tools enabling the activation of inhibited user knowledge via flexible prototyping supporting agile business processes and learning by doing.

Justifying that more than 99% of European enterprises are SMEs, Balzert, Burkhart, Werth et al in "State of the Art Solutions in Enterprise Interoperability" state that although collaboration with other enterprises provides potential for improving business performance, enterprise interoperability research has yet to produce results which can be used by SMEs without the need for high start-up costs, e.g. learning, infrastructure and installation costs. The chapter introduces the Commius project (funded by the European Union) that aims the development of such a "zero costs of entry" interoperability solution for SMEs, allowing them to reuse existing and familiar applications for electronic communication. Based on a four layer interoperability framework, it will be examined which technical, process-based and semantic solutions for enterprise interoperability are available at the moment and which strategic motives drive or prevail SMEs to engage in E-business activities.

Chapter 13

 Mirjana D. Stojanovic, University of Belgrade, Serbia
 Vladanka S. Acimovic-Raspopovic, University of Belgrade, Serbia

Chapter 13, "Communication Issues for Small and Medium Enterprises: Provider and Customer Perspectives," by Stojanovic and Acimovic-Raspopovic, considers communication issues for SMEs from both provider and customer perspectives. SME communication infrastructure at the individual site should usually be built around Ethernet-based local area network with a remotely manageable integrated access device that enables high speed Internet access, virtual private networking, Voice over Internet Protocol (VoIP) functionality and collaborative services. The authors further address several open quality of service (QoS) issues that include: service level agreements, signaling for quality of service and management aspects. The proposed framework for service management encompasses interfaces for QoS-aware and legacy applications, generic service level specification, functional model of service negotiation and management policies.

Chapter 14

 Hélder Fanha Martins, Lisbon Polytechnic Institute - Lisbon School of Accounting and
  Administration, Portugal
 Maria João Ferro, Lisbon Polytechnic Institute - Lisbon School of Accounting and
  Administration, Portugal

Accomplishing creative tasks collaboratively is particularly problematic when team members who are attempting to achieve the creative results are geographically dispersed throughout the globe in a virtual team. Therefore, sound communication tools are needed to ensure communication does not hamper team creativity. Martins and Ferro, in Chapter 14, "Selecting Appropriate Communication Tools to Support Teams' Creative Processes in SMEs" highlight the communication tools available for doing creative work, offering a short analysis of the most relevant synchronous and asynchronous communication tools. Some rules and tips are given to allow for a better choice of the communication tools to use according to both the nature of the team and the work it is performing in terms of creative processes in SMEs. Authors also present how knowledge experts and knowledge-based companies consider whether it would be any benefits on applying "Web 2.0" in their organisational architecture to strengthen collaboration.

Section 3
Managerial and Organizational Issues

Chapter 15

The implementation of Enterprise Information Systems is a difficult task, even for large companies. It can be even more so for SMEs, for most are seriously constrained in terms of time, money and skills. According to Paul Kidd, author of Chapter 15, "Enterprise Information Systems: Aligning and Integrating Strategy, Technology, Organization and People," the key to successful implementation lies in achieving an alignment between strategy, technology, organization and people, and also in achieving commitment to the new technologies. An implementation method called HiSTOP, which stands for High Integration of Strategy, Technology, Organization and People, is described in the chapter. This method provides a means of adjusting all four elements so that each is appropriate and also so that all four elements fit together. Although the method was initially designed with SMEs in mind, the method is also suitable for larger companies, hence the chapter considers both types of enterprises. The method places emphasis on development of internal implementation competencies. The key foundational principles of the method are discussed along with some key findings from early trials.

Chapter 16

From chapter 16, "Developing and Customizing Federated ERP Systems" by Lübke and Gómez, we understand that SMEs need to further reduce costs and optimize their business in order to stay competitive. Larger enterprises utilize ERP systems and other IT support for reducing costs and time in their business processes. SMEs lack behind because the introduction and maintenance of ERP systems are too expensive, the return on investment is achieved too late and the associated financial risks are too high. However, SMEs would like to have IT support for their business. The authors introduce the Federated ERP System (FERP) that addresses the problems SMEs face with conventional ERP systems and offers reasonable and scalable IT support. This is done by decomposing the whole business logic of the ERP system into Web services, which are linked at run-time. The service composition is realized by a workflow system that is also responsible for creating and managing the user interfaces and the data-flow. By integrating only the Web services that are needed (possibly from third parties) the cost is reduced and the functionality can be scaled to the actual needs.

Chapter 17

In "EIS systems and Quality Management," Bart Gerritsen discusses the support of quality management by Enterprise Information Systems. After a brief introduction in ISO9001, one of the principle and most widespread quality management frameworks, this chapter discusses the design and implementation of a typical QMS and in particular of key performance indicators, indicating the present state of performance in the organization. While analyzing design and implementation issues, requirements on the supporting EIS system will be derived. Finally, the chapter presents an outlook onto future developments, trends and research. This chapter reveals that key performance indicators can be well integrated in EIS systems, using either relational or object-oriented storage technology.

Chapter 18

In Chapter 18 "e-Impresa: A System Dynamics Strategic Model to Evaluate SME Marketing On Line Investment," Habib Sedehi introduces a System Dynamics (SD) model developed to give a support in better understanding the process of the Web marketing and so to have more elements to decide to "dive" into the virtual world. The model has the aim to support strategic decisions, for a SME involvement in E-commerce, pointed out to guarantee sustainable growth and medium-long term success. The project of e-Impresa analyses the whole process of the investment in building and maintaining a Web site, taking into account the main variables of E-commerce. Through a case study, a SD business game model has been developed. The model gives the opportunity to users to evaluate different what-if analysis through the simulation period time (2 years) at each model step time (4 weeks). The chapter will explain the overall architecture of the model and will present some results of use of the model in different conditions.

Chapter 19

In "Preparedness of Small and Medium-Sized Enterprises to Use Information and Communication Technology as a Strategic Tool," Klara Antlova emphasizes issues connected with adoption of information and communication technology (ICT) as a strategic tool contributing to further organizational growth. This understanding is based on the results of a qualitative analysis of a group of SMEs. Gradual development of a group of 30 organizations has been monitored over the last fifteen years during their co-operation with the Technical University of Liberec. The research focused on SME management's approach to ICT, its utilization for competitive advantage and its relation to and defining of business strategy. Other aspects of the study looked at the effect of ICT on organizational performance, knowledge and skills of the employees, training and organizational culture. The results indicate that successful and growing companies have gradually established business, information and knowledge strategies and make strategic use of ICT.

Section 4
Critical Success Factors and Case Studies

Jeffrey Chang, London South Bank University, UK
Margi Levy, University of Warwick, UK
Philip Powell, University of Bath, UK and University of Groningen, The Netherlands

The factors that lead to business process re-engineering (BPR) success in SMEs are not clearly understood. In chapter 20, "Process Re-Engineering Success in Small and Medium Sized Enterprises," Chang, Levy and Powell review the main contributing factors to BPR success using a framework that considers culture, structure, technology and resource. Eight Taiwanese case studies are used to explore issues contributing to, or impeding, successful process re-engineering in small firms. The analysis shows that BPR success is empowered by innovation, employee empowerment, top management commitment and strategic direction and is dependent upon customer relations, IS involvement and financial resources.

Dimitrios Gagalis, Technological Educational Institute of West Macedonia, Greece
Panayiotis Tahinakis, University of Macedonia Economic and Social Sciences, Greece
Nicolaos Protogeros, University of Macedonia Economic and Social Sciences, Greece
Dimitrios Ginoglou, University of Macedonia Economic and Social Sciences, Greece

"Challenges and Trends Towards an Effective Application of ERP and SCM Systems in SMEs" by Gagalis, Tahinakis, Protogeros and Ginoglou, has as purpose to present international trends and challenges on the field of ERP and SCM systems, thus to: (a) record background information on legacy and current supply chain IT systems for SMEs, (b) discuss the importance of both ERP and SCM systems and the complementarities of ERP and SCM systems, (c) present survey conclusions of ERP and SCM systems adoption in various industries and countries, mainly in Europe and reveal the most prominent trends and barriers, (d) identify the technologies that are used to provide integrated view of information for SMEs, with emphases on both technological and organizational dimensions and recommendations to SMEs and (e) provide future trends, possible future areas of work and conclusions. Contemporary SMEs must carefully examine integration approaches and their technological and organizational issues such as hidden integration costs and management of change considered with human organizational concerns, cultures and business objectives. Application service providers, Web services and Service Oriented Architecture as well as ERP and SCM application's maturity and open source software solutions, especially for SMEs requirements, are amongst the anticipating future trends in the field.

Lorraine Warren, University of Southampton, UK
Ted Fuller, Lincoln University, UK

Chapter 22, "Contrasting Approaches to Preparedness: A Reflection on Two Case Studies" by Warren and Fuller, reflects on ongoing research in SMEs in the manufacturing and service sectors. It contrasts different approaches to the issue of preparedness from an organisational and social perspective in two cases where new enterprise-wide business processes were implemented and integrated in different settings. In both cases, the emergence of new systems presented a huge challenge to companies hard-pressed to marshal the resources to mount effective change and implementation projects on this scale. The cases presented enable a comparison of different strategies used, one firm responding to organic growth, and the other to rapid industry-driven change. The chapter focuses not on the implementations *per se*, but instead on the issue of preparedness for change. The chapter concludes by drawing out general lessons concerning how to support and maintain organisational preparedness for enterprise wide change in different industry settings.

Chapter 23

    Simona Sternad, University of Maribor, Slovenia
    Samo Bobek, University of Maribor, Slovenia
    Zdenko Dezelak, University of Maribor, Slovenia
    Ana Lampret, SRC.SI, Slovenia

ERP solution implementation is a complex process, that requires substantial resources and efforts, and yet the results are very uncertain. The ERP hype has already reached SMEs, so Sternad, Bobek, Dezelak and Lampret in "Critical Success Factors (Csfs) For Enterprise Resource Planning (ERP) Solution Implementation In SMEs – What Does Matter For Business Integration" examine the strategies, methods and critical success factors from SMEs point of view. The results of their survey of SMEs in Slovenia have shown that SMEs have to pay attention to different critical success factors in different phases of the implementation process. Moreover, there are differences in implementation process as opposed to large companies. Case studies of two SMEs have shown similar results. The chapter also includes recommendations for future SME implementations.

Chapter 24

    Dominique Vinck, Université P. Mendès, France
    Igor Rivera-Gonzales, Instituto Politécnico Nacional, México
    Bernard Penz, Institut National Polytechnique, France

In chapter 24, "Enterprise Resource Planning (ERP) Embedding: Building Of Software/Enterprise Integration," Vinck, Rivera-Gonzalez and Penz analyse the mutual processes according to which the tool (ERP) and the organization adapt to each other. The chapter documents the live experience of technological change during the introduction of ERP in a medium-sized enterprise. Focusing on the election of the new tool and its appropriation by firm members, it does not simply reduce the process to a handful of factors (of success or failure), but analyses the different negotiations between actors leading to the reconstruction of both the tool and the organisation. It thus takes an in-depth look at the role of technology rather than just resorting to a simplistic and deterministic search for causal connections. Tracing the construction and meshing of the performance of both organisation and tools within the company, it reviews a set of dichotomies between technology and society, initial project and "impact," but also action and submission to constraints. Hence, the chapter explores the learning processes and the redefinition of actors, organisation and tools.

Chapter 25

The new communication and information systems have significantly increased the possibilities offered to professional companies for developing and maintaining long-term customer relationships. However, technology alone cannot ensure the success of CRM strategies. The implementation of a customer-centred culture, shared by the entire professional organisation, requires the combination of human resources, expertise and technology in order to identify and satisfy the needs of the existing customers. Considering a sample of French and UK professional SMEs, Călin Gurău in "The Management of CRM Information Systems in Small B2B Service Organisations: A Comparison between French And British Firms" investigates the type of CRM strategy implemented by these firms, as well as the usage intensity of various communication channels, both by companies and clients. The satisfaction of client organisations is analysed from a multi-level perspective and a diagnostic procedure is proposed in order to identify the gap between the perceptions service provider firms and clients on various dimensions of the CRM process.

Chapter 26

Chapter 26, "Elements that can Explain the Degree of Success of ERP Systems Implementation" by Carmen Heredero and Mónica Heredero, discusses that the implementation of an ERP is a risky and high cost action, even more when we are dealing with SME. Although many studies have shown the importance of paying attention to critical success factors in ERP implementations, there is still a high degree of failures and bad experiences around ERP implementations. Most literature review has shown experiences of success and failure coming from big sized firms. But there is a lack of information of what has happened in the area of small and medium size firms, and for some economies, they are essential. The authors show a model containing the main elements that can better explain the degree of success and of failure in ERP implementations by providing examples mainly affecting to the circumstances of small and medium size firms. In the model the authors propose five main groups of variables affecting final results in ERP implementations.

Chapter 27
Özalp Vayvay, Marmara University, Istanbul, Turkey
İlhan Derman, ABH, Istanbul, Turkey
Ergin Beceren, ABH, Istanbul, Turkey

SMEs differ from large firms in terms of environmental uncertainty, dependency, centralization, specialization, strategy, systems, resources and flexibility. Because of these distinguishing characteristics, the results of research carried out in large firms cannot be transferred directly to small firms. This is particularly true for the critical success factors for change management and technology implementation. The case study in Turkey, presented and discussed by Vayvay, Derman and Beceren in "Change Management Strategies For ERP Implementation in SME and a Case Study in Turkey: ABH Success Story" represents the change management activities on ERP implementation by a consultancy firm (ABH) on an international corporation (a SME) located in Turkey.

Preface

ABOUT THE SUBJECT

An enterprise system has the Herculean task of seamlessly supporting and integrating a full range of business processes by uniting functional islands and making their data visible across the organization in real time. (Strong & Volkoff, 2004, p. 22).

For the last decades, it is being recognized that that enterprise computer-based solutions no longer consist of isolated or dispersedly developed and implemented MRP solutions, electronic commerce solutions, ERP solutions, transposing the functional islands to the so-called island of information. Solutions must be integrated, built on a single system, and supported by a common information infrastructure central to the organization, ensuring that information can be shared across all functional levels and management, so that it lets users instantly see data entered anywhere in the system and, simultaneously, seamlessly allows the integration and coordination of the enterprise business processes.

These suites of solutions are no longer designed for large enterprises, multinationals, with high turnover, etc. They are tools for small businesses of all types and sectors of activity. This book is concerned with Enterprise Information Systems (EIS) as drivers of competitiveness for Small and Medium Enterprises (SME) of every economic sector, in their quest for agility, flexibility and responsiveness.

The topic of Enterprise Information Systems (EIS) is gaining an increasingly relevant strategic impact on global business and the world economy, and organizations of all sort are undergoing hard investments (in cost and effort) in search of the rewarding benefits of efficiency and effectiveness that this range of solutions promise. But as we all know, this is not an easy task—it is not only a matter of financial investment. It is much more, as the book will show. EIS are responsible for tremendous gains and even result in tremendous losses.

Responsiveness, flexibility, agility and business alignment are requirements of competitiveness that enterprises search for. And we hope that the models, solutions, tools and case studies presented and discussed in this book can contribute to highlight new ways to identify opportunities and overtake trends and challenges of EIS selection, adoption and exploitation, in particular targeting SME.

ORGANIZATION OF THE BOOK

This book is a compilation of 27 contributions to the discussion of the main issues, challenges, opportunities and developments related with Enterprise Information Systems as tools for competitiveness for SME from the social, managerial and organizational perspectives, in a very comprehensive way, in order to disseminate current achievements and practical solutions and applications.

These 27 chapters are written by a group of 66 authors that includes many internationally renowned and experienced authors in the EIS field and a set of younger authors, showing a promising potential for research and development. Contributions came from USA, Latin America, several countries of Eastern and Western Europe, Asia and Australia. At the same time, the book integrates contributions from academe, research institutions and industry, representing a good and comprehensive representation of the state-of-the-art approaches and developments that address the several dimensions of this fast, evolutionary theme.

"Enterprise Information Systems for Business Integration in SMEs: Technological, Organizational and Social Dimensions" is organized in four sections:

- "Section 1 – Models, Applications and Solutions" presents the main frameworks, approaches, methodologies and models that support Enterprise Systems.
- "Section 2 – Supporting Technologies and Tools" introduces some tools associated to the development of EIS
- "Section 3 – Managerial and Organizational Issues" discusses challenges, opportunities and concerns related to the managerial, social and organizational aspects of EIS adoption and exploitation.
- And finally "Section 4 – Critical Success Factors and Case Studies" describes and discusses motivations, trends, cases studies, successful cases of EIS implementation and exploitation in SME.

The first section, "*Models, Applications and Solutions,*" includes ten chapters summarized below.

In the first chapter, "*Measuring the Impact of an ERP Project at SMEs: A Framework and Empirical Investigation*", Maria Argyropoulou, George Ioannou, Dimitrios N. Koufopoulos and Jaideep Motwani analyze and test a novel framework for the evaluation of an ERP project. The framework incorporates specific performance measures, which are linked to a previously developed model, (the "six-imperatives" framework) and are relevant to ERP implementation. Two case studies illustrate the use of the framework in two Greek companies aiming to measure, in practical terms, the impact of the ERP project on their operations. The main results indicate that the "six-imperatives" provide a comprehensive methodology based on the profound exploration and understanding of specific business processes and objectives that should be met in order to assess an ERP project.

Chapter 2

Information system conversion has been with us since users of punch-card tabulating systems first moved to vacuum-tube computers. However, it is often seen as an afterthought: once the "interesting" work of analysis, design and so on is done, it will somehow happen. Efrem Mallach, in the second chapter, "*Information System Conversion in SMEs,*" attempts to view the process holistically, from both the technical and human viewpoints, reflecting the fact that information systems have both technical and human components. It shows how ignoring one side or the other can lead to problems, which can be avoided if all aspects are considered together. It proposes a systematic approach to considering these issues and points out benefits of using it.

Nowadays, the implementation of business process management modern tools in companies becomes a matter of acceptation of an effective organization management. The first ultimate precondition for achieving this goal is a properly structured company. Vladimír Modrák, in "*Business Process Management as a Critical Success Factor in EIS Implementation,*" places the focus on business process reengineering due to preparing preconditions for smooth implementation of EIS. Since there are differences between tools of business processes redesign and information systems development, then a main focus was on overcoming existing semantic gaps. With the aim of solving this problem, the specific modeling method has been used that was clear for company's staff and usable for EIS designers.

For Wai M. Cheung and Dirk Schaefer, in "*Product Lifecycle Management: State-of-the-Art and Future Perspectives,*" while most SMEs in general are willing to invest into Product Lifecycle Management (PLM) systems, many are still apprehensive to the sometimes large initial investment to be made in terms of both software cost and the time needed to implement and integrate such system into their digital enterprise technology infrastructure. In light of this, it is crucial for decision makers not only to understand the current PLM market, but also to become familiar with emerging trends and future developments in order to select a PLM solution that best fit the needs of their enterprise. In this chapter, the authors summarize a detailed analysis of the PLM market with the aim of providing educators, students, and decision makers in industry with an overview of the current PLM market as a whole. In addition, emerging trends and future developments are addressed.

In chapter five, *"ERP Systems Supporting Lean Manufacturing in SMEs"* and according to Pritish Halgeri, Roger McHaney and Z. J. Pei, the explosive growth of e-business methodologies and the resulting pressure to become nimble and embrace rapid change forced many SME to rethink their production approaches, particularly in regard to where they stand in relation to these two methodologies (ERP systems and Lean Manufacturing). Over time, ERP vendors recognized the power and advantages of Lean manufacturing and developed ways to incorporate Lean-related features into their software. The main objective of this chapter is to explore how ERP and Lean methodologies can coexist in SMEs. The chapter discusses misconceptions about the fit between ERP and Lean then summarizes differences and synergies between the two methodologies. It also emphasizes how linking ERP and Lean methods can lead to competitive advantage then explores key Lean toolsets available in leading ERP systems used by SMEs. Further focus is provided with additional insight on several leading ERP vendors offering Lean-enabled software modules.

Planning and management of Virtual Organisations (VOs) depends on accurate prognosis and forecasting of several organizational aspects. New and innovative business models such as the VO offer a variety of new options for SME to do business. In the sixth chapter, *"A Forecasting Concept for Virtual Organisations Supporting SMEs,"* Jens Eschenbacher and Heiko Duin present a system-oriented view to understand planning and forecasting needs in VOs. The strategic issues in planning will be elaborated by using the cross-impact analysis. For the medium-term planning the focus lies on investigations based on the so-called collaborative network analysis. An industrial case study is introduced to demonstrate the application of the concept.

In the seventh chapter, *"Business Integration Model in Services Sector SMEs,"* Snežana Pantelić shows the importance of integration business processes and information systems for service sector SMEs and presents an opportunity of synchronous and simultaneous development of both business process integration (BPI) and enterprise information system (EIS) utilizing the introduced Business Integration Model (BIM). BIM approach is based on modeling core business processes, which are supported by modern IS. Process centric and customer centric modern organization relies on enterprise management standards like ISO 9000 family. The task is to achieve the business goal of the process measured by defined Key Performance Indicator (KPI) and to improve the processes continually. The presented "Autotransport" case describes BIM design and implementation for the core process "Transport services management." The critical factor of the success of implementation of Business Integration Model (BIM) is undoubtedly the readiness of employees to accept a process approach in the execution of their tasks.

Multi-project business operations in SMEs require adaptation of management processes and, consequently, revision of information systems. Present ERP solutions are not suitable in a multi-project environment. Chapter eight, *"Conducting Multi-Project Business Operations in SMEs and IS Support"* by Igor Vrečko, Anton Hauc, Vesna Čančer and Igor Perko presents a newly designed IS model that supports strategic and commercial multiple project operations. The importance of connecting business goals with project performance and upgrading operational CRM into multi-partner management technology is considered. Significant added functions of IS in a multi-project environment should support project evaluation and management of project portfolios, intra- and inter-project communication, and mastering multi-task workflow. To reduce the need to spend limited SMEs' resources, technological development of the designed IS model must assure its simplicity for use and deployment.

In chapter nine, *"An ERP Adoption Model for Midsize Businesses,"* Fahd Alizai and Stephen Burgess theorize the development of a conceptual ERP adoption model, applicable to midsize businesses, identifying the general business factors associated with ERP implementation along with the corresponding organisational benefits. This chapter also highlights the constraints that confront midsize businesses whilst implementing sophisticated applications. The needs for ERP adoption can occur due to an attempt to be more competitive or due to an external pressure from large businesses to adopt an ERP application. The proposed conceptual model uses a strategic approach containing; ERP implementation processes, stages, factors & issues associated with ERP adoption in midsize businesses. This research also focuses on identification of strategies in the organisational, social and technical domains that could be influential for ERP adoption.

The importance of SMEs today is far beyond any discussion in countries all over the world - in European countries as well as in Asia and in USA, in Africa as well as in Latin America. In chapter 10, *"Enterprise Information Systems for Business Integration in Global International Cooperations of Collaborating Small and Medium Sized Organisations"* and according to its authors, P. H. Osanna, N. M. Durakbasa, M. E. Yurci and J. M. Bauer, to meet market demands in present and future global industrial world, manufacturing enterprises of any kind and any size must be flexible and agile enough to respond quickly to product demand changes. With the support of artificial intelligence and modern information technology, it is possible to realise modern cost-effective customer-driven design and manufacturing taking into account the importance and basic role of quality management and metrology. This will be especially possible on the basis of the innovative concept and model for modern enterprises the so-called "Multi-Functions Integrated Factory - MFIF" that makes possible an agile and optimal industrial production in any kind of industry and especially in up-to-date SMEs.

Section two, *"Supporting Technologies and Tools"* is composed of the following four chapters.

SME have specific requirements on the software systems (SWS) they use, described by Jaroslav Král and Michal Žemlička in *"Software for Small-to-Medium Enterprises."* The solution to this issue or overtaking of its consequences can be based on the variant of service-oriented architecture (SOA) discussed in the chapter. A proper use of modern software systems depends on the skills and knowledge of (end) users of the systems. The extent of a new software-oriented knowledge of the users needed to specify, install, and use the systems depends on the architecture of the system. Authors further show that a properly used SOA can substantially reduce the need to learn new knowledge at users' side. The kernel of the solution should be based on the SOA-based generalization of the concept of usability and on a technical turn enabling agility of business processes. The solution can simplify the development of tools enabling the activation of inhibited user knowledge via flexible prototyping supporting agile business processes and learning by doing.

Justifying that more than 99% of European enterprises are SMEs, Sike Balzert, Thomas Burkhart, Thomas Werth et al., in *"State of the Art Solutions in Enterprise Interoperability"* state that although collaboration with other enterprises provides potential for improving business performance, enterprise interoperability research has yet to produce results which can be used by SMEs without the need for high start-up costs, e.g. learning, infrastructure and installation costs. The chapter introduces the Commius project (funded by the European Union) that aims the development of such a "zero costs of entry" interoperability solution for SMEs, allowing them to reuse existing and familiar applications for electronic communication. Based on a four layer interoperability framework, it will be examined which technical, process-based and semantic solutions for enterprise interoperability are available at the moment and which strategic motives drive or prevail SMEs to engage in E-business activities.

Chapter 13, *"Communication Issues for Small and Medium Enterprises: Provider and Customer Perspectives,"* by Mirgana D. Stojanovic and Vladanka S. Acimovic-Raspopovic, considers communication issues for SMEs from both provider and customer perspectives. SME communication infrastructure at the individual site should usually be built around Ethernet-based local area network with a remotely manageable integrated access device that enables high speed Internet access, virtual private networking, Voice over Internet Protocol (VoIP) functionality and collaborative services. The authors further address several open quality of service (QoS) issues that include: service level agreements, signaling for quality of service and management aspects. The proposed framework for service management encompasses interfaces for QoS-aware and legacy applications, generic service level specification, functional model of service negotiation and management policies.

Accomplishing creative tasks collaboratively is particularly problematic when team members who are attempting to achieve the creative results are geographically dispersed throughout the globe in a virtual team.

Therefore, sound communication tools are needed to ensure communication does not hamper team creativity. Hélder Fanha Martins and Maria João Ferro, in Chapter 14, *"Selecting Appropriate Communication Tools to Support Teams' Creative Processes in SMEs"* highlight the communication tools available for doing creative work, offering a short analysis of the most relevant synchronous and asynchronous communication tools. Some rules and tips are given to allow for a better choice of the communication tools to use according to both the nature of the team and the work it is performing in terms of creative processes in SMEs. Authors also present how knowledge experts and knowledge-based companies consider whether it would be any benefits on applying "Web 2.0" in their organisational architecture to strengthen collaboration.

Section three, *"Managerial and Organizational Issues"* includes Chapters 15 to 19.

The implementation of Enterprise Information Systems is a difficult task, even for large companies. It can be even more so for SMEs, for most are seriously constrained in terms of time, money and skills. According to Paul T. Kidd, author of the Chapter 15, *"Enterprise Information Systems: Aligning and Integrating Strategy, Technology, Organization and People,"* the key to successful implementation lies in achieving an alignment between Strategy, Technology, Organization and People, and also in achieving commitment to the new technologies. An implementation method called HiSTOP, which stands for High Integration of Strategy, Technology, Organization and People, is described in the chapter. This method provides a means of adjusting all four elements so that each is appropriate and also so that all four elements fit together. Although the method was initially designed with SMEs in mind, the method is also suitable for larger companies, hence the chapter considers both types of enterprises. The method places emphasis on development of internal implementation competencies. The key foundational principles of the method are discussed along with some key findings from early trials.

From Chapter 16, *"Developing and Customizing Federated ERP Systems"* by Daniel Lübke and Jorge Marx Gómez we understand that SMEs need to further reduce costs and optimize their business in order to stay competitive. Larger enterprises utilize ERP systems and other IT support for reducing costs and time in their business processes. SMEs lack behind because the introduction and maintenance of ERP systems are too expensive, the return on investment is achieved too late and the associated financial risks are too high. However, SMEs would like to have IT support for their business. The authors introduce the Federated ERP System (FERP) that addresses the problems SMEs face with conventional ERP systems and offers reasonable and scalable IT support. This is done by decomposing the whole business logic of the ERP system into Web services, which are linked at run-time. The service composition is realized by a workflow system that is also responsible for creating and managing the user interfaces and the data-flow. By integrating only the Web services that are needed (possibly from third parties) the cost is reduced and the functionality can be scaled to the actual needs.

In *"EIS systems and Quality Management"*, Bart H. M. Gerritsen discusses the support of quality management by Enterprise Information Systems. After a brief introduction in ISO9001, one of the principle and most widespread quality management frameworks, this chapter discusses the design and implementation of a typical QMS and in particular of key performance indicators, indicating the present state of performance in the organization. While analyzing design and implementation issues, requirements on the supporting EIS system will be derived. Finally, the chapter presents an outlook onto future developments, trends and research. This chapter reveals that key performance indicators can be well integrated in EIS systems, using either relational or object-oriented storage technology

In Chapter 18 *"e-Impresa: A System Dynamics Strategic Model to Evaluate SME Marketing On Line Investment,"* Habib Sedehi introduces a System Dynamics (SD) model developed to give a support in better understanding the process of the Web marketing and so to have more elements to decide to "dive" into the virtual world. The model has the aim to support strategic decisions, for a SME involvement in E-commerce, pointed out to guarantee sustainable growth and medium-long term success. The project of e-Impresa analyses the whole process of the investment in building and maintaining a web site, taking into account the main variables of the E-commerce. Through a case study, a SD business game model has been developed. The model gives the opportunity to users to evaluate different what-if analysis through the simulation period time (2 years) at each model step time (4 weeks). The chapter will explain the overall architecture of the model and will present some results of use of the model in different conditions.

In "*Preparedness of Small and Medium-Sized Enterprises to Use Information and Communication Technology as a Strategic Tool,*" Klara Antlova emphasizes issues connected with adoption of information and communication technology (ICT) as a strategic tool contributing to further organizational growth. This understanding is based on the results of a qualitative analysis of a group of SMEs. Gradual development of a group of 30 organizations has been monitored over the last fifteen years during their co-operation with the Technical University of Liberec. The research focused on SME management's approach to ICT, its utilization for competitive advantage and its relation to and defining of business strategy. Other aspects of the study looked at the effect of ICT on organizational performance, knowledge and skills of the employees, training and organizational culture. The results indicate that successful and growing companies have gradually established business, information and knowledge strategies and make strategic use of ICT.

The last section of the book, section four "*Critical Succes Factors and Case Studies*" integrates eight chapters.

The factors that lead to business process re-engineering (BPR) success in SMEs are not clearly understood. In Chapter 20, "*Process Re-Engineering Success in Small and Medium Sized Enterprises,*" Jeffrey Chang, Margi Levy and Philip Powell review the main contributing factors to BPR success using a framework that considers culture, structure, technology and resource. Eight Taiwanese case studies are used to explore issues contributing to, or impeding, successful process re-engineering in small firms. The analysis shows that BPR success is empowered by innovation, employee empowerment, top management commitment and strategic direction and is dependent upon customer relations, IS involvement and financial resources.

"*Challenges and Trends Towards an Effective Application of ERP and SCM Systems in SMEs*" by Dimitrios Gagalis, Panayiotis Tahinakis, Nicolaos Protogeros and Dimitrios Ginoglou, has as purpose to present international trends and challenges on the field of ERP and SCM systems, thus to: (a) record background information on legacy and current supply chain IT systems for SMEs, (b) discuss the importance of both ERP and SCM systems and the complementarities of ERP and SCM systems, (c) present survey conclusions of ERP and SCM systems adoption in various industries and countries, mainly in Europe and reveal the most prominent trends and barriers, (d) identify the technologies that are used to provide integrated view of information for SMEs, with emphases on both technological and organizational dimensions and recommendations to SMEs and (e) provide future trends, possible future areas of work and conclusions. Contemporary SMEs must carefully examine integration approaches and their technological and organizational issues such as hidden integration costs and management of change considered with human organizational concerns, cultures and business objectives. Application Service Providers, Web Services and Service Oriented Architecture as well as ERP and SCM application's maturity and Open Source software solutions, especially for SMEs requirements, are amongst the anticipating future trends in the field.

Chapter 22, "*Contrasting Approaches to Preparedness: A Reflection on Two Case Studies*" by Lorraine Warren and Ted Fuller, reflects on ongoing research in SMEs in the manufacturing and service sectors. It contrasts different approaches to the issue of preparedness from an organisational and social perspective in two cases where new enterprise-wide business processes were implemented and integrated in different settings. In both cases, the emergence of new systems presented a huge challenge to companies hard-pressed to marshal the resources to mount effective change and implementation projects on this scale. The cases presented enable a comparison of different strategies used, one firm responding to organic growth, and the other to rapid industry-driven change. The chapter focuses not on the implementations *per se*, but instead on the issue of preparedness for change. The chapter concludes by drawing out general lessons concerning how to support and maintain organisational preparedness for enterprise wide change in different industry settings.

ERP solution implementation is a complex process, that requires substantial resources and efforts, and yet the results are very uncertain. The ERP hype has already reached SMEs, so Simona Sternad, Samo Bobek,

Zdenko Dezelak and Ana Lampret in *"Critical Success Factors (Csfs) For Enterprise Resource Planning (ERP) Solution Implementation in SMEs: What Does Matter for Business Integration"* examine the strategies, methods and critical success factors from SMEs point of view. The results of their survey of SMEs in Slovenia have shown that SMEs have to pay attention to different critical success factors in different phases of the implementation process. Moreover, there are differences in implementation process as opposed to large companies. Case studies of two SMEs have shown similar results. The chapter also includes recommendations for future SME implementations.

In Chapter 24, *"Enterprise Resource Planning (ERP) Embedding: Building of Software/Enterprise Integration,"* Dominique Vinck, Igor Rivera-Gonzalez and Bernard Penz analyse the mutual processes according to which the tool (ERP) and the organization adapt to each other. The chapter documents the live experience of technological change during the introduction of ERP in a medium-sized enterprise. Focusing on the election of the new tool and its appropriation by firm members, it does not simply reduce the process to a handful of factors (of success or failure), but analyses the different negotiations between actors leading to the reconstruction of both the tool and the organisation. It thus takes an in-depth look at the role of technology rather than just resorting to a simplistic and deterministic search for causal connections. Tracing the construction and meshing of the performance of both organisation and tools within the company, it reviews a set of dichotomies between technology and society, initial project and "impact," but also action and submission to constraints. Hence, the chapter explores the learning processes and the redefinition of actors, organisation and tools.

The new communication and information systems have significantly increased the possibilities offered to professional companies for developing and maintaining long-term customer relationships. However, technology alone cannot ensure the success of CRM strategies. The implementation of a customer-centred culture, shared by the entire professional organisation, requires the combination of human resources, expertise and technology in order to identify and satisfy the needs of the existing customers. Considering a sample of French and UK professional SMEs, Călin Gurău in *"The Management of CRM Information Systems in Small B2B Service Organisations: A Comparison between French and British Firms"* investigates the type of CRM strategy implemented by these firms, as well as the usage intensity of various communication channels, both by companies and clients. The satisfaction of client organisations is analysed from a multi-level perspective and a diagnostic procedure is proposed in order to identify the gap between the perceptions service provider firms and clients on various dimensions of the CRM process.

Chapter 26, *"Elements that Can Explain the Degree of Success of ERP Systems Implementation"* by Carmen de Pablos Heredero and Mónica de Pablos Heredero, discusses that the implementation of an ERP is a risky and high cost action, even more when we are dealing with SME. Although many studies have shown the importance of paying attention to critical success factors in ERP implementations, there is still a high degree of failures and bad experiences around ERP implementations. Most literature review has shown experiences of success and failure coming from big sized firms. But there is a lack of information of what has happened in the area of small and medium size firms, and for some economies, they are essential. The authors show a model containing the main elements that can better explain the degree of success and of failure in ERP implementations by providing examples mainly affecting to the circumstances of small and medium size firms. In the model the authors propose five main groups of variables affecting final results in ERP implementations,

SMEs differ from large firms in terms of environmental uncertainty, dependency, centralization, specialization, strategy, systems, resources and flexibility. Because of these distinguishing characteristics, the results of research carried out in large firms cannot be transferred directly to small firms. This is particularly true for the critical success factors for change management and technology implementation. The case study in Turkey, presented and discussed by Vayvay, Derman and Beceren in "Change Management Strategies For ERP Implementation in SME and a Case Study in Turkey: ABH Success Story" represents the change management activities on ERP implementation by a consultancy firm (ABH) on an international corporation (a SME) located in Turkey.

EXPECTATIONS

The book provides researchers, scholars, professionals with some of the most advanced research developments, solutions and discussions of Enterprise Information Systems adoption in SME under the social, managerial and organizational dimensions.

This book is expected to be read by academics (teachers, researchers and students of several graduate and postgraduate courses) and by professionals of Information Technology, IT managers and responsible, Information Resources managers, Enterprise managers (including top level managers), and also technology solutions developers.

Maria Manuela Cruz-Cunha
Editor
Barcelos, February 2009

REFERENCES

Strong, D. M., & Volkoff, O. (2004). A Roadmap for Enterprise System Implementation. *Computer-Aided Design & Applications, 37*(6), 22-29.

Acknowledgment

Editing a book is a quite hard but compensating and enriching task, as it involves an set of different activities like contacts with authors and reviewers, discussion and exchange of ideas and experiences, process management, organization and integration of contents, and many other, with the permanent objective of creating a book that meets the public expectations. And this task cannot be accomplished without a great help and support from many sources. As editor I would like to acknowledge the help, support and believe of all who made possible this creation.

First of all, the edition of this book would not have been possible without the ongoing professional support of the team of professionals of IGI Global. I am grateful to Dr. Mehdi Khosrow-Pour, President, and to Jan Travers, Vice President, for the opportunity. A very very special mention of gratitude is due to Julia Mosemann, Development Editor, for her professional support and friendly words of advisory, encouragement and prompt guidance.

Special thanks go also to all the staff at IGI Global, whose contributions throughout the process of production and making this book available all over the world was invaluable.

We are grateful to all the authors, for their insights and excellent contributions to this book. Also we are grateful to most of the authors who simultaneously served as referees for chapters written by other authors, for their insights, valuable contributions, prompt collaboration and constructive comments. Thank you all, authors and reviewers, you made this book! The communication and exchange of views within this truly global group of recognized individualities from the scientific domain and from industry was an enriching and exciting experience!

I am also grateful to all who accede to contribute to this book, some of them with high quality chapter proposals, but unfortunately, due to several constraints could not have seen their work published.

A special thanks to my institution, the Polytechnic Institute of Cávado and Ave, for providing the material resources and all the necessary logistics.

Thank you.

Maria Manuela Cruz-Cunha
Editor
Barcelos, Febrary 2009

Section 1
Models, Applications and Solutions

Chapter 1
Measuring the Impact of an ERP Project at SMEs:
A Framework and Empirical Investigation

Maria Argyropoulou
Brunel University, UK

George Ioannou
Athens University of Economics and Business, Greece

Dimitrios N. Koufopoulos
Brunel University, UK

Jaideep Motwani
Grand Valley State University, USA

ABSTRACT

This article analyses and tests a novel framework for the evaluation of an ERP project. The framework incorporates specific performance measures, which are linked to a previously developed model, (the 'six-imperatives' framework) and are relevant to ERP implementation Two case studies illustrate the use of the framework in two Greek companies aiming to measure, in practical terms, the impact of the ERP project on their operations. The main results indicate that the "six-imperatives" provide a comprehensive methodology based on the profound exploration and understanding of specific business processes and objectives that should be met in order to assess an ERP project.

INTRODUCTION

An Enterprise Resource Planning (ERP) system is an integrated enterprise information system to automate the flow of material, information, and financial resources among all functions within an enterprise on a common database. ERP systems are meant to replace the old systems usually referred to as 'legacy systems' in order to help organizations integrate their information flow and business processes (Abdinnour-Helm et Al., 2003). ERP provides two major benefits that do not exist in non-integrated departmental systems: (1) a unified enterprise view of the business that encompasses all functions and departments; and (2) an enterprise database where all business transactions are entered, recorded, processed, monitored, and reported. This unified view increases the requirement for, and the extent of, interdepartmental cooperation and coordination. Moreover, it enables companies to achieve their objectives of increased communication and responsiveness to all stakeholders (Dillon, 1999). This is the most important point raised when it comes to the ERP systems and integration of information flows and business processes as they can support information sharing along company value chain and help in the achievement of operating efficiency (Law & Ngai 2007).

After over a decade of applications, the implementation of ERP systems is still considered a complex project with many problems concerning budgets and expected benefits. Given the possibility for success and failures, it is reasonable to expect that organisations should be able to assess the implications of the ERP adoption on their overall performance. Until recently most ERP researchers and practitioners generally talk about ERP critical success factors (CSFs) and implementation models based on CSFs that address key implementation issues (Holland and Light, 1999; Motwani et al., 2005; Umble et al., 2003). Top management involvement, business plans, vision, vendor support, change readiness, teamwork, team composition, and communication were found to be critical factors to ensure a smooth introduction for successful ERP implementation (Ramayah et al., 2007). It seems that very few multi-disciplinary studies have been conducted in an attempt to conclude on the impact of ERP system on organisational performance. Moreover, the topic of assessing the benefits of ERP systems

has not been fully addressed mainly because the justification process is a major concern for organisations investing in IT, and managers are unable to evaluate the holistic implications of adopting new technology, both in terms of benefits and costs (Gunasekaran et al., 2006). Questions like how do we define a successful ERP project have not yet been answered.

Motivated by the ERP benefits concept, in this article we suggest that ERP success is achieved when the organisation is able to better perform all its operations and when the integrated information system can support the performance increase of the company. This comprises of the benefits that the company has reaped from the implementation of the ERP or the achievement of ERP objectives. This is often called benefits management (Willcocks, 1994) and is defined as 'the process of organising and managing such that potential benefits arising from IT are actually realised'. According to Coleman and Jamieson (1994) benefits management encourages manager to focus on exactly how they will make the system pay off and contribute to the business objectives. Based on our recently developed methodology called the *"six-imperatives"* methodology (Argyropoulou et al., 2008a; 2008b) for ERP system evaluation, we measured the impact of the ERP implementation project on two Greek SMEs.

ERP System Implementation and SMEs

Existing literature suggest that SMEs may be differentiated from larger enterprises by a number of key characteristics such as personalised management, severe resource limitations, flat and flexible structures etc. (Berry, 1998; Burns & Dewhurst, 1996; Huin, 2004; Marri et al., 1998). Another major characteristic of SMEs is the absence of proper and formal IS practices and skills. In the present era of globalisation, it is obvious that the survival of SMEs will be determined by their ability to understand and acknowledge the importance of IS and their accessibility to the right information at the right time (Sharma & Bhagwat, 2006). Thus far, ERP adoption has been attempted by larger organizations, thus consulting and implementation methodologies are specified for their operations. Following a study in 150 Italian SMEs, Morabito at al., (2005) concluded that the risks associated with investments in ERP software are many and resellers should be able to offer end-to-end business management solutions addressing specific requirements before and after implementation of the solution. According to Sun et al., (2005) few SMEs have the resources to adequately address every Critical Success Factor as they should and they are forced to make implementation compromises according to resource constraints, subsequently putting the success of their ERP project at risk. Thus to improve the increased use of ERP systems and the overall business performance, necessitates suitable ERP project management strategy. With limited financial resources and in most cases insufficient managerial and technical skills SMEs need a simple and comprehensive methodology to evaluate the ERP implementation throughout the whole ERP life cycle. Although there is no company to accept or justify an unsuccessful investment, it is obvious that large companies can afford the damages better than SMEs as they have more resources available. It is imperative for smaller companies to embrace ERP projects with great care (Argyropoulou et al., 2007; 2008a).

The organisation of the article is as follows: Section 2 reviews the related literature on performance measures. Section 3 discusses the theoretical background of the recommended framework, as well as the methodological deployment describing the proposed performance metrics. Then, the findings are discussed and the article finishes with a discussion, limitations, and future research directions.

LITERATURE REVIEW

This work draws on three areas: a) Supply Chain performance measures, b) IS performance measures and c) ERP performance measures. The next paragraphs discuss briefly these areas as they apply to our analysis.

Supply Chain Performance Measures

The literature review on the area of supply chain performance measures revealed three important frameworks: a) the Supply Chain Operations Reference (SCOR) Model, developed by the Supply Chain Council (SCC) in 1996 and b) the Oliver Wight ABCD checklist and c) the Balanced Scorecard for SCM evaluation (Bhagwat & Sharma, 2007). The SCOR model provides a common process oriented language for communicating among supply-chain partners in the following decision areas: plan, source, make and deliver. It contains 12 metrics which fall into four categories: a) delivery reliability metrics, b) flexibility and Responsiveness metrics, c cost metrics and d) assets metrics: The Oliver Wight ABCD 20 point checklist, on the other hand, is a guide used by manufacturing professionals to improve their company's performance. It addresses the following business areas: strategic planning, people and team systems, product development, continuous improvement, planning, and control. Both frameworks do not cover every area of ERP performance, but they give an indication about the company's overall business performance. In a recent study Bhagwat and Sharma (2007) propose a balanced approach for SCM performance evaluation. The authors used the Balanced Scorecard (Kaplan & Norton, 1992) four perspectives and developed a new framework structurally similar to SBSC with corresponding metrics that reflect SCM strategy and goals.

IS Performance Measures

Many researchers focused on measuring IS performance (Cha-Jan, Chang, & King, 2005; DeLone & McLean, 1992; 2003; Jiang & Klein, 1999; Mirani & Lederer 1998; Pitt et al., 1995; Saarinen, 1996; Sharma & Bhagwat, 2006; Torkzadeh & Doll, 1999) All these studies have substantially contributed, in that they advocate the importance of performance measurement for the improvement of business activities and they identified a number of metrics for the IS function. However, most of them have developed and tested general survey instruments, which measure IS performance without focusing on a specific system being evaluated and its purpose.

ERP Systems Performance Measures

The review of recent literature covering the particular area of ERP systems impact on overall performance allowed us to identify the following significant papers: a) Wieder et al., (2006) who conducted a field study to find the impacts of several aspects of ERP adoption using IT measures, business process performance measures and firm performance and b) Chand et al., (2005) who carried out a case study research where a balanced-scorecard based framework for valuing the strategic contributions of an ERP system was applied. Motivated by these two researchers but mainly by the Information Systems Functional Scorecard (Cha-Jan, Chang, & King, 2005), last year we introduced a new framework called the *"six-imperatives"* framework which provides a solid methodology for the identification and incorporation of the necessary metrics for ERP system post implementation review (Argyropoulou et al., 2008b).The purpose of this article is to apply the 'six-imperatives' framework on two Greek SMEs that were aiming at the assessment of their ERP implementation project. The next section describes briefly the theoretical background as well as the

methodological deployment of the *"six-imperatives"* framework, for the readers to comprehend the rational of the analysis that follows.

THE "SIX-IMPERATIVES" FRAMEWORK FOR MEASURING THE IMPACT OF AN ERP PROJECT

The theoretical background of the framework is based mainly on two previously developed methodologies: The *Information Systems Functional Scorecard* developed by Cha-Jan Chang & King, (2005) and the *'six imperatives'* framework for ERP system selection and evaluation developed by Argyropoulou et al., (2008a; 2008b). Both frameworks are briefly described in the remainder of this section (detailed theoretical information in Argyropoulou et al., 2008a; 2008b).

The (ISFS) Information Systems Functional Scorecard

The Cha-Jan Chang and King (2005) scorecard is based on the models suggested by Pitt et al., (1995) and Delone & McLean (2002) and has been designed to measure the performance of the entire IS function. The authors developed an instrument consisting of three major dimensions: systems performance, information effectiveness and service performance. These dimensions constituted the basic constructs for their field study research. These are briefly discussed in the next paragraph, whereas the ISFS sub-constructs are presented in table 1 (For detailed discussion, see Cha-Jan Chang and King, 2005).

Systems performance: Measures of the systems performance assess the quality aspects of the system such as reliability, response time, ease of use, and so on, and the various impacts that the systems have on the user's work.

Information effectiveness: Measures of the information effectiveness assess the quality of information in terms of the design, operation, use,

Table 1. Sub-ISFS Constructs, adapted from Cha-Jan Chang and King, (2005)

Systems performance	Information effectiveness	Service performance
Impact on job	Intrinsic quality of information	Responsiveness
Impact on external constituencies	Contextual quality of information	Reliability
Impact on internal processes	Presentation quality of information	Service provider quality
Effect on knowledge and learning	Accessibility of information	Empathy
Systems features	Reliability of information	Training
Ease of use	Flexibility of information	Flexibility of services
	Usefulness of information	Cost/benefit of services

and value provided by information as well as the effects of the information on the user's job.

Service performance: Measures of service performance assess each user's experience with the services provided by the IS function in terms of quality and flexibility.

The Six Imperatives Framework For ERP System Implementation in SMEs

According to figure 1, the ERP system's evaluation should commence well before implementation, during the selection process, where necessary ERP objectives are identified, and determined (Argyropoulou et al., 2008a). Any SME that wishes to implement an appropriate ERP system should primarily conduct an in depth analysis of their strategy and needs based on six imperatives which represent the building pillars on which the investigation is actually performed and are critical for implementation and operative success. These are analysed briefly in the following paragraph, to draw attention to the main activities, issues, dynamics, and complexities involved in the ERP project implementation cycle (detailed analysis in Argyropoulou et al., 2007; 2008a).

The strategy analysis imperative implies that companies should look for ERP implementation options and objectives concerning the package's alignment with the corporate strategy and com-

petitive priorities such as expansion, alliances, or other competitive priorities.

The investment concerns imperative emphasizes the importance of investment justification in an ERP project and the two associated objectives are: a) adherence to time schedule, and b) contingency budgetary planning which can reduce the issues relating to increased financial expenses that may label the project as a 'black hole' or failure.

The process assessment imperative suggests that the ease of customisation and systems functionality should constitute the basic ERP objectives because a better fit between the packaged software functionality and user organisation requirements leads to successful implementation and usage.

The user needs identification imperative recommends that the future system should be designed to support business processes based on the needs and capabilities of the current and future users. The ERP objectives stemming from this imperative are the development and communication of an *easy system*, which fulfils a range of specific user needs, and expectations that will be covered under the term '*usefulness*' of the system.

The technology requirements imperative considers the technical characteristics as well as the system's integration with other information technologies within the supply chain. Moreover,

Figure 1. The 'six imperatives' framework for the assessment of an ERP project (adapted from Argyropoulou et al, 2008b)

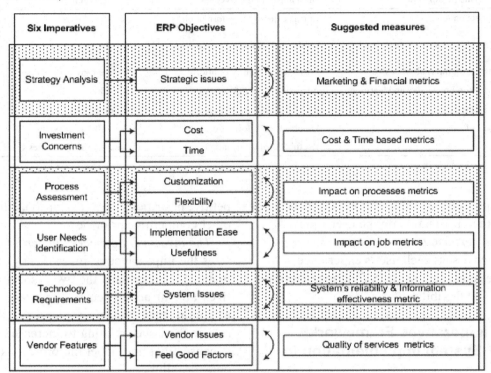

it implies that the ERP must produce the required information when needed, and that control over both the information and the information systems is maintained.

The vendor features imperative commands an effective supplier relationship management (SRM) by implementing specific supplier selection practices

An organizational analysis based on the these imperatives leads to a number of ERP objectives to be achieved, which integrate all the expected benefits pursued in order to derive value from the new system (Figure 1). The specific objectives, that are determined pre-project, can serve as a guidance tool throughout the whole ERP life cycle and especially for post-implementation review (Argyropoulou et al., 2008b; Nicolaou, 2004).

Combining the Sub-ISFS Constructs (see table 1), and the 'six imperatives' framework,

Argyropoulou et al., (2008b) provided a set of performance metrics which can actually measure to which extent the pre-determined ERP objectives have been achieved (see Appendix 1). The strategy analysis and the investment concerns measures were drawn from the recent literature (i.e Hunton et al., 2003; Irani et al., 1997, 2002; Poston & Grabski and the SCOR model as it was used by Weider et al., 2006).The remaining metrics were based on the ISFS sub constructs. At this point it should be mentioned that any organisation might choose amongst a number of metrics available in the literature. The important issue is their direct relationship to the ERP implementation objectives and the degree to which the latter have been achieved.

TESTING THE 'SIX IMPERATIVES' FRAMEWORK

This section describes a practical example of the use of the 'six –imperatives' framework in two Greek SMEs. The *'action research'* strategy has been followed as the whole project focused on action, promoting change in the company (Cunningham, 1995; Marsick & Watkins, 1997) and involved academics with a genuine concern for the expected findings (Eden & Huxham, 1996: 75).

Data Collection

We contacted two pharmaceuticals: Company A with 100 employees, had successfully applied the *"six-imperatives"* analysis prior to ERP selection and adoption. They implemented a customised Oracle ERP system. Company B, with 200 employees, had implemented SAP without any prior analysis /reengineering of their processes. The measures from our framework in Table 2 were provided to the IT managers one week prior to the scheduled interview allowing them to look for answers not readily available. Finally, some modifications were incorporated to include particularities of the pharmaceutical sector. In the following paragraph, we discuss the performance metrics that were selected for application in the two case organisations (table 2).

Findings

The results from both cases are presented in Table 2 whereas a brief explanation is discussed in the remaining of the section.

Comments on financial metrics: The reduction of COGS/revenues in both cases was due to a reduction in production costs. For Company A., labour hours and raw material costs were significantly reduced due to a more effective production schedule that followed the ERP (MRP in particular) implementation. Company B reported much lower reduction of the ratio COGS/revenues

which according to their managers was within their strategic objectives. The inventory holding cost remained the same in both companies as pharmaceuticals are obliged by legislation to hold 2 months stock.

Comments on marketing metrics: Company A reported that the percentage of missed orders/ total orders reduced from 4% before ERP to 2% after ERP adoption because of the specific marketing /sales module implementation. Company B explained that this had always been low due to a specific CRM software they had been using and they did not really witness any significant improvement following SAP adoption. The reduction of delivery time is not applicable in pharmaceuticals as they are obliged to keep stock. Extraordinary outbursts like flew might affect the delivery time but these are not incorporated in the production schedule. In such cases both companies resorted to imports from abroad.

Comments on investment metrics: Company A explained that they replaced their legacy systems almost immediately, following a two months period of training. The preparatory needs analysis based on the 'six-imperatives' guidance had already guaranteed a smooth adoption of a suitable software. Moreover, the whole project finished within budget. Indirect human costs exceeded budgets by 10% due to additional training and motivation schemes. Indirect organisational costs overruns were not reported. Company B reported a three years' implementation project with parallel use of the previous systems and 25% overruns mainly due to unplanned configuration. Indirect human costs exceeded budgets by 15% for additional technical support and expert advice. Indirect organisational costs incurred and over exceeded budgets by 15% due to the organisational restructuring that followed ERP adoption.

Comments on process metrics: Both companies explained that manufacturing cost is considered confidential information and that the whole production process is subject to strict

Table 2. Actual performance measures

Imperative	Measure	COMPANY A	COMPANY B
Strategy analysis			
Financial	% reduction of COGS/revenues	15%	4%
Marketing	% reduction of missed orders/total orders	50%	15%
	% reduction of delivery time	N/A	N/A
Investment concerns			
Time-based	Processing time along critical path	6 months	3 years
Cost-based	Direct Project Costs	Within budget	25% overruns
	Indirect Human Costs	10%	15%
	Indirect Organisational Costs	-	15%
Process assessment			
Impact on internal processes	Reduction in order fulfilment time	41%	N/A
	Reduction of order cost	22%	5%
User needs			
Impact on job	% of errors per function/department	0.1%	0
Ease of use	Number of training hours per user	90 days	120 days
	Number of consultant days per user	in-house	60 hours
Impact on knowledge/ learning	productivity	40% increase	5% reduction
Technology requirements			
Systems reliability	Number of restoration hours	N/A	N/A
	Number of maintenance hours	N/A	N/A
Information effectives			
Accessibility	Number of hours that the information was not received in timely manner.	never	rarely
Accuracy	Number of errors in reports	Limited	Limited
Flexibility	Number of hours for parameterization- customization	4 man months	20 man months
Vendor Features			
Service Responsiveness	Response time and maintenance fees	N/A	N/A

Note: COGS: Cost of goods sold

legislation. However, Company A explained that the time for order fulfilment was reduced from 17 minutes to 10 minutes, whereas the order cost reduced to 470.000 euros from 600.000 before ERP implementation (attributed mainly to a reduction in raw materials, warehousing and distribution costs). Company B reported that they had always performed efficiently due to previous warehouse software and automated picking and packing that they had been using prior to SAP. Warehousing and distribution had always been under control. The order cost that was further reduced by 5% was attributed to better inventory management.

Comments on users' metrics: Company A manager reported that labour hours reduced from an average of 2.833/employee to 1850 hours/

employee (the legal working time is about 1800 hours/employee on a yearly basis). The ensuing productivity index was calculated as labour hours/total orders and decreased from 2,833/10,000 = 0.28 to 1,850/10,000 = 0.185 resulting in 40 % increase in productivity. Company B reported a productivity reduction of 5%. However, they argued that this concerned a sudden increase in administrative costs as they hired technically skilled people to support the new system. Errors in both companies were measured as a percentage of returns. In company A, errors were reduced to 0.1% from 0.4% before ERP adoption. Company B had always had zero defects due to strict Statistical Process Quality Control Schemes.

Comments on technology metrics: System's reliability measures were not available because both companies were bounded by the Service Level Agreement (SLA) they had signed with their IT subcontractors. Information effectiveness measures for both companies were satisfactory. The parameterization-customization period in Company A lasted for 4 man months; this period lasted 20 months in company B which was actually expected due to the installation of very sophisticated software and the lack of any prior reengineering.

Comments on vendor metrics: These measures were not available. Nonetheless, both managers were triggered to explore the issue for internal use.

DISCUSSION AND PRACTICAL IMPLICATIONS

The purpose of this study was to test the framework and to explore whether it could become a useful tool for the actual measurement of the ERP impact on company performance. Both companies confirmed that the methodology was comprehensive albeit simple and straightforward. Nonetheless, taking a stance, we could argue that project A was definitely successful because the

company had reaped the benefits that they were actually looking for, focusing on how they could make the system pay off and contribute to the ERP business objectives.

We asked both managers to weigh up their ERP implementation. Company A managers were confident about the success of the ERP venture because they had met to a great extent the ERP objectives that had determined pre-project such as: optimisation of business processes, standardisation of operations flow, establishment of customer-centric policies and better organisational performance. Finally, they commented that the real contribution of the 'six-imperatives' framework lies on the learning process and the profound exploration and understanding of specific business processes and goals that had been translated into tailor-made ERP objectives, which, in turn, were largely met. Company B managers explained that they could consider it a successful project since it was finally up and running and the overall results were satisfying. After all, they had always been doing well and the SAP adoption was meant to replace their legacy systems.

LIMITATIONS

The acceptability of case study research suffers from a lack of ability to generalise the findings. However, based on Yin (1994) and Walsham (1995) arguments that case studies findings can be used to develop the concepts identified from the literature, we believe that our framework needs only to be tested in a wider range of situations to fine-tune the details and draw implications form the data. Nonetheless, our 'before and after' analysis is straightforward and can compare and eventually control the factors that are related to ERP implementation and affect its use and performance. All suggested metrics are simple to measure, and can continuously be monitored. In this way, the framework can be easily used in SMEs, offering valuable insight regarding the

ERP performance by comparing specific areas of operation before and after implementation. In addition, the 'before and after' analysis can be very useful for internal benchmarking.

CONCLUSION AND FUTURE DIRECTIONS

The research reports on a comparative case study of 2 Greek SMEs that implemented an ERP system. Using established approaches in the literature of IS performance measurement, in this article we tested the 'six-imperatives' framework for the evaluation of an ERP project. The framework consists of six key measures, each of which contains a set of metrics, expressed in time or monetary units and/or percentages. The holistic approach of the framework is simple and can be used by managers. The suggested metrics can be objective, and can provide SMEs with valuable information in a fast and accurate way, to ensure the comprehensiveness in their decision making which in most cases can strengthen their competitive position. The six imperatives framework for ERP performance measurement contributes to the ERP evaluation literature because it integrates the necessary factors to be considered in this process. Conclusively, this framework illustrates the critical factors/issues that need to be addressed at all three phases of the implementation process: pre-implementation or setting-up phase, implementation, and post-implementation or evaluation phase.

Future research might compare the 'six-imperatives' framework with the balanced scorecard and/or other performance measurement frameworks. Moreover, it can be further expanded and used as an instrument for field study research.

REFERENCES

Abdinnour-Helm S., Lengnick-Hall, M.L., & Lengnick-Hall, C.A. (2003). Pre-implementation attitudes and organizational readiness for implementing an Enterprise Resource Planning system. *European Journal of Operational Research, 146*(2), 258-273.

Berry, M. (1998). Strategic planning in small and high tech companies. *Long Range Planning, 32*(3), 455-466.

Burns, P., & Dewhurst, J. (1996). *Small Business and Entrepreneurship* (2nd ed.). London: Macmillan Press.

Argyropoulou, M, Ioannou, G., & Prastacos, G.P. (2007). ERP implementation at SMEs: an initial study of the Greek market. *International Journal of Integrated Supply Management, 3*(4) 406-425.

Argyropoulou, M., Ioannou, G., Soderquist, K.E., & Motwani, J. (2008a). Managing ERP system evaluation and selection in SMEs using the 'six-imperatives' methodology. *IJPM, 1*(4), 430-452.

Argyropoulou, M., Ioannou, G., Koufopoulos, D., & Motwani, J. (2008b). Performance drivers of ERP systems in small and medium-sized enterprises. *International Journal of Enterprise Network Management, 2*(3), 333-349.

Bhagwat, R., & Sharma, M.K. (2007). Performance measurement of supply chain management: a balanced scorecard approach. *Computers and Industrial Engineering, 53*, 43-62.

Cha-Jan Chang, J., & King, W.R. (2005). Measuring the Performance of Information Systems: A Functional Scorecard. *Journal of Management Information Systems, 22*(1), 85-115.

Chand, D., Hachey, G., Hunton J., Owhoso, V., & Vasudevan, S. (2005). A balanced scorecard besed framework for assessing the strategic impacts of ERP systems. *Computers in Industry, 56*, 558-572

Colleman, T., & Jamieson, M. (1994). Beyond return of investment. In L. Willocks (Ed.), *Information Management: The Evaluation of Information Systems Investments* (pp 189-205). Chapman & Hall London.

DeLone, W.H., & McLean, E.R. (2003). The DeLone and McLean model of information systems success: a ten-year update. *Journal of Management Information Systems, 19*(4), 9–30.

DeLone, W.H., & McLean, E.R. (1992). Information systems success: The quest for the dependent variable. *Information Systems Research, 3*(1), 60-95.

Eden, C., & Huxham, C. (1996). Action research for management research. *British Journal of Management, 71*(1), 75-86.

Gunasekaran, A., Ngai, E. W. T., & McGaughey, R.E. (2006). Information technology and systems justification: A review for research and applications. *European Journal of Operational Research, 173*(3), 957-983.

Cunningham, J.B. (1995). Strategic considerations in using action research for improving personnel practices. *Public Personnel Management, 24*(2), 515-529.

Heizer, J., & Render, B. (2003). *Operations management*—International edition (7th ed.). Pearson Education Inc, Upper Saddle River, NJ .

Holland, C.P., & Light, B. (1999). A critical success factors model for ERP implementation. *IEEE Software, 16*(3), 30-35.

Huin, S.F. (2004). Managing deployment of ERP systems in SMEs using multi-agents. *International Journal of Project Management, 22*(6), 511-517.

Hunton, J.E., & Bieler, J.D. (1997). Effects of User Participation in Systems Development: A Longitudinal Field Experiment. *MIS Quarterly, 21*(4), 359-388.

Hunton, J.E., Lippincott, B., & Reck, J.L. (2003). Enterprise resource planning systems: comparing firm performance of adopters and nonadopters. *International Journal of Accounting Information Systems, 4*(3), 165–184.

Irani, Z., Ezingeard, J.N., & Grieve, R.J. (1997). Integrating costs of manufacturing IT/IS infrastructure into the investment decision-making process. *Technovation, 17*(11/12), 695-706.

Irani, Z. (2002). Information systems evaluation: Navigating through the problem domain. *Information and Management, 40*(1), 199–211.

Kaplan, R.S., & Norton, D.P. (1992). The Balanced Scorecard-measures that drive performance. *Harvard Business Review, 70*(1), 71-80.

Jiang, J.J., & Klein, G. (1999). User evaluation of information systems: By system typology. *IEEE Transactions on Systems Man and Cybernetics, 29*(1), 111-116.

Lin, C., & Pervan, G. (2003). The practice of IS/IT benefits management in large Australian organisations. *Information and Management, 41*(1) 13-24.

Marri, H., Gunasekaran, A., & Grieve, R. (1998). An investigation into the implementation of the computer integrated manufacturing in small and medium sized enterprises. *International Journal of Advanced Manufacturing Technology, 14*, 935-42.

Marsick, V.J., & Watkins, K.E. (1997). Case study research methods' in Swanson, R.A. and Holton, E.F. (eds), *Human Resource Development Research Handbook* (pp 138-157). San Franscisco, CA: Berret-Koehler.

Mirani, R., & Lederer, A.L. (1998). An instrument for assessing the organisational benefits of IS projects. *Decision Sciences, 29*(40), 803-838.

Morabito, V., Pace S., & Previtali, P. (2005). ERP marketing and Italian SMEs. *European Management Journal, 23*(5), 590-598.

Motwani, J., Subramanian, R., & Gopalakrishna, P. (2005). Critical factors for successful ERP implementation: Exploratory findings from four case studies. *Computers in Industry, 56*, 529-544.

Nicolaou, A. (2004). Quality of post implementation review for enterprise resource planning systems. *International Journal of Accounting Information Systems, 5*(1), 25-49.

Pitt, L.F., Watson, R.T., & Kavan, C.B. (1995). Service quality: A measure of information systems effectiveness. *MIS Quarterly, 19*(2), 173-185.

Poston, R., & Grabski, S. (2001). Financial impact of enterprise resource planning implementations. *International Journal of Accounting Information Systems, 2*(4), 271-294.

Ramayah, T., Roy, M.H., Arokiasamy, S., Zbib, I., & Ahmed, Z.U. (2007). Critical success factors for successful implementation of enterprise resource planning systems in manufacturing organisations. *International Journal of Business Information Systems, 2*(3), 276-297.

Saarinen, T. (1996). An expanded instrument for evaluating information systems success. *Information and Management, 31*(2), 103-118.

Sharma, M. K., & Bhagwat, R. (2006). Performance measurements in the implementation of information systems in small and medium-sized enterprises: A framework and empirical analysis. *Measuring Business Excellence, 10*(4), 8-21.

Sun, A. Y. T., Yazdani, A., & Overend, J.D. (2005). Achievement assessment for enterprise resource planning (ERP) system implementations based on critical success factors (CSFs). *International Journal of Production Economics, 98*(2), 189-203.

Torkzadeh, G., & Doll, W.J. (1999). The development of a tool for measuring the perceived impact of information technology on work. *Omega- The International Journal of Management Science, 27*(3), 327-339.

Umble E., Haft, R., & Umble, M. (2003). Enterprise resource planning: Implementation procedures and critical success factors. *European Journal of Operational Research, 146*(2), 241-257.

Walsham, G. (1995). Interpretive case studies in IS research: Nature and method. *European Journal of Information Systems, 4*, 74-81.

Wieder, B., Booth, P., Matolcsy, Z. P., & Ossimitz, M.L. (2006). The impact of ERP systems on firm and business process performance. *Journal of Enterprise Information Management, 19*(1) 13-29.

Willcocks, L. (1994). Introduction of capital importance. In L.Willcocks (1994) (Ed.), *Information Management: The Evaluation of Information Systems Investments* (pp. 1-27). London: Chapman & Hall.

Yen, R., & Sheu, C. (2004). Aligning ERP implementation with competitive priorities of manufacturing firms: an exploratory study. *International Journal of Production Economics, 92*(3) 207–220.

Yin, R.K. (1994). *Case Study Research Design and Methods* (2nd ed.). Sage, Thousand Oaks.

APPENDIX

Methodological Deployment of the Six Imperatives Framework

Imperative	Measure	Relevant Literature
Strategy analysis		
Financial DeLone and McLean, (2003)	% reduction of COGS/revenues	Net benefits proposed by DeLone and McLean , (2003)
	% reduction of inventory holding cost	SCOR model
	% reduction in logistics costs	SCOR model
Marketing Mirani and Lederer, (1998)	% reduction of defects	Total Quality Management Theory
	% reduction of lead time	SCOR model
Investment concerns		
Time-based Heizer & Render, (2003)	Processing time along critical path	Project management theory
Cost-based Heizer & Render, (2003)	Direct Project Costs	Irani et al., (1997); Irani, (2002)
	Indirect Human Costs	Irani et al., (1997); Irani, (2002)
	Indirect Organisational Costs	Irani et al., (1997); Irani, (2002)
Process assessment		
Impact on internal processes (Cha-Jan Chang & King, 2005)	Reduction in process time	Cha-Jan Chang & King, (2005)
	Reduction of process cost	Cha-Jan Chang & King, (2005)
User needs		
Impact on job Cha-Jan Chang & King, (2005)	Number of errors per function/ department	Cha-Jan Chang & King, (2005)
Ease of use (Cha-Jan Chang & King, 2005)	Number of training hours per user	Cha-Jan Chang & King, (2005)
	Number of consultant days per user	Cha-Jan Chang & King, (2005)
Impact on knowledge/learning Cha-Jan Chang & King, (2005)	Rate of sick leave, or staff turnover	New
	% increase in employees' productivity	SCOR model
Technology requirements		
Systems reliability DeLone and McLean, (2003) Cha-Jan Chang & King, (2005)	Number of restoration hours	New
	Number of maintenance hours	New
Information effectives		
Accessibility Cha-Jan Chang & King, (2005)	Number of hours that the information was not received in timely manner.	Cha-Jan Chang & King, (2005)
Accuracy (Cha-Jan Chang & King, 2005)	Number of errors in reports	Cha-Jan Chang & King, (2005)

APPENDIX CONTINUED

Flexibility (Cha-Jan Chang & King, 2005)	Number of hours for customization and enhancements	Cha-Jan Chang & King, (2005)
Vendor Features		
Service Responsiveness Cha-Jan Chang & King, (2005)	Response time and maintenance fees	Cha-Jan Chang & King, (2005)
Service Flexibility Cha-Jan Chang & King, (2005)	Response time and maintenance fees	Cha-Jan Chang & King, (2005)

This work was previously published in the International Journal of Enterprise Information Systems, vol. 5, issue 3, edited by A. Gunasekaran, pp. 1-13, copyright 2009 by IGI Publishing (an imprint of IGI Global).

Chapter 2
Information System Conversion in SMEs

Efrem G. Mallach
University of Massachusetts Dartmouth, USA

ABSTRACT

Information system conversion has been with us since users of punched-card tabulating systems first moved to vacuum-tube computers. However, it is often seen as an afterthought: once the "interesting" work of analysis, design and so on is done, it will somehow happen. This chapter attempts to view the process holistically, from both the technical and human viewpoints, reflecting the fact that information systems have both technical and human components. It shows how ignoring one side or the other can lead to problems, which can be avoided if all aspects are considered together. It proposes a systematic approach to considering these issues and points out benefits of using it.

INTRODUCTION

Conversion from one information system (IS) to another is common in all organizations. Small-medium enterprises (SMEs) are no exception. On the information technology (IT) side, conversion can involve hardware, operating system, database management system and the database it supports, and/or applications. On the human side, procedures must be changed and people must be, if not changed, at least moved (in the sense of change theory, e.g., Schein 1990, not geographically) and retrained.

Effective management of this conversion is vital to IS success. The choice of conversion strategy from one information technology environment to a new one is not easy. A conversion effort may affect any of the four IT components to varying degrees, as well as the human and procedural components of the IS as a whole. It thus involves both technological and organizational/social dimensions, the theme of this book.

This chapter provides a current view of information system conversion, with a focus on small/medium organizations, to provide guidance to professionals faced with a new conversion situation.

BACKGROUND: IT CONVERSION METHODS

The literature (e.g., Palvia, 1991; Mallach, 2006) discusses the coverage in ten MIS and eight systems analysis textbooks) generally recognizes four IT conversion methods:

Direct cut-over: an entire organization stops using the old system at one time and begins using the new one immediately thereafter (perhaps after a natural break in activity, such as over a weekend). This is the riskiest method. The other methods exist to reduce conversion risks. (Direct cut-over is sometimes called *plunge* conversion, for the sake of alliteration and/or to mimic the "four Ps"—Product, Price, Promotion, Placement—that constitute the marketing mix.)

Pilot conversion: Part of an organization uses the new system while the rest continues to use the old. This localizes problems to the pilot group so problem-solving resources can focus on it. However, it can create interface difficulties when organizational units share data.

Phased (modular) conversion: The new system is put into use one module at a time, while the rest of the old system remains in place. This localizes problems to the newly introduced module and its interfaces, so problem-solving resources can focus on it. However, it can create interface difficulties when modules pass data from one to another.

Parallel conversion: The new system is introduced while the old one is still in use. Both systems process business activity, and the results are compared. Once there is confidence that the new system operates properly, the old one is shut down.

As Palvia et al. (1991) point out, the variations on direct cut-over can be combined. This creates four more methods: pilot-phased, pilot-parallel, parallel-phased and pilot-phased-parallel, for a total of eight.

These strategies address the technology side of conversion. However, it also has a human side.

The two are usually treated separately, for the understandable but unfortunate reason that managers' and researchers' interests tend to focus on either technology or people. Reduced risk tends to go hand in hand with increased complexity of the human transition. Effective management of the conversion process requires considering both together.

A Note on Terminology

Some writers use the word *conversion* to refer only to the technological (IT) aspects, calling either the human side or the entire process *implementation*. In this article "conversion" will refer to the entire process. We will use more specific terminology (such as "IT conversion") as appropriate for its subsets, unless the meaning is clear from the context.

Concerns with Parallel IT Conversion

Parallel IT conversion has been a staple of the literature, including textbooks, for decades. Few writers (Rainer & Turban, 2009, among textbooks, is an exception) recognize that it is no longer appropriate. This is for two reasons (Mallach, 2006):

1. When both old and new systems are online, today's usual case, it is impractical to expect users (especially customers) to enter transactions twice.
2. Timing differences can lead to different outputs. Consider a bank whose old system processed checks overnight, but whose new one will handle them as they arrive. A $100 check arrives at 9 am on an account with a balance of $150, whose holder tries to withdraw $100 at noon. The old system would dispense the cash, then bounce the check at night. The new one will pay the check immediately, then refuse the withdrawal.

Either system can be used by itself, but their outputs differ.

As a result, parallel conversion is practical today in only a few situations:

1. Advisory (decision support) systems, where multiple and perhaps differing sources of advice can be reconciled by a human decision-maker.
2. The decreasing number of situations in which the older system is manual.
3. Systems with critical financial or legal implications, where certainty of identical output is required. These are hardly ever customer-facing. Input timing differences cannot be allowed to affect their results.

Parallel conversion is not the same as keeping an older system around as insurance. If the two don't process the same work, with the results compared, it is not parallel conversion.

Therefore, outside these special cases, four of the eight possible IT conversion methods are used today:

1. Direct cut-over;
2. Pilot conversion;
3. Phased conversion; and
4. Pilot-phased conversion: phased, with a pilot group for some or all phases.

An example of pilot-phased conversion is the move by the University of Massachusetts to PeopleSoft's integrated software in the early 2000s. Modules were introduced via pilot groups: for example, its Lowell campus was the first to use the student registration module. After it had been used there for one term, the others moved. The purchasing module was introduced at a different time, with a different pilot campus. Yusuf et al. (2004) give another example in the adoption of ERP by Rolls-Royce.

Of these strategies, direct conversion poses the highest technical risk. Lee (2004) discusses how the Nevada (U.S.) Department of Motor Vehicles created problems for itself by using it. At the same time, it is the simplest transition on both the technical and human sides. The other strategies exist to reduce this risk, but at the expense of additional technical and/or human complexity.

FACTORS AFFECTING CHOICE OF IT CONVERSION STRATEGY

There is no "best" IT conversion strategy. This section gives considerations in choosing an approach. They must be taken as a group, along with other factors that are specific to an organization or system and which therefore cannot be covered here.

Impact of Conversion Type on IT Conversion Strategy

System conversions tend to fall into three main categories:

Manual to automated. This is no longer common, as manual candidates for automation grow increasingly rare, but may arise in small organizations or with specialized functions.

Manual systems are typically easy to partition because physical records limit data sharing. For example, in converting from paper to electronic voting systems, it is easy to use different methods in different polling places. This lends itself to the pilot approach.

Parallel conversion can work here, if all system users are within the organization and duplicate outputs going forward don't create problems. (A restaurant kitchen shouldn't receive duplicate orders on both slips of paper and overhead displays.) Presumably a new computerized system involves less work than the previous manual one, so the incremental work of processing each transaction twice may be acceptable. This can help alleviate employee concerns about the accuracy of a newly computerized way of doing business.

Unlike systems. This might involve, for example, moving from functional "silo" systems to ERP. A major issue here is data conversion: the collection of older systems plus the new one usually use, together, a variety of different files and databases.

In this situation the new system is typically more integrated than the old one was. This suggests phased IT conversion. Each part of the older system can be converted individually to the corresponding module of the new one. However, despite efforts on the part of integrated software vendors to adapt their offerings to SMEs' needs, they remain used primarily by large organizations.

Like systems. An example of this would be CRM to CRM, perhaps moving from hosting the application on a firm's own servers and clients to software-as-a-service or vice versa.

Like systems can be converted via any approach. The best one to use depends on other factors. If one or more pilot groups can be identified, their use is recommended.

Impact of System Type on IT Conversion Strategy

Whether a system is automated or advisory affects IT conversion strategy.

The issue here is whether or not a system updates an organizational database. Advisory systems (decision support, business intelligence, data mining, information retrieval, etc.) do not.

Advisory systems offer more conversion flexibility than automated systems. Something resembling parallel conversion is practical, as two advisory systems need not produce identical outputs; the new one need only produce output at least as useful as the old. This is analogous to asking two human investment advisors for recommendations. Furthermore, since usage

of advisory systems tends to be more sporadic than that of automated systems, and the volume of data entered into them tends to be small, the disadvantage of having to enter input twice is less of a concern. When the U.S. Securities and Exchanges Commission converted its EDGAR system (SEC 2008) from an OS/2-based to a Windows NT-based network in 1999, it used this approach (Messmer, 2000).

Such systems can also use a pilot approach. The pilot group can be self-selected: those who like to be early adopters of new technologies try the new system while the rest of the organization continues to use the old one. All can easily revert to the older one if the new system doesn't meet their needs. If decision-making consistency in an area is important, which would argue for a single advisory system, a pilot group can convert as a unit without impacting others. However, few SMEs have enough decision makers to split off a meaningful pilot group.

Impact of Organization Size on IT Conversion Strategy

Organization size is correlated with other factors. Smaller organizations, such as SMEs on which this book is focused, are more likely than large ones to convert from a manual system, less likely (as noted above) to convert to an unlike system. They are also less likely to use advisory systems than are large ones, since the benefit of such systems is proportional to the size of the organization using it but their cost goes up more slowly. It is important not to confuse the size factor with other factors with which it is correlated.

Small organizations typically have fewer organizational units than large ones, often just one. Data are likely to pertain to all geographic locations or lines of business. This makes it harder to create self-contained pilot groups.

Small organizations have less data in total than larger ones, making it practical to recover from a bad conversion and reducing the value of risk-mitigating strategies. This can make direct cut-over practical.

Smaller organizations also have, obviously, fewer people. People in different areas are more likely to know each other personally and to have developed informal relationships. This gives managers in different work areas personal credibility that their equivalents in a large organization would not have. Small firms may be able to relax some of the "IS managers do this; user managers do that" guidelines given below.

Table 1 that follows summarizes the above guidelines. These should be taken as generalizations, which may be overridden by the circumstances of a specific organization when those are known.

HUMAN FACTORS IN CONVERSION

An information system, as Kroenke (1981) points out, consists of five components: hardware, software, data, procedures and people. Conversion involves all five. Managers ignore any of them at their peril. IS professionals must therefore think about human issues, which may not come easily. That doesn't mean they must become experts on them or manage that aspect of conversion—there are some tasks IS managers cannot do, regardless of ability or competence—but they must be aware of them and work with user managers in the overall process.

Organizational change was studied well before information systems entered the management picture. One seminal work was (Lewin, 1947). It led to the well-known "unfreeze-move-refreeze" model of change management, later expanded upon by Schein (1990) and others, and known today as the Lewin/Schein model. Other models have up to at least eight steps (e.g., Kotter, 1990). The ADKAR method (Hiatt, 2006) describes five required building blocks for successful change (and is named for their first letters):

1. **Awareness** of why change is needed
2. **Desire** to support and participate in the change
3. **Knowledge** of how to change
4. **Ability** to implement new skills and behaviors
5. **Reinforcement** to sustain the change

The first, second and fifth stages are often considered to be in the realm of change management while the third and fourth may be grouped as "training," but they are all needed if the change is to succeed.

The second and fifth stages must be driven by user management. No amount of exhortation by IS experts can create a desire for change. Only users' peers and managers have the required credibility. Knowledge and ability can come from IS in the form of trainers. Awareness of the need for change can come from either side, though the support of users' managers can help technical reasons carry weight. If change is to succeed, user and IS managers must coordinate their activities to cover all five building blocks. IS managers must thus recognize the importance of human factors

Table 1.

System Type	Conversion Type	M/L organizations	Small organizations
Operational	Manual to Automated	Pilot; parallel if duplicate system output is avoided	Direct also practical
	Unlike	Phased or pilot/phased	(Less common)
	Like	Any; pilot usually a good choice	Direct also practical
Advisory		Pilot; parallel	(Less common)

in a conversion and must enlist the support of business unit managers in obtaining it.

For example, a study of ERP implementation in China (Yusuf et al., 2005) found that state-owned enterprises (SOEs) had more difficulty implementing ERP systems than non-SOEs. Technical factors (hardware, software, previous systems, etc.) were similar in both groups. Organizational culture was not. Had the (presumably technical) managers who led SOE conversions been aware of the human factors that led to difficulties in their environment, they could have dealt with them more successfully.

As another example, consider a common employee reaction to impending system replacement: fear.

This reaction is a variation on the misunderstanding that Theodore Levitt pointed out in "Marketing Myopia" (Levitt, 1960). It showed how organizations often misunderstand their strengths, focusing instead on specifics of what they do. The classic example is railroads. They could have become successful airlines, had they recognized the value of understanding passenger handling, baggage handling, ticketing and so on rather than seeing their business (mistakenly, in retrospect) as just rolling large boxes along steel rails.

If large corporations with experienced managers make this error, it is not surprising that information system users do as well—and without realizing it. Employees who fear an IS conversion often see their value to their employer in the specifics of their work, in knowing an existing system at a functional level, rather than in their true underlying strengths. Since any new hire will know the specifics of a new system as well as they do, they fear that their value to their employer will drop—with obvious consequences.

This is, of course, not the case. Experienced employees are valued because they understand when to give a customer a discount, not because they know which screen or sub-menu lets them do it. Unfortunately, few people see the true underlying business value of their day-to-day work that clearly.

"Conversion myopia" can disable a department or more. In extreme cases it can lead to slow-downs, even sabotage. Managers in charge of a conversion must prevent this by discussing with employees what their real value to the organization is based on.

RELATIONSHIPS BETWEEN TECHNICAL AND HUMAN CONSIDERATIONS

A successful conversion must take into account both technical and human factors. They are parts of a single process, though managers often focus on one or the other. As a minimum, the manager responsible for each must be aware of the other and must work closely with the person responsible for that side of the process.

Part of the interrelationship becomes evident when task precedences of the entire process are looked at together. If the unfreezing stage of managing change begins too early, people will be left in limbo: unsatisfied with the status quo, but having no alternative to it. If it begins too late, the moving part will of necessity start before unfreezing is complete. That leads to incomplete movement. Similarly, training must be scheduled at the right time: not too soon, not too late. If the pilot approach to IT conversion is used, it may be necessary to train different employee groups at different times.

Another aspect of pre-conversion training differs from training in other situations: *trainees already know how to do what they're being trained in; they just know how to do it differently.* Trainers must understand their existing mindset in terms of how things are done and reflect that in their approach to the training. That, in turn, may call for them to spend time learning the current system though they don't really have to know it, therefore to start work on a course earlier than they'd otherwise have to, and (if, say, they work for a software supplier whose customers now use different systems) to develop different materials for different audiences even though the content to be taught is the same.

Beyond those, the approaches to the technical and human sides of conversion have implications for each other. For example:

- If direct cut-over is used, procedures may be needed to maintain an audit trail of some or all work in case it is necessary to revert to the previous system and re-enter it. (This may be a good idea in any case, but the lower risk associated with other IT conversion strategies may make it less necessary.)

If such procedures require extra work on the part of some users their purpose, their likely duration and the way those who will work overtime (if any) were selected must be explained. If practical, some indication of management appreciation beyond overtime pay is appropriate.

- If pilot conversion is used, it is important not to create status distinctions on the basis of being, or not, first to use the new system. IS managers are most likely not sensitive to how users read unintended messages in such things.

Example: In converting a nationwide network of distribution centers, it is natural to convert the closest one to headquarters first for proximity to IT support in case of problems. If this is not explained, staff of other centers may think "They always get the good stuff first; we're second-class citizens." Few IS managers will anticipate this reaction or even recognize it when it happens.

- If parallel conversion is used, the need for extra work should be explained even if overtime is compensated.

As with the extra work that may be required for an audit trail in direct cut-over, its purpose, its *likely duration and the way those who will work overtime were selected must be explained. If practical, some indication of appreciation beyond overtime pay is appropriate here as well.*

- If phased conversion is used, the issue is a bit more subtle. Here the problem is that people will use parts of the old system and parts of the new concurrently. The unfreezing-moving-refreezing process will, if carried out in the usual fashion, create dissatisfaction with the old system modules that people are still required to use.

This makes it necessary to approach unfreezing delicately. Enthusiasm for the new system must be created without at the same time creating too much dissatisfaction with the old one. It is impossible to provide general rules for this, as the specifics will vary from case to case. Sensitivity to the issue is the best guide.

Change management, as handled by user managers, must suit the technical IT conversion process. User managers must therefore understand the reasons that led to the technical choices. This can only happen through interaction with the IT personnel who made those choices.

In the other direction, the technical approach must be organizationally (or operationally) as well as technically and economically feasible. No matter how desirable a pilot approach may be on technical grounds, for example, it won't work if the organizational division of labor does not lend itself to the creation of a pilot group.

RECOMMENDATIONS

We recommend this sequence for conversion planning:

1. Study the organization to see which technical approaches are organizationally feasible.

This comes first because the purpose of any information system is to facilitate the work of the organization, not vice versa. It is far more difficult to change how an organization works, especially informal processes rooted deep in its culture, than to do almost anything on the technical side.

This stage must be led by a user manager or a user-focused systems analyst, in close consultation with IS experts who can explain what the different technical strategies imply (for example, for database conversion).

2. If more than one technical approach is feasible, make cost, time and risk estimates for feasible approaches so that one can be chosen. This may involve a one-minute meeting ("We can do direct or pilot, direct is too risky, does everyone agree? OK, then, that settles it.") or an in-depth study.
3. Draw up a project plan showing both the human and technical aspects of the conversion with their interrelationships and dependencies. Those are fundamental, since only through them is it possible to adjust one side of the process if the other goes awry and thus manage the conversion as a whole.
4. Carry out the conversion itself. Organizational culture permitting, and assuming suitable candidates exist, this can be co-managed by two people: one for its technical aspects, one for its human side.

This sequence will lead to fewer implementation failures resulting from a conversion approach which is inappropriate for technical reasons, human reasons, or both. In other words, the probability of a successful system—since a system whose implementation fails has failed as surely as one whose software doesn't work, or whose hardware takes ten minutes to respond to simple queries—is increased.

This approach also forces cooperation between IS and user managers. In environments where this would not happen otherwise, which are unfortunately not rare, this cooperation removes another potential cause of implementation failure.

CONCLUSION

- Conversion must be approached from the technical, human, and economic sides. This is analogous to the requirement, familiar to every systems analyst, that a feasibility study address these aspects.
- Since conversion has technical and human aspects, some tasks must be done by those who are competent in each area. In all but the smallest organizations these are unlikely to be the same managers. Managers in both areas must therefore cooperate to develop a joint plan that addresses both sets of needs.
- An IS or user manager must "own" each aspect of the process. Some technical parts can't be managed from the user side. Some user issues can't be addressed effectively by technically-oriented IS managers.
- Those responsible for the two aspects must coordinate their work throughout the conversion process.

REFERENCES

Hiatt, J. (2006). *ADKAR: a model for change in business, government and our community*. Loveland, Colo: Prosci.

Kotter, J. (1990). *Force for change: How leadership differs from management*. New York, NY: Free Press.

Kroenke, D. (1981). *Business Computer Systems*. Santa Cruz, CA: Mitchell Publishing, (and more accessibly in his more recent books; e.g., *Using*

MIS, Prentice-Hall, 1st ed., 2007, and 2nd ed., 2009)

Lee, O. (2004, March). A case study of Nevada DMV system. *Journal of the Academy of Business and Economics.*

Levitt, T. (1960, July–August). Marketing Myopia. *Harvard Business Review, 82*(7–8), 138.

Lewin, K. (1947). Frontiers in Group Dynamics. Part II-B: Feedback problems of social diagnosis and action. *Human Relations 1,* 147.

Mallach, E. (2006, April–June). System Conversion: Teaching versus Reality. *International Journal of Information and Communication Technology Education 2*(2), 17.

Messmer, E. (2000). Thanksgiving no holiday for EDGAR. *Network World, 17*(42), 18.

Palvia, S., Mallach, E., & Palvia, P. (1991, October). Strategies for Converting from One IT Environment to Another. *Journal of Systems Management, 42*(10), 23.

Rainer, R. K., & Turban, E. (2009). *Introduction to Information Systems: Supporting and Transforming Business* (2nd ed.). Hoboken, NJ: John Wiley & Sons.

Schein, E. (1990). Organizational culture. *American Psychologist, 2,* 109.

SEC Web page. *SEC Filings and Forms* (EDGAR). Accessed at http://www.sec.gov/edgar.shtml on Jan. 5, 2009, last modified Dec. 15, 2008

Yusuf, Y., Gunasekaran, A., & Abthorpe, M. (2004). Enterprise information systems project implementation: A case study of ERP in Rolls-Royce. *International Journal of Production Economics, 87,* 251.

Yusuf, Y., Gunasekaran, A., & Wu, C. (2005, December). Implementation of enterprise resource planning in China. *Technovation.*

This work was previously published in the Journal of Enterprise Information Systems, vol. 5, issue 1, edited by A. Gunasekaran, pp. 44-54, copyright 2009 by IGI Publishing (an imprint of IGI Global).

Chapter 3
Business Process Management as a Critical Success Factor in EIS Implementation

Vladimír Modrák
Technical University of Košice, Slovakia

ABSTRACT

Nowadays, the implementation of business process management modern tools in companies becomes a mater of acceptation of an effective organization management. The first ultimate precondition for achieving this goal is a properly structured company. An attention in the study is placed on business process reengineering due to preparing preconditions for smooth implementation of enterprise information system (EIS). Since there are differences between tools of business processes redesign and information systems development, then a main focus was on overcoming existing semantic gaps. With aim to solve this problem the specific modeling method has been used that was clear for company's staff and usable for EIS designers. Used modeling approach was supported by QPR software.

INTRODUCTION

It is no doubt that the business process management (BPM) gives companies the fundamentals they need to continuously improve enterprise processes and structure and get more from their existing ERP investments. It also known, that many approaches have been evolved from research on BPM. On the other hand there is agreement that business process modeling must be an integral part of the methods for business process management (Hess & Brecht, 1995; Scheer & Nüttgens, 2000; Scheer, 1998). The effective business process management depends on how well it defines responsibilities and forces an employee to take control of their own performance. The first ultimate precondition for achieving this goal is a properly structured company.

Since management of Original Equipment Manufacturing (OEM), where presented study was conducted, was not confident whether company's internal and external activities are univocally defined, this reality motivated given company to change this situation. Particularly, in coherence with ISO 9000:2000 their focus had been oriented

DOI: 10.4018/978-1-60566-892-5.ch003

Figure 1. Phases of enterprise reengineering

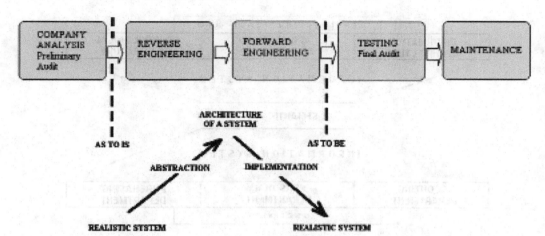

on gradual transformation of functionally oriented management to process-oriented management system. In this effort they went through more developmental periods that are described in this study. A concurrent attention had been placed on business process redesign due to preparing preconditions for smooth implementation of enterprise information system.

The Company pays special attention to the technical innovations by promoting a modern quality management style. Similarly as many other small and medium enterprises (SMEs), company started with the traditional vertically arranged organizational structure that was represented in a graphical form by an organizational chart. It was a hierarchical structure with a chief executive officer and other executive at the top, small number layers of management below this, with the majority of employees at the bottom of the pyramid. The jobs in given organizational structure was grouped by function into departments such as accounting, sales, human resources, and so on.

The chapter is structured in the following way. A theoretical background on an interrelation of organization models and IS architecture-designing issues are described in the following section. Current directions in business process modeling are dealt in section 3. Then selected methodological

aspects of the process modeling technique used for the creation of business process models in real case are presented. The final sections discuss future trends and some decisive findings from the case study.

BACKGROUND

It is common knowledge that the introduction of Enterprise Information Systems in SMEs requires a principal restructuring of the Business processes (BP) and management systems of an organization, simply Enterprise Reengineering with its typical steps (see figure 1).

Usually, reengineering project in organization presents a complex task, normally assigned to external consultants, with the aim to transform the current functionally-oriented organizational model to process-based organizational pattern. Greasley (2004) states that a process-based approach plays crucial role in the implementation of an information system and claims that process mapping and business process simulation support of current process design. When we want to get the pertinent information elements into the information system, we should name the unnamed, make them explicit, and organize them into a simple

Figure 2. Different views of users and designers to IS

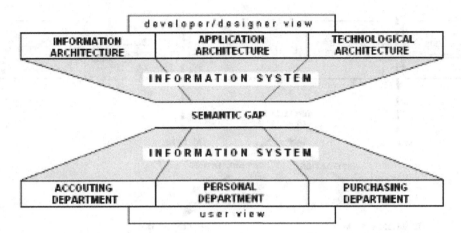

structure and process. Accordingly, it could be seemed that process based approach is implicit in each IS designing technique. In reality, process based approach in IS design rather means a transformation of process-oriented organizational model into a IS design model.

Accordingly, organizational structure models might correspond with the architecture of an EIS as much as possible. According to Vasconcelos et al. (2005), application architecture of enterprise IS has to be a part of an enterprise organizational model. In reality, a consistency of enterprise organization models and architectures of enterprise information system is more or less unusual. In this connection Kalnins et al.(1998) compared tools and languages for business process reengineering and found out that 'higher level business goals have not got a real semantic link with other parts of modeling'. The reason of inconsistency of enterprise organization models and architectures of enterprise information system is that information system development methodologies have traditionally been inspired by programming concepts, not organizational ones, leading to semantic gaps between the system and its environment (Castro et al., 2002). Zhuang et al. (2007) define a semantic gap in an information system as 'the inefficacy in information transmission through representation,

especially when an information bearer is unable to carry the information that it is supposed to. Accordingly, semantic gaps between IS users and designers is one of the potential realm in the deployment of the enterprise information systems applications. Basically, this phenomenon results from different views of users and designers to IS and their different knowledge levels. The users of IS understand it in simplified way as an operation automation tool, mainly used in data processing and accessing. Designers of IS or its part understand it principally as HW/SW subsystems and their interaction. These contradictory notions are shown in Figure 2, in which chosen components are used as an example (Modrák, 2007).

It is obvious that outlined semantic gap cannot be replaced completely. The goal should be to reduce it to a level allowing relieving the shortage made by it, when creating and deploying IS. The way of minimizing this semantic gap is possible through process modeling approach leading up to merge of process models to process maps in the phase before IS design and development. A precondition for exploitation of such process maps is understandability for users and simultaneously usability for IS developers (consultants). In opposite way, even though the EIS is sophistically designed, possible deficiencies are practically anticipated. In other words, to ensure better operability of enterprise activities through IS without detailed knowledge of process relations in various levels of decomposition of enterprise activities is rather complicated. This potential risk is not a crucial issue for designers of IS, moreover if they know that client/user is responsible for information requirement determination. But companies are not fully known of this reality. It confirms the fact that companies mostly use simple models of organization structures without formal determination of work and information flows and reflects a lack of process management in organization. By this thesis, IS architecture and subsequently effectiveness of EIS strongly depends on maturity of process management in organization. This is a role of Business Process Management that presents systematically managing all of a company's business processes and attempts to continuously improve processes in organization.

A successful transformation of process-oriented organizational model into a IS design model requires being accepted two basic conditions:

- process based model of organization has to be continuously optimized and sufficiently unambiguous,
- notation of process based model of organizational will be equally familiar for two sides,
- involved company's staff and designers of IS.

Then such models form the basis of comprehensive business reference, detailing how the entire operation in company fits together (White & Miers, 2008).

CURRENT DIRECTIONS IN BUSINESS PROCESS MODELING

According to Farnken et al. (1997) models of business processes can be dividing into exten-

sive and intensive model structures. In *extensive model structures* of the business processes are the processes described as an integrated whole. With such a model, investigation is not concentrated on internal process structure and its behavior. An extensive model describes the process from the viewpoint of its environment, which usually consists of external or internal suppliers and customers. On the contrary, *intensive structures models* of business processes are used to describe the entities interactions inside the part of the system that is being investigated. Such models describe business processes from the viewpoint of their internal objects, sources and other entities such as the staff, technological components, protocols, etc..

Intensive models of processes structures can be additionally divided into:

- Workflow-oriented model structures, which represent the behavior of a business process from the perspective of a single item that crosses through the process.
- Functional-oriented model structures that reveal the behavior of functional units (departments) from the viewpoint of subsequent business functions. These models represent the obsolete functional approach of organization structuring.

Technically, horizontal structuring and vertical structuring of business process models are mostly recognized (Jonkers, 1997). Horizontal structuring helps to handle each customer engagement with guaranteed service. Vertical structuring serves to distinguish different levels of details, or abstraction levels.

In developing business process management notation by the Object Management Group were differentiated the following levels of process modeling (White & Miers, 2008):

- **Process maps:** Simple flow charts of the activities; a flow diagrams without a lot of

Figure 3 Process maturity model

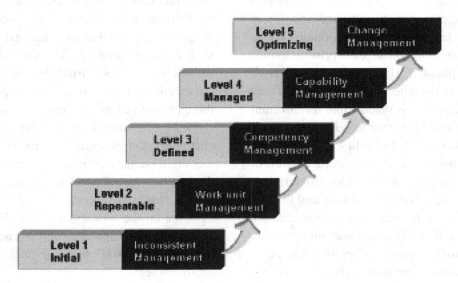

details others than names of the activities and the broad decision conditions.

- **Process descriptions:** Provide more extensive information on the process, such as the roles of involved actors, the data, information and so on.
- **Process models:** Detailed flow charts encompassing sufficient information such that the process is amenable to analysis and simulation.

Process models can be created or presented using many different methodologies. Basically, each business process model is built for a different purpose. In this context can be identified many potential uses of process models (Browning, 2002):

1. Program planning,
2. Baseline for continuous improvement,
3. Knowledge retention and learning,
4. Process visualization,
5. Training,
6. Framework for metrics,
7. Compliance, audit, and assessments,
8. Program execution.

In the framework of this chapter it is focused on process based models of organization that helps organizations in transitioning to the advanced and efficient BPM practices. Accordingly, it is pertinent to mention Process Maturity Model (PMM) approach, which was built on success with software Capability Maturity Model (CMM). A modified version of PMM describing main development phases is shown in Figure 3.

For the Level 1 is symptomatic that processes are usually ad hoc and chaotic. At this stage, business processes need to be studied identified and catalogued. Work unit management (Level 2) assumes that basic standards and tools in business process management are adopted. Key attributes of Process Maturity Level 3 include that all management processes are well defined, established and controllable. At maturity Level 4, processes are quantitatively managed and the non-conformances of process are known. According to Reitzig et al. (2002) 'A critical distinction between a defined process and a quantitatively managed process is the predictability of the process performance'. Organization at maturity Level 5 is expected to document continuous improvement action plans for both innovation and *process* improvement.

Figure 4. Process-oriented model of organization

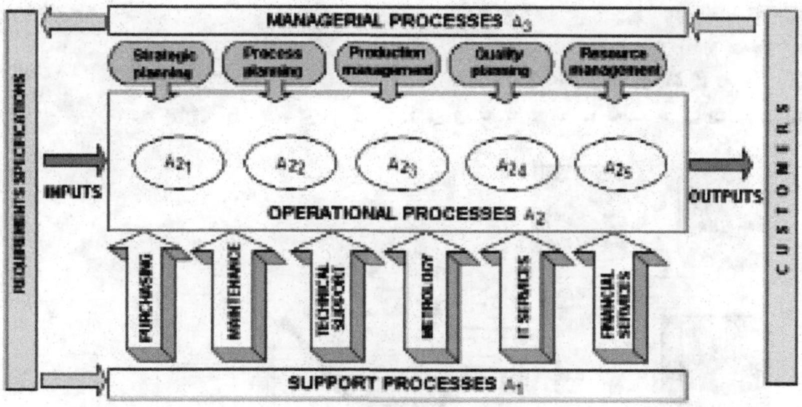

Moreover, it is assumed to employ the continuous transfer of work experiences across the organization (Kováč & Svač, 2007).

THE CASE ON BUSINESS PROCESS MODELING

Due to the company's focus on ISO 9000 series standards company's quality management team originally prepared first version of process-oriented model of organization based on a gradual decomposition, which is shown in figure 4.

It copies a typical known approach to the categorization of business processes into operational, support, and managerial processes.

In a proposed approach a hierarchical classification framework for the systematic rebuilding of business processes was used. The classification of processes is based on splitting up them to three hierarchical levels, which are represented by (Modrák & Manduľák, 2008):

• so called Unified Enterprise processes (UEP),
• so called Integrated Processes (IP),
• so called elementary processes (EP).

Smaller objects than Elementary Processes are hierarchically (top to bottom) divided to two groups:

• Complex Tasks (CT),
• Activities (A).

Substantial problem concerning originally applied approach to process-oriented model of organization lied in practical impossibility to create overall network of interaction between connected processes. It was due to a lack of unequivocal methodological rules. In further presented approach is applied the hierarchical classification framework to built up process based organizational model that will allow previously segregated business units to work in synthesis and enable business units to integrate processes with external entities and consolidates redundant processes across functional areas. It closely corresponds to business process integration approach (Ulrich, 2001), which results in an enterprise that is more efficient and effective, which in turn drives up revenues and drives down costs. It was a ground of motivation to develop the following method for business processes mapping and modeling that is based on a process decomposition resulting in a set of business structure models, which are represented by diagrams in the order given (Modrák, 2005):

Figure 5. System diagram

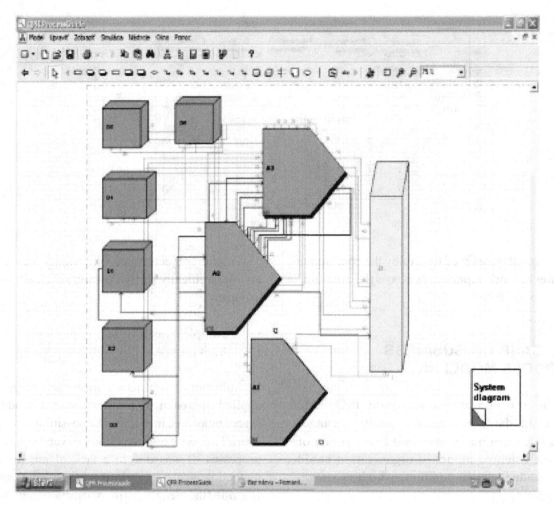

- System diagram,
- Context diagrams,
- *Commodity flow diagrams* of the first and second decomposition stage,
- *State transition diagrams* of the first and second decomposition stage.

In the sense of the outlined procedure of redesigning business processes, the first step of this method is the creation of a System Diagram. Its purpose is to separate so-called Unified Enterprise Processes (UEP) from the original arrangement of processes. Subsequently, relations between them and the environment of the enterprise are

specified. The environment is represented in a System diagram by External Entities, with which the system communicates, while their content is not a subject of analysis in the following steps. They usually represent the initial source of commodity flows, or their end consumer. In fact it represents the starting base of modelling processes, from which other diagrams are derived using the principle of process decomposition. Based on the transformation of previous process-oriented model of organization (showed in figure 4) has been created System diagram (see figure 5).

Subsequently are created the Context diagrams for each Unified Enterprise Process depicted in

Figure 6. Context diagram of the process A2

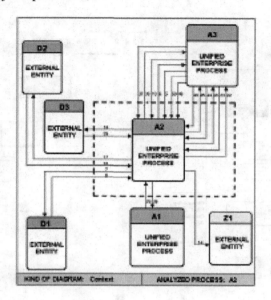

a System diagram. Individual Context diagrams express relations only of the given UEP with its environment. All surrounding elements of the given UEP in Context diagram, irrespective of whether they represent objects outside the enterprise or internal processes, are considered as External entities. Supplier/customers rules might be the same as for external as for internal subjects. An example of the Context diagram of the process A2 is depicted in figure 6.

Consecutively, Commodity flow diagrams of the first stage are designed for A1, A2 and A3 processes, which describe relations usually between integrated processes. Two of them for the A2 and A3 processes are shown on Figure 7. The purpose of the Commodity flow diagrams is gradual decomposition of UEP, up to the level of Elementary Processes. Commodity flow diagrams of the second stage are constructed in an analogous way as Commodity flow diagrams of the first stage. It is the last stage of Commodity flow diagrams because the Elementary Processes, which present the objects of modeling in this diagram's class, are considered to be the primitive processes.

The objective of the state transition diagrams (STDs) is the description of an internal structure and mutual relations of tasks and/or activities of Elementary Processes. State transition diagrams describe all of the states that an object can have, the events under which an object changes state and the conditions that must be fulfilled before the transition will occur. State Transition Diagrams are basically used for describing the behavior of individual objects. Hoverer, STDs have limited possibilities for describing the collaboration between objects that cause the transitions. This level of modeling is also pertinent for IS designers, through which proper form modelling technique is selected. The most popular variety of STD in the programming area of OOD (Object Oriented Design) is the Harel state chart (Harel, 1987). Example of one STD drawn by QPR software in this study is described in Figure 8.

In analogical way, "STDs of the first stage" are sequentially decomposed to the level of State Transition Diagrams of the second stage.

An important condition in the designing and subsequent modeling of process diagrams is to maintain the consistency of inputs and outputs, so that it is possible to create process maps, starting at the level of Commodity flow diagrams of the first stage, up to the level of state transition diagrams.

Figure 7. (a) Commodity flow diagram (CFD) for the process A2; (b) CFD for the process A3

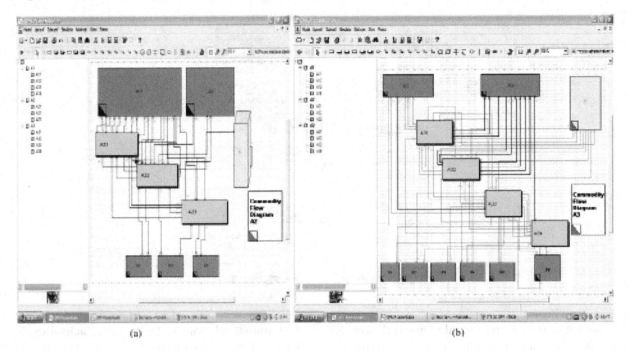

(a)　　　　　　　　　　　　　　　　(b)

An example of the creation of the process map from two Commodity flow diagrams of the first stage specified in the previous charts (showed in Figure 6) is depicted in Figure 9.

Such maps are defining where the business process starts and ends and are identifying the specific activities that need to be performed by the process owners. From those maps the managers

Figure 8. STD of the first decomposition stage for the process A211

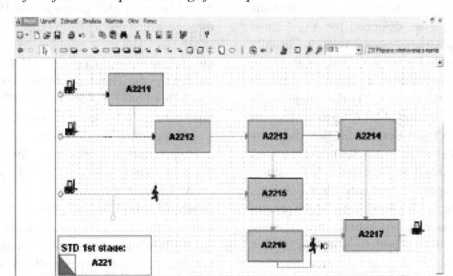

Figure 9. Process map fragment by the merging of two CFDs at the first level of decomposition.

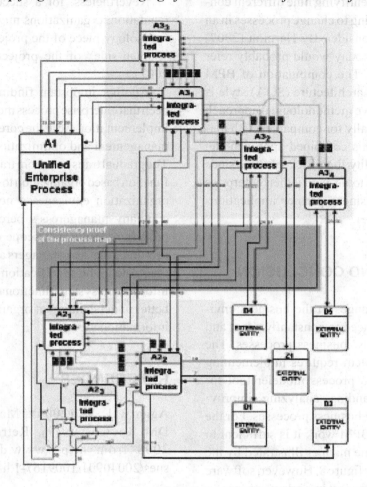

can easily define critical processes and analyze them in detail. This approach evidently differs from the method with which the company accomplished requirements of standard for quality management system.

FUTURE TRENDS

According to Van der Aalst (2003) in BPM using information technology dominated data-driven approaches during the last decades. Consequently, the modeling of business processes was often neglected and existing process structures had been directly adapted to information technology. In the

present time, more and more company's processes are being conducted under the external supervisors of information systems that are driven by process models. However, the role of IS supervision does not aim at taking on the duties of company management alike as IS supervision can not guarantee avoiding problems arising from organizational changes. When spiking about process based IS, one of the most important aspects is the selection of techniques for process architecture. White & Miers (2008) states that functional decomposition should be definitely avoided and recommend thinking of processes as a dynamic network of interacting process instances. Rummler & Brache (1990) introduced important framework of business methodology identifying nine different concerns that anyone trying to change processes in an organization must consider. By Harmon (2007) 'software architects today would probably refer to it as framework'. The combination of BPM and service-oriented architecture (SOA) style is considered as effective methodological approach for the future, especially for companies with major ERP systems. This combined approach can bring greater flexibility than ERP systems since integration of these tools with other enterprise applications and business partner applications can be achieved easier.

DISCUSSION AND CONCLUSION

Competition and changes in the business environment induce the need to constantly adapt and improve the company' business processes. The solution of this problem requires implementing an effective business process modeler tool for visualizing, understanding, analyzing, improving and documenting business processes. For the beginning phase of BPM work it is sufficient to model processes in the manner illustrated by the schemes in figure 5 or figure 8. However, software is often considered the most important in successfully implementing BPM initiatives (Aggarwal, 2004). For this purpose we implemented QPR software that supports all key elements of business processes management - from modeling and documentation, communicating, measurement and analysis, to continuous process management and improvement. It served us to create comprehensive business process models with accordance to the presented approach illustrating the current status of operations. Due to the fact that QPR software enables to generate process maps, equally as was shown in figure 8, it opens a further door to modern business process management. Moreover, this software tool can be integrated with other systems using a web-based portal that provides an effective means for communicating, monitoring and continuously improving business processes.

Nevertheless, for a successful BPM implementation, organizations might look beyond the technology piece of the project and focus on the "human-side" of the project as well (Deepak, 2007).

Another important finding in this work has been that enterprise process modeling; analysis and implementation are at the core of business process management and optimization of EIS designing. The gradual transition from traditional hierarchical function based organization to the process-oriented organization envisages a noticeable change in company manageress's perception of business process redesign in a scope of reengineering. It presumes that key managers are not only aware of their role in the specification of requirements on information system functionalities, but they have better understanding of organizational context of information system.

REFERENCES

Aggarwal, R. (2004). Making BPM work. *DM Review*, *14*(9), Retrieved October 1, 2008 from http://www.dmreview.com/issues/20040901/1009167-1.html

Browning, T. R. (2002). Process integration using the design structure matrix. *Systems Engineering*, *5*(3), 180–193. doi:10.1002/sys.10023

Castro, J., Kolp, M., & Mylopoulos, J. (2002). Towards requirements-driven information systems engineering: Rhe Tropos project. *Information Systems*, *6*, 365–389. doi:10.1016/S0306-4379(02)00012-1

Chrissis, M., Konrad, M., & Shrum, S. (2003). *CMMI: Guidelines for process integration and product improvement*. Boston: Addison-Wesley.

Davenport, T. H., & Short, J. E. (1990). The new industrial engineering: Information technology and business process redesign. *Sloan Management Review*, 11–27.

Deepak, V. (2007). *Simplifying BPM implementations: Business process management*. Executive Insights Gordian Transformation Partners Inc. Retrieved October 1, 2008 from http://www.bptrends.com/resources_publications

Franken, H. M., de Weger, M. K., & Jonkers, H. (1997). Structural and quantitative perspectives on business process modelling and analysis. In *Proceedings of the 11th European Simulation Multiconference, Istanbul, June 1-4, 1997* (pp. 595-599). Ghent, Belgium: Society for Computer Simulation International.

Greasley, A. (2006). Using process mapping and business process simulation to support a process-based approach to change in a public sector organization. *Technovation, 26*(1), 95–103. doi:10.1016/j.technovation.2004.07.008

Harel, D. (1987). A visual formalism for complex systems. *Science of Computer Programming, 8*(3), 231–274. doi:10.1016/0167-6423(87)90035-9

Harmon, P. (2007). *Business process change: A guide for business managers and BPM and Six Sigma* (2nd ed). San Francisco, CA: Morgan Kaufmann Publishers Inc.

Hess, T., & Brecht, L. (1995). *State of the art des business process redesign*. Wiesbaden, Gabler-Verlag.

Jonkers, H. (1997). *The application of hybrid modeling techniques for business process* performance *analysis*. In Kaylan & Lehmann (eds.), *Proceedings of the 11th European Simulation Multi-conference, Istanbul, Turkey, 1-4 June* (pp. 779-786).

Kalnins, A., Kalnina, D., & Kalis, A. (1998) Comparison of tools and languages for business process reengineering. In *Proceedings of the Third International Baltic Workshop on Databases and Information Systems, Riga, July, 24-28.*

Kováč, M., & Švač, V. (2007). Knowledge sharing in project Equal. In *EQUAL for Automotive* (pp. 10-12). Technical University of Košice.

Lopez, H., Massacci, F., & Zannone, N. (2007). Goal-equivalent secure business process re-engineering for e-health. In J. Sztipanovits, et al. (eds.), *Workshop on model-based trustworthy health information systems.* September 28 - October 3, Toulouse, France.

Modrák, V. (2005). Business process improvement through optimisation of its structural properties. In L. Fischer, (Ed.) *Workflow handbook 2005* (pp. 75-90). Lighthouse Point, FL: Future Strategies.

Modrák, V. (2007). Bridging organizational structure and information system architecture through process (LNCS 4537, pp. 445-455).

Modrák, V., & Manduľák, J. (2008). LPH Vranov n/T-Case study. In L. Fischer (Ed.), *BPM excellence in practice 2008 – Using BPM for competitive advantage* (pp. 51-62). Lighthouse Point, FL: Future Strategies.

Reitzig, R. W., Miller, J. B., West, D., & Kile, R. L. (2003). *Achieving capability maturity model integration maturity level 2 using IBM Rational software's* [White Paper]. Retrieved October 1, 2008 from http://www.cognence.com/pdfs/CMMI_ProcessAndRequirementsManagement_WhitePaper%20v1.0.pdf

Rummler, G., & Brache, A. (1990). *Improving performance: How to manage the white space on the organization chart*. San Francisco: Jossey-Bass.

Scheer, A.-W. (1998). *ARIS – Business process frameworks* (2nd ed.). Berlin.

Scheer, A. W., & Nüttgens, M. (2000). ARIS architecture and reference models for business process management (LNCS 1806, pp. 301-304).

Ulrich, M. (2001). *Critical success factors in a business process integration initiative* [Tactical Strategy Group White Papers]. Retrieved October 1, 2008 from http://www.ebizq.net/topics/ bpm/ features/2602.html.

Van der Aalst, W. M. P. (2003). *Business process management: Past, present, future* [BPTrends White Papers]. Retrieved October 1, 2008 from http://www.bptrends.com/resources_publications

Vasconcelos, A., Sousa, P., & Tribolet, J. (2005). *Information system architecture evaluation: from software to enterprise level approaches.* Paper presented at 12th European Conference on Information Technology Evaluation (ECITE 2005), Turku, Finland.

White, S., & Miers, D. (2008). *BPMN Modeling and reference guide.* Lighthouse Pt, FL: Future Strategies Inc.

Zhuang, Q., Feng, J., & Bao, H. (2007). Measuring semantic gap: An information quantity perspective. *5th IEEE International Conference on Industrial Informatics, 2*, 669-674.

Chapter 4
Product Lifecycle Management:
State-of-the-Art and Future Perspectives

Wai M. Cheung
University of Bath, UK

Dirk Schaefer
Georgia Institute of Technology, USA

ABSTRACT

While most SMEs in general are willing to invest into PLM systems, many are still apprehensive to the sometimes large initial investment to be made in terms of both software cost and the time needed to implement and integrate such system into their digital enterprise technology infrastructure. In light of this, it is crucial for their decision makers not only to understand the current PLM market, but also to become familiar with emerging trends and future developments in order to select a PLM solution that best fit the needs of their enterprise. In this chapter, the authors summarize a detailed analysis of the PLM market with the aim to provide educators, students, and decision makers in industry with an overview of the current PLM market as a whole. In addition, emerging trends and future developments are addressed.

INTRODUCTION

Due to continuously increasing complexity in product development, more and more Small and Medium-sized Enterprises (SMEs) need to utilize a wide range of technological tools to document and manage their product development activities throughout the entire product-life cycle chain. One type of software systems to aid this process is Product Lifecycle Management (PLM). PLM is a term used to describe the process of managing the entire life cycle of a product from its conception, through design and manufacturing, to service and disposal. PLM is also considered a set of capabilities that enable an enterprise to effectively and efficiently innovate and manage its products and related services throughout the entire business life cycle (Stark, 2004). Due to the rate at which the PLM industry is evolving, there is a widespread confusion with regards to what PLM systems actually are capable of. Unfortunately, there is no unique definition of PLM. Any potential definition of PLM in broader

DOI: 10.4018/978-1-60566-892-5.ch004

terms needs to account for both the main purpose of these systems and the PLM market's rapid evolution and development.

Two widely used definitions introduced by two well established PLM research companies, namely *AMR Research* and *CIMdata*, read as follows: According to AMR (Burkett, 2002), PLM systems cover five core functionalities, which are useful in identifying the quality of the management support they provide:

(i) Product Data Management (PDM), the predecessor of PLM, provides functionalities that manage and publish product data;

(ii) Collaborative Product Design, which provides functionalities that apply to product design and manufacturing process design;

(iii) Direct Material Sourcing, which handles the product data that is relevant to the suppliers and vendors of the product;

(iv) Customer Needs Management, which Deals with the data of the product with regards to the customers; and

(v) Product Portfolio Management, which consists of the management, reporting and presentation of product data as needed for a general overview of all products a user may be interested in.

According to CIMdata (2007), PLM systems can be classified into two sub-groups:

(1) Tools that help facilitate fundamental intellectual property creation including all the applications that are used to create, analyze and simulate products and plants e.g.; and

(2) Collaborative Product Data Management (cPDm), which consists of the intellectual property management including collaboration, visualization, vaulting, and sharing of product information e.g. content and document management, product data management and digital manufacturing.

While most SMEs in general are willing to invest into PLM systems, many are still apprehensive to the sometimes large initial investment to be made in terms of both software cost and the time needed to implement and integrate such system into their digital enterprise technology infrastructure. In light of this, it is crucial for their decision makers not only to understand the current PLM market, but also to become familiar with emerging trends and future developments in order to select a PLM solution that best fit the needs of their enterprise.

In this chapter, the authors summarize a detailed analysis of the PLM market with the aim to provide educators, students, and decision makers in industry with an overview of the current PLM market as a whole. In addition, emerging trends and future developments are addressed. The uniqueness of the overview presented lies in the way the PLM market analysis was conducted. The authors carried out three different types of analysis:

(1) An analysis of the commercial PLM market detailing its movements as well as requirements of specific industries within the PLM market;

(2) A state-of-the-art analysis depicting the variety and types of products available in the market today as well as the direction in which they are likely to move in the near future; and

(3) A detailed analysis of five major PLM products describing a method of analysis that can be used by decision makers to gain a better understanding of the functionalities of specific PLM systems with the prospect of investing in one of them.

BACKGROUND

In the late 1990's, there was a shift of focus in Product Data Management (PDM) technology. Rather than focusing on individual companies as before, PDM systems were enhanced in order to address companies supply chain areas as well. At the time, this was referred to as Collaborative Product Data Management (cPDM) and Collaborative Product Commerce (CPC). Despite of this, on a broader scale, PDM was still the common term used in industry and academia (Hameri, 1998). Later, a new generation of software systems, so-called Product Lifecycle Management (PLM) system, evolved from the PDM systems. Portella (2002) described PLM systems as an enterprise-wide Information Technology, "an infrastructure to support management of product definition throughout its complete lifecycle from initial concept to product obsolescence". Including workflow management, PLM systems, as a single source of product information, ensure that up-to-date information are available and accessible for the right people in the right format at the right time. PLM is also viewed as "an effective tool in managing the product definition supply chain by serving as an informational bridge connecting OEMs, partners, subcontractors, vendors, consultants and customers" (Miller, 2003).

In recent years there have been relatively few comprehensive reviews on PLM-related topics. Ming (2005) conducted a survey on how world-leading academics pioneered in product lifecycle research. Rangan (2005) discusses the evolution of PDM/PLM over the past two decades, issues in PLM implementation, as well as future development directions. In order to close this gap in the literature available, an overview a three-phase analysis of the commercial PLM market is presented.

Commercial PLM Markets Analysis

In this section, a first analysis of the commercial PLM market is presented. The focus is on the development and growth of the PLM market in various industrial sectors.

PLM Market History

In 2003, which was a particularly competitive year for PLM system vendors due to severe price pressures, vendors were heard to be gaining strategic deals by offering discounts of up to 50% from the list prices for the traditional PDM systems they were offering the years before. The market mood improved substantially over 2004 and 2005 and exceeded CIMdata expectations with the cPDm market showing 16% growth and tools showing 6% (Miller, 2005). PLM investments were forecasted to continue their climb over the next five years, reaching an estimated $26.3 billion by 2010 Five top vendors began to dominate the market: Dassault Systémes, UGS, PTC MatrixOne, SAP and Agile. These companies were achieving high returns due to steady sales of new licenses and good application of services to current customers. There were also a growing number of niche companies appearing, many of them being bought out by larger companies for their specialist functionalities. In summary, PLM investments regained momentum, the PLM economy is developing and the market is expanding. (Miller, 2005; CIMdata, 2007; Burkett et al., 2007).

Industry-Sector Specific PLM Requirements

In the following sections, industry-sector specific PLM requirement with regard to Aerospace, Defence, Automotive, High-tech, Telecom, Petrochemical, Pharmaceutical, and Consumer Packaged Goods are discussed. The purpose is to point out that one-size-fits-all does apply to the market of PLM systems development.

Aerospace and Defence

Aerospace and Defence (A&D) develop products with extremely complex product lifecycles that must be traceable for several decades. Their designs are usually based on latest technological breakthroughs and must be documented precisely to ensure that the intended product quality and associated performance is achieved. In this industry sector, testing and validation of design and materials are crucial parts of the overall process and high accuracy is required throughout. The vast amount of changes that occur throughout the product design and development process must be reliably communicated to all parties involved to ensure correct implementation. In particular, mechanical design related geometry is of utmost importance because both material and tooling requirements are critical. In Aerospace and Defence, appropriate PLM support is crucial. While ERP systems still provide much of the assistance to procurement and manufacturing operations in this industrial branch, PLM is more suitable for managing the product lifecycle in both its entire breadth and depth (Burkett et al, 2002; Burkett et al, 2003, CIMdata, 2004).

Automotive Industry

According to CIMdata (2007), there are four overall trends that the automotive industry faces:

(1) Globalization of markets;
(2) The need to innovate faster and more cost effectively;
(3) Mandated local production to penetrate growing markets; and
(4) Reducing total manufactured vehicle cost.

This industry needs feature-level engineering control because of the high cost and lead times associated with production tooling. Their CAD 3D geometry must translate from the computer to metal with very high accuracy so that accurate predictions on manufacturing costs can be made. In addition, sharing design detail is a high priority to gain efficient communication and collaboration with all companies and suppliers involved in the product lifecycle.

High-Tech and Telecom

These industries offer utilities that require a high degree of asset tracking and maintenance. They serve virtually the entire population of a region and consequently have a large complex network of systems to maintain. These industries need to have good configuration rule sets for selling and making to order. Efficient bill of materials management is also of key importance. Variable performance levels in basic components such as processors or I/O devices means that substituting parts is very doable and can be an arbitrage opportunity from a sourcing perspective. In the High-tech and Telecom industry, PLM needs to serve as an asset management tool that is very important for both of these sectors. In particular, it is essential to have efficient document management capabilities in order to deal with the vast amount of consumer information coming in after product launch (Burkett et al, 2002; Burkett et al, 2003, CIMdata, 2004).

Petrochemical Industry

The facilities used within this industry are extremely capital-intensive and have major safety and environmental factors involved in their design, operation and maintenance. According to CIMdata (2007), there are three constituencies in the petrochemical process industry that are interested in PLM:

- Engineering Procurement and Construction contractors (EPC)
- Suppliers to EPC's
- Owner/operators of plants or facilities

In this industrial sector it is important to maintain reliable records of plant design and maintenance information, thereby enabling access to that information quickly in the event of an equipment breakdown. By providing people of the three constituencies mentioned above context-specific access to the same plant information, work in each of these areas can be done concurrently thus reducing the time for a new plant to come on line. PLM support with regard to asset management and plant management is also critical. Document management, engineering change management, configuration management and program management are also important functionalities that PLM systems need to cover for this industrial branch (Burkett et al, 2002; Burkett et al, 2003, CIMdata, 2004).

Pharmaceuticals and Consumer Packaged Goods

The requirements to PLM systems in these industrial branches are similar to those of the petrochemical industry both during plant design/ construction and in managing assets after the plant is in operation. This industrial sector also has its own unique requirements. During product development, there is a need to design packaging, labelling and delivery devices (such as inhalers). Regulatory compliance has a key influence on these industries e.g. the product approval stage of a new drug, truth in labelling for food and beverage or emissions controls management.

Pharmaceuticals have to support high-stakes development and test processes, including clinical trials and basic research and development. Here, the major focus is on discovery. Unfortunately, the features of current PLM systems do not address this directly. Clinical trials management systems and labelling are areas that these companies require their PLM solution to cover, including integrated documentation management.

While in the Consumer Packaged Goods (CPG) industry, product information is not systematically independent, it still must be managed in minute details such as recipes and labels. Specification management has started to emerge as a very useful PLM application, bringing together products that are purchased from the same suppliers. That way, bulk purchases make substantial savings on

raw materials (Burkett et al, 2002; Burkett et al, 2003, CIMdata, 2004).

Discussion of the Commercial PLM Market Analysis

The PLM market is maturing yet still evolving. New smaller producers of PLM systems are appearing with focused systems for specific niche markets. While more SME's are becoming more willing to invest in PLM systems they are still apprehensive of the large initial investment for the implementation of these systems. A potential solution to this is to either sell a modular system or a hosted system that can be "rented" for a certain amount of time. Such a modular system would provide base functionalities with specialized add-ons that can cater to specific industries. This would require less customization and thus less capital investment. A "rented" system could be used by small companies to test the system and identify potential benefit gains before making a substantial investment in IT. However, this second solution might lead to issues with security as the PLM system would not be owned by the company using it.

More recently, the cPDm (non-CAD) part of the PLM market has shown high growth and a number of vendors have seen solid increases in sales of cPDm offerings. These offerings target the mid-market more than the larger investors, and many vendors are seeing this as an area of expected growth. Investments in cPDm enabling technologies and solutions have consistently increased since CIMdata began tracking the market in 1989 (CIMdata, 2003). More and more vendors are entering the market targeting the mid-market sector with mainly cPDm based PLM solutions. According to AMR Research, the highest growth rates are in non-traditional industries, including Pharmaceuticals, Apparel, Retail and Petrochemical. This fact has proved that the utilization of PLM systems is not limited to companies that require PLM 'tools' but also require improved management capabilities (AMR Research PLM Team, 2004; CIMdata, 2003).

New license sales drive future services and maintenance revenues, leading to a continuing overall growth. As PLM services have grown so have the services associated with implementation of these programs. However, the rate of growth of services may not match the growth of sales as closely as it has in the past because of poorer companies investing in PLM system. "Services growth will be less in the mid-market as small to midrange companies cannot afford significant service fees (CIMdata, 2003; Miller, 2005).

Overall, the PLM market is reaching a mature stage. The first few industries to implement PLM solutions on a larger scale were Transportation, Aerospace and Defence. Their markets still continue to grow, however, at a slower rate compared to the other industries. The older maturity of the Transportation, Aerospace and Defence industries makes them less attractive for current PLM system vendors. A common area in which the other before mentioned industries requires strong PLM functionalities is that of plant management. There will be much more research being conducted by PLM vendors into this area in the near future, and new PLM products that address this demand are likely to appear on the market soon. Asset Management is another area of PLM that was not of key importance to the older industries but is more important for new industries. It is likely that this area will see increased vendor investment so that they can capitalize on the extra growth predicted in these industries.

Even more detailed PLM system improvements that target specific industries are likely. An anticipated growth rate in this sector will further shift the focus on specific niche markets for PLM system vendors (Burkett et al, 2003, CIMdata, 2003).

PLM Systems: State-of-the-Art Analysis

In Figure 1, the key functionalities of the forty-five different PLM systems that were analyzed in the research project leading to this study are shown. Five of the PLM systems were selected for further analysis and will be covered in detail at a later point. The data presented was collected by 'ticking a box' whenever a particular PLM system possessed a specific functionality. Each tick was given the value of 'one', a total of the number of ticks each PLM product received was then calculated to provide a score for each system. The five specific areas that were chosen for 'highest relevance to the PLM market' were: Databases, Operating Systems, Industry Standards, Target company size and Scripting languages. For each of the areas a graph showing their current proportion of support by the PLM market as well as a brief discussion follows. In addition, a final overall discussion of the results recognizing recurring themes in industry specific discussions is provided.

In the following sections, summaries of key characteristics of the systems analyzed will be presented.

Support of Databases

According to Figure 2 for most PLM vendors SQL Server is more popular than Oracle. This can be viewed as a sign of increasing maturity within the market. As the mid-market begins to mature, this will likely have a positive impact on the demand for Microsoft's SQL server (AMR Research PLM Team, 2004). It also shows that the market is preparing itself for the growth expected within the mid-market by making PLM systems that support SQL server as well as the more substantial Oracle databases. The other two databases mentioned in the chart, namely Access and IBM SB2, are likely to show larger growth within the mid-market as they offer lower price solutions. Since the mid-

Figure 1. Detailed analysis of forty five PLM systems (Yarrow (2006)).

	Position	Target companies, Size in Millions$						5 core Functionalities of PLM the systems cater for					Databases					Operating systems					Industry standards that system conforms to							Scripting language used for customization						Total Score
		Less Than 50	50-100	101-200	201-500	500-1 billion	More than 1 billion	Collaborative Product Design	Product Data Management	Product Portfolio Management	Direct Material Sourcing	Customer Needs Management	Oracle	Access	SQL	IBM SS2	Other	Windows	Unix	Linux	HP	Other	XML	J2EE	STEP	IGES	ISO 9000	Six-sigma	Other	Java	Visual Basic	C++	Javascript	UML	Other	
Aras Corp Innovator	1	1	1	1	1	1		1	1	1	1	1	1	1	1	1		1	1				1	1	1	1				1	1					25
IBM SPL Software Suite	2	1	1	1	1	1		1	1	1			1	1	1	1		1	1				1	1	1	1				1	1					21
Adobe Systems PLM software suite	3					1		1	1		1	1	1	1	1	1		1	1	1		1	1	1	1	1				1	1					20
MatrixOne Matrix10	4	1	1	1	1	1		1	1	1	1		1			1		1	1	1	1	1							1	1	1	1	1	1	1	20
SmarTeam SmarTeam Suite	5			1	1	1		1	1				1			1		1	1		1		1	1	1				1	1			1			19
Spicer Corp. Imagenation	6	1	1	1	1	1		1	1		1		1	1	1	1		1	1				1						1	1						19
Spicer Corp. ViewCafe 3.2	7	1	1	1	1	1		1	1		1		1	1	1	1		1	1				1						1	1						19
Autodesk Inc. Inventor Series	8	1	1	1	1	1		1	1		1				1			1	1				1						1	1	1	1	1	1	1	18
QS Solutions Iced*CAD	9		1	1	1			1	1			1	1	1	1	1		1	1				1						1	1	1	1	1		1	18
Web4 eReview	10			1	1	1							1	1	1	1		1	1	1			1					1		1	1				1	18
Spicer Sorp. Image a*X	11	1	1	1	1	1		1		1			1	1	1	1		1	1				1						1	1	1				1	18
eQuotum Corp ImageSite	12	1	1	1				1					1		1	1		1					1	1	1	1	1	1	1	1	1					16
Synergis Synergis adept	13	1	1	1	1	1	1								1	1	1	1				1		1	1	1			1	1	1					16
Ninatek Nilighten	14				1	1		1	1				1		1							1	1						1	1	1	1	1	1	1	16
Delmia Corp.	15	1	1	1	1	1		1	1				1					1	1				1						1	1	1	1	1	1		16
Mystic Management DCS 6.0 Professional	16	1	1	1	1	1		1	1	1	1	1			1	1		1	1				1			1			1							16
Product Sight Corp. PLM Product Suite	17		1	1	1	1		1	1	1	1	1			1	1		1	1				1							1	1	1			1	16
Pragmax Software Pragmax	18		1	1	1			1	1		1	1			1			1	1				1							1	1	1		1		15
Fast Design Fast Automation	19	1	1	1	1	1						1	1	1	1	1		1	1				1							1	1				1	15
IBM PLM/ Dassault CATIA Version 5	20	1	1	1	1	1		1					1		1	1		1	1	1			1		1	1				1						15
Vistagy Inc. Encapta	21	1	1	1	1	1		1	1				1		1	1		1	1				1							1						15
Auto-Trol KONFIC CM	22				1	1		1	1	1			1	1				1					1				1		1	1	1	1	1	1	1	15
SAP MySAP PLM	23		1	1	1			1	1	1	1	1	1					1	1				1						1	1					1	14
Fast Design Warranty Management	24	1	1	1	1	1		1	1		1	1	1	1				1	1				1							1	1				1	14
Polyplan CmPM Solution	25					1							1	1	1	1	1	1		1		1	1							1	1				1	13
Omnify Software PLM Product Shuit	26		1	1	1			1	1	1	1				1			1					1							1	1	1			1	13
UGS PLM Solutions Solid Edge	27	1	1	1	1			1	1						1	1		1					1							1	1	1			1	13
Alibre Inc Alibre Design	28	na	na	na	na	na	na	1	1				1	1	1	1	1	1					1							1	1	1				12
Cmstat Cmstat PLM Soltuion	29	1	1	1	1			1	1					1	1	1		1					1							1	1				1	12
CoCreat OneSpaceDesigner	30	1	1	1	1			1	1				1				1	1					1							1	1					12
CoCreate Model Manager	31	1	1	1	1			1	1				1				1	1					1							1	1					12
Thetis Technologies ThetisPro	32	1	1	1	1			1	1		1				1			1					1											1		11
Arena Solutions Arean PLM	33				1			1	1		1						1					1	1							1	1	1	1			11
MTS Systems Corp. Etim	34		1	1	1	1				1					1			1					1							1	1	1			1	11
Telelogic Telelogic DOORS	35		1	1	1	1						1	1	1	1			1					1							1	1				1	11
ImpactXoft IX Speed Suite	36	1	1	1				1						1	1	1		1					1								1	1			1	10
IFS Applications 2004	37		1	1	1	1							1	1	1			1					1							1	1				1	10
BetaSphere Inc ReviMax suite	38					1					1	1			1			1					1		1	1	1			1	1					10
Prodicka PLM Solutions	39				1			1	1		1	1			1							1	1							1					1	10
Empresa Solutions eChange Solutions	40	1	1	1	1			1	1						1			1					1							1					1	10
CoCreate OneSpace.net	41	1	1	1				1	1		1							1					1							1						10
Fast Design Fasr configurator	42	1	1	1				1	1						1			1					1							1	1					8
Sopheon Accolade	43				1							1		1	1	1		1					1												1	7
Cuco Cotware AutoManager	44		1	1											1	1		1					1													7
SolidWorks Corp. PDM Works	45	1						1	1									1	1																1	6
Total		27	31	35	31	26	3	31	30	19	14	13	26	11	28	15	13	42	20	13	7	7	37	5	5	5	6	3	14	24	24	22	14	8	24	

market puts less emphasis on high-end CAD data, they do not require some of the expensive offerings. Oracle do offer similar options as the other less established databases, however, it earns a huge amount of capital from implementation with larger computer systems, which means they better serve the PLM mid-market (Urman, 2004). This may raise some concerns about the level of service they would receive among some investors and thus encourage investment into one of the less established database systems.

Support of Operating Systems

In 2003, UNIX systems showed a dominant 52% PLM market share. Since then, PLM manufacturers have prompted an unprecedented increase in the amount of Windows based operating systems for the PLM market as shown in Figure 3 (AMR Research PLM Team, 2004). MS Windows™ has a huge amount of support from the PLM system vendors. Out of the forty-five systems that were investigated, only three do not support a Windows operating system. This concurs with the comments made by AMR research; therefore, investors are likely to increase their Microsoft support.

The only three PLM solutions that do not support the Windows operating system are: Arena Solutions (Arena PLM), Nina Tek (Nlighten), Prodika (PLM solutions). Each of these systems do not support any of the other named systems that were investigated either. However, they do offer their own proprietary operating systems along with their PLM solutions. An example of this is the system that Prodika provided to the food products manufacturers Heinz™ with the implementation of project VIPER. This was a fully customized solution that was run on a Prodika operating sys-

Figure 2. Pie Chart showing the market distribution of database support of the 45 systems analyzed

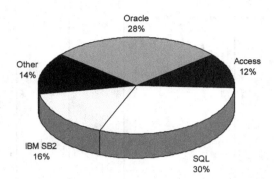

tem, and saw a very successful implementation in 2002-2003. A fully customized operating system is a very useful feature for any PLM solution. However, it requires a large amount of investment for set-up and maintenance and only companies with dispensable budget can afford it. With the predicted growth of the mid-market and the slowing down of PLM sales to the larger companies, these three PLM providers require less initial investment to make them more attractive to the lucrative mid-market (Brown, 2003).

UNIX sales are also being affected by Linux systems which have seen steady growth as manufacturers look for a cost-effective alternative to running on the expensive UNIX workstations (AMR Research PLM Team, 2004). However, the Linux system is less supported by the PLM products than may have been expected, but there are other predictions that the future will see an increase in the amount of Linux operating systems in the world. "It's one of the fastest growing markets and is projected to exceed $35.7 billion by 2008" (Keizer, 2004). Linux has gained the reputation of being mainly for computational experts (Negus, 2005). The producers of the PLM systems are waiting for further improvement upon Linux's general user interface before it gains the same popularity as that of Windows.

Figure 3. PLM systems operating systems support

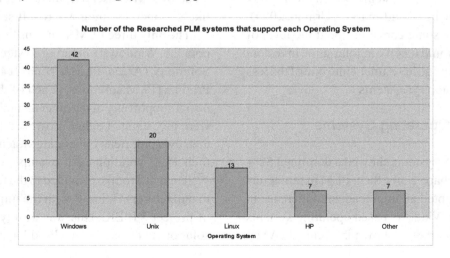

Figure 4. Industry standards supported by PLM systems

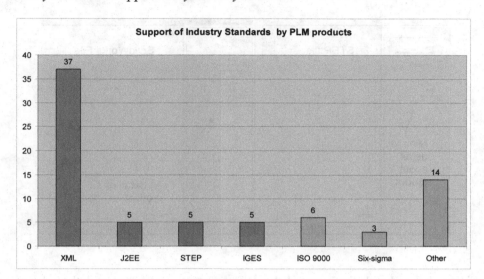

Support of Industry Standards

In Figure 4 the PLM systems that support relevant industry standards are shown. In this regards, XML is the most popular standard format supported (Harold, 2004). It is widely recognized as one of the most flexible data formats and therefore has a justified popularity. It is recognised by W3C as a "recommended general-purpose markup language for creating special-purpose markup languages". This is an ideal description for a file format that is to be used in a PLM system. Other industry standards of relevance are underrepresented with only five PLM products supporting them. This poor support for the more specialized data formats shows that the industry doesn't believe there is much use for them in the future of PLM.

The PLM market is very competitive and each company is likely to use any possible method to gain an advantage over its competitors.

One of the most common methods is to use a personalized file format for the storage of data. This means that any first time buyer of the new system (for example CAD) saves all the data in this personalized data format. The downfall is that when a new CAD system with better func-

tionalities appears in the market, investors will have difficulty transferring existing data formats into new ones. Ideas such as industry standards to prevent this problem have been proposed, however, these standards do not offer the same functionality that the daughter files of the original program can offer as illustrated in Figure 5. The industry standards available are not yet widely accepted as a useful form of data storage due to the lack of information they can hold.

STEP and IGES are two specific standardized data exchange formats that are more focused on the exchange of CAD data. All of the systems analyzed support at least one of these standards. There is a substantial amount of growth likely to occur outside of the CAD based PLM market. A major problem of industry standards in CAD is that they do not contain as much information as the actual CAD files. For example, if a CATIA user were to save a STEP document and load it up in SolidWorks they would not gain the full design history from the file. Additional detail is available in the SolidWorks file compared to the STEP file, even though they are referring to exactly the same part. This is a very basic example and therefore doesn't fully cover the amount of detail that can

Figure 5. Limitations of STEP and IGES files

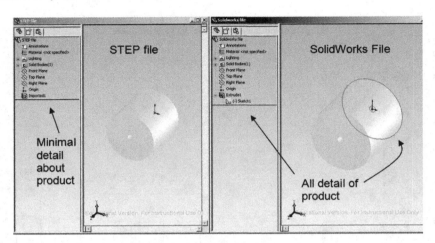

be lost. In Figure 4 the sketch that created the cylinder is not available in the STEP file whereas the SolidWorks file can show it. The SolidWorks file also shows that it was created by extruding the sketch, another detail that is not available from STEP or IGES format. If more complex designs are used, a considerable amount of data is lost and the ability to alter parts is badly affected. This means that companies using a PLM system are still keen to provide all lifecycle managing parties involved access to the same CAD package. As a result, from a PLM perspective, industry standards for CAD systems are not as popular as expected. (See Figure 5)

The quality management system ISO9000 shows twice as much support compared to six-sigma. Six-sigma and ISO9000 are only two of the many quality management processes that can be implemented within PLM systems. While some quality management systems offered within PLM systems may be customized, they still may not comply with industrial requirements with regard to supporting either Six-sigma or ISO9000 (Tubbs, 2005). There are organizations such as ISO (International Organization for Standardization) that were formed to recommend different file formats as industry standards. There are so many advances in computer technology that many new standards need to be brought out constantly to keep up with the industry's evolution. Some products are so successful that their data format can become an unofficial industry standard, which can have the result of decreasing the respect of the ISO. ISO needs to improve the speed with which standards are recognized so that they can keep up with the rapid speed of market change.

Target Company Size

Figure 6 shows the size of the target companies of the forty-five PLM systems. The least amount of support in this area is provided to companies that are valued higher than $1 billion. This is due to the very small potential market that is available to the PLM suppliers. Firstly, there are not many companies of this size in the world market as a whole; secondly, if they were to invest in a PLM system they would probably develop an in-house PLM system. For example, Heinz used Prodika to create VIPER which is not available for the market to buy as a product but was created specifically for Heinz (Brown, 2003). As indicated on the chart, most popular target companies are the ones valued between $101-200 million. This is due to the vendors recognizing that PLM is most successful in companies that are willing to invest the resources in implementing the PLM systems.

Figure 6. Size of the target companies of the 45 PLM systems

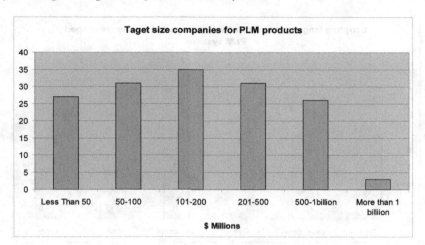

The companies that are worth less than $101-200 million are less likely to take such a large risk on a system that requires such a large investment. These companies are going to become more likely to invest as soon as they can see for certain that PLM is worth the risk or if they can make smaller steps to investment instead of paying for the full implementation.

Support of Customising Scripting Languages

Figure 7 shows the number of products that can be customized using specific languages. The number of PLM systems that support each language is a portrayal of the overall popularity for each language in the computing world. Both Java and Visual Basic are the most popular languages understood and used within the market.

Discussions of Analysis

A weighting method is not implemented in this research. However, this analysis method may be useful for companies looking for customized PLM system. A weighting analysis could be used to gain a better list of top performers depending on the requirements of an investigating company. For example, if a company wanting to invest in PLM has a large number of employees that are able to write code in JavaScript but none who can write code in C++, they need to give higher scoring value to the PLM products that support JavaScript and lower scoring for C++. If this method were implemented throughout the analysis, it is a reliable and accurate list of top products specific to a company that could be produced.

There is an expected growth in the mid market that is affecting the types of PLM systems available in the market. The fact that only three of the PLM products are targeting the largest companies is a demonstration of where the PLM vendors see the market investment coming from in the future. With this expected increase of popularity in the mid-market for PLM, PLM vendors need to start offering cheaper and more SME specific solutions to improve the attractiveness of the market. "Large companies with sizeable IT staffs spend months creating systems. Small and midsize companies did not and do not have the people or time to do that. Such companies need real solutions to management problems they can implement more or less immediately" (Elliott, 2006). Ready made systems need to start appearing on the market, these would be far more likely to attract the mid-market. One method of achieving this would be

Figure 7. Number of products that can be customised using specific languages

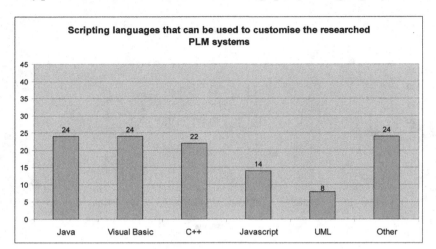

to offer a basic PLM platform that can be built upon in a modular fashion. Instead of forcing the companies to invest in every type of functionality, the companies would be able to choose certain modules that are required for a specific area. With time their investment in PLM would increase and spread to the other areas that were not part of the initial implementation, thus allowing investors to enter the PLM market gradually and not affect such a sudden change within their business (CIMdata, 2006).

IT infrastructure is another dilemma faced by the mid-market. "The cost of IT infrastructure is a big issue of SMEs, and vendors are looking for ways that allow midrange companies to absorb the functional aspects of PLM without big investments in infrastructure." (Elliott, 2006). One method that could be adopted by more PLM vendors is to offer hosted systems. Thus, when a company wants to use the PLM system they would pay an amount of capital per unit of time. This prevents the issue of IT infrastructure affecting the smaller businesses. However, the fact that another company who owns the PLM system may create certain trust issues about the data stored on the system, the more sensitive industries (e.g. Defence) will be more likely to invest in a more secure PLM system. (AMR Research PLM Team, 2004; CIMdata, 2006)

Detailed Analysis of Five Major PLM Systems

In the following, an in-depth analysis of five selected PLM systems is presented. The five PLM systems chosen to be looked at more closely are: SAP (mySAP), MatrixOne (Matrix 10), Auto-trol Technology (KONFIG CM), CoCreate (OneSpace.net) and IBM Dassault Systémes (SmarTeam).

Two of the five chosen products are ranked among the top systems: Matrix10 is ranked 4th and SmarTeam is 5th. Two systems that ranked in the middle of the field are: KONFIG CM (22nd) and mySAP (23rd) places. OneSpace.net ranked 41st. These products were also chosen due to their strength in the market compared to the other extremes available. Companies such as SAP and IBM Dassault Systémes are well established in the PLM market and therefore are more likely to survive than the others such as Aras Corp or Cuco Software Auto Manager. The data presented in the following tables was collected from the PLM vendor's various sources including websites and brochures. The five core areas of investigation are (Burkett et al, 2003):

(i)   Product Data Management;

Figure 8. Results of detailed analysis of PDM

	Vendors	SAP	MatrixOne	Auto-trol Technology	CoCreate	IBM DS
	Products	mySAP	Matrix 10	KONFIG CM	OneSpace.net	Smarteam
	Vendor Offering	6	5	4	4	4
Product Data Management (PDM)	Capabilities					
	Product Structure	y	y	y	y	y
	CAD Integration	y	y	y	y	y
	Engineering Change	y	y	y	y	y
	Specification Management for Process	y	y			
	Recipe Management	y				
	Configuration Management	y	y	y	y	y

(ii)   Collaborative Product Design;

(iii) Direct Material Sourcing;

(iv) Customer needs management; and

(v)   Product Portfolio Management.

Each of the main five core areas is divided into more detailed capabilities. Each of the PLM products is checked to see if it has this specific offering.

PDM

Figure 8 and Figure 9 show the PLM systems that scored highest in terms of PDM capabilities. PDM is strongly supported across the vendors and seen as a major foundation for a successful PLM system. Therefore, this area is reaching maturity in the market with each PLM system containing high quality PDM capabilities. SAP is the front-runner among this group of vendors as it caters for Recipe Management. Matrix 10 offers specification management which puts it in second place to mySAP and ahead of the others in the short-list.

Collaborative Product Development

The most important aspect of cPDm is to effectively connect engineers and other technical members of the enterprise to other, less technology savvy staff. PLM vendors who already had a history in the CAD market usually do well in this regards due to the key role that CAD can have in creating this connection. As shown in Figure 10, all chosen PLM vendors support CAD visualisation. This is because it is widely recognised that "visualisation is critical to extend value" (Miller, 2005) and it helps to explain more technical details to those in an organisation. Both mySAP and OneSpace.net do well in this functional area showing support for systems engineering and formulation. All of the selected products lack process designing capabilities as this is an area of recent work along with systems engineering, and PLM vendors are currently working on solutions for these areas. "Systems Engineering and process designing are critical new frontiers for PLM strategy" (Burkett et al, 2003). Since most contemporary products or systems comprise of a combination of hardware, electronics and software, there is also an increased demand for PLM systems to support the management of cross-disciplinary aspects of systems design as well.

Figure 9. Results of detailed analysis for product data management

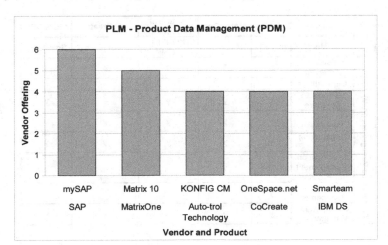

Direct Materials Sourcing

Figure 11 shows the results of our detailed analysis with regard to DMS. While there has been significant focus on strategic sourcing in the purchasing community, it has primarily been targeted at indirect or commodity direct materials. This functional area requires different capabilities as the design content and dependence on supplier engineering expertise increases (Burkett, 2002). Matrix10 and mySAP posses all the capabilities that were analyzed and gained the maximum score possible. KONFIG CM and OneSpace.net do not posses purchasing integration capabilities. Finally SmarTeam, which does have the capability of purchasing integration, does not show any RFQ workflow or Quote Analytics capability causing it to have the lowest score in this core functionality.

Customer Needs Management

This functional area is regarded as the weakest area in the PLM footprint, but CNM has had a lot

Figure 10. Results of detailed analysis of cPDm

	Vendors	CoCreate	SAP	Auto-trol Technology	IBM DS	MatrixOne
	Products	OneSpace.net	mySAP	KONFIG CM	Smarteam	Matrix 10
	Vendor Offering	5	5	3	3	3
	Capabilities					
Collaborative Product Development (cPDm)	Product Design Tool	y	y	y	y	
	Process design Tool					
	Visualization	y	y	y	y	y
	CAD Interoperability	y	y		y	y
	Formulation	y	y	y		
	Systems Engineering	y	y			y

of improvement in the recent past with regards to customer influence, order error tracking, and warranty expenses (Burkett, 2003). Matrix 10 meets all of the capabilities that are mentioned for this functional area and mySAP only lacks a decent requirements management capability. The weakness of this area in the PLM market is made more obvious by both KONFIG CM and OneSpace.net which do show the requirements management capability; however, do not have four of the six capabilities mentioned in Figure 12.

Product Portfolio Management

PLM is not a transaction environment, but rather a creative atmosphere in which projects are the basic unit of work. These application parts of a PLM system manage projects that are part of larger programs which in turn are part of an overall portfolio. Portfolio management is a very useful tool for executives and presentations as it gains all the general data from projects and makes it easier to view. Project/Program management has many dimensions based on the type of data being managed and the point in the product's lifecycle. (Figure 13)

Matrix 10 and mySAP again score high and do not lack any of the capabilities mentioned. However, SmarTeam lacks all of the PPM capabilities and gains the lowest possible score of zero. Project/Program Management and Stage Gate processing are the most represented in this area, that is because they are the very basic fundamentals of PPM and for any system to have any PPM it will probably have at least Project/Program Management if not both of these capabilities.

Overall Results and Discussion of Detailed Analysis

As can be seen from Figure 14 mySAP has achieved the highest score out of the shortlist of investigated products, with MatrixOne second highest. These two products showed the most substantial amount of functionality in the areas that were investigated. Therefore it would be the judgment of the person in charge of choosing the PLM system, to use the top scoring product, in this case mySAP, or to gain a further opinion.

The analysis presented is easy to understand and very useful for short listing PLM systems a company may consider to purchase. The fact that it is easy to understand makes it applicable to almost any other selection of systems to be considered. Hence, it can be regarded an important factor for the success of implementing any strategic IT system (SofTech et al, 2005; Tubbs, 2005). Of course, the analysis presented in this

Figure 11. Results of detailed analysis of DMS

	Vendors	MatrixOne	SAP	Auto-trol Technology	CoCreate	IBM DS
	Products	Matrix 10	mySAP	KONFIG CM	OneSpace.net	Smarteam
	Vendor Offering	4	4	3	3	2
	Capabilities					
Direct Material Sourcing (DMS)	RFQ Workflow	y	y	y	y	
	Quote Analytics	y	y	y	y	
	Purchasing Integration	y	y			y
	Part Database Access	y	y	y	y	y

Figure 12. Results of detailed analysis of CNM

	Vendors	MatrixOne	SAP	IBM DS	Auto-trol Technology	CoCreate
	Products	Matrix 10	mySAP	Smarteam	KONFIG CM	OneSpace.net
	Vendor Offering	6	5	3	2	2
	Capabilities					
Customer Needs Management (CNM)	Configurator	y	y	y		y
	Service Feedback	y	y	y		
	Concept BOM	y	y	y		
	Requirements Management	y			y	y
	Web Market Test	y	y		y	
	Preference Analytics	y	y			

chapter could have been covered in greater detailed by rating the quality of coverage of each system functionality.

As mentioned earlier under *Collaborative Product Development*, the general product market is becoming more advanced and includes work from different areas of expertise, electronics and software as well as mechanical design. These new complex products fall under the umbrella term "Mechatronics". PLM users require better communication between these different areas so that the product development can maintain a high

standard with the increasing complexity. Collaborative Product design is the functional area that covers this new and more complex process and therefore it is a key element that PLM systems show a high level of coverage in this area for the future (Miller, 2005).

Future Directions for the PLM Market and Features in the Systems

According to Hojlo et al, (2007) that the PLM market is now more matured in terms of support-

Figure 13. Results of detailed analysis of PPM

	Vendors	MatrixOne	SAP	CoCreate	Auto-trol Technology	IBM DS
	Products	Matrix 10	mySAP	OneSpace.net	KONFIG CM	Smarteam
	Vendor Offering	5	5	3	2	0
	Functions					
Product Portfolio Management (PPM)	Executive Dashboard	y	y			
	Portfolio Analytics	y	y			
	Project/ Program Management	y	y	y	y	
	Resource Management	y	y	y		
	Stage Gate Process	y	y	y	y	

Figure 14. Overall results for detailed analysis

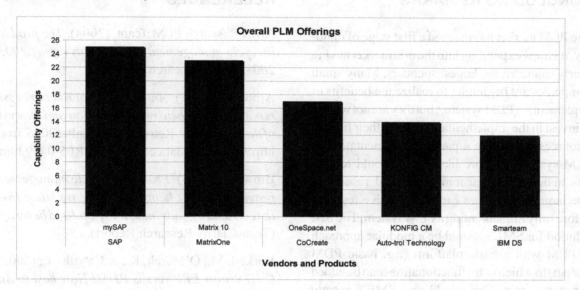

ing design-to-manufacturing planning. The only opportunity left for PLM applications is in the business layer, i.e. to allow end users to utilize PLM more than just managing CAD data and concurrent engineering processes. A new generation of PLM should allow closer collaboration with global value chain.

However, Rowe (2007) argued that one further improvement of modern PLM is 'digital manufacturing' as showcased by Siemens PLM Software Digital Manufacturing Symposium. Rowe states that "digital manufacturing is about collaborative process planning, which allows companies to define the manufacturing processes to produce their products. In effect, digital manufacturing creates an environment in which manufacturing process definition is conducted concurrently with product design activities".

Finally, Rouse-Talley (2007) has completed a survey concerning the predictions of where PLM technology will lead us to in the near future. The survey concluded by a list of panellists, here are some of the comments:

- Customers are increasingly looking for solutions that allow them to better manage product lifecycle business processes and use embedded decision support and analytics. — *Chris Farinacci, Agile Software*

- PLM vendors are expanding functionality that is useful across many industries with capabilities like strategic sourcing, requirements management, or portfolio management. — *Ed Miller, CIMdata*

- Many companies build products with high electrical and mechanical content, and no software vendor exists serving both of these CAD markets, it is very important for the leading PLM vendors to support an open data-management strategy. — *Jonathan Gable, Dassault Systemes*

- Neither the ERP companies nor the CAD companies are doing a good job with enterprise PDM software, so there is room for independent firms, even open source firms to innovate. — *L. Stephen Wolfe, PE*

CONCLUDING REMARKS

The PLM market has reached a first stage of maturity. It is now expanding into the mid market having nearly saturated the largest spenders. Many small companies are beginning to realize the benefits of implementing PLM systems, but they are not willing to invest in the implementation due to their limited resources. Therefore a partial implementation of PLM systems is more likely; this would require less maintenance, customization and resources. The largest companies can do extensive research before fully implementing a PLM system. The best solution for SME's would be a modular approach to PLM with a basic platform (e.g. basic PDM system) to which extra functionalities can be added at separate cost. This would give SME's exactly what they require in terms of specific functionality whilst keeping costs down.

The pace at which the PLM market is evolving stands for both its strength and weakness. New or significantly improved PLM solutions make inroads into the market on a regular basis. While innovation in general is considered highly beneficial, the variety of new solutions and the speed at which this innovation takes place makes it very difficult for companies to keep track of the state-of-the-art.

ACKNOWLEDGMENT

The authors would like to thank the following institutions: (1) AMR Research for providing their *The Product lifecycle Management Applications Report 2003-2008* Market Analytics Report (2004) which was used as a basis for an undergraduate research project at Durham University, UK, in 2006. (2) Technology Evaluation Centres for providing their daily newsletters and weekly summaries. (3) The Editors of DE magazine (Desktop Engineering) and CIMData for providing their weekly newsletters and finally Guy Yarrow from the University of Durham.

REFERENCES

AMR Research PLM Team. (2004). *The product lifecycle management applications report 2003-2008*. AMR Research Inc.

Arbor, A. (2005). *Annual PLM market analysis report: Comprehensive information and analysis of the plm market*. Retrieved December 2006, from http://www.cimdata.com/press/PR05-0809.htm

Brown, J. (2003). *Product lifecycle management proving value at heinz: A PLM case study from the consumer goods industry - Food and beverage* (Tech-Clarity Research Report).

Burkett, M., O'Marah, K., & Carrillo, L. (2003). *CAD versus ERP versus PDM: How best to Anchor a PLM strategy* (AMR Research Report). Retrieved September 27, 2008, from http://www. ptc.com/WCMS/files/17636en_file1.pdf

Burkett, M., O'Marah, K., & Karofsky, E. (2007). *MatrixOne acquired by Dassault Systemes – PLM consolidation close to an end*. Retrieved September 27, 2008, from http://www.amrresearch.com/content/View.asp?pmillid=19236

Burkett, M., O'Marah, K., & Kemmeter, J. (2002). *Product lifecycle management: What's real now?* (AMR Research Report). AMR Research Inc.

CIMdata. (2002). *Product lifecycle management: Empowering the future of business*. Retrieved September 27, 2008 from http://www.ariondata.es/servicios/documentacion/PLM_Definition_0210.pdf

CIMdata. (2003). *PDM to PLM: Growth of an industry*. CIMdata Research Document. Retrieved January 2005, from http://www.cimdata.com/press/PR03-0325.htm

CIMdata. (2004). *PLM and ERP integration: Business efficiency and value* (CIMdata Research Report). Retrieved January 2005, from http://www.cimdata.com/php/download_reports.php

CIMdata. (2007). *Defining Mid-market PDM* (CI-Mdata Research Report). Retrieved May 2007, from http://www.cimdata.com/publications/PDM_and_MidMarket_Final.pdf

Elliott, L. (2006). *PLM - Does one size fit all?* Retrieved September 27, 2008, from http://www.deskeng.com/articles/aaabzm.htm

Hameri, A. P., & Nihtila, J. (1998). Product data management - Exploratory study on state-of-the-art in one-of-a-kind industry. *Computers in Industry*, *35*, 195–206. doi:10.1016/S0166-3615(98)00064-5

Harold, E. R., & Means, W. S. (2004). *XML in a Nutshell* (3rd ed.). O'Reilly Media, Inc.

Hojlo, J., Burkett, M., & Verma, K. (2007). *PLM market landscape: Evolving To Enable value chain excellence*. 2007 Technology and Vendor Landscape Series. AMR Research Inc.

Keizer, G. (2004). *Linux to ring up $35billion by 2008*. TechWeb news article. Retrieved September 27, 2008 from http://www.techweb.com/wire/showArticle.jhtml?articleID=55800522.

Miller, E. (2003). *State of the PLM industry*. CIM Data PLM Conference 2003, MI, USA, July 23, 2003.

Miller, E. (2005). *Ask the Expert Ed Miller: Dec 16 2005 Innovative Forum*. Retrieved August 21, 2008, from http://cimdata.com/newsletter/2005/51/02/51.02.01.htm

Miller, E. (2005). *PLM – State of the PLM industry- October 2005*. Retrieved September 29, 2008, from http://www.perceptionsoftware.com/ama/orig/PLM_State_of_Industry_October_2005.pdf

Ming, X. G., Yan, J. Q., Lu, W. F., & Ma, D. Z. (2005). Technology solutions for collaborative product lifecycle management – Status review and future trend. *Concurrent Engineering . Research and Applications*, *13*(4), 311–319.

Negus, C. (2005). *Linux Bible* (2nd ed.). John Wiley & Sons.

Portella, J. (2000). *Collaborative management of the product definition lifecycle for the 21st century*. CD-Rom Proceedings, PDT Europe Conference, Noordwijk, Netherlands, May 2000.

Rangan, R. M., Rohde, S. M., Peak, R., Chadha, B., & Bliznakov, P. (2005). Streamlining product lifecycle processes: A survey of product lifecycle management implementations, directions, and challenges. *Journal of Computing and Information Science in Engineering*, *5*, 227–237. doi:10.1115/1.2031270

Rouse-Talley, N. (2007). *PLM Roundtable, Part 2*. Retrieved November 16, 2008, from http://66.195.41.10/Articles/Feature/PLM-Roundtable%2C-Part-2-200703161743.html

Rowe, J. (2007). *Digital manufacturing's growing PLM role*, Retrieved November 16, 2008, from http://manufacturing.cadalyst.com/manufacturing/article/articleDetail.jsp?id=477580

SofTech Inc. & John Stark Associates (2005). *Top 10 PLM pitfalls to avoid*. Retrieved September 27, 2008, from http://www.softech.com/plm-whitepapers/plm-pitfalls-to-avoid.php

Stark, J. (2004). *Product lifecycle management: Paradigm for 21st Century Product Realisation*. Springer.

Tubbs, A. (2005). *Top ten risks to a configuration project and how to avoid them*. Retrieved September 27, 2008, from http://whitepapers.businessweek.com/detail/RES/1203446022_342.html

Urman, S., Hardman, R., & McLaughlin, M. (2004). *Oracle Database 10g PL/SQL Programming*. McGraw-Hill Osborne Media.

Yarrow, G. (2006). *BEng Thesis: Product lifecycle management systems (PLM) - state-of-the-art report*, University of Durham, UK.

Chapter 5
ERP Systems Supporting Lean Manufacturing in SMEs

Pritish Halgeri
Kansas State University, USA

Roger McHaney
Kansas State University, USA

Z. J. Pei
Kansas State University, USA

ABSTRACT

Small and medium enterprises (SMEs), more than ever, are being forced to compete in a global economy with increasingly complex challenges. This new economy has forced SMEs to become more responsive and agile in operational, tactical and strategic areas while requiring thoughtful integration between business functions and manufacturing/ production/ service operations. Enterprise Resource Planning (ERP) and Lean manufacturing are two production control methodologies that have been implemented in various ways. In early incarnations, ERP systems were considered a hindrance to Lean manufacturing efforts and were criticized for encouraging large inventories and slower production. The explosive growth of e-business methodologies and the resulting pressure to become nimble and embrace rapid change forced many SMEs to rethink their production approaches, particularly in regard to where they stand in relation to these two methodologies. Over time, ERP vendors recognized the power and advantages of Lean manufacturing and developed ways to incorporate Lean-related features into their software. The main objective of this chapter is to explore how ERP and Lean methodologies can coexist in SMEs. The chapter discusses misconceptions about the fit between ERP and Lean then summarizes differences and synergies between the two methodologies. The chapter emphasizes how linking ERP and Lean methods can lead to competitive advantage then explores key Lean toolsets available in leading ERP systems used by SMEs. Further focus is provided with additional insight on several leading ERP vendors offering Lean-enabled software modules. These include Oracle, TTW WinMan and Pelion Systems.

DOI: 10.4018/978-1-60566-892-5.ch005

INTRODUCTION

Small and medium enterprises (SMEs), more than ever, are being forced to compete in a global economy with increasingly complex challenges. This new economy has forced SMEs to become more responsive and agile in operational, tactical and strategic areas while requiring thoughtful integration between business functions and manufacturing/production/service operations. When faced with similar pressures, larger firms migrated to expensive ERP systems. As early as 1999, researchers (Gable & Steward, 1999) suggested SMEs would follow suit and suggested reasons motivating this phenomenon. First, the larger enterprise market for ERP systems was becoming saturated and ERP vendors were hungry for new markets. Secondly, these larger firms were pushing ERP vendors to create software to leverage inexpensive Internet technologies that would promote closer integration with their SME partners along the supply chain to obtain a variety of efficiency-based benefits. Thirdly, SMEs made up a large portion of regional economies and represented a high percent of overall manufacturing and service firms. And finally, ERP packages designed for SMEs had become more sophisticated, cost efficient and upwardly scalable for growth oriented firms.

In spite of these obvious incentives many SMEs were slow to adopt ERP technologies. According to Aladwani (2001) two fundamental sources of resistance to innovations like an ERP exist: perceived risk and habit. According to Aladwani (2001), perceived risk refers to one's *perception of the risk associated with the decision to adopt the innovation*, i.e. the decision to accept an ERP system and habit refers to *current practices that one is routinely doing*. Koh & Simpson (2005) suggest this is pronounced in SMEs due to widespread informal culture and a disregard for formalizing business processes. Often in SMEs, a worker wears many hats and as a result, operations are conducted on the fly and without formal procedures or documentation. Aladwani (2001)

suggests this can be hard to overcome and for some time, that appeared to be the case.

In recent years, SMEs involved in the business-to-business (B2B) market have worked hard to develop delivery performance capability compatible with larger corporate customers. In many cases this means that the SME is required to interface with their clients' ERP systems. Larger enterprises rely on big ERP system vendors such as SAP, ORACLE, and others (Rashid, Hossain & Patrick, 2002). The implementation cost of these systems is high and installation complex making it difficult for SMEs to follow suit. In response, midrange and less complex systems have been developed both by the large ERP vendors and by smaller software companies. In order to continue taking advantage of being, smaller nimble companies, and satisfy the needs of the larger corporate partners, SMEs may need to use their ERP software in conjunction with other proven systems and methodologies such as Lean planning and control tools. SMEs may need to combine capabilities to continue using other concepts such as just-in-time (JIT) and optimized production technology (Cheng & Podolsky, 1993; Deep, et al. 2008; Koh & Simpson, 2005). This article specifically looks at progress made in integrating Lean production methodologies with ERP systems.

BACKGROUND

Competing Philosophies

Over the past couple decades, philosophies related to the most effective manner to run manufacturing operations have been debated and evolved greatly (Nakashima, 2000). Added to the mix has been increased competition and expectations for rapid production changes and retooling. This has intensified the need for more efficient and cost effective manufacturing and put pressure on managers and production engineers to develop new and better solutions.

The methodology debate has not been without controversy and opposing philosophies have emerged as different means to address the same basic problem (Spearman & Zazanis, 1992). Nowhere is this situation more apparent than where manufacturers are torn between two camps concerning production control (Piszczalski, 2000). One embraces Enterprise Resource Planning systems (ERP) where for the past two decades, organizations have spent billions of dollars and countless hours installing enterprise wide systems (Bradford, Mayfield & Toney, 2001). The other camp is Lean manufacturing (Piszczalski, 2000), pioneered in Japan by Toyota Motor Corporation but now embraced in the U.S. by literally thousands of firms, particularly SMEs (Bartholomew, 1999).

ERP and Lean have emerged from fundamentally different approaches to production. As a result, misconceptions that Lean and ERP approaches do not mix well have emerged (Steger-Jensen & Hvolby, 2008). In some cases, these misconceptions have gone as far to argue that ERP systems are actually the antithesis of Lean manufacturing and are largely responsible for a variety of inefficiencies (Nakashima, 2000). Others say ERP is a waste of money and time in no uncertain terms. For instance, in 1999, Bartholomew reported opponents of ERP as saying: *We are staying away from ERP* because *it doesn't work. To do both ERP and Lean jeopardizes the success rate of either* (Bartholomew, 1999).

This opinion is one side of many arguments both pro and con. Others have said: *only by using computer systems (ERP) manufacturers can possibly get their arms around the Herculean task of recognizing the multitude of constraints and issues that inevitably impact operations and planning* (Piszczalski, 2000). To them, it is obvious that ERP systems have an important purpose in gathering enterprise data that can and should be used in conjunction with Lean methodologies (Bradford, Mayfield & Toney, 2001).

Added to competitive pressures, the explosive growth of information and telecommunications technologies and the resultant rise of e-business (Kent, 2002) have forced most SMEs to revisit their production control methodologies and re-evaluate where they stand in relation to ERP use and Lean manufacturing implementation. As attitudes have changed and information exchange increased, Lean practitioners have begun to adopt supportive ERP software to facilitate their advanced Lean manufacturing initiatives and allow the rich compilation of organizational data and production history take them to a new level of operational excellence (Bragg, 2004).

Lean Enabled ERP Development

The area of Lean enabled ERP software has become the subject of many recent and important, ongoing developments. However, very few researchers have examined this area to discuss the availability of Lean enabled ERP systems (Halgeri, et al, 2008). Additionally, not many researchers describe the Lean toolset features offered by ERP vendors. This article will attempt to rectify that by discussing the differences between ERP and Lean methodologies and then examining available Lean toolsets provided by several ERP vendors. The article will go on to provide a list of ERP vendors offering support in Lean manufacturing then provide additional details on several selected vendors together with the expected benefits of their software solutions.

Enterprise Resource Planning (ERP)

ERP is defined as a method for the effective planning and controlling of all the resources needed to take, make, ship and account for customer orders in a manufacturing, distribution or service company (Miller, 2002). ERP software attempts to integrate all departments and application modules into one computer system to serve each department's needs from a central repository.

ERP effectively eliminates standalone computer systems for each functional business silo or software module (e.g. manufacturing/production, warehousing, accounting, marketing, logistics, human resources, finance, etc.) and replaces them with an integrated program composed of various modules representative of required components of an organization's business. The primary difference is that these components are now linked with a common database therefore giving all entities within the organization the ability to share and view desired information while eliminating data entry and update redundancies, and effectively enhancing communication with easy access to work flows. (Koch, 2008). Additionally, ERP solidly integrates all necessary business functions, such as production planning, accounting, purchasing, inventory control, marketing, sales, finance, and human resources, into a single system with a shared database (Li, Liao & Lei, 2006) which enables a variety of automatic data collection not previously possible.

As a direct result of ERP systems' abilities to collect data and improve the ease of information sharing, several other advantages generally result from its use. For example, ERP systems consistently improve SMEs' productivity, as the systems eliminate the need for multiple entries of identical data, reduce the possibility of errors and inconsistencies, and reduce time spent on needless phone calls and inquiries to other departments. Other advantages provided to SMEs using ERP systems include improved tracking and forecasting abilities, better customer service, ability to standardize manufacturing processes more easily, and in some instances, cost savings after initial start-up costs are recouped (Jacobs, 2007).

While ERP systems possess numerous advantages, key disadvantages also exist. For instance, ERP systems require extensive installation and configuration processes that may take from three months to a year or more depending on the size and complexity of the organization. For some SMEs this may be less of an issue since less customiza-tion may be required. ERP systems often demand reengineering business processes. Installing the software without changing the business model to match encoded best practices can result in fewer benefits, and may even decrease efficiency and productivity. Additionally, employees must be trained to use both new software and new business processes in the conduct of their work tasks. Another disadvantage relates to cost factors. ERP systems can be expensive to install and run. Hidden costs also exist. For example, training, data conversion, testing, and updates all add to the price tag. Of course, these costs are generally part of any organizational information system and should be viewed within that perspective.

Lean Manufacturing

Lean manufacturing is a term given to a family of related methodologies that seek to streamline production processes. Sometimes Lean is referred to as Just-in-Time (JIT) manufacturing, kanban system, Toyota Production System, or flow manufacturing. A primary feature of Lean manufacturing how it uses demand to pull items into inventory and through the manufacturing process. Lean attempts to sequence these items on flow lines to maximize resource utilization (Kent, 2002). A key goal of Lean manufacturing is the continuous reduction and even eventual elimination of all waste in the production process (Mekong Capital, 2004; Strategosinc, 2008).

In general, Lean manufacturing seeks to minimize all the resources (including time) used in various enterprise activities. A key aspect of Lean is to identify and reduce or eliminate non-value-added activities in design, production, supply chain management, and streamline customer interaction. Lean principles and practices aim to reduce cost through the relentless removal of waste and through the simplification of all manufacturing and support processes (Miller, 2002) consistent with continuous quality improvement techniques.

Key Principles of Lean Manufacturing

Several key principles lay behind the development and use of Lean manufacturing techniques. Among these are:

(1) **Elimination of Waste:** Lean thinking offers a definition of value and therefore allows an organization to determine what activities and resources are needed to create and maintain this value (Poppendieck, 2002).

(2) **Pull Production:** In its most basic form, downstream activities inform upstream activities when replenishment is required.

(3) **Value Stream Identification:** To deliver products as specified by customers, an assessment of required actions to move through purchasing, production, distribution and other parts of the value stream are necessary (Burton & Boeder, 2003; Paez, et. al. 2004)

(4) **Standardization of Processes:** Lean manufacturing seeks to develop standardized work processes to eliminate variation in the way individual workers may perform their tasks. Lean may use a combination of training techniques and process design to ensure this is possible (Mekong Capital, 2004).

(5) **Quality at the Center:** At the center of Lean manufacturing is a commitment to quality improvement. Lean encourages the elimination of defects at the source and strives to ensure quality inspection is completed by workers during in-line production process (Poppendieck, 2002).

(6) **People Add Value:** Lean manufacturing values the human component and seeks to add value to processes through human interaction (Arc Strategies, 2007).

(7) **Continuous Improvement:** Lean manufacturing is never content with the status quo. It seeks to improve and enhance efficiency and production practices. So Improvement is never truly complete (Turbide, 2005).

(8) **Continuous Flow:** Lean manufacturing seeks to implement continuous production flows free of any interruptions, bottlenecks, detours, backflows, unwanted changes or waiting (Mekong Capital, 2004)

Lean Manufacturing Shortcomings

Lean manufacturing is not without shortcomings. Key features in Lean can only be used to their fullest potential in situations where a stable master schedule exists. This means that current processing must match with capacity. Unexpected changes or an influx of unexpected orders can be difficult to accommodate. Further, changes in lead times can result in problematic changes. Many manufacturers expecting these situations may not use Lean methodologies in the first place. Another potential shortcoming is the inability to share and communication electronic transaction data with business operations and other parts of the enterprise. In Lean, information flow is minimized (Nagendra & Das,1999).

ERP AND LEAN: CAN THEY COEXIST?

ERP and Lean Compared

Although both ERP and Lean manufacturing seek to provide a similar outcome to an organization, the conflict between the methodologies can be attributed to implementation and philosophical difference in general (Bartholomew, 2003). One of these differences involves the way goods and services are viewed in the two methodologies. For instance, Lean promotes a "pull" environment as the operative principle whereby goods or services are not purchased or produced until demand exists. Meanwhile in traditional ERP systems, the primary focus is on the "push" principle where forecasts are developed from historic data and orders, and then goods are produced to meet expected demand (Nakashima, 2000).

Figure 1. Typical push system (Halgeri, 2008)

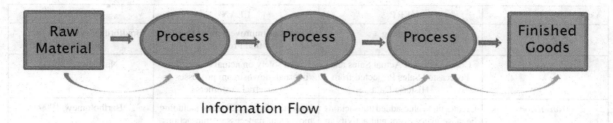

While not sounding too different, the basic philosophy between these two approaches is significant. First, in a push system, a production job begins on a start date computed by subtracting an established lead time from the date the goods are required, usually for shipping or for assembly (Spearman & Zazanis, 1992). A push system schedules the release of work based on demand. The key factor here is access to historic data that aids in the development of forecasts for items to be produced. Release time has to be fixed and cannot be modified easily for unexpected changes in the manufacturing system or product being manufactured. Figure 1 represents a general push production system.

In a push system, information from the master production schedule (MPS) flows downstream toward the finished goods inventory and is computer generated (Kent, 2002) based on history and current orders. The MPS becomes the plan used by a company for production. The MPS considers all work currently in-house and develops an aggregate plan based on forecasts for individual parts, actual orders on hand, expectations for orders, and available capacity (Lee & Adams, 1986).

A pull system takes the opposite approach and at its center is inherent flexibility. Pull systems use the actual end customer demand to drive the manufacturing process as much as possible. Pull systems attempt to match the rate of production for each product to the rate of customer consumption (Steger-Jensen & Hvolby, 2008) as it occurs. This has the net effect of reducing inventories and holding down costs throughout the supply chain. A pull system is characterized by the practice of downstream work centers pulling stock from previous operations (Spearman & Zazanis, 1992). In other words, nothing is produced by the upstream supplier until the downstream customer signals a need (Kent, 2002). Work is coordinated by using an information flow up the supply chain, having originated with the end consumer of the product (Spearman & Zazanis, 1992). Figure 2 shows a typical pull system.

Information flows from the finished goods inventory (the customer) upstream towards the raw material inventory and in many SMEs can be conveyed visually by the use of a kanban (Kent, 2002). Many systems are now completely run by automated computer-driven systems. Other differ-

Figure 2. Typical pull system (Halgeri, 2008)

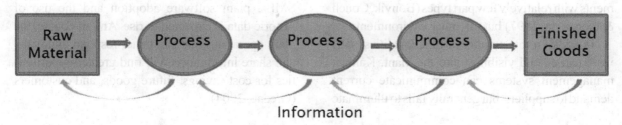

Table 1. Differences between ERP systems and lean manufacturing

Aspect	ERP	LEAN	Reference
Emphasis	Planning	Continual Improvement of Production Process	Bradford, Mayfield & Toney, 2001
Production Plans	Combination of Actual Sales and Forecasted Sales Projected from Historic Data	Based solely on actual orders from internal, downstream processes or external customers	Nakashima, 2000
Transaction	Creates non value-added transactions because every event and activity in entire business is tracked (although most are done automatically)	Seeks to eliminate all waste including movement, unnecessary transactions, and materials. Seeks to speed and smooth production	Bartholomew, 1999
Traditional Approach	Top-down	Bottom-up	(Nakashima, 2000)
Time Horizons	As short as a few weeks but as long as a year or more. Average around 12-week mark.	Based on daily production capacity and actual orders received	(Nakashima, 2000)
Basic Focus	Forward-looking planning, communication, and scheduling tool	Cost reduction and process improvement methodology	Bartholomew, 2003
Platform	Computer dependent	Shop Floor oriented (often with computerization	(Piszczalski, 2000)
Production Concepts	Loaded machine work centers	Balanced production lines with synchronized Takt and cycle times	(Nakashima, 2000)
Information Philosophy	More is better. For example, more information, more flexibility, more functions and more features are desirable	Less is best. For example less variability, less material, less movement, less floor space are desirable	(Piszczalski, 2000)
Product Movement	Product moves in batches with specified operations being performed on the complete batch before moving on to the next operation	Each operation is completed on a single unit with specific unit moved to next operation in a continuous flow	(Nakashima, 2000)

ences between traditional ERP systems and Lean manufacturing are summarized in Table 1.

Advantages of ERP over Lean

ERP can provide advantages over Lean. For instance, researchers have claimed ERP, in general, is more applicable to more manufacturing firms than Lean (Spearman, Woodruff & Hopp 1990) and that Lean should be used in high volume production environments with relatively few part types (Bonvik, Couch & Gershwin, 1997) but not other environments.

In addition to a number of functionalities, software can extend visibility into the plant. Kanban management systems can communicate current demand to suppliers, but generally fails to illuminate quality or other shop floor issues. Lean manufacturing's line-of-sight management can also fall short since it typically also does not help internal departments serve customers beyond their immediate point of interaction. This can inhibit the design of better products.

Lean can create the low cost, efficient operations needed for survival. However, that is not the only goal of most companies where long term survival is also an important consideration. Thus, in many SMEs, plant software adoption and the use of historic data is expected to rise. And of course, the plant operations that can better respond, innovate, and share information will find greater opportunities for cost savings, future goods, and customers (Greene, 2004).

Software can bring capabilities to the plant environment that are difficult or even impossible to achieve by any other mechanism. Of course, not every production operation will require all of the capabilities available in software systems, but for those needing to achieve specific goals, certain features can be crucial. It is possible SMEs not specifically interested in implementing Lean may still acquire software tools typically found in ERP or other enterprise systems for use in their environments. Several examples of these features are:

- **Track and Trace:** Many industries require full product histories that track all materials back to their sources for quality and other reasons. Required or not, a track and trace feature makes great business sense. Not only can warranty costs be reduced but brand image can be protected. Additionally, recall costs can be better controlled and supply problems can be identified and suppliers rated and ranked. Most ERP software systems include this feature.
- **Performance Dashboard:** Managers need access to performance data and a performance dashboard provides access to information as it is acquired. Timely and accurate views of data are essential to improving business performance.
- **Work Instruction Tools:** Lean manufacturing relies on work standardization. In many new software systems developed to support Lean and in many ERP systems, best practices down to the work instruction level are maintained. An easy way to ensure quality and efficiency is through the maintenance of up-to-date work instructions. This functionality often comes from specialized vendors and ERP software providers.
- **Resource Allocation Tools:** Production systems with responsibility to produce multiple products often face resource

allocation problems. This may include work fixtures, capital equipment, or even skilled workers. Finite capacity scheduling systems and other resource allocation tools have been developed to aid with these situations.

Potential for Linking ERP and Lean

Some academics and industry analysts have implied that ERP is old school and Lean manufacturing has replaced it. Others, of course, disagree, saying those claims are akin to saying the automobile chassis is obsolete because a new engine has been invented (Miller, 2002). It is important to make a distinction between an ERP and Lean manufacturing. ERP can be thought of as a large scale software system for linking all parts of the firm and encouraging best practice business processes. Lean manufacturing is one of these best practices mostly focused in the manufacturing area. At least, that's one productive way of viewing the synergy that may emerge from a marriage of the two methodologies.

As an example of how the broader set of organizational data can benefit Lean manufacturing, consider a shortcoming of many Lean initiatives. Often, these initiatives make rapid progress then the rate of improvement plateaus. The difficulty of managing pull operations in an environment where demands and product mix widely fluctuate is partly responsible for this plateau (Bragg, 2004). Another difficulty might be related to incomplete data. Imagine a 30% reduction in process cycle time resulting from a Lean kaizen event that does not get formally communicated to marketing, procurement, material planning, customer order management or the capacity planning functions (Metzger, 2008). What is perfectly obvious in manufacturing may not be communicated up the supply chain to other business operations. Visual pull systems developed for a local process must be communicated and linked through ERP to sustain the Lean program results across the SME

(Metzger, 2008). This is especially important when the SME maintains separate production and business facilities.

Having access to additional business data may lead to understanding where bottlenecks may still occur, or what operations may be further optimized. Without historic data combined with analytic tools, this can become increasingly difficult or even impossible. The data associated with an ERP can help identify these constraints to optimize demand flow manufacturing (Bragg, 2004).

Other challenges to Lean include trying to modernize manual kanban methods that use printed cards, which work well within SMEs with contained environments or "line of sight" manufacturing facilities. Major difficulties can result when these systems are extended across the plant and to suppliers, since breakdowns in manual kanbans get lost at the local level (Bragg, 2004). Typical approaches for Lean used by most SMEs today do not provide an optimal return on investment for companies (Steger-Jensen & Hvolby, 2008) and financial data regarding each part of the operation may not be collected.

Lean enabled modules offered by ERP suppliers and specialist suppliers may help overcome many of these challenges (Bragg, 2004). In fact, ERP vendors are starting to offer new solutions aimed to bridge the gap between the shop floor and ERP (Nakashima, 2000; Bradford, Mayfield, & Toney, 2001). These solutions may be offered in the form of Lean modules or add-on components (Bradford, Mayfield & Toney, 2001).

Benefits gained by implementing Lean-enabled ERP modules can be illustrated by the following example provided by Nakashima (2000). Cerberus, a New Jersey-based manufacturer of commercial fire detection systems, and division of Siemens, implemented Lean techniques and American Software's Flow Manufacturing application to achieve significant increases in both flexibility and productivity. Before implementing Flow Manufacturing application, a new model would be produced every 15-30 days. After implementing Flow Manufacturing, multiple models come off the production line every 20 seconds (Nakashima, 2000). Productivity increased by as much as 15-20%, floor space was reduced by 25-30%, finished goods inventory was reduced by 50%, while sales volumes increased by 35% (Nakashima, 2000). These improvements are by no means insignificant.

ERP Vendors Offering Lean Tools

Many ERP vendors have introduced "enablers" that incorporate Lean manufacturing best practices into their systems. These enablers include a variety of new modules, database items, toolsets, and business process modifications that create new functionality in existing software (Nakashima, 2000). The following sections describe these features in more detail (Halgeri, 2008):

Toolset # 1: Just-in-Time

A key difference between ERP implementation and Lean manufacturing has been the approach to production. Since ERP has traditionally used a push production system, adopting a philosophy of pull production has been a challenge. Many ERP vendors have begun to add a JIT toolset to their best practices procedures as a step in this direction. A primary functionality of this tool extends the pull concept through the entire supply chain from suppliers to customers. Of course, incorporating just-in-time features encourages flexible, small lot deliveries of parts and materials without the need for traditional purchase orders and this can be difficult to implement in an ERP system (Nakashima, 2000).

One vendor, Oracle, and its Flow Manufacturing software includes multiple component replenishment routines that support multiple component demand patterns. This flexible approach to JIT procurement helps eliminate stock-outs. The software automates material replenishment processes through the creation of a self-regulating pull production system. Oracle also offers Feeder Line Synchronization processes that can create specific JIT schedules for complex, dependent demand to ensure parts are delivered when needed. This is ideal for products that must be built specifically for customer orders, or are highly customized or variable. Using additional features, required components and parts can be ordered to ensure delivery at the perfect time to become available during production. Stable, predictable demand can use kanban management processes but more complex demand can access both ERP data and use JIT concepts for delivery (Oracle, 2006).

Toolset # 2: Convertors to Transform Multi-Level Bills-of-Material into Flat Bills with Event Sequencers

Many ERP vendors have begun to offer functionality intended to eliminate traditional MRP-based bills-of-material that simulate the manufacturing process and establish start and due dates for each department. These time-phased and shop floor control routings are converted into flat bills without sub-assemblies or parent assembly product routing. These converters transform multilevel bills-of-material into flat bills with event sequencers, emulating processes used in Lean manufacturing (Nakashima, 2000).

Toolset # 3: Analysis and Mapping Tools

Lean manufacturing initiatives often begin with an analysis phase used to identify potential and existing production problems. The goal is to determine "quick wins" to immediately and dramatically improve production performance (Bragg, 2004). These quick wins may come about because of production practices or when Lean principles are used to examine other business practices (McManus & Richard, 2002). Several methods are used to accomplish this including Value Stream Analysis (VSA).

VSA is used to ensure the product specified by the customer is delivered in a cost effective way and value is added throughout the supply chain (Paez, Dewees, Genaidy, Tuncel, Karwowski, & Zurada, 2004). Womack & Jones (1996) suggest several business methodologies including: problem solving (from design to product launch), information management (from order taking to delivery), as well as material transformation (from incoming raw materials to finished goods) are all key to conducting a value stream analysis. VSA demonstrates process steps for elimination, modification or improvement both with and without investment. A Value Stream Mapping (VSM) tool can be implemented to further improve this analysis by graphically illustrating current and desired processes in the value stream. This makes it easier to understand and implement recommendations derived from earlier or ongoing Value Stream Analysis activities (McManus & Richard, 2002).

Several vendors offer both VSA and VSM support in their ERP software systems. First, Pelion's ERP system is noted for its strengths in VSM. Their EASYVSM workbench software adapts to specific production environments to reduce manufacturing cycle times and to streamline work processes. Additionally, non-value added work can be identified and eliminated. This helps increase customer responsiveness and satisfaction (Pelion Systems, 2008). The following features of EASYVSM have been documented as mechanisms to improve product and material flows (QSG Team, 2006):

- Current and future state maps
- Collaborative, enterprise-wide value stream maps
- VSM presentation material
- Visual communication boards in multiple locations
- Cycle time organization features
- Features to manage changeover times, production volumes, information flows, staffing requirements and inventory strategies

- Calculation tools for value-added and non-value added times
- Visualization for high leverage projects, kaizen events and operating programs

Oracle's Flow Manufacturing software also offers VSA and VSM support. Flow Manufacturing offers Graphical Line Designer to aid in visualization of current value streams and to create maps which can be redesigned into balanced line operations and in ways that eliminate waste and redundancy. Graphical Line Designer defines standard processes and associates them with configurable models, product families, and networks or processes. Each individual process is linked to a set of primary and feeder processes and can be identified as rework where relevant. Overall, users are able to focus on events important to quality improvement initiatives (Oracle, 2006).

Toolset # 4: Demand Smoothing

The focus of demand smoothing tools are to accumulate forecasts and customer demands and then provide graphical analyses of requirements for daily production. This functionality is a natural fit for ERP systems since forecasting is often based on historical data. Most demand smoothing tools also consider important resources needed to complete the recommended production (Nakashima, 2000). An ERP package that offers demand smoothing is Manugistics. It specializes in support for dynamic pricing techniques. Additionally, it can be integrated with production planning software modules. Manugistics smoothes demand through dynamic pricing. So if demand exceeds production capabilities, pricing is raised and vice versa. This helps manufacturers proactively stabilize demand so production rates more closely mirror sales (Bragg, 2004). Other ERP vendors offering demand smoothing include Oracle, SAP, and IFS.

Toolset # 5: Engineering Change Orders

Engineering change orders can be a huge disruption to workflow. Workflow or other similar technology to communicate engineering changes to the production line can be implemented using an ERP system to more easily and more immediately signal the factory floor. This can be important since changes can impact the work process as much as the bill-of materials (Nakashima, B. 2000). Many ERP systems have begun to implement this feature.

Toolset # 6: Kanban Control and Management

Simple flow manufacturing, particularly in SMEs, often will not require enterprise software. Many successful manufacturers use kanban tags instead of work orders, however, this works best only in situations where production is steady and product demand stable with few changes (Turbide, 2005). As production becomes more complex with greater variation, changes, and customers, specialty kanban will be required. Special situations such as promotional peaks, seasonal demand, long lead-time supplies, and highly customized orders can lead to difficulties in the kanban environment (Bragg, 2004). As demand changes, manual kanbans can become more difficult to manage thus changes harder to track (Garwood, 2002).

According to Bragg (2004) another difficulty associated with manual kanban relates to loss. He reports that up to 1% of manual kanbans gets lost every day (Bragg, 2004). Manual kanbans are also hard to track and often labor intensive (Bragg, 2004). Simplicity can come at a cost.

ERP software vendors have created support modules that address many kanban control and management problems. A promising solution has been to offer electronic kanbans that continue to allow plant floor operations to capitalize on the advantages of kanban but at the same time provide access to a greater range of organizational data and intelligence to optimize the use of resources. This enables smarter scheduling together with the benefits of kanban. A much larger segment of the manufacturing community can benefit (Turbide, 2005). Additionally, ERP systems can provide additional analysis tools which can help recalculate the size and number of kanban bins required. This can be done on-the-fly and used to alert key personnel of expected changes. Manual kanbans can then be changed. Of course, if electronic kanbans are being used, then the changes can be done automatically (Nakashima, 2000).

Pelion's ERP software offers a variety of functions to extract updated requirements from the organizational data repositories and uses this information to send out new kanban levels to the plant floor. This can be done on a continual or at least regular basis to avoid production over-or-under estimates. These tools allow for proper sizing and timing of material deliveries together with electronic release signals. This ensures vendors provide timely delivery of needed supplies and parts (Garwood, 2002).

Oracle also provides kanban functionality in its Flow Manufacturing software. Oracle's approach has been to support all kanban transactions with its Mobile Supply Chain Applications (MSCA) module. Kanban replenishment becomes more sophisticated with access to enterprise data. Therefore kanban can be based upon anticipated volumes based on historical data and the optimal number of kanbans and their sizes can be calculated based on anticipated and actual demand. This also protects against errors that may be attributable to varying demands (Oracle, 2006).

Toolset # 7: Line Design / Sequencing

In multiple product production lines, minimizing changeovers can become a difficult and tricky problem. In production lines with the capability to simultaneously produce multiple parts, it becomes necessary to not only minimize changeovers, but also sequence them in a logical order that maximizes overall production (Bragg, 2004).

Some ERP vendors now offer Line Design and Sequencing toolsets adapted from Lean manufacturing. These software tools are designed so flow logic can be used to maximize specific customer-ordered variations of offered product mixes and the key components required to meet the demand. This is particularly true when products are configure-to-order (Nakashima, 2000).

In a configure-to-order, products are assembled from modules based on pre-constructed components that are then finished and configured to meet customer demand (Bradford, Mayfield & Toney, 2001). A line design tool helps to synchronize related work activities and ensure that raw material consumption is considered and planned in a way to reduce or eliminate queue time, inventory, and work-in-process. This helps support continuous improvement efforts by ensuring the facility has a continually balanced manufacturing line (Bradford, Mayfield & Toney, 2001).

Oracle offers a tool called Sequencing Rules to perform these functions. Oracle uses ILOG's optimization engine in conjunction with enterprise data to develop optimal production sequences. ILOG is a third-party software vendor specializing in resource optimization, resource allocation and network management among other areas. Oracle's Sequencing Rules toolset offers a variety of features relating to Lean (Bragg, 2004). Among these are:

- **Groupings:** Allows products with common attributes to be placed together
- **Spacing between Products:** Ensures hard-to-manufacture variants not bunched in production sequence
- **Required / Disallowed Transitions:** Transitions are monitored and tracked so changeover-related costs can be reduced.

In another ERP package from SYSPRO (ARC Strategies, 2007), a "rules based" Product Configurator software module has been developed to specifically address the needs of assemble-to-order or engineer-to-order SMEs. The main premise is that products comprised of varying combinations of predefined components, subassemblies, and operations can be configured from within the Sales Order, Quotation/Estimating and/or Work-In-Process modules. This gives a salesperson or estimator the ability to immediately configure a product based on a client's answer to questions.

The Configurator software can be used to select a number of pre-finished products, to create a sales kit, or a standard bill of material to request the manufacture of a custom product (CTS, 2008).

Backflush is the deduction from inventory records of the component parts used in an assembly or subassembly by exploding the bill of materials by the production count of assemblies produced (Cox and Blackstone, 2008). In other words, inventory can be backflushed to remove raw material from inventory, instead adding to finished goods inventory or to inventories of stocked sub assemblies. In Lean manufacturing, backflushing should be a routine transaction for material issues. Activity reporting and inventory level updates can be replaced by the performance of all inventory transactions upon completion of a single unit (Nakashima, 2000). In some plants, the replenishment signal for a bin is generated from a backflush, since this saves the waste of creating Kanban cards and scanning them.

Oracle Flow Manufacturing backflushes all the components and performs resource and overhead transactions upon recording the assembly completion. Oracle Flow Manufacturing allows scrapping assemblies and returning from scrap at any operation using either scheduled or unscheduled flow schedules. A scrap transaction will cause all the components through the scrap operation to be backflushed (Oracle, 2006).

Toolset # 8: Orderless Flow Manufacturing

Traditional batch production is controlled through work orders which, by Lean standards, include too much waste (Turbide, 2005). Kanban-based flow manufacturing is conducted without work orders – and therefore without the waste associated with work orders. Flow manufacturing is characterized by production lines and/or cells in which work is pulled or moves piece-by-piece through the process and not in batches (Turbide, 2005). This pull based work flow in the production line is generally achieved by using visual Kanban cards that can be tags, labels, containers, or electronic signals (Turbide, 2005).

One of the available ERP systems offering support in Orderless Manufacturing is TTW's WinMan software. It uses an empty container as a signal to trigger internal replenishment. These empty containers further indicate completion of a finished product and backflushing of the component material. In order to help complete the transaction, TTW has designed a set of internal Kanban cards which can be bar code scanned. (WinMan, 2003). Oracle Flow Manufacturing records completions of assemblies without having to create work orders (Oracle, 2006).

ERP Vendors Offering Lean Support

As is evident from the list of Lean-enabled features now being supported in ERP systems, a number of vendors have begun to enter the marketplace. Table 2 provides a list of some of these vendors and their primary Lean-enabled software modules. Three of these vendors are then explored in more detail.

Vendor #1: Oracle

Oracle is considered a leader in Lean-manufacturing implementation within its ERP system. According its research, Oracle had over 100

Table 2. Lean enabled ERP systems

Lean-Enabled Software	Vendor	Website
Alliance/MFG	Exact Software	www.alliancemfg.com
American Software Enterprise Version 3	American Software	www.amsoftware.com
Demand Point	Pelion Systems	www.pelionsystems.com
E2	Shoptech	www.shoptech.com
e-Intelliprise	American Software, Inc	www.amsoftware.com/marketing/intelliprise-home.asp
Fourth Shift	Softbrands Manufacturing Solutions	www.fourthshift.com
Global Shop	Global Shop Solutions	www.globalshopsolutions.com/product.htm
IFS Applications	IFS	www.ifsworld.com
Infor ERP VISUAL	Infor Global Solutions, Inc.	www.infor.com
Made2Manage	Consona	www.made2manage.com
MFG/PRO	QAD	www.qad.com
Manugistics	JAD Software Group, Inc.	www.jda.com
MISys	MISys	www.misysinc.com/mi2kover.htm
Oracle E –Business Suite	Oracle	www.oracle.com
PeopleSoft Enterprise	Oracle	www.oracle.com/applications/peoplesoft-enterprise.html
Seradex ERP Solutions	Seradex	www.seradex.com/ERP/Lean_Manufacturing_ERP.php (Seradex, 2007)
Sage ERP X3	Adonix	www.adonix.com
SYSPRO Enterprise	SYSPRO	www.syspro.com
Ultriva	Ultriva (ebots)	www.ultriva.com
Vista	Epicor	www.epicor.com
WinMan	TTW	www.winmanusa.com
xApp	SAP	www.sap.com/solutions

companies using its Flow Manufacturing module, and as many as four times that amount used its Kanban software (Bragg, 2004). Oracle Flow Manufacturing has been implemented as part of the Oracle E-Business Suite (Oracle, 2006). Oracle considers Flow Manufacturing as crucial to its e-commerce strategy. Because of this, Flow Manufacturing has been promoted as effective in the reduction of product cycle times, inventories, and process complexity. In addition, Oracle claims the software will simplify production, and help meet production demand at affordable prices (Kent, 2002). Of course, none of these features would be possible without the synergy offered

by coupling Lean with the wide array of ERP enterprise data.

Additionally, Oracle's software allows users to create simulations of expected Lean environment changes. Several simulation tools allow experimentation with line balancing, optimized product flows, and Heijunka sequencing (Wheatley, 2007). Oracle's software not only supports kanban from assembly to the supplier base, it also includes tools to provide users with the capability to view historic demand and optimize the size and number of system kanban cards (Wheatley, 2007). Various researchers and practitioners have reported a great deal of success with Oracle's Lean enabled ERP

Table 3. Lean-enabled tools from Oracle

Feature	Description
Value Stream Mapping	Identifies opportunities for improvement
Value Stream Analysis	Visualizes opportunities for improvement
Line Design and Balancing	Supports mixed model production of standard or configured products
Just-in-Time Procurement	Pull-based, kanban replenishment chain supported to improve inventory turns. Also, supports synchronized component replenishment for configured or build-to-order components.
Electronic Work Methods	Lean manufacturing execution workstation supported for operators thus enabling move toward paperless shop floor.
Backflushing	Scrap transaction generated automatically causing all components to be backflushed
Kanban	Supports kanban transactions with Mobile Supply Chain Applications (MSCA) module
Orderless Flow Manufacturing	Allows recording of completions of assemblies without having to create work orders
Sequencing and Scheduling Capability	Produces directly to customer order

systems (Lee & Adam, 1986; WinMan, 2006). Table 3 provides a list of several Lean-enabled tools offered by Oracle (Oracle, 2006):

Vendor #2: TTW

TTW's Windows ERP product, WinMan is particularly suited for use by SMEs. This product features an integrated manufacturing management system designed specifically for the needs of small to midsized enterprises. Since it manages both manufacturing and business operations, including bill of materials, purchasing, material requirements planning (MRP), inventory planning and control, and master production scheduling (MPS), it can help control all aspects of an SME (Global Shop Solution, 2008).

TTW reports several success stories related to WinMan implementations including Lantech being about to grow its share of the stretch-wrap machinery market from 35 percent to 50 percent. Capricorn Cars Parts increased its inventory turnover by 188% and increased its parts portfolio from 1,800 to 15,000 while experiencing

Table 4. Lean-enabled tools from TTW's WinMan

Feature	Description
Support for Just-in-Time	External Kanban generates bar coded kanban cards for pre-selected suppliers and allows manufacturers to pull inventory on demand from the shop floor
Demand Driven Manufacturing	Eliminates non-value added activities and reduces inventory by using pull manufacturing techniques
Push/Pull Flexibility	Ability to process back to back orders in both purchasing and manufacturing and simulates the pull concept while still utilizing traditional push purchase orders and manufacture orders
Line Design and Sequencing.	Product Configuration workbench allows selection of various options on the fly during the sales order process. Guided by pre-selected logic. May offer inclusion and/or exclusion rules.
Orderless Flow Manufacturing	Uses an empty container as a signal to trigger internal replenishment. Empty containers may signal completion of finished product and trigger backflushing of the component material
Backflushing	Backflushing is deduction from inventory records of component parts used in an assembly or subassembly

Table 5. Lean-enabled toolsets from Pelion Systems

Feature	Description
Value Stream Analysis	EasyVSM workbench determines key breakthrough improvement opportunities, helps distinguish between value-added and non value-added activities.
Value Stream Mapping	Delivers visual roadmap of Kaizen and other improvements, increases visibility and aids in communication
Lean Engineering:	Defines flow as a means of driving Lean process layouts and aids in continuous improvement effects
Lean Material Flow	Aids in material flow design, strategic inventory decisions, stock out reductions, pull signal methods in all parts of production, inventory turnover. Supports rapid analysis of dynamic material requirements
Line Design and Sequencing	Matches product mix with demand volume (both actual and forecast) with factory resources. Provides alerts to potential resource allocation bottlenecks
Kanban Control and Management	Enables real-time coordination on dynamic demand-pull requirements; tracks fulfillment performance and ensures production goals met in effective, timely fashion

a marginal increase in overhead costs (WinMan, Athena Controls 2008).

Since many SMEs utilize the benefits offered with Lean practices, WinMan provides a number of related tools. Table 4 illustrates (CTS, 2008; WinMan, 2006).

Vendor #3: Pelion Systems

Unlike other ERP vendors, Pelion Systems' suite of products is developed as third party software to augment existing ERP applications. The primary objective of Pelion's software is to reduce excessive lead time and lot size obstacles through the use of Lean manufacturing practices (Garwood, 2002). Pelion calls its primary software Demand Flow Technology. The approach is to combine a kanban execution system with value stream mapping capability. Full integration occurs within the line design and balancing tools inside Pelion's Lean module, Collaborative Flow Manufacturing (CFM). This further offers support for kanban size determination in flow lines. Pelion provides functionality that gives users the capability to work on four time horizons simultaneously (Bragg, 2004). For instance a production planner can use an annual time horizon to develop a plant layout, a quarterly horizon to implement new product introductions together with expected kanban sizes and takt time, monthly horizons for work schedules and other

plans, and finally daily horizons to monitor and manage work output (Bragg, 2004).

Bragg (2004) reports a number of success stories associated with Pelion software. For instance, Husqvarna reduced its inventory by more than a million dollars and was able to improve order fulfillment within a predetermined time frame from less than sixty percent to more than ninety-five percent. Brooks Automation reported a twenty million dollar inventory reduction. Nissan Forklift reported a twenty percent reduction in final assembly direct labor, a forty-seven percent reduction in inventory and nearly five and half million in annual savings. Table 5 provides a look at the Lean-enabled toolsets provided by Pelion Systems.

FUTURE TRENDS

The near saturation of ERP sales in large organizations has encouraged software vendors to seek additional venues for development and growth. SMEs provide a natural fit for a new focus of ERP software development. A problem in marketing software within this arena has been the widespread focus on Lean manufacturing used by many SMEs. This problem becomes complicated since most ERP software is based on push methodologies and Lean practice revolves around pull

Table 6. Software comparison

Lean Initiative	Oracle Flow Manufacturing (Turbide, 2005)	TTW's Winman (Wheatley, 2007)	Pelion systems Demad Flow (Bragg, 2004; Pelion, 2008)
Analysis Tools	√	-	√
Mapping Tools	√	-	√
JIT Procurement Support	√	√	√
Kanban Control	√	√	√
Sequencing	√	√	√
Demand Smoothing	√	√	√

methodologies. Software vendors have addressed this through a variety of new software modules and ERP add-ons.

This in turn has encouraged additional manufacturers to adopt Lean practices and experience the synergy offered by using Lean-enabled ERP software. However, manufacturers face a variety of issues when making the transition to Lean (Michel, 2002).

Although the primary question, can ERP software be used to support Lean has been answered by a variety of organizations with their software solutions (See table), many Lean purists believe only visual signals and shop floor implementation provide a true implementation of this philosophy and the added functionality of ERP flies in the face of basic Lean premises. Others believe ERP systems provide additional transactional foundations and historical data collection and analyses that can further improve Lean practices. Added then are benefits associated with having business software integrated and tied to the same database.

ERP vendors are competing with best-of-breed software vendors to understand and offer solutions to support best practice implementations of Lean production (Michel, 2002). A Lean-enabled ERP implementation must necessarily include a variety of new modules, procedures, practices and toolsets to add new functions to existing ERP software (Nakashima, 2000). These modules often include: value stream analysis, value stream mapping, lean engineering, lean material flow, line design

and sequencing, backwash capability, kanban management, and others.

A variety of software packages and functionality have emerged. Table 6 adapted from Halgeri (2008) provides a glimpse at these cross referenced with the three vendor solutions this article explored in more depth.

Certainly the future of ERP systems will include more Lean-enabled tools and continue to capitalize on the synergy derived from the using best Lean practices within an environment of automatic data collection and access. SMEs will continue to derive benefits from appropriate scaled versions of ERP systems without losing their edge in terms of nimbleness and ability to react to their customers' needs. Larger organizations will gain greater access to the methods developed in smaller organizations and will find closer links and better communication along the entire supply chain possible. More ERP vendors will add Lean tools and continue to improve those already in use.

CONCLUSION

Overall, this research suggests Lean manufacturing has been successfully integrated with ERP software as a best-of-breed approach useful to many SMEs and other manufacturers. With global competition heating up, small and medium enterprises (SMEs), more than ever, must have access to superior software systems and tools.

This article has described how ERP (Enterprise Resource Planning) and Lean manufacturing have been implemented in various ways. In early incarnations, ERP systems were considered a hindrance to Lean manufacturing efforts and were criticized for encouraging large inventories and slower production. In more recent years, it has become apparent that SMEs must seek the best of both worlds and use the benefits of ERP and retain the nimbleness provided by Lean. Linking ERP and Lean methods can lead to competitive advantage as demonstrated in a number of software solutions offered by vendors such as Oracle TTW, and Pelion. These tools represent the future of SMEs and their use of ERP systems.

REFERENCES

Aladwani, A. M. (2001). Change management strategies for successful ERP implementation. *Business Process Management Journal, 7*(3), 266–275. doi:10.1108/14637150110392764

Bartholomew, D. (1999). Lean vs. ERP. *Industry Week, 248,* 1–6.

Bartholomew, D. (2003). ERP: Learning to be Lean. *Industry Week.* Retrieved July 19, 2008, from http://www.industryweek.com/ReadArticle. aspx?Article ID=2289.

Bonvik, A. M., Couch, C. E., & Gershwin, S. B. (1997). A comparison of production-line control mechanisms. *International Journal of Production Research, 35*(3), 789–804. doi:10.1080/002075497195713

Bradford, M., Mayfield, T., & Toney, C. (2001) Does ERP fit in a Lean world? *Strategic Finance, May,* 28-34.

Bragg, S. (2004) Software solutions taking Lean manufacturing to the next level. Retrieved July 20, 2008, from http://www.oracle.com/lean/arc_leanmfg.pdf

Burton, T. T., & Boeder, S. M. (2003). *The Lean extended enterprise: Moving beyond the four walls to value stream excellence.* Fort Lauderdale, FL: J. Ross Publishing.

Cheng, T. C. E., & Podolsky, S. (1993). *Just-in-time manufacturing: An introduction* (2nd ed.). London: Chapman & Hall.

Cox, J., & Blackstone, J. (Eds.). (2008). *APICS dictionary* (12th ed.). Chicago, IL: APICS Educational Society for Resource Manage.

CTS. (2008). *Manufacturing software reviews.* Retrieved July 20, 2008 from http://www.cts-guides.com/manufacturing.asp

Deep, A., Dani, S., & Burns, N. (2008). Investigating factors affecting ERP selection in made-to-order SME sector. *Journal of Manufacturing Technology Management, 19*(4), 430–446. doi:10.1108/17410380810869905

Gable, G., & Stewart, G. (1999). SAP R/3 implementation issues for small to medium enterprises. In W.D. Haseman & D.L. Nazareth (Eds.), *Proceedings of the 5th Americas Conference on Information Systems* (pp. 779-781), Milwaukee, WI.

Garwood, D. (2002). ERP or flow manufacturing? Collaboration, not separation. *R.D. Garwood, Inc.* Retrieved July 22, 2008 from http://www.rdgarwood.com/archive/hot56.asp.

Global Shop Solutions. (2008). Global solutions products. Retrieved August 30, 2008 from http://www.globalshopsolutions.com/erp-software/default.asp.

Greene, A. (2004). Toyota production systems: Lean goes mainstream. *Managing Automation* (April). Retrieved July 20, 2008, from http://www.managingautomation.com/maonline/magazine/read/view/Toyota_Production_Systems__Lean_Goes_Mainstream_3874.

Halgeri, P., Pei, Z. J., Iyer, K. S., Bishop, K., & Shehadeh, A. (2008). *ERP systems supporting Lean manufacturing: A literature review*. 2008 International Manufacturing Science & Engineering Conference (MSEC), Evanston, IL, USA.

Jacobs, R. (2007). Enterprise resource planning (ERP) - A brief history. *Journal of Operations Management*, *25*(2), 357–363. doi:10.1016/j.jom.2006.11.005

Kent, J. F. (2002). *An examination of traditional ERP and Lean manufacturing production control methods with a view of flow manufacturing software as an alternative*. MS thesis, University of Oregon.

Koch, C. (2008). ABC: An introduction to ERP. *CIO*. Retrieved March 18, 2008, from http://www.cio.com/article/40323/ABC_An_Introduction_to_ERP/1

Koh, L., & Simpson, M. (2005). Change and uncertainty in SME manufacturing environments using ERP. *Journal of Manufacturing Technology Management*, *16*(6), 629–653. doi:10.1108/17410380510609483

Lee, T. S., & Adam, E. E. Jr. (1986). Forecasting error evaluation in material requirements planning (MRP) production-inventory systems. *Management Science*, *32*(9), 1186–1205. doi:10.1287/mnsc.32.9.1186

Li, Y., Liao, X. W., & Lei, H. Z. (2006). A knowledge management system for ERP implementation. *Systems Research and Behavioral Science*, *23*(2), 157–168. doi:10.1002/sres.751

McManus, H. L., & Richard, L. M. (2002). Value Stream analysis and mapping for product development. In *Proceedings of 23rd ICAS Congress* (pp. 6103.1-6103.10). Toronto, Canada.

Mekong Capital. (2004). Introduction to Lean manufacturing for Vietnam. Retrieved August 30, 2008 from http://www.mekongcapital.com/Introduction%20to%20Lean%20Manufacturing%20-%20English.pdf

Metzger, B. (2008). *Linking Lean and ERP systems together for sustained advantage* [White paper of TriMin Systems, Inc.]. Retrieved August 30, 2008 from http://www.triminmfg.com/images/KnowledgeBase/Metzger.pdf

Michel, R. (2002). Multiple paths to Lean: Detector Electronics, Norlen turn to specialized Lean manufacturing solutions. *Manufacturing Business Technology*. Retrieved July 20, 2008 from http://www.mbtmag.com/article/CA254538.html?q=Lean+ERP+software

Miller, G. J. (2002). Lean and ERP: Can they co-exist? Retrieved July 19, 2008 from http://facilitatorgroup.net/pdf/LeanERPCoExist.pdf

Nagendra, P. B., & Das, S. K. (1999). MRP/SFX: A kanban-oriented shop floor extension to MRP. *Production Planning and Control*, *10*(3), 207–218. doi:10.1080/095372899233172

Nakashima, B. (2000). Lean and ERP: Friend or foe? *Advanced Manufacturing (September)* Retrieved July 20, 2008 from http://www.advanced-manufacturing.com/index.php?option=com_stati cxt&staticfile=informationtech.htm&Itemid=44

Oracle (2006). *Oracle Flow Manufacturing datasheet*. Retrieved July 19, 2008 from ttp://www.oracle.com/applications/manufacturing/flow-manufacturing-data-sheet.pdf.

Paez, O., Dewees, J., Genaidy, A., Tuncel, S., Karwowski, W., & Zurada, J. (2004). The Lean manufacturing enterprise: An emerging socio-technological system integration. *Human Factors and Ergonomics in Manufacturing*, *14*(3), 285–306. doi:10.1002/hfm.10067

Pelion Systems. (2008). *Pelion Systems Solutions*. Retrieved July 22, 2008 from http://www.pelionsystems.com/solutions.asp

Piszczalski, M. (2000). Lean vs. information systems. *Automotive Manufacturing & Production, 112*(8), 26–28.

Poppendieck, M. (2002) *Principles of Lean thinking* (pp. 1-7). Poppendieck LLC.

Rashid, M. A., Hossain, L., & Patrick, J. D. (2002). *The evolution of ERP systems: A historical perspective*. Hershey, PA: Idea Group.

Seradex. (2007). Lean Manufacturing - Seradex ERP Solutions. Retrieved September 3, 2008 from http://www.seradex.com/ERP/Lean_Manufacturing_ERP.php

Spearman, M. L., Hopp, W. J., & Woodruff, D. L. (1999). A hierarchical control architecture for constant work-in-process (CONWIP). *Journal of Manufacturing and Operations Management, 2*(3), 147–171.

Spearman, M. L., & Zazanis, M. A. (1992). Push and pull production systems: Issues and comparisons. *Operations Research, 40*(3), 521–532. doi:10.1287/opre.40.3.521

Steger-Jensen, K., & Hvolby, H. (2008). Review of an ERP System Supporting Lean Manufacturing. In T. Koch (Ed.), *International Federation for Information Processing (IFIP)*, Volume 257, *Lean Business Systems and Beyond* (pp. 67-74). Boston, MA: Springer.

Strategies, A. R. C. (2007). The when, why and how of ERP support for Lean. *SYSPRO*, 1-22. Retrieved July 18, 2008 from http://www.syspro.com

Strategosinc (2008). *Origins & history Lean Manufacturing*. Retrieved July 18, 2008 from http://www.strategosinc.com/just_in_time.htm

Team, Q. S. G. (2006). *Manufacturing can actively manage their value streams with Pelion's next generation EasyVSM tool*. Retrieved July 20, 2008 from http://www.qsoftguide.com/cm/index.php?blog=2&p=254&more=1&c=1&tb=1&pb=1

Turbide, D. A. (2005). *Five ways ERP can help you implement Lean*. EPICOR Software. Retrieved July 16, 2008 from http://whitepapers.zdnet.com/abstract.aspx?docid=351964.

Wheatley, M. (2007). ERP is needed to sustain the gains of Lean programs. *Manufacturing Business Technology*. Retrieved July 18, 2008 from http://www.mbtmag.com/article/CA6450623.html

WinMan. (2003). *WinMan and Lean systems - A white paper on integrating WinMan with Lean systems*. Retrieved August 20, 2008 from http://www.winmanusa.com/PDF/WinMan_Lean_Systems.pdf

WinMan. (2006). *Athena Controls*. Retrieved August 20, 2008 from http://www.winmanusa.com/success.asp

Womack, J. P., & Jones, D. T. (1996). Beyond Toyota: How to root out waste and pursue perfection. *Harvard Business Review*, (September-October): 140–158.

Chapter 6
A Forecasting Concept for Virtual Organisations Supporting SMEs

Jens Eschenbächer
BIBA GmbH, Germany

Heiko Duin
BIBA GmbH, Germany

ABSTRACT

Planning and management of Virtual Organisations (VOs) depends on accurate prognosis and forecasting of several organisational aspects. New and innovative business models such as the VO offer a variety of new options for SME to do business. This chapter presents a system-oriented view to understand planning and forecasting needs in VOs. The strategic issues in planning will be elaborated by using the cross-impact analysis. For the medium-term planning the focus lies on investigations based on the so-called collaborative network analysis. An industrial case study is introduced to demonstrate the application of the concept.

INTRODUCTION

Virtual Organisations and Forecasting

The organisational form of the Virtual Organisation (VO) can be considered as some type of business model innovation (Gassmann & Sutter, 2008). Consequently a VO can be seen as answer to the enormous market pressures due to the ever changing market environments showing e.g. discontinuities in trends, cost pressures and globalisation (Camarinha-Matos & Afsamarnesh, 2008; Mertens,

1993; Boutellier & Gassmann, 2008). Any kind of manufacturers – and especially small and medium sized enterprises (SMEs) – have responded to these conditions by forming collaborative relationships with suppliers, distributors and even customers (Camarinha-Matos & Afsamarnesh, 2008; McInerney, 2008) called Collaborative Networked Organisations (CNOs).

In the context of CNOs prognosis and forecasting have been discussed several years (e.g. Gassmann, 2008; Sturm et al, 1994), especially in the context of strategic management (Mintzberg, 1994). Wild (1982) pointed out that decision making on the issue forecasting and prognosis is indeed the most impor-

DOI: 10.4018/978-1-60566-892-5.ch006

tant information, which will be collected and used in the process of enterprise planning. Regarding the strategic management of SMEs all aspects of enterprise analysis and environment analysis are subject of prognosis and measurements. Trends in the macro environments, such as investments in new ICT (Information and Communication Technologies) solutions (e.g. Krauth, 1982), changes in competitive situation, and the evolving changes in resource and competence management of companies, do call for new forecasting methods and instruments. A classical systematisation of these methods and instruments differentiates quantitative and qualitative approaches (Bircher, 1976, Makridakis & Wheelwight, 1990; Götze, 1993). All these approaches have been developed for the usage in large companies. But are they also applicable for collaborating SME in Virtual Organisations?

Up to now, forecasting of business developments in Virtual Organisations has got some interest from both practitioners and academia (Gassmann & Sutter, 2008; Mertens, 1993). But, especially within harsh competition it becomes a key competence to better understand and foresee future developments. Boutellier et al (2008) have shown that a systematic planning of innovation processes can support the competitiveness dramatically. Also, McInnerney showed that forecasting can provide an enormous benefit to better understand customer requirements (McInnerney, 2007). Several other authors also state that the general trend towards more decentralization and cooperation towards virtual organisation can be observed (Gassmann & Sutter, 2008). To summarise: SME are faced with tremendous pressure from the market and they need to better understand their own business models in terms of planning on a short, medium and long term basis. This chapter will interlink these subjects and will present first conceptual results supporting SME in their forecasting activities.

Objectives of the Chapter

The main objective of this chapter is to set a basis for forecasting and prognosis concepts which could stimulate SMEs in their planning activities. The authors believe that this is very important because major trends such as continuous networking via Internet, new enterprise information systems and permanently changing market conditions are especially critically for non-prepared SME. This means that accurate strategic and operational planning and forecasting is essential for their survival (Gassmann & Sutter, 2008). Unfortunately the usage of EIS (Enterprise Information systems) tools for systematic planning and forecasting in SME is still in its beginning when comparing it with multinational companies (Rank, 2003; Wald, 2003; Boutellier et al, 2008). Especially here the usage is mostly limited to shop-floor oriented approaches such as production planning and control. This requires stabile production forecasts depending on an accurate planning of the business itself. Within these developments heavy debates about the organisational form of SME and their role in enterprise collaborations have started. The SME have to accept the shift from a limited environment to a global dynamic collaboration and competition within connected networks. Indeed this also implies a set of new challenges which need to be understood (Wildemann, 2008). SME have to coordinate a much higher number of inter-organisational relationships between each other and they have to understand business developments in forefront.

The aeronautical industry delivers a useful example (Airbus production network) in which a high number of SME have been disconnected to the original equipment manufacturer (OEM). This causes the establishment of new relationships and new planning schemes with other companies. Here new system or module suppliers become new integrators. Such integrators somewhere placed in the supply chain do not have to the SME long-term stabile relationships. Consequently the planning and forecasting work formerly done by Airbus is now divided to the members on the supply chain as well. This means that the SME have to better understand upcoming business trends and developments because it is not Airbus anymore providing exact information about their demands. The last point will be taken up by this chapter. How can the need to have a more accurate forecast be achieved by using new forecasting approaches?

This chapter addresses the forecasting and management of SME-based VOs. First, a system theoretic view on analysing SME-based VO is presented. This is followed by a pragmatic presentation on the both quantitative and qualitative forecasting approaches. Thirdly, a scenario is presented and will be used to illustrate the forecasting needs. Following, the two methods developed to support forecasting will be presented and discussed. Finally the discussion of the results so far concludes this chapter.

ENTERPRISE PLANNING AND FORECASTING APPLIED TO VIRTUAL ORGANISATIONS

SME-based VOs have to understand their relationships in order to foresee future developments. So far many SME have neglected their forecasting because they were directly linked to companies on a long-term basis and received concrete planning from the OEM. As indicated in the introduction this is slowly changing which creates a dramatic change for SME which need to be reflected in the application of new methods and tools.

System-Oriented Forecasting Approaches

Theoretical Foundation

The task of the network analysis lies in the investigation of relationship patterns within one or more organisations. In general the network analysis is a method to describe structure, relationships and functions between actors (Weyer, 2000).

A network is formally considered as a limited amount of nodes and elements and the number of connecting edges between those (Jansen, 2006). In an enterprise network the nodes and edges display the various relationships. Considering actors of an enterprise network we see them as company units (individuals, groups, departments, factories, etc.). Their relationships can be of very different nature such as legal, personnel or financial. The smallest possible unit of the network analysis is the Dyad which consists out of two nodes and their respective relationships (Wassermann & Faust, 1994). Structural investigations are carried out by breakdown of a complete network in single dyads.

A Triad represents a network with three nodes that considers elements with the respective relationships (Wassermann & Faust, 1994). In the same manner as for the Dyade the Triad will be investigated in the frame of the complete network. The graphical representation of networks depends on fact that actors are presented (company units) in form of nodes and the course of relationships or relations as edges. Figure 1 visualizes a network with three nodes (Triad) and respective three actors. Referencing Wiendahl altogether four elements to analyse can be differentiated (Wiendahl, 1997).

The "**node analysis**" specifies the analysis of the willingness to cooperate of single nodes (organisations). In this respect nodes can be defined as a set of activities that are interlinked by complex social networks to fulfil a common task. The "**node analysis**" considers activity bundles which are provided from individual partners for the network in order to investigate strength and weaknesses (Weber, 2005).

The "**edge analysis**" specifies the analysis of collaborative relationships between the nodes. In contrast to the "node analysis" the "edge analysis" focuses on the interpretation of the interactions on the level of the collaborative relationship (Sydow,

Figure 1. Elements to analyse

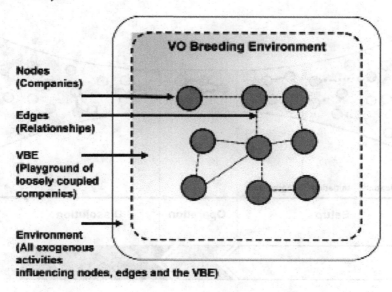

1992; Ulrich, 2004). Especially for SME cooperation on the level of innovation processes such as analysis can deliver a very good understanding about the prognosis of the common work.

Additionally the analysis of **Virtual Organisation Breeding Environments** is stressed in Figure 1. The aim of this form of analysis is the identification and interpretation of all issues concerning legal, organisational and technical organisation of the network. This enables the collaboration on the level of partnerships (Seifert, 2007; Camarinha-Matos, 2005.).

Finally the analysis of the **network environment** is stressed. This form of analysis goes down to the business oriented "stakeholder-analysis" descried e.g. by Welge and Al-Laham (2008). In the context of this chapter the authors define that virtual organisation are subject to similar influences as single enterprises. Indeed they have a high flexibility to anticipate and coordinate the influence of stakeholder environments. Against this background it is important to better understand the particularities of virtual organisations on the classical elements of the environment analysis.

On the basis of Figure 1 the ideas of analysing

scope, relationships and developments over time is fundamental for the chapter. Consequently Figure 2 shows the life-cycle of a Virtual organisation which interlinks the three elements mentioned before. Basically the lifetime of a VO is generally short and depends on the complexity of the value creation process and could be described by the three phases of setup, operation and dissolution. The setup phase can be further divided into identification, initiation and agreement. In comparison, the lifetime of the VBE is generally long-term. From a perspective of planning, the VO needs operational planning during its operation phase supported by some tactical planning during the set-up and dissolution phase. In difference to a VO the VBE needs strategic planning due its long-term existence.

Once in operation the main task of a VBE is to prepare and to react on occurring business opportunities. It continuously creates VOs in different configurations and for different durations. Each VO goes through the three phases of setup, operation and dissolution.

After presenting basic elements and their interconnections in the life-cycle this chapter will

Figure 2. Life cycle of a virtual organization

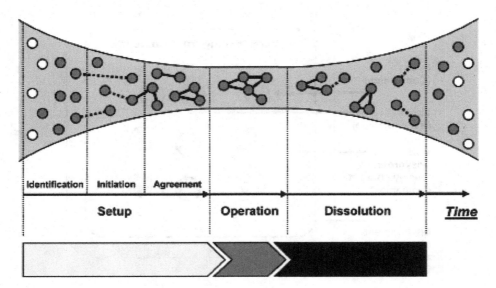

be summed up by presenting some kind of overall view. This view summarises the complex structure in which SME-based VO can be integrated. This structure can be summarised as follows:

- Network nodes are represented by system **elements** and edges describe the **relations** among the nodes.
- A number of elements which are connected by relations describe a **system**. A subgroup of elements and relations can be a **subsystem**, if all elements and relations also belong to the system.
- Finally, a system is embedded in a **supersystem** which creates a framework for the bigger picture. The actors and their relationships are supplemented by roles – both together is characterized by the structural dimension.

Virtual Organisation Breeding Environments as Source Networks for Virtual Organisations

The concept of the VO Breeding Environment (VBE) has been developed during the ECOLEAD research project. The two basic types of enterprise collaborations are represented by VOs and by VO Breeding Environments (Camarinha-Matos &Afsamarnesh, 2008). The connection between these two forms is that the Breeding Environment prepares the instantiation of VOs (Jagdev & Thoben, 2001). It acts as an incubator for a VO. From the VO point of view, the VO is created when a business opportunity occurs. In order to perform the actual value creation task, the VO can be created from scratch (collecting cooperating partners from an "open universe" of enterprises) or through a VO Breeding Environment (VBE). This situation is shown in Figure 3. In short the following aspects can be divided:

- The open universe illustrates organisations which might be SMEs.
- The breeding environment delivers an additional structure to the SME in which they agree to certain instruments such as cooperation agreements and common processes.
- WAY 1: The selection of cooperation partners is not supported by any organisational structure.
- WAY 2: The selection of SME is led by the VO breeding environment.

Figure 3. Creation options for virtual organisations

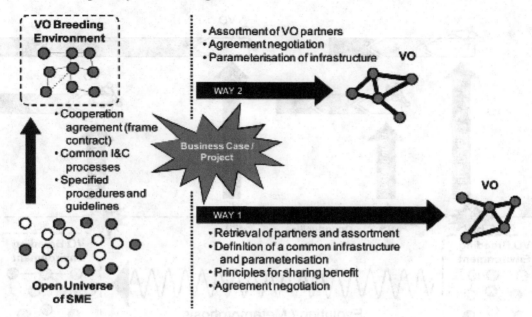

In this chapter we are focussing on the second way, meaning the creation of a VO buy through a VBE. Figure 4 shows a VBE during the operation phase. It continuously creates VOs in different configurations and for different durations. Each of the VOs go through the three phases of setting it up, operation and dissolution.

Evolution and metamorphosis of the VBE may be driven by random or in a planned and controlled way. Camarinha-Matos and Afsarmanesh do mention a long-term strategy behind the VBE, but the responsibility to develop and implement the strategy has not yet been assigned to one of the roles identified within a VBE. Duin (2007a) proposes to define a steering committee for strategic management tasks. Several other roles have already been identified including the member, administrator, opportunity broker, VO planner and coordinator (Camarinha-Matos & Afsarmanesh, 2006). The VBE Administrator is a role performed by a member organisation, which is responsible for the VBE operation and evolution, which includes promotion of coopera-

tion among the VBE members, filling the skill/competency gaps in the VBE by searching and recruiting/inviting new organisations into the VBE and the daily management of the VBE general processes, conflict resolution, preparation of a bag of VBE assets, and making common VBE policies, among others. The responsibility of the VBE administrator needs to be extended by strategic management tasks, when the long-term evolution and metamorphosis of the VBE should occur in a planned and controlled way.

From this perspective of continuously creating VOs from a VBE it becomes clear that two different kinds of planning and forecasting are needed:

- **Vertical Forecasting:** In this respect the planning of a concrete VOs including all types of necessary interactions between the partners of the VO is planned.
- **Horizontal Forecasting:** The horizontal forecasting supports the strategic development of the VBE and defines the gveneral conditions for a concrete VO life cycle.

Figure 4. Continuous instantiation of VOs by a VBE in operation phase

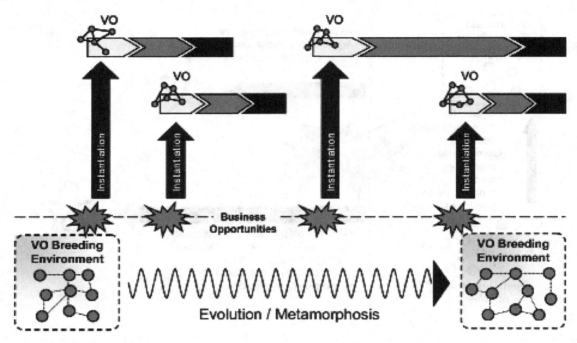

In principle the authors will develop two forecasting approaches: one for the vertical development of the VO (CNA) and one for the evolution and metamorphosis of the VBE (CRIMP)

Quantitative and Qualitative Forecasting Methods

Quantitative forecasting methods deliver on the basis of mathematical and statistical operations results regarding the forecasting of developments. A short overview about the quantitative methods and instruments, including a short characteristic and application fields is shown in several publications (e.g. Welge & Al-Laham, 2008).

The second group is called qualitative forecasting methods. Those methods have been highlighted in strategic management due to the high uncertainty which continuously increases in companies. They are suited for application in enterprise and network contexts in which either past data is not available or in which data cannot be easily quantified. Simon (1985) differentiates quantitative from qualitative forecasting methods with the help of the following characteristics:

- The application is limited on worse structured situations, which are labeled by imperfect information.
- They deliver no guarantee for solutions, but they can be used to reduce the complexity by focusing on a view on most suitable solutions.

Qualitative methods imply subjective assumptions on individuals or groups. To summaries, qualitative methods shall be seen as forecasting approaches which are based on a subjective evaluation of the respective prognosis issue. Both, qualitative and quantitative methods have been developed for the usage in enterprises. As an addition, this chapter shows how two approaches can be applied in the dynamic context of smart and virtual organisations. These two methods have been developed towards demonstration of forecasting in VOs.

Quantitative Methods

Description
The application area of the network analysis is very broad (Hollstein, 2006). Especially the developments in the social network analysis led to many approaches (Wassermann & Faust, 1994) and a high number of tools (CASOS, 2008). Meanwhile business oriented study results are available focussing on the application of the methods of the network analysis in companies (Rank, 2003; Wald, 2003). The two authors were analyzing intra-organisational networks from the BASF corporate group. A recent study discusses the analysis of ICT aspects in the Siemens Corporation (Ellmann, 2008). Ellmann has analysed two indicators out of many in the framework of the quantitative network analysis. Specifically she has studied the density and centrality of nodes within a network. Consequently the methods of the social network analysis arrived in the framework of business management.

In general the quantitative network analysis is divided into three phases: data acquisition, data representation and data analysis (Renz, 1998).

Indeed there are different methods available to collect, structure and evaluate quantitative data. For more information different authors discuss the diver's issues (Seifert, 2007; Welge & Al-Laham, 2008).

Potential and Limits
The quantitative network analysis captures network structures by using mathematical calculations, which implies a very formalistic way of handling network relationships. In fact this has been the basis for a lot of criticism towards quantitative procedures of the network analysis (Renz, 1998). Basically two points can be summarised:

- **Too static:** Due to the different measurement of various characteristics, the procedures of network analysis are able to construct networks in deep according to their structure but content, and dynamics of relationships cannot be captured (Sydow, 1992). Additionally, lacking consideration of context awareness seems to be a problem (Renz, 1998).

- **Difficult translation from experiences into numbers:** As a matter of fact the quantitative description necessary to operational qualitative characteristics by using indicators is to a certain extent impossible. Indeed an actor which is acting a long time already in the network can be a layman considering network analytic methods. But – and this is important – such a layman can most probably understand and translate the network behaviour due to his experience better the every network analyst.

The quantitative methods for network analysis can be used specifically in those situations in which already a lot of knowledge about the behaviour of the network is available. This knowledge can be used within a precise analysis leading to concrete results. Additionally a narrow and precise research question should be formulated to make it understandable. In case of rough investigated research fields and non precise research questions the quantitative methods and not recommended. The research field should not have many explorative elements.

Qualitative Methods

Description
Indeed it is a question of the massive criticism towards the quantitative network research that qualitative network analysis is getting increasing attention. In comparison to quantitative approaches the usage of qualitative approaches is still in its beginning.

Qualitative methods for network analysis aim to transfer the layman theories of members of the virtual organisation about relationship constellations in the network analytical outward perspective. Exactly this transfer can be seen as the main objective of qualitative network research methods.

When it is made possible to interpret the actor's behaviour in networks for outsiders in a transparent manner, then the network analysis touches ground, which were closed so far (Renz, 1998). For this reason the qualitative network analysis can give direction for the network analytical research in general (Sydow, 1995). Instruments which can capture and analyse both dynamic and temporal changes in the network can be seen as biggest conceptual challenge for research (Jansen 2006). The qualitative network research offers opportunities for doing this (Hollstein,, 2006).

The qualitative network analysis can in the same manner as for the quantitative be divided in data acquisition, data representation and data analysis. The main difference lies in the kind of instruments and the respective questions. Naturally the qualitative network approaches are analyzing different instruments focusing less on mathematical accuracy but more on gathering and understands layman theories.

A nice overview about more qualitative tools for network analysis can also be found at Casos. Additionally, Hollstein (2006) discusses the whole range of tools.

Potential and Limits

In order to achieve transparency by using qualitative research methods, the network researcher must enter the subsurface structure and the social reality of the network actors. This complex task gets even more difficult, because there is no common language between network actor and network researcher. While the network researcher is able to capture emotional and systematic characteristics of networks and transfer that to a comprehensive language, actors within the network might not understand this. Contrariwise it will be very difficult to translate layman theories into a network describing formal language. This is especially true because there is no commonly accepted network language which offers much room for interpretation (Renz, 1998).

The qualitative network analysis highlights context conditions such as trust and emerging standards. The analysis can be used as a form for exploring new issues such as innovation processes. Additional qualitative network analysis methods can be used for interpreting each actor, subjective perceptions and guided orientations (Hollstein, 2006). However the results of the qualitative network analysis are always subjective because there are based on prognosis and estimates. In the case of this chapter both procedures such be sued to investigate innovation processes.

Scenario Technique as the Basic Approach

Scenario technique (Götze, 1993) or scenario planning (Walton, 2008) is a widely used tool for strategic planning, risk and sensitivity analysis and organisational learning. When dealing with hard (quantitative) approaches of forecasting, the result is often just one single scenario connected with a specific probability of occurrence. But, to anticipate the full range of possible future states, other approaches (like narrative storytelling, simulations with varying parameters) should be applied.

The natural time frame for scenario techniques is mid- to long-range. Concerning the planning of the VOs to be created from a VBE two aspects are important: First, the long-range trends and developments of the VBE and its environment, which form the frame for the VOs, and second the VO itself with focus on the collaboration. Figure 5 shows how different factors constituting a scenario are varied to generate (forecast) different future states. The task of VO planning is to be prepared in each of these anticipated scenarios.

Figure 5. Analyse future systematically with scenario oriented forecasting approaches

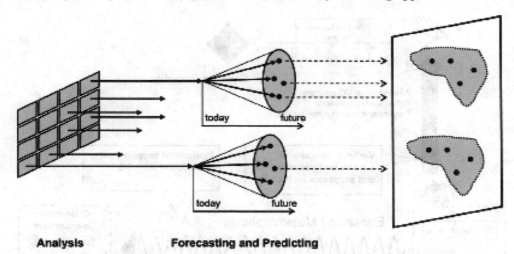

Analysis   **Forecasting and Predicting**

A SCENARIO BASED FORECASTING APPROACH TO SUPPORT SMES

Industrial Case Study: The CeBeNetwork Case

In European IST research project ECOLEAD structure, processes, needs, requirements and ICT-Systems for VOs have been analysed. The main focus was constantly on the development and usage of ICT. For some reason the analysis of forecasting methods were only subject in the ECOLEAD project, where the following descriptions are based on. One of the ECOLEAD cases, the CeBeNetwork scenario, is described in full length in Eschenbächer et al (2007). This case is used for relevant aspects for this chapter.

Specification of the Demonstration Case

The "CeBeNetwork cooperation group" exists and is proven since 2002 as an international aerospace subcontractor network of more than 20 mainly SME-based partners with over 20 years of experience in aerospace. It provides competitive services for the aviation sector in France, Germany, UK and Spain and additionally in some low-cost countries. The cooperating SME try to create new business in automotive and other industries. CeBeNetwork accomplishes the central management of the co-operation obtaining the role of consortium coordinator. So it is a highly sophisticated network of professionals specialising in IT and management solutions in the area of product development as well as in full service packages for the entire engineering process in the automotive and railroad industries, mechanical engineering and in the aircraft industry. The "CeBeNetwork cooperation group" is highly motivated by achieving a high level of customer satisfaction and innovation. The pre-selection has taken place with the help of the VBE so that no unknown partners will become part of a VO. This ensures that trust and business processes are established on a agreed understanding. This makes planning and forecasting much easier. Figure 6 provides a more detailed view on the example SME network example. The strategic analysis shall support the selection of the right candidates by forecasting the basic conditions and strategic situation in which the cooperation shall be created. The vertical, operational support gives SME a better planning basis. The horizontal support delivers detailed information about the evaluation of the VBE.

Figure 6. Closer view on the ECOLEAD demonstration case

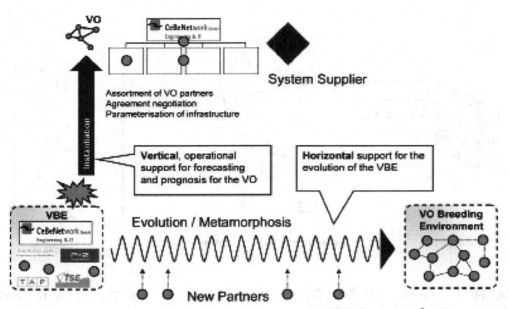

Basically Figure 6 can be understood as a specification of Figure 4. The vertical and horizontal approach is shown within the grey boxes alongside to the black arrows. The CeBeNetwork case explained before in Figure 6 has shown the two main conceptual routes the authors will follow. In Figure 7 the ECOLEAD demonstration case scenario is further elaborated. The first aim by analysing the case is the evolution and metamorphosis of a VBE and the creation to a VO. In principle the strategic planning will not only support the metamorphosis of the VBE but will also deliver basic information such as trends, number of partners and basic conditions for creating the VO. For doing this CeBeNetwork would need a strategic planning tool to identify the right SME and their collaboration. The second aim is to further investigate the collaborative relationships by identifying and forecast the collaboration intensity of the respective relationships. For doing this CeBeNetwork would need a method which supports accurate forecasting of the forthcoming collaboration intensity between the companies.

The subject of forecasting virtual organisations as shown in Figure 7 implies a high number of unsolved questions. These questions can be structured into three different levels which show a rough model (we call it bird's eye view, representing strategic knowledge), detailed model (we call it system model level) and the picture of the real world which includes all the complexity. Our approach is to use the rough model – the bird's eye view – to understand the most important structural elements of the system and to forecast the tendencies within its functional behaviour.

Application of the Forecasting Methods in the CeBeNetwork Case

The conceptual description of Figure 8 shows that the authors do follow two aims. The CeBeNetwork group is interested to have a better overview about their planning of activities both on strategic and operational level. In our example most of the SME are forced to completely change their planning activities (Tiefensee, 2008). The reason for doing so is the Power 8 program which can be summarised in the following points (Müller, 2007):

Figure 7. Forecasting and prognosis demand in the demonstration case scenario

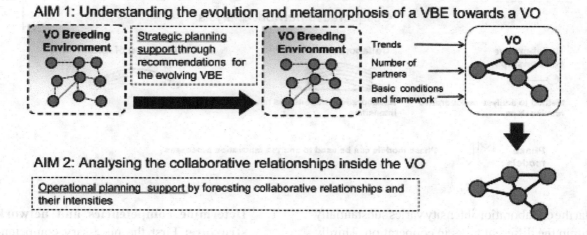

- M1: Develop faster,
- M2: Maximise cash,
- M3: Smart buying,
- M4: Lean Manufacturing,
- M5: Reduce overhead cost,
- M6: Restructure industrial set-up
- M7: Streamline supply chain and
- M8: Focus on core
- CUSTOMER FIRST and profit maximization

All these measures do have an implication of the CeBeNetwork case we have introduced. The most serious measure however is highlighted in bold – restructure industrial set-up. One of the main reasons to create the CeBeNetwork VBE was to respond to this challenge. Restructure industrial set-up means reducing the total number of suppliers and the creation of system and/or module suppliers. In principle this is the same ideas copied from the automotive industry. This causes that a high number of SME are not interacting directly with Airbus anymore. The decoupling from Airbus does have serious implications of SME takes place which led to new situations. Planning and forecasting the own resources becomes more difficult for SME because of the missing detailed airbus forecast. The new structure via system suppliers

interacting with Airbus and coordinating a supply chain will evolve – but this will take time. In a transition period all SME cannot rely anymore on detailed plans but must rather find their role in the new structure. The both approaches presented in this chapter show that both tactical and operational as well as strategic issues can be addressed by methodological approaches.

Collaborative Network Analysis: A Method to Plan and Forecast the Collaboration within SME-Based VO

Concept and Method

The concept of collaborative network analysis is based on some assumptions and basic conditions. The main assumption is that a group of companies have the intention to cooperate. In other words they are not carefully analyzing "make-or-buy" or deciding if collaboration is the right way to do the things. The SME have simply decided to collaborate in order to bring together resources, Knowledge and core competencies. The basis for the collaborative network analysis is the identification of the needed collaborative relationships (see Figure 9). In a second step the collaboration intensity have to be specified. Another assumption is

Figure 8. Concept of the collaborative network analysis

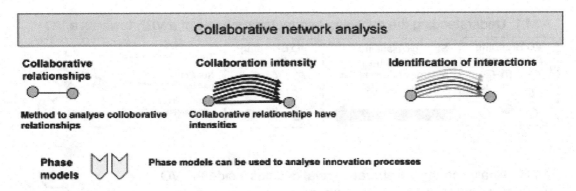

that the collaboration intensity varies substantially within the different tasks in cooperation. Thirdly it is necessary to forecast the needed interactions differentiated in 6 categories. Finally these issues have been supplemented by a model to analyze innovation processes.

Based on the concept of Figure 8 the collaborative relationships have to be forecasted and analyzed. The aim is to identify all three the relationships, the interactions within these relationships and the optimal collaboration intensity between the partners. Based on these conceptual ideas the collaborative network analysis method has been proposed which is shown in Figure 9.

Basically the method differentiates three phases:

- Planning phase: in this phase the stage for cooperation is being set.
- Configuration phase: In this phase stage-gate model will be build on the basis of collaborative relationships and ICT system will be selected.
- Usage/Evaluation phase: In this phase the success of the forecasting results will be evaluated.

In the following the three sub-phases of the planning phase of the method is briefly described:

1. **Determine competencies and network structure:** First the necessary competencies and the network structure need to be identified. This is done based on the identification of collaborative relationships, their respective interactions with their divers' intensities.

2. **Present cooperation partners:** In this step a value chain model is being used to analysis the competencies of the nodes.

3. **Derive cooperation intensities:** In this step the deduction of cooperation intensities is taking place which finally led to the specification of cooperation intensities on the level of interactions.

In the following two sub-phases of the configuration phase of the method is briefly described:

1. **Configure stage-gate model:** In this step the stage gate model is build on the basis of collaborative relationships, intensities and interactions.
2. **Select and assign ICT-systems:** Select appropriate ICT-tools to support the innovation processes.

Finally the evaluation phase – sub-phase 6 – use and evaluate applications – analysis if the forecast and planning of the VO was successful

Figure 9. Method of collaborative network analysis (CNA)

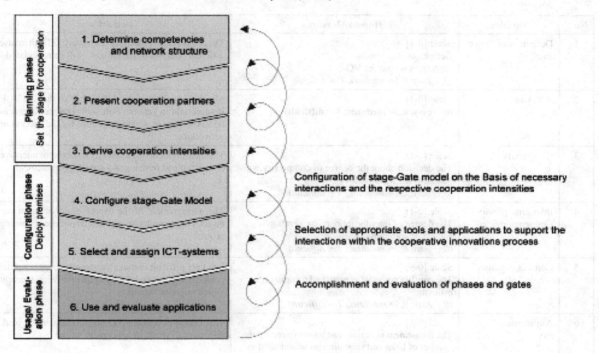

or not. Here the focus is on the quality of the forecast of collaborative relationships and the forecast of ICT tools.

Sub-Phase 3 within the CNA Method

The basis for sub-phase 3 within the CNA method are variables which shall be used to evaluate the collaboration intensity. Table 1 discussed 8 variables which have been used in the context of the CNA model.

The ideas of collaborative relationships have been introduced in the previous section. In order to use the variables of Table 1 a five-step approach has been developed which links the needed information towards the identification. Figure 10 shows the developed approach to specify the collaborative relationships.

1. All identified interactions within the forecasted VO are collected. Additionally the interactions will be specified towards one of the six categories.

2. The variables defined in Table 1 are selected.

3. The variables are evaluated by using a simple method. An estimated about the collaboration intensity is investigated by a simple scoring system. This scoring provides ideas about the potential difficulty to conduct the interaction.

4. The collaboration intensity will be specified on the basis of the scoring result from the previous step.

5. Finally the collaborative relationships are specified by using the evaluated interactions.

Innovation Project at CeBeNetwork as Example for the Planning Phase within the CNA Method

Based on the description of the previous section an example for the application of the CNA method is presented here. In sub-phase 1 the competencies and the number of network partners have been

Table 1. *Documentation of the variables used for the CNA model*

No	Variable	How to Measure	Remarks
1	Definition of Objectives	Scale [0-1] Definition of common objectives within the VO *(0 = easy, 0,5= medium, 1 = difficult)*	The discussion of objectives can be very difficult in case different interests of the partners will be articulated.
2	ICT Admin	Scale [0-1] **(0 = easy, 0,5= medium,, 1 = difficult)**	Members need the right skilled staff so that the VBE is successful in general. Soft skills (e.g. communication skills) are of great importance for the success of networking.
3	Complexity	Scale [0-1] The decision about the degree of complexity will be discussed within the VO. *(0 = easy, 0,5= medium,, 1 = difficult)*	The measurement of complexity is subject of intensive discussion and remains as a qualitative statement.
4	Inter-Disciplinary Cooperation	Scale [0-1] The degree of interdisciplinary cooperation is subject of common discussion. *(0 = easy, 0,5= medium,, 1 = difficult)*	The measurement of the degree of cooperation can be seen as a qualitative estimate about the upcoming project.
5	Conflict Potential	Scale [0-9] The conflict potential is matter of a common estimate. ***(0 = easy, 0,5= medium,, 1 = difficult)***	It is very difficult to make statements about potential conflicts so this can be seen as qualitative judgement which might be wrong.
6	Adjustment Necessity	Scale [0-1] The adjustment necessity can be measured by the number of links and relationships which need to be coordinated. *(0 = easy, 0,5= medium,, 1 = difficult)*	This variables tells the VO upfront how much work they have to spend in adjustment work.
7	Dependency of Planning	Scale [0-1] This measurement will again be measured via qualitative statement. *(0 = easy, 0,5= medium,, 1 = difficult)*	The dependency of planning shows clearly that the different partners of the VO must understand the dependencies of the various activities they are conducting.
8	Information Deformation	Scale [0-1] This measurement can be measured via qualitative statement. *(0 = easy, 0,5= medium,, 1 = difficult)*	The information deformation variable indicated the problem that different partners of the VO do understand topics differently.

investigated. The result is shown in Figure 11. Four partners collaborate within an innovation project. Altogether five competencies have been selected. The different partners do bring in such competencies in the collaboration as shown in the middle of Figure 11. In the first place such competencies are based on interactions which are so far neither coupled nor further specified.

The logical structure of the connections between the different competencies is shown in Figure 11. Here the interactions are not evaluated in a quantitative or qualitative manner. Finally Figure 12 presents the result of sub-phase 3 of the planning phase. Basically the approach shown in

Figure 12 has been applied to identify the type of interactions, the intensity of interactions as basis for and the interaction value chain. This Figure illustrates the forecasting approach clearly. The main objective is the identification of the needed competencies with the SME collaboration and to evaluate them.

The collaborative network analysis provides a detailed way to better understand and forecast collaborative relationships. From an application point of view the method focuses on an operational support for innovation project. The results provide a detailed overview about the concept of collaboration intensity on the level of edges between nodes.

Figure 10. Approach to specify the collaborative relationships

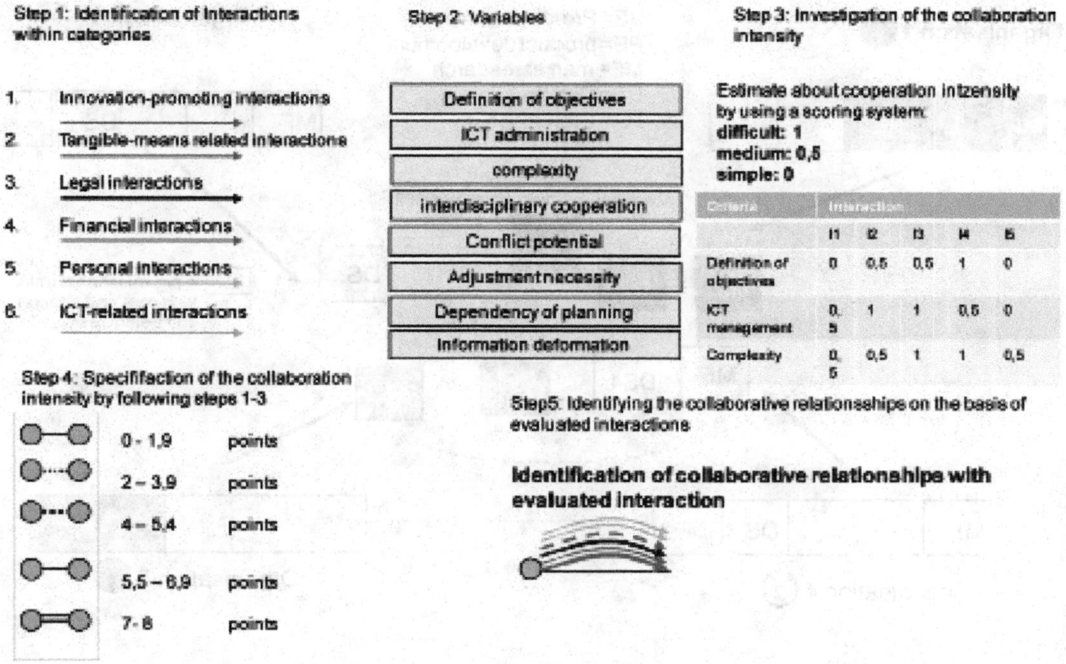

Causal Cross-Impact Analysis: A Method to Plan and Forecast the Framework

Historic Development

Cross-Impact Analysis has been developed in the late sixties of last century by Olaf Helmer and Theodore Gordon. Gordon and Hayward were the first to publish experiences of initial experiments by inter-relating event occurrence probabilities (Gordon & Hayward, 1968). Since then, several enhancements and developments have been taken under the label of Cross-Impact Analysis. Banuls and Salmeron (2007) provide an overview on the main milestones in the history of the development cross-impact method, which has been extended by Duin (2007b, see Table 2).

During the 90ies, the research institute BIBA has implemented a cross-impact modelling and simulation software package called CRIMP for Windows, which allows the interactive set-up,

simulation and evaluation of causal cross-impact models (Krauth, 1992; Krauth et al., 1998; Duin, 1995; Duin et al., 2005) based on Helmer's approach (1977). Currently, the model editor is re-newed to employ and/or support new technologies like Java SWING, XML, etc.

The purpose of the causal cross-impact analysis approach is to "give expression to the interdisciplinary connections which we all sense to exist among widely disparate aspects of the world around us, even though in most instances we are still far removed from the point where we can articulate such vaguely perceived causalities in the from of law-like regularities" (Helmer, 1977, p 19).

Illustrative Example

Before introducing an illustrative example, the elements of a Cross-Impact Analysis Model are introduced:

Cross-Impact Analysis is based on a discrete time model. The time period under investigation

Figure 11. Competencies and network

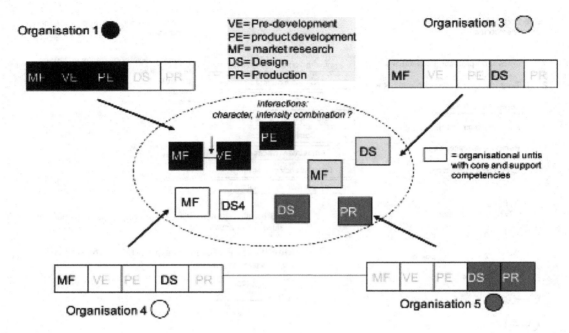

is divided into single time steps called scenes. Each scene represents a time span, e.g. a year, a quarter or a month. The end of the total time period under consideration is called the time horizon. The length of a scene must be specified carefully, because it represents the shortest time an effect needs to transfer from cause to effect.

Trend Variables

A trend variable defines a system variable, which changes its value continuously over time (like levels or stocks in system dynamics model). For each trend variable the user is asked to provide a lower and upper limit and an estimated business-as-usual development coupled with an uncertainty factor called volatility. The fluctuations from the

Figure 12. Step 3: Specification of intensity

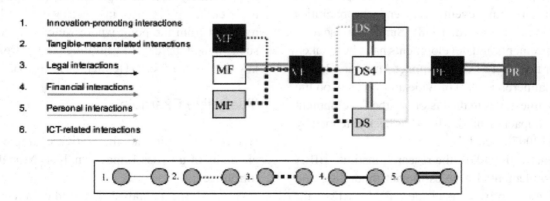

Table 2. Main Cross-Impact-Analysis Approaches (after Duin, 2007b)

Year	Authors	Approach
1966	Gordon and Helmer	Initial developments
1968	Gordon and Hayward	First paper about cross-impact analysis
1972	Helmer	Cross-impact gaming (causal cross-impact analysis)
1972	Kane	Proposal of KSIM
1972	Turoff	Alternative approach (based on physics principles)
1974	Duval, Fontela and Gabus	Proposal of EXPLOR-SIM
1975	Duperrin and Godet	Proposal of SMIC
1980	Enzer	Proposal of INTERAX
1981	Helmer	Re-assessment of causal cross-impact analysis
1995	Duin	Scenario management for cross-impact models
1995	Sapio	Proposal of SEARCH
2003	Chon and Kwon	Proposal of CHP

expected business-as-usual values in one scene will affect the values of impacted trends in subsequent scenes.

Event Variables

Event variables in a causal cross-impact model describe events which are not under the control of actors of the model, but which might have a strong influence on other variables (trends or events) in the case of their occurrence. The user is asked to provide occurrence probabilities for event variables.

Actors and Action Variables

Actors are some kind of players who are equipped with instruments called Actions. By default, the actors have a marginal budget, representing the amounts available above the business-as-usual operations and which they can spend on actions available for them. Actions represent the instruments of an actor (player). The intensity with which an action influences other variables depends on the amount of the budget spend on it. In a model, there might be cheap and expensive actions when compared to their intensity.

Cross-Impacts

Trends, events and actions are inter-related by defining cross-impacts between them spawning up the cross-impact matrix as demonstrated in Figure 13. The cross-impact matrix consists of six different areas (see the numbered areas of Figure 13) or sub-matrices: One sub-matrix collects all impacts having a trend variable as source and destination, one for events on trends and so on.

Each cross-impact has strength and a direction of its effect. Small impacts might cause strong effects, when the cross-impact is large. The direction could be positive or negative as mentioned above. Also, a cross-impact has a timely delay. The shortest time a cross-impact needs to demonstrate its effect is one scene, but it might take longer or distributed its effects over several scenes. Normally, a cross-impact is given by a constant value (coefficient), but in some cases this value might change over time or changes in dependence from some other trend developments in the model.

Illustrative Sample Model

Due to the dynamics of the external (e.g. fast changing or disruptive trends) and the internal (e.g.

Figure 13. Structure of the Cross-Impact Matrix

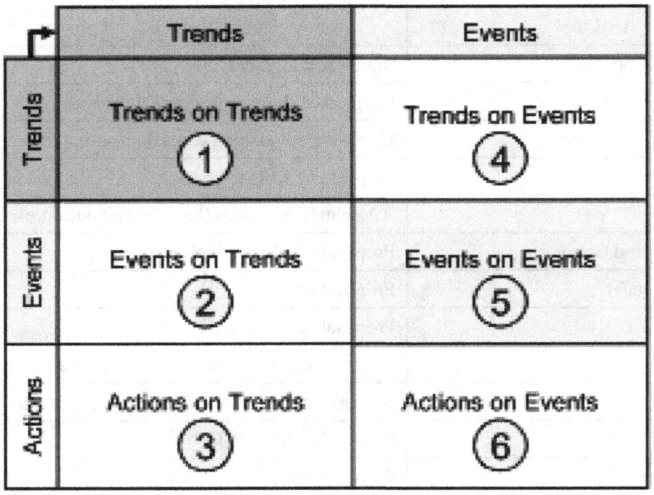

	Trends	Events
Trends	Trends on Trends ①	Trends on Events ④
Events	Events on Trends ②	Events on Events ⑤
Actions	Actions on Trends ③	Actions on Events ⑥

development of skills connected with new member entrance) factors an approach is needed, which allows the adaptation of plans to changing situations during the course into the future. This is fulfilled by scenario techniques. A well known method to create scenarios is Cross-Impact Analysis. An illustrative example model is used for the introduction of the causal cross-impact analysis method based on the systemic view explained earlier. The model development has been carried out as a group work of scientists and students at the German research institute BIBA. Initial results are published in (Kirik, 2007). The focus has been set to a thought VBE acting in the mechanical engineering sector covering the following influencing areas:

- Enterprise Network Factors
- Market
- Technology
- Society
- Politics

Application of the CRIMP Method

Table 3 describes the variables of that reduced model, which has been implemented using the JCrimp software developed at BIBA.

As the variables defined in Table 3 describe a generic model there is a need to adapt it the specific situation of the example – the CeBeNetwork case. The application of the model is done in six steps by a project team:

Step 1: Problem Analysis. Within this step the problem area has to be defined precisely and bounded to the model environment. The team has to decide what should be included and what should not be part of the model. A good result is achieved by merging different views of the group members to one model. It is important that the boundary of the model is not too tight. E. g. to describe a networked enterprise as a socio-economic system both the internal and the external factors have to be considered.

Step 2: Trend Variable Definition. The goal of this step is to define a set of trend variables aggregating all the aspects of the problem identified in step 1. This is done by varying the variables of the generic model or by defining new trends. When defining new variables often the meaning of a variable is ambiguous. Different experts have a different understanding of a specific variable. Often the necessity arises to go back one step to the problem analysis and to change the semantic of variables until a common understanding within the team is reached.

Table 3. Documentation of variables used for the CIA model

No	Variable	How to Measure	Remarks
1	Number of VBE Members	Counting the number of participating enterprises	The number of members can have an optimum: many enough to provide additional value on the market, but not too many, because planning complexity will grow.
2	Capabilities of Staff	Scale [0-9] **(0 = badly skilled, 9 = very good skills)**	Members need the right skilled staff so that the VBE is successful in general. Soft skills (e.g. communication skills) are of great importance for the success of networking.
3	Market Share	%	The market share of the VBE.
4	R&D	Ratio of R&D-Investments to Turnover	Research and Development is important to develop new business models and value added services for the product portfolio.
5	Product Quality	Scale [0-9] **(0 = very bad, 9 = very good)**	The product quality as considered by the customers. Here the product is considered as an extended product (physical product and support services).
6	Complexity of Planning	Scale [0-9] (0 = low complexity, 9 = high complexity)	High complexity of planning influences many other factors, e.g. product quality, price, and timeliness of delivery.
7	Product Program	Size in % relative to start year	The size of the product program is important for many factors like the size of the VBE, etc.
8	Image	Scale [0-9] (0 = very bad, 9 = very good)	The image of the VBE as seen by the customers concerning quality of products, timeliness of delivery, level of support, etc.
9	Competition	Number of competing organisations	The level of competition described by the number of competing networks and/or companies.
10	Earnings	% relative to start year	This is an indicator for the financial success of the members of the VBE.

Step 3: Interconnection. The results of the first two steps are static. These steps are important to understand the problem as an integral whole. The goal of this step is to create from the static models a dynamic one by interconnecting the identified variables by cross-impacts. For each variable it has to be checked if a change in this variable will cause changes in other variables. During the discussion of influences of variables disagreement about such impacts can occur among team members. This is normally an indicator for different meanings connected with the variables. In such cases the group has to go back one or more steps to refine the variable definitions until consensus is reached. The result of this step is a network of variables, describing the problem as an integral whole, as a system. Simulation can be employed to analyse the behaviour of this system.

Step 4: Strategy Analysis. The goal of this step is the definition of strategies and the simulation of the effects of how the application of the selected strategies will affect the model. Within this step action variables are defined which have an impact on the up to now defined network of trend variables. Simulation demonstrates how the application of such actions influences the defined system. The results of this step are evaluated (see step 6) and used for further refinement and verification. The application of each selected strategy defines a possible scenario.

Step 5: Event Analysis. The goal of this step is the analysis of how external events influence the future development of the system under consideration and how these effects disturb the success of the selected strategies. Within this step event variables are defined which have an impact on the up to now defined network of trends. The event variables can also be impacted by actions or other variables (e.g. the application of an action can reduce the probability of some event occurrences). Simulation demonstrates how the occurrence (or absence) of events is influencing the defined scenarios. The results of this step are also evaluated (see step 6) and used for further refinement and verification. The defined strategy scenarios can be refined by the introduction of events which support specified strategies or which will act as a brake for the strategies.

Step 6: Evaluation. The last step is for the evaluation of the stepwise generated model. Evaluation takes part after the steps Interconnection, Strategy Analysis and Event Analysis. The results of evaluation give feedback for further efforts in model verification and refinement. For example, the results for applying a specific strategy are not satisfying the expectations of the members of the team. In such cases the team has to check whether the strategy is not able to gain the expected result or if there is something wrong in the model definition up to now. The same procedure is performed for the Event Analysis step.

Applying theses steps in a systemic approach, the members of the team often run through loops which are necessary to get a common understanding of the subject among all team members. Step by step the model under investigation is refined until the results of this process are accepted by the whole team. A side effect of this approach is that the minds of all team members are opened for different sights from different perspectives to the same problem. This ensures that the model is not generated one sided, moreover the model seems to be more complete and correct.

DISCUSSION OF RESULTS

Contributions of Methods

The methods shall be used to support the forecasting of SME. Here the cross-impact analysis is more focused on high-level strategic support whereas the CNA focuses more on the forecasting of business developments. However both methods deliver ex ante suggestions of potential developments so they can be considered as explorative approaches. In general the CNA supports endogenous elements whereas the cross-impact analysis supports the exogenous interactions.

The results of the CNA can be summarised as follows:

- **Structural dimension:** Short-term / mid term planning of actors and their relationships; Network structure; Specification of necessary relationships, Roles of VO partners; Value chain structure
- **Functional dimension:** Design of distributed business process by using Porter Value chain model; Stage-Gate-Process; Collaboration intensity, Understanding of secondary value chain processes

The results of the cross-impact analysis can be summarised as follows:

- **Structural dimension:** Consortium balance; Network size, Strategic planning; Assessment of market niche / business opportunity; Competition
- **Functional dimension:** Efficiency and effectiveness; Best competence fit; Process performance, Adequacy of auxiliary processes

In general the CeBeNetwork case did illustrate a major improvement in their planning and forecasting activities by using the proposed approaches. This can be summarised in the following points:

- More transparency about log, mid- and short term planning,
- Awareness about the usefulness about the usage of a VBW,
- Clear scenarios about potential developments of cooperation projects by using the CNA an
- Better understanding about the evolution and metamorphosis of VBE and their respective partners.

It can be summarised that the proposed concepts do support SME-based VO in their ability to conduct planning and forecasting in an open, collaborative environment.

Expected Business Benefits

Collaborative networks are going to become the major driver for European industry (COIN IP 2008). Especially SME are forced to learn to play their role in such networks in order to achieve a sufficient quality in their planning activities. So far the real support and understanding of such organisational forms are still lacking far behind expectations (Eschenbächer, 2008). The authors claim that one reason is the missing knowledge and understanding about accurate forecast and planning. By using the two approaches the following business benefits can be summarized:

- Better strategic understanding of the potential actors relationships and / or roles within the Virtual Organisation –leads to improvements,
- Better operational and tactical planning of the activities taking place in the VO,
- Better definition of partner roles before starting the operation phase,
- More efficient business process management.

Feasible Results

The application of the Causal Cross-Impact Analysis and the Collaboration Network Analysis at CeBeNetwork shows remarkable results. Regarding the collaboration Network Analysis the following points can be summarised:

- Due to the results of the CNA business risks about future demands can be earlier apprehended. As an example the current economic crises came totally surprising for many market participants – especially SME – which would be different when applying the CNA. This would have highlighted that the collaborative relationships are changing.
- The partners of the Virtual Organisation can a transparent view of the early phase of the respective business processes. The CNA delivers trustful information about the potential evolution of business processes as shown in chapter 3.2.
- Finally, the CeBeNetwork Case shows the enormous problem to understand the upcoming processes. It happens many times that the future has not been properly understood. This leads to misallocation of resources, late deliveries and so forth. Thanks to the collaboration network analysis these issues can be identified earlier.

The application of the cross impact analysis shows the following results:

- The main strategic developments within innovation processes can be forecasted. For CeBeNetwork the careful analysis of the Power 8 program of Airbus indicated dramatic changes within the aeronautical industry.
- The demonstration on alternative scenarios showed CeBeNetwork different alternative routes for the behaviour of the

collaboration which provided important support the decision making.

To summarise: The application of the two forecasting methods provides a decision support for the CeBeNetwork cooperation which gained into future business benefits.

FUTURE TRENDS AND CONCLUSIONS

Future Trends for SME

Forecasting and prognosis of business developments is a very hot topic industry. Especially for SME which are faced with continuous changing market conditions should be prepared for such challenges. In contrast to multinational companies in which forecasting has become a function in the company (Gassmann & Sutter, 2008; Boutellier et al, 2008; McInerney, 2007, p. 50 ff.) SME companies are still far away from having instruments for doing this work. The two approaches presented in this chapter do focus on operative and strategic support of decision making when entering into collaborations.

The following future trends which have been touched inside this chapter can be summarised:

- Investments in new ICT solutions: During the past 20 years a high majority of large companies has heavily invested into new ICT solutions such as SAP. SME are slowly catching up with this.
- Changes in the competitive situation: As discussed in chapter two the competitive situation for SME is changing dramatically. Trends towards supply chain integration in automotive and aeronautical industry did have a large impact on the forecast activities of every company. Stabile processes within supply chains are changing towards less suppliers and complexity. As

for the case of CeBeNetwork in chapter 3.1 the SME is transforming towards a system supplier with different obligations.

- Evolving chances in resource competence management of companies: Due to the changing market situation the competence management in companies evolves dramatically towards higher specialization.
- Tremendous change from dealing with innovation processes in the own organisation to distributed innovation management (Eschenbächer, 2008): The innovation processes are changing from intra-organisational towards inter-organisational or distributed innovation processes.
- Virtual Breeding environments supporting long term collaboration between SME

Conclusion

One major requirement to deepen the understanding of forecasting in Virtual Organisation is the creation of a conceptual knowledge. With this chapter we have tried to introduce basic concepts and understanding. The authors have learnt that there is still work to do to create a common understanding of forecasting in the research community.

Furthermore the chapter has discussed how the cross-impact analysis and the collaborative network analysis can be used to support the forecasting in Virtual Organisations. The methodologies have been conceptually applied in an aeronautical case study. The business benefits clearly show the importance of such approaches in everyday business.

The discussion has shown that SME do face a changing business environment which suggests thinking about new methods and tools supporting their business planning. Furthermore, the collaborative network analysis has shown that a prognosis of the intensity of collaborative relationships can have a major positive impact.

ACKNOWLEDGMENT

The authors thank the partners and the European Commission for support in the context of the COIN project under contract number EU-FP7-216256. For more information see http://www.coin-ip. eu/.

REFERENCES

Banuls, V. A., & Salmeron, J. L. (2007). Benchmarking the information society in the long range. *Futures*, *39*(1), 83–95. doi:10.1016/j.futures.2006.03.006

Bircher, B. (1976). *Langfristige Unternehmensplanung*. Bern, Stuttgart: Haupt.

Boutellier, R., Gassmann, O., & Zedtwitz, M. (2008). *Managing global innovation – Uncovering the secrets of future competitiveness*. Berlin, Heidelberg: Springer.

Camarinha-Matos, L., & Afsamarnesh, H. (2008). *Collaborative networks: Reference modelling*. New York: Springer.

Camarinha-Matos, L. M., & Afsamarnesh, H. (2007). A comprehensive modelling framework for collaborative networked organisations. *Journal of Intelligent Manufacturing*, *18*(5), 529–542. doi:10.1007/s10845-007-0063-3

CASOS. (2008). *Computational models and social network tools*. Retrieved December 12, 2008, from http://www.casos.cs.cmu.edu/computational_tools/tools.html.

COIN. (2008). *Enterprise collaboration & interoperability*. Retrieved December 12, 2008, from http://www.coin-ip.eu.

Duin, H. (1995). Object-oriented scenario management for simulation models. In *Proceedings of IMACS European Simulation Meeting, 28-30 August 1995, Gyor, Hungary* (pp. 38-44).

Duin, H. (2007a). Causal cross-impact analysis as strategic planning aid for virtual organisation breeding environments. In L.M. Camarinha-Matos, H. Afsarmanesh, P. Novais, & C. Abalide (Eds.), *Establishing the foundation of collaborative networks* (pp. 147-154). New York: Springer.

Duin, H. (2007b). Causal cross-impact analysis as a gaming tool for strategic decision making. In K.-D. Thoben, J. Baalsrud Hauge, R. Smeds, & J.O. Riis (Eds.), *Multidisciplinary research on new methods for learning and innovation in enterprise networks* (pp. 79-93). Aachen: Verlag Mainz.

Duin, H., Schnatmeyer, M., Schumacher, J., Thoben, K.-D., & Zhao, X. (2005). Cross-impact analysis of RFID scenarios for logistics. In R. Lasch, & C.G. Janker (Eds.), *Logistik Management 2005* (pp. 363-376). Wiesbaden: Deutscher Universitätsverlag (DUV), Gabler Edition Wissenschaft.

Duperrin, J. C., & Godet, M. (1975). SMIC74 - A method for constructing and ranking scenarios. *Futures*, *7*(4), 302–312. doi:10.1016/0016-3287(75)90048-8

Ellmann, S. (2007). *Management komplexer internationaler Projekte: Netzstrukturen, Governance und Handlungsempfehlungen*. Dissertation at the Universiy of Bremen.

Eschenbächer, J. (2008). *Gestaltung von Innovationsprozessen in Virtuellen Organisation durch kooperationsbasierte Netzwerkanalyse*. Dissertation at the Universiy of Bremen.

Eschenbächer, J., Graser, F., Thoben, K.-D., & Tiefensee, B. (2007). Management of dynamic virtual organisations: Conclusions from a collaborative engineering case. In M. Taisch, K.-D. Thoben, & M. Montorio (Eds.), *Advanced manufacturing: An ICT and systems perspective* (pp. 275-284). London: Taylor & Francis.

Gassmann, O., & Sutter, P. (2008). *Praxiswissen Innovationsmanagement – Von der Idee zum Markterfolg*. München: Hanser Verlag.

Gausemeier, J., Fink, A., & Schlake, O. (1998). Scenario management: An approach to develop future potentials. *Technological Forecasting and Social Change*, *59*(2), 111–130. doi:10.1016/S0040-1625(97)00166-2

Gordon, T., & Hayward, H. (1968). initial experiments with the cross impact matrix method of forecasting. *Futures*, *1*(2), 100–116. doi:10.1016/S0016-3287(68)80003-5

Götze, K. (1993). *Szenario-Technik in der strategischen Unternehmensplanung*. Wiesbaden: Deutscher Universitäts-Verlag.

Helmer, O. (1972). Cross-impact gaming. *Futures*, *4*(2), 149–167. doi:10.1016/0016-3287(72)90039-0

Helmer, O. (1977). Problems in futures research: Delphi and causal cross-impact analysis. *Futures*, *9*(1), 17–31. doi:10.1016/0016-3287(77)90049-0

Helmer, O. (1981). Reassessment of cross-impact analysis. *Futures*, *13*(5), 389–400. doi:10.1016/0016-3287(81)90124-5

Hollstein, B. (2006). *Qualitative Netzwerkanalyse: Konzepte, methoden, anwendungen*. Wiesbaden: VS Verlag für Sozialwissenschaften.

Jagdev, H. S., & Thoben, K.-D. (2001). Anatomy of enterprise collaborations. *Production Planning and Control*, *12*(5), 437–451. doi:10.1080/09537280110042675

Jansen, D. (2006). *Einführung in die Netzwerkanalyse – Grundlagen, Methoden, Forschungsbeispiele*. Wiesbaden: VS Verlag für Sozialwissenschaften.

Jarimo, T., & Korpiaho, K. (2008) Networked partner selection with robust portfolio modeling. In L.M. Camarinha-Matos, & H. Afsarmanesh (Eds.), *Collaborative networks: Reference modelling* (pp. 215-226), New York: Springer.

Kane, J. (1972). A primer for a new cross-impact language - KSIM. *Technological Forecasting and Social Change*, *4*(2), 129–142. doi:10.1016/0040-1625(72)90010-8

Kirik, S. (2007). *Ermittlung von strategischen Einflußfaktoren für die strategische Planung in kollaborativen Produktionsnetzwerken*. Diploma Thesis at the University of Bremen.

Knoke, D., & Kuklinski, J.-H. (1982) *Network analysis*. Beverly Hills: Sage University Chapter.

Krauth, J. (1992). Simulation for the evaluation of CIM Investments as Part of an enterprise strategy. In *EUROSIM '92 Simulation Congress Reprints* (pp. 295-300), North Holland.

Krauth, J., Duin, H., & Schimmel, A. (1998). A comparison of tools for strategic simuation and scenario generation with special emphasis on 'soft factors'. *Simulation Practice and Theory*, *6*(1), 23–33. doi:10.1016/S0928-4869(97)00005-0

Makridakis, S., & Wheelwright, S. C. (1990). *Forecasting methods for management*. Winchester.

McInerney, F. (2008). *Panasonic the largest corporate restructuring in history*. New York: Truman Talley Books St. Martin Press.

Mertens, P. (1993). *Prognoserechnung*. Heidelberg: Physica-Verlag.

Mintzberg, H. (1994). *The Rise and fall of strategic planning*. Eaglewood Cliffs: Prentice Hall.

Müller, C. (2007). *Sanierungsprogramm Power 8 und die Auswirkungen auf die Marktteilnehmer*. Presented at the Collaborative Business Workshop, Hamburg, Germany.

Rank, O. (2003). *Formale und informelle Organisationsstrukturen- Eine Netzwerkanalyse des strategischen Planungs- und Entscheidungsprozesses multinationaler Unternehmen.* Wiesbaden: Gabler Verlag.

Seifert, M. (2007). *Unterstützung der Konsortialbildung in Virtuellen Organisationen durch prospektives Performance Measurement.* Dissertation at the University of Bremen.

Serdült, U. (2005). Anwendung sozialer Netzwerkanalyse. In *Zürcher Politik- & Evaluationsstudien,* No. 3.

Simon, D. (1985). *Die Früherkennung von strategischen Diskontinuitäten durch Erfassung von "Weak Signals".* Dissertation at the University of Vienna.

Sturm, F., Kemp, J., & Wendel de Joode, R. (2004). Towards strategic management in collaborative network structures. In Camarinha-Matos (Ed.), *Collaborative networked organisations* (pp. 131-138). Boston: Kluwer Academic Publishers.

Sydow, J. (1992). *Strategische netzwerke: Evolution und organisation.* Wiesbaden: Gabler Verlag.

Tiefensee, B. (2008, September). *Power8 und die Auswirkungen auf die Luftfahrtzulieferindustrie - Erfolgreiche Kooperationen in der Luftfahrtzulieferindustrie.* Presentation at the BIBA Kolloquium.

Turoff, M. (1972). An alternative approach to cross impact analysis. *Technological Forecasting and Social Change, 3*(3), 330–341.

Ulrich, C. (2004). *Die Dynamik von Coopetition – Möglichkeiten und Grenzen dauerhafter Kooperation.* Wiesbaden: Deutscher Universitätsverlag.

Wald, A. (2003). *Netzwerkstrukturen und -effekte in Organisationen: eine Netzwerkanalyse in internationalen Unternehmen.* Mannheim: Gabler Verlag.

Walton, J. S. (2008). Scanning beyond the horizon: Exploring the ontological and epistemological basis for scenario planning. *Advances in Developing Human Resources, 10*(2), 147–165. doi:10.1177/1523422307304101

Wassermann, S., & Faust, K. (1994). *Social network analysis – methods and applications.* Cambridge University Press.

Weber, D. (2005). *Strategische Planung im Unternehmensnetzwerk am Beispiel industrieller Dienstleistungen im Industrieanlagenbau.* Aachen: Shaker Verlag.

Welge, M. K., & Al-Laham, A. (2008). *Strategisches management – Grundlagen, prozess implementerung.* Wiesbaden: Gabler Verlag.

Weyer, J. (2000). *Soziale Netzwerke - Konzepte und Methoden der sozialwissenschaftlichen Netzwerkforschung.* München: Oldenbourg Verlag.

Wiendahl, H.-P. (1997). *Betriebsorganisation für Ingenieure.* München: Carl Hanser Verlag.

Wild, J. (1982). *Grundlagen der Unternehmensplanung.* Wiesbaden: VS Verlag für Sozialwissenschaften.

Wildemann, H. (2008). *Innovationsmanagement –Leitfaden zur Einführung eines effektiven und effizienten Innovationsmanagementsystems.* München: TCW Verlag.

Wührer, G. *(1995).* Internationale Allianz- und Kooperationsfähigkeit österreichischer Unternehmen: Beiträge zum Gestaltansatz als Beschreibungs- und Erklärungskonzept. *Linz: Trauner.*

Chapter 7
Business Integration Model in Services Sector SMEs

Snežana Pantelić
The Mihailo Pupin Institute, Serbia

ABSTRACT

The objective of this chapter is to show the importance of integration business processes and information systems for service sector SMEs and to present an opportunity of synchronous and simultaneous development of both business process integration (BPI) and enterprise information system (EIS) utilizing the introduced Business Integration Model (BIM). BIM approach is based on modeling core business processes, which are supported by modern IS. Process centric and customer centric modern organization relies on enterprise management standards like ISO 9000 family. The task is to achieve the business goal of the process measured by defined Key Performance Indicator (KPI) and to improve the processes continually. The presented "Autotransport" case describes BIM design and implementation for the core process "Transport services management." The critical factor of the success of implementation of Business Integration Model (BIM) is undoubtedly readiness of employees to accept a process approach in the execution of their tasks.

INTRODUCTION

Every manager wants his/her company to be flexible, agile, innovative, competitive, efficient, customer oriented and profitable. In order to achieve that, it is essential to implement modern organizational approaches, information technologies, management methods and techniques and to strive for permanent company improvement. But keep in mind that, according to Wheatley (2005, p. 1), "Processes—not applications—make the company go 'round".

A successful business performance in contemporary conditions is unachievable without enterprise integration, i.e. "end-to-end" – business processes integration (BPI), and integration of all organizational units.

Business process management requires gathering and managing a vast amount of data. It must be

DOI: 10.4018/978-1-60566-892-5.ch007

supported with modern **enterprise information systems (EIS)** which spread through the entire company. These information systems are based on modern information and communication technologies (ICT) and modern IT architecture. EIS must be integrated.

Quality of business and increase in profitability are dependent on «flat organization» and «consumer centric» business processes.

Concepts and fundamentals of Quality Management System (QMS), based on ISO 9000 standard (International Organization for Standardization (ISO), 2005), support customer centric and process centric approach in enterprise management.

Business processes can be divided into "core" and "supporting".

Core business processes can be used as a basis for process model of a company organization and for the model of company information system. Core processes are, also, excellent bases for the organizational design and planning of the development of Enterprise Information System (EIS). Integrated planning for business processes and IS development is a prerequisite of an agile and flexible enterprise capable of responding quickly to continuously changing market requirements.

The objective of this chapter is to show:

- the importance of integration of business processes and information systems for service sector SMEs and
- an opportunity of synchronous and simultaneous development of both BPI and EIS based on introducing a **Business Integration Model (BIM)**.

A case study of "Autotransport" d.o.o. Kostolac, a Serbian company, a transportation services SME, will be presented.

BACKGROUND

Concepts and Definitions

Business always tends to be oriented towards goal delivery and therefore it demands goal oriented structures. Only a process can submit a request to achieve enterprise-wide integration, because a process, by definition, is initiated with the triggering event which evokes an action and does not end until it delivers the valuable result for appropriate stakeholders. Those are core business processes. All other structures of a company should be set up in such a manner to solely serve to core processes (Burlton, 2001).

Business processes and process oriented business model of a company, based on systems approach and holistic view of a company, are becoming a common approach in business organization and management in modern market environment.

Business integration is a notion that will be used for the integration of business processes of a company that is realized through the usage of principles of management, modern organization and information technology aimed at its customer benefits and earning a profit for itself. Further on, business integration will stand for business process integration and will be noted as BPI.

What will we be exploring and talking about?

We will talk about:

- business process modeling,
- information systems design and
- business integration model ("marriage of two").

Business Process Modeling is aimed at explaining how to structure and run a business.

It is the activity of representing both the current ("as-is") and future ("to-be") processes. It is usually being used as a method for understanding and analysis of existing processes and their improvement, as well as for designing new ones. The central concept used for process modeling is the business process consisting of business activities. It describes how business activities relate to and interact with resources in the business to achieve a goal for the process (Eriksson & Penkar, 2000).

The result of the activities of business process modeling is a business process model that should be directed towards the description of core business processes and tasks as well as the key mechanisms of business. It can be the basis of the design of appropriate supporting information systems. This model can also be used for the specification of key requests for these information systems.

The process improvements identified by Business Process Modeling (BPM) may not require IT involvement, but IT is a common driver for the need to model a business process. Often IT impact on business processes is not even consciously recognized without BPM. Business process change "just happened" due to IT "required activities". This is a common practice when management wants to avoid "democratic" discussions regarding business process modeling and possible conflict of interest within various groups. It seems to be easier to get "forgiveness" (acceptance of an IT driven change) than a permission (consent for BPM) of those who will be impacted with the change. Change management programs are implemented to put the improved business processes into practice.

BPM abbreviation could cause some doubt because it is often being used as an abbreviation for "*Business Process Management*" and therefore we will not use it further in this paper with that meaning. This notion, according to Burlton (2001) describes a process that ensures continuous improvement in company's performance. Processes are assets of company that synchronize other assets and aspects of changes. Only processes can be measured in a sense of business performance.

Business Process Management focuses on a company as a whole and creates continuous

work flow, integrates functional silos, eliminates repetition of tasks and often makes a true sketch for automation (Walford, 1999).

Information System Modeling is an activity whose products are models, as various views on developing an information system. Modern information systems are being developed by object-oriented method. Object-oriented modeling and Unified Software Development Process (Jacobson, Booch & Raumbaugh, 1999), development process of software-intensive systems, enable achieving a stable architecture that allows iterative and incremental system development. Therefore, with the implementation of additional functionalities, the system is being upgraded without significant change in its architecture.

The Unified Modeling Language (UML) is being used as a standard language for object-oriented modeling. It is a language that enables visual modeling and supports concepts and methods of the entire Unified Software Development Process. The UML has an extension mechanism that uses stereotypes. This has enabled stereotype development for business modeling objects (Eriksson & Penkar, 2000).

We will address „marriage of two"– Business Process Modeling and Information System Modeling. We shall introduce it here and call it Business Integration Model.

Business Integration Model is an integrated model of business process and information system which shows that business process and information system interact and realize a business goal.

In a contemporary enterprise, business goals cannot be realized if business processes are not supported by today's IS. This means that a business process (BP) and an information system (IS) have to be integrated in the sense of the simultaneous 'participation' (from business process 'input' to its 'output') in the realization of a business goal (BG). However, a goal cannot be realized without a permanent interaction between the BP and the IS in the sense of data exchange. It is therefore necessary to provide interactions between the BP and IS through their coupling in business process execution. In the execution of a business goal, business processes and the information system contain the same business objects on which activities/events take place (for example, a shipping document is provided by the IS, transport cannot be realized without a shipping document, after transport realization a shipping document is processed by the IS).

This writing will address *service sector SMEs*.

Services as non material products of a work process have distinctiveness which refers to the activities of interaction between a service customer and service provider, as well as to the fact that services cannot be stored and are dominantly intangible.

Services are being characterized by the following variables: Place, People, Equipment, meaning:

- *Place*, is a physical setup where the services are provided,
- *People,* is a direct contact between customer/user and organization,
- *Equipment,* which has to be standard to facilitate fast and efficient service provision (Lovelock & Wright, 2002).

According to ISO 9004-2 standard (ISO, 1991) *Service* is the result created by activities realized between the service supplier/provider (supplies with a service) and the customer/user (receives a service) and by service supplier/provider internal activities in order to satisfy customer/user needs. A service provider or customer can be represented in this interaction by people or equipment. Activities of the customer in relationship with the provider can be crucial for service delivery.

In ISO 9001 standard (ISO, 2008), concerning QMS requirements, there is no difference in requirements for quality assurance in a company, no matter of the field of work, i.e. whether the organization provides products or services.

According to their nature, SMEs are initially being organized around some "end-to-end" process – an initial event/outcome pair in the business field they are in (e.g., from a request of the customer for a transport service to the response - delivery of service). Human resources involved (workers) perform various tasks and have more than one role in a team that realize a customer request. Managers (often owners as well) "see" the integral process execution and optimize necessary resources for its execution.

When the number of requests increases and so does the volume of production/realization, the focus is still on the "end-to-end" process and horizontal relations between the processes, but the management of service realization process becomes more complex. Efficient resource management for service request realization is necessary in order for people (workers) and resources (equipment) to be available for realization of service.

It is important for a service based SME to integrate customer relation management, resource management, service providing and financial management into a unified management process.

BUSINESS PROCESS MATURITY AND IS MATURITY

WHEN and WHY would BPI and EIS integration come to our Attention?

Companies are Constantly Changing to Meet Demands

Capability Maturity Model (CMM) is usually used to define the characteristics of a mature, capable process in different fields. It provides basic elements of effective process improvement. CMMI is abbreviation used for Capacity Maturity Model Integration that is developed by the Carnegie Mellon Software Engineering Institute. This model consists of best practice for system and software development and maintenance. It helps an organization in software engineering and organizational development to achieve process performance during its lifecycle. In this text "business process maturity" and "IS maturity" will be used in a less formal way considering a few specific business situations for a SME beginning.

Various stages of business maturity of a SME bring various issues both for BPI and EIS and the methodology to address them is not the same ("one suit doesn't fit all"):

- *"start-up" company* without established business processes and without IS,
- *"spin-off" company* – a company is established in the restructuring process of a large company (the core business remains in the existing company, and new companies have business activities that used to support the core business) – in new companies, new processes are established, existing processes are being reevaluated, and there is no modern IS,
- *mergers* (one company buys another, two companies join, creating a third company – a new company) – in this case, there are two business process models and two ISs that should share and exchange information or a new IS should be designed and new business processes created.

This text will be dealing with "spin-off" companies.

Various stages of IS maturity bring various issues both for BPI and EIS and the methodology to address them is not the same (again "one suit doesn't fit all"):

- *a non-existent IS* creates its own challenges and business processes to work around and offset the lack of automation,
  ◦ *an outdated IS* becomes an obstacle for business development. New EIS must replace the old one. Business

processes changes are needed to optimize utilization of a new technology.

It should be kept in mind that some of the new business processes do exist because information systems are a "cause" and fully integrated into business processes. For example, e-commerce like eBay-inspired SMEs, or e-gaming-inspired SMEs would not exist in that number in brick and mortar environment.

Still, we have to keep in mind that "Processes—not applications—make the company go 'round'" (Wheatley, 2005, p. 1). *People* make changes of processes, not IS/IT. Even when one makes IS renewal, it is most important to start with the changes of business processes that are run by people and IT systems. Or even when a SME starts because of an opportunity created by IS, soon the SME faces human and organizational issues, process and other issues like any other company.

Business Process Integration Issues

One can distinguish two main directions to solve the problem of efficient connecting of business processes:

- *Technological* – introduction of IT solutions that connect business processes in the company with hierarchy functional organization and the existence of vertical silos of automation,
- *Organizational* - redesign of organization structure towards "process-centric" organization with reduction of the number of managing layers (towards a "flat" organization).

The first one undoubtedly gives the results in practice, but what remains is the problem of inefficiency of business processes (ones without value-added steps and workers who are not directed towards the result of the entire process). Even when Business Process Management promises dramatic time and cost savings and output increases (without increasing human resources), there is still a human factor issue. In addition to the human factor, there are the other key issues to be considered like technology infrastructure, KPIs, policies and regulations, and physical facilities (Berg, 2006).

Organizational direction requires a way of IT support different from that of organizations with a hierarchical structure. Process oriented companies are being characterized with organizing workers into teams that share focus of the entire process results. This requires IT support to collaboration and availability of information from the entire process to the workers.

In both cases, business process modeling is a method used to define "to-be" business processes in a clear way.

Current practice in modeling of business process is representation of a business process through a diagram and a map of process. Depending on a view on the process that should be represented, various techniques and diagrams are being used. The most commonly used are: flow charts, Pareto charts, control charts, cause-and-effect diagrams. These are only some of many different types of diagrams. Similarly, in the UML (Unified Modeling Language), a standard modeling language used in software development, the activity diagram, which is a type of flowchart, is just one of many different diagram types.

Recommended approach: New practice for business process modeling with UML. UML activity diagrams and analysis diagrams (UML extension for business modeling) are usually used.

Modeling as a method and technique and UML as a language for object-oriented modeling of information systems and software are convenient for the representation of concepts, significant for business integration (e.g., business objects, activities, actors).

Integration of an organization process model and IS demands an efficient approach to the integration of business processes and it does not include IT aspects only, but organizational, managerial and QMS demands as well.

It is obvious that, if a business process and the model of its elements are placed in the focus, they are not sufficient for efficient integration on the company level, i.e. company business.

Therefore, high level business processes should be modeled with those elements that are significant for achievement of business goals of a company (company performance indicators) and they are used as a basis for development, integration of operational processes in and outside a company.

IS Integration Issues

Aiming at efficient business process integration, a company must solve following problems:

- *Data integration,*
- *Application integration (within organization),*
- *Integration of new IT applications that support new business concepts (external integration e.g., B2B, B2C, e-commerce).*

Data integration permits a user to have a unified view of the enterprise data residing at different resources. This process emerges in a variety of situations. For example, acquisition & merging of companies, when they need to merge their databases, or when management makes a decision based on cross data from different information systems in the company. An approach usually used in merging of needed data is Data Warehousing. In management practice, data integration is frequently called enterprise information integration.

Application integration (within organization) helps avoiding significant changes in the existing application or data structure. It also ensures automation of business processes in a way easier for a user.

Solutions for better integration of business processes have been found in:

- Implementation of Business Process Management solution,
- Design and implementation of Web portals enabling access to data in various applications and systems,
- Using middleware to connect software components or applications, enabling connection of two or more software applications, allowing them to exchange data and solving the problem of how to link newer applications to older legacy systems.

Without integration of application and data in a company, enterprise computing often becomes a set of islands of automation.

New business models such as <u>B2B, B2C, e-commerce emerged thanks to the expansion of Internet infrastructure and services. They would have advanced much slower if there had been no</u> middleware which became indispensable in the development of web-based applications. Middleware enables seamless integration of applications with various types of databases.

New software is being developed in new architectures and technologies (e.g., SOA-Service Oriented Architecture, with Web services and ESB-Enterprise Service Bus), with new development concepts supported by CASE tools for e.g., MDA-Model Driven Architecture and MDD-Model Driven Development. The ultimate goal is to have all IT solutions aligned with company's business development and to protect investment in software (Huberts & Petten, 2007).

Looking into advances in technology from a larger platform vendors viewpoint, the mission – making business process models fully executable, with capability of round-trip engineering – seems to be accomplished. Supporting technologies include Unified Modeling Language (UML), a model-driven development and service-oriented architecture (Peleg, 2007).

Recommended approach: New practice for modeling IS towards EIS which spreads through the entire company.

Software Ownership and SMEs

Global communication infrastructure and open architecture application software enable new business models for software utilization, besides traditional purchasing. This is of a great importance for SMEs that do not have enough money to buy software. Furthermore, the main characteristics of the most commonly used models are being presented:

1. On demand
   - Software installed at vendor's location,
   - Software ownership with vendor,
   - End user has „power users" but not developers,
   - Utilization paid as it is used.

This type of business relation for software usage is being developed towards a concept **Software as a Service (SaaS)**.

2. Outsourcing (development or whole operations)
   - End user has software ownership,
   - Software installed at vendor's location or at end user's location,
   - End user has "power users" but not developers,
   - Utilization paid per fixed price.
3. Lessening
   - Software installed at end user's location,
   - Software ownership with vendor,
   - End user has in house developers,
   - Utilization paid per fixed price.

Integration of Business Process and IS

It is important for a service based SME to integrate customer relation management, resource management, service providing and financial management

Figure 1. Global business integration model

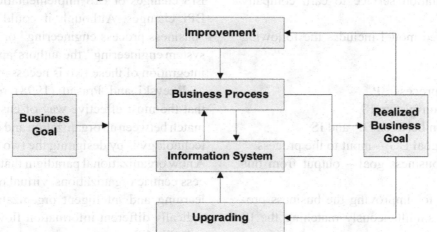

into a unified management process. All these processes generate and use large sets of different data to facilitate efficient enterprise's operations and development. Integration of business process and information system has to be achieved.

In order to achieve the best business results of process oriented organization that builds modern IS, the author's stand is that design and implementation of process model and IS should be done synchronized. That approach and model shall be called Business Integration Model (BIM).

For the development of this model, it is important to identify key business processes of a company and to identify key objects that maintain the structure of these processes.

Furthermore, it should be analyzed how the activities of those processes are executed and what the roles of their executor in the realization of activities are. This is the basis for the development of the object-oriented information system that will be coupled with business processes and organizational structure of a company. It will enable efficient implementation of business processes and achievement of company's business goals.

BIM concept of integration of business process and IS can be distinguished from the automation of business processes in the following sense: this

concept takes care of people who perform business tasks, who are result oriented and who share a common business goal. IS and IT help people to cooperate, to share data, to do tasks successfully producing the result of the process.

BIM APPROACH AND MODEL

Business Integration Model is an integrated model of business process and information system which shows that a business process and information system interact and realize a business goal (Figure 1).

The realization of a business process represents the essential integration of BP_i and IS_i, because the business goal cannot be realized without **the simultaneous execution of the activities/events** of the business process BP_i (for example, goods transportation) and information system IS_i (that the IS contains a requirement for goods transportation registered in the IS). This realization involves permanent interactions between the BP_i and IS_i. These interactions allow starting the activity/event by following how a business process proceeds. It may be concluded that contemporary business conditions require the integrated BP_i and IS_i to enable the business goal to be realized (performing a transportation service to earn company income).

An integrated model includes the following elements:

- business process BP_i
- information system IS_i
- interaction between BP_i and IS_i
- business goal BG_i – input to the process
- realized business goal – output from this process
- feedback for improving the business process and simultaneously matching the IS with this.

The given BIM statement conditions the interacting business process and IS to be designed simultaneously. The implementation of BP_i and IS_i has to be synchronized and simultaneous to permit the designed effects to be realized.

The interaction between the business process and information system during the execution of business process allows the execution of the business process and the information system and the achievement of the enterprise business goal.

The business goal of business process includes criteria for evaluating the achieved goal in limited time (KPIs of the business process).

All we have said refers to the realization of one business goal of an enterprise. Since an enterprise has several business goals, these goals may be connected into a global integrated model, i.e., an enterprise BIM. Business Integration Model enables synchronized and simultaneous development of business processes and information systems for services sector SMEs.

Synchronized or not Synchronized (Challenges What Comes First)

Although it is believed that integration in BIM is necessary and possible, it is important to understand the issue of timing ("what comes first - chicken or egg") and whether BPI is driving

EIS changes or EIS implementation is causing BPI changes. Although it could be disputed "business process engineering" or "information system engineering", the authors' approach is that integration of these two is necessary.

Rzevski and Prasad (1998) recommended that the most effective way of ensuring a close match between an organization and its supporting technology is by designing the two concurrently. A new organizational paradigm that refers to process centric organizations, virtual organizations, learning and intelligent organizations requires radically different information flows and thus a radically different supporting technology. Flexible and distributed organizations cannot be supported effectively by the traditional centralized information systems, corporate databases, large mainframe application programs and data-driven structured methodologies.

A practice, very frequent nowadays, is that modeling of business processes is done without full synchronization with EIS or that EIS renewal is not synchronized with essential changes of business processes. Namely, an IS is rolled out without business engineering and business engineering is done without IS renewal.

New integrating approaches are emphasizing that business engineering must be supported by IS and IS must not be developed without business engineering. This can be reached easier in SMEs than in large enterprises. This integration is of great importance for running business of SMEs. Initially, it requires greater efforts in a company and holds a greater risk for success. These problems can be overcome through a company's management structure that has a clear goal of new, process-centric organizational structure and a clear plan of development and introduction of new or renewed IS. Further, employees should be involved in those changes from the very beginning, i.e., from the planning activities. The practical solution presented in the auto transport case study demonstrates that this approach has been successfully implemented.

Figure 2. Processes of QMS in service sector

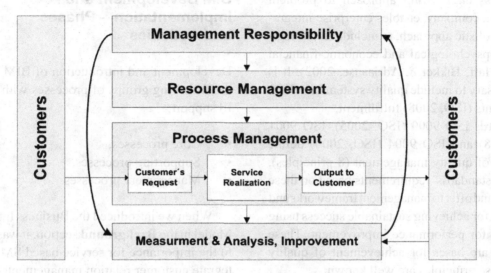

Insight to ISO 9000

The ISO 9000 family consists of a core of three ISO standards and many associate quality standards. Having in mind topic of the chapter, we shall point out to: ISO 9000 (ISO, 2005), ISO 9001 (ISO, 2008) and ISO 9004 (ISO, 2000).

ISO 9000 standard (ISO, 2005) defines quality management systems approach, introducing the process approach. ISO 9001 standard (ISO, 2008) defines quality system requirements. It requires that a business entity follows the process approach when running its business and towards that goal, maps of business processes help a company to manage its processes in an effective way (a process is executed successfully even the first time), and efficiently (continuous improvement that ensures that the processes use the least volume of resources). ISO 9004 (ISO, 2000) gives a broader view of QMS, than ISO 9001 (ISO, 2008). It includes expectations of all stakeholders in performance improvement. Figure 2 shows key processes of process-based QMS applied to service sector.

ISO 9001 standard requirements (ISO, 2008) are grouped as follows:

- **Managerial responsibility:** every company has management with its specific tasks.
- **Resource management:** every company must manage its human, material and technical and financial resources.
- **Product/service realization:** every company must create products and/or services that are the essence of its existence and that are sold to customers/users.
- **Measuring, analysis, improvements:** every company has to monitor the effects of its activities, to solve problems, remove obstacles and correct mistakes, but to prevent their appearance as well.
- **Quality management system (QMS):** every company uses documents, technical, commercial and other and has to manage them.

For SME in service sector, EIS provides document generation through process execution, by gathering all data and information for the service realization process, resource management, etc. Based on these data, a company can trace the effects of its work, evaluates the success of single process and solves problems during the work.

Business engineering approach to problem solving in a company, enables enterprise integration, as a holistic approach, to include technological, socio-psychological and economic-financial aspects. (Haff, Bikker & Adriaanse, 2002). It is also necessary to include quality system ISO 9001 requirements (ISO, 2008) fulfillment.

Standards ISO 9000 (ISO, 2005), ISO 9001 (ISO, 2008) and ISO 9004 (ISO, 2000) define principles of quality management (8 principles), formulate standards' requirements based on these principles and offer to management frameworks and guidelines for achieving sustainable success using guidelines for performance improvement. These principles are bases for achievement of quality goals. These principles are well known:

- Customer oriented organization,
- Leadership,
- Staff inclusion,
- Process oriented approach,
- System approach to management,
- Continual improvement,
- Decision making based on facts,
- Mutually beneficial relationships of customers with service providers.

Some principles like *Process oriented approach, System approach to management and Continual improvement* reflect orientation to an organization/company as a whole, that efficiently realizes an expected result (outcome) for a customer, with constant company performance improvement as its permanent goal. Decision making based on facts is a principle that reflects that effective decisions are based on data and information analysis.

Practice has shown that SMEs might not be ready to implement BIM approach as a holistic approach of business success assurance, as it is the case with Quality Management System. That is so, usually, because of lack of money and lack of resources within an organization, but also because of management that has no overall view of the company as a system.

BIM Development and Implementation - Phases and Activities

Development and introduction of BIM includes the following groups of processes with relevant IS support:

- Core processes,
- Supporting processes,
- Management processes.

When we introduced the Business Integration Model in the **Background** section, it was pointed to the importance for service based SMEs to integrate customer relation management, resource management, service realization and financial management into a unified management process. Having that in mind, as a guiding idea – BIM approach is realized through the phases:

- Planning,
- Design,
- Implementation.

Starting from positive experience in iterative and incremental software development approach (Pantelić, Avramović, Conić & Samardžija, 2002), when end-users were involved in all phases of software development, in BIM approach, methods and techniques of visual modeling with UML (use case diagrams, activity diagrams with swim lines, test cases description) were implemented. Those diagrams and models enabled efficient communication with users during the development and implementation of business processes and information systems. The idea was to have participants involved in the realization of a single process and to accept the main characteristics of process oriented company and to accept new business environment for business processes whose activities are supported by information system (Pantelić, Zeljković, Simeunović, Conić & Laćimić, 2001).

Planning Activities

Planning phase is common to all business processes and as the result-output has:

- Enterprise business process model,
- Conceptual model of IS and
- Plan of development and implementation of business processes and IS.

All processes identified in Enterprise business process model will be called high level business processes, while operations processes will be identified in the design phase.

Planning phase steps/activities are:

- Step 1. Business modeling – identifying a set of high level business processes (business processes and their relations, business goals, KPIs)
- Step 2. Defining relevant IT
- Step 3. Defining QMS requirements that will be implemented
- Step 4. Defining conceptual EIS object model
- Step 5. Defining functional requests of high level for IS
- Step 6. Defining functional structure of EIS
- Step 7. Defining logical components of EIS architecture (key business processes are supported by information systems within EIS infrastructure)
- Step 8. Defining starting process organization structure of a company (who is responsible for what in process structured organization)
- Step 9. Defining priorities and development planning and introduction of business processes and IS
- Step 10. Plan of development and implementation of business processes and IS.

It is important to identify business processes in a value added chain (Robson, 1997). These are

customer centric end-to-end processes that should be supported by information systems, because they are crucial for business of the enterprise. For service sector SMEs, priorities in business process development and IS development are:

- Fulfillment of a customer request for service realization as a core business process (the process that delivers outcomes that make company's income),
- Resource management supporting core business process,
- Accounting management supporting the calculation of income and costs of service(s) and business units (e.g., usually a vehicle is a business unit of income in transportation enterprise).

Defined priorities are aligned aiming at creating a common ground for integration of customer relation management, resource management, service realization and financial management into a unified management process in order to decrease costs and increase revenue of the enterprise.

Development and implementation of BIM are being done in iterations. Every iteration has a defined goal to develop and/or implement a core business process and IS that supports it. For each core business process, a BIM is realized through phases: Design and Implementation.

Design and Implementation Activities

Design and Implementation phases are realized in viterations that include steps from both phases for a single business process or a group of business processes. The goal of one such iteration is to develop and/or introduce a single core business process with the smallest number of steps, supported by an information system that will facilitate management of business process. Steps and activities of business process design and information system design are conducted alternatively or in parallel but are always synchronized. One iteration can encompass the following steps in design and implementation for a number of business processes from appropriate groups: core processes, supporting processes, management processes.

- Step 1. Designing core business processes
- Step 2. Defining a detailed requests specification for IS: Use case (UC) model, conceptual model of business objects support, activity diagram for business processes
- Step 3. IS development based on the decision "buy or develop"
- Step 4. IS implementation
- Step 5. Introducing designed core business process in new IS environment.

Those steps/activities are not always sequential. They are comprised of smaller steps within steps 4 and 5 that take turns or are performed simultaneously. (E.g., during the testing phase of application software, in the new business environment supported by IS, users are being prepared for execution of activities in innovated processes).

Similar steps are taken for all core business processes, i.e. groups of business processes. Every above mentioned step represents a set of activities that require different methods and techniques for implementation, depending on whether a critical factor of success is organizational, technological or socio-economic in character.

The majority of activities of business process are performed supported by IS, but the procedures are changed. Integration of business process and IS which stores data and documents, forces an employee to use applications of IS to execute an activity. A positive motivation factor is that employees "see" the whole process and information system helps them to see the results of their activities and know how the execution of the entire process affects the realization of business goals of a company.

However, as with any change, there is initial resistance of employees because the new way of work requires a change in employees' behavior

as well. A work process is realized in a smaller number of steps and every participant/employee or a team has a clearly defined responsibility in the execution of a business process.

Meanwhile, in IS it is recorded who and when executed each critical activity on which the process performance and quality of service depend. It helps solving operations' problems that improve quality of service.

Phase development of integrated business processes and IS is enabled because a high level business process model of a company is defined at the beginning of BIM development, as well as conceptual EIS model that contain models of common business objects. The iterative and incremental methodology of IS development that characterizes software development process, enables development by phases also. This is very important to SMEs because of the amount of financial and human resources that SME should engage for projects of this kind.

A good example that illustrates convenience of the integration of business process development and the development of application software of an IS, relates to a product that is delivered in roll-out phase of application software of IS implementation. It is concerned with the technological manual for users, instead of a conventional user manual.

The technological manual for the realization of business process activities in new IS environment is created based on use case scenarios that define functional demands of IS. In the phase of defining functional requirements, users verify the description of UC scenarios and in testing phase they verify test cases for these use cases. In the roll-out phase, when users' training is also delivered, users are prepared for changes to come. This makes the whole process of development and implementation of business processes and IS effective and less risky.

"Autotransport" Case Study – BIM in Practice

Company Profile

The application of developed BIM approach and model is realized in the enterprise for transport services and maintenance of motor vehicles "Autotransport" d.o.o. Kostolac, Serbia (further referred to as AT).

It is a „spin-off" enterprise, established within a process of restructuring the Electric Power Industry of Serbia, by separating organizational divisions that were providing support to core business processes in the field of transportation of passengers, goods, materials and freight, back in 2003.

Main AT resources are the assets of the fleet of:

- Freight vehicles and small freight vehicles,
- Passenger transportation vehicles, buses,
- Work machines.

AT offers services such as:

- Transport of goods and freights,
- Transport of passengers.

AT has had a rapid growth from 90 to 150 transportation units and from 100 to 200 employees. By 2007, AT doubled the number of kilometers and increased significantly its revenue and it continuously increases profit.

BIM planning phase was in 2005. Realization of the plan started in the mid 2006. The first phase of implementation lasted for 8 months. The second phase of implementation also lasted for 8 months and ended in 2007 (Ivanović, Pantelić, Stefanović & Mojović, 2008).

This case study will include design of Business Process Model (core processes) and software development (IS) as well as the implementation of both for transport services management business process.

Challenges

"Transport services management" (further shortened to "Transport") is a core business process that is an "end-to-end" process and it includes activities from receiving and processing requests for a transport service to the specification and calculation of the costs of a realized service. As a high level process, it has the following characteristic elements: a request for a transport service (input) and a performed transport service with the calculation of the realized service cost (output).

As the core process it has one of defined (measurable) goals for process performance – increase in vehicles production expressed by a performance indicator (KPI-key performance indicator) that is measured in "number of kilometers driven * the amount of freight" [km*t] for freight vehicles and so called "passengers' kilometers" [km*passenger] for passengers vehicles. One more goal should be mentioned: increase in income per vehicle.

For the realization of this process, resources are needed (available vehicles and drivers). It is a responsibility of the support process "Vehicle fleet" which has a relation with the support process "Maintenance". The former has a responsibility to provide transport with available vehicles and available drivers with appropriate documentation on a vehicle and driver (registration, driving license, etc.). The latter is responsible for the high level of availability and readiness of vehicle fleet.

Figure 3 is a graphical interpretation of this high level process model according to the notation of Eriksson-Penkar (Eriksson & Penkar, 2000): Event "Received request from a customer" initiates process, Input is "Service request from a customer", Resources that supply process are Vehicles and Drivers, Outputs are Specification of (delivered) transport service, Report on monthly consumption of fuel, Report on monthly realization of vehicles and drivers. One of the measur-

Figure 3. Transport services management process

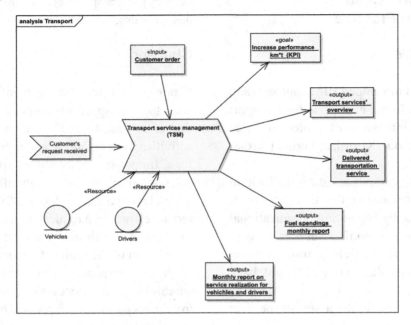

able goals, marked with KPI, is presented in the model in Figure 3.

"Transport" is a business process of high priority for the BIM realization for the following reasons:

- Enterprise makes revenue with transport services,
- This process realizes contacts with a customer and it is in contact with a customer during service realization,
- This process must "know" how many resources are available (relation with "Vehicle fleet" and "Maintenance" process) when accepting a customers' request and whether it needs to rent resources by outsourcing,
- This process must perform a service,
- This process must gather data for the cost calculation of realized service.

BIM Applied to Address the Challenges

Assumption was that *Customer request* is available through EIS.

The business process model of this core process is identified by the following business requirements for information system:

- Identified relations of this process with other processes of enterprise are significant for operational execution and calculation of realized service,
- Identified main operational sub processes/ activities for the process realization
- Identified roles and responsibilities for main activities realization (e.g. commercial staff, staff in charge of fuel consumption, financial staff, manager)
- Identified business documents significant for commercial business of Autotransport (e.g., Travel order for a vehicle, a document that traces transportation of goods...),
- Identified main business objects (e.g., Buyer, Contract/Order, Vehicle, Driver, Service, Document).

In this manner all requests of quality system related to the realization of service processes and measuring efficiency of processes have been integrated into the business process model. Information support to quality management principles, stated in the **Insight to ISO 9000** section of this chapter, is also provided.

The main activities (sub processes) of this process are:

Registration and processing of customers' requests,

Transport service realization consisting of:

Transport organization,

Transport service cost calculation,

Calculation of *income and* costs per driver and vehicle,

Fuel consumption calculation.

Description of Process Realization

Based on a customer contract or an ad hoc request, a driver and a vehicle are assigned. When the transport service is performed, delivered service details are generated (both commercial and financial) to be billed. Various reports, standard or «query by example», are available including: fuel utilization per vehicle, vehicle performance, driver performance or service details.

"Transport" process is realized through use cases gathered in 2 groups: Realization of transport services – passengers and Realization of transport services – freight. Use cases present the functionalities of application software that are being realized through collaboration between business objects. This application software is realized within the designed, developed and implemented EIS of AT.

Documents, Reports and Business Decision Making

In order to run business processes based on quality principles and requirements, the following documents are defined and implemented through application software:

- Input documents (e.g., Contract, Customer order),
- Process documents (e.g., Travel order for vehicle),
- Reports (data on KPIs and other management data in real time)

E.g., Report on transported freight with a freight vehicle, Financial reports of vehicle performance, Financial report on a Contract realization, etc.

Based on *operational and economic indicators on realized services* and direct insight into the status of service realization, it is possible to efficiently manage the process of transport service realization.

Integration of the process "Transport service management" with other processes ("Vehicles fleet", "Maintenance", "Financial management") supported by other application software is based on data integration through a data access layer of the software system "Transport services" and is implemented through a technical solution.

Some of adopted software systems are "off the shelf" solutions, like ERP system. Software systems that facilitated the complete integration of "Transport" business process with others, in order to provide all relevant data and documents for operational processes to its actors through IS are (Figure 4):

- "Vehicle fleet maintenance" (i.e. "Maintenance"),
- "Vehicle fleet availability" (providing data on availability of drivers and vehicles),
- "ATK_Admin" – administration of access rights of users,
- Common business objects ("ATK_OSP") – business partners (e.g. customers, buyers), employees etc.
- Calculation of income and costs per vehicle ("Income and expenditure calculation").

Figure 4. "Transport services" software system in Autotransport's EIS

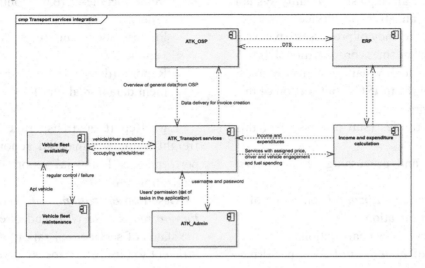

Integration of "Transport services" system with ERP system, as well as "Common business objects" with "Transport services" is technically realized using MS DTS (Microsoft Data Transformation Services).

Business integration model for the key business process "Transport", for which an IS was developed, has been presented (Figure 4). This system (ATK_Transport services) is interrelated to the following systems: an off-the-shelf ERP system, "Vehicle fleet availability" system (for managing vehicles and drivers), "Income and expenditure calculation" system, Common business objects system ("ATK_OSP") and IS administration system ("ATK_Admin").

In Autotransport, the organizational structure follows streamline business processes, in which, the data on business objects, activities and documents are available through EIS and a modern ICT infrastructure. It is a dynamic component of a modern enterprise and enables flexibility and agility, which for an SME in service sector means "survival" and development.

It is observed that actors' responsibilities in business processes increased when business process is supported by IS.

It is also observed that better cooperation between actors and more efficient flow of documents/data from the processes through EIS is achieved when business process integration is supported by an information system.

Lack or irregularity of data or documents in EIS is quickly noticed in the business process realization, and requires a special data update in EIS. That makes operational data for management process complete and of good quality.

A new business process of subcontracting vehicles and drivers was defined and implemented when the need for outsourcing occurred and their success is monitored like they are company's own resources. This happens in the case when own capacities are not enough. The next example of a new process refers to efficient provision of maintenance service to third parties using Autotransport's assets and facilities. The enterprise business model and EIS have become the pillars of enterprise business.

Lessons Learned from this Case

It is recommended that integration of business process and IS should be realized through performing the planning, design and implementation activities of BIM.

It is recognized that people are changing their behavior and easier accept process changes if they are involved in the design and implementation of business processes and IS, according to BIM approach.

It is important that actors in a business process actively participate in the design of a business process – business environment in which the application software will be used. This enables faster implementation of application software in a business process, along with the application of business process modeling methodology and software development methodology.

BIM approach has confirmed that with a process KPI data in EIS, a significant managing value for management structure is achieved.

In Autotransport, the development and implementation of BIM resulted in an increase in business flexibility.

FUTURE TRENDS

Since utilizing integrated planning of business processes and IT support is not fully achieved today, it is to expect that the future trend will be just that - a wide use of BIM. Likewise, BIM will be supported with better planning tools (new visual oriented process/software presentation tools) and new process/software education tool including role play and gaming.

Future trends in software architecture utilized in the development of application software will include more of Open Source, MASHUP, new database management systems and multimedia platforms, and tools for hand held device programming.

Specific for transportation industry, since that was a subject of our study, application software will include but not be limited to: transportation predictive analytics and simulation; real time routing; various location software and increased

Radio Frequency Identification (RFID) presence. Managing relationship with customers or vendors may include some of currently popular social software (blog, wiki,...) or integrated voice/hand held device communication tools (schedule changes or cargo tracking pushed to mobile devices or being able to pull information per customer request).

Since SME will always have a problem with lack of in house resources, SaaS/outsourcing may expand its presence.

CONCLUSION

To reach business integration based on developed and implemented Business Integration Model is NOT ONLY an ultimate goal, but just the beginning of changes and the opportunity to improve the business.

A critical factor of a SME success is the identification and establishment of streamline "end-to-end" business processes in order for SME to "survive" and develop.

A critical factor of the success of implementation of BIM is undoubtedly the readiness of employees to accept a process approach in the execution of their tasks. It is recognized that people are changing behavior more easily if they are involved in design and implementation of business processes and IS, according to BIM approach.

It is necessarry for management to have continous access to KPIs that evaluate process performance so corrective measures can be applied immediately.

It is recommended to create business procedures manuals with referencing how to use IT support.

It is important to see that BIM approach enables phase development and implementation, although it is assumed that business processes and information systems design and implementation according to BIM design and implementation are synchronized and simultaneous. This is very important to

SMEs because of the limited amount of financial resources and human resources hours that SME should engage for projects of this kind.

Since transportation industry is evolving toward heavy information dependency, the goal for SME should be that there is NO ACTIVITY without serious IT support including maintenance as well as all resources management, business partner management and customers' management.

REFERENCES

Berg, R. (2006). Empowerment, productivity and profit: The promise of business process management. *Insurance News Net Magazine.* Retrieved September 25, 2008 from http://insurancenewsnet. com/article.asp?=top_news&id=73920

Burlton, R. T. (2001). *Business process management: Profiting from process.* Indianopolis, Indiana: SAMS.

Eriksson, H. E., & Penkar, M. (2000). *Business Modeling with UML: Business patterns at work.* New York: John Wiley & Sons.

Haff, W. T., Bikker, H., & Adriaanse, D. J. (2002). *Fundamentals of business engineering and management: A systems approach to people and organizations.* Retrieved July 24, 2008 from http://vssd.nl/hlf/b001.htm#FBEM

Huberts, A., & van Petten, A. (2007). *Trends in business process management.* Retrieved September 3, 2008 from http://scribd.com/doc/2335647/ Trends-in-Business-Process-Management.

International Organization for Standardization. (1991). *Quality management and quality system elements – Part 2: Guidelines for services.* (ISO 9004-2:1991). (Date of withdrawal: 2001-04-26). Geneva, Switzerland: International Organization for Standardization.

International Organization for Standardization. (2000). *Quality management systems – Guidelines for performance improvements.* [Geneva, Switzerland: International Organization for Standardization.]. *ISO, 9004,* 2000.

International Organization for Standardization. (2005). *Quality management systems – Fundamentals and vocabulary.* ([). Geneva, Switzerland: International Organization for Standardization.]. *ISO, 9000,* 2005.

International Organization for Standardization. (2008). *Quality management systems – Requirements.* [Geneva, Switzerland: International Organization for Standardization.]. *ISO, 9001,* 2008.

Ivanović, G., Pantelić, S., Stefanović, B., & Mojović, P. (2008). Processes and software of maintenance management system for vehicles. In *XIV International Scientific Conference on Industrial Systems – IS'08, Proceedings* (pp. 379-386). Novi Sad, Serbia: University of Novi Sad, Faculty of Technical Sciences, Industrial Engineering Department.

Jacobson, I., Booch, G., & Raumbaugh, J. (1999). *The Unified Software Development Process.* Reading, Massachusetts: Addison-Wesley Longman.

Lovelock, Ch., & Wright, L. (2002). *Principles of service marketing and management* (2nd ed.). New Jersey: Prentice Hall.

Pantelić, S., Avramović, Z. Ž., Conić, M., & Samardžija, N. (2002). Modern software development for bus station activities, In *Proceedings of Transport Systems Telematics, II International Conference* (pp. 339-343). Katowice – Ustron, Poland: Silesian University of Technology, Faculty of Transport.

Pantelić, S., Zeljković, V., Simeunović, D., Conić, M., & Laćimić, L. (2001). Different types of testing during development phase to achieve software high reliability and quality. In *12th MIRCE International Symposium, Proceedings* [CD-ROM]. Exeter, England: MIRCE Akademy.

Peleg, E. (2007). *Model driven development (MDD) for service oriented architecture (SOA) using UML and Metaphor Builder*. Retrieved September 11, 2008 from http://www-05.ibm.com/il/news/events/ruc/pdf/uml_and_metaphor_builder.pdf.

Robson, W. (1997). *Strategic management & information systems*. London: Pitman Publishing.

Rzevski, G., & Prasad, K. (1998). The synergy of learning organizations and flexible information technology. *AI and Society, 12*, (87-96). Retrieved August 20, 2008 from http://www.rzevski.net

Walford, R. B. (1999). *Business process implementation for IT professionals and managers*, Norwood, MA: Artech House.

Wheatley, M. (2005, November). Processes—not applications—make the company go 'round, *Manufacturing Business Technology*. Retrieved August 9, 2008 from http://www.mbtmag.com/archive/2005/20051101.php.

Chapter 8
Conducting Multi–Project Business Operations in SMEs and IS Support

Igor Vrečko
University of Maribor, Slovenia

Anton Hauc
University of Maribor, Slovenia

Vesna Čančer
University of Maribor, Slovenia

Igor Perko
University of Maribor, Slovenia

ABSTRACT

Multi-project business operations in SMEs require adaptation of management processes and, consequently, revision of information systems. Present ERP solutions are not suitable in a multi-project environment. This chapter presents a newly designed IS model that supports strategic and commercial multiple project operations. The importance of connecting business goals with project performance and upgrading operational CRM into multi-partner management technology is considered. Significant added functions of IS in a multi-project environment should support project evaluation and management of project portfolios, intra- and inter-project communication, and mastering multi-task workflow. To reduce the need to spend limited SMEs' resources, technological development of the designed IS model must assure its simplicity for use and deployment.

INTRODUCTION

The growing dynamics of project implementation and the appearance of multi-project business operations in all types of organizations, including Small to Medium Enterprises (SMEs), requires adaptation of their management processes at all levels. The increasing complexity of SMEs' multi-project business operations leads to greater complexity among different business relationships. SMEs can cooperate in one project and compete in another,

DOI: 10.4018/978-1-60566-892-5.ch008

while sharing resources only when necessary. The business systems[1] (BSs) role differs in projects: for instance, it can be project management, a coordinator, a subcontractor, or a consultant. The use of diverse communication standards can lead to inefficient project coordination among partners and can result in sub-optimal project portfolio performance. Dealing with the multi-project business operations conducting process, therefore, has to be holistic enough. New tools and concepts have to be developed to support the management of multi-project business operations. Among this support, special attention is given to assuring appropriate information and information system (IS) suitability.

In general, information systems provide the means for the BS to change and adapt to the business environment. Many ISs, are available to help plan and execute business processes, which will result in better product and services quality, a better response to clients' requests, and recognizing and mitigating the risks. For standard business processes suites of pre-prepared business applications, such as Enterprise Resource Planning (ERP) applications are available.

Present Enterprise Resource Planning (ERP) solutions do not support multi-project business operations appropriately because they are more or less adapted to the continual – therefore non-project oriented – business operations. Among those solutions are some ERP versions, partly adapted to the needs of project-oriented SMEs; there are also some supplemental ERP modules supporting project management in non-project-oriented SMEs. But mostly all of them assist the conduction of individual projects instead of entire (multi)project-oriented business operations, which deal with contemporary and strategically oriented BSs.

Because of some differences in informational needs, we outlined the differences between project-oriented BSs, which deal mostly with commercial projects representing their core business, and BSs, which deal mostly with developing strategic and

other on-going projects. To support the informational needs of them all, the new IS should be developed, assuring state-of-the-art support for challenges arising in a multi-project environment. It should upgrade existing independent applications and deliver greater interconnectivity with the BSs' ERP and decision support systems. In this chapter we propose a model for such IS in the form of *Project Oriented Enterprise Application Suite* – PREAS.

We wanted to make it possible for SMEs to use the information resources provided in the most efficient way and to efficiently focus on the management of complex business workflow. The model supports project evaluation and the selection process required for managing project portfolios using multi-criteria decision-making methods. It upgrades the operational CRM into multi-partner management technology to manage project partnership relations. Furthermore, the model connects information about the SMEs' business goals and business results with project performance and supports intra- and inter-project communication, as well as connecting project members and partners from within and outside the company. It also supports multi-task workflow planning and processing with limited resources. In developing the applicable IS model, especially in SMEs, we wanted to ensure it would be easy to use and deploy, reducing the need to spend limited resources on IS. Another objective in developing the model was to ensure an environment that stimulates innovative processes and reduces the costs and risks of converting the innovation into projects.

Since new technologies can easily outperform and substitute current mainstream technologies, we tried to avoid and replace as many information application terms as possible (including email and intranet) with content-related terms such as communication.

BACKGROUND

The contemporary business environment, which is characterized by quick and constant change, is the perfect setting for the growth of new projects (Shenhar & Dvir, 2005; Leintz & Rea, 1995; Dietrich & Lehtonen, 2005). Artto & Wikström (2005) as well as Hauc & Kovac (2000) connect the concepts of "business" and "project" together and emphasise the strategic importance of projects to the overall business of a BS. They suggest that "projects are part of overall business and a central part of the development, strategic sight and maintaining of the firm's competitiveness". Modern methods of project management can be adapted and altered to suit the needs of smaller organizations (Murphy & Ledwith, 2006). For the sake of strongly limited resources in SMEs in comparison to larger BSs, the need for efficient and especially effective implementation of many strategic and other projects is very important. But it is not an easy job (Shenhar & Dvir, 2005; Lycett & Rassau & Danson, 2004; Morris & Pinto, 2004; Shenhar & Dvir, 2004; Morris & Jamieson, 2004).

The problem becomes much more complex where there are multiple projects ongoing at the same time and within the same organization (Turner & Speiser, 1992; Platje, Harald & Wadman, 1994). And that is the case in the contemporary business environment. According to some estimates, up to 90% of all projects occur in a multi-project context (Payne, 1995). Fricke & Shenbar (2000) and similarly Engwall (2001) support this cognition.

In such an environment an additional set of management problems emerges in comparison to managing individual or single projects (Turner & Speiser, 1992; Platje, Harald & Wadman, 1994; Pellegrinelli, 1997). They relate to issues such as the mix of projects (Elonen & Artto, 2003), the portfolio's resource management (Engwall & Jerbrant, 2003; Eskerod 1996, Lee & Miller 2004), aligning the portfolio to achieve optimization (Dooley, 2000), etc.

The area of multi-projects is still largely un-researched (Van Der Merwe, 1997; Fricke & Shenbar, 2000; Anavi-Isakow & Golany, 2003). Because the potential for improvement in management of simultaneous multiple projects is significant (Payne, 1995), recent studies on project management have been redirected toward multi-project management (Meredith & Mantel, 1995; Shtub, Bard & Globerson, 1994; Van Der Merwe, 1997; Levy & Globerson, 1997; Fricke & Shenbar, 2000; Engwall, 2001; Chan & Chung, 2002; Anavi-Isakow & Golany, 2003; Gray & Larson, 2003; Nilsson, 2004).

For BSs to respond adequately to ever-increasing demands, management requires a new framework of tools to address the needs of multiple project management (Duoley, Lupton & O'Sullivan, 2005). Among the tools required we would like to put out the project selection and project portfolio formation supporting tools and the information extraction and delivery tools.

When selecting, evaluating and prioritising suitable projects, decision making is important. In practice, a number of important decisions are often made without methodological decision support. Namely, even the use of well-defined traditional quantitative procedures can oppress effective decision making. For example, it is hard to evaluate probabilities because the assumptions do not hold in a given situation or they cannot be verified. Besides, many decision theories are based on the assumption that a decision maker is always perfectly rational. Therefore, Raiffa (1994) suggests a so-called prescriptive approach to decision making: instead of regarding people as perfect rational individuals, we develop systematic ('systematic' considers a concept, taking care of all steps of a process in a hierarchy of succession) decision-making procedures supportive of decision-making, and completed with intuition. Systematic approaches to complex problem solving are intended for decision makers in BSs as practical working tools to help them resolve complex problems. Rational action on the one hand, and intuitive experience-supported action on the other, complements each other when solutions to problems are developed in real life. Therefore, finding the solution to decision-related problems must in practice incorporate the sensible use of intuition and experience – see, e.g. Grünig & Kühn (2005). Evaluating and forecasting methods, as well as creative thinking methods can enlarge capacities of decision-making procedures, as well.

It has already been demonstrated that modern operational research (OR) methods can help managers much more than traditional ones (Jackson, 2003; Perrin, 2002)2. They can well support their requisite holism, i.e. diminish the danger of making oversights, as well as the danger of being overwhelmed by data, hence losing their focus and requisite holism. Mulej (2005) concluded that systems thinking have always helped people fight oversight.

Appropriate information support is another prerequisite for successfully conducting a contemporary multi-project business environment. Basic business functions are supported by ERP applications, while special needs, such as those for multiple project management and decision support are contented separately. The use of multiple software tools to support business needs often forces the BS to use its valuable resources to focus on IS issues, which represents a particularly large problem in SMEs.

Different analysis confirms the significant contribution of project management information systems (PMIS) to successful project management. Research by Light & Rosser & Hayward (2005) estimates that 75% of large IT projects managed with the support of a PMIS will succeed, while 75% of projects without such support will fail. For the architectural, engineering and construction industry, Fischer, Waugh and Axworthy (1998) showed benefits of suitable information support on project work and especially multi-project work. According to Raymond and Bergeron (2008) PMIS plays a central role in a successful project management system. Project management software usage

has also been found to have many drawbacks and limitations, both in theory, when compared to an ideal PMIS by researchers (Jaafari & Manivong, 1998) and in practice, as perceived by project managers (White & Fortune, 2001).

Software systems that exist to assist management are generally not adequate to cope with the additional complexity of the multi-project situation (Payne, 1995). Information solutions are insufficiently holistic and are not integrated into BSs basic information systems (Fischer, Waugh and Axworthy 1998). Support from existing decision systems incorporated into PMIS (Jaafari & Manivong, 1998) is not adequate in a multi-project environment. It should be widened and also incorporate support for projects' selection process and making the project portfolio. Multi-project management requires a central monitoring platform involving the whole project portfolio, observing all the projects in all phases of development.

PROJECTS AND PROJECT PROCESSES IN DIFFERENT TYPES OF SMES

BSs implement projects in order to reach strategic, developmental and business objectives. All projects in those systems represent **multiple project operations,** which can be divided, with regard to BS needs, into:

- **multiple projects implementation of developmental strategies of BS**, which comprises projects for the implementation of strategic developmental programmes (SDP) in order to attain strategic goals;
- **on-going multiple project operations** for the implementation of projects, which arise from annual business plans and urgent projects implemented for various reasons, e.g. projects aimed at solving crises, projects which arise in reaction to the influences

Figure 1. Multi-project business operations in BSs

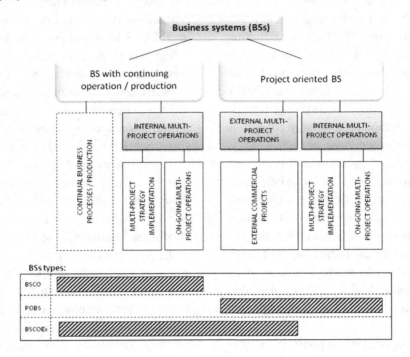

of present changes, business actions of competitors, opportunities in the market, etc. Such projects represent projects of ongoing adaptation of BS to their business environment and are not the consequence of the process of strategic planning;

- **external multiple project operations**, within which ordered (commercial) projects are being implemented, typically on the basis of concluded agreements (in civil engineering, engineering services, production of tools, R&D institutions, IT companies, service-providing companies, etc.).

According to their business operations and organization, BSs can be divided into (Figure 1):

- **BS with continuing operation/production (BSCO)**, characteristic of series and mass production;
- **BS with project operations;** these are **project-oriented BS (POBS)**, which

implement a number of external commercial projects for external customers.

In the above BS the implementation of multiple project operations has to be carried out for various purposes. In BSCO, in addition to basic business and production processes (e.g. production of electrical appliances, parts, food etc.), there are also project operations, which are related to the implementation of strategies and on-going adaptation to the business environment, which together form **internal multiple project operations**. In POBS, in addition to internal multiple project operations, there are also **external multiple project operations**, which comprise all projects the BS carries out for its customers.

When dividing multiple project operations in BSCO, we can come across, mainly in SMEs, special project operations within continuing operations/production in cases in which a BS, for instance, is a supplier of a large corporation and has to supply a special order within its production activities (e.g. a certain limited amount of special parts the customer ordered, for which this company supplies parts on a permanent basis), which represent an **urgent production project**. A number of such projects form a special multiple-project activity, which should be organized within existing business activities and production. In such case we can speak about BSCO with external multiple project operations – BSCOEx.

For internal multiple project operations we have to ensure project organization for integrated project management. An increasing number of projects appearing in BS require inbuilt project organization, because of permanent **project production** (Hauc, 2007; Hauc & Vrečko, 2006).

Regardless of the type of BS and the type of multiple project operations, it is necessary to establish a **multiple project organizational and information environment** in the BS to successfully manage total operations management. In BSCO it is also necessary to ensure an environment for continuing operations/production management. To understand informational needs in different types of BS, we have to be acquainted with project processes going on in such systems. Further on, we present the process of multiple project implementation of strategic development and the process of multiple project implementations of external commercial projects.

The Process of Multiple Project Implementation of Strategic Development

The process of project implementation of strategic development, defined in the SDP[3], is a dynamic process of strategy formation in accordance with mission and vision, project definition, programme and project portfolio (further on we shall discuss projects in general, and, where necessary, put special emphasis on the programme or project portfolio), with which strategies are implemented according to a strategic plan, with the choice of suitable projects followed by project implementa-

tion. The projects execution has to be in line with planning and implementation of annual operation plans, because project implementation involves the use of all available BS resources (Vrečko, 2007). At the same time, growth projects ensure modified and/or new scope of operations. Through the development projects, development of the organization, informatization, human resources, quality, etc. is ensured. With regard to the increasing number of changes in the BS environment, which cannot be forecast either by risk analyses or by influence factors analysis, it is necessary to implement the process of SDP according to the principles of **strategy start-up.** Strategy start-up is the process of transforming strategies into projects in which strategic decisions – when it is not possible to reach a high degree of strategy definition – are transferred into project start-up preparation and its implementation to a previously defined point in project implementation while permanently integrating measures related to change impact (Hauc & Kovač, 2000). The process of strategic development projects implementation includes:

- **Initial project identification:** In accordance with adopted strategies, initial identification or project identification, and the selection of appropriate projects in relation to strategic goals and implementation possibilities is performed, which represents **initial project selection**. Selected projects are incorporated into a strategic project plan (SPP). The process of project start-up documentation preparation follows. The project owner, project management and team for the creation of project start-up documentation are selected. For decision making, controlling and implementation of this part of the process of SDP implementation we have to ensure, in addition to project organization, not only a project management information system (PMIS) for individual projects, but also an integrated multiple-project management information system (MPMIS).

- **Preparation of project start-up:** Project start-up documents (which include input project strategies, goals, project content, project economy, risk analysis, project organization, influential factor analysis, implementation plan, control plan, etc.) have to be in line with SDP and approved by the top management of a BS. Within PMIS a project database should be created. On the basis of prepared start-up documents, a **second project selection** is implemented, which includes the preparation of the project portfolio and the inclusion of project plans in SPP as well as in the annual plan of internal projects. The preparation of a project's start-up is concluded with its implementation.

- **Project implementation:** During project implementation strategic controlling (checking conformity with the strategy) and project controlling (checking conformity of project implementation with the implementation plan) is carried out. In case of deviations, the project start-up documents are revised. When deviations are considerable, changes of SPP are needed, e.g. the inclusion of new projects, change of existing projects and/or termination of currently implemented projects, which necessitates repeated selection of projects. In this case we speak about a **third project selection**, during which a new portfolio should be prepared.

- **Project handover and completion:** On completion of the project, the handover project activities and completion are carried out as well as the start-up of its exploitations in accordance with the ongoing annual operation plans. PMIS and MPMIS ensure a database upgrade for the needs of ERP (for example, with the product development project completion, the project result is not only production and sales, but also a database, which enables this production and sales – data on products, technological procedures, calculations, fixed assets, current assets, suppliers, etc.).

- **Start-up and controlling of exploitations:** Depending on the project, the start-up of exploitations is carried out in different forms (in product development projects it may take the form of the aforementioned production and sales with all accompanying processes; in IT projects it may take the form of regular use of information solutions; in projects of reorganization the implementation of processes in a newly set up organization, etc.). The start-up of exploitations is usually included in annual operations and other business plans. Controlling should ensure monitoring of exploitations in accordance with the strategy and project goals and in light of the business and other project effects achieved.

Multiple project strategy implementation is thus a dynamic process of determining projects and programmes, identifying and forming the initial project portfolio, called the **portfolio of identified projects**; the preparation of project and programmes start-up with the second selection, which ensures implementation of SPP, results in the **start-up implementation portfolio;** and a dynamic process of project implementation, including controlling, which may lead to a repeated selection, called **dynamic implementation portfolio;** this is followed by project implementation after revised strategic project plans.

On-going multiple project operations (Figure 1) are, in principle, carried out in a similar way as the process of multiple project strategy implementations, but with fewer selections and are highly determined with regard to objectives and effects.

Multiple project operations require appropriate PMIS and its connection with MPMIS.

The Process of Multiple Project Implementation of External Commercial Projects

In POBS, in addition to internal multiple project operations, external multiple project operations are also carried out. Such projects are carried out for external customers, who request proposals for the implementation and/or project management of various degrees of complexity. It is also possible that customers – on their own or in agreement with project providers or other parties (e.g. banks) establish a **project enterprise** (BS of limited duration), which operates until the project is concluded and whose main task is project implementation control and management. After the project has been completed such BS is liquidated and a new BS is set up to manage exploitations. In SMEs such projects' offerings and implementations are less frequent due to limited financial and other resources.

In the field of external multiple projects operations we come across different external commercial projects, ranging from civil engineering projects, production investment projects, telecommunication networks projects, and projects in the tooling industry, to R&D projects, etc. Project locations may also differ, which requires a number of logistic solutions in project implementation, management and organization with regard to project location, etc. Regardless of the type of external commercial project, the process of such projects is as follows:

- **Acquiring market information:** this is a permanent process of obtaining information about bids;
- **Invitation for bid:** in which offers are made on the basis of bids, which is the basis for concluding a contract between the customer and supplier;
- **Project implementation:** which follows the bidding procedure and ends with the handover of the project to the customer;

- **Guarantee:** with which the supplier ensures uninterrupted use of the project and the time during which the customer has the right to corrections, usually at the cost of the supplier;
- **Maintenance:** if the project object enables or requires it and when this is in the interest of the customer.

As a rule, POBS submit a larger number of offers, than the actual number of projects that are signed for in contracts. Management should accept decisions if a bidding procedure are adopted for certain requirements. This is a special project selection called **bidding portfolio**.

External multiple project operations represent the basic activity of POBS. In order to control such operations not only PMIS for individual projects should exist but also an **external multiple project management information system – EMPMIS,** which represents the main part of the business information system – ERP. External commercial project databases are formed with the decision that the bidding procedure should start. If the contract is signed, the database is built for both POBS and the customer. PMIS for each project, EMPMIS and ERP form an integrated information system.

THE MULTI-PROJECT SMES IS CHALLENGES

To support the needs of a multi-project SME, the information system should deal with both the internal processes and the communication flow with the SMEs' business environment. It should also deliver state-of-the-art support for core BSs operations and projects. We propose the IS model in the form of *Project Oriented Enterprise Application Suite* (*PREAS*).

To find out which attributes need attention when developing a general IS model for SMEs dealing in a multi-project business environment, common business issues need to be examined.

Focusing on the multi-project SMEs and closely examining issues a BS is confronted with enables us to elaborate the IS features needed for their solution. Issues provide challenges for the IS model development and a base for building a framework of an IS for a multi-project SME.

Some of the main issues worth focusing on when developing IS for supporting multi-project business operations are:

- **Supporting the management of limited resources,** such as a budget and human resources;
- **Supporting project evaluation and decision making** in project portfolio management, upgrading project management tools to project portfolio management tools;
- **Supporting intra- and inter-project communication** as well as connecting the project members and partners from within and outside the company;
- Providing an **environment for innovative processes**, reducing the costs and risks in using and reusing innovations;
- **Connecting business goals and business results with project performance** information;
- **Managing multi-project business parties' relations** by upgrading operational Customer Relationship Management (CRM) technology into multi-project partner relation management suite,
- **Supporting multi-task workflow** planning and processing;
- **Enabling multi-project management.**

In the next sections we will focus on every one of these issues, and try to extract the challenges for the IS to help the BS achieve its business goals.

Managing Limited Resources

Due to their size SMEs have to cope with limited financial resources, human capital, management knowledge, and organizational structures. Diverse options were researched to overcome weaknesses arising from these issues, mainly related to connecting multiple SMEs (Vonortas, 2000; Havnes & Senneseth, 2001). Not enough research though was focused on IS support for: automation of information exchange processes, reducing complex organizational structures, and providing the know-how needed to conduct the business.

Using appropriate IS knowledge and organizational shortcomings can be turned to a company's advantage. To do so, we provide some IS challenges:

- The **IS TCO** (total cost of ownership) reaches reasonable levels;
- **Out of the box** products, should have simple installation procedures and minimal administration requirements, and provide external **know-how** and **best practices** in standard business processes management, reducing supporting staff requirements;
- Complex project **processes** in project management should be automated, reducing the need for complex organization structures;
- The ERP, project development, communication, and documentation building processes should be integrated; and
- **State-of-the-art technologies,** which are key business processes, should be used to facilitate diversity from the competition.

In other words: a cheap, easy to manage IS should support all the standard business processes, ensuring standard business execution, enabling the staff to focus on state-of-the-art supported key performance products.

Managing Multi-Project Business Parties' Relations

In BSCOs diverse multi-project business parties are represented. Among them are:

- project owner;
- project management (as project manager, project management organization, project office, etc.);
- internal and external performers;
- project receivers;
- project stakeholders;
- project controllers; and
- others with different roles – from making partial decisions to giving information about the project.

The upper composition in POBS involves the following additional parties:

- customers who order the project;
- competitors; and
- project approvals, e.g. institutions for issuing building permits and operating permits, inspection authority, auditor, etc.

SMEs operate in environments that should be divided into a business partners' environment and a social environment, where relationships are usually related to external information systems (EIS) legislation, e.g. tax IS, IS state statistics, etc. Business partners can be divided into:

- business partners for the implementation of multiple project operations of strategy implementation;
- business partners for the implementation of external multiple project operations; and
- business partners for continuing operations.

Many studies elaborate on the type of SMEs' relations with business parties. Some focus on collaboration, competition, client-server relations, and on the SME's role in supply chains etc. In a multi-project environment where all of these types of relations can occur, even with one party playing multiple roles in company projects, managing multi-project business parties' relations is a key issue.

For example:

- **When competing:** for creating an optimal project proposal, business intelligence supports planning the project results, while competition intelligence explains the competitors' abilities to execute the project;
- **When recruiting team members:** in the recruiting process diverse sources can be used to assess the partner's competences. These include the partner's resume and references, references of collaboration from previous mutual cooperation, or ratings from external agencies. To avoid risks in the recruiting processes, the quality of the data is an important issue;
- **For managing external partners relations:** typically, external project team members have special, time-limited roles in the project, different business goals, and special communication needs. The time variance of external team members is usually limited, therefore the activities they execute must remain on schedule. Because they don't share the goals of the project managers, quality issues may arise, which must be addressed at a higher level of control. Communication by external team members, which is discussed further in the following sections, must comply with official project protocols. The project goals, rules, the members' role in the project and specific tasks external partner must perform, must be extensively explained (Highsmith 2004).

The IS challenges in the management of multi-project business parties' relations are:

- connecting **business intelligence** and **competition intelligence**;
- providing **partner intelligence**, supporting the recruiting process;
- organizing **proactive reporting of the**

project's execution to face the project parties' special requirements; and

- **executing and documenting** formal communication and **supporting** the exchange of informal information communication.

Supporting Communication

The goal of communication is to keep all parties informed, providing the receiver with relevant information. Communications should follow some common rules: the messages must have an agreed formal structure, they should focus on an issue, comments of the parties involved should be recorded, and communication conclusions and results should be stored for later use.

To avoid project communication issues some aspects should be considered:

- **The receivers** should be selected according to the value of information delivered. Information overflow can be avoided by sending the information only to the involved receivers. On the other hand, all participants should possess all the relevant information concerning their work;
- **The communication purpose:** if the message doesn't have an impact on the receivers' activities on the project it probably doesn't have to be sent. Continuous delivery of information that has no value for the receiver diminishes the receiver's attention;
- **A standard communication format** should be used, with emphasis on the important parts of the communication. The format of the communication should enable the receiver to use automated processing to minimize the administrative tasks;
- **Standard agreed communication channels** should be used. Formal communication is often supported by informal exchange of information. Using informal communication channels (Portny 2007)

can keep formal information exchange simple and issues focused;

- Formal communication should be **documented** (Wysocki & McGary 2003). The sender, receiver and the project documentation should keep a communication log, allowing swift resolution of issues. In the case of multiple levels of external project participants, the hub's organizational structure can emerge (Highsmith 2004); and
- **Project reporting** (Project Management Institute 2004): The messages from the project's participants can inform about potential or actual changes to project development, and should be easily processed by the project planning or execution management software. The project participants should be informed about the project's performance and modifications in the original plans, concerning their execution.

To summarize, a project's communication software should enable optimal delivery of information to the receivers, minimizing the administrative tasks of cataloguing information received in the repositories. Information affecting the project's status should be easily applicable, allowing successful project management.

The communication aspect in SMEs is concentrated on three major IS challenges:

- **Complying** with communication standards accepted in a BS business environment;
- **Automating** the administrative tasks in documenting the communication, and connecting communication channels with the PMIS;
- **Proactive reporting**, delivering the recipients the information they need, reducing the information overload.

Enabling Innovation Processes

Standard project management techniques presume the implementation of planned activities in project execution, while innovations often post the need for adaptation, and are therefore hardly welcome. Since innovations can cut costs and raise the quality of a product, they should be considered, even if they change the project execution plans.

As Highsmith (2004) states, BSs have to deliver better products geared to what customers want at the time of shipment, which may or may not resemble what the team guessed they wanted when the project was initiated. BSs that have the ability to quickly and inexpensively adapt to changes in customer demands during the development life-cycle will have a competitive advantage.

The reason to highlight the innovation process is to produce more desirable products faster and cheaper by modifying them, their design, or the production process. Agile project management (ibid) states a BS should deliver innovative results to customers within cost and schedule constraints.

Innovation is mostly about involving new tools, making the processes faster and cheaper, and the products better. IT can be regarded as a tool, providing documentation, communication, research and analyses methods services.

An example of IT innovation is the evaluation of the probability of default in a commercial bank, where data-mining technologies are used, producing more accurate results than the manual evaluation, and greatly reducing the cost and time of the evaluation process (Perko & Bobek 2008).

To successfully involve the innovation process in the project processes two aspects must be considered: the project team members' development process and the management process of the innovation proposals (Khazanchi et al., 2007):

- **Building the team members' competences**: This is crucial for the project's success, especially in agile, small dynamic teams (Portny, 2007). Team member intelligence enables successful team member selection and supports the member building process.
- **The innovation process** starts with the innovation notification and innovation impact evaluation. The innovation, the planned results and the actual innovation impact are recorded in the knowledge structures, providing means for the successful re-use of innovation.

The IS should support the innovation management process by:

- Providing **team member intelligence**, supporting team building and upgrading team members' competences;
- Supporting the **innovation registration process**, reducing administrative costs;
- Using **IT-supported simulation and modeling** techniques in the innovation evaluation and execution process; and
- **Providing access** to the innovation status, results and background data, making the innovation available for further use.

Relating Projects and Business Performance

The economic appraisal of the project outcome involves identifying options and assessing the benefits and costs to determine the options' net present values or the highest benefit-cost ratios (Cooper et al. 2004). The direct project benefits can mostly be numerically evaluated, while indirect effects can often only be described. On the cost side, the uncertainties must be evaluated and risk mitigation strategies elaborated. A detailed economic appraisal of the project is the basis for making decisions regarding the execution and funding of the project.

Economic outcome planning is resumed by controlling the project's progress (Wysocki &

McGary 2003). Project progress controlling involves proactive reporting on regular project progress, deviations in the plan, and exceptions. Change management, supported by these reports, uses risk-mitigation strategies, which result in modifications of project time and cost plans.

Both project planning and controlling project results are very complex, knowledge-intensive and time-consuming occurrences. The reporting process is very intensive, both for the project manager in creating the reports, and for the audience, especially when the audience comes from diverse companies, and assuming a lack of informal information communication. Because of the complexity of planning, the planning often isn't developed to the micro level; therefore some effects can only be evaluated.

Project planning delivers expected economic benefits and costs, later measured during project execution. These should be tightly connected to the BS business intelligence (BI) systems. BI performs business performance reporting. Complete BI systems involve the planning process and support project execution performance reporting.

The tight integration of PMISs and BI systems is essential to minimize duplicate data entry and administrative costs, and raise information quality. The planning process is usually executed using project management software integrated with the BI systems. The economic effects of project execution, evidenced in the BI systems, provide the basis for the automated economic effects progress reports.

To successfully evaluate the execution of the project schedule, the economic effects must be interlinked with the project execution data. For example: a cost reduction in the economic report, usually considered a cost-cutting success, can be explained by shifting one of the cost-intensive project tasks. Therefore, to provide comprehensive, informative reports, the economic results must be associated with the project content. The IS should connect business performance to projects by:

- **Integrating ERP and project management software** to support the planning processes and deliver control support in the project execution phases;
- **Automating data synchronization** between the project management systems and intelligence suite during project planning and execution, and especially on project modifications;
- Establishing a **proactive reporting system**, linking project execution information with financial business performance effects stored in the BI systems.

Decision Support

Decisions concerning project management include selecting the projects, selecting the appropriate project resources, evaluating the project change effects, and others. In SMEs, coping with limited resources is combined with high availability of external resources, and dynamic organization, enabling the use of new technologies in the project execution process. Therefore the uncertainty evaluation and risk-mitigation processes need to be involved in project planning and execution. For project evaluation, a cost-benefit comparison (Lawson et al. 2006) can be used, though the project selection process can be divided into several steps. For instance:

1. Project **potential benefits evaluation:** arranging project according to its value for the BS;
2. **Feasibility evaluation:** evaluating potential ways the project will be executed. Feasibility evaluation includes analyses of the availability of internal and external resources, as well as the availability of new technologies, lowering project execution costs, and raising the product customer value (Highsmith 2004);
3. **Cost assessment:** calculating the planned costs of the project execution.

The project selection process results in absolute numbers and can be calculated. The issues in calculating the results are in the uncertainty evaluation and potential-risk assessment, and their complexity arises when evaluating a multi-project portfolio. Multi-criteria, based on decision models, are required for their structural resolution.

Computer-supported methods can help manage complexity by facilitating individual or group research, supporting and solving important complex decision-making problems. The following facts contribute to the applicability of the Multi-Criteria Decision-Making (MCDM) methods in dealing with complex problems:

- Their role is to complement intuition and experience.
- In MCDM we take into account multiple, often conflicting criteria.
- In this type of decision-making process we structure the problem.
- The most useful approaches are conceptually simple and computer supported.
- The aim of MCDM is to help decision makers learn about the problem, express their judgments about the importance of the criteria and their preferences for alternatives, confront other participants' judgments, understand the value of the final alternatives, and use them in problem-solving activities.

Due to complexity, efficient conducting of multi-project business operations, including suitable approaches to further IS development of MPBP, and projects selection to determine the most suitable project portfolio can, therefore, be supported with contemporary MCDM methods. They enable SMEs to select the most suitable form of ERP solutions (to reach the standards of the competition) and to elevate standards above this level by building, evaluating and selecting a differential approach in managing their performance. They enable requisitely holistic dealing with the multi-project business operations conducting process. They can well support the process for the selection of the most appropriate projects and thus the formation of the most suitable project portfolio.

The costs and complexity of the project selection process force SMEs to prefer intuitive selection over structured ones. The implications of such project selection are an unbalanced project portfolio and badly assessed project costs and project risks, resulting in the failure of project assessment. We believe the complexity and costs of multi-project portfolio management can be reduced significantly by using appropriate IT tools (Leopoulos et al. 2006).

IS challenges, concerning the SMEs multi-project portfolio management are:

- using **creative thinking presentation technology** to support problem definition presentations;
- using **business intelligence** to access information on current and projected internal resources;
- using **project parties' intelligence** to evaluate the costs and expertise of external resources;
- using **scorecards and performance-indication hierarchies** stored in knowledge structures to evaluate the project's contributions to the portfolio's goals;
- creating easy-to-use **project comparative fact sheets**, based on existing project and product know-how, stored in knowledge structures;
- **re-using** the project sections and using **best practices** from the business environment and executed projects, stored in knowledge structures.
- using **business rules and automated decision logic,** enabling repeatable, unified and swift evaluation of criteria and alternative simulations, eliminating unacceptable alternatives;

- using **out of the box simulation models and methodologies**, successfully predicting the project attributes, and supporting sensibility analysis in the project portfolio.

Supporting Multi-Project Workflow

Managing multiple projects requires optimizing the use of common resources, conducting parallel processes, and achieving semi-overlapping goals. When comparing the management of multiple projects to the management of a single project, optimizing efforts multiply, but so do the potential advantages in the form of available reusable components, semi products and, of course, accumulated knowledge.

The administrative tasks discussed in the preceding paragraphs are mainly focused in reducing communication costs and facilitating the company information resources required for the management of a single project. For the IS to support the multi-project workflow, it should:

- provide standard views to the **portfolio scorecards** according to the project's alignment with portfolio strategy;
- share a **common project management software** with the external partners or **enable the exchange of automated content** to minimize external communication administration costs;
- **impose strong coordination mechanisms** to minimize the risk of project change caused by external partners;
- optimize multi-project execution by **joining parallel processes**.

Enabling Multi-Project Management

In preparing the project start-up and implementation phase we must cater for the information needs of all project system elements. PMIS should meet those needs. Basic information support in SME is, as a rule, based on diverse ERP solutions, and PMIS should be appropriately connected with them.

For established ERP systems, appropriate computer and communication equipment, software and everything else needed for permanent use is available. Similarly, PMIS requires the adaptation of appropriate computer and communication hardware, software and other equipment to the project's requirements. As a rule, in PMIS we can use existing computer and communication hardware, but it is often necessary to install additional software, which supports project management processes, from the identification of the project until it is completed.

In multiple project operations, project-adapted PMISs, supporting the management and implementation of individual projects, should be connected with multiple project processes creating multiple project-management information systems (MPMIS). The MPMIS database needs to be integrated from the databases of individual projects. Annual operation plans can be prepared, carried out and controlled based on data stored in appropriate databases.

Projects need to be connected with other processes in a SME – they need to be planned, and the plans should be integrated into SMEs operational plans, etc. This requires that MPMIS is integrated with the ERP. In BSCO, PMIS is connected with the ERP system through MPMIS until the completion of the project's start-up preparation, whereas in POBS MPMIS is connected with the ERP from the bidding procedure, through start-up preparation and project execution until completion of the project and providing data for the customer's ERP system databases.

The IS should support multi-project management by:

- ensuring responsible project management and project controllers with needed information from **integrated PMIS with (internal and external) ERPs**;
- enabling project owners holistic planning

and control with **integrated MPMIS with (internal and external) ERPs**;

- **developing an MPMIS database** embracing all technical, organizational and experience data concerning progress and concluded projects.

Combining the IS Challenges

Some of the issues mentioned in the previous sections are fully supported by existing ISs, some have partial solutions, while some don't have the appropriate solutions presented. The SMEs multi-project issues emerging from diverse business viewpoints all present some IS- related challenges. Some challenges are related, some even identical, while all together they try to cover the issues preventing successful multi-projects in SMEs.

The issues and challenges stated in the previous paragraphs can be grouped in the form of technologies used (See Table 1)

The IS challenges, presented in Table 1, have the premise to resolve the business issues in multi-project SMEs:

- Out of the box IS with implemented know-how resolves the limited resources issue and supports decision making, using existing knowledge stored in IS.
- Business processes automation eliminates complex organization needs and supports the innovation registration processes, the first step in creating new knowledge.
- Automated data transfer resolves inner data transfer, settles inconsistencies in the SME's IS subsystems and external data sources, lowering the cost of documenting simplified communication among the project partners.
- The SME's limited resources should be used on the company's key business activities, distinguishing the SME from its competition. State-of-the-art software supports exceptional results in these fields.

- The intelligence should provide quality information on business performance, partner relations, and innovation processes, by providing proactive reports. This would support project and project portfolio decisions.
- Existing components in the form of best practices and innovation results, accessible in knowledge management structures, can be used in the project decision process and in optimizing the multi-project flow by joining parallel processes.
- Compliance supports mitigating the risks of project change and reducing administration costs, complying with communication standards and imposing strong communication mechanisms.
- Using R&D progress in advanced analyses and simulation technologies, supporting the innovation process and simplifying the decision process by using out of the box simulation models.

The resulting challenges support some key attributes of business success:

- **Low resources input** in standard business processes, using existing know-how and automated best-breed business processes, optimizing communication, and documenting management processes;
- **Supporting the project decision process** and project portfolio management, using balance sheets, simulation technologies, and linking project planning and execution with business performance;
- **Focusing on key business processes**, using state-of-the-art software and supporting the innovation process;

Achieving these IS challenges, an SME's weakness of limited resources, know-how and organizational skills can be avoided, while supporting the advantages of agility and adaptability to changes in the business environment.

Table 1. Challenges to the IS

Issue	IS Challenge	Solutions
Communication	**Complying** with acceptable communication standards in the company business environment	Communication flow
Workflow	**Imposing strong coordination mechanisms**	Communication flow, Proactive reporting
Business performance	**Automating data synchronization** between the project management systems and intelligence suite	Data flow
Business performance	Establishing a **proactive reporting system**, linking project execution information with the effects of business financial performance	Data flow, Intelligence suite, Proactive reporting flows
Decision support	Using a **creative thinking presentation technology**	Decision support flow
Managing relations	**Executing and documenting** formal communication, and **supporting** the informal exchange of information communication	Documentation flows
Communication	**Automating** administrative tasks in documenting the communication	Documentation flows
Limited resources	**Integrating** the ERP, project development, communication and documentation-building processes	ERP, MPMIS integration
Business performance	**Integrating ERP and project management software**	ERP, MPMIS integration
Managing relations	Connecting **business intelligence** and **competition intelligence**	Intelligence Suite
Managing relations	Providing **partner intelligence**	Intelligence Suite
Innovation	Providing **team member intelligence**	Intelligence Suite
Decision support	Using **Business intelligence** to access information on current and projected internal resources	Intelligence Suite
Decision support	Using **project parties' intelligence** to evaluate the costs and expertise of external resources	Intelligence Suite
Decision support	Creating easy-to-use **project comparison fact sheets**	Intelligence Suite
Innovation	Using IT-**supported simulation and modeling** techniques in the innovation evaluation and execution process	Intelligence Suite, Decision support flow
Decision support	Using **out-of-the-box simulation models and methodologies**	Intelligence Suite, Decision support flow
Decision support	Using **scorecards and performance indication hierarchies** to evaluate the projects' contributions to portfolio goals	Intelligence Suite, Knowledge structures
Limited resources	Using **state-of-the-art technologies** in key business processes	Intelligence Suite, MPMIS, Knowledge structures
Limited resources	Providing external **know-how** and **best practices** in standard business processes management	Knowledge structures
Innovation	Supporting the **innovation registration process**	Knowledge structures
Innovation	**Providing access** to the innovation status, results and background data	Knowledge structures
Decision support	**Re-using** the project sections and using the **best practices** from the business environment and executed projects	Knowledge structures
Decision support	Using **business rules and automated decision logic**	Knowledge structures
Workflow	**Joining parallel processes.**	Knowledge structures, MPMIS
Multi-project management	Integrating PMIS with internal and external ERPs	ERP, MPMIS integration
Multi-project management	Integrating MPMIS with internal and external ERPs	ERP, MPMIS integration

continued on following page

Table 1. continued

Issue	IS Challenge	Solutions
Multi-project management	Developing MPMIS database	MPMIS
Workflow	Sharing a **common project management software** with the external partners or **enabling automated content exchange**	MPMIS, Communication flow
Limited resources	The **IS TCO** reaching reasonable levels	PREAS
Limited resources	**Out of the box** products	PREAS elements
Limited resources	**Automating** complex project **processes** in the project management	PREAS elements
Managing relations	Organizing **proactive reporting** on **project execution**	Proactive reporting flows
Communication	**Proactive reporting**	Proactive reporting flows
Workflow	Providing standard views to the **portfolio scorecards**	Standard reporting flows

In the following section a simplified model of a multi-project SME's IS is presented, based on existing premises and regarding the described challenges.

THE PREAS MODEL

The IS model addresses the IS challenges and represents the Project Oriented Enterprise Application Suite (PREAS).

Employees engaged in project management plan and execute the projects, conduct innovation, and communicate with partners, while their actions are fully documented. Decision support is information supported by the business, partners' and employees' intelligence in the form of proactive reporting, analyses, decision support, and simulation technologies.

Partners are supported in formal and informal communication and their communication is documented. They receive proactive reports about the status of their part in project reports.

The project management suite and ERP are integrated. The planning and changes in the project's portfolio are evidenced by the ERP, and available

Figure 2. The project oriented enterprise application suite – PREAS model

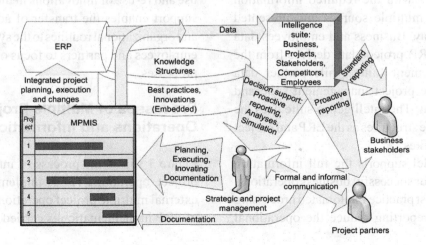

Figure 3. Multiple-project processes in BSs and information system

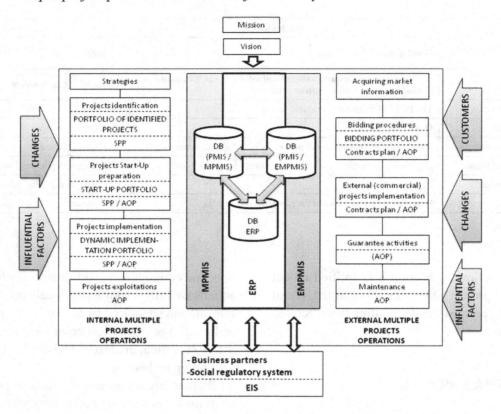

resources can be used by the project management suite. Both share the same knowledge structures, holding information on business and project best practices and innovation.

The intelligence suite is crucial for central and comprehensive reporting, empowering the decision makers with the required information gathered from multiple sources and presented in a uniform way. Business and employees data derives from ERP, project data derives from the project management suite, while partner data comes from the project management suite and the environment. The intelligence suite uses the same knowledge structures as the ERP and project management suites.

The IS model supports the full information cycle required for successful business operations. The involved best practices, automated processing and proactive reporting reduce the operational costs in executing multiple processes. Advanced decision support, based on standard data enables project portfolio management, including planning, execution monitoring and change management. Embedded knowledge structures empower the use of recognized best practices and the development, use and re-use of innovations in the projects. Full support enables the transfer of administrational and organizational routines to the system, allowing employees and partners to focus on key business processes.

Processes of Multiple Project Operations and Information Systems

Figure 3 shows the process of internal multiple project operations (SDP implementation) and external multiple project operations. The process of SDP implementation is carried out in steps of strategy formation, projects identification with the portfolio of identified projects and their inclusion in a strategic project plan (SPP), the projects start-up preparation with start-up portfolio and with the integration of projects into SPP. SPP is integrated into current annual operation plans (AOP). This is followed by the implementation of projects with integrated dynamic implementation portfolio and by connecting SPP with AOP. The process is concluded with the start-up of projects exploitations. To manage this process, MPMIS should exist with a database (DB) obtained by PMIS of individual projects or programmes, if the strategies are implemented with them.

The process of external multiple projects operations begin with the process of acquiring market information. This is followed by bidding procedures, with an integrated bidding portfolio, and after successful negotiations with customers and signed contracts start-up of project implementation is conducted. Project implementation is the central process of external project operations. When the projects are concluded and handed over to the customer, the guarantee activities follow. In some projects POBS can sign a contract related to maintenance of project objects, which represents project or regular operations and is planned within AOP.

To manage the process of project-oriented strategy implementation MPMIS should be built on the basis of PMIS of individual projects. To manage external multiple projects operations, EMPMIS has to be established. For the successful conducting of BS operations, an appropriate ERP should exist and be connected with MPMIS and EMPMIS by virtue of databases (DB). In addition to this, information and data connection of ERP, MPMIS and EMPMIS with external information systems (EIS) should exist, comprising of IS of the different business partners and certain IS of the social regulatory system.

In SMEs carrying out multiple projects operations it is critical to establish such integrated IS which connects MPMIS, EMPMIS with

ERP and all these ISs with EIS. This means it is necessary to treat SMEs' databases in a multiple project environment as an integrated database connecting MPMIS, EMPMIS, ERP and EIS databases.

Multiple-Project Information System and Project Databases

Projects ensure certain project results, which during the project implementation phase build a **database** and, after the project is completed, supplement the integrated BS database. In the event of BSCO, bases are needed to manage, implement and finish projects. In the case of POBS, databases are needed for the preparation of bidding procedures, management, implementation and hand-over of project objects to the customer. These represent the basis for guarantee management (if needed after the project has been completed) in accordance with the agreement, as well as regulatory and other provisions. Project databases are a part of PMIS and can be divided according to their purpose into:

- **Start-up project database.** This includes input project requirements (e.g. input project strategy or other business plans), project identification data, tasks for project start-up, information regarding the start-up portfolio and other documentation that appeared during the project start-up. It can also include the creation of the start-up plan, all control reports, meeting decisions, minutes, job orders, cost accounts for the preparation of project start-up, solutions for the preparation of the start-up plan, decisions of start-up meetings, strategic conferences, etc. The database includes all input documentation used for the preparation of project start-up, documentation that is the result of this preparation, documentation related to the management of the project start-up preparation, and all the documentation that was necessary to start project implementation.

- **Project management database.** This represents the project start-up database, which is constantly upgraded with regard to the implementation progress. It includes all documentation related to project management until completion and project handover, e.g. job orders, minutes of start-up and control meetings, control reports, cost accounts, revised start-up plans, correspondence, schedules, planned expenses, financial plans, technical control reports, auditing, operations controlling, hand-over of documentation, project management costs, etc. It includes documentation that is necessary for executing project management tasks.
- **Project content database.** This includes all project documentation and depends on project type. In a building project this database, for instance, includes all project documentation: ranging from preparation plans, project identification document, design, project design documentation, investment programmes, bids, offers made by outsourcers, agreements signed with outsourcers, auditing documentation, preparation tasks documentation, executive documentation, building permits, handover documentation, the analysis of environmental impacts, assents, permits, documentation related to measurements, building site documentation, work projects control documentation, handover documentation, inspection examination documentation, documentation permitting the operation, etc. In a product development project it includes: design, construction documentation, prototype production documentation, prototype testing documentation, outsourced parts approval documentation, technological documentation, marketing concepts, documentation

related to new market entrance, launched products documentation for test and zero series, etc.

Project content database is the basis for the preparation of all databases necessary for the exploitation start-up after the project has been completed. In new bridge construction projects this only includes handover documentation, obligatory archive documentation or documentation regarding regular maintenance work. In product development projects, the project results in a content database, which ensures regular production of the new product, sales, purchases, production tender documentation, including production and sales plans, sales price calculations selling price, product databases, technological procedures, supplier database, planning database, databases for calculating company operations, etc., if these databases were agreed upon as objectives – results, which should be achieved on completion of the project. Project content database or a part of it is gradually transformed into ERP database. A certain part of a project content database derives from technical databases, e.g. construction solutions, design solutions, construction statics and dynamics calculations, computer simulations of construction rigidity and a number of other »technical« results, calculated with various computer programmes. Project content databases can also include technical databases. A project content database can be divided into:

- **Integrated content project database**, which includes all documentation documenting the project result.
- **Exploitation database**, which includes all data or documentation, on which exploitation is planned and then implemented (e.g. regular production, sales, warehousing and distribution to retailers in product development projects, and all documentation for sales start-up and operations relating to new shopping mall construction, etc.)

- **Completed project database.** A final database is prepared when a project is completed, which is mainly used as an archive database, but which can also play a different role.
- **Learning and experience project database.** This is a preparation for the experience and knowledge database, which can be used in preparation, management and implementation of subsequent projects and in project organization models in general.

Each project brings new knowledge and experience. New knowledge is related to the preparation of project start-up, planning, organization of implementation, content solutions, solving crises during implementation, risk control, negotiation with suppliers, controlling, motivating or improving project culture, managing influencing factors, lobbying, cost control, setting up project databases, handovers, managing administrative procedures, international regulation, standards, communication, etc. When the project is completed, the acquired knowledge and experience can quickly disappear. In new projects, especially when they involve new employees who have never worked on projects and do not have project work experience, this knowledge and experience have to be newly acquired. This requires a lot of time and can lead to mistakes, conflict situations, loss of time, etc. This could be prevented, if the knowledge and experience involved in successfully and effectively implemented projects as well as unsuccessful projects were collected. It is not only the personnel involved in project management who are important, but also all those employees who are a part of the project system. **A learning and experience project database is thus a good basis for a learning enterprise**, as employees can learn from project cases. Such a database is developed simultaneously with the implementation of the project. It is upgraded by all employees who participate in the project and can contribute towards the preparation of such a database, which

ensures the formation of a **project-based learning enterprise** or other organization.

From the above it can be concluded that project databases are connected with existing databases in BS within ERP and through ERP with external databases, e.g. bank databases (when applying for loans), databases of external suppliers, databases of project customers, public administration databases, etc. We can also speak about the connectedness of internal and external IS, of which project databases are the basis.

A Case of Multi-Criteria Decision-Making Frame Procedure and Criteria

Considering the prescriptive approach to decision-making[4], we present the frame procedure for multi-criteria decision-making[5]. When applying MCDM methods to several decision-making problems, we concluded that they should be approached step by step. On the basis of our implementing this process in real-life applications at the micro and macro level, we concluded it should include the following steps (Čančer & Mulej, 2008):

1. **Problem definition.** When the problem arises, we should describe it accurately. We should define relevant criteria and alternatives. Creative thinking methods can be applied when developing alternatives.
2. **Elimination of unacceptable alternatives.** We should define requirements for the alternatives. We assess all possible alternatives; when the alternative does not fulfil the requirements, it is defined as unacceptable and should therefore be eliminated.
3. **Problem structuring.** We structure a complex situation in a hierarchical model. Each problem consists of a goal, criteria, very often some levels of sub-criteria, and alternatives. In a hierarchy, criteria can be structured into more levels so that lower levels specify sets of sub-criteria related to the criterion of a

higher level. When structuring a problem, the law of requisite holism should be considered (Mulej & Kajzer, 1998).

4. **Measuring local alternatives' values.** This step involves judgments about the alternative preferences and calculation of the values of alternatives with respect to each criterion on the lowest level. We can measure the local alternatives' values by making pair-wise comparisons or by using value functions (Čančer, 2003). In this step, professionals of several fields should be involved; namely, skills in their own professions as well as the ability of interdisciplinary co-operation are of great importance when making pair-wise comparisons or defining value functions.

5. **Criteria's weighting.** We have to establish the criteria's importance in order to define the weights of the criteria: by using the methods based on the ordinal (e.g. SMARTER), interval (e.g. SWING and SMART) and ratio scale (e.g. AHP), or by direct weighting (for details see e.g. Belton and Stewart, 2002; Helsinky University of Technology, 2008; Saaty, 1994). Again, professionals in several fields that are capable of interdisciplinary co-operation should be involved in this step.

6. **Synthesis and Ranging.** In synthesis, we obtain the final alternatives' values. By alternatives' ranging, we can select the most appropriate alternative(s), eliminate the alternative(s) with the lowest final value, or compare the alternatives with respect to their final values.

7. **Sensitivity analysis.** Sensitivity analysis is used to investigate the sensitivity of the goal fulfillment to changes in the criteria weights. It enables decision makers to detect the key success or failure factors for goal fulfillment.

The frame procedure for MCDM was followed in the selection of a suitable approach to further information system development of multi-project

business processes in a Slovenian building business system (Čančer, 2006). Participants in this application were an outside expert (a tutor), experts in the company and the head of a computer department with the appropriate knowledge about the methods used.

In steps 1-3 of the frame procedure for MCDM, experts determined possible software solutions as alternatives: renovation, internal development, external development, purchase – Add-On and purchase of the standardized program solution; they determined relevant criteria and structured the problem. The criteria structure is presented in Figure 4. In step 4, they measured the alternatives' values with respect to each attribute by pair-wise comparisons, direct input and value functions. To measure alternatives with respect to criteria by value functions, experts should know the characteristics of each criterion. Value functions enable decision makers to understand the problem (as a whole and in detail) better and provide insight into the structure of values for the decision. In step 5, the method based on an ordinal scale, SMARTER was evaluated as convenient in decision situations, in which it is possible to evaluate only the rank of the criteria's importance. They evaluated the methods based on interval scale SWING and SMART as more convenient because a basis of sufficient information enables the assessment of the criteria's importance and preferences to alternatives. Further, they are convenient for both quantitative (in this case investments, rate of return, automation, savings, information needs, risk, compatibility, complexity) and qualitative (in this case functionality, robustness, support, further development, upgrade) criteria. In this practical case, the AHP method based on a ratio scale was found applicable when expressing judgments about the criteria's importance, mainly on the basis of the experts' experience. Pair-wise comparisons enabled decision makers to achieve a better understanding of the criteria's meaning and importance; they gave decision makers the opportunity to confront other participants' judg-

Figure 4. The criteria structure for the selection of a suitable approach to further information system development of multi-project business processes.

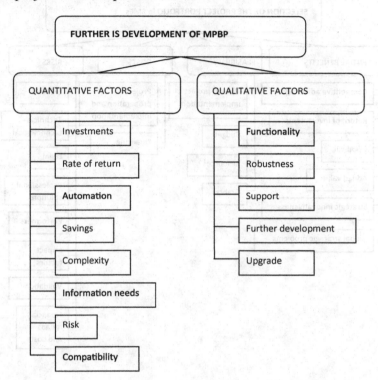

ments. The enterprise's experts that evaluated the information systems found multi-criteria decision methods and appropriate software as excellent tools in solving complex problems.

The frame procedure for MCDM can be followed in the selection of the most appropriate project portfolio in SMEs as well. Again, participants in this application should be an outside expert (a tutor), managers/experts in the SME and an employee with the appropriate knowledge about the methods used.

In steps 1-3 of the frame procedure for MCDM, possible projects that could form the project portfolio should be determined; furthermore, the criteria describing the project's potential benefits, feasibility, costs and risks should be structured into the model. It is good enough to assess the projects kept in the first record with respect to the criteria on the first level only (see Figure 5). For the final assessment of the projects, in order to form the project portfolio, criteria should be structured in more levels. Figure 5 includes the sub-criteria

that received special attention in SMEs. In step 4, experts can measure the alternatives' values with respect to each attribute by pair-wise comparisons, direct input and value functions. It is good enough to evaluate the values of the projects kept in the first record with respect to the criteria on the first level only (see Figure 5). However, requisite data (and evaluations) about the projects should be considered when measuring local alternatives' values with respect to each sub-criterion in order to form the project portfolio. In step 5, experts have to establish the criteria's importance in order to define the weights of the criteria. Considering our experiences in real-life applications, managers in SMEs attached special importance to the return on investments, strategic innovativeness and grants. Final alternatives' values can be easily obtained with appropriate computer programs in step 6; ranging helps decision makers detect the projects with the highest final values – they form the project portfolio. Using sensitivity analysis, decision makers can detect the key success and

Figure 5. The criteria structure for the selection of the project portfolio in SMEs

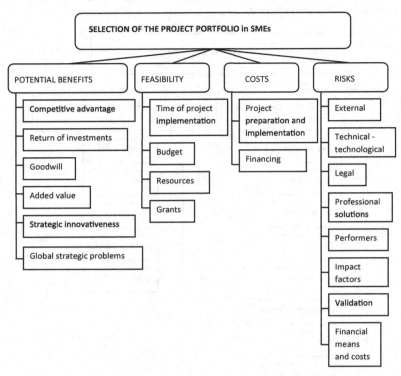

failure factors of the projects included in the project portfolio as well as the sensitivity of its structure to changes in the criteria's weights.

CONCLUSION AND FUTURE TRENDS

Up to this point, companies use IS mainly to execute business processes, organize business functions, and comply with regulators' requirements. IS implementation and administration involves valuable resources, with the operational workload remaining mainly unchanged. In this chapter the new role IS plays in empowering SMEs to conduct multi-project business is elaborated on.

First two SMEs production types are presented: one implementing multiple strategic projects and one implementing multiple external commercial projects, explaining the project steps and roles.

Next, business and multi-project SMEs' business issues are evaluated, identifying the SMEs' IS challenges. To create a multi-project IS model, some solutions are identified: MPMIS and ERP integration, automated communication, intelligence suite, and decision support. These form the key elements in the featured PREAS model, providing low resources input in standard business processes, supporting the project decision process and project portfolio management and enabling focus to be kept on key business processes. The PREAS model is further elaborated by explaining MPMIS models and databases, providing the insight in databases required for successful multi-project management and underpinned by a case of multi-criteria decision-making frame procedure and criteria.

The IS, holding and executing the best practices in standard business processes, can help diminish the organizational and knowledge-based competitive advantage of large companies compared to SMEs. The SMEs' advantages in innovativeness, adaptation and flexibility can then be heavily supported by collaboration automation, decision support, and knowledge- development systems.

Since systematic procedures cannot compensate for the lack of knowledge or limited abilities of decision makers, an important task is given to the requisitely holistic use of decision logic, heuristic principles, information and practical experience – the main characteristics of informal systems thinking. The limitations of systematic procedures can be overcome by informal systems thinking, emphasizing interdisciplinary creative co-operation of mutually different specialists: it includes synergies more probably.

REFERENCES

Adler, P. S., Mandelbaum, A., Nguyen, V., & Schwerer, E. (1995). From project to process management: An empirically-based framework for analyzing product development time. *Management Science*, *41*(3), 458–484. doi:10.1287/mnsc.41.3.458

Adler, P. S., Mandelbaum, A., Nguyen, V., & Schwerer, E. (1996). Getting the most out of your product development process. *Harvard Business Review*, (March-April): 134–152.

Amami, M., & Beghini, G. (2000). Project management and communication of product development through electronic document management. *Project Management Journal*, *31*(2), 6–19.

Amami, M., Beghini, G., & La Manna, M. (1993). Use of project management information system for planning information systems development projects. *International Journal of Project Management*, *11*(1), 21–28. doi:10.1016/0263-7863(93)90006-9

Anavi-Isakow, S., & Golany, B. (2003). Managing multi-project environments through constant work-in-process. *International Journal of Project Management*, *21*, 9–18. doi:10.1016/S0263-7863(01)00058-8

Archer, N., & Ghasemzadeh, F. (1999 b). An integrated framework for project portfolio selection. *International Journal of Project Management*, *17*(4), 207–216. doi:10.1016/S0263-7863(98)00032-5

Artto, K. A., & Wikström, K. (2005). What is project business? *International Journal of Project Management*, *23*, 343–353. doi:10.1016/j.ijproman.2005.03.005

Belton, V., & Stewart, T. J. (2002). *Multiple criteria decision analysis: An integrated approach*. Boston, Dordrecht, London: Kluwer Academic Publishers.

Brackett, S.W., & Isbell, A-M. (1989). PMIS – an integrated approach for the management and distribution of project information. *Project manage journal*, *20*(3), 5-10.

Čančer, V. (2003). *Analiza odločanja: izbrana poglavja (Decision Analysis: Selected Chapters, in Slovenian)*. Maribor: Faculty of Economics and Business.

Čančer, V. (2006). Selection of the information systems' development in enterprises by multi-criteria decision-making. *Manažment v teórii a praxi [Online ed.]*, Vol. 2, No. 2, 10-18. Consulted in February 2008. Retreived from http://casopisy.euke.sk/mtp/clanky/2-2006/cancer.pdf

Čančer, V., & Mulej, M. (2008). Informal systems thinking in the form of operations research. Managing the unmanageable – 16th Interdisciplinary Information Management Talks, Linz.

Chan, K. C. C., & Chung, L. M. L. (2002). Integrating process and project management for multi-site software development. *Analysis of Software Engineering, 14*(1-4), 115–143. doi:10.1023/A:1020553624256

Comstock, G., & Sjolseth, D. (1999). Aligning and prioritizing corporate R&D. *Research Technology Management, 42*(3), 19–25.

Cooper, D., Grey, S., Raymond, G., & Walker, P. (2004). *project risk management guidelines.* Chichester: John Wiley & Sons Ltd.

Cooper, R. (2001). Winning at new products— Accelerating the process from idea to launch. Massachusetts: Perseus Publishing.

Cooper, R., & Edgett, S. (2003). Overcoming the crunch in resources for new product development. *Research Technology Management, 46*(3), 48–58.

Cooper, R., Edgett, S., & Kleinschmidt, E. (1997). Portfolio management in new product development: lessons from the leaders I. *Research Technology Management, 40*(5), 16–28.

Dietrich, P., & Lehtonen, P. (2005). Successful management of strategic intentions through multiple projects – Reflections from empirical study. *International Journal of Project Management, 23*(5), 386–391. doi:10.1016/j.ijproman.2005.03.002

Dooley, L. (2000). *Systems innovation management.* PhD thesis, Galway, National University of Ireland.

Elonen, S., & Artto, K. A. (2003). Problems in managing internal development projects in multi-project environments. *International Journal of Project Management, 21*(6), 395–402. doi:10.1016/S0263-7863(02)00097-2

Elonen, S., & Artto, K. A. (2003). Problems in managing internal development projects in multi-project environments. *International Journal of Project Management, 21*, 395–402. doi:10.1016/S0263-7863(02)00097-2

Engwall, M. (2001). *Multi-project management: Effects, issues and propositions for future Research* (Fenix Working Paper Series). Stockholm: Stockholm School of Economics.

Engwall, M., & Jerbrant, A. (2003). The resource allocation syndrome: the prime challenge of multi-project management. *International Journal of Project Management, 21*(6), 403–409. doi:10.1016/S0263-7863(02)00113-8

Eskerod, P. (1996). Meaning and action in a multi-project environment. Understanding a multiproject environment by means of metaphors and basic assumptions. *International Journal of Project Management, 14*(2), 61–65. doi:10.1016/0263-7863(95)00038-0

Fiscehr, M. A., Waugh, L. M., & Axworthy, A. (1998). IT support of single project, multi-project and industry-wide integration. *Computers in Industry, 35*, 31–45. doi:10.1016/S0166-3615(97)00082-1

Fricke, S. E., & Shenbar, A. J. (2000). Managing multiple engineering projects in a manufacturing support environment. *IIE Transactions on Engineering Management, 47*(2), 258–268. doi:10.1109/17.846792

Geraldi, J. G. (2008). The balance between order and chaos in multi-project firms: A conceptual model. *International Journal of Project Management, 26*, 348–356. doi:10.1016/j.ijproman.2007.08.013

Graves, S., Ringuest, J., & Case, R. (2000). Formulating optimal R&D portfolios. *Research Technology Management, 43*(3), 47–51.

Gray, C. F., & Larson, E. W. (2003). *Project management: The managerial process*. Irwin: McGraw-Hill.

Grünig, R., & Kühn, R. (2005). *Successful decision-making: A systematic approach to complex problems*. Berlin, Heidelberg, New York: Springer.

Hall, D., & Nauda, A. (1990). An interactive approach for selecting IR&D projects. *IEEE Transactions on Engineering Management, 37*(2), 126–133. doi:10.1109/17.53715

Hansen, K. F., Weiss, M. A., & Kwak, S. (1999). Allocating R&D resources: A quantitative aid to management insight. *Research Technology Management, 42*(4), 44–50.

Hauc, A. (2007). *Projektni management (Project management)*. Ljubljana, GV Zalozba.

Hauc, A., & Kovac, J. (2000). Project management in strategy implementation - experiences in Slovenia. *International Journal of Project Management, 18*, 61–67. doi:10.1016/S0263-7863(98)00071-4

Hauc, A., & Vrečko, I. (2006). Strategy start-up and strategy implementation through the production of multiple projects. *Value management - how to ensure value for project stakeholders - 1st ICEC and IPMA Global Congress on Project Management and 5th World Congress on Cost Engineering, Project Management & Quantity Surveying, Ljubljana, Slovenia*.

Havnes, P. A., & Senneseth, K. (2001). A panel study of firm growth among SMEs in networks. *Small Business Economics, 16*(4), 293–302. doi:10.1023/A:1011100510643

Helsinki University of Technology. (2008) *Web-HIPRE help*. Consulted in May 2008, available: http://www.hipre.hut.fi.

Henriksen, A., & Traynor, A. (1999). A practical R&D project-selection scoring tool. *IEEE Transactions on Engineering Management, 46*(2), 158–170. doi:10.1109/17.759144

Herroelen, W. (2005). Project scheduling–theory and practice. *Production and Operations Management, 14*(4), 413–432.

Highsmith, J. (2004). *Agile project management creating innovative products*. Boston: Pearson Education.

Huin, S. F. (2004). Managing deployment of ERP systems in SMEs using multi-agents. *International Journal of Project Management, 22*, 511–517. doi:10.1016/j.ijproman.2003.12.005

Jaafari, A. (1996). Time and priority allocation scheduling technique for projects. *International Journal of Project Management, 14*(5), 289–299. doi:10.1016/0263-7863(96)84512-1

Jaafari, A., & Manivong, K. (1998). Toward a smart project management information system. *International Journal of Project Management, 16*(4), 249–265. doi:10.1016/S0263-7863(97)00037-9

Jackson, M. (2003). *Systems thinking. Creative holism for managers*. Chichester: Wiley.

Khazanchi, S., Lewis, M. W., & Boyer, K. K. (2007). Innovation-supportive culture: The impact of organizational values on process innovation . *Journal of Operations Management, 25*(4), 871–884. doi:10.1016/j.jom.2006.08.003

Lawson, C. P., Longhurst, P. J., & Ivey, P. C. (2006). The application of a new research and development project selection model in SMEs . *Technovation, 26*(2), 242–250. doi:10.1016/j.technovation.2004.07.017

Lee, B., & Miller, J. (2004). Multi-project software engineering analysis using system thinking. *Software Process Improvement and Practice, 9*, 173–214. doi:10.1002/spip.204

Leintz, B. P., & Rea, K. P. (1995). *Project management for the 21st Century*. London: Academic Press.

Leopoulos, V. N., Kirytopoulos, K. A., & Malandrakis, C. (2006). Risk management for SMEs: Tools to use and how. *Production Planning and Control*, *17*(3), 322–332. doi:10.1080/09537280500285136

Levy, N., & Globerson, S. (1997). Improving multi-project management by using a queuing theory approach. *Industrial Project Management*, *28*(4), 40–47.

Liberatore, M. J., & Pollack-Johnson, B. (2003). Factors influencing the usage and selection of project management software. *IEEE Transactions on Engineering Management*, *50*(2), 164–174. doi:10.1109/TEM.2003.810821

Light, M., Rosser, B., & Hayward, S. (2005). *Realizing the benefits of projects and portfolio management*. Gartner. *Research ID, G00125673*, 1–31.

Loch, C. (2000). Tailoring product development to strategy: Case of a European technology manufacturer. *European Management Journal*, *18*(3), 246–258. doi:10.1016/S0263-2373(00)00007-4

Love, P. E. D., & Irani, Z. (2003). A project management quality cost information system for the construction industry. *Information & Management*, *40*, 649–661. doi:10.1016/S0378-7206(02)00094-0

Lycett, M., Rassau, A., & Danson, J. (2004). Programme management: A critical review. *International Journal of Project Management*, *22*(4), 289–299. doi:10.1016/j.ijproman.2003.06.001

Macheridis, N., & Nilsson, C. H. (2006). *Management of Multi-projects in a Process Oriented Organization*. Lund Institute of Economic Research, Working Paper Series No. 8.

Martinsuo, M., & Lehtonen, P. (2007). Role of single-project management in achieving portfolio management efficiency. *International Journal of Project Management*, *25*, 56–65. doi:10.1016/j.ijproman.2006.04.002

Meissner, J. O., Schweikert, S., & Wolf, P. (2007). Making SME know, what they don't know: Archetypes of central Swiss innovation profiles and challenges for innovation support. *ESSHRA-Conference 2007 'Towards a Knowledge Society: Is Knowledge a Public Good? Dynamics of Knowledge Production and Distribution'*, Berne.

Meredith, J. R., & Mantel, S. J., Jr. (1995). *Project management: A managerial approach*. New York: John Wiley & Sons, Inc.

Morris, P., & Jamieson, A. (2004). *Translating corporate strategy into project strategy: realizing corporate strategy through project management*. Pennsylvania, USA: Project Management Institute.

Morris, P., & Pinto, J. K. (Eds.). (2004). *The Wiley guide to managing projects*. London: Wiley.

Mulej, M. (2005). New roles of systems science in a knowledge society: Introductory provocation. In J. Gu & G. Chroust (Eds.), *Proceedings of the first world congress The new roles of systems science for a knowledge-based society*. Kobe: International Federation for Systems Research.

Mulej, M., & Kajzer, S. (1998). Ethics of interdependence and the law of requisite holism. In M. Rebernik & M. Mulej (Eds.), *STIQE '98. Proceedings of the 4th International Conference on Linking Systems Thinking, Innovation, Quality, Entrepreneurship and Environment* (pp. 129-140). Maribor: Institute for Entrepreneurship and Small Business Management, at Faculty of Economics and Business, University of Maribor, and Slovenian Society for Systems Research.

Murphy, A., & Ledwith, A. (2006). Project management tools and techniques in high-tech SMEs in Ireland. *High Technology Small Firms Conference 2006*, Ireland: Department of Manufacturing and Operations Engineering, University of Limerick.

Payne, J. H. (1995). Management of multiple simultaneous projects: A state-of-the-art review. *International Journal of Project Management, 13*(3), 163–168. doi:10.1016/0263-7863(94)00019-9

Pellegrinelli, S. (1997). Programme management: Organizing project-based change . *International Journal of Project Management, 15*(3), 141–149. doi:10.1016/S0263-7863(96)00063-4

Perko, I., & Bobek, S. (2008). Supporting Business Intelligence in a Knowledge Intensive Environment: BIMAS, a Multi Agent System. *EMCSR 2008*, Wienna.

Perrin, B. (2002). How to – and how not to – Evaluate innovation. *Evaluation, 8*(1), 13–29. doi:10.1177/1358902002008001514

Platje, A., Harald, S., & Wadman, S. (1994). Project and portfolio planning cycle: project-based management for the multiproject challenge . *International Journal of Project Management, 12*(2), 100–106. doi:10.1016/0263-7863(94)90016-7

Portny, S. E. (2007). *Project management for dummies* (2nd ed.). Indianapolis: Wiley.

Project Management Institute. (2004). *A guide to the project management body of knowledge* (3rd ed.).Pennsylvania: Project Management Institute.

Raiffa, H. (1994). The prescriptive orientation of decision making: A synthesis of decision analysis, behavioral decision making, and game theory. In S. Rios (Ed.), *Decision theory and decision analysis: Trends and challenges*. Boston: Kluwer Academic Publishers.

Raymond, L., & Bergeron, F. (2008). Project management information systems: An empirical study of their impact on project managers and project success. *International Journal of Project Management, 26*, 213–220. doi:10.1016/j.ijproman.2007.06.002

Ringuest, J., & Graves, S. (1999). Formulating R&D portfolios that account for risk. *Research Technology Management, 42*(6), 40–43.

Saaty, T. L. (1994). *The fundamentals of decision making and priority theory with the analytic hierarchy process*. Pittsburgh: RWS Publications.

Shenhar, A. J., & Dvir, D. (2004). Project management evolution: Past history and future research directions. In D.P. Slevin, D.I. Cleland, & J.K. Pinto (Ed.), *Proceedings of the PMI research conference 2004*, London, UK.

Shenhar, A. J., & Dvir, D. (2005): *Project management research - Challenges and opportunities*. Stevens Institute of Technology, Hoboken. [Electronic version].

Shtub, A., & Bard, J. F. (1995). *Globerson Shlomo: Project management engineering, technology and implementation*. Prentice Hall International Editions.

Spradlin, C., & Kutoloski, D. (1999). Action-oriented portfolio management. *Research Technology Management, 42*(2), 26–32.

Turner, J. R., & Speiser, A. (1992). Programme management and its information system requirements. *International Journal of Project Management, 10*(4), 196–206. doi:10.1016/0263-7863(92)90078-N

Van Der Merwe, A. P. (1997). Multi-project management-organizational structure and control. *International Journal of Project Management, 15*(4), 223–233. doi:10.1016/S0263-7863(96)00075-0

Vonortas, N. S. (2000). Multimarket contact and inter-firm cooperation in R&D. *Journal of Evolutionary Economics, 10*(1-2), 243–271. doi:10.1007/s001910050014

Vrečko, I. (2007). Mastering strategic crisis with project management usage as a holistic invention-innovation process. In A.W. Małgorzata, J.S. Erich, & M. Mulej (Eds.). *Entrepreneurship and innovation in Europe, Klagenfurt.* Klagenfurt University, Department of Innovation Management and Entrepreneurship.

Wang, Q., Yung, K. L., & Ip, W. H. (2004). A hierarchical multi-view modeling for networked joint manufacturing system . *Computers in Industry, 53*(1), 59–73. doi:10.1016/S0166-3615(03)00124-6

White, D., & Fortune, J. (2001). Current practice in project management – an empirical study. *International Journal of Project Management, 20,* 1–11. doi:10.1016/S0263-7863(00)00029-6

Wysocki, R. K., & McGary, R. (2003). *Effective project management* (3rd ed.). Indianapolis: Wiley.

ENDNOTES

[1] In this chapter, we use the term *business system* to describe all companies and other organisations that have to carry out (also) necessary operational processes (e.g. cost management, marketing, organisation, leadership, etc.) to exist and develop in the future. Because this is valid not only for profit-oriented enterprises, but also for individuals, public sector, non-profit and other organisations, we address them all from a common perspective, namely that they have to carry out similar business functions. As we emphasise the business component of these enterprises and organisations, we define them as business systems and not as social, personnel, technological, legal, environmental, or any other systems.

[2] Traditional evaluation and forecasting methods seek to replace intuition and can oppress creative thinking. For example, Perrin (2002) even argues that traditional evaluation methods inhibit, rather than support, innovation.

[3] In theory and in practice we come across different names for strategic development documents. Expressions such as strategic development plan, strategic long-term plan, strategic business plan, etc. are used. The document is about mission, vision, strategic goals, global business, functional strategies and all long-term projects that are constantly being upgraded with regard to their operations and adaptation strategies in the business and strategic environment of a BS.

[4] Namely, we put forward suggestions for the improvement of decision making in situations where practical problems are encountered.

[5] For the theoretical bases of MCDM, see e.g. Belton & Stewart (2002).

Chapter 9
An ERP Adoption Model for Midsize Businesses

Fahd Alizai
Victoria University, Australia

Stephen Burgess
Victoria University, Australia

ABSTRACT

This chapter theorizes the development of a conceptual ERP adoption model, applicable to midsize businesses. The general business factors associated with ERP implementation along with the corresponding organisational benefits are identified. This chapter also highlights the constraints that confront midsize businesses whilst implementing sophisticated applications. The needs for ERP adoption can occur due to an attempt to be more competitive or due to an external pressure from large businesses to adopt an ERP application. The proposed conceptual model uses a strategic approach containing; ERP implementation processes, stages, factors & issues associate with ERP adoption in midsize businesses. This research also focuses on identification of strategies in the organisational, people and technical domains that could be influential for ERP adoption.

INTRODUCTION

The importance of midsize businesses has been recognised in recent decades due to their role of creating jobs, enhancement of global economic activity and most importantly higher growth rate, regardless of their size (Rovere, L & Lebre, R (1996); Acs 1990). To increase their production capabilities, they should be vigilant towards adoption of the latest technology (Barad, M & Gien, D. 2001)

DOI: 10.4018/978-1-60566-892-5.ch009

as use of Information Technology (IT) could result in an increase in innovative activities, resulting in improved productivity and efficiency in business operations (Correa 1994). Therefore, it is appropriate for midsize businesses to utilize their resources and adopt means of automated data transfer both internally and externally (Caillaud 2001). Business applications such as ERP systems could provide a better way to execute business operations in an effective, organised and sophisticated way.

The adoption of ERP applications in a modern day organisation has been described as being one of the most innovative developments associated with the IT sector (Al-Mashari 2002). ERP systems can be viewed as sophisticated business applications that integrate major functions of different departments (Koch 2003) as its modules allow organization to improve the functionality of its business processes (Chung 1999). Hence, ERP software modules have the ability; once implemented, to integrate major activities across the organisational departments using one integrated software solution (Koch 2003). Amoako-Gyampah (2007) suggests that ERP systems are integrated software developed to handle multiple corporate functions, allowing companies to synchronise activities, eliminate multiple data sources with provisioning of accurate and timely information, obtaining better communication among different units to meet expectations and reducing cost required to manage incompatible legacy systems. In effect, this can greatly assist organisations to carry out their operations in more effective and efficient ways and allow the workforce to interact and collaborate in an information-enabled environment.

ERP systems have been developed in the last two decades to replace the common legacy and Material Requirement Planning (MRP) systems that have traditionally been associated with larger enterprises. As the ERP market has evolved and matured, so have the related hardware and infrastructure technology. The cost of ERP solutions have been reduced to the point where it has now become viable for the midsize business sector to consider ERP implementation (Aberdeen 2006). Arguably, the implementation of ERP systems in midsize businesses could be viewed simply from the perspective of applying the success factors already identified for larger businesses to a different set of smaller entities. However, midsize businesses are unlike their larger business counterparts. They have a diverse range of separate adoption issues that need to be considered when it comes to ERP— issues such as limited finance availability, technology understanding and human resources constraints (Rao 2000).

Assuming the pending shift of ERP adoption to smaller-sized business entities, this chapter examines the relevant literature on ERP implementation as well as highlighting the characteristics of midsize businesses to propose an adoption model for implementing ERP systems in that business sector.

BACKGROUND

ERP Systems

ERP applications were built primarily to integrate different department functions and business processes to form a collaborative view of business operations in a single IT architecture (Klaus, H., Rosemann, M, Gable, G. 2000). Modern day ERP applications are business process centric, evolved to address diverse aspects of corporate business requirements. One aspect of this evolution has been the ability of ERP systems to be a replacement for IT legacy systems that were developed in different functional areas of the business. Another aspect of ERP success has been the importance of such systems to integrate the supply chain so as to facilitate information flows across all business areas— in effect allowing the large corporation to be managed in real time (Turban 2006). The manner in which ERP has applied industry standards to organisational business processes has also been recognised as a significant ERP feature (Keller & Teufel 1998)— allowing a corporation to espouse enterprise wide best practices.

Given the evolving nature of ERP systems, there are different point-of-views on how to explore ERP implementations. One view is to focus on ERP as a product or commodity in terms of software application (Klaus, H., Rosemann, M, Gable, G. 2000) where ERP modules are integrators of all business processes and data under one inclusive umbrella. ERP systems are equipped with features that embrace costing, finance, sales, contact management, customer relationship management and human resources issues (Rooney et al. 2000). Arguably, each application area becomes a central focus in order to understand and facilitate the ERP implementation process. It is important to note that getting a desired outcome from ERP applications can be difficult task due to related constraints involved in its implementation and customisation (Marnewick, C. & Labuschagne, L. 2005). Therefore, it is advisable to focus on long term business objectives associated with ERP implementation to understand the complex nature of integration processes (Boubekri 2001). A strategic approach could also be a suitable by addressing business needs with respect to the organisational, technical and people (human) aspects of ERP implementation.

Some Benefits of ERP

Turban et al. (2006) highlighted the internal and external nature of systems integration associated with introduction of an ERP system. The internal integration of systems allows different functional areas of business to be presented under a 'single umbrella' leading to many operational benefits. External integration benefits promote cross-collaboration and data exchanges between a firm's allied partners, enhancing significant business-to-business (B2B) information exchanges as well as improving partner relationship management (PRM).

ERP systems standardize business operations and automate business functions such as production, planning, manufacturing, purchasing, marketing and human resources into number of operational modules. These modules are integrated with each other, forming a relationship chain and can provide significant benefits across the enterprise (Boubekri, 2001). Indeed the selection of an ERP module is related to the factors such as business attributes, specific operational needs and the characteristics of the company. The ability of ERP systems to integrate business functions does provide significant tangible and intangible benefits

(Sandoe, K. Corbitt G. Boykin R. 2001). The tangible benefits include reduction in employee numbers and inventory stock; improvements in productivity, order management and timely deliveries – all of which can lead to increased profitability. The intangible benefits are associated with new/improved business processes; information supply chain visibility; process standardization and enhanced globalization opportunities.

ERP systems also allow an organization to become more 'customer centric', where more accurate/up to date information about customers results in enhanced customer services (Rao 2000). A study conducted by Kennerley et al. (2001) identifies benefits and shortcomings of ERP systems implementation in an organisation. The benefits across four distinct areas were evaluated relating to; corporate organisation, operational plant, functional divisions and the individual employees. Kennerley et al. (2001) alludes to the benefits of ERP systems implementation being:

- Improved efficiency and control
- An ability to rationalize inventories
- Enhanced cross border capacity and optimization
- Increased leverage opportunities with suppliers
- Improved resource and management planning

Keller & Teufel (1998) describes the standardization imposed on business processes as being another benefit of ERP system implementation. Arguably, standardization may come at the expense of business process flexibility, however business process standardization allows industry best practice to be adopted by a business with the commensurate benefits. The level of standardization resulting from the adoption of best practice standards set by ERP packages might increase concerns regarding competitive advantage. For successful implementations, existing business knowledge must be translated into application knowledge by mapping existing business processes with ERP package embedded processes and defining new processes that should fit with both new system and organisational needs (Vandaie 2008).

ERP System Implementation

A conceptual model for ERP implementation (the '4p' model) was proposed by (Marnewick, C. & Labuschagne, L. 2005), addressing four fundamental aspects of implementation. The model derived its structure from the well-known marketing '4Ps' (people, product, process and performance). The ERP areas associated with 4Ps entities are;

- *People* as the customers that represent organisational requirements/mindset,
- *Product* as software modules that are to be implemented across the business,
- *Process* as representing the project's change management issues
- *Performance* that is analogous to data flows associated with business process.

Every aspect in this model has a direct or indirect impact on ERP implementation processes. This includes identification of organizational requirements, customization of selected software, the installation and subsequent operations and finally the important needs of system training for personnel. All various proposed levels are important for ERP system adoption, allowing organisations to progress through implementation processes that require all relevant factors to be considered (Marnewick, C. & Labuschagne, L. 2005).

Another approach for ERP implementation has been alluded to by Al-Mashari (2002) who suggests that an intense effort is required to highlight business and technological requirements of a company before ERP systems should be implemented. Al-Mashari (2000) also indicates that successful

ERP implementation is directly related to organizational preparedness. Success could be defined as a favourable results or satisfactory outcomes in accordance with user expectations. Outcomes of ERP system projects could be evaluated on the basis of different factors, such as technical, effectiveness and user experience related factors (Wei 2008). According to Rao (2000) there is a certain level of competence that should be achieved that reflects organizational preparedness when it comes to ERP system adoption— these levels related to areas associated with technical, human and management aspects of the organisation.

A number of other approaches for ERP system adoption exist. Wilhelm et al., (2000) indicated certain traditional information systems modelling methods that could be used to reduce the persistent cost of ongoing ERP implementation. As ERP is defined as integrated business software, the modelling required for ERP implementation should detail the aspects relating to all abstraction layers in integration management. The prime objective should be progressing from upper to lower abstraction levels such as enterprise modelling to final coding with complete existing business process information (Monnerat, Carvalho and Campos 2008). Edward et al, (2003), (drawing from the work of Esteves & Pastor (1999)) uses the system life cycle model to explain six different stages of ERP systems adoption— such as adoption, decision-making, acquisition, implementation, use & maintenance, evolution and retirement.

ERP has become a strategic survival instrument for businesses using information technology to conduct their operations. ERP implementation requires a huge investment and greater initiative towards engaging resources such as time, money and people (Yang, Wu and Tsai 2007). The use of multi-factor business strategies (as identified) has been suggested as a suitable approach for adoption or upgrade of an ERP system. According to Aladwani (2001), a firm needs to identify the various organizational, technical and people strategies that could be used with the introduction of ERP systems. The *organizational strategies* include proper project management, recognition of organizational structure and business ideology, change strategy development and deployment, appropriate managerial style and available communication mechanisms. The *technical strategies* address the technology challenges of ERP installation and include gaining a thorough understanding of systems configuration, hardware complexity, the capabilities of technical staff to handle pending challenges; and access to sufficient resources (time and cost associated factors). The *people strategies* associate with ERP systems implementation include the ability to identify and manage staff attitudes towards change, inclusion and involvement of all staff in the implementation process as well as an appropriate ERP training regime. Aladwani (2001) suggest that these strategies have significant importance in the ERP implementation process with adherence and use of these strategies reducing the likelihood of project failure.

ERP in Midsize Business

ERP systems have been historically associated with implementation projects in large businesses. However; there has been a recent trend for **midsize business** to also consider adopting ERP systems. In this research an organization with 200-500 employees and/or an annual turnover of less than US$75 million is defined as a midsize business (Gefen et al. 2005, Yates 2004, APEC 2003, Duxbury et al. 2002).

Midsize businesses are considered to be the backbone of a country's economy and play a vital role in economic development. They create job opportunities, accelerate economic revival and support industry to boost up economic progress (Pramukti 2003). Midsize businesses are also vulnerable and exposed to threats due to their size and operability (Sarbutts 2003). The risks associated with midsize businesses could be related to the availability of adequate resources such as time, money and skills to run business operations (Barad

et. al 2001). For instance, the literature suggests that the following affects the decision making process of introducing latest IT applications in midsize businesses: lack of resources, availability of accurate information, lack of skilled labour and management's ability to adopt new change (Rovere, L. & Lebre, R. 1996). An ERP implementation with a more strategic focus should be of greater importance to senior management that has firm control over its IT operations. This would enhance management's supervision of ERP, resulting in better performance (along with improved operational and strategic control) (Ragowsky and Gefen 2008). Another more strategic issue faced by midsize businesses include their continuous growth requirement and consistency to update their technological level to meet with the existing technology standards (Rauof, 1998). The future growth of midsize businesses depends upon the use of advanced technologies for enhancement of their production capabilities. Use of the latest technology can help enhance the production capabilities by producing good quality products at cheaper cost and efficient delivery to its customers (Barad et. al 2001).

It has been suggested that information technology in general has created opportunities for midsize businesses to be more competitive in the marketplace (Rovere, L & Lebre, R (1996). However, midsize enterprises, because of their limited available resources can find it difficult to improve IT support services (such as increasing the number of educated IT professionals on staff and/ or expanding their IT departments). In the midsize business arena several internal and external factors also can govern technology adoption behaviour. Kennerley et al. (2001) identified internal factors such as lack of training and insufficient information/documentation about IT systems as being problematic; external factors were associated with the level of support provided by implementation professionals and also the nature of on-going technology upgrades. According to Rao (2000), an ERP solution is expensive and some midsize companies may not be able to afford them. Given this observation, Rao (2000) further indicates that information integration can be a major motivational factor for midsize businesses to implement ERP systems, allowing them to approach a level of business flexibility similar to large enterprises. There is some suggestion that smaller type businesses are unaware of the advantages of ERP technology and how the technology has become necessary for global interaction— an issue that, if not addressed, may eventually push these businesses out of the market (BRW, 2002).

In terms of successful ERP adoption, Lee (2000) highlights the concerns of **small manufacturers**, finding that the benefits associated with ERP software had yet to be derived. According to Alison (2002), ERP systems users are not technological experts and ERP software tends to be less than user-friendly because of challenging interfaces— these findings potentially posing a significant user training issue for resource limited midsize businesses. With respect to ERP systems adoption several criteria have been proposed for small and midsize business to select and implement an appropriate ERP system solution that includes affordability, supplier knowledge, local support, technical upgradeability and the availability of the latest technology (Rao 2000).

According to Saccomano (2003) the initial target market for ERP vendors was big companies that could afford solutions costing millions of dollars at project start up. In recent times, many multinational companies have restricted their operations to partnering only those midsize companies that are using compatible ERP software. Hence, it becomes essential for many midsize companies to adjust their business model and adopt ERP software that is compatible with the large enterprises with which they deal (Rao 2000). Thus, midsize enterprises are increasingly finding themselves attracted to ERP solutions and their associated benefits. Additionally, ERP systems are becoming a necessity in order to maintain relations with larger enterprises (Rao 2000).

Section Summary

Enterprise Resource Planning (ERP) has changed the way of doing business by re-engineering and redesigning business processes in accordance with standardised business operations. The literature highlights the main objective of having an ERP application implemented is to obtain and facilitate best practice in the business operations. Evidence also suggests that midsize business play a vital role toward collective productivity of a nation. Midsize Business often lacks leadership, strategic vision and they mainly focus on day to day operations. Implementing a new information system in a midsize business can be a cumbersome process as there is not much information available for these businesses to decide what could be a better solution for them. Midsize business are also tend to be influenced by number of factors while selecting an information systems; these could be relate to lack of resources such as knowledge and skill, availability of time and money. Midsize businesses have also adopted a cautions approach towards ERP applications due to the lack of information with strategic direction and associated risks involved in ERP implementation.

ERP IMPLEMENTATION ISSUES AND MIDSIZE BUSINESS

There is considerable amount of evidence suggesting that companies face problems while implementing ERP applications. Millions of dollars are spent every year to purchase and implement ERP products with problems relating to customisation and resulting in over budgeted delayed implementation (Martin 1998). The nature of problems faced during ERP implementation is quite abnormal comparative to implementation of other IT products (Parr et. al. 2000). Some of the important aspects in relation to ERP implementation are discussed below;

ERP Adoption

Mostly large businesses have already adopted ERP applications to meet with their growing business needs. Midsize businesses found themselves attracted to these applications due to their cost effectiveness and collaborative requirements to do business with larger enterprises (Klaus, H., Rosemann, M, Gable, G. 2000).

Some of the growth factors for ERP in mid-market bracket (midsize businesses) includes; continuous industrialisation and its reliance on small & midsize business, adoption of new technologies such as client server and availability of small & medium business centric ERP applications and so forth (Rao 2000). There is a general understanding that ERP implementation is an expensive process and midsize businesses cannot afford it but this does not mean midsize businesses do not need to have ERP applications. Information integration could be one of the major triggering points for midsize businesses to implement ERP applications and achieve high levels of business flexibility with their larger counterparts (Rao 2000).

Another important aspect of ERP implementation is to understand business needs and customise ERP products to mould application(s) according to existing business processes or altering business function in accordance with ERP standards. Research indicates that customisation in ERP application increases the risk of failure and cost of the project significantly increases comparative to none customised implementation (Wilhelm et al. 2000). Higher levels of dissatisfaction amongst ERP application users have been observed due to customisation and BPR (business process re-engineering) related issues, impacting mainly on cost and duration of the project. ERP vendors have also admitted that generally a customer spends more to implement than to buy the software itself (Wilhelm et al. 2000).

ERP Vendors & Midsize Businesses

The benefits from ERP applications have been realised by small manufacturing concerns (Lee 2000). As indicated earlier, the initial target market for ERP vendors was large enterprises that could afford to implement a costly application. Later, when large enterprise market for ERP systems dried up by the year 2000 (Saccomano 2003) ERP vendors started focusing on the mid-market bracket. ERP application developing companies such as, SAP and PeopleSoft have sought to increase their market share in the mid-market bracket by boosting their offers and developing business specific applications. PeopleSoft have also offered database, storage and hardware bind options along with customer support features and introducing self service portal with features to access system availability, account, billing and invoicing visibility (Ferguson, et al. 2004). ERP companies are offering extensive support with the help of their service partners (outsource companies) in relation to business application strategy, implementation integration and optimisation services and so forth. Small and midsize business centric packaging is another strategy adopted by some of the ERP vendors to capture major market share such as, SAP Business by Design; an on demand business solution for midsize businesses.

ERP Implementation in Midsize Business

It is not necessary that small & midsize businesses should go for 'high brand' and costly ERP products. They could consider other cheaper alternate ERP solutions that could serve their business needs (Lee 2000). It is also important to note that selecting an appropriate solution for small and midsize businesses can be difficult; depending upon their existing information technology management and business needs (Wilhelm et al. 2000).

Rao (2000) presented criteria for midsize businesses to select an appropriate ERP application consisting of following five points;

- **Product affordability:** A decision should be made according to the affordability of a product and its price.
- **Knowledge about supplier:** An experienced supplier should be selected with a deep understanding of ERP implementation issues.
- **Domestic support:** ERP applications are highly sophisticated requiring greater degree of hands on knowledge and expertise; it would be beneficial to choose a supplier who provides domestic/local support.
- **Technically upgradeable:** Product with upgradeability features should be selected that will allow the company to upgrade applications with changes in technology. A contract should be established with the vendor to provide annual upgrade software support.
- **Latest Technology:** An easily implementable product should be selected with user friendly interface with capability to adopt any future modifications. It would be better if product is designed on object oriented technology and GUI interface.

According to Wilhelm et al., (2000), ERP affordability could be increased by reducing the cost of implementation and increasing the user acceptance. Certain modelling approaches could be used to reduce the cost of implementation such as; (Wilhelm et al., 2000)

- Use a reference model to select best practice case for implementation.
- Modelling techniques to be used while documenting requirement definition details.
- To make the business logic more understandable, the system requirements should be documented with help of conceptual modelling methods.
- A conceptual model should be used as starting point for system automation, configuration and customisation (if required).

There are some strategies suggested by Aladwani (2001) for improving ERP implementation processes. These strategies could be categorized as;

- *Organisational strategies* comprising of project management, organizational structure, change strategy development and deployment, managerial style, ideology, communication and so forth.
- *Technical strategies* contain technical aspects of ERP implementation such as, ERP installation, configuration, complexity and capable technical staff to handle the complexities, time - cost factors and so forth.
- *People strategies* including management and staff related issues towards change management, training and level of staff engagement in a project.

As mentioned earlier, Marnewick et al., (2005) ERP conceptual model that comprises of four components. These components are derived from marketing 4P's model (People, Product, Process, and Performance) and maps on ERP components; People as Customers mindset, Product as Software, Process as Change Management and Performance as Process flow. Change management strategies are vital to promote steps necessary for adaptability to change. Therefore, it is important to identify factors that influence ERP user acceptance (Bueno and Salmeron 2008). Similarly, every other component also has an impact on ERP implementation process (direct or indirect), starting from identification of organisational requirements to customisation of software, installation to make software operational and training for successful adoption. These levels have significant importance and every organisation has to go through them.

Barriers to Implement ERP in Midsize Business

The adaptability of ERP applications is one of the major constraints faced by businesses implementing ERP applications. Mostly ERP users are not their experts and they do not desire to be due to the complex and non user friendly nature of these applications (Alison 2002). To increase the adaptability of ERP applications, vendors introduced different integration techniques such as Enterprise Application Integration (EAI) and also improved application design and modules to facilitate implementation handling capabilities of business, regardless of its size (Alison, 2002). Gable (1999) identified some of the potential barriers that could cause implementation hazards to midsize businesses;

- Lack of resources and less control over business operations.
- Managers/owner might be more influential towards strategic policy making issues and could make a biased choice
- The decision maker's background could be less or none technical and could result in lesser understanding of technology and its implications on the business
- Business might try to resolve sophisticated technical issue with less technological understanding.

Aladwani (2001) indicated some crucial issues in relation to ERP implementation that includes mainly the possible resistance from staff toward adaptability of the product. If staff considers ERP applications as threat to their job, they will develop negative attitude towards it. The ERP literature does not provide sufficient help to cope with this problem and it should be considered as a major threat to ERP implementation.

To overcome the possible resistance (to change) problem, management could engage and communicate with its employees in a more effective manner. Communication strategies could be useful to educate prospective users about benefits of ERP applications. In many cases ERP projects fails due to lack of communication and if problems are addressed appropriately, positive benefits could be entertained (Al-Mashari et. al., 2000).

ERP Implementation Models

Some researchers have categorised ERP implementation into stages and tried to standardize the processes for successful implementation. Bancroft (1996), Ross (1998), Markus and Tanis (2000) and Parr et al. (2000) proposed models of ERP implementation to obtain much deeper understanding of implementation processes and the purposed models could be used as an initiating point to create a similar model for midsize business.

1. Bancroft et al., (1998) developed a model as result of a comprehensive study carried out on ERP implementation in three anonymous multinational companies and with consultations of 20 ERP practitioners. This model consists of five phases including; four pre-implementation phases ('focus', 'as is', 'to be', 'construction and testing') and one actual implementation phase ('go live'). This model covers all major ERP implementation activities, starting from 'focus' to 'go live' and is briefly described below;
   - The *Planning (focus) phase* consists of initial project activities such as, formation of steering committee, project team selection, project guide development and project plan creation.
   - The *Analysis (as is) phase* consists of business process analysis, initial ERP system installation, business process mapping on ERP functions and project team training etc.
   - The *Design (to be) phase* includes, high level and detailed designing for user acceptance, interactive

prototyping with constant communication with ERP users.

- The *Construction (construction & testing) phase* consists of comprehensive configuration development, population of real data in test instance, interfaces building and testing, creation and testing of reports, system and user testing.
- The *Actual implementation phase (go live)* includes, network building, installation of desktops and organising the user training and support.

2. Ross (1998) presented another model after analysing ERP implementations at 15 case study large organisations. This model comprises of five phases; Design, implementation, stabilization, continuous improvement and transformation.

- The *Design phase* (which could be rephrased as *planning*) includes critical guidelines and decisions made towards ERP implementation.
- The *Implementation phase* includes several phases of Bancroft *et al.*'s (1998) model such as; 'as is', 'to be', 'construction & testing' and actual implementation ('go live').
- The *Stabilisation phase* comes after cut-over (final sign off) and if problems identified are fixed, consequently improves the organisational performance.
- The *Continuous improvement phase* includes any functionality added to the system.
- Finally, the *Transformation phase* covers achievement of maximum system flexibility up to organisational boundaries (system's operability on every organisational level).

3. Markus et al's (2000) theory concentrates on sequences of activities that lead to successful implementation of ERP systems in large size businesses. Markus et al. (2000) specified four major phases in the implementation life cycle; Chartering, Project, Shakedown and Onwards & upwards.

- The *Chartering phase* starts before Bancroft et al.'s (1998) focus and Ross' (1998) design phases. It comprises of decisions that lead to financial approval of an ERP project and it includes development of a business case, package selection, identification for the project team, budget and schedule approval and so on.
- The *Project phase* is similar to Ross' implementation phase and it covers all Bancroft's model phases except focus ('as is', 'to be', 'construction & testing' and 'actual implementation' phases). In this phase system configuration and rollout occurs and major activities such as, software configuration, system integration, testing, data conversion, training and roll-out takes place.
- The *Shakedown phase* refers to the period when system is beginning to operate normally by removing all glitches and implementing standards.
- The *Onward and upwards phase* is a combination of Ross' (1998) continuous improvement and stabilization phases. This phase refers to continuing maintenance, user support, upgrade or enhancements required by ERP system and focuses on any further system extensions.

4. Parr et al. (2000) Project Phase model (PPM) synthesizes previous models (Bancroft *et al.* (1998), Ross (1998), Markus and Tanis (2000)) and includes the planning and post implementation stages. The focus of this model is on project implementation & factors that influence a successful implementation at each phase. Parr et al. (2000) indicated that

for an organisation it is important to have significant amount of knowledge regarding unsuccessful projects and an experienced "Champion" should be appointed with well defined responsibilities. One large project should be partitioned into several sub-projects that can be identified as vanilla implementation. The PPM model consists of three major phases; planning, project and enhancement.

○ The *Planning phase* comprises of selecting an ERP application, formation of steering committee, project scope determination and broad implementation approach, selection of project team and determination of resources.

○ The *Project phase* includes a range of activities from identification of ERP modules to installation and cut-over. As the prime focus of this model is on implementation, therefore, this phase has been divided into five sub-phases: set-up, re-engineering, design, configuration and testing, installation.

▪ *Setup* comprises of project team selection and structuring with suitable mix of technical and business expertise. The team(s) integration and reporting processes are established and guiding principles are established or re-affirmed.

▪ *Re-engineering* comprises of analysis of current business process and to determine the level of process engineering required. This phase also includes, installation of ERP application, mapping of business processes on ERP functions and training the project teams.

▪ The *Design sub-phase* includes high level designing with

additional details for user acceptance. It also includes interactive prototyping through constant communication with users.

▪ The *Configuration & testing sub-phase* includes, development of comprehensive configuration, real data population in test instance, building and testing interfaces, writing and testing reports and finally system and user testing.

▪ The Installation sub-phase includes building networks, installation of desktops & managing user training and support. (Last four sub-phases are similar to the phases described in Bancroft et al. (1998) model)

○ The Enhancement phase comprises of stages of system repair, extension and transformation and it may extend over number of years. This phase encapsulates the Ross (1998)'s continuous improvement and stabilization phases and Markus et al. (2000) onwards and upwards phases.

Section Summary

ERP implementation has been described as unique and different from other software implementations due to its strategic impact over business. There are number of attempts made to produce an effective model, providing an appropriate strategic direction for large enterprises while implementing sophisticated business applications.

Based on existing research work, sequence of events outlined as stages could be represented as follows, (See Figure 1)

Figure 1. Sequence of events outlined as stages

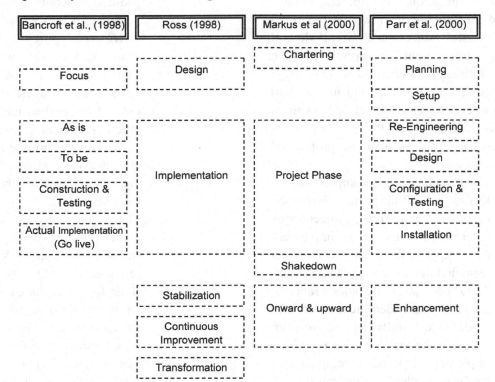

SOLUTIONS AND RECOMMENDATIONS

It cannot be assumed that ERP implementation by midsize business can directly use the existing ERP implementation frameworks that have traditionally been used during application assessment, implementation and evaluation processes in large enterprises (Rao 2000).

The adoption of technology by midsize businesses tends to be influenced by a number of associated factors. These factors could be summarized as a lack of experience in adopting new technology and its implementation, access to decision making information and availability of general resources (i.e. skill, time & money). Midsize businesses also face a number of other challenges during ERP implementation such as, selection of an effective IT solution, cost of implementation and customisation, staff training, business process standardisation and post production application maintenance (Barad et. al 2001, Rao 2000, Gable 1999, Rovere et. al 1996). Thus, the midsize business environment (with its limitations) is an important governing aspect of research that is associated with ERP adoption and needs to be part of a conceptual working model.

Companies adopt precautionary measures while implementing ERP applications and attempt to mitigate associated risks. It is suggested that midsize businesses should adopt an implementable strategy with proper planning and should resolve related problems to increase project success rate. Taylor (1999) discussed solution to nine challenges faced by small and midsize business while implementing an ERP application;

- Scalable software that could meet future growth requirements.
- Finding a best way to implement solutions with minimum cost.

- Realistic and achievable expectations from the application and implementation.
- The correct level of resources should be allocated to achieve maximum outcomes.
- Reduce possible staff resistance by overcoming the fear of change by consistent communication and staff engagement.
- Mapping out key business processes to a negotiable point where software could be implemented easily.
- Data conversation (data reformation from one application to another) should be performed appropriately.
- Avoid taking short cuts or quick fixes.
- Technical and hands on training must be provided.

Different research approaches have also been used to examine and identify factors that are critical for successful implementation of ERP applications. For example, ERP implementation models (Bancroft (1996), Ross (1998), Markus and Tanis (1999), Parr et al. (2000)) identify factors associated with ERP implementation stages and the degree of importance of each factor to every implementation stage, as do the traditional system approach (Edward et al 2003) and marketing derived 4Ps model (Marnewick, C. & Labuschagne, L. 2005). Arguably these methods are reliant on resource intense activities that are necessary in larger and change resistant organizations. Another approach to ERP research is to focus on business strategies that allow an understanding of ERP implementation as business progresses from one implementation stage into another (Aladwani 2001). The three core strategies (organisational, technical and people strategies) could be crucial for an organization to adopt ERP application and indeed these three are tangibly identifiable within the midsize business environment and less problematical to investigate if the study was to focus purely on business processes.

Clearly, there is a difference between issues that need to be considered while examining ERP adoption by midsize businesses and their large business counterparts. It is important to adopt a collaborative approach based upon existing research work to provide a road map (in form of ERP implementation models for large scale businesses) and also the strategic approach across organizational, technical and people domains and their resource limitations for midsize businesses. This forms a strong base for the proposed ERP adoption model described below.

An ERP Adoption Model for Midsize Business

A need to investigate ERP implementation issues in relation to their applicability in midsize business is apparent. The literature outlines implementation models and strategies for large enterprises to have successful ERP implementation. This existing knowledge base could be beneficial to develop a strategic ERP adoption model for midsize businesses that should provide a workable solution for their ERP implementations. In the past, much of ERP research was described as 'factor research' that mainly focused upon identifying *factors or variables* critical to ERP implementation. More recent research focus has been on *processes* that helps understand 'how' an implementation takes place (Aladwani, 2001). To take advantage of both perspectives, it is important to focus on an integrated approach to have a better understanding about issues relating to ERP implementation. The link between factors and stages is crucial to analyse the importance of different factors with the change in each stage during ERP implementation (Markus et al. 2000). This will help to assess what factors are affecting which process during certain periods of time and what impact is seen on the process itself. Parr et al's (2000) Project phase model and Markus et. als' (2000) process theory are useful tools to conduct the factor impact analysis while developing an ERP adoption model for midsize businesses.

The major focus of this research is to develop

Figure 2. ERP adoption model for midsize businesses

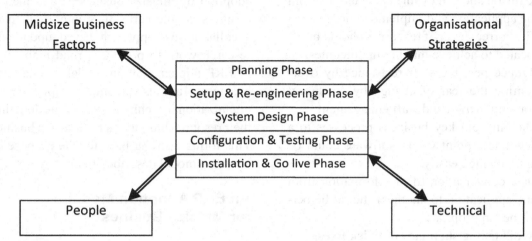

an ERP adoption model for midsize businesses by critically evaluating the strategic factors and issues with respect to different stages of implementation. Given the various resource limitations associated with midsize businesses and the potential challenges of ERP systems adoption, this study is important in focusing on specific business sector (midsize) as a basis for proposing a model. The resultant model will contribute to an increased understanding of implementation processes, factors, strategies and issues in relation to midsize business, enabling them to determine appropriate solution in accordance with their operational needs.

Figure 2 provides a 'bird's eye' view of the complex relationship that exists between the project implementation phases and strategies (organisational, people, technical) with issues relating to midsize business.

This model is developed by identifying the ERP implementation stages; defined in Parr et al.'s (2000) Project Phase model (PPM) (*also presented byBancroft et al. (1998),Ross (1998), andMarkus and Tanis (2000)ERP implementation models*) and the three major strategies impacting ERP implementation including organisational, technical and people strategies identified by Al-

dwani (2001). It also includes the midsize business specific issues (Barad et. al 2001, Rao 2000, Gable 1999, Rovere et. al 1996) identification and their management to mitigate any risks associated with them. Thus this model adopts an integrated approach of identifying factors critical to ERP implementation along with the processes crucial to every stage of ERP implementation.

Table 1 provides a detailed view of issues in relation to implementation stages and strategies during the implementation process. The model is designed to identify key factors associated with ERP implementation processes. The intent is to adopt a best practice theoretical base approach by encapsulating existing literature to propose a strategic ERP adoption model specifically designed to facilitate the needs of midsize businesses. There is an enormous amount of research that has been conducted in relation to ERP implementation in large enterprises; that is used to help identify many of the ERP implementation issues faced by midsize businesses. However, we are also introducing those factors that relate specifically to midsize businesses because they are different from large size businesses. Midsize businesses are strategically fragile and economically less stable with limited operability.

Table 1. ERP adoption model for midsize businesses – Detailed diagram

Stages Bancroft *et al.* (1998), Parr et al. (2000)	Activities **Bancroft *et al.* (1998)**, Parr et al. (2000)	Factors			
		Organisational Aladwani (2001)	People Aladwani (2001)	Technical Aladwani (2001)	Midsize Business (Barad et. al 2001, Rao, 2000, Gable 1999, Rovere 1996)
Pre-Planning		* Change strategies development; * Risk Management;			* Business & Technology Issues; * Strategic Management Issues; * Criteria of Selecting an IS;
Planning	* ERP Application Selection, * Project Scope determination, * Project team selection, * Resource determination	* Change strategies development; * Project management; * Risk Management;	* Training strategies; * Change Management;	* Time & Cost of implementation	* Accurate Information; * Limited Resources (Time, Budget);
Setup & Re-engineer	* Team Structure & integration, * Guiding principles, * Business process analysis, * Installation of ERP app, * BP mapping, * Team training	* Organizational resources, * Organisational structure; * Managerial style; * Organisational Ideology;	* Staff attitude to change; * Management attitude;	* ERP complexity; * In house expertise; * Cost of implementation	* Limited Resources (Budget, Skill);
System Design	* High level designing * Additional details for user acceptance * Interactive prototyping * User Communication	* Organizational resources; * Communication & * Coordination; * Risk Monitoring;	* Staff Involvement;	* ERP complexity; * In house expertise; * Cost of implementation	* Business & Technology Issues;
Configuration & Testing	* Comprehensive configuration, * Real time data in Test instance, * Build test interfaces, * Write & test reports, * System & User testing	* Information System Function * Communication & * Coordination;	* Staff Involvement;	* ERP installation aspects; * In house expertise; * Cost of implementation	* Limited Resources (Budget, Skill);
Installation & Go live	* Building Network, * Desktop installation, * User training, * System Support	* Change strategies (**Update**); * Risk Management (**Update**);	* Staff attitude to change (**Update**); * Management attitude (**Update**);	* ERP implementation issues (**Update**);	* Business & Technology Issues (**Update**); * Strategic Management Issues (**Update**);

Now we shall discuss the proposed composition of the model and the importance of the strategic mixture being proposed.

The Model

The model is divided into two major dimensions, *ERP implementation stages* and *factors impacting implementation*, which are represented as a matrix in Table 1. The objective is to underline the interrelationship between these two modules and to suggest activities, strategies and tasks to execute the project efficiently. Midsize businesses often lack leadership and strategic vision and they mainly focus on day to day operations. Midsize businesses also tend to be influenced by number of factors while selecting an information system and are often limited by their lack of knowledge and skill. Our model will provide midsize business a broader picture of issues that they could encounter during the ERP implementation processes and will assist them to have a controlled implementation.

ERP Implementation Stages

As shown earlier, different researchers have identified planning, set up, engineering, system design, configuration, testing and installation as separate stages but we have consolidated these to align in accordance with midsize implementation. Markus et al. (2000) identified 'chartering' as a crucial stage that contains decision making processes leading up to selection of an ERP application. This has been reflected as a pre-planning phase in our model to highlight the need for activities that are important for decision making processes leading up to selection of a suitable ERP application.

1. **Pre-Planning:** It is important for midsize businesses to perform comprehensive pre-planning analysis of their existing financial and operational performance indicators. At the organisational level; strategic planning for projects becomes vital when risks are high and resources are limited. All important decisions leading to financial approval, the development of a business case, gathering appropriate business, technical & architectural information should be obtained and shared with the appropriate people for an informed decision. Midsize businesses should assess the operational significance and collective business benefits of the proposed application before making any judgements. Change management and risk management plans should be developed to underline areas that should be considered during implementation.

2. **Planning:** This is the first official stage of the project in which initial project activities should be performed, such as the identification of key stakeholders and formation of a governing body and project team selection (including hiring new staff). Change and risk

management strategies should be revisited and updated if necessary. A project management plan should be developed to scope the project activities, project tasks should be scheduled and resources should be identified and allocated (including time and money). Accurate and timely information is very important for midsize businesses to execute project plans in accordance with their desired expectations. Therefore it is important that information should be accurate during entire planning process.

3. **Setup & Re-engineer:** To execute the project effectively, it is important to structure the project team with the correct mix of technical and business professionals. As midsize businesses lack resources, it is crucial for them to decide whether they need to *hire* or *acquire* the necessary skills. Midsize businesses should identify and reassess their available resources (in-house expertise and money) to structure the project team according to the standard required for ERP implementation. The cost of implementation could be significantly high if there is a need of customisation in the application. Therefore, the organisation's ideology should be examined to assess the staff and management's attitude to change before taking any decisions. The guiding principles of the project should be identified and a business case analysis should be completed to underline the expectations. The ERP application should be installed in the development environment and business process mapping should take place with gap analysis. Internal team training should occur to equip existing organisational staff with the appropriate skill levels. For midsize businesses it would usually be wise to have right mix of in-house and third party technical expertise to avoid any surprises in the 'post go-live' phase.

4. **System Design:** This is an important stage in which higher level design should be

completed and approved. Extensive communication and coordination is required to address organisational expectations and users should be engaged consistently during development process. Details in relation to user acceptance should be captured and documented. Staff and management's attitude to change should be examined and the change management plan should be updated to cater for resistance to change. ERP applications are complex in nature, therefore, associated risks should be analysed and addressed by developing a suitable risk mitigation plan. An initial application *interactive prototype* should be completed to demonstrate application functionality. This functionality should also be compared with the midsize business expectations to ensure that it is addressing the business and technology needs.

5. **Configuration & Testing:** Once the interactive prototype is completed, its comprehensive configuration should be executed in accordance with the requirements identified in the design document. Real data should be populated in *test instances* for system testing, test interfaces should be developed and reports should be documented and tested accordingly. During the entire testing process, staff should be engaged and extensive communication should be conducted at the organisational level. Information system functions should be assessed and prospective change should be coordinated. The project budgetary estimates should be assessed and existing staff skill levels should be reassessed. System and user testing should be completed in this stage.

6. **Installation & Go live:** In this stage, all post testing activities should be executed, such as building the production environment, building the network (if required) and desktop installation (if required). User training should be completed and the system should go live in the production environment. The lessons learned from the implementation should be documented, including change and risk management strategies, management of staff attitudes to change, ERP implementation, business technology issues and so forth. The system support should be ongoing to perform post production *glitch* analysis.

FUTURE RESEARCH

Developing and Refining an ERP Adoption Model

In order to refine the ERP adoption model for midsize businesses a research study containing quantitative and qualitative data collection stages is proposed (Leedy et al. 1997). The data collection focus in this study will primarily be based upon Australian midsize businesses; however it is also applicable to midsize businesses around the world. Stage one of the methodology roadmap will use surveys to provide an understanding of what is happening in midsize business market in relation to ERP adoption. The second stage of roadmap utilises case studies that will help to further refine the adoption model by determining the important reasons as to way midsize businesses should adopt ERP applications.

Stage One— Industry Survey

Stage one of research methodology explores the implementation stages with reference to overall strategies that are important while implementing an ERP application and also the midsize business specific issues. In this stage, activities to be performed in each implementation stage, impact of relating strategies and midsize business relating issues, problems and benefits will be explored. The survey instrument will concentrate on around 200 midsize companies using ERP applications along with 200 non ERP using companies in Australia in an endeavour to determine the various operational

& implementation factors, strategic issues associated with ERP implementation. The questionnaire will investigate the level of usage of ERP systems in mid-market and specially examine; the strategies that led to smooth implementation of ERP applications; selection of business solutions for a business type; issues and impact of proposed strategies during implementation process; factors affecting the implementation processes and sequence of activities performed in each implementation stage.

The outcome of this survey will be used to generate a first iteration or revised version of ERP adoption model.

Stage Two— Industry Case Studies & Expert Panel

The stage two of investigative methodology will consist of multiple case studies. The respondents of industry survey (stage one) will be asked to state their interest in a follow up interview. The purpose of this exercise is to conduct a qualitative analysis to examine each case in depth in order to understand the individual experiences of midsize businesses. This will provide an opportunity to obtain first hand knowledge about organisation and their understanding of issues in relation to ERP implementation in midsize businesses. The strategies adopted by these businesses to overcome issues relating to their implementation of ERP applications will also be discussed. This data collection stage will help to identify specific strategies that these businesses have adopted to help them address certain issues and problematic situations. The case studies will be categorised into three levels;

- Midsize businesses that have performed ERP implementation,
- Midsize companies that tried to implement an ERP application but 'rolled back' and
- Midsize businesses that have not tried but considering ERP solution for their problems

A total of fifteen to eighteen businesses will be interviewed and they will be selected depending upon responses received and their ERP implementation results. The results of second iteration of the model will be presented to ERP system experts to ascertain technological and managerial implications. The feedback gauged from ERP experts will confirm the industry findings and potentially also identify new or undocumented strategies that are directly related to the area of research.

The data received from different sources will be evaluated and result will be used in further refinements of ERP adoption model. The resultant ERP adoption model derived from this two stage methodology will provide a road map for midsize businesses, incorporating strategies that should be considered in accordance with their situation, background, financial situation and applicability to implement ERP applications successfully.

CONCLUSION

This chapter examines the impact of ERP implementation on midsize businesses by discussing factors with reference to strategies and processes that are important for ERP implementation in midsize businesses. There are many constraints being identified in relation to ERP implementation, especially when there is a need of their customisation. Sometimes businesses need to customise these applications to add or delete features to serve their business needs, hence it would be beneficial to identify business requirements and scope the project objective before its initiation. The chapter also examines the nature of midsize businesses and argues that ERP adoption is likely to be an important consideration for these businesses in the near future. Midsize businesses are mainly dependent upon many internal (organisational) and external (wider economic) influential factors. Arguably, some internal or external factors might force midsize businesses to adopt ERP applications, not only to make them more competitive but also due to pressures associated with their larger counterparts. Therefore, it is important to underline factors that could impact midsize businesses during sophisticated application adoption processes.

Implementation of an ERP system is different from any other software application due to its impact on business operations and requirement to facilitate business needs. There have been a number of attempts made by different researchers to produce an effective framework, enabling businesses to have a strategic direction for ERP implementation. ERP implementation models were developed specifically to focus on the identification of large enterprise implementation requirements and activities/ stages that are crucial for their implementation. It would be beneficial to utilise existing knowledge base while developing a strategic model for ERP adoption in midsize businesses. This model should focus on strategic issues faced by midsize businesses providing guidelines that could help to mitigate associated risks to ERP implementation.

ERP adoption is also discussed from aspect of number of different implementation methodologies that are traditional, process focussed, marketing enabled, strategy or process oriented. It is argued that a strategic approach focusing on organisational, technical and people area alongside with midsize business factor analysis would be desirable while outlining the activities to be performed in each implementation stage. Hence, a conceptual ERP adoption model would include a strategic approach to investigate and deliver a road map to a limited midsize business environment.

To test and reform the proposed ERP adoption model, a methodological roadmap is documented that embraced quantitative and qualitative data collection stages and will be tested on Australian midsize business market. The quantitative stage will be associated with the capture of business characteristics that detail the scope of ERP systems adoption and identification of salient aspects of strategy across the three areas of interest (organisational, people, organisational). The qualitative stage of the roadmap involves the capture of individual experiences of midsize businesses adoption through the case study method in order to gain first hand knowledge about the organisations and the ERP strategies they implemented. Each stage of the roadmap will allow the progressive development and refinement of the proposed ERP adoption model.

REFERENCES

Aberdeen Group. (2006). *ERP in the mid-market*. Boston: Aberdeen Group, Inc.

Al-Mashari, M. (2002). ERP Systems: A research agenda. *Industrial Management & Data Systems*, 165–170. doi:10.1108/02635570210421354

Al-Mashari, M., & Zairi, M. (2000). Information and business process equality: The case of SAP R/3 implementation. *Electronic Journal on Information Systems in Developing Countries, 2*.

Aladwani, A. M. (2001). Change management strategies for successful ERP implementation. *Business Process Management Journal*, *7*(3), 266–275. doi:10.1108/14637150110392764

Alison, C. (2002, Dec). Works management. *HortonKir by*, *55*(12), 30–33.

Amoako-Gyampah, K. (2007). Perceived usefulness, user involvement and behavioural intention: an empirical study of ERP implementation. *Computers in Human Behavior*, *23*, 1232–1248. doi:10.1016/j.chb.2004.12.002

APEC Profile of SMEs. (2003). What is an SME? Definitions and statistical issues. *Journal of Enterprising Culture*, *11*(3), 173–183. doi:10.1142/S021849580300010X

Bancroft, N., Seip, H., & Sprengel, A. (1998). *Implementing SAP R/3* (2nd ed.). Greenwich: Manning Publications.

Barad, M., & Gien, D. (2001). Linking improvement models to manufacturing strategies – A methodology for SMEs and other enterprises. *International Journal of Production Research, 39*(12), 2675–2695. doi:10.1080/00207540011005182

Boubekri, N. (2001). Technology Enablers for supply chain management. *Integrated Manufacturing Systems, 12*(6), 394–399. doi:10.1108/EUM0000000006104

BRW. (2002, November). *Fast 100 Issue*. Cited by Business Technologies for SMEs, October 2003, Conference at Sydney.

Bueno, S., & Salmeron, J. (2008). TAM-based success modelling in ERP. *Interacting with Computers, 20*, 515–523. doi:10.1016/j.intcom.2008.08.003

Caillaud, E., & Passemard, C. (2001). CIM and virtual enterprises: A case study in a SME. *International Journal of Computer Integrated Manufacturing, 14*(2), 168–174. doi:10.1080/09511920150216288

Chung, S. H., & Synder, C. A. (1999). *ERP initiation- A historical perspective*. Americas Conference on Information Systems, August 13-15, Milwaukee, WI, 1999

Correa, C. (1994). cited by Aladwani (2001). Change management strategies for successful ERP implementation. *Business Process Management Journal, 7*(3), 266–275.

Duxbury, L., Decady, Y., & Tse, A. (2002). Adoption and use of computer technology in Canadian small businesses: A comparative study. In *Managing Information Technology in Small Business: Challenges & Solutions* (pp. 22-23). Hershey, PA: Information Science Publishing.

Edward, W. N., Bernroider, N., & Tang, K. H. (2003). A preliminary empirical study of the diffusion of ERP systems in Austrian and British SMEs. *Working Papers on Information Processing and Information Management.*

Ferguson, R.B. (2004). *ERP targets the midmarket. eWeek, 21*(6), 41.

Gable, G., & Stewart, G. (1999). *SAP R/3 implementation issues for small to medium enterprises.* Americas Conference on Information Systems, August 13-15, Milwaukee, WI.

Gefen, D., & Ragowsky, A. (2005). A multi-level approach to measuring the benefits of an ERP system in manufacturing firms. *Information Systems Management Journal, 22*(1), 18–25. doi:10.1201/1078/44912.22.1.20051201/85735.3

Keller, G., & Teufel, T. (1998). *SAP R/3, process oriented implementation.* Harlow: Addison-Wesley.

Kennerley, M., & Neely, A. (2001). Enterprise resource planning: Analysing the impact. *Integrated Manufacturing Systems, 12*(2), 103–113. doi:10.1108/09576060110384299

Klaus, H., Rosemann, M., & Gable, G. G. (2000). What is ERP? *Information Systems Frontiers, 2*(2), 141–162. doi:10.1023/A:1026543906354

Koch, C. (2008). The ABC of ERP. *Enterprise Resource Planning Research Center.* Retrieved from http://www.cio.com/research/erp/edit/erp-basics.html

Lee, T. T. (2000). Apt ERP alternatives. *New Straits Times-Management Times.*

Leedy, P. D. (1997). *Practical research – Planning and design* (6th ed.). NJ: Prentice-Hall, Inc.

Markus, M. L., Axline, S., Petrie, D., & Tanis, C. (2000). Learning from adopters' experiences with ERP: problems encountered and success achieved. *Journal of Information Technology, 15*, 245–265. doi:10.1080/02683960010008944

Markus, M. L., & Tanis, C. (2000). In R. W. Zmud (Ed.), *The enterprise systems experience – From adoption to success, in framing the domains of IT management: Projecting the future……. through the past* (pp. 173-207).

Marnewick, C., & Labuschagne, L. (2005). A conceptual model for enterprise resource planning (ERP). *Information Management & Computer Security, 13*(2). doi:10.1108/09685220510589325

Martin, M. (1998). An electronics firm will save big money by replacing six people…… not every company has been so lucky. *Fortune, 137*(2), 149–151.

Monnerat, R., Carvalho, R., & Campos, R. (2008). Enterprise systems modeling: The ERP5 development process. [Fortaleza, Ceara, Brazil]. *SAC, 08*(March), 16–20.

Parr, A., & Shanks, G. A. (2000). Model of ERP project implementation. *Journal of Information Technology, 15*, 289–303. doi:10.1080/02683960010009051

Pramukti, S. (2003). Establishing synergy between small companies and banks. *JAKARTA POST 06/03/2003.* Accession Number: 2W81194803776, Business Source Premier

Ragowsky, A., & Gefen, D. (2008). What Makes the Competitive Contribution of ERP Strategic. *The Data Base for Advances in Information Systems, 39*(2).

Rao, S. S. (2000). Enterprise resource planning: business needs and technologies. *Industrial Management & Data Systems, 100*(2), 81–88. doi:10.1108/02635570010286078

Raouf, A. (1998). Development of operations management in Pakistan. *International Journal of Operations & Production Management, 18*(7), 649–650. doi:10.1108/01443579810217602

Rooney, C., & Bangert, C. (2000). Is an ERP System Right for You? *Adhesives Age, 43*(9), 30–33.

Ross, J. W. (1998). *The ERP revolution: Surviving versus thriving.* Centre for Information Systems Research, Sloan School of Management.

Rovere, L., & Lebre, R. (1996). IT diffusion in small and medium-sized enterprises: Elements for policy definition. *Information Technology for Development, 7*(4), 169–181.

Saccomano, A. (2003). ERP vendors consolidate. *Journal of Commerce, 4*(24), 46.

Sandoe, K., Corbitt, G., & Boykin, R. (2001). *Enterprise Integration.* New York: Wiley.

Sarbutts, N. (2003). Can SMEs 'do' CSR? A practitioner's views of the ways small-and medium-sized enterprises are able to manage reputation through corporate social responsibility. *Journal of Communication Management, 7*(4), 340–348. doi:10.1108/13632540310807476

Taylor, J. (1999). *Management Accounting.*

Turban, E., Leidner, D., Mclean, E., & Wetherbe, J. (2006). *Information Technology Management: Transforming Organisations in the Digital Economy* (5th ed.). New York: John Wiley & Sons.

Vandaie, R. (2008). The role of organizational knowledge management in successful ERP implementation projects. *Knowledge-Based Systems, 21*, 920–926. doi:10.1016/j.knosys.2008.04.001

Wei, C. (2008). Evaluating the performance of an ERP system based on the knowledge of ERP implementation objectives. *International Journal of Advanced Manufacturing Technology, 39*, 168–181. doi:10.1007/s00170-007-1189-3

Wilhelm, S., & Habermann, F. (2000). Making ERP a success. *Communications of the ACM, 43*(4), 57–61. doi:10.1145/332051.332073

Yang, J., Wu, C., & Tsai, C. (2007). Selection of an ERP system for a construction firm in Taiwan: A case study. *Automation in Construction, 16,* 787–796. doi:10.1016/j.autcon.2007.02.001

Yates, I. (2004). 2004 Proved Successful for SAP Latin America. *Caribbean Business, 33*(10).

Chapter 10
Enterprise Information Systems for Business Integration in Global International Cooperations of Collaborating Small and Medium Sized Organisations

P. H. Osanna
Vienna University of Technology, Austria

N. M. Durakbasa
Vienna University of Technology, Austria

M. E. Yurci
YILDIZ Technical University, Turkey

J. M. Bauer
National University of Lomas Zamora, Argentina

ABSTRACT

The importance of small and medium sized enterprises (SMEs) is today far beyond any discussion in countries all over the world - in European countries as well as in Asia and in USA, in Africa as well as in Latin America. To meet market demands in the present and future global industrial world, manufacturing enterprises of any kind and any size must be flexible and agile enough to respond quickly to product demand changes. With the support of artificial intelligence and modern information technology, it is possible to realise modern cost-effective customer-driven design and manufacturing taking into account the importance and basic role of quality management and metrology. This will be especially possible on the basis of the innovative concept and model for modern enterprises the so-called "Multi-Functions Integrated Factory – MFIF" that makes possible an agile and optimal industrial production in any kind of industry and especially in up-to-date SMEs.

DOI: 10.4018/978-1-60566-892-5.ch010

THE GLOBAL IMPORTANCE OF SMES

To meet high-level demands both from industrial and from private customers in the future, manufacturing enterprises must be flexible and agile enough to respond quickly to product demand changes. New models for alternative configurations of future industrial organisations in general which are usually applied and especially for small and medium sized enterprises (SMEs) need to be investigated.

Those new models can be developed on the basis of intelligent production technologies and extensive use of the internet, of **distributed computing environment (DCE)** technology, parallel-processing computing and advanced engineering data exchange techniques - Osanna & Si (2000). By these means global competitive associations of factories as well as of collaborating SMEs with intelligent, associative, concurrent, interactive, modular, integrative, learning, autonomous, self optimising and self organising functions are already under development and the world wide application of such associations and cooperations will be possible in the near future.

COOPERATION AND COLLABORATION OF MODERN INDUSTRIAL PLANTS

Multi-Functions Integrated Factory MFIF is an innovative concept and model for future enterprises and collaborations which is initiated with the aim to provide cost-effective, agile and optimal ways to produce customer-driven Multi-Functional Products MFPs in the near future (see Figure 1). By means of information technology and artificial intelligence, factories which for instance produce cars, aircrafts and ships respectively could be linked to form a new kind of collaboration with all three functions according to needs. The product - MFP - will be produced in such a way that the above mentioned different function tasks of the product should be manufactured in adequate function factory or function SME, and then assembled and integrated to realize the combination of the functions. The collaboration works by using its advantages of multi-functions, and produces high efficiently and agilely low cost high quality customer-driven multi-functional products - Si & Osanna (1995).

Such MFIF or SME collaboration has the potential to improve industrial competitiveness. Additionally comprehensive manufacturing automation and optimal production of customer-driven MFPs will be made possible worldwide. **Intelligent manufacturing systems (IMS)** are the basis for realization of such a collaboration in which individual functional enterprises or functional SMEs are functionally and configurationally integrated with other functional units located in different parts of the world to produce MFPs respectively. This new concept of SME collaborations or MFIFs will come into existence in the near future and will be realised step by step. One of its specific features is the use of cross-functional design and manufacturing teams, in which the small engineering teams or single engineers of the units or SMEs with different skills and expertise work together on a MFP project concurrently and interactively.

Such a system is based on the assumption that it works under the condition that each single-functional factory or SME has a possible full-scale IMS working environment and is an integration of intelligent manufacturing machines, cells and systems for manufacturing and other tasks to be carried out. Concurrent, interactive, modular, integrative, learning, autonomous, self optimising and self organising functions are the main features of the MFIF or SME cooperation respectively.

The factories are reconfigurable to take advantages of agile manufacturing production for the MFPs. The system provides a function-business-shared feature to create new customer-driven markets. It is controlled and arranged by

Figure 1. Integration of intelligent computer aided quality control (ICAQ) and intelligent computer aided metroloy (ICAM) into the model of MFIF and SME collaboration respectively

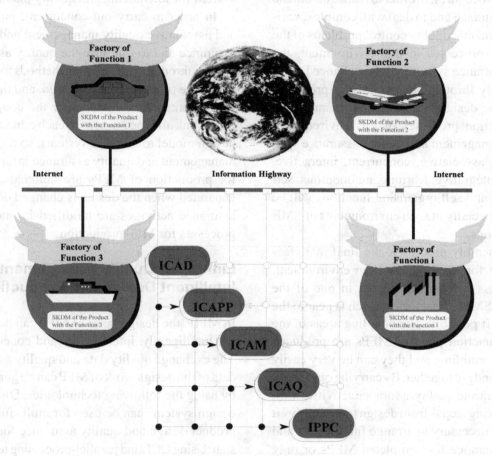

Multi-Functions Integrated Factory

collaborative activities between the individual factories or SMEs. Cooperative activities between all units of the system can also be concurrently on-line carried out. Learning is carried out step to step by using the methods of evolution, and is used to optimise process control. It is possible that all the systematisation knowledges for design and manufacturing (SKDM) of each module of the system and all production information between ICAx systems of MFIF can be exchanged simultaneously on-line.

Failurefree concurrent exchange of production information and data, concurrent processing and executing of production processes through distributed computing environment DCE and learning of all collaborative production processes are also features in global systems as there are MFIF or SME collaborations.

QUALITY MANAGEMENT AND METROLOGY FOR DESIGN AND PRODUCTION

The Support of Artificial Intelligence

The quality assurance process will be carried out simultanously in all product realisation steps in future factories - from the design process to the assembly procedures. In order to realise automatic quality assurance and to deal with complex, variable and dynamic quality control problems of the production processes in this environment, the quality assurance system will be enhanced comprehensively through self-optimising processes thrust in the design system and all manufacturing production processes of this environment. Quality management and quality assurance with intelligent, associative, concurrent, interactive, modular, integrative, learning, autonomous, self optimising and self organising functions will be realized especially in such environments of SME collaborations.

The assembly process is the final manufacturing step for MFPs in such an environment. This process will be carried out in one of the individual SMEs or factories which is near to the customers if possible. The coupling areas of the different function parts of MFPs are produced for ease-assembling, and they can be very easily combined and put together. By carrying out quality management and quality assurance activities in all manufacturing steps - from design to assembly - it will not be necessary to arrange final checks and quality assurance for completed MFPs or only few and very short such activities.

The way to scrap free and zero defect production will be made possible by learning with self improving ability, a goal which at least can be realised partly. Improvement and optimization of production processes is possible based on the supervision of quality in the process chain as well as by means of knowledge and learning management systems and self-learning systems. This method permits to learn stepwise from deviations and to improve the used processes continuously.

In the ICAQ system **Fuzzy Logic** will be applied for Quality Function Deployment (QFD) and for monitoring and forecasting of maintenance of measuring instruments - Durakbasa & Osanna

(2002) - furtheron for CAD and for an **expert system** for tolerancing and quality planning.

In order to carry out concurrent, interactive and associative quality management and quality assurance and to optimise the quality assurance process through itself, learning methods for quality assurance processes must be used, and the ICAQ components of the factories or the cooperating SMEs link all process steps to each other from the design model to all other systems, so the quality management and quality assurance informations for production of MFPs are automatically re-generated when the design is changed or quality assurance activities are modified in one of the processes for MFP production.

Linking of Quality Management to Intelligent Design and Production

In MFIF, the design tasks of MFP can be carried out intelligently, interactively and concurrently. The exchange quality data and quality assurance data of the design work of MFP can be guaranteed by using the following technologies. Distributed design systems can be used for multi-functional product design and quality assurance for the design. Using DCE and parallel-processing technologies, the engineers and experts can work on parts of a design task, but the content of the design as a whole is a corporate resource to be managed and secured. This system makes it possible that the product designers of different function SMEs or factories can work parallelly on all the subtasks of the product.

Collaborative working method in MFIF has the goal to realise not only electronic data exchange function but also an interactive working function on-line, and to work at the different places and at heterogeneous systems out the same product model. Transmission of words, figures and sound by means of multimedia will also be integrated in such interactive CAD systems which could recognise manual drawings, learn the design process of the product, even understand the natural language instruction for the design, and optimise the design process and design quality. This kind of process would be guaranteed by modern data communication technologies and intelligent quality management and quality assurance as described in above. The design quality and quality assurance data exchange of the design work of MFP can be guaranteed by using the already mentioned techniques.

An effective use of analysis, simulation and visualisation tools gives several advantages for MFP design and quality assurance of the design. In this system the designers from the different single-functional enterprises use typically parallel-processing, virtual reality and virtual prototyping technologies, to design and simulate the customer-driven MPFs and their systematical function activities as well as to create a fully digital MFP production and programs for the entire manufacturing process.

In the ICAM system, the quality management and quality assurance information and programs will also be on-line exchanged and modified concurrently, interactively and collaboratively. It runs autonomously according to the adequate functional qulity assurance tasks and organises all manufacturing quality activities and units optimally in adequate factories. Learning the processes from the processes, the quality assurance parts of the ICAM units improve the all manufacturing process quality assurance parameters continously.

The implemetation of all these properties in an intelligent quality management and quality assurance architecture is a great challenge, and distributed, decentralised, self-organised and self-optimised concepts will be the main approach for this goal.

METROLOGY AND QUALITY MANAGEMENT IN GLOBAL FACTORIES

Intelligent Metrology and Intelligent Quality Assurance

In the already described computer-integrated and intelligent manufacturing environment, the integrated ICAQ system with intelligent **coordinate metrology** ICM is utilised to test the product or to scan and digitise complex product models with **freeformsurfaces**. This is in order to obtain the digital model of the product and to modify it in ICAD system and then to create a new modified surface model and CNC programs for manufacturing of the final product by machine center in the workshop.

Intelligent **coordinate metrology** is a very important tool to solve various problems of quality management and quality assurance in MFP production especially when high flexibility and high accuracy are demanded simultanously. This way of metrology is the uptodate measuring method for complex dimensional and geometrical measuring problems.

The following Figures 2 and 3 illustrate a non-conventional application of intelligent **coordinate metrology** to support the improvement and optimisation of musical instruments. This is a typical task for metrology and manufacturing in a small producing enterprise. Figure 2 illustrates the schematics of the mouth piece of a clarinet whereas Figure 3 shows the measurement and evaluation of such a mouth piece. The correct sound of the instrument depends of the numerically defined exact form of both the side ribs and the tip rib of the mouth piece.

In a system or compound of SMEs as described above, CNC-controlled intelligent CMMs are connected by using networks with design and manufacturing. The goal is to mutually use the data stored in ICAD, ICAM and ICAQ systems, and to realise data parallel-processing. For the

Figure 2. Mouth piece of a clarinet, schematic view

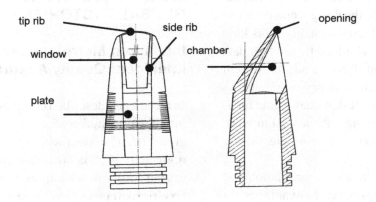

concurrent production and the quality management system, it is suitable to use off-line programming technique, through which CNC inspection programs can be worked out without using the CMMs and the products. By means of this technique, the quality assurance data and inspection CNC programs can be generated simultaneously during the product design.

Because of world wide needs for customer-driven MFPs, a global concurrent quality assurance system must be used with the support of internet and parallel processing computer technology. Internet makes it possible to establish a global quality assurance information highway for simultaneous on-line MFP quality assurance data exchange in global environment of collaborating SMEs or MFIF, and to interact with suppliers and customers world wide.

Off-line programming for ICMM in ICAD system and in special programming software is the basis for simultaneous quality assurance in the individual enterprises but also in global MFIF. Many off-line programming packages as well as ICAD/ICAM/ICAQ system architechture are typical combinations in the integrated factory. ICAD/ICAQ data communication technique will be widely used in MFIF. On the basis of computer aided measurement technique and especially co-ordinate metrology quality management is integrated in the production information network.

Off-line programming packages based on 3D-CAD model that represents nominal data of products can be used for the application. The probe configurations can be selected through the created probe database. The operator can call all regular element measuring functions and the actual data evaluation functions, using main dialog menu of the package. On this basis measuring programs and the probe paths can be simulated, edited and optimised. During the simulation a CNC measuring program is generated in a specific format. Additionally a collision control function is realised through simulating the measuring processes on the computer monitor.

Application of Non-Conventional Metrology

Besides coordinate metrology modern optoelectronic methods are important measurement tools in computer integrated production plants and also as basic tools for global quality management and quality assurance activities. Their efficient use and correct calibration are crucial requirements for quality management in this environment.

Presently exists the general development from micro technology to "nano technology". Nano technology describes new innovative manufacturing technologies, finishes, tolerances and especially measurement technique in the nanometer range - Taniguchi (1974), Whitehouse (1991) & Whitehouse (2002).

In persecution of this aim since about 1982 new high resolution and high precision measuring devices have been developed, especially **Scanning Tunnelling Microscopy (STM)** and **Atomic Force or Scanning Probe Microscopy (AFM, SPM)** - Binnig & Rohrer (1982). For highest demands these methods make it possible to explore atomic structures and in general very accurate and small industrially produced parts and structures. With scanning tunnelling and scanning probe microscopes lateral resolutions up to 10 nm

Figure 3. Measurement and evaluation of the mouth piece of a clarinet

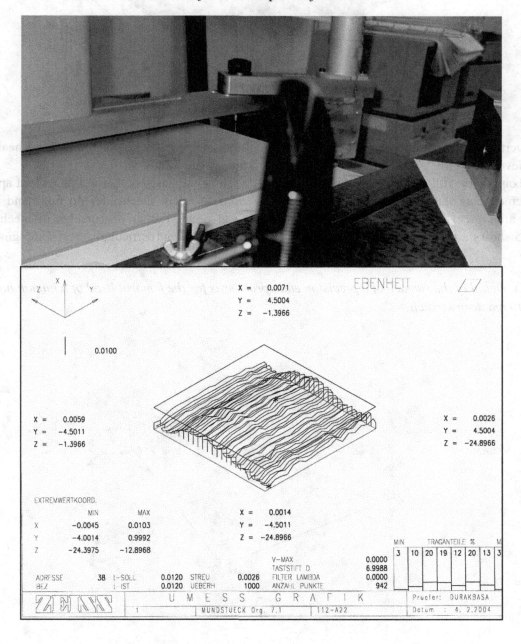

Figure 4. Structure of precision machined workpiece surface

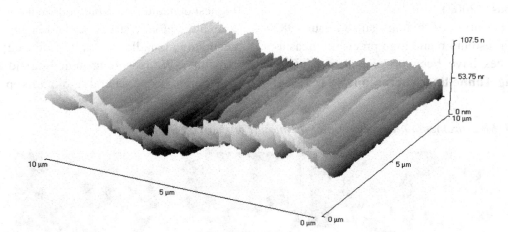

and in vertical direction up to atomic resolution are achieved.

As example the following Figure 4 shows the measurement data of the structure of a workpiece surface after precision turning. The following Figure 5 shows a part of the surface of a preci-sion endo prosthesis for the femoral head of a human hip joint.

It is emphasised, that in this respect applications in micro electronics do not stand in the focal point. Rather instruments of mechanical engineering and particularly precision engineering

Figure 5. Detail of the surface of a precision endo prosthesis for the femoral head of a human hip joint with a 40 nm deep scratch

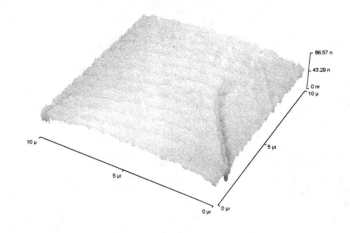

Figure 6. Configuration of an intelligent quality sssurance cell

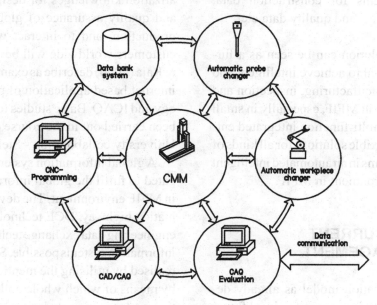

are addressed in the first hand. Extremely high accuracy demands deposit presently already at highly developed instruments for everyday use as there are VCRs or CD-players and in the sensor technique in automotive engineering and even in the home appliance if we think on one-hand mixing taps which demand ultra precision form tolerances.

PROPOSAL FOR AN INTELLIGENT QUALITY ASSURANCE SYSTEM

For the intelligent flexible automation of quality management and quality assurance, data collection and evaluation in single functional enterprises a proposed system in the form of an intelligent measuring cell can solve the following tasks:

- automatic intelligent measurement by using CNC metrology,
- off-line CNC programming of measuring instruments,
- automatic changing of workpieces,

- automatic changing of probes and snesors,
- automated evaluation of measuring results.

Figure 6 shows the principal structure of such an Intelligent Quality Assurance Cell according to the above given definition. It consists of a series of devices and components:

- a local area network of various PCs especially for ICAD, ICAE and ICAQ evaluation,
- a precision intelligent CNC dimensional measuring instrument with control computer,
- a probe changer with interface and control computer,
- a robot for workpiece manipulation,
- various measuring instruments, for instance a small CMM and other devices,
- a scanning probe microscope to evaluate surfaces in the submicrometer and atomic range,
- printers for data and graphic output,

- database systems for construction data, measuring results and quality data etc.

The proposed solution can be seen as a further step with the goal to achieve intelligent and economical MFP manufacturing, inspection and quality management in MFIF, especially in small and medium sized multi-function integrated enterprises, and to find flexible solutions for all kinds of measurement problems in an automated intelligent manufacturing environment in MFIF.

GLOBAL CONCURRENT QUALITY MANAGEMENT

The data communication model as already described in paragraph 2 is proposed as ideal future solutions in global and intelligent manufacturing environment. By means of a common data model and powerful communication network established among ICAD/ICAQ and all other manufacturing processes, it is possible to realise the concurrent quality management and quality assurance activities and other production activities in modern manufacturing environment and especially in a global international cooperation of collaborating SMEs., e.g. all production processes, for example design and development, process planning, manufacturing, quality assurance and quality management etc., which are traditionally carried out sequentially, can be carried out parallelly in such a system. The quality management and assurance production knowledge can be stepwise parallelly established and refined. If a modified quality activity is made in a process, a correspondent quality assurance activity change will be simultaneously carried out in all other intelligent CAx systems.

The establishment of a global information highway for simultaneous on-line exchange of production data for collaboration on the design, quality assurance and all production processes, for concurrent communication of all the system-

atization knowledges for design, manufacturing and quality assurance of global and intelligent production, and to interact with suppliers and customers worldwide will be made possible. Fu & Raja (2000) describe as example an appropriate internet based application of production metrology and ICAQ. Basic studies for that system have been carried out in the course of an international University collaboration - Steindl (1999).

A global information system has to be investigated to fulfil the global information connection in MFIF environment. The development of information highway, DCE technology and advanced engineering data exchange technique make global information systems possible. Such systems can be realised by utilising the mentioned technologies, by means of which whole collaborative, interactive and concurrent design and manufacturing processes of products in global and intelligent production environment can be achieved. STEP provides an unambiguous representation and an exchange mechanism for computer-interpretable product data throughout the whole life cycle of a product, independent from any particular system.

Through global information connection a quality assurance process could be so carried out, that during the CAD modelling the quality assurance planning, modeling, programming and simulating processes which cooperate with the customers and suppliers could also be simutaneously carried out. The design, quality assurance planning and the quality assurance programming can be carried out at one place and the quality assurance simulating, measuring and evaluating processes can concurrently be carried out at another place in the world.

FINAL STATEMENTS AND OUTLOOK TO FUTURE DEVELOPMENTS

In this contribution global competitive associations of factories as well as of collaborating SMEs have been presented as an innovative concept and a new model for manufacturing enterprises developed to meet demands for cost-effective customer-driven design and production. This concept can be used with success to realize agile and optimal global international cooperations of collaborating SMEs. The quality assurance process will be used in all product production processes in such a system - from the design stage to the final assembly. Quality management and quality assurance in individual activities of different function enterprises - big factories as well as SMEs - in such a collaboration structure play a basic role to ensurse the realisation of the concept, e.g. through the intelligent production systems based on quality management and quality assurance in the system to create, to realize and to present the features, such as, concurrent, interactive, modular, integrative, learning, autonomous, self optimising and self organising functions.

In this presentation, the intelligent quality assurance system in MFIF, an off-line programming technique for ICMM as basis for simultaneous quality assurance and an intelligent measuring cell for the flexible automation of quality assurance and management, data collection and data evaluation in multi-function integrated factory was proposed and discussed. Optoelectronic and Nanotopographic quality assurance methods and a global data communication model for the future that is investigated to realise the concurrent quality management and quality assurance activities and other production activities in MFIF, e.g. all production processes, for example design and development, process planning, manufacturing and quality assurance and management etc., which are traditionally carried out sequentially, can be parallelly carried out in MFIF in global and intelligent manufacturing environment, are introduced.

Quality management systems with intelligent, associative, concurrent, interactive, modular, integrative, learning, autonomous, self optimising and self organising functions will be realized in global international cooperations of collaborat-

ing small and medium sized enterprises in the near future.

REFERENCES

Binnig, H., & Rohrer, H. (1982). Scanning Tunnelling Microscopy. *Helv. Phys. Acta, 55,* 726–731.

Durakbasa, N. M., & Osanna, P. H. (2002). The role of co-ordinate metrology in the hierarchical structure of metrology and the system for measurement instruments confirmation. In *Proceedings of the 5th International Scientific Conference: Coordinate Measuring Machines, Bielsko-Biala, PL* (pp. 55-62).

Fu, S., & Raja, J. (2000). Internet based roundness and cylindricity analysis. In M.N. Durakbasa, P.H. Osanna, & A. Afjehi-Sadat (Eds.), *IMEKO 2000 Proceedings, Vol. VIII* (pp. 83-88).

Osanna, P. H., & Si, L. (2000). Multi-functions integrated factory mfif - a model of the future enterprise. In *Proceedings of "Internet Device Builder Conference", Sta. Clara, May 2000, 1-16.*

Si, L., & Osanna, P. H. (1995). Multi-functions integrated factory. In *Proceedings of 11th ISPE/IEEE/IFAC International Conference on CARS&FOF'95, Colombia* (pp. 578-586).

Steindl, K. G. (1999). *Development of a Software package for the internet based analysis of roundness data.* Master Thesis, TU-Wien, A, and UNC Charlotte, USA, 32-37.

Taniguchi, N. (1974). On the basic concept of nanotechnology In *Proceedings of the. Int. Conf. Prod. Eng., Tokyo: JSPE, part 2* (pp. 18-23).

Whitehouse, D.J. (1991). Nanotechnology Instrumentation. *Measurement + Control, 24* (2), 37-46.

Whitehouse, D. J. (2002). Surface and Nanometrology, Markov and Fractal Scale of Size Properties. In Y.V. Chugui, S.N. Bagayev, A. Weckenmann, & P.H. Osanna (Eds.), *Proceedings of 7th International Symposium on "Laser Metrology Applied to Science, Industry and Everyday Life - LM-2002", Nowosibirsk, Russia* (pp. 691-707).

Section 2
Supporting Technologies and Tools

Chapter 11
Software for Small-to-Medium Enterprises

Jaroslav Král
Charles University, Czech Republic and Masaryk University, Czech Republic

Michal Žemlička
Charles University, Czech Republic

ABSTRACT

Small-to-medium enterprises (SME) have specific requirements on the software systems (SWS) they use. SME have a limited possibility to design stable business processes as they have limited resources and data to design the processes properly. Moreover, SME must be able to adapt itself dynamically to changing business conditions and must, due to limited resources, reuse legacy systems and third-party products. SME cannot apply the higher levels of CMM and to define precisely its business processes, as SME cannot have enough data and experience. The solution of this issue or weakening of its consequences can be based on the variant of service-oriented architecture (SOA) discussed next. A proper use of modern software systems depends on the skills and knowledge of (end) users of the systems. The extent of a new software-oriented knowledge of the users needed to specify, install, and use the systems depends on the architecture of the system. We further show that a properly used SOA can substantially reduce the need to learn new knowledge at users' side. The kernel of the solution should be based on the SOA-based generalization of the concept of usability and on a technical turn enabling agility of business processes. The solution can simplify the development of tools enabling the activation of inhibited user knowledge via flexible prototyping supporting agile business processes and learning by doing. The solution further enables new business turns and has many technical advantages. Our solution is especially preferable for small-to-medium enterprises, but it should be applied in very large enterprises for different reasons.

DOI: 10.4018/978-1-60566-892-5.ch011

INTRODUCTION

Small to medium enterprises (SME) are strongly influenced by global challenges and business conditions changes. SME is rather an object than a subject of the business challenges. Any SME must be – due to its size and consequently due to its openness – even more dynamic than large enterprises. SME have insufficient resources to update or develop their software resources from scratch. Under these conditions the necessary preconditions of success is a proper reuse of software systems.

Software systems supporting SME must support the dynamics of modern business. It follows that such software must itself be open and dynamically changeable. A classical solution was a quick development of new software editions or updates. Growing complexity of software systems makes such a solution continuously less feasible. This problem is especially severe for SME due the following reasons:

1. SME have not enough resources and IT experts to apply repeated software development from scratch or quick software enhancement.
2. It can be too difficult for SME employees to use quickly changing systems.
3. It is difficult for SME to develop reliable and stable business processes. SME have not enough business data to design repeatable or even optimized processes in the sense of CMM. The business processes must be often even on-the-fly changed due to changed outer business conditions.
4. SME have a limited possibility to apply fully the complex software standards like the standards of IEEE, ISO, W3C, or OASIS (OASIS, 2008) and complex considerations like the ones from special issues of IBM Systems Journal (IBM, 2005 and 20082008). The complexity of the standards can be one of the substantial reasons of falling interests

of the new SOA developments (Sholler, 2008). SME need, however, not apply complex standards provided they apply a proper pragmatic based on the fact that SME can use small systems and are unable to use the huge ones.

The only feasible solution of these challenges is the (re)use of legacy systems, integrate them together and with (purchased) third-party systems to obtain a system providing a new quality. It is a crucial issue for SME.

Service orientation (SO) and service-oriented architecture (SOA; Erl, 2004) offer a framework for doing it. We, however, must apply specific techniques that are applicable in SME; it is a specific version of SOA – a subclass of confederations (Král & Žemlička, 2003a, 2003b). Confederations are SOA having core subnetwork of services knowing each other. In SME the core consists of quite small number of services being almost independent. It leads to solutions not involving Enterprise Service Bus (ESB; Chappell, 2004). We call such systems *unions* for short[1]. Note that unions are in fact broadly used outside SME, for example in e-government, municipal systems, or health-care systems. SME often pragmatically use techniques used in SOA but they are afraid to apply highly-standardized SOA in the form supported by large software vendors.

SOA SYSTEMS FOR SME

The problems listed above can be solved if we integrate applications such that the resulting system has the service-oriented architecture of the following properties: SOA use wrapped legacy systems, third-party systems, and, may be, newly developed applications such that they can behave like real-world services, i.e. such that technically they can be peers of a virtual peer-to-peer (p2p) network. The middleware of such a network can be based on different tools or frameworks – Enterprise Service Bus, www, or other transport means. The tools can be combined. In unions the ESB-based solutions are rarely used. A small number of core services in SOA supporting SME reduces the need for ESB.

The systems can be integrated together with their client tiers, if any. It is desirable (often necessary) to integrate the systems as wrapped black boxes such that they are equipped by a new interface (tier, adaptor) enabling communication with other peers being applications or even systems. Such a solution enables it that the "old" users of the systems, if any, are not too influenced by the fact that "their" systems have been already integrated.

The number of core applications or systems is usually quite small. As obviously the systems influence business the behavior of them must be well understood by users (i.e. businessmen).

It – together with above discussed facts – implies that the kernel of the integrated system must be a not too large group of components knowing each other. In such a group communication protocols and formats can be "agreed" if necessary. It opens the way not to use expensive tools like ESB and complex standards.

The crucial design pattern in such SOA systems (unions) applied in SME but also in e-government and so on is the (re)use of existing systems and the possibility to choose or design the formats of the messages used by the service interfaces. It gives the possibility to design the interfaces to be "usable" by other (sub)systems and by users. It generalizes the common concept of usability (Nielsen, 1993 and 1999, Nielsen 1999 and Loranger 2006, Leventhal and Barness, 2008, Král & Žemlička, 2007d).

USABLE INTERFACES IN GENERALIZED SENSE AND SME

The development and the use of modern information systems depend on knowledge of user knowledge domains and on IT knowledge. The processes of knowledge gaining, combining, and using can be difficult, time consuming, and expensive. They require specific abilities and usually inclusive user involvement. The development process must be therefore "user friendly" or agile, i.e. it must have properties enabling/simplifying the user involvement.

An example of the solution of the problem is the principles of agile programming (Beck et al., 2001, Beck, 1999). The principles of agile programming can be fully applied during the development of non-critical applications of moderate size only.

Modern business processes, especially the processes in SME must have specific properties:

1. They must admit "supervision" by responsible businessmen – "process owners". This principle should be always applied in business supporting systems.
2. They are subject of frequent changes due to outside turbulences and the fact that solutions in SME are rarely repeated. Such turbulences are for SME difficult to predict and change. SME must therefore adapt to the changes and to new task types quickly.
3. The processes are in principle based on a very limited set of data (SME has a limited number of business cases). As such they must be adaptable, i.e. they can be used in agile way using intuition. There is a limited space for the methods proposed by CMM or CMMI.
4. The process must be able to use third-party products and legacy systems.

To summarize: The development and use of software systems in SME suffers by lack of data and knowledge, lack of properly trained experts[2], limited resources, sometimes also by deficiencies in management. It is known to be a common problem of software development but in SME it is more severe. We will see that the solution can be software having a specific variant of service-oriented

Figure 1. Portal SOA

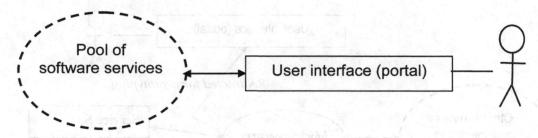

architecture (SOA) – software confederations (Král & Žemlička, 2003a, Král et al., 2006). Systems having SOA are (virtual) peer-to-peer (p2p) networks where peers are autonomous software components implementing permanently active processes called services. As peers in a p2p network the services must be able to communicate asynchronously. Synchronous communication is also possible but usually not preferable or even not applicable. We attempt to show that the solution can be SOA based on a generalization of usability (Nielsen, 1993) supporting (re)use of legacy systems and third-party products.

UNIONS IN SME

Small or middle-sized enterprises usually have a limited number of business partners. They use a limited set of operations. The partners tend to be local. The majority of the partners are known for a longer period of time and the partners are often SME too. SME's consists of a limited number of constituent autonomous organizational units and use a limited number of autonomous legacy systems, third party software products, and can afford (modernize or update, i.e. purchase or develop) a very limited number of large software units at a time. It implies that the communication partners of services "are known", i.e. they need not be looked for possibly all over the world before a communication with them is to be started using tools like UDDI (UDDI Initiative, 2003).

Note further that the communication partners must be acceptable for the businessmen responsible for business processes (business process owners). It implies that the communication with the partners must be transparent and well understood for the owners.

All these conditions taken together imply that the communication protocols can be as a rule agreed using proprietary ad hoc standards, if necessary. The protocols can be and should be based on coarse-grained messages inspired by the interfaces of real-world services. In many cases the communication is powered by a system portal. The system then can be viewed as portal commanding a pool of services (Figure 1). Such architecture is called *portal SOA*.

Coarse grained interfaces have substantial technical (Cohen, 2003) as well as practical advantages (Král & Žemlička, 2007b). We say that the services have user-oriented or usable interfaces. An issue is that such protocols have a little chance to be (properly) standardized – at least for the time being. As mentioned above, it is no crucial drawback (compare (Král & Žemlička, 2007b)).

We can therefore assume that information system supporting SME is a union and that the messages communicated among services are user oriented. The applications can be integrated with their client tiers. The systems are not too large, so the service governance is a quite simple task. The development of a SOA system should benefit from it to have any chance to succeed. A pragmatic

Figure 2. Prototyping in SOA. The prototype can be used as temporal replacement of S.

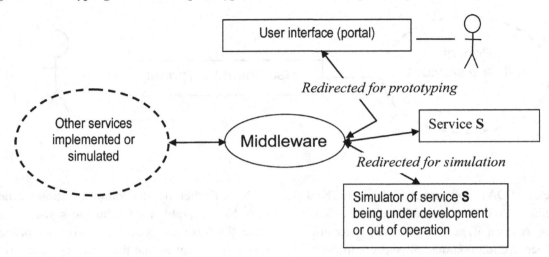

implementation of union at SME taking properly into consideration that the union is not too large can avoid the problems that people at SME have not enough SOA-related expertise. Under such conditions the need to study thick standards and books like (Bell, 2008, Earl, 2004 and 2008) is not ultimate.

PROTOTYPES AND INHIBITED OR NOT ACHIEVABLE KNOWLEDGE

One of crucial issues of the development of information systems is the problem of inhibited or not accessible knowledge at users' side and the problem of its activation (Král & Žemlička, 2004). The knowledge can be activated using software prototyping. The prototype is used to simulate real-world situations.

Using modern method of communication of software services based on e.g. SOAP-message encoding (W3 Consortium, 2000) and modern browsers we can get mock-up prototypes of software services by redirecting the SOAP messages to the user interface of the system, e.g. to a browser (Král & Žemlička, 2004), see also Figure 2.

Such a method is especially effective of the messages have format mirroring real-world communication of humans (i.e. of real-world services). Such messages are then well understood by users. We say that they are user-oriented (UO). UO messages are coarse grained and from IT (or programming languages) point of view declarative – stating rather what to do than how to do it. UO service interfaces have many functional as well as technical advantages. Properly designed UO substantially simplifies prototyping. It is based on stable user domain languages. It hides implementation details. It is preferable for the activation of user knowledge. It can even be used to train users to use the system and to apply effective development process.

Using a specific service and the possibility to save the value of system clock it is possible to test response times in real-time systems (Král & Žemlička, 2004). The proposed solution further enables to test middleware, message formats, and service interfaces. The prototypes can be used as a replacement of failed (temporarily out of operation) services during the system use. It is good to use a log system producing human readable log file for future analysis. These properties can be used to develop business processes in try-and-test-result style. It admits to develop new (business) knowledge. For the development of business processes we can apply a yet more powerful solution discussed below.

AGILE BUSINESS PROCESSES

Modern business in global economy is very dynamic. The business processes must be dynamic too – i.e. they must be on-the-fly changeable. They must be agile. The extent of the agility must be usually greater at SME than in large enterprises.

1. Large enterprises have the power to influence the business processes in (global) economy. It can reduce the need to adapt frequently their behavior, business processes inclusive.
2. Large enterprises only have enough data to be able to apply higher levels of Capability Maturity Model (CMM, (SEI Institute, 2005))[3] and generally the application of sophisticated methods of mathematical statistics.
3. Small and medium firms do not have enough resources (investments, experts) to be able to develop reliable models of their business processes. A solution can be application of the processes and tools of system learning (partly as trial-and-error process). The processes/tools supporting the learning how to use the system are discussed below.
4. The business of SME vary so much that it is meanless to invest large volume of resources into the development of the models of business processes. Such models can be moreover contraproductive as they tend to reduce one of the most important advantages of SME – business flexibility and intuitive management.
5. Business processes of SME must be highly open and the requirement of agility implies that agility must be the property of the cooperation with business partners all over the world; i.e. it must be included into

SCM (Lowson et al., 1999), CRM (Dyché, 2002). It implies service oriented software architectures based on user-oriented message formats.

Agility of business processes is necessary for all enterprises. It is, however, crucial, for SME's. In SME it should be enabled even in the case when business process steps are performed by legacy systems.

INTEGRATION TOOLS FOR LEGACY SYSTEMS AND THIRD-PARTY PRODUCTS

As we have seen the limited IT resources of SME imply that SME must reuse existing software as much as possible. It implies that SME must reuse legacy systems. If there is no appropriate one a cheap system must be purchased and integrated to achieve the required capabilities of the system.

There are further reasons why integrate existing applications. The integration of legacy systems can be implemented – if made properly – so that the users of the formerly not integrated legacy systems need not even notice that the systems were integrated. The condition is that the legacy systems are integrated so that their (local) interfaces (Fig. 3) or client tiers are preserved.

The third-party services need not be suited to the user needs and SME culture. For example, SAP systems are inspired by large enterprises. Such systems need not meet the SME needs and culture. It can be one of the reasons why SAP is less successful at SME's than expected.

It is often necessary that the used system should be developed and updated incrementally.

It replaces the modernization in big-bang style being too expensive and often risky.

The incrementality can be implemented by the stepwise integration, enhancement, or replacement of legacy systems and third-party software components.

Figure 3. Integration of legacies and applications into SOA

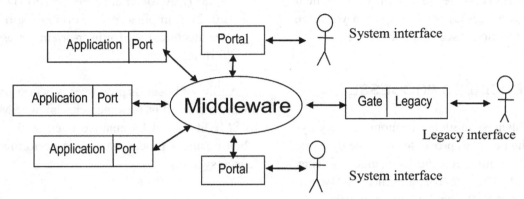

The collaboration with the systems of business partners should be very similar with the collaboration of services inside the "own" system. It has many technical advantages (Král & Žemlička, 2005, 2007a, 2007b) as well as organizational advantages as it simplifies insourcing, outsourcing, and collaboration with business partners in general. The only known way of easy implementation is the design of the system as a system having SOA, i.e. as a system being a virtual peer-to-peer system where peers are (wrapped) legacy systems, wrapped third-party products, and even information systems of organizational components.

The peers of the network collaborate via exchange of messages. We have shown that it is preferable if the messages have appropriate formats well understandable by users – if the services have usable interfaces. It implies that if SOAP is used, it should be the SOAP-message encoded variant. The messages should be coarse grained. In other words the kernel of the solution is a service-oriented system with services having usable interfaces, i.e. such SOA should be a union.

BUSINESS PROCESSES AND USER ORIENTED INTERFACES OF SERVICES

Let us now summarize the requirements on the implementation of business processes at SME:

1. The (atomic) steps of the processes are provided by software services that often are wrapped legacy systems or third-party systems.
2. Every business process must have its human supervisor (process owner) responsible for business consequences of the process and able to modify the process.
3. The software services can have client tiers, if appropriate. Legacy systems can retain their original (local) user interfaces or whole client tiers besides the interfaces allowing them to communicate directly with other software services.
4. There should be tools enabling flexible integration of software services into business processes.
5. It should be possible to group the services easily into composite services.
6. Business processes can be composed into composite processes.

Figure 4. SOA with service adapters implemented as Front End Gates (F).

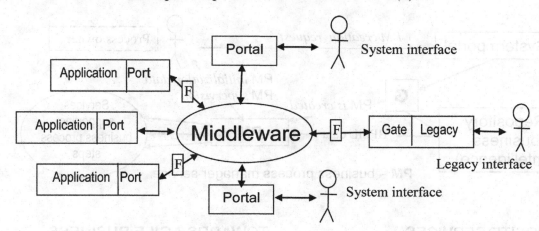

The technical solution can be following: The services to be integrated are equipped by a port (gate) satisfying above conditions. It has the drawback that the implementation requires substantial change of the service source code. It need not be the case. Even if the source code of the service is available, the code changes can be dangerous and expensive.

In the case when a legacy system has client-server architecture (or a three-tier one) it is not difficult to redirect the messages between client and server tiers. In many cases the involved applications have programmer-oriented interfaces instead. Such interfaces will probably have no satisfactory properties – it will be fine-grained, often RPC (remote procedure call) oriented. It is not user oriented (usable).

In this case we can use the tools like XSLT engine for transforming the messages into user-oriented (usable) ones. We have two possibilities – integrate the engine as API or to include it into a newly created service (front-end gate, FEG) working as a service adapter (see Fig. 4). The second solution is more flexible. A service can have none, one, or more FEG's – each serving different group of communication partners. A slight generalization of FEG can provide a tool for service composition. Logically FEG is a newly developed service (white box) standing between

a legacy system and the rest of the system. The tools like XSLT can be used for FEG development in some cases.

FEG is a service having specific properties:

- it is usually developed from scratch;
- it facilitates the collaboration of other services;
- it provides no basic business operations.

We call services having such property *architecture services* (ArS). Unions are SOA formed by architecture services integrating *application services* (ApS). Application services are often reused legacy systems.

Figure 4 gives the logical view of the system with adapters. Physically the messages (service requests) are sent using middleware services to some FEG and the FEG sends them (after some transformation) via middleware to their target services (Figure 4).

The architecture services can provide information for enterprise managers in the form legible for them. It can be used for the flexible supervision of enterprise activities as a logging tool and as a source of data for the long-term analysis of enterprise behavouour.

Figure 5. Implementation of agile business processes.

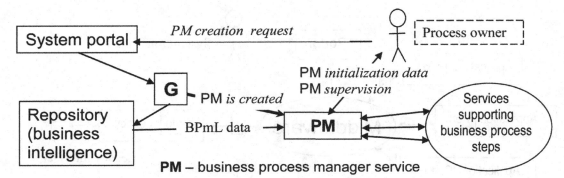

COMPOSITE SERVICES

FEG has one distinguished service for which it is an adapter. The concept of FEG can be generalized so that there are several distinguished services hidden behind the gate. It can be used to build composite services. We call the generalized front-end gates service heads. More formally:

A service H is the head of a composite service C consisting of H and services S_1, S_2, ..., S_k if any message from any service S different from S_1, S_2, ..., S_k, and H to any service S_1, S_2, ..., S_k must pass H and any message from any service S_1, S_2, ..., S_k to S must also pass H.

The head H can be from S viewed as a service having the capabilities of all the services S_1, S_2, ..., S_k. It opens the possibility to build composite services composed from composite services. We can generalize the concept of the head of composite service so that a group of services can have several heads. Each head then behaves like a specific peer – portal of the composite service. Such feature can be useful for specific groups of communication partners (compare the case of multiple FEG's supporting single service). H is jet another example of an architecture service.

TOWARDS AGILE BUSINESS PROCESSES

The implementation principles discussed above enables us to assume that the integrated services have usable interfaces. An agile business process P is in our proposal represented by:

1. A business process engine called Process Manager *PM*. *PM* is a service providing a user interface to human beings (process owners) responsible for the process P, i.e. *PM* has some features of the portal for P – see Figure 5.

2. *PM* can use a control structure S that defines the business process P. S can be defined using the form of textual information. It can be written e.g. in BPEL (Andrews et al., 2003).

3. S is interpreted and *PM* sends messages to the services. The process owner can agree or modify the process steps, delete or add them. If necessary, S can be empty and then the process owner must explicitly state the service requirements corresponding to business steps.

4. *PM* uses a data store to log the communication traffic. The logs can be used to construct business process models.

The process manager *PM* with the control structure *S* is generated using business intelligence data – i.e. data on processes that have been already enacted, their business effects and business process models (e.g. in BPML or in some more informal language(s)).

P is initiated (see Figure 4; compare (Král & Žemlička, 2005) in the following way:

1. The process manager *PM* for *P* with empty control structure *S* is generated on the request of process owner *O*. The request is addressed via system portal to a service *G* able to generate *PM*.
2. *G* generates *PM* and provides *O* with an interface to *PM*.
3. *O* with the help of *G* using a business intelligence data repository updates *S*, if required. If a business process model is used, the model is firstly updated and then transformed into *S* using business data (like numbers of products, scheduling, responsibilities, and assigned resources). Note that process model is chosen under (possible) supervision of process owner *O*.
4. *PM* in cooperation with *O* using *S*, if it is not empty, generates messages (commands) for the messages providing the actions of the process steps.

As *PM* is a service the process of its generation and use can be easily generalized. *PM* can be generated on a request of another process manager (or its owner) and then used. *PM* together with the services it communicates with form a virtual portal of the SOA subsystem implementing the business process. Note that usable interfaces are of crucial importance here.

Different strategies determining who is the owner of the nested (called) process can be used. It is an issue for a further study.

UNIONS IN LARGE ENTERPRISES

The properties of unions are preferable for SME. They are preferable for large enterprises as well. The reasons are, however, partly different. Large enterprises have more sources and are less influenced by outer business conditions. They still must, however, require their businessmen to be responsible for business processes they own. Their businessmen must be therefore able to supervise the processes and to modify them in an agile way. Otherwise no responsibility is possible.

It implies that the software services should have usable interfaces. This requirement is not ultimate but it is quite strong as otherwise tit can be difficult to require the responsibility of the process owners for business effects of the processes they supervise.

Large enterprises have more resources to re-develop or to buy whole systems. But there are strong reasons why it is usually not feasible. It is in fact practically impossible. Such big-bang changes are too time consuming and they imply too great burden to system users.

There are yet more important problems. Large human organizations acquire or sell their organizational units. Fusions of enterprises are not exceptional. The organizations sometimes must or see advantageous to outsource some activities and to in source others. In this case it is crucial not to disclose too much about the enterprise and its information system(s) or business during outsourcing or selling. User-oriented coarse grained message formats enable it.

These problems can be solved if large pieces of software, e.g. information systems of integrated organizations or organizational units (e.g. of particular offices during the development of e-government) are integrated. Involved software components should/must be integrated "as such" and as black boxes – often together with their "native" user interfaces. The process owner must supervise their processes and occasionally use agile attitude. So the kernel of the software system of such organization must have properties quite similar to the kernel of software supporting SME. The main difference is that the integrated software artifacts of large organizations tend to be very large and agility is to a lesser extent necessary.

CONCLUSION

Service orientation is often denounced to be a buzzword intended to hidden the fact that it is only a packet of old often obsolete practices in a new packaging. It is mainly due to fact that there are different variants of service-oriented architectures (SOA) and different technical ways of SOA implementation. Different SOA variants and different implementations are good for different purposes. We believe a pragmatic application of attitudes known from SOA is a great challenge as well as a great promise for SME. It allows putting long existing practices on a solid base. It moreover simplifies the enhancement of the systems being in use for a long time and to apply new software business philosophies like SaaS (software as a service).

Principles of SOA in the form discussed above (unions) are quite simple and understandable in principle as they mirror real-world life. Unions are only one variant of confederations, though broadly used. Unions are not good for hard real time process control, for pure e-commerce, etc. Unions in SME enable to tune and enhance the service integration practices currently used in a "catch-as-you-can" style.

It does not imply that unions are simple from technical, management, and marketing point of view. The problem is that people, especially software developers, are mainly trained to act according to object-oriented philosophy inducing sometimes the application of object-oriented design patterns being antipatterns in service-oriented environment. An example is the ban to reuse of legacy systems. There are different marketing politics of software vendors. Under these conditions the application of the above mentioned techniques in not easy to start with. It is, however, a good way to meet the challenges of dynamic global turbulent business and to develop extreme large systems.

ACKNOWLEDGMENT

This research was partially supported by the Program "Information Society" under project 1ET100300517 and by the Grant Agency of Czech Republic under the project 201/09/0983.

REFERENCES

W3 Consortium. (2000). *Simple object access protocol. A proposal of W3 Consortium*. Retrieved from http://www.w3.org/TR/SOAP

Andrews, T., Curbera, F., Dholakia, H., Goland, Y., Klein, J., Leymann, F., et al. (2003). *Specification: Business process execution language for web services version 1.1*. Retrieved January 2005 from http://www-106.ibm.com/developerworks/library/ws-bpel

Beck, K. (1999). *Extreme programming explained: Embrace change*. Boston: Addison Wesley.

Beck, K., Beedle, M., van Bennekum, A., Cockburn, A., Cunningham, W., Fowler, M., et al. (2001). *Agile programming manifesto*. Retrieved from http://www.agilemanifesto.org

Bell, M. (2008) *Service-oriented modeling: Service analysis, design, and architecture*. Hoboken, NJ, USA: John Wiley & Sons.

Chappell, D. A. (2004). *Enterprise service bus*. Cambridge, MA: O'Reilly.

Cohen, F. (2003). *Java testing and design: From unit testing to automated web tests*. Prentice Hall Publishing.

Dyché, J. (2002). *The CRM handbook: A business guide to customer relationship management.* Boston: Addison Wesley Professional.

Erl, T. (2004) *SOA – principles of service design.* Upper Saddle River, NJ: Prentice-Hall.

Erl, T. (2008) *Service-oriented architecture – A field guide to integrating XML and Web services.* Upper Saddle River, NJ, USA: Prentice-Hall.

IBM (2005). *IBM Systems Journal – Special issue on Service-Oriented Architecture, 44*(4), 651-905.

IBM (2008). *IBM Systems Journal – Special issue on SOA: From Modeling to Implementation, 47*(3), 355-473.

Institute, S. E. I. (2005). Capability maturity model, home page. A methodology of the SEI institute. Retrieved January 10, 2005 from http://www.sei.cmu.edu/cmm/cmm.html

Král, J., & Žemlička, M. (2003a). Software confederations – An architecture for global systems and global management. In S. Kamel (Ed.), *Managing globally with information technology* (pp. 57-81). Hershey, PA: Idea Group Publishing.

Král, J., & Žemlička, M. (2003b). Software confederations and alliances. In *CAiSE'03 Forum: Information Systems for a Connected Society.* Maribor, Slovenia: University of Maribor Press.

Král, J., & Žemlička, M. (2004). Service orientation and the quality indicators for software services. In R. Trappl (Ed.), *Cybernetics and Systems,* volume 2 (pp. 434-439). Vienna, Austria: Austrian Society for Cybernetic Studies.

Král, J., & Žemlička, M. (2005). Implementation of business processes in service-oriented systems. In *Proceedings of 2005 IEEE International Conference on Services Computing,* volume II (pp. 115-122). Los Alamitos, CA, USA: IEEE Computer Society.

Král, J., & Žemlička, M. (2007a). Crucial patterns in service-oriented architecture. In *Proceedings of ICDT 2007 Conference* (pp. 24). Los Alamitos, CA: IEEE CS Press.

Král, J., & Žemlička, M. (2007b). The most important service-oriented antipatterns. In *International Conference on Software Engineering Advances (ICSEA'07)* (pp. 29). Los Alamitos, CA: IEEE Computer Society.

Král, J., & Žemlička, M. (2007c). Requirements specification: What strategy under what conditions. In *Proceedings of 5th International Conference on Software Engineering Research, Management and Applications (SERA2007)* (pp. 401-408). Los Alamitos, CA: IEEE CS Press.

Král, J., & Žemlička, M. (2007d). Usability issues in service-oriented architecture. In *ICEIS 2007: Proceedings of the Ninth International Conference on Enterprise Information Systems, Volume DISI* (pp. 482-485). Setúbal, Portugal: EST Setúbal.

Král, J., & Žemlička, M. (2008). Engineering education – a great challenge to software engineering. In R. Lee (Ed.), *7th IEEE/ACIS International Conference on Computer and Information Science* (pp. 488-495). Los Alamitos, CA: IEEE Computer Society.

Král, J., Žemlička, M., & Kopecký, M. (2006). Software confederations – an architecture for agile development in the large. In P. Dini (Ed.), *International Conference on Software Engineering Advances (ICSEA'06)* (pp. 39). Los Alamitos, CA: IEEE Computer Society.

Leventhal, L., & Barnes, J. (2007) *Usability engineering. Process, products & examples.* Upper Saddle River, NJ: Prentice Hall.

Lowson, B., King, R., & Hunter, A. (1999). *Quick response: Managing the supply chain to meet consumer demand.* New York: John Wiley & Sons.

Morello, D. (2005). The IT professional outlook: Where will we go from here? Nielsen, J. (1993). *Usability engineering*. New York: Academic Press.

Nielsen, J. (1999). *Designing Web usability*. Berkley, CA: Peach Pit Press.

Nielsen, J., & Loranger, H. (2006). Prioritizing Web usability. Indianapolis, IN: New Riders Publishing.

OASIS. (2008). OASIS Standards and other approved work. Retrieved from http://www.oasis-open.org/specs

Sholler, D. (2008, September). *2008 SOA user survey: Adoption trends and characteristics*. Retrieved from http://www.gartner.com/DisplayDocument?id=765720.

UDDI Initiative. (2002-2003*). Universal definition, discovery, and integration, version 3. An industrial initiative*. Retrieved from http://www.oasis-open.org/committees/uddi-spec/doc/tc-specs.htm#uddiv3.

ENDNOTES

[1]   There are different types and different variants of SOA. This fact is the reason why there are misunderstanding regarding SO. SOA used to control a NC machine tool center or aviation of an airplane are quite different from the SOA type applied in e-commerce. Both variants are different from the SOA discussed in this paper.

[2]   Note that the experts involved in the development of information system for SME must posses a broad knowledge and be versatile – i.e. they must be able to understand quickly various knowledge domains (Morello, 2005) and some skills can be trained in real-world projects only. It is very difficult to educate such people as academia develops towards very narrow scientific specializations (Král & Žemlička, 2008).

[3]   It implies that SME can benefit substantially less from CMM than large enterprises do as they have too little data to apply statistical methods, e.g. statistical optimization, effectively. This fact having the form of a scientific rule is often overlooked.

Chapter 12
State of the Art Solutions in Enterprise Interoperability

Silke Balzert
Institute for Information Systems at German Research Center for Artificial Intelligence, Germany

Thomas Burkhart
Institute for Information Systems at German Research Center for Artificial Intelligence, Germany

Dirk Werth
Institute for Information Systems at German Research Center for Artificial Intelligence, Germany

Michal Laclavík
Institute of Informatics, Slovak Academy of Sciences, Slovakia

Martin Šeleng
Institute of Informatics, Slovak Academy of Sciences, Slovakia

Nikolay Mehandjiev
University of Manchester, UK

Martin Carpenter
University of Manchester, UK

Iain Duncan Stalker
University of Teesside, UK

ABSTRACT

More than 99% of European enterprises are SMEs. While collaboration with other enterprises provides potential for improving business performance, enterprise interoperability research has yet to produce results which can be used by SMEs without the need for high start-up costs (e.g. learning, infrastructure and installation costs). Therefore the Commius project (funded by the European Union) aims towards the development of such a "zero costs of entry" interoperability solution for SMEs, allowing them to reuse existing and familiar applications for electronic communication. This chapter provides an overview of the research field "Enterprise Interoperability." Based on a four layer interoperability framework, this

DOI: 10.4018/978-1-60566-892-5.ch012

chapter will examine which technical, process-based and semantic solutions for enterprise interoper-ability are available at the moment and which strategic motives drive or prevail SMEs to engage in E-business activities.

INTRODUCTION

The widespread use of modern Information and Communication Technologies (ICT) nowadays results in highly competitive markets. Companies of all sizes have to cope with a changing busi-ness environment, where former entry barriers are not existing any more and product and price competition increases steadily. Therefore more and more companies try to meet the challenge by concentrating on their core competencies and cooperating with other companies to complete the value chain (Wirtz & Vogt, 2003). However, before and while working together, cooperating companies have to coordinate their activities. This coordination generates costs which are to be minimised to maximise the cooperation benefit. Especially for **SMEs** (**S**mall- and **M**edium-sized **E**nterprises) with their usually very restricted financial resources it is necessary to minimise these coordination costs.

Moreover, the technology-induced global competition makes time a critical success fac-tor forcing enterprises to quickly react on new business opportunities. Therefore a concentrated effort to be always prepared to initiate or join new businesses will become a mandatory management task, going beyond the classical core competence orientation. This ability is a constitutional element of the term Interoperability, which is e.g. defined by the Institute of Electrical and Electronics Engineers as "the ability of two or more systems or components to exchange information and to use the information that has been exchanged" (IEEE, 1990).

There are several comparable definition ap-proaches of this technical kind – however, Enter-prise Interoperability is more than interoperability between technical systems. Therefore, this article begins with a definition of the term "Enterprise Interoperability", which goes beyond the technical perspective. To clarify the different perspectives, a framework will be introduced which describes the four most important aspects of Enterprise Interoperability. Based on this framework an analysis will be executed, presenting and evaluat-ing current approaches to support interoperability between enterprises with special focus on SMEs. This analysis will be supported by facts and figures from an European survey. The article closes with a summary of the results.

DEFINITION OF ENTERPRISE INTEROPERABILITY

Following the understanding of the IEEE defini-tion given in the introduction, interoperability is defined as a property of a technical system and is being strictly regarded as a technological phe-nomenon. Even though this appears to be only a partial perspective, there are several definitions that mainly describe interoperability as an aspect of technical systems (Lewerenz, 1999). From a tech-nical point of view, the main prerequisite to enable interoperability is the possibility to exchange data based on a common gateway enabling interactions (Roser, 2008). This leads to the conclusion that in this pure technical coherence, interoperability just constitutes a system feature.

The reference object of enterprise interoper-ability however is not such a technical system but rather a complex organisational system: the co-operating enterprise itself. An enterprise however can not be seen as a pure system-based object; strategic, social and market related issues have to be considered as well. Thus it becomes necessary to transfer the understanding of a mainly technical interoperability into a new business-oriented domain, which also emphasizes economic aspects of interoperability. Nevertheless, in the context of enterprise interoperability the technical understanding can be considered as the foundation on which interoperability occurs. Hence a shared base in the meaning of common standards and gateways is a crucial requirement to enterprise interoperability (Gerst & Bunduchi, 2007).

A business-orientated understanding of interoperability on the other hand consists of several aspects beyond purely technological interoperability. So enterprises are no self-contained systems with predefined gateways: the most decisive requirements to enable enterprise interoperability are less the technical circumstances than the ability of business partners to collaborate. Besides the fact that the given technical landscape must support collaboration in general, business partners furthermore need to have a common understanding why they seek a partnership.

This leads to a fundamental precondition in order to facilitate enterprise interoperability. Business partners are required to have a common goal which can only be achieved with a collaboration. From an economic point of view, this corresponds mainly in generating added value for all partners involved. Based on this pre-condition, enterprise interoperability can be summarized as follows: Enterprise Interoperability is the ability of multiple firms to perform self-coordinated division of labour within an overlapping process, based on the exchange of coherent information with the common goal of generating added value, without fundamental changes to the initial organisational, procedural and technical landscapes of an enterprise.

FRAMEWORK FOR ENTERPRISE INTEROPERABILITY

Based on the definition given above, enterprise interoperability can be decomposed into smaller concepts – more precisely, four main pillars can be identified. Strategic or Business interoperability is an organisational concept, describing if enterprises are able to interwork from a strategical point of view. It comprises questions of cultural compatibility, of the validity of a combined business model as well as of trust and human relationship between the main decision makers. Process interoperability on the other hand is a concept of control and steering. It describes the state in which the enterprise is able to steer activities within other firms or vice versa, to be partially steered by others. Therefore, process interoperability is highly related to distributed and/or modular coordination and synchronization. Application system interoperability is the founding base for operations. It comprises mechanisms and structures allowing enterprise systems to interwork, i.e. to exchange information and to process information accordingly to the (common) business purposes.

These three interoperability perspectives are linked by a fourth one, called the semantic perspective. The achievement of working collaboration partnerships and creation of added value demands more than just exchanging pure data and information. The exchanged information has to be brought into the correct context in order to successfully create a benefit for all members of a partnership. Since the Strategic, the Process as well as the Application perspective are in need of semantic information, the Semantic perspective has a comprehensive character and conducts all three other perspectives. This fragmentation of interoperability is shown in figure 1 as an interoperability framework which denotes that collaboration between enterprises takes place on each of the four interoperability layers.

Figure 1. Interoperability framework

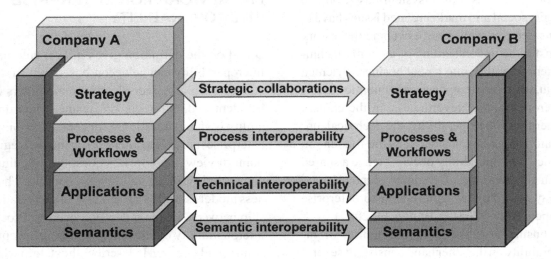

ENTERPRISE INTEROPERABILITY FORM THE STRATEGIC PERSPECTIVE

The strategic perspective of enterprise interoperability deals with a variety of management tasks, which have to be considered to ensure a successful collaboration. These management tasks comprise questions concerning the definition of common goals or the level of trust between the collaborating partners for example. These problems refer to human interactions and decisions, incorporating highly creative processes which can be hardly analysed or formalized. Furthermore, the strategic decision to take part in collaborations and the selection of possible partners usually precedes all further actions on the layers of the above mentioned interoperability framework. It can thus be regarded as a precondition for collaboration rather than an operative element in enterprise interoperability.

The scope of this analysis is not to provide information about Management Information Systems or Decision Support Systems which try to support strategic decisions, but with information concerning operational interoperability solutions supporting single, cross-organisational busi-

ness processes. Consequently, a state-of-the-art analysis concerning these strategic aspects will be omitted from the further considerations in this article. However, the reasons why companies and especially SMEs decide in favour or against a collaboration are very important for the design and acceptance of an interoperability solution. Therefore, the next two subsections deal with drivers and barriers of eBusiness from a more market-oriented point of view.

Barriers for eBusiness: the Market Point of View

SMEs feature a lot of competitive disadvantages due to their company size which could be compensated or at least diminished by cooperations. Companies directly and indirectly affected by globalization, stand a chance only if they achieve an adequate company size for example. Likewise, **LSEs (Large-Scale Enterprises)** rather have the ability to realise economies of scale than SMEs. However, according to relevant empirical studies for Germany, the strategic option "cooperation" is chosen much more infrequently by SMEs than by LSEs (Schmidt & Kiefer, 2005).

Nevertheless, the ongoing development of

Figure 2. Barriers to eBusiness (Data Source: European Commission, 2006)

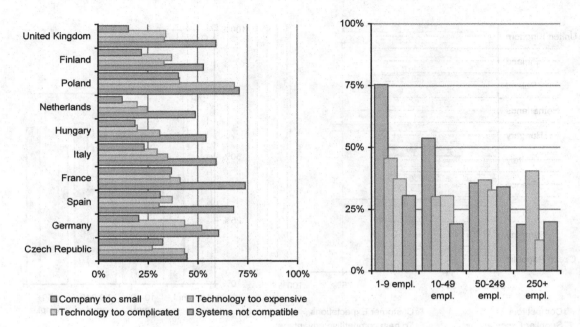

Company too small
Technology too complicated
Technology too expensive
Systems not compatible

internet technologies opens more and more ways for communication and cooperation – not only for LSEs but also for SMEs. By overcoming geographical and temporal barriers, business processes can be enlarged across company borders. Via this creation and the necessary optimisation of cross-company value-added processes, the support of these processes in every stage of the value chain by eTechnologies (which is meant by the term eBusiness) becomes an important economic factor (Kersten, Kern & Held, 2003).

Nevertheless, especially SMEs seem to be very careful and reserved when it comes to the participation in eBusiness activities. The question is, why SMEs refuse to do (at least some part of their) business electronically and which circumstances are considered as barriers for eBusiness respectively.

The majority of small companies with 49 or less employees within the European Union see their size and the corresponding lack to benefit from eBusiness as the main barrier. As shown in Figure 2, also the complexity and expensiveness of technologies underlying eBusiness transactions are regarded as obstacles. Very interesting in this context is the percentage of companies stating that the incompatibility of systems is an important reason for not practising eBusiness - more than 30 percent of micro- and medium sized companies indicated this factor as important (European Commission, 2006).

The above mentioned statements from a European survey confirm the necessity for a zero-cost-of-entry solution for SME interoperability. More than one third of the participants indicated a too expensive technology as main reason for not participating in eBusiness. Except from this cost factor, SMEs demand easy-to-implement and easy-to-use solutions for their eBusiness activities. Otherwise, if the technology is too complicated, they just refuse to use it.

Taken the statements concerning the incompatibility of systems into account, SMEs also expect a common understanding between the

Figure 3. Drivers of eBusiness (Data Source: European Commission, 2006)

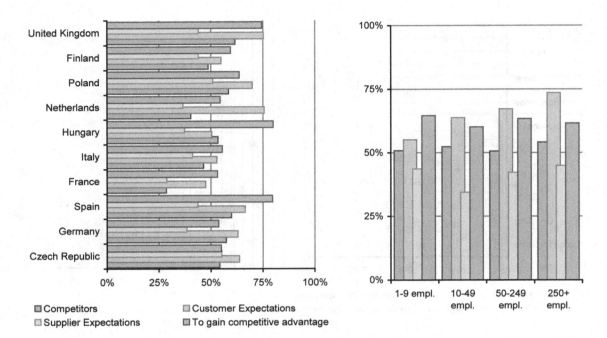

different IT systems which support the eBusiness transactions. Therefore an approach which provides an easy-to-use solution based on existing ICT infrastructure of eMail and Web could be very promising to overcome the main barriers of eBusiness described above.

Drivers of eBusiness: the Market Point of View

Besides of the noticed barriers, it is also interesting to examine which are the motives driving companies to engage in eBusiness. As shown in Figure 3, the majority of enterprises in the European Union either tries to fulfil customer expectations or gain competitive advantage with eBusiness activities. Appropriate to the latter case, many companies also react to eBusiness activities of other market participants by establishing corresponding own activities.

The main intention behind this behaviour is probably to avoid falling behind potential or actual competitors. Last but not least, the expectations of suppliers are another important reason why European enterprises of all sizes engage in eBusiness (European Commission, 2006).

However, a remarkable point is the percentage of companies stating competition as reason for engaging in eBusiness because it does not significantly vary between different company sizes: from the smallest to the largest size range, the percentage remains around 50%. Competitive reasons are realised as a driver for eBusiness to nearly the same extent among small, medium-sized and large companies for example (European Commission, 2006), which is evidence for the assumption that not only globally active LSEs but also SMEs have to cope with increased competition in their markets.

Given this information it can be assessed that the pressure to establish collaboration partnerships between European SMEs is growing and a system which easily supports ebusiness collaboration at low costs would fulfil exactly this market driven need.

ENTERPRISE INTEROPERABILITY WITH FOCUS ON BUSINESS PROCESSES

After the consideration of several motives which drive or prevail enterprises to engage in eBusiness activities, the objective of the following sections is to provide an analysis of relevant commercially oriented approaches in the field of process interoperability. This issue concerns Frameworks, standards, languages and some specific ERP solutions developed by SAP AG. The determined approaches within this section have been preselected based on their use for the Commius project, hence the list is not exhaustive. In order to sufficiently evaluate the different approaches and their usability for an SME interoperability solution, the following five characteristics with different occurrences have been developed:

Startup-Costs: Comprises costs to establish a technology or standard, etc. A solution for SMEs forces an easy interoperability approach with low start-up costs, which is the reason for the analysis of this requirement.

Running Costs: Most SMEs might not be able to afford expensive interoperability solution with high running costs, which is the reason to consider this factor as well.

In both of the characteristics mentioned above, a high compliance in this coherence means very low start-up costs or running costs, while a lower rating implicates that a huge amount of monetary resources has to be invested to either start or run the solution.

Implementation effort: European SMEs usually do not possess sophisticated IT-systems and also do not employ IT-experts. Hence, an interoperability approach especially for SMEs needs to be tailored to these necessities. Approaches which are easy to implement will receive high ratings in this category accordingly.

Direct use for an SME interoperability solution: In this category, the analysis is focussed to the question whether an approach might be of direct use for an interoperability solution fulfilling the special needs of SMEs. Following this idea, a high rating stands for high usability for such a solution.

Conceptual input for an SME interoperability solution: Additionally to their direct use, it will also be analysed to what degree the different approaches might be used as a conceptual input for a SME interoperability solution. High ratings stand for concepts which should be highlighted more closely while low ratings show that the reviewed concepts are too far away from the basic idea to satisfy further research in the field of SME interoperability.

Each approach will be assessed by three occurrences. Solutions which exhibit attributes of high relevance for a SME interoperability solution will receive high ratings. For example, solutions applicable with low costs will be rated high since this characteristic is of high relevance for SMEs. Should only parts of a reviewed approach be of use for a solution, only average ratings will be awarded – this would be the case if only concepts could be adapted for example. Finally, solutions which are not adaptive for SME interoperability, e.g. due to very high start-up costs, will be classified as not applicable. The evaluation will symbolized using the notation given in the Table 1.

The UN/CEFACT Business Collaboration Framework

One of the major achievements of UN/CEFACT, the Geneva based Centre for Trade Facilitation and Electronic Business sponsored by the United Nations, is the so called Business Collaboration Framework (BCF). It allows for business process models to be specified independently from technologies or standards as well as their implementation in software using the information exchange syntax and structures of choice.

The primary goal of the BCF is to systematically capture business and administrative process knowledge which will enable the development of

Table 1. Overview notation

●	High relevance for SME interoperability solution
◉	Partly relevant for SME interoperability solution
○	Not applicable for SME interoperability solution

low cost software components for SMEs adopting eBusiness practices. By first focusing on defining the business process and information models, the BCF itself is technology-neutral. However, it facilitates eBusiness implementations based on the technology of choice (i.e. XML/EDI based). The BCF mainly consists of four steps (United Nations Centre for Trade Facilitation and Electronic Business, 2008):

- **Knowledge Transfer:** based on UMM (UN/CEFACT Modelling Methodology) worksheets, relevant business processes, objectives, requirements and constraints can be identified and analysed.
- **Create the Business Model:** based on the information of the *Knowledge Transfer* step, a Business Collaboration Model can be created, which will still be technology and implementation neutral. Once business models are created, they are stored in BCF Libraries which can be used as a repository for further models. Additionally, a Core Component Library (which consists of industry proven information) may be used as a reference for the Business Collaboration Model.
- **Transform to Business Model:** the developed model above reflects all requirements which have to be implemented on the one hand, but on the other hand it is not specific enough to be directly implemented. Therefore, a Business Collaboration Specification Schema (BCSS) is being used to transform the model into a (still technology neutral) form which can be implemented easily.

- **Implement the Business Model:** in this fourth stage specific technologies are applied on the created business model in order to implement the model for its final concrete use.

The BCF provides a foundation, on which business models can be developed independently from the applied technologies. In this way, a proprietary solution matching exactly the collaboration partner's needs can be established. Even though the BCF and the BCSS provide enormous support in establishing eBusiness collaborations, such solutions will always be combined with high startup-costs. Furthermore, BCF solutions make use of already existing, often expensive software and hardware in order to enable interoperability – an infrastructure which is inexistent in most SMEs. Nevertheless the idea of the Core Component Library as well as the BCF Libraries could be used as a template for a Reference Model Directory within a SME interoperability solution in which adaptable standard processes are being stored. The four steps of the BCF which create a running process could be also considered as a raw model for the deployment of process templates dealing with cross-organisational business processes.

WFMC

The Workflow Management Coalition (Workflow Management Coalition, 2008), founded in 1983 is a non-profit, international organization of workflow vendors, users, analysts and university/research groups. The Coalition aims at promoting and developing the use of workflows by establishing standards for software terminology, interoperability and connectivity between workflow products. Besides the known ERP solutions, many workflow products exist such as FlowMark (IBM), Lotus Notes (IBM/Lotus), Ad hoc or WorkMAN (reach software).

A Workflow Management System provides procedural automation of a business process by management of the sequence of work activities and the invocation of appropriate human and/ or IT resources associated with the various activity steps. At the highest level, all WFM systems may be characterized as providing support in three functional areas:

- the *build-time functions* concerned with defining and possibly modelling the workflow process and its constituent activities
- the *run-time control functions* concerned with managing the workflow processes in an operational environment and sequencing the various activities to be handled as part of each process
- the *run-time interactions* with human users and IT application tools for processing the various activity steps.

The most important work done by the WFMC is the development of the Workflow Reference Model, which identifies individual characteristics, terminologies and components and thereby allows to build a workflow management system based on this specifications within the framework of an overall reference model. Furthermore, the WFMC introduced XPDL (XML Process Definition Language) which is the language proposed by the WFMC for interchange process definition between workflow system, process definition repositories and business processing modelling tools.

Workflow Management Systems exhibit many similar characteristics with SME interoperability solutions. Given the three main characteristics of a WFMS listed above, all of them could be used in an interoperability solution. During build-time, processes can be customized and adapted, while during run-time, the defined processes can be executed, triggered either by human or by machine, based on the determined sequence and the requirements of the process. Despite the usually high costs of workflow management systems, which are not affordable for most SMEs, the concept of WFMS in general and the Workflow Reference Model in particular offer a high value of benefit and thus should be considered notably when developing a SME interoperability solution.

RosettaNet

RosettaNet (RosettaNet, 2008) is a non-profit consortium of more than 400 of the world's leading Information Technology (IT), Electronic Components (EC), Semiconductor Manufacturing (SM) and Solution Provider (SP) companies working to create, implement and promote open eBusiness process standards. It aims at overcoming technology barriers due to specific infrastructures by creating common standard processes for the electronic sharing of business information. Since the RosettaNet standards have been developed in collaboration with leading high-tech companies, they are mainly market driven.

RosettaNet standards offer a robust non-proprietary solution, encompassing data dictionaries, an implementation framework, and XML-based business message schemas and process specifications for eBusiness standardisation. These public standards are mainly aiming at connecting existing solutions by providing data formats and implementing tools in order to support eBusiness based on existing solutions. The RosettaNet standards include three major components: Partner Interface Processes (PIPs), the RosettaNet dictionaries and the RosettaNet Implementation Framework.

Since the RosettaNet consortium aims at enabling collaboration between different technical solutions rather than developing a proprietary standard, the idea of RosettaNet is highly relevant for an SME interoperability solution. However, besides the conceptual ideas, RosettaNet does not exhibit characteristics which are of special use for SMEs. Moreover, current RosettaNet solutions are mostly implemented within ERP solutions, for example from SAP, Seeburger or Oracle, which mainly address LSEs. So at present, the use of RosettaNet comes along with high start-up and operating costs.

ebXML

ebXML (Electronic Business Extensible Markup Language) (ebXML Website, 2008) is a modular set of specifications, enabling businesses of any size and location to collaborate over the internet. The vision of ebXML is to establish a foundation for a global electronic marketplace in which enterprises can safely and securely conduct business through the exchange of XML-based messages. Therefore its major goal is the standardization of the secure exchange of business data using XML. The language was initiated by UN/CEFACT and OASIS with the idea to provide:

- an infrastructure which ensures data communication interoperability
- a semantics framework which ensures commercial interoperability
- a mechanism which allows enterprises to find each other.

ebXML basically consists of four major parts: an ebXML Technical Architecture Specification, a Business Process Specification Schema which is basically a XML-Schema for business processes, a Registry Services Specification and a Registry Information Model.

Unlike other standards and interoperability solutions, ebXML especially addresses collaboration partners of smaller size. Additionally, since ebXML is a widespread known standard, its use can have a positive impact on the implementation effort of an SME interoperability solution.

UN/EDIFACT

UN/EDIFACT (Electronic Data Interchange For Administration/Commerce and Transport) is an international EDI standard developed by the United Nations Centre for Trade Facilitation and Electronic Business (UN/CEFACT) (United Nations Centre for Trade Facilitation and Electronic Business, 2008). EDIFACT is kind of an opposing standard to all XML-based interoperability standards and issues the same information in much (up to 10 times) smaller messages. To allow an interchange between EDIFACT and XML standards, XML/EDIFACT was developed to allow EDIFACT to be used with XML-systems. It is currently used for example in Microsoft BizTalk.

Especially the connectivity feature of XML- and EDI- based systems is of high interest for an SME interoperability solution. Since such a solution should aim at enabling interoperability for all applicant SME collaboration scenarios, XML/EDIFACT could be an archetype in order to enable interoperability between partners of which one is already using a determined technology.

BPMN and EPC

The standard Business Process Modeling Notation (BPMN) was developed by the Business Process Management Initiative (BPMI). The primary goal of the BPMN effort was to provide a notation which is readily understandable by all business users, from business analysts creating the initial drafts of the processes and technical developers responsible for implementing the technology performing those processes, up to businessmen managing and monitoring those processes. Since the focus of BPMN is on the notational elements, it also supports an internal model enabling the user to create executable BPEL4WS on base of the created BPMNs.

Core part of BPMN is the Business Process Diagram (BPD), which is based on a flowcharting technique specific to create graphical models of business processes. The notation contains four main notational element categories: flow object, artefacts, swimlanes and connecting objects. These elements may be used to model internal processes as well as B2B collaborations in cross-organisational interoperability scenarios (White, 2008).

The EPC (Event driven Process Chain) has especially established itself for the construction of process models at a conceptual level. It basically consists of an alternating sequence of events and functions which are triggered by each other. At present the EPC is one of the most popular and widely-accepted modelling method for business processes. It was developed at the Institute for Information Systems (IWi) in Saarbruecken in cooperation with the SAP AG (Keller, Nüttgens & Scheer, 1992) and is the central modelling language for the architecture of integrated information systems (ARIS). Owing to its application orientation and comprehensive tool support, it is widely used and accepted in practice. An extension of this modelling method to satisfy SMEs requirements within collaborative business scenarios has been elaborated within several projects.

Both languages should be considered for an SME interoperability solution, since both are easy to use modelling languages which can be used to align process templates for example. BPMN can give some insight in how business models have to be described in order to transform them later on into executable processes based on the BPD concept. The EPC on the other hand is a possible foundation for a drag and drop process customization tool due to its ease of use.

BPEL

The Business Process Execution Language (BPEL) was first conceived in 2002 as a joint effort by IBM, Microsoft and BEA. BPEL is an XML based language used to specify automated business processes that orchestrate the activities of multiple Web Services (Afshar et al., 2004).

Those implemented processes can be interpreted and executed by compliant engines. The language itself encompasses methods to specify complex process control flows, including error-handling, compensation behaviour and parallel or sequential process flows. A BPEL process itself is a container where relationships can be declared within external partners, process data, handlers for various situations and most importantly, executable actions.

BPEL itself only focuses on business processes executed by Web Services, not incorporating any human interactions. To solve this problem, the BEPL extension BPEL4People was developed. This extension allows for the participation of people in a BEPL process from the simple "approval" up to complex actions like the input of data.

The fundamental idea of BPEL seems quite applicable for an SME interoperability solution, since the idea of process containers which can be specified to any collaboration scenario offer flexibility. Even though the idea aims at the same direction, BPEL is only applicable for LSEs, since currently the use of BPEL engines and corresponding processing tools premises expensive technologies, like for example ERP-systems. Nevertheless, especially the idea of BPEL4People could be of high use in the conceptual phase of an SME interoperability solution. Since some business processes could be human triggered through link enhanced emails, the BPEL4People concept could be used as a foundation for processes which are not fully automated. Similar to ebXML, BPEL is widely known which implies its usage could have a positive impact on the implementation effort.

ERP Solutions

SAP Business Connector

The SAP Business Connector is an internet- and XML-based technology to provide a link between SAP/R3 systems and other applications, enabling businesses with heterogeneous IT infrastructure to employ internet technologies to interchange business data. Business Connector requires no proprietary software as it is completely based on open technologies like XML and HTTP (Enterprise Resource Planning Portal, 2008).

Application Link Enabling

Application Link Enabling (ALE) is an interface integrated in SAP/R3 Release, which allows the linking of distributed application like other R3, R2 instances or third party application systems.

SAP Business Workflow

SAP Business Workflow, a production workflow system which is based on R/3 offers standard workflow templates delivered by SAP, which can be used out-of-the-box or can be customized until it matches the customers needs and can be seamless integrated into SAP systems (SAP Business Workflow, 2008).

Although the three solutions above postulate expensive ERP-systems, they feature interesting concepts and approaches disposable for an SME interoperability solution. In particular the extensive connection functionalities of the Business Connector and the customizable workflow templates of the Business Workflow system are promising approaches.

Overview and Summary

Table 2 gives an overview of the results of the analysis done in this section. As shown in the passages above, a huge amount of commercial endeavours have been made on the market. Besides the fact, that tremendous amounts of knowledge, relevant for a special SME interoperability solution might be extracted from other interoperability solutions, the analysis pointed out one important fact. The current situation is mainly embossed by interoperability solutions matching the needs

of LSEs. Hardly any of the introduced solutions was developed for or tailored to the needs of SMEs. Accordingly, solutions which support either intra-organisational or inter-organisational business processes are mostly used by LSEs. To substantiate this statement, the next two subsections will clarify the situation with facts & figures from the European Union.

Support of Intra-Organisational Processes

One of the most extensive application to support internal business processes is an ERP software system. The use of ERP-systems in European enterprises seems to be dependent on the particular company size. While the vast majority of SMEs in Europe do not use such a system, almost half of LSEs with 250 and more employees manage their internal business processes by ERP software. Interesting in this context are the statistics for the different European countries; with only 17%, Spain is the leader while in the United Kingdom only 2% of all companies use ERP-systems (European Commission, 2006).

This means, only a minority of companies within the European Union use ERP software and thereby support their internal business processes in a comprehensive way. An explanation for these findings could be the fact that the implementation and maintenance of ERP-systems is complex and expensive. Thus, SMEs in particular avoid this investment and focus on the use of special software which is covering only partial aspects. In the European Union for example, the vast majority of SMEs (between 70% and 85%) without an ERP-system use an accounting software, which supports only the financial aspects of corporate management but therefore is also much more easier and cheaper to use and maintain than an ERP software (European Commission, 2006).

Table 2. Overview of analysed approaches

	Startup-Costs	Running Costs	Implementation effort	Direct relevance for an SME solution	Conceptual input for SME solution
BCF	○	◉	○	○	●
WFMC	○	○	○	◉	●
RosettaNet	○	○	○	◉	●
ebXML	◉	◉	○	●	●
EDIFACT	○	○	○	◉	●
BPMN	◉	◉	◉	◉	●
EPC	◉	◉	◉	●	◉
BPEL	○	◉	○	◉	●
SAP	○	○	○	○	●

Support of Inter-Organisational Processes

In the mid-eighties, corporate management gave priority to organisational aspects and corporate functions or departments like procurement, production and sales. In the meantime, the management focuses on business processes, which proceed along the value chain to create internal and external outputs. Until the mid-nineties, most of the companies concentrated on the examination and reorganisation of internal business processes. However, with cooperations becoming more and more an important strategic factor of success, the examination focus shifts from internal to cross-organisational business processes.

Depending on the degree of cross-linking, the support of cross-organisational business processes can range from simply placing or accepting orders online to the use of specific software solutions for Supply Chain Management (SCM) along the complete value chain. Therefore, the following considerations will be organised from very "simple forms" to support cross-organisational business processes to more complex ones.

In the European Union, about 50% of all SMEs place orders for supplies online, but only a minority uses this possibility for more than 25% of their total orders. Those SMEs ordering online do this mainly from national suppliers (about 65%), while only a minority (about 10%) orders from international suppliers. (European Commission, 2006). As can be seen in figure Figure 4, the rate of SMEs using specific ICT solutions for eProcurement is also rather slight.

From a customer's point of view, most SMEs in Europe do not support external business processes very well. Indeed, the majority of enterprises provide a website, but only a minority (less than 30%) accept orders from customers online. Finally, this means a customer can gather information about a product or service 'online' but has to contact the SME vendor 'offline' to close the purchase actually. Even less enterprises use specific ICT solutions, either for eMarketing and Sales or for Customer Relationship Management (CRM). Only about 25% of LSEs in the European Union use such software products, while the statistics for SMEs are still much lower (European Commission, 2006) (see Figure 5).

Closely connected to procurement and sales is the question, if corresponding invoice processes are handled traditionally, i.e. paper-based or electronically. In the European Union, far more LSEs than SMEs send and receive eInvoices. However, even 14% of micro-sized enterprises (with 9 or

Figure 4. Use of eProcurement (Data Source: European Commission, 2006)

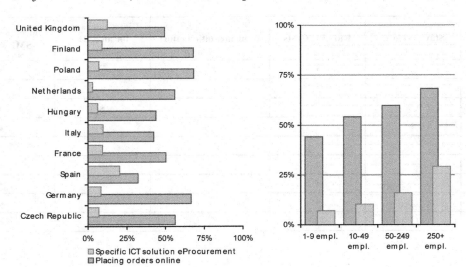

less employees) send and 17% of them receive eInvoices respectively (European Commission, 2006).

Apparently, the most common way to exchange documents in the European Union seems to be sending them by eMail. Only 10% to 31% of European SMEs and 47% of European LSEs use online applications other than eMail for sharing documents (European Commission, 2006) (see Figure 6).

As can also be derived from the figure above, similar statements can be made for collaborative demand forecasting or collaborative design activities in the European Union. If at all, LSEs use special online applications other than eMail to support such activities. For SMEs the figures are

Figure 5. Online marketing and sales (Data Source: European Commission, 2006)

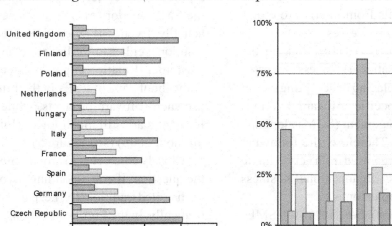

Figure 6. E-collaboration tools (other than eMail) (Data Source: European Commission, 2006)

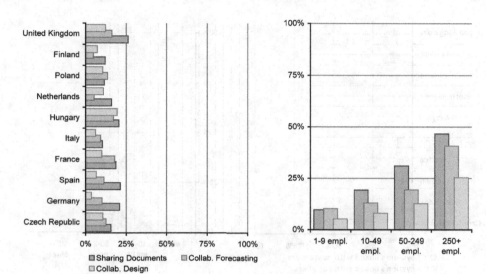

much lower, less than 20% use special software to support collaborative demand forecasting and even less than 15% to support collaborative design activities (European Commission, 2006).

After the description of solutions used by European enterprises to support cross-organisational business processes, it is interesting to focus on the question, which of these solutions are used across enterprises actually. As can be seen from Figure 7, only a minority of all European companies have linked their ICT system with suppliers or customers respectively. Especially for SMEs, this task seems to be very problematic or unattractive – less than 10% make use of the possibility (European Commission, 2006).

Apart from these figures, a second aspect can be consulted to examine the degree of cross-organisational business activities, namely the use of SCM systems. SCM can be understood as the planning, steering and controlling of all flows of materials, goods, money, services and information. Thus, SCM ranges from the procurement of raw materials to the end customer (Krcmar & Klein, 2003). Most of the time, SCM-Software is used to support and manage external business

processes of large enterprises only, because a complex customizing is necessary to ensure a comprehensive control along the supply chain. This proposition can be substantiated by figures for the European Union, where only 8% to 14% of all SMEs but about 34% of LSEs use a SCM system (European Commission, 2006) (see Figure 8). Concerning the figures for SMEs, one should take into consideration that they contain also those small enterprises, which are forced to install and use the SCM software of their main supplier. Thus, in general it can be stated that available SCM solutions are not interesting for SMEs, because their implementation is too complex and expensive.

ENTERPRISE INTEROPERABILITY FROM A TECHNICAL POINT OF VIEW

System interoperability includes standards, protocols and also architectures which are built on top of protocols and interoperability standards. These necessarily overlap with basic technical interoperability to enable seamless communication. In short, system interoperability refers to the ability to con-

Figure 7. Connections to external ICT Systems (Data Source: European Commission, 2006)

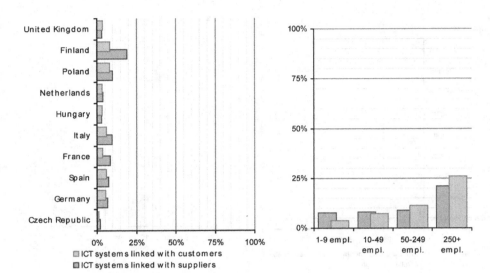

ICT systems linked with customers
ICT systems linked with suppliers

nect systems by defining standard protocols (e.g. SOAP, HTTP, IP) and data formats. Nowadays, the following crucial technologies are taken into account when dealing with system interoperability:

- Service-Oriented Architectures (SOA)
- Peer-to-peer (P2P)
- Mash-up technologies based on Web 2.0

Service-Oriented Architecture is a natural evolutionary step from Object and Component based approaches. The main value of SOA approaches is that it provides a framework for matching and combining needs, as well as capabilities to address those needs.

There are three major trends in Service Oriented Computing (SOC): Web Services, Grid Services and peer-to-peer services. Web Services build on XML standards to provide a platform for building many distributed applications. New Web Services can be created on-the-fly using any existing Web Services (software components). Grid Services came originally from the Grid Computing needs which are accessing distributed computational

(grid) resources. Nowadays, this has moved slightly away from original Grid definition and includes software, data and knowledge capabilities. P2P has much success and has potential to be the most powerful trend, however, it still lacks any consensus on how applications should be built and what semantics should be supported.

Several middleware solutions on the market include parts of integration brokering, business process management, and application development platform functionality based on an SOA framework. Commercial solutions include IBM WebSphere (IBM Workplace and IBM Tivoli), Microsoft BizTalk, Oracle Fusion, BEA AquaLogic and SAP Net Weaver. Also, the open source community offers some solutions such as JBoss by the Red Hat, JOnAS by the Object Web consortium, Tomcat and Geronimo by the Apache Software Foundation, Eclipse by the Eclipse Foundation, and LogicBlaze FUSE by LogicBlaze Inc. Interoperability solution is also provided by Web Service Interoperability Organization (WS-I). WS-I is an open industry organization chartered to promote Web Services

Figure 8. Use of SCM and ERP-Systems (Data Source: European Commission, 2006)

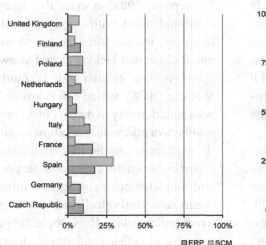

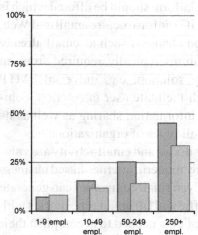

interoperability across platforms, operating systems and programming languages. This organization includes many industrial organization described upper like: SAP, BEA Systems, Fujitsu, HP, Sun Microsystems, IBM, Intel, Oracle, Microsoft, Hitachi and webMethods.

Other interoperability approaches come under "Web 2.0", which is characterised by the development of "lightweight" software (from standard technology building blocks) that can be released quickly over the Web using HTTP protocol. In addition, "mash-up" technologies use public APIs of (mostly big) firms with given infrastructures or databases to provide new services. These developments offer the means for an SME to significantly lower its "cost barrier" to entry into new businesses and markets.

Email Communication and Interoperability

Findings from 2003 show that 80% of users prefer e-mail (Meta Group, 2003) for business communication similarly some case studies (Blumberg, 2008) point that Web 2.0 businesses often depend on email.

One of the main drawbacks of email usage today is its insufficient integration into the collective environment. Email is rarely a standalone information source, but often contains pointers to further information such as files (e.g. saved attachments), links to items on the web, and references to other resources. Email is currently used as a conduit for many functions (Whittaker et al., 1996, Fisher et al., 2006) including alerting, archiving, task management, collaboration and interoperability. By integrating it with other external information (both on the desktop and on distributed servers), it could support workers with information needed to fulfil interoperability tasks on manual or semi automatic level depending on how well the system is configured and customized. Thereby, the problem of interoperability and collaboration could be addressed and users could get an integrated access to needed information within their usual working tool. Currently, there is much research in the area of both personalised and business information management, but very little research that focuses on email as the primary information source, despite its ubiquity.

Architectures or solutions for a specific business sector cannot fulfil the generic interoperability needs of SMEs. Thus, an interoperability and collaboration platform should be offered which is using standard ICT infrastructure email and Web. Communication channels such as email already have some features typically required from an interoperability solution, e.g. universal SMTP protocol, which facilitate user interaction, communication or information sharing as well as its availability in all types of organizations.

Email repositories and email activity are valuable assets in any modern, internet-based business organisation. Even small companies can generate large email traffic and fill email repositories with high volumes of data needed to accomplish their daily tasks. Email is the second most-used internet service after the Web. The following features are common in the use of emails in enterprises and communities of all sizes (Schwartz & Te'eni, 2000):

- Every organisation, without exception, will have an eMail infrastructure before it reaches the stage of developing or adopting any interoperability solution.
- email communication in a modern organisation is over 78% action-oriented, according to a study (Te'eni & Schwartz, 1999). Communication is perhaps the foundation for most organisational actions.
- Managers, and knowledge workers of all kinds, interact with their email systems on a daily basis.
- When building a solution on top of email communication, an organisation does not have to change its work practices when such a solution is installed and set up in an organisation. Users simply receive emails as before, but additional information or knowledge relevant to the interoperability or collaborative aspects is attached, as appropriate to the email.

Work to connect knowledge or context-sensitive information with emails has been done in several projects such as the kMail (Kontact Homepage, 2008) system: this integrates email communication with organisational memories, however, it also forces users to use a special email client and lacks a closed knowledge cycle loop. Another related tool is Zimbra (Zimbra Website, 2008), which offers a web-based client with functionality to detect objects such as phone numbers or addresses and allows some actions on these objects. Similar to kMail, Zimbra requires a particular email client and server application and thus changes existing ICT infrastructure in organization on both client and server side. Gmail, a webmail developed by Google, supports content-sensitive advertising and some actions such as "add event to calendar" with the email. Additionally, extensive work on email processing and active context-sensitive information and knowledge provision has been undertaken by IISAS, where the ACoMA (Laclavik, Seleng & Hluchy, 2007) and EMBET frameworks were developed. The following R&D prototypes have been developed, which are focused on solving problems of email communication to handle various tasks such as task management, information archiving or collaboration aspects: Telenotes, ContactMap, TaskMaster, Snarf, Remail or Priorities.

Commercial Effort

Email communication is envisaged as valuable source of information and knowledge also by many industry players. In this section solutions build on top of email communication in the commercial area are summarized.

MarkMail (MarkMail Website, 2008) is a community-focused searchable message archive service which allows an organisation with large amounts of email to leverage the large amounts of collective knowledge accumulated over time through email discussions. Users can find technical information, research historical decision making, spot trends, and locate the subject matter experts for any topic. While it provides extensive search facilities for email, it does not combine information in email with other desktop knowledge or context. MarkMail thus focuses on finding information rather than connecting it with other forms of data.

iWantSandy is an email-based tool aimed at helping with the organisation of tasks in a person's daily life. Essentially it operates as a reminder service to a person or group of people (e.g. family, colleagues etc.), based on the user sending emails to the service containing details of the information to be reminded about, and the service sending reminders by text or email at the appropriate time. While it is a very useful tool in assisting with organisational activity, it does not integrate information from external sources, and operates only on a fairly restricted language as far as the instructions go.

The Attent solution from Seriosity (Seriosity Website, 2008) is one of the few commercial applications which really attempt to address the information overload problem resulting from the enormous amount of email found in business. It works by prioritising a user's email based on perceived importance. While this is very useful in some situations, there are again a number of drawbacks. First, the perceived importance of an email may differ wildly between sender and recipient: the recipient therefore has no real control of importance or of topics of interest to themselves. Second, there is no importance attached to other information other than the email itself. Third, it only deals with importance but offers no possibilities for searching and navigating information, nor of relating information either with other emails or with other kinds of information.

Both iWantSandy and Attent operate on a user-input basis: they require the user (either the sender in the case of Attent or the recipient in the case of iWantSandy) to be pro-active in deciding what they consider important or what they want to be notified about. Neither use any form of understanding of information or intelligent analysis.

Xobni (Xobni Website, 2008) is a recent Outlook plug-in, which supports extended search capabilities, a better organization of the inbox and management of the media and contacts within emails by integrating social networking aspects into the email communication. Xobni does not support any intelligent analysis or understanding of the email communication and relies heavily on the integration with social networking standards.

Twine (Twine Website, 2008) is another recent effort by Radar Networks, which aims to provide semantic understanding of the email communication by combining the existing methods of Semantic and Social Web. Twine is more focused towards implementing a feature-rich social web site and therefore does not address any email infrastructure integration.

System Interoperability in a Solution Especially for SMEs

Technical or system interoperability needs to be build around well established internet protocols and standards. Nowadays, interoperability solutions focus mainly on HTTP protocol and related standards such as Web Services (WS), XML or mesh up technologies. Especially in SMEs however, other important requirements are needed for interoperability. First of all, they need to have tools to interoperate – HTTP is supported only by web browsers and no other eBusiness or eCommerce solutions are present in most SMEs. Furthermore, it is hard for an SME and especially for a micro-SME to interoperate synchronously, because they have neither the financial nor the personnel resources to maintain adequate systems which keep track of business processes including interoperability tasks.

Therefore, from a technical point of view an adequate solution for SME interoperability should be based on SMTP, because

- SMTP is a well established communication protocol available in most enterprises.
- Email clients are available in most

219

enterprises, so an SMTP-based approach provides interoperability within nearly any email client and device.

- Email communication is asynchronous, information send over email can comply with established interoperability or industry standards and stay human readable (e.g. XML with XSL templates). Thus emails can be processed either manually or automatically. Human can keep track, confirm or achieve interoperability communicated via email.

The facts and figures from the European Union presented in the next to sections will substantiate the prospects of success for such an interoperability approach.

Internet Access and Employment of ICT Practitioners

The definition of interoperability introduced in chapter 2 includes the aspect of information exchange. In today's global business environment, this information exchange proceeds electronically via the internet, which provides " [...] the infrastructure for collecting, distributing and sharing information." (Shaw, 2000) Therefore, internet access is a prerequisite for companies to be actually interoperable. Figure 9 shows that most of the European companies are connected to the internet, mostly over broadband connections. Solely a minor part of the micro-enterprises with nine or less employees have no access to the internet at all (European Commission, 2006). In general, it can be assumed that almost every SME in the European Union fulfils this basic requirement for interoperability, namely to be online.

However, fulfilling this prerequisite of interoperability does not mean that European SMEs can easily interoperate with each other. Most of the current available interoperability solutions work under the precondition that individual software has to be installed. This software needs to be implemented and maintained by skilled personnel. However, Figure 10 shows that especially SMEs face the problem of not employing ICT practitioners while larger companies within the European Union can resort to such specialists (European Commission, 2006).

Use of Technical Standards

The foundation to enable enterprise interoperability is the use of technical standards which allow electronically data interchange between two collaboration partners. Within this technical background, a "standard" and be defined as a "technical specification approved by a recognised standardisation body or continuous application, with which compliance is not compulsory" (European Commission, 2006/2007).

Most currently existing standards on the market can be divided into EDI- and XML-based standards. Furthermore there are solutions for data exchange agreed among a limited number of companies within the same supply chain, here referred to as proprietary standards.

As shown in Figure 11, EDI-based standards are only used to a very small part within European countries. Leader in this category is Spain with a 6% usage. Over all only 3% of European Firms use EDI to collaborate electronically (European Commission, 2006).

While EDI occurred to be the most popular standard during the last past years, the deployment of XML-based standards has lately become more and more dynamic and has by now even displaced EDI as the most popular interoperability standard.

Even though the overall use of XML-based standards with an average 5% usage rate is slightly higher than the one of EDI, Figure 11 shows clearly that the major part of European SMEs rather make use of proprietary solutions than of common standards (European Commission, 2006). Reasons might be found in the fact

Figure 9. Internet and broadband access (Data Source: European Commission, 2006)

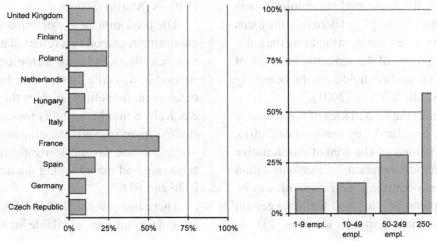

that most standards are implemented in standard software solutions, which are too expensive to implement for European SMEs.

ENTERPRISE INTEROPERABILITY FROM A SEMANTIC POINT OF VIEW

The basic problem facing any semantic interoperability approach is to ensure that companies in communication with each other possess a shared understanding of the meaning of this communication. An especially important case of this comes when two companies share documents with each other.

The first approach to suggest itself is to define certain standards governing both the structure of the information being exchanged and the manner in which this information should be processed. The semantics of any communication using such standards will then be fully understood. Indeed this approach is the principle one seen in practical solu-

Figure 10. Companies employing ICT practitioners (Data Source: European Commission, 2006)

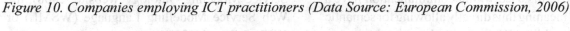

Figure 11. Use of technical standards (Data Source: European Commission, 2006)

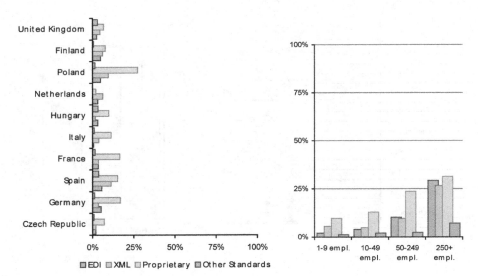

tions to semantic interoperability. Major practical examples include RosettaNet (RosettaNet, 2008) and ebXML (ebXML Website, 2008).

In general this approach to providing semantic interoperability can be characterised as relying on mutual commitment to a shared ontology. Probably the most widely used definition of an ontology is that given by Gruber (1993): "a formal, explicit specification of a shared conceptualisation". A commitment to a single shared ontology ensures that the terms used within communication have a shared meaning thus directly allowing for semantic interoperability. While the study of ontologies has deep roots within philosophical domains, the focus of much recent interest has been enabling the automatic comprehension of the semantic meaning of terms. The evolution of this field is comprehensively discussed by Smith & Welty (2001).

In recent times the related idea of the semantic web, originally popularised by Berners Lee (2001), has risen to prominence. The goal of this initiative is to place semantic annotations on elements within web pages thus permitting their semantics to be machine interpretable. This will facilitate certain features such as intelligent web searches.

Many proponents of the Semantic Web seek a universal medium for information exchange based upon XML syntax. This has given rise to such standards as the Resource Description Framework (RDF) (Resource Description Framework Website, 2004) and its elaboration in RDF Schema or the Web Ontology Language (OWL) (W3C Semantic Web, 2008) and is also reflected in the vision of Semantic Web Services and related standards, namely, the Web Service Modelling Ontology (WSMO) (Web Service Modeling Ontology Website, 2008), the Web Service Modelling Language (WSML) or OWL-S (Martin, 2004).

The predominant use of ontology to foster semantic interoperability is reflected by the numerous research efforts, and software tool development and support in this area. In response to approaches to ontological modelling, such as those cited above, e.g. RDF, a number of tools for ontology editing, storage, querying and reasoning are now available. These include several semantic frameworks for accessing and manipulating documents in OWL, RDF and RDFS.

There are several RDF/RDFS-based reasoners and repositories, available including OWLIM

(Ontotext Semantic Technology Lab Website, 2008), Sesame, Jena (Jena, 2008), Joseki (Joseki, 2008), Kowari (Kowari Metastore Website, 2008) and 3store (Advanced Knowledge Technologies, 2008). While most of the repositories are based on triples, some of them additionally implement scalable inferencing for RDF/RDFS documents, or alternatively for OWL-Lite (SHIF(D) description logic).

The most prominent semantic framework is Jena (Jena, 2008) which provides a wide range of functionality through its APIs. There are also several existing OWL-DL reasoners, which can be used to check consistency and infer relevant facts from OWL-DL documents. Current tableaux-based description logic reasoners include Racer (Racer Website, 2008), Pellet (Pellet Website, 2008) and Fact++ (FaCT++ Website, 2008). All implement various optimisations for tableau-based inferencing for SHOIQ(D) class of description logics. An alternative reasoner for the SHIQ(D) subset of OWLDL is KAON2 (KAON Website, 2008), which implements a novel resolution-based description logic reasoning. Ontologies can be created using ontology editors, such as Protégé (Protégé Website, 2008), an open source development environment for ontologies and knowledge-based systems which was developed at Stanford University (USA). OWL plug-ins for Protégé support the editing of OWL ontologies and the ongoing CO-ODE project (CO-ODE Website, 2008) provides valuable support for user modelling in OWL. Many other ontology editors exist (Denny, 2002), including OntoEdit, which supports translating the ontology from its own XML-based storage format to others, such as F-Logic and RDF; and OilEd, which allows the users to build ontologies using OWL and its precursor DAML+OIL. Finally, tools such as DUET (DAML UML Enhanced Tool) support visualisation and management of ontologies, as indeed do a number of web-based editors, such as OntoWiki or POWL (OntoWiki Website, 2008).

A basic requirement for the realisation of the semantic web is that the documents within it must contain tags identifying the semantic meaning of their concepts. In light of the enormous quantity of web pages already in existence it is not feasible to expect their manual annotation, so the semi-automated annotation of Web documents is a key challenge for the realisation of the Semantic Web. Several systems for performing such annotation through annotation protocols exist, including Annotea (Annotea Project Website, 2008), Rubby and RDF annotation. As discussed by Uren (Uren et al., 2005), annotation solutions can be manual, such as CREAM and Magpie, or semi-automatic based on natural language processing (NLP), a document structure analysis or a learning approach (which requires training sets or supervision). Moreover, there exist pattern-based semi automatic solutions, such as GATE (Cunningham et al, 2002) with its Annie or KIM extentions, PANKOW and C-PANKOW (Cimiano et al., 2005), SemTag or pattern based approach Ontea (Laclavik et al., 2007).

Ontology Sharing

The above discussion has assumed the existence of a single centralised ontology to which all parties involved in communication subscribe thus providing shared meaning. In practice however it is more likely that multiple differing ontologies will coexist.

Indeed in a situation where many SMEs must interact the existence of multiple standards is inevitable. Naturally, many have recognised that the use of a single ontology is untenable in a distributed environment and this has led to research in "ontology alignment". There are several techniques for aligning ontologies: an extensive survey can be found e.g. within Kalfoglou & Schorlemmer (2003).

Two prominent techniques are the creation of local rules for translating concepts between the different ontologies and creating some "meta-structure" to relate the ontologies. In principle these techniques hold out the promise of enabling distributed ontology interactions: each document is defined according to the ontology used by its creator, the local rules of every receiver then map them into terms known by the reader of the document.

The major difficulty with this approach lies in the need to create the mapping rules. An obvious possibility is to support users in the manual creation of mapping rules between two ontologies, an approach used for example in the OntoMerge project (Dou et al., 2005). A notable feature of such techniques is that in order to define such rules, complete descriptions of the two ontologies to be mapped between must be available. In addition a human expert is required to define the mapping rules. While this is reasonable for a pair of static ontologies, it may not be feasible for more dynamic situations, so the investigation of approaches for automatically deriving such rules was motivated.

However such approaches have tended to solely focus on identifying situations where concepts within two ontologies can be identified and – as noted in Kalfolglou & Schorlemmer (2003) – typically still require some human input. This human input is required to solve perhaps the harder half of the problem, i.e. creating rules relating how the information within the attributes of the concepts of one ontology should be mapped into the attributes of the class identified as equivalent within the other ontology.

This problem is closely related to that of database schema integration which has been well studied e.g. by Rahm & Bernstein (2001) who demonstrate that the formation of translation rules to deal with such syntactic matters represents a substantial problem.

Evaluation for an SME Interoperability Solution

A primary driver of an interoperability solution especially for SMEs should be the goal of achieving "zero-cost-of-entry". In particular a new company must be able to easily configure their software locally before using it to provide interoperability. The previously outlined techniques fail to facilitate such behaviour.

In particular both the initial creation of appropriate ontologies and the adoption of these ontologies impose substantial costs on the SME in question. Further such ideas make the implicit assumption that all parties within the communication will subscribe to the same central ontology.

In the case of a large company who can control it's interactions with its suppliers this is reasonable. However an individual SME has no such leverage and the problem becomes one of interpreting incoming documents of arbitrary formats in terms that the SME can locally understand.

Moreover a new company using an existing interoperability solution might bring new concepts with it which must then be inserted into the main centralised ontology. This might not only require substantial work on the centralised ontology itself but also requires the other companies using the same interoperability solution to learn the new concepts introduced.

Similar problems are encountered when considering approaches which use mapping rules – every time a new company started to use the interoperability solution, appropriate mapping rules or "metastructures" for mapping from and to every other ontology within this solution to their local ontology would have to be created. This process would obviously be far from "zero-cost" and would indeed increase rapidly as more businesses started to use the interoperability system.

An alternative, promising approach to this

problem which could be oriented on the investigation already done as part of the MaBE (MaBE, 2005) and Crosswork (CrossWork Website, 2008) European research projects.

This approach advocates abstracting from matters of syntax to focus on the information passed within a concept. When a concept is passed to a recipient with a local ontology, the approach compares the atomic items of information within this concept to those within existing concepts within the receivers ontology.

The results of this comparison can trigger a range of actions, starting from only retaining the subset of the concepts overall information which that recipient will understand, up to a decision by the recipient to learn the complete new concept because of the future utility of this concept. This permits actors/trading partners to meaningfully communicate without the need for potentially expensive ontology agreement or alignment. A more complete account of this approach can be found e.g. within Stalker & Mehandjiev (2006).

Within the context of SMEs communicating this approach can be developed to allow the local interpretation of document arriving in unspecified formats. This approach will be investigated within the Commius project.

SUMMARY AND CONCLUSION

In this article, the term Enterprise Interoperability has been analysed and a four layer framework has been introduced to clarify the different perspectives of interoperability. The strategic layer reveals that in order to establish stable collaborations, a minimum of common concepts and interests between the collaboration partners has to exist. In the field of process interoperability, different already existing interoperability solutions like the UN/CEFAT Business Collaboration Framework, the Workflow Reference Model as well as standards like RosettNet, ebXML and EDIFACT, languages like BPEL, BPMI and the EPC and ERP solutions have been examined with respect to their relevance for an SME interoperability solution.

It has been stated that even though much effort is currently done in this field, hardly none of the present approaches particularly matches the exigencies of SMEs. From a technical perspective, SME interoperability could be best achieved using an SMTP based solution, because SMTP as well as appropriate eMail clients are available in most SMEs. Furthermore eMail communication is of asynchronous nature and does not require specialized end systems which are always online, it can be processed using a mixture of automated or manual process steps and stays human readable, even if one collaboration partner does not use an interoperability system. The results concerning the three perspectives of strategic, process and technical interoperability have been substantiated with facts and figures from an European survey.

Concerning the fourth semantic perspective of Enterprise Interoperability, this article has shown that research in this field is mainly embossed by ontologies. Relevant approaches for semantic interoperability have been eluded and reviewed concerning their potential use for an SME interoperability solution. As derived in the previous sections, current solutions in this area are not applicable for SMEs due to their high costs which make them not affordable in most cases. Hence an interoperability solution especially for SMEs should follow another approach – in the Commius Project for example, it will be an approach which concentrates more on the information passed within a concept, than focusing on the syntax of information.

In summary, it can be stated that most of the work done in the field of interoperability is not tailored for the adaption within the domain of SMEs. Nevertheless this article showed that SMEs need and are willing to use interoperability solutions – but only if they are adapted to their special needs.

REFERENCES

W3C Semantic Web. (2008). *Web Ontology Language (OWL)*. Retrieved October 15, 2008, from http://www.w3.org/2004/OWL

Advanced Knowledge Technologies. (2008). *3 store – Scalable storage solutions for next generation knowledge services*. Retrieved October 15, 2008, from http://www.aktors.org/technologies/3store

Afshar, M., et al. (2004). *Process-centric realization of SOA*. Retrieved October 15, 2008, from http://soa.sys-con.com/node/46870.

Annotea Project Website. (2008). Retrieved October 24, 2008, from http://www.w3.org/2001/Annotea

Berners-Lee, T., Hendler, J., & Lassila, O. (2001)... *Scientific American, 284*(5), 34.

Blumberg, M. (2008). *Case study: Web 2.0 runs on Email*. Retrieved December 15, 2008, from http://www.returnpath.net/blog/2008/07/case-study-web-20-runs-on-emai.php

Business Workflow, S. A. P. (2008). Retrieved October 14, 2008, from http://help.sap.com/saphelp_46c/ helpdata/en/c5/e4a930453d-11d189430000e829fbbd/content.htm

Cimiano, P., et al. (2005). Gimme' the context: context-driven automatic semantic annotation with cpankow. In *WWW '05*, (pp. 332-341). New York: ACM Press.

Collaborative Open Ontology Development Environment CO-ODE project webpage. (2008). Retrieved October 07, 2008, from http://www.jisc.ac.uk/index.cfm?name= project_coode&src=alpha

CrossWork Website. (2008). *Cross-Organisational Workflow Formation and Enactment*. Retrieved October 14, 2008, from http://www.crosswork.info/.

Cunningham, H., Maynard, D., Bontcheva, K., & Tablan, V. (2002). GATE: A framework and graphical development environment for robust NLP tools and applications. In *Proceedings of the 40th Anniversary Meeting of the Association for Computational Linguistics (ACL'02), Philadelphia*.

Denny, M. (2002). *Ontology building: A survey of editing tools*. Retrieved October 07, 2008, from http://www.xml.com/2002/11/06/Ontology_Editor_Survey.html

Dou, D. (2005). Ontology translation on the semantic Web. *Journal on Data Semantics II (. LNCS, 3360*, 35–57.

ebXML Website. (2008). Retrieved October 15, 2008, from http://www.ebxml.org/geninfo.htm

Enterprise Resource Planning Portal. (2008). Retrieved October 14, 2008, from http://www.erpgenie.com/mysap/bus_connector.htm.

European Commission. (2006). *Table Report e-Business Survey, Version 2.1*. Retrieved May 20, 2008, from http://www.eBusiness-watch.org

European Commission. (2006/2007). *Enterprise directorate-generals, The European e-Business Report 2006/07 edition*. Retrieved June 26, 2008, from http://www.eBusiness-watch.org.

FaCT++ Website. (2008). Retrieved October 15, 2008, from http://owl.man.ac.uk/factplusplus/.

Fisher, D., Brush, A. J., Gleave, E., & Smith, M. A. (2006). Revisiting Whittaker & Sidner's "email overload" ten years later. In *CSCW 2006*. New York: ACM Press.

Gerst, M., & Bunduchi, R. (2007). The analysis of standardised technology in the automotive industry. In P. Cunningham & M. Cunningham (Eds.), *Exploiting the knowledge economy: Issues, applications and case studies*. Amsterdam: ISO Press.

Gruber, T. R. (1993). Towards principles for the design of ontologies used for knowledge sharing. In N. Guarino (Ed.), *Proceedings of the International Workshop on Formal Ontology, Padova/ Italy.*

Homepage, K. (2008). Retrieved October 14, 2008, from http://kontact.kde.org/kmail/.

In Shaw, et al. (Eds.), *Handbook on electronic commerce* (pp. 431-444), Berlin/ Germany: Springer.

Institute of Electrical and Electronics Engineers. (1990). *IEEE Standard Computer Dictionary: A Compilation of IEEE Standard Computer Glossaries.* New York, NY.

Jena – A Semantic Web Framework for Java. (2008). Retrieved October 14, 2008, from http://jena.sourceforge.net

Joseki - A SPARQL Server for Jena. (2008). Retrieved October 14, 2008, from http://www.joseki.org.

Kalfolglou, Y., & Schorlemmer, M. (2003). Ontology mapping: The state of the art. *The Knowledge Engineering Review, 18*(1), 1–31. doi:10.1017/S0269888903000651

Keller, G., Nüttgens, M., & Scheer, A.-W. (1992). Semantische Prozeßmodellierung auf der Grundlage "Ereignisgesteuerter Prozeßketten (EPK)." In A.-W. Scheer (Ed.), *Veröffentlichungen des Instituts für Wirtschaftsinformatik, Nr. 89.* Saarbrücken: Universität des Saarlandes.

Kersten, W., Kern, E.-M., & Held, T. (2003). Auf dem Weg zur E-Collaboration – Entwicklungslinien im Electronic Business. In W. Kersten (Ed.), *E-collaboration* (pp. 5-27). Wiesbaden/Germany: Gabler Verlag.

Kowari Metastore Website. (2008). Retrieved October, 14, 2008, from http://www.kowari.org.

Krcmar, H., & Klein, A. (2003). Collaborative commerce und CSCW – Zum Nutzen der CSCW-Forschung für das collaborative E-Business. In W. Kersten (Ed.), E-collaboration (pp. 5-27). Wiesbaden/Germany: Gabler Verlag.

Laclavik, M., et al. (2007). Ontology based text annotation – OnTeA. *Information Modelling and Knowledge Bases XVIII* (Frontiers in Artificial Intelligence and Applications, Vol. 154, pp. 311-315). Amsterdam: IOS Press.

Laclavik, M., Seleng, M., & Hluchy, L. (2007). ACoMA: Network Enterprise Interoperability and Collaboration using E-mail Communication. In P. Cunningham & M. Cunningham (Eds), *Proceedings of eChallenges 2007; Expanding the Knowledge Economy: Issues, Applications, Case Studies* (pp. 1078-1085). Amsterdam: IOS Press.

Lewerenz, J. (1999). On the use of natural language concepts for the conceptual modeling of interaction in information systems. In G. Fliedl, & H.C. Mayr (Eds.), *Proceedings of the 4th International Conference on Applications of Natural Language to Databases, NLDB'99,* (pp. 61-75). Klagenfurt/ Austria: Österreichische Computer Gesellschaft.

Lücke, F., & Webering, J. (2003). Gegenwart und Zukunft von Online-Kooperationen. In M. Büttgen,& L. Fridjof (Eds.), *Online-Kooperationen* (pp. 3-14). Wiesbaden/Germany: Gabler Verlag.

MaBE. (2006), The MaBE Middleware. In *Emerging Solutions for Future Manufacturing Systems* (pp. 53-60). Boston: Springer.

MarkMail Website. (2008). Retrieved October 14, 2008, from http://markmail.org

Martin, D., et al. (2004). OWL-S: Semantic markup for Web services. Retrieved October 15, 2008, from http://www.w3.org/Submission/OWL-S/.

META Group, Inc. (2003). *80% of users prefer E-Mail as business communication tool.* Retrieved December 15, 2008, from http://www.mariosalex-androu.com/technology-trends/2003/80-percent-of-users-prefer-email.asp.

O'Leary, D. (2000). Supply chain processes and relationships for electronic commerce.

Ontotext Semantic Technology Lab Website. (2008). Retrieved October 15, 2008, from http://www.ontotext.com/owlim/index.html.

OntoWiki Website. (2008). Retrieved October 15, 2008, from http://aksw.org/Projects/OntoWiki.

Rahm, E., & Bernstein, P. A. (2001). A survey of approaches to automatic schema matching. *The International Journal on Very Large Data Bases, 10,* 334–350. doi:10.1007/s007780100057

Resource Description Framework Website. (2004). Retrieved October 15, 2008, from http://www.w3.org/RDF

Roser, S. (2008). *Designing and enacting cross-organisational business process: A model-driven, ontology-based approach.* Retrieved October 14, 2008, from http://www.opus-bayern.de/uni-augsburg/volltexte/2008/805/pdf/Diss_Roser_Business_Processes.pdf.

RosettaNet Website. (2008). Retrieved October 15, 2008, from http://www.rosettanet.org/cms/sites/RosettaNet.

Scheer, A.-W., Grieble, O., & Zang, S. (2003). Collaborative business management. In W. Kersten (Ed.), E-collaboration (pp. 29-57). Wiesbaden/Germany: Gabler Verlag.

Schmidt, A., & Kiefer, C. (2005). Kooperationen zwischen mittelständischen Unternehmen. In J. Zentes, B. Swoboda, & D. Morschett (Eds.), *Kooperationen, Allianzen und Netzwerke* (pp. 1357-1381). Wiesbaden/Germany: Gabler Verlag.

Schwartz, D., & Te'eni, D. (2000). Tying knowledge to action with kMail. In *IEEE Knowledge Management* (pp. 33-39), Bar-Ilan University.

Seriosity Website. (2008). Retrieved October 14, 2008, from http://www.seriosity.com/products.html

Shaw, M. (2000). Electronic commerce: State of the art. In Shaw, et al. (Eds.), Handbook on electronic commerce (pp. 431-444). Berlin/Germany: Springer.

Smith, B., & Welty, C. (2001). FOIS introduction: Ontology---towards a new synthesis. In *Proceedings of the international Conference on Formal ontology in information Systems - Volume 2001* (pp. 3-9). Ogunquit, Maine/USA. FOIS '01. New York: ACM.

Stalker, D. I., & Mehandjiev, N. (2006). *A devolved ontology model for the pragmaticweb,* Paper presented at the First International Conference on the Pragmatic Web, ICPW.

Te'eni, D., & Schwartz, D. (1999). Contextualization in computer-mediated communication. In L. Brooks, & C. Kimble (Eds.), *Information systems—The next generation* (pp. 327-338). New York: McGraw-Hill.

United Nations Centre for Trade Facilitation and Electronic Business. (2008). Retrieved October 14, 2008, from http://www.unece.org/cefact/.

Uren, V. (2005). Semantic annotation for knowledge management: Requirements and a survey of the state of the art. *Journal of Web Semantics: Science . Services and Agents on the WWW, 4*(1), 14–28. doi:10.1016/j.websem.2005.10.002

Web Service Modeling Ontology Website. (2008). Retrieved October 15, 2008, from http://www.wsmo.org/.

Website, K. A. O. N. (2008). Retrieved October 14, 2008, from http://kaon.semanticweb.org

Website, P. (2008). Retrieved October 14, 2008, from http://pellet.owldl.com/

Website, P. (2008). Retrieved October 15, 2008, from http://protege.stanford.edu/

Website, R. (2008). *Racer - Renamed Abox and Concept Expression Reasoner*. Retrieved October 15, 2008, from http://www.sts.tu-harburg.de/~r.f.moeller/racer/

Website, Z. (2008). Retrieved October 14, 2008, from http://www.zimbra.com/.

White, S. A. (2008). *Introduction to BPMN*. Retrieved October 14, 2008, from http://www.bpmn.org/Documents/Introduction%20to%20BPMN.pdf.

Whittaker, S., & Sidner, C. (1996). Email overload: Exploring personal information management of Email. In *Proceedings of ACM CHI'96* (pp. 276-283).

Wirtz, B., & Vogt, P. (2003). E-Collaboration im B2B-Bereich: Strategien, Strukturen und Erfolgsfaktoren. In M. Büttgen, & L. Fridjof (Eds.), *Online-Kooperationen* (pp. 265-284). Wiesbaden/Germany: Gabler Verlag.

Workflow Management Coalition Website. (2008). Retrieved October 15, 2008, from http://www.wfmc.org/.

Chapter 13
Communication Issues for Small and Medium Enterprises:
Provider and Customer Perspectives

Mirjana D. Stojanovic
University of Belgrade, Serbia

Vladanka S. Acimovic-Raspopovic
University of Belgrade, Serbia

ABSTRACT

This chapter considers communication issues for small and medium enterprises (SMEs) from both provider and customer perspectives. SME communication infrastructure at the individual site should usually be built around Ethernet-based local area network with a remotely manageable integrated access device that enables high speed Internet access, virtual private networking, Voice over Internet Protocol (VoIP) functionality and collaborative services. We further address several open quality of service (QoS) issues that include: service level agreements, signaling for quality of service and management aspects. The proposed framework for service management encompasses interfaces for QoS-aware and legacy applications, generic service level specification, functional model of service negotiation and management policies.

INTRODUCTION

Recent trends in enterprise networks are radically changing the communication infrastructure of these systems. Instead of having diverse data networks, each of which is dedicated to a single class of applications, corporations are moving to a unified Internet Protocol (IP) based intranet. The main prerequisites for building a multiservice IP-based enterprise communication infrastructure include

quality of service (QoS) support and differentiation, certain level of mutual service isolation and implementing the appropriate security policy.

Advances in networking technologies create a new opportunity for small and medium enterprises (SMEs) to become more efficient and competitive by interconnecting sites, deploying collaborative applications, increasing remote access of telecommuters and mobile users, deploying collaborative applications and integrating heterogeneous telecommunication services (voice, data, video) over the same network. Benefits of such approach include:

DOI: 10.4018/978-1-60566-892-5.ch013

(1) deployment of new natural communication services (see and listen); (2) use of person-to-person and person-to-machine real-time and non-real-time multimedia and mobile data services; (3) services can easily be self-configured and personalized (same look and feel on various devices) and (4) service mobility (access of home services in visited networks; any service on any access, any device, any location, any time).

Unlike large enterprises, SMEs typically don't have the necessary IT resources to deploy, integrate and manage these services. For that reason, they need preconfigured, fully integrated equipment that can be easily installed, used and maintained by non-IT experts. The requirements for such equipment encompass a variety of features such as high speed Internet access, QoS support, virtual private networks (VPN), voice over IP (VoIP) gateway, as well as a variety of security mechanisms.

On the other side, fulfillment of such requirements poses a number of new issues to service providers, including: variable bandwidths, high bandwidth business services, absolute and/or relative QoS guarantees, specific support for IP applications (e.g. VPNs and multicasting), service management, as well as security of user and management interfaces (DSL Forum, 2007). High reliability and availability is required to support business and voice services. Besides, service providers need to define appropriate strategies quickly to address the business market, increase revenue, stay competitive, and increase market share (Mordelet, Festraets, & Wang, 2006). Providers should achieve revenue increase by offering a wide spectrum of new services, particularly multimedia services. Cost reductions are achieved by sharing network infrastructure and systems. Savings are also a function of network scenario, equipment modernization status and customers grow speed. Another important fact is simplification of network management due to use of integrated operation platforms

In this article we first address QoS issues (from the perspectives of both provider and customer),

since QoS support represents a basic requirement for service integration. Providing end-to-end QoS in IP-based networks requires implementation at the network level a variety of mechanisms and algorithms dealing with the call and packet handling, as well as network resource management. They should operate at different time scales, from picoseconds to milliseconds for handling packets in the routers up till hours and days, for performing certain control and management operations. Furthermore, a signaling system is extremely required to inform the network about the user application needs.

The starting point is a proper definition of service level agreement (SLA) between the user and the provider, together with its associated service level specification. Deployment of IP QoS-enabled networks requires a change of traditional concept of static SLA negotiation, due to necessity to redefine SLAs more frequently, according to changes of network resource availability and conditions for provisioning of different QoS levels. In other words, dynamic SLA negotiation is needed, through an appropriate QoS signaling protocol. We address signaling issues and briefly present the two predominant signaling protocols standardized by the Internet Engineering Task Force (IETF).

Deployment of the end-to-end QoS architecture assumes the use of appropriate QoS interfaces by end users and applications, by which they can access the QoS parameters offered by the service provider.

Further, providing automated service management to SME is a mandatory requirement for service providers. For that purpose, we propose a framework that encompasses interfaces for QoS-aware and legacy applications, generic service level specification, functional model of service negotiation and management policies. The prototype implementation has also been addressed.

Finally, we briefly discuss future trends with respect to technologies, features and applicability of the commercially available SME equipment and also the requirements for evolution of the providers' backbones towards fully automated, QoS-enabled networks.

BACKGROUND

SMEs vary from tens to hundreds of employees, located on a single or multiple sites. What they have today are a few pre-paid or post-paid mobile phones for managers and team leaders, and a few fixed lines or a small private branch exchange (PBX) with tens of extensions and a few analogue or digital trunks connected to the public network (Mordelet, Festraets, & Wang, 2006). Dial-up, leased line or DSL (Digital Subscriber Line) for Internet access is often limited to management or administrative use.

The virtual enterprise paradigm relying on reliable and secure communication infrastructure has been recognized years ago as a basis for enhancing business models in SMEs (Camarinha-Matos & Afsarmanesh, 1999). Some available market solutions have pointed to the establishment of VPNs for connecting different sites from the same enterprise or even different enterprises on a bilateral technological agreement. Another approach has been focused towards offering SMEs a flexible and reliable proprietary platform to participate in virtual enterprises (Osório & Barata, 2001).

Klincewicz, Schmitt, and Wong (2002) address the problem of interconnecting enterprise branches and offices, i.e. wide area networking (WAN). They distinguish WAN providers from local access providers. WAN providers are telecommunications services companies that provide long-haul transmission links between widely separated locations. Local access providers are telecommunications services companies that provide transmission links within a local area. Further, they propose a design methodology for IP enterprise networks that takes into account the technologies and techniques that can provide QoS.

In the past few years, IP-based **VPNs**, in several forms and based on different network technologies, have become a leading solution for a wide range of corporate network services. Comprehensive overviews of standardization efforts and solutions for IP VPNs can be found in works of Carugi and De Clercq (2004), Knight and Lewis (2004), and Mohapatra, Metz and Cui (2007). Resource management and QoS provisioning framework for IP VPNs have been addressed in recent publications by Raghunath and Ramakrishnan (2007), and Stojanovic and Acimovic-Raspopovic (2008), respectively.

QoS Issues in Next Generation Networks: Provider Perspective

Next generation network (NGN) refers to an architectural concept of future telecommunication core and access networks, which assumes transport of all information and services over a common network, typically built around the IP. A single network, reduced costs, innovative, converged, IP-based applications and increased competitive advantage are just some of the benefits of NGNs. Providing different levels of end-to-end QoS guarantees is one of the key requirements for deployment of NGN. However, this requirement introduces complexity in several areas including user applications, network architecture, as well as network management and business models.

The IETF has defined the Differentiated Services (DiffServ) framework (Blake, Black, Carlson et al., 1998), which has been widely accepted as a basis for QoS implementation in the backbone IP-based network. The framework assumes that incoming packets belonging to different traffic flows, but with similar QoS requirements, may be associated to the same traffic class and processed in the same manner at network nodes. Complex processing operations, including packet classification and traffic conditioning, are performed at the edge routers, while core routers perform simple forwarding operations based on the traffic class code in packet header that defines the specific per-hop behavior (PHB). The basic DiffServ model provides edge-to-edge QoS guarantees with rather coarse service level granularity.

Besides, the maturity of the IETF Multi Protocol Label Switching (MPLS) technology (Rosen, Viswanathan, & Callon, 2001) that integrates a scheme for label swapping/tagging with layer 3 routing makes it easier to manage a backbone network for QoS.

Access networks may implement other QoS models like per-flow based Integrated Services – IntServ (Braden, Clark, & Shenker, 1994) in wired networks and services defined in the Universal Mobile Telecommunication System – UMTS (Third Generation Partnership Project (3GPP), 2003) in wireless environment.

The International Telecommunication Union – Telecommunication standardization sector (ITU-T) defines an architectural framework for support of quality of service in packet networks in its recommendation Y.1291 (ITU-T, 2004). The framework specifies a number of QoS building blocks (mechanisms) that are organized into three logical planes: the data, control and management planes. Mechanisms in the date plane deal with user traffic and encompass buffer management, congestion avoidance, packet marking, queuing and scheduling, traffic classification, traffic policing and traffic shaping. Mechanisms in the control plane are related with paths that carry data traffic, i.e., admission control, QoS routing, and resource reservation. Mechanisms in the management plane deal with operation, administration and management (OAM) aspects of the network and include SLA, traffic restoration, metering and recording, and policy.

In spite of intensive research work and existing of commercially available QoS-enabled solutions, there are several open issues that slow-down widespread deployment of end-to-end QoS architectures. They include: signaling for QoS, lack of standards for SLA formats, QoS routing, inter-provider QoS, automated service and net-work management, pricing for QoS and security of information and network infrastructure.

Service and Network Management Aspects

Today, functionality of the widespread Simple Network Management Protocol (SNMP) enables only management of individual network elements that implement appropriate manageable agents and corresponding management information bases (MIBs). SNMP is mainly used to obtain the status of individual network devices and for reporting the alarm events.

Requirements for end-to-end QoS, reliability and network survivability cause new approaches to design and development of network management system with respect to definition of new management architectures, developing of new methods and software tools for management automation and developing of hardware and software platforms that allow for efficient implementation of fault, configuration, accounting, performance and security (FCAPS) functionality.

Unification of service level specification formats is an important prerequisite for management automation and interoperability between providers. Development of systems that implement sets of abstractly defined rules – **policies** (Policy Based Management, PBM) is a direction to build flexible and highly-automated management platforms. The IETF Distributed Management Task Force (DTMF) suggested a framework for PBM, with the objective to provide management through standardized solutions and improve network scalability. The framework encompasses conceptual, functional and informational models (Verma, 2002).

Administrator, through appropriate application programming interface uses policy management tool to define policies that should be enforced in the network. The device that implements and performs different management policies is called Policy Enforcement Point (PEP). Policy reposi-

Table 1. Typical requirements of applications (adapted from Kazovsky, Gutierrez, Shaw, & Wong, 2008)

Application	Download speed	Delay requirements	Other
Voice over IP (VoIP)	64 kbit/s	200ms	Protection
Video conferencing	2 Mbit/s	200ms	Protection
File sharing	3 Mbit/s	1s	–
Standard-definition television (SDTV)	4.5 Mbit/s/channel	10s	Multicasting
Real time video	10 Mbit/s	200ms	Content distribution
Video on demand (VoD)	20 Mbit/s	10s	Low packet loss
High-definition television (HDTV)	20 Mbit/s/channel	10s	Multicasting
Network-hosted software	25 Mbit/s	200ms	Data security

tory is a data base in which different policies are stored. It can be implemented as SQL (Structured Query Language) directory server that is accessed through a standardized protocol, e.g. Lightweight Directory Access Protocol (LDAP). Policy Decision Point (PDP) is responsible for communication with the policy repository, interpretation of policies and their forwarding to PEPs, by means of management protocols like SNMP or Common Open Policy Service (COPS). Scopes of PBM application include: QoS control and management (Flegkas, Trimintzios, & Pavlou, 2002), security management (Li, 2003), wireless networks (Hadjiantonis, Charalambides, & Pavlou, 2007), etc.

From the provider perspective, the most important open issues encompass: (1) the scope and structure of management functions that should be integrated in the network; (2) the extent of measuring and collected data that are needed to enhance reliability and efficiency and (3) accounting management in a multi-domain network (Ahmed, Asgari, Mehaoua et al., 2007; Pras, Schönwälder, Burgess et al., 2007).

SME COMMUNICATION REQUIREMENTS AND INFRASTRUCTURE

Depending on user applications, traffic demands on enterprise intranets may include a multitude of diverse requirements: delay-sensitive traffic, low packet loss probability, high bandwidth, multicasting, security, etc.

In Table 1, requirements of typical user applications have been summarized.

There is a need to provide an efficient network for all types of applications while satisfying individualized performance requirements. This general concept is embodied in the term "quality of service". Another important issue is related with security. Best practices for data security alone do not provide total protection for applications like VoIP and video conferencing. For example, to deploy secure IP PBX, enterprises need real-time security solutions that offer comprehensive threat protection, strict policy enforcement, robust access control, and privacy of confidential data.

SME communication infrastructure at the individual site (office or branch) is usually built around local area network (LAN) based on the Ethernet technology. Today, Ethernet technology brings with it numerous advantages:

Figure 1. SME business gateway functionality

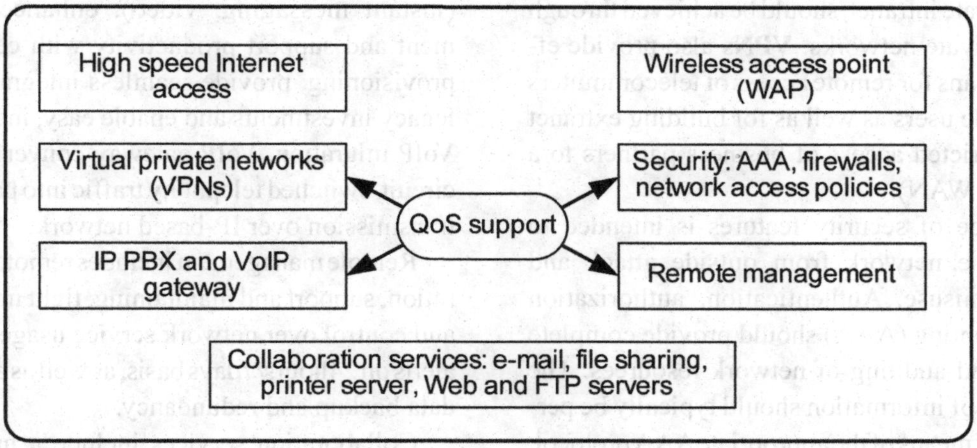

Figure content:
- High speed Internet access
- Wireless access point (WAP)
- Virtual private networks (VPNs)
- Security: AAA, firewalls, network access policies
- QoS support
- IP PBX and VoIP gateway
- Remote management
- Collaboration services: e-mail, file sharing, printer server, Web and FTP servers

- 10 Mbit/s, 100 Mbit/s, 1 Gbit/s, 10 Gbit/s and growing speeds;
- Support for copper, fiber optic and wireless media;
- Network redundancy and fault tolerance by automatic reconfiguration of the active topology as a result of the failure of LAN components, through Rapid Spanning Tree Protocol (Institute of Electrical and Electronic Engineers (IEEE), 2004);
- Support for quality of service through definition of traffic types and classes, queuing rules and extended filtering services (IEEE, 2004);
- Virtual LANs which allow for traffic isolation and system security (IEEE, 2005).

Ethernet is the world's most widely adopted LAN technology and is now migrating into the wide area networking space (Sánchez, Raptis, & Vaxevanakis, 2008). In the near future we could see a total Ethernet solution from the WAN via metropolitan area network (MAN) to the LAN.

The other essential enterprise communication requirements may encompass:

- Interconnecting offices and branches;
- Increasing access to data inside and outside the office (telecommuters, mobile users);
- Deploying collaborative applications;
- High-speed Internet access.

In considering fulfillment of the aforementioned requirements, two essential features that distinguish SMEs from large enterprises and corporations should be outlined.

First, SMEs typically do not employ ICT experts for purpose of network planning, building and maintenance. For that reason, they need cost-effective, fully integrated, preconfigured equipment that might be monitored and managed remotely. In other words, an integrated access device is needed that is called "SME business gateway".

Second, SMEs usually do not build their own switching and transmission infrastructure for achieving WAN capabilities between sites. For building the corporate intranet, different forms of IP VPN services, offered by operators or Internet Service Providers, should be used.

Functionality of **SME business gateway** is illustrated in Figure 1.

High speed Internet access should be achieved via Asymmetric Digital Subscriber Line (ADSL), Cable, UMTS or other access technology that is interoperable with the Ethernet.

WAN capabilities between sites, i.e. building the corporate intranet, should be achieved through virtual private networks. **VPNs** also provide efficient means for remote access of telecommuters and mobile users as well as for building extranet (e.g., restricted access of business partners to a corporate WAN).

A range of security features is intended to protect the network from outside attack and internal misuse. Authentication, authorization and accounting (AAA) should provide complete control and auditing of network resources. The exchange of information should typically be performed by means of the appropriate AAA protocol, like Remote Authentication Dial In User Service (RADIUS), Terminal Access Controller Access Control System (TACACS) and Diameter. The latter has been recommended by the IETF as a preferred protocol for NGNs, since it provides a framework for applications such as network access (Calhoun, Zorn, Spence, & Mitton, 2005) and IP mobility (Calhoun, Johansson, Perkins, Hiller, & McCann, 2005). Firewall management is needed for each external link and VPN to protect the network from all common types of threat such as suspicious packets, and denial of service (DoS) attacks. Network access policies provide fully configurable and audited internet access policies for the intranet and extranet by user/machine/group. Each may have different QoS classes, access restricted to specific time periods, restrictions on service access (e.g., VoIP, e-mail, Web).

Wireless access point (WAP) should be integrated together with security and authentication.

IP PBX should support advanced capabilities for inbound and outbound call management. Those capabilities include centralized voice mail, automatic call distribution (ACD) and support for remote and mobile workers. With the advent of IP voice communications, it is now possible for IT organizations to easily extend standard and advanced PBX capabilities, enforce headquarters audio, video and web conferencing resources,

provide real time communications capabilities (instant messaging, video), enhance deployment and support productivity with centralized provisioning, provide seamless integration with legacy investments and enable easy, incremental VoIP migration. VoIP gateway converts normal circuit-switched telephony traffic into packets for transmission over IP-based network.

Remote management includes remote configuration, support and maintaining, tight monitoring and control over network service usage, security alerts on 24hours/7days basis, as well as automatic data backup and redundancy.

Collaboration services include a number of services that assume sharing of data and network resources, like e-mail services, file sharing, printer server, Web server and File Transfer Protocol (FTP) server. E-mail services assume the use of the available protocols such as Simple Mail Transfer Protocol (SMTP), Post Office Protocol (POP3), Internet Message Access Protocol (IMAP), Webmail, for e-mail hosting or relaying as well as anti-virus and anti-spam capabilities. File sharing enables sharing of files by acting as FTP, Hyper Text Transfer Protocol (HTTP) or Windows file server with configurable disk quotas. Printer server functionality enables installation and management of shared printers between customer sites. Web and FTP servers are needed for deployment of internet and intranet pages including default user home pages.

QoS support is tightly related with most of device functions: VPNs, security, VoIP and management. Typical QoS requirements for **SME business gateway** include:

- Support for LAN quality of service (IEEE, 2004) and virtual LANs (IEEE, 2005);
- Support of the basic DiffServ, i.e. packet classification, traffic conditioning as well as packet queuing and scheduling;
- Bandwidth management;
- Support of remote QoS monitoring and control;

- QoS negotiation, including support of access signaling protocol and predefined SLA format.

SERVICE LEVEL AGREEMENT

Service level agreement (SLA) is a contract between the service provider and the user (either end user or another domain), which defines provider's responsibilities in the sense of QoS guarantees, performance metrics, measurement methods, tariffs and billing principles, as well as penalties for both the user and the provider in the case of contract violation. Regardless of the applied QoS model, SLA should consist of two parts: the technical part and the administrative part. The technical part encompasses set of descriptors and associated attributes that describe the particular **service class** and the **traffic profile**. Administrative part covers financial and legal aspects: information about pricing, charging, billing and payment; penalties for both the user and the provider in the case of contract violation, etc.

The technical part of the SLA is usually denoted as **service level specification (SLS)**. The IETF defines SLS for the DiffServ model as "a set of parameters and their values which together define the service offered to a traffic stream by a DiffServ domain" (Grossman, 2002, p.2). In the same document, the notion of traffic conditioning specification (TCS) has been introduced and defined as "a set of parameters and their values which together specify a set of classifier rules and a traffic profile"(Grossman, 2002, p.2). A TCS is an integral element of an SLS. Possible structures and formats of the DiffServ SLS and its associated TCS have been addressed in literature (Bouras & Sevasti, 2005; Bostjancic & Stojanovic, 2007), where a similar SLS contents (set of descriptors and their associated parameters) has been recognized. Stojanovic and Acimovic-Raspopovic (2008) propose the VPN SLS format consisting of the generic part, which describes IP service

for individual traffic flow, and the VPN-specific part. The latter encompasses descriptors of VPN tunnel, reachability, Network Address Translation (NAT), routing and security.

Deployment of NGNs assumes mapping of QoS requirements between different types of networks and QoS models. Interoperability in a multi-domain network with different QoS models inside particular domains assumes mapping of service classes and their associated QoS parameters at domain boundaries. For that purpose, specification of generic service class is needed, which allows administrators to describe service classes in their own domains independently of the network technology and the applied QoS model. Maniatis, Nikolouzou, and Venieris (2004) proposed generic service specification (GSS) framework for end-to-end QoS provisioning across multiple administrative domains in the backbone network and different types of access networks. The basic idea of GSS framework is to express QoS requirements by means of universally accepted format, which also facilitates automatic translation of QoS requirements to appropriate internal QoS policies. Bostjancic, Timcenko, and Stojanovic (2008) proposed a common framework for inter-provider IP QoS specification, which encompasses a generic service level specification format and an efficient conformance matching scheme that allows administrators to assess the degree of correspondence between the required and offered QoS. An example of generic **SLS**, illustrated in Figure 2, encompasses both traffic profile specification and QoS specification.

Traffic profile descriptor includes: packet size, bit rate, burst size, TTL (time to live), adaptability and treatment of the excess traffic. Adaptability denotes the ability of application to adjust bandwidth consumption to network conditions. If adaptive, ingress flow can be elastic or non-elastic. Elastic flow can tolerate certain delay variations but poses strict requirements with respect to low packet loss. Non-elastic flow can tolerate

Figure 2. Example of generic service level specification (adapted from Bostjancic, Timcenko, & Stojanovic, 2008)

```
BEGINNING OF SLS:
 Traffic flow:
  - Communication type: <1□ 1> <1□ N> <N□ N>
  - Addresses: <source and destination addresses>
  - Interfaces: <source and destination port IDs>
  - Transport protocol: <TCP> <UDP> <RTP> ...

 Traffic profile:
  - Packet size: <minimum> <average> <maximum>
  - Bit rate: <peak> <average>
  - Burstiness: <peak> <average>
  - Time To Live: <value>
  - Adaptability: <elastic> <non-elastic> <no>
  - Excess traffic: <dropping> <re-marking> <shaping>

 Performance metrics:
  - Maximum delay: <value> <not specified>
  - Maximum round trip delay: <value>  <not specified>
  - Maximum jitter: <value> <not specified>
  - Maximum packet loss probability: <value> <not specified

 Reliability:
  - MTBF: <value> <not specified>
  - MTTR: <value> <not specified>

 Availability: <value>

 Service schedule:
      <day/beginning - end of period> <7days/24h>

 Service re-negotiation: <yes> <no>
END OF SLS
```

certain degree of packet loss, but implies strict requirements in the sense of delay guarantees. Treatment of the excess traffic refers to dropping, re-marking or shaping of the traffic that exceeds negotiated profile. Performance descriptor encompasses performance metrics like delay, round trip delay, jitter and packet loss probability (all values are defined from ingress to egress point). Availability descriptor describes percentage of total time of service availability. Reliability descriptor encompasses parameters like mean time between failures (MTBF) and mean time to repair (MTTR). Service scheduling descriptor specifies time interval in which the service is available. QoS renegotiation descriptor explicitly defines whether administrator is allowed to offer service of worse characteristics if the network can not meet user's requirements.

SIGNALING FOR QUALITY OF SERVICE

Signaling for quality of service (**QoS signaling**) is a mechanism responsible for "conveying application (or network) performance requirements, reserving network resources across the network, or discovering QoS routes" (ITU-T, 2004, p.11). Classification of QoS signaling is presented in Figure 3.

In-band QoS signaling assumes that signaling information is associated with data traffic. Signaling information is typically present in the appropriate field of IP packet header, for example differentiated services code point (DSCP) in the DiffServ architecture. Inherently, this type of signaling is not suitable for resource reservation or QoS routing, which have to be defined statically before the data transfer phase. Out-of-band QoS signaling assumes that signaling information is carried in appropriate messages, by means of a

Figure 3. Classification of QoS signaling

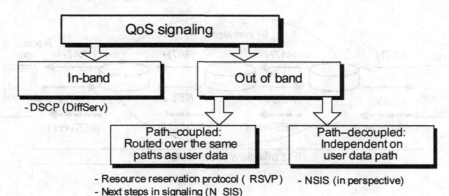

separate protocol, which allows dynamic resource reservation and QoS routing. Path-coupled QoS signaling assumes that signaling messages can be routed only through the nodes that are potentially on the data path. In path-decoupled QoS signaling, signaling and data paths are independent.

Requirements for signaling information regarding IP-based QoS encompass the interface between the user and the network (UNI), across interfaces between different networks (NNI), including access networks (ITU-T, 2005, p.1). Specification of mandatory and optional QoS parameters in signaling messages includes:

- Expected numerical values of performance metrics for specific **service class**, like packet loss ratio, maximum delay, etc.;
- Parameters that describe traffic flow, including peak and/or average rate, peak and/or average burstiness, maximum packet size;
- PHB code, i.e. the value of DSCP in IP packet header (optionally);
- Parameters that specify service priority and reliability.

Standardization of **QoS signaling** protocols is still in progress. Until the end of this Section, a brief overview of two predominant IETF standards is presented: the Resource Reservation Protocol and the Next Steps in Signaling framework.

Resource Reservation Protocol

Resource reservation protocol – RSVP (Braden, Zhang, Berson et al., 1997), which has originally been designed as a companion standard of the IntServ model, has also been considered as QoS signaling protocol. RSVP is a path-coupled protocol, which supports multicast reservations and "many-to-many" communication. RSVP was the first protocol that formalized the use of so-called soft signaling states – nonpermanent control states in network nodes that will expire unless refreshed.

The basic principle of RSVP operation is illustrated in Figure 4.

Sending host specifies IP traffic flow in a signaling message *PATH*. After receiving *PATH* message, RSVP entity in each router stores the address of preceding RSVP router, creates or refreshes "path" state and forwards the message towards the receiver. Receiving host answers by *RESV* message, which contains request for a certain type and amount of resources. Each RSVP router which receives *RESV* message creates or refreshes its reservation state ("resv"), and then forwards the message towards sending host. *RESV* message may contain the optional confirmation request object, which causes generating of messages *RESVconf* from sending to receiving host.

The original variant of RSVP has been modified

Figure 4. RSVP basic protocol operation

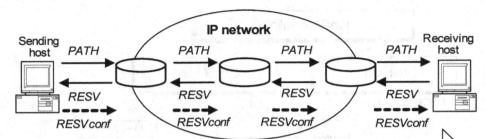

and extended for purpose of service differentiation over aggregate traffic flows (Baker, Iturralde, Le Faucheur, & Davie, 2001) as well as label distribution and explicit traffic routing in MPLS networks (Awduche, Berger, Gan et al., 2001).

However, RSVP suffers from several drawbacks which make it unsuitable for application in NGNs (Manner & Fu, 2005). First of all, RSVP was designed at the time when mobile communications were still at the beginning and it does not support node mobility. Second, the use of unreliable, connectionless transport protocol (User Datagram Protocol, UDP) without message segmenting poses limitations to network architectures and signaling applications. Finally, RSVP does not provide any framework for security mechanisms, particularly authentication and key management. The general need of path-coupled signaling is to discover a chain of signaling nodes on a hop-by-hop principle, along data path. However, in RSVP node discovery and delivery of signaling messages are performed in a single protocol operation. That feature also makes it difficult to use the existing security mechanisms (for example, IP Security), which is particularly unsuitable for end-to-end addressed signaling messages (for example *PATH*).

Next Steps in Signaling (NSIS) framework

Due to the shortcomings of RSVP and its extensions, the IETF Next Steps in Signaling (NSIS) working group began to work on a new protocol suite in order to meet new signaling requirements and create a general purpose signaling framework (Hancock, Karagiannis, Loughney, & Van den Bosch, 2005). The NSIS framework is primary focused to specification of path coupled point-to-point two-layer signaling protocols. The main NSIS objectives are: (1) to achieve applicability in different network parts, i.e., access signaling, end-to-end signaling, edge-to-edge signaling and (2) to enable interactions between signaling and the other network layer functions, including address translation, routing and mobility.

In order to meet those objectives, the NSIS framework separates functions such as reliability, congestion control and integrity of signaling messages from signaling applications. Hence, two-layer NSIS architecture consists of:

*   NSIS Transport Layer Protocol (NTLP), which is responsible for transport of signaling messages between applications. Although the option of building a monolithic protocol at the NTLP layer is stated in the framework, the preferred approach is to build NSIS specific functions in the General

Figure 5. Logical structure of NTLP and the role of GIST

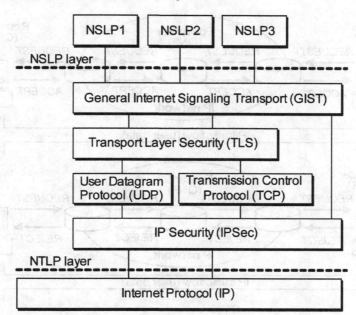

Internet Signaling Protocol (GIST), which makes use of the existing transport and security protocols (Fu, Schulzrinne, Bader et al., 2005).

- NSIS Signaling Layer Protocols (NSLPs), each of which performs signaling functions that are specific for particular applications, including formats and processing rules of signaling messages. Examples of NSLPs include QoS NSLP for signaling with resource reservation, NSLP for configuration of metering entities, etc.

Similar like RSVP, NSIS protocols use a soft state approach. The NSIS framework introduces concept of session identifier, which is carried in signaling messages to uniquely identify installed state, instead of reusing the flow identifier. The concept enables flexible flow-session relationships particularly with respect to mobility, multihoming, tunneling and IPv4/v6 traversal.

NSIS builds upon the GIST protocol. The basic GIST responsibility is efficient upstream and downstream peer-to-peer message delivery, in a wide variety of network scenarios. Message delivery includes peer discovery, i.e., locating and/or selecting which NTLP peer should carry out signaling exchanges for a specific data flow. Decoupling of peer discovery from the signaling message transport mechanism is a key design concept that enables GIST to use existing transport and security protocols. The peer discovery component in GIST can rely on IP router alert options or routing tables. Logical structure of NTLP and the role of GIST are illustrated in Figure 5.

At the NSLP layer, QoS NSLP is responsible for signaling for QoS. With regards to direction of data flow, QoS signaling may be either sender-oriented or receiver-oriented. QoS NSIS Initiator (QNI) is the signaling entity that makes the resource request, usually as a result of user application request. QoS NSIS Responder (QNR) is the signaling entity that acts as the endpoint for the signaling and that can optionally interact with applications as well. QoS NSIS Forwarder (QNF) is a transit signaling entity between a QNI

Figure 6. Basic principle of QoS NSLP operations:

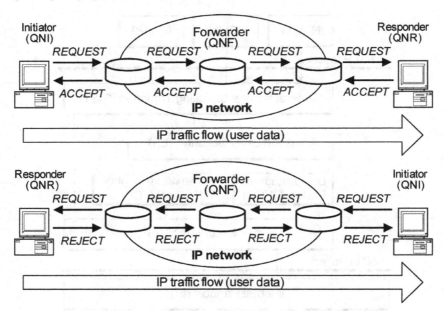

and QNR that forwards NSIS signaling through the network. The basic principle of QoS NSLP operation is illustrated in Figure 6.

At the node, QoS request may originate either from local application (user application or network management system) or the incoming QoS NSLP message. In the latter case, NSIS messages must be extracted during input packet processing and forwarded to the GIST entity.

QoS NSLP processes only the messages related with QoS provisioning, independent on the QoS model (IntServ, DiffServ, UMTS, other models). Parameters related with resource reservation (available bandwidth, traffic conditioning parameters) are encapsulated in NSLP and exchanged between QoS NSLP nodes. Resource management function is responsible for processing of QoS request. A local QoS model determines the interpretation of QoS request, as well as resource provisioning and configuring. Resource provisioning encompasses two additional processes: admission control procedure and policy control. Finally, QoS NSLP node generates the indication that the requested resources have been configured,

i.e., the acknowledgement message. The node may also forward QoS request toward the data receiver.

a) Sender-oriented signaling – example of successful establishment of signaling connection

b) Receiver-oriented signaling – example of signaling set-up failure

The NSIS framework has been designed taking into account security issues by assuming integration with standard transport and network layer security protocols such as Transport Layer Security (TLS) and IP Security (IPSec). Since the NSIS protocol suite is split into two layers, the security solution needs to offer protection for both NTLP and NSLPs. Tschofenig and Fu (2006) have identified the following basic requirements for securing NSIS protocols:

• Ability to run an authentication and key exchange protocol between neighboring NSIS peers;

- Security association establishment to provide integrity, confidentiality and replay protection for signaling messages exchanged between neighboring peers;
- Denial of service protection;
- Lightweight protection for the discovery mechanism;
- Authorization of the NTLP signaling peers;
- Flexible authorization at the NSLP layer including the interworking with the existing AAA infrastructure.

A FRAMEWORK FOR SERVICE MANAGEMENT

In this Section, we propose a framework for service management. First, requirements for user application design have been considered. Further, a functional model of QoS negotiation has been proposed. We also consider management policies and finally briefly describe a prototype implementation.

Requirements for User Application Design

Deployment of QoS architectures and associated mechanisms supporting end-to-end QoS guarantees assumes development of QoS oriented applications, i.e. "QoS aware" applications. Highly portable QoS application programming interface (API) should provide interactions of application with QoS signaling protocol, as well as independency of application from network technology or details of applied QoS architecture and associated mechanisms.

Chassot, Auriol, and Lozes (2003) describe an example of generic API functionality in IPv6 network. Programmable API parameters encompass sequence of IP traffic flows inside a domain and between domains together with logical constraints in flow synchronization, availability,

maximum allowed delay, maximum number of consecutively lost packets, etc. The semantics of QoS guarantees includes establishing of logical relationship between application requirements and service classes. QoS API is also responsible for establishing of signaling channel between applications in end systems. Selection of transport protocol is performed depending on selected service class.

API should be based on object-oriented design, very high level programming languages and advanced information technologies, in order to guarantee efficient usage and portability (Schantz1, Loyall, Rodrigues et. al, 2003).

On the other side, in order to provide interoperability for legacy applications, an appropriate access interface to QoS parameters offered by the provider is needed. Such interface is typically installed at the end user's host, allows manual configuration of QoS parameters and does not require any changes of the existing applications (Engel, Granzer, Koch et al., 2003). Similar approach has been proposed by Bostjancic and Stojanovic (2007), assuming DiffServ provider's network and an appropriate service level specification. The latter approach has recently been extended by a framework for QoS specification in an all-IP environment (Bostjancic, Timcenko, & Stojanovic, 2008).

A Functional Model of Service Negotiation

We further propose a functional model of service negotiation, which is illustrated in Figure 7. At the customer premises, coexistence of both QoS-aware and QoS-unaware (legacy) applications has been supposed. QoS-aware applications access to QoS signaling protocol entity through QoS API to forward their requirements to the provider. For legacy applications, QoS access interface should be manually configured. User requirements are typically specified in an informal manner (e.g., qualitatively rather than quantitatively). The

Figure 7. QoS negotiation: a functional model

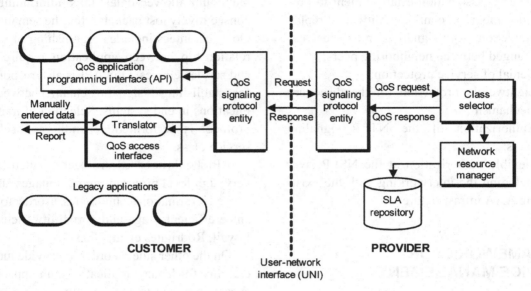

translator entity within QoS access interface is responsible for mapping informal user requirements to a formal request and vice versa.

It should be emphasized that this functional model does not assume any particular signaling protocol (e.g., RSVP, NSIS or some proprietary protocol). Instead, we make use of the fact that all **QoS signaling** protocols rely on "Request/Response" paradigm and suppose a generic protocol with two basic types of messages: *Request* and *Response*. *Request* message carries user requirements for particular service in terms of service level specification, with parameters and descriptors described in Figure 2. *Response* message carries either the answer from the provider: positive, negative or request for service re-negotiation. For example, in RSVP *Request* corresponds to *PATH*, while *Response* corresponds to *RESV* message. In QoS NSLP, *Request* and *Response* correspond to *REQUEST* and *ACCEPT/REJECT* messages, respectively.

At the provider's side, QoS signaling protocol entity accepts *Request* message, extracts relevant traffic and QoS parameters and forwards them to the Class selector, through the internal primitive *QoS request*. Class selector is responsible for

evaluating user requirements with the set of **service classes** offered by the provider and finding the most suitable class for ingress traffic flow that will provide required QoS level. Network resource manager decides about the admission of new traffic flow and allocates resources (bandwidth, buffer space etc.), according to QoS requirements and the state of network resources. Based on that decision, Class selector generates the appropriate internal primitive *QoS response*, which is further mapped to *Response* message in QoS signaling protocol entity. All negotiated SLAs are stored in the SLA repository.

It should be noted that the proposed framework is applicable to management of layer 3 provider provisioned IP VPN services (Stojanovic & Acimovic-Raspopovic, 2008), assuming appropriate VPN specific service level specifications.

Management Policies

Management policies may encompass set of rules concerning service classification, network devices, admission control, bandwidth allocation, pricing, security, etc. They should be defined, through the appropriate entity, for different net-

Figure 8. An example of pricing policy scheme

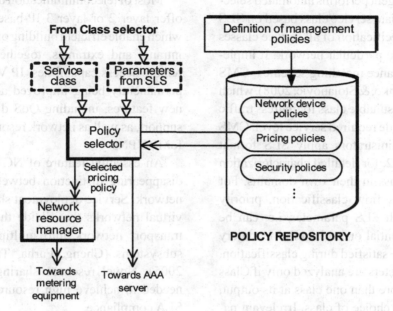

work devices and different classes of service. For each network device or group of devices a specific number of policies is defined, which depends on QoS architecture deployed in network. For example, for DiffServ ingress routers policies are defined with respect to IP traffic conditioning, bandwidth allocation and configuring of queues, while for core routers there are only policies defined for bandwidth allocation and configuring of queues.

An example of pricing **policy** scheme is presented in Figure 8. The inputs to Policy selector are parameters obtained from the Class selector: service class and parameters from SLS, e.g., service scheduling. Based on these inputs, Policy selector fetches the appropriate policy from the policy repository. It further forwards the policy to AAA server and to Network resource manager, which translates it to corresponding configuration parameters for metering equipment.

The Prototype Implementation

The prototype of proposed framework has been developed for PC Windows environment, using object oriented design and C++ programming language. Modular design provides high level of portability and also enables efficient upgrade and customization. The application consists of the set of windows that appear alternatively after selection of appropriate commands (menu items, program buttons or shortcuts from the keyboard).

At the moment, the prototype supports manual configuration of QoS parameters through access interface that is called User agent. It allows: (1) creating of user entry, with selection of user name, password and registering with personal data; (2) negotiation of a new SLA, with the possibility to specify QoS and **traffic profile** parameters; (3) service re-negotiation through modification of the existing SLA; (4) inspection of the existing SLAs, through suitable reports and (5) cancellation of the SLA.

Class selector agent performs automated selection of the appropriate service class based on **SLS** parameters and specification of all service classes that are available in particular network. It implements the conformance matching scheme – CMS (Bostjancic, Timcenko, & Stojanovic, 2008), which discovers the most suitable class for ingress traffic flow that will provide required service level. CMS assumes that administrators apply SLS format depicted in Figure 2, for detailed characterization of each service class in their own domains. For purpose of ingress flow classification, priority is assigned to each SLS parameter, i.e. can be mandatory, preferential or irrelevant. Mandatory parameters must be satisfied during classification. Preferential parameters are analyzed only if Class selector returns more than one class at its output, to facilitate proper choice of class. Irrelevant parameters are ignored during conformance matching. Class selector also establishes the most appropriate degree of correspondence between the requirements for particular session and a class from the available set of service classes.

Finally, Administrator agent implements search engine by defined criteria like user name, service class, etc. It allows network administrator to access to all user entries and SLA repository and inspect all of data related with users and their associated SLAs, as well as to cancel user entries and/or their associated SLAs.

FUTURE TRENDS

Existing commercial solutions for building SME communication infrastructure encompass advanced Ethernet-based equipment as well as **SME business gateways** from different vendors, at reasonable prices. They typically support a number of collaborative services, high-speed Internet access, different forms of VPNs, range of security features, VoIP gateway functionality, and basic QoS support (mainly limited to data plane mechanisms).

Most of telecommunication operators and ISPs offer layer 2 or layer 3 IP-based **VPN** services, which enable efficient building of secure enterprise intranet and extranets, together with enhanced remote access capabilities. IP VPN solutions are permanently being improved and enriched with new features, including QoS differentiation and support, as well as network resource management for IP VPNs.

An essential feature of NGNs should be the disappearing distinction between users and the network. Service deployment should be based on virtual networks that divide the DiffServ-based transport network into multiple self-managed subsystems (Cheng, Farha, Tizghadam et al., 2005). Novel resource sharing techniques are needed to achieve high resource utilization and SLA compliance.

At the moment, standards for SLS formats (either generic or related with particular QoS models) are still missing, as well as a recommendation for formal descriptive language that should be used for representation of SLS. Those issues are of the key importance for developing of QoS-aware applications and access interfaces, for achieving the inter-provider QoS and also for facilitating an automated service and network management.

The extensibility, interworking with the existing transport and security protocols as well as mobility support of the NSIS protocols should speed their deployment. However, more detailed validation and verification of these protocols, together with experiences from test bed environments are still missing.

Policy based management is foreseen as a solution to build flexible and highly-automated management platforms in **NGNs** (ITU-T, 2006). Another important issue is related with specification and development of new, sophisticated management protocols. Research is also needed on scalable distributed data aggregation and event correlation mechanisms.

Finally, there is a strong need for deploying pricing schemes that take into account network resource utilization, with different tariffs per each service class (Acimovic-Raspopovic & Stojanovic, 2008; Gupta, Stahl, & Whinston, 2005; Shakkottai & Srikant, 2006). On the other side, providers require simple pricing schemes with which they can fairly recover costs from their users and effectively allocate network resources. Novel, usage-based pricing schemes together with accounting management systems are needed for providers to build their business models with regards to different profiles of customers and to enforce customers to wisely select the most appropriate **traffic profiles** and to properly adjust to them.

CONCLUSION

This article discusses communication requirements for small and medium enterprises (SMEs) from both provider and customer perspectives. The basis for SME communication infrastructure at the individual site should be Ethernet-based LAN equipped with so called SME business gateway, which is a remotely manageable access device that integrates a variety of communication functions needed to achieve wide area networking between sites.

We further emphasize QoS issues in control and management planes, particularly SLA, QoS signaling and service management. The proposed policy-based framework for service management encompasses interfaces for QoS-aware and legacy applications, generic service level specification, functional model of service negotiation and management policies.

The generic SLS format should contain a set of descriptors and their associated parameters that describe the required service class independently of the network technology (e.g. wired, wireless) and the applied QoS model. Further, an appropriate algorithm is needed for mapping of QoS requirements across multiple administrative IP domains and different types of access networks.

The functional model of QoS negotiation assumes generic signaling protocol, which relies on "request/response" paradigm and is applicable with standard protocols (RSVP, NSIS) as well as with proprietary protocols. Selection and enforcement of different management policies has also been addressed. The proposed framework is generally applicable to provider provisioned layer 3 VPN services.

The future work should be focused towards specification and development of business models for service providers, suitable to stay competitive in the growing SME market.

ACKNOWLEDGMENT

This work has partially been funded by the Serbian Ministry of Science and Technological Development (project TR 11002).

REFERENCES

Acimovic-Raspopovic, V., & Stojanovic, M. (2008). Pricing quality of service in DiffServ IP networks. In G. Putnik & M. Cuncha (Eds.), *Encyclopedia of Networked and Virtual Organizations*, Vol. II (pp. 1245-1251). Hershey, PA: Information Science Reference.

Ahmed, T., Asgari, A., Mehaoua, A., Borcoci, E., Berti-Équille, L., & Georgios, K. (2007). End-to-end quality of service provisioning through an integrated management system for multimedia content delivery. *Computer Communications, 30*(3), 638–651. doi:10.1016/j.comcom.2006.10.009

Awduche, D., Berger, L., Gan, D., Li, T., Srinivasan, V., & Swallow, G. (2001). RSVP-TE: extensions to RSVP for LSP tunnels. *IETF RFC 3209 (Standards Track)*. Retrieved October 31, 2006 from http://www.rfc-editor.org/rfcsearch.html

Baker, F., Iturralde, C., Le Faucheur, F., & Davie, B. (2001). Aggregation of RSVP for IPv4 and IPv6 reservations. *IETF RFC 3175 (Standards Track)*. Retrieved October 31, 2006 from http://www.rfc-editor.org/rfcsearch.html

Blake, S., Black, D., Carlson, M., Davies, E., Wang, Z., & Weiss, W. (1998). An architecture for Differentiated Services. (1998). *IETF RFC 2475 (Proposed standard)*. Retrieved April 26, 2003 from http://www.rfc-editor.org/rfcsearch.html

Bostjancic, S., & Stojanovic, M. (2007). SLAM: an object-oriented application for IP Quality of Service negotiation. In B. Milovanovic (Ed.), *Proceedings of the 8th International Conference on Telecommunications in Modern Satellite Cable and Broadcasting Services – TELSIKS 2007, Vol. 1* (pp. 87-90). Serbia: University of Nis, Faculty of Electronic Engineering.

Bostjancic, S., Timcenko, V., & Stojanovic, M. (2008). A common framework for inter-Provider IP Quality of Service specification. In B. Milovanovic (Ed.), *Proceedings of the XLIII International Scientific Conference on Information, Communication and Energy Systems and Technologies - ICEST 2008, Vol. 2* (pp. 429-432). Serbia: University of Nis, Faculty of Electronic Engineering.

Bouras, C., & Sevasti, A. (2005). Service level agreements for DiffServ-based services provisioning. *Journal of Network and Computer Applications, 28*, 285–302. doi:10.1016/j.jnca.2004.07.001

Braden, R., Clark, D., & Shenker, S. (1994). Integrated services in the Internet architecture: an overview. *IETF RFC 1633 (Informational)*. Retrieved April 26, 2003 from http://www.rfc-editor.org/rfcsearch.html

Braden, R., Zhang, L., Berson, S., Herzog, S., & Jamin, S. (1997). Resource reservation Protocol (RSVP) – version 1 functional specification. *IETF RFC 2205 (Standards Track)*. Retrieved April 26, 2003 from http://www.rfc-editor.org/rfcsearch.html

Calhoun, P., Johansson, T., Perkins, C., Hiller, T., & McCann, P. (2005). Diameter mobile IPv4 application. *IETF RFC 4004 (Standards Track)*. Retrieved July 25, 2007 from http://www.rfc-editor.org/rfcsearch.html

Calhoun, P., Zorn, G., Spence, D., & Mitton, D. (2005). Diameter network access server application. *IETF RFC 4005 (Standards Track)*. Retrieved August 30, 2007 from http://www.rfc-editor.org/rfcsearch.html

Camarinha-Matos, L. M., & Afsarmanesh, H. (1999). *Tendencies and general requirements for virtual enterprises*. In L. Camarinha-Matos & H. Afsarmanesh (Eds.), *Proceedings of the IFIP TC5 WG5.3 / PRODNET Working Conference on Infrastructures for Virtual Enterprises: Networking Industrial Enterprises* (pp.15-30). Boston, MA: Kluwer Academic Publishers.

Carugi, M., & De Clercq, J. (2004). Virtual private network services: Scenarios, requirements and architectural constructs from a standardization perspective. *IEEE Communications Magazine, 42*(6), 116–122. doi:10.1109/MCOM.2004.1304246

Chassot, C., Auriol, G., & Lozes, A. (2003). QoS management protocol for end-to-end communication architecture implemented over a differentiated IPv6 network. In J. Charzinski, R. Lehnert, & P. Tran-Gia (Eds.), *Proceedings of the 18th International Teletraffic Congress*, Vol. 5b (pp. 1251-1260). Berlin, Germany: Elsevier Science.

Cheng, Y., Farha, R., Tizghadam, A., Kim, M. S., Hashemi, M., & Leon-Garcia, A. (2005). Virtual network approach to scalable IP service deployment and efficient resource management. *IEEE Communications Magazine, 43*(10), 76–84. doi:10.1109/MCOM.2005.1522128

Engel, T., Granzer, H., Koch, B. F., Winter, M., Sampatakos, P., & Venieris, I. S. (2003). AQUILA: Adaptive resource control for QoS using an IP-based layered architecture. *IEEE Communications Magazine, 41*(10), 46–53. doi:10.1109/MCOM.2003.1166653

Flegkas, P., Trimintzios, P., & Pavlou, G. (2002). A policy-based quality of service management system for IP DiffServ networks. *IEEE Network, 16*(2), 50–56. doi:10.1109/65.993223

Forum, D. S. L. (2007). Broadband multi-service architecture & framework requirements. *Technical Report TR-144*. Retrieved September 19, 2008 from http://www.broadband-forum.org/technical/trlist.php

Fu, X., Schulzrinne, H., Bader, A., Hogrefe, D., Kappler, C., & Karagiannis, G. (2005). NSIS: a new extensible IP signaling protocol suite. *IEEE Communications Magazine, 43*(10), 133–141. doi:10.1109/MCOM.2005.1522137

Grossman, D. (2002). New terminology and clarifications for DiffServ. *IETF RFC 3260 (Informational)*. Retrieved April 5, 2005 from http://www.rfc-editor.org/rfcsearch.html

Gupta, A., Stahl, D. O., & Whinston, A. B. (2005). Pricing traffic on interconnected networks: issues, approaches and solutions. In S. K. Majumdar, I. Vogelsang & M. E. Cave (Eds.), *Handbook of Telecommunications Economics*, vol. 2 (pp. 413-439). North-Holland.

Hadjiantonis, A. M., Charalambides, M., & Pavlou, G. (2007). An adaptive service management framework for wireless networks. *IEEE Vehicular Technology Magazine, 2*(3), 6–13. doi:10.1109/MVT.2008.915322

Hancock, R., Karagiannis, G., Loughney, J., & Van den Bosch, S. (2005). Next steps in signaling (NSIS): framework. *IETF RFC 4080 (Informational)*. Retrieved March 19, 2007 from http://www.rfc-editor.org/rfcsearch.html

Institute of Electrical and Electronic Engineers (IEEE). (2004). IEEE standard for local and metropolitan area networks: media access control (MAC) bridges. *IEEE Std 802.1D-2004*.

Institute of Electrical and Electronic Engineers (IEEE). (2005). IEEE standard for local and metropolitan area networks: virtual bridged local area networks. *IEEE Std 802.1Q-2005*.

International Telecommunication Union – Telecommunication Standardization Sector (ITU-T). (2004). An architectural framework for support of quality of service (QoS) in packet networks. *ITU-T recommendation* [Geneva, ITU-T.]. *Y (Dayton, Ohio),* ▪▪▪, 1291.

International Telecommunication Union – Telecommunication Standardization Sector (ITU-T). (2005). Signaling requirements for IP-QoS. *Supplement 51 to ITU-T Q-series recommendations*. Geneva, ITU-T.

International Telecommunication Union – Telecommunication Standardization Sector (ITU-T). (2006). Converged services framework functional requirements and architecture. *ITU-T recommendation* [Geneva, ITU-T.]. *Y (Dayton, Ohio),* ▪▪▪, 2013.

Kazovsky, L. G., Gutierrez, D., Shaw, W.-T., & Wong, G. (2008). *Broadband fiber access*. A tutorial from IEEE Communications Society. Retrieved September 25, 2008 from http://www.comsoc.org/freetutorials

Klincewicz, J. G., Schmitt, J. A., & Wong, R. T. (2002). Incorporating QoS into IP enterprise network design. *Telecommunication Systems, 20*(1-2), 81–106. doi:10.1023/A:1015441400785

Knight, P., & Lewis, K. (2004). Layer 2 and 3 virtual private networks: taxonomy, technology and standardization efforts. *IEEE Communications Magazine, 42*(6), 124–131. doi:10.1109/MCOM.2004.1304248

Li, M. (2003). Policy-based IPsec management. *IEEE Network, 17*(6), 36–43. doi:10.1109/MNET.2003.1248659

Maniatis, S., Nikolouzou, E., & Venieris, I. (2004). End-to-end QoS specification issues in the converged all-IP wired and wireless environment. *IEEE Communications Magazine, 42*(6), 80–86. doi:10.1109/MCOM.2004.1304236

Manner, J., & Fu, X. (2005). Analysis of existing Quality-of-Service signaling protocols. *IETF RFC 4904 (Informational)*. Retrieved July 15, 2008 from http://www.rfc-editor.org/rfcsearch.html

Mohapatra, P., Metz, C., & Cui, Y. (2007). Layer 3 VPN services over IPv6 backbone networks: requirements, technology, and standardization efforts. *IEEE Communications Magazine, 45*(4), 32–37. doi:10.1109/MCOM.2007.343609

Mordelet, N., Festraets, E., & Wang, M. (2006). The enterprise: A high-value market for broadband services. *Alcatel Telecommunications Review* (3rd Quarter 2006). Retrieved September 5, 2008 from http://www.alcatel-lucent.com

Osório, A. L., & Barata, M. M. (2001). Reliable and secure communications infrastructure for virtual enterprises. *Journal of Intelligent Manufacturing, 12*, 171–183. doi:10.1023/A:1011204627577

Pras, A., Schönwälder, J., Burgess, M., Festor, O., Martínez Pérez, G., Stadler, R., & Stiller, B. (2007). Key research challenges in network management. *IEEE Communications Magazine, 45*(10), 104–110. doi:10.1109/MCOM.2007.4342832

Raghunath, S., & Ramakrishnan, K. K. (2007). Resource management for virtual private networks. *IEEE Communications Magazine, 45*(4), 38–44. doi:10.1109/MCOM.2007.343610

Rosen, E., Viswanathan, A., & Callon, R. (2001). Multiprotocol label switching architecture. *IETF RFC 3031 (Standards Track)*. Retrieved April 26, 2003 from http://www.rfc-editor.org/rfcsearch.html

Sánchez, R., Raptis, L., & Vaxevanakis, K. (2008). Ethernet as a carrier grade technology: developments and innovations. *IEEE Communications Magazine, 46*(9), 88–94. doi:10.1109/MCOM.2008.4623712

Schantzl, R. E., Loyall, J. P., Rodrigues, C., Schmidt, D. C., Krishnamurthy, Y., & Pyarali, I. (2003). Flexible and adaptive QoS control for distributed real-time and embedded middleware. In M. Endler & D. Schmidt (Eds.), *Middleware 2003* (LNCS 2672, pp. 374-393). Springer Berlin/Heidelberg.

Shakkottai, S., & Srikant, R. (2006). Economics of network pricing with multiple ISPs. *IEEE Transactions on Networking, 14*(6), 1233–1245. doi:10.1109/TNET.2006.886393

Stojanovic, M., & Acimovic-Raspopovic, V. (2008). QoS provisioning framework in IP-based VPN. In G. Putnik & M. Cunha (Eds.), *Encyclopedia of Networked and Virtual Organizations*, Vol. III (pp. 1317-1324). New York: Information Science Reference.

Third Generation Partnership Project – 3GPP. (2003). End to end quality of service concept and architecture. *Technical specification 23.207, Release 5*. Retrieved July 7, 2007 from http://www.3gpp.org

Tschofenig, H., & Fu, X. (2006). Securing the next steps in signaling (NSIS) protocol suite. *International Journal of Internet Protocol Technology*, *1*(4), 271–282.

Verma, D. C. (2002). Simplifying network administration using policy-based management. *IEEE Network*, *16*(2), 20–26. doi:10.1109/65.993219

KEY TERMS AND DEFINITIONS

Authentication, Authorization and Accounting (AAA): A system in IP based networking that provides a secure network connection and a record of user activity, by identifying who the user is, what the user can access, and what services and resources the user is consuming. AAA represents the three primary services required by a network access server (NAS), which are typically implemented by means of a common protocol.

Differentiated Services (DiffServ): A scalable IP QoS architecture, which assumes marking and grouping of packets with similar QoS requirements to the same traffic aggregate (class), which is then processed in the same manner at the network nodes. Complex processing of individual traffic flows is performed at the edge routers, while simple and fast forwarding operations are performed at the core routers over aggregate flows.

Next Generation Network (NGN): An architectural concept of future telecommunication core and access networks, which assumes transport of all information and services over a common network, typically built around the IP.

Next Steps in Signaling (NSIS): The IETF framework, which is intended to specification of path coupled point-to-point two-layer signaling protocols. The main NSIS objectives are: (1) to achieve applicability in different network parts, i.e., access signaling, end-to-end signaling, edge-to-edge signaling and (2) to enable interactions between signaling and the other network layer functions, including address translation, routing and mobility.

Policy Based Management (PBM): IETF framework that encompasses conceptual, functional and informational models for development of highly-automated management systems that implement sets of abstractly defined rules – policies.

QoS Signaling: A mechanism responsible for conveying application (or network) performance requirements, reserving network resources across the network, or discovering QoS routes.

Service Level Agreement (SLA): A contract between the service provider and the user (either end user or another domain), which defines provider's responsibilities in the sense of QoS guarantees, performance metrics, measurement methods, tariffs and billing principles, as well as penalties for both the user and the provider in the case of contract violation.

SME Business Gateway: An integrated, remotely manageable access device that implements a variety of communication functions, including high-speed Internet access, wireless access point, virtual private networks, IP PBX and VoIP gateway, QoS support, as well as security mechanisms.

Traffic Profile: Description of the temporal properties of a traffic stream such as rate and burst size.

Virtual Private Network (VPN): A service that enables restricted communication between a set of sites, making use of a backbone that is shared with other traffic not belonging to that communication.

Chapter 14
Selecting Appropriate Communication Tools to Support Teams' Creative Processes in SMEs

Hélder Fanha Martins
Lisbon Polytechnic Institute - Lisbon School of Accounting and Administration, Portugal

Maria João Ferro
Lisbon Polytechnic Institute - Lisbon School of Accounting and Administration, Portugal

ABSTRACT

Accomplishing creative tasks collaboratively is particularly problematic when team members who are attempting to achieve the creative results are geographically dispersed throughout the globe in a virtual team. Therefore, sound communication tools are needed to ensure communication does not hamper team creativity. This chapter highlights the communication tools available for doing creative work, offering a short analysis of the most relevant synchronous and asynchronous communication tools. Some rules and tips are given to allow for a better choice of the communication tools to use according to both the nature of the team and the work it is performing in terms of creative processes in SMEs. This chapter also presents how knowledge experts and knowledge-based companies consider whether it would be any benefit to apply Web 2.0 in their organisational architecture to strengthen collaboration.

INTRODUCTION

In collaborative work, communication is essential. If there is faulty or no communication or inadequate information exchange, team creativity is hampered. Accomplishing creative tasks collaboratively can become particularly problematic when the very team members who are attempting to achieve the creative results are geographically dispersed throughout the globe in a virtual team.

This chapter highlights the communication tools available for doing creative work, offering a short analysis of the most relevant ones. We start by pointing out some of the challenges faced by virtual teams when team members need to communicate with each other before digging into an analysis of synchronous and asynchronous communication

DOI: 10.4018/978-1-60566-892-5.ch014

tools. We then proceed to offer some general rules and tips to select the appropriate communication tools and after that we examine the situations when those tools are used. Before the final remarks, some words on creative work are said.

The main purpose of this chapter is to provide some general insight into the existing communication tools to allow the best alternative according to both the nature of the team and the work it is performing in terms of creative processes in SMEs.

BACKGROUND

The following background defines what a virtual team is and its importance for the integration of IT in SMEs. It explains the collaborative process, with the knowledge workers being at its center. The term virtual is fairly new and is associated with concepts such as the virtual knowledge network, the virtual organization, the virtual team, the virtual community of practice, and the virtual workplace, to name just a few. Basically, the virtual team is defined as a group of knowledge workers who are geographically dispersed but not necessarily distributed across expansive geographic locations. They are working together toward a common purpose and goal and using electronic communication as their primary medium. The virtual team is interested in explicit and tacit knowledge management using integrated technologies from synchronous and asynchronous communication, knowledge management functionalities, discussion forums, and much more. The virtual team may have little or no face-to-face contact. Therefore, it must build a foundation of teamwork and trust for collaboration to truly happen and for performance to be achieved. Among the characteristics of a virtual team is the type. Fisher and Fisher (2001) define the type based on three criteria: time, space, and culture:

1. Time refers to *when* people work. Virtual team members may be assigned different hours, different shifts and different days to work. They may also work at the same moment but in a different time zone.

2. Space refers to *where* people work. Virtual team workers may work in close proximity to one another or be quite remote. They may share the same office or a different one on the same floor or another floor in a given building. Or they may also be located in different buildings, in different cities, and even in different countries.

3. Culture refers to *how* people work together-- the ways in which they deal with each other. Elements of culture include languages, races, nationalities, professions, and education, as well as religious, political, social, and economic factors. In a way, even gender can influence culture.

For their part, Duarte and Snyder (2001) present seven types of virtual teams based on boundaries and membership:

1. The virtual corporation lacks clear boundaries with the organization and has a fluid membership; that is, members come and go as needed.

2. The parallel team has clear boundaries and distinct membership and works in the short term to develop recommendations for an improvement in a process or system.

3. The project or product development team has a fluid membership with clear boundaries and a defined customer, technical requirement, and output.

4. The work or production team has a distinct membership and clear boundaries, where members perform regular and ongoing work, usually in one functional area.

5. The service team has a distinct membership and aids in ongoing customer and network activity.

6. The management team has a distinct membership and works on a regular basis to lead corporate activities.
7. The action team has a fluid or distinct membership. It deals with immediate action and emergency situations.

Challenges

Each member of an effective team possesses a needed element to contribute. Effective communication behavior pulls in all these elements so that problems are collectively solved. Communication is the vehicle for creating synergy and for keeping a team together and moving it forward. However, communicating with one's team members can become problematic when those team members are geographically dispersed throughout the globe, reside in different time zones, possess different levels of technological proficiency, and come from different cultural backgrounds. Thus, one of the key challenges facing virtual teams is how to effectively communicate with one another across distance.

Why is it difficult to communicate and exchange information virtually? One answer might be the rate or speed at which communication flows. People who are able to send electronic messages at a rapid speed may not take adequate time to clearly encode and process their thoughts and messages. In addition, because electronic information can be exchanged so quickly, information overload is a danger for those on the receiving end. As virtual team members attempt to deal with information overload, they may block out potentially important communication exchanges. In addition, much communication between virtual team members is asynchronous (not at the same time). Feedback and confirmation, then, may be delayed, leading to potentially disruptive misunderstandings and miscommunications and to time not well spent. Finally, a key answer to why communication poses such a challenge for virtual teams lies in the difficulty of transmitting complete messages and

multiple cues, and offering immediate feedback through the electronic communication methods often used by virtual teams, methods that are limited in information richness. Face-to-face communication is considered the richest form of communication, but for virtual teams, where face-to-face interaction is not frequent and, in some cases, non-existent, the inherent limited richness in communication exchanges can lead to further misunderstandings and miscommunications among team members.

Thus, there is a real need for virtual team members to learn how to be active and effective communicators and to design and utilize an effective communication plan that supports and does not detract from their creative process. Indeed, the very survival of virtual teams depends on individual team members' ability to exchange critical information despite the challenges of time and place.

Time and Place

Information technology supporting communication between virtual team members is frequently categorized along the two dimensions of time and place (O'Hara-Devereaux and Johansen, 1994). The dimension of time refers to whether the communication tool supports communication that occurs synchronously (at the same time) or asynchronously (at different times). Communication that is synchronous allows members to communicate with one another simultaneously or at the same time, as in a face-to-face conversation, telephone call, videoconferencing session, or chat room discussion. For computer-mediated communication to be synchronous, computers must be linked together in real time. Asynchronous communication occurs when communication between team members is not simultaneous and does not occur at the same time. Common asynchronous forms of communications are e-mail, shared database systems, and bulletin boards (an electronic notice board where users post notices).

Figure 1. Dimensions of time and place

Same Place and Same Time:	Different Place and Different Time:
• Face-to-face meetings	• Audioconferencing
• Computer meetings	• Videoconferencing
	• Chat technology (IRC)

Same Place and Different Time:	Different Place and Different Time:
• Bulletin board	• Voice mail
• Shared databases	• E-mail
• Web pages	• Intranets
	• Threaded discussions

The dimension of place refers to whether the tool allows for co-located (same place) communication or dispersed (different places) communication. Combining these two dimensions together yields four separate categories in which some common technologies used by virtual teams can be classified, as shown in Figure 1.

For most individuals, communicating at the same time in the same place is the most comfortable type of interaction, as in face-to-face meetings. Virtual teams may incorporate varying amounts of face-to-face interaction, especially early on to develop a sense of trust among team members before they begin working together at a distance. However, this mode of communication is not the predominant form of communication for virtual teams. Thus, virtual team members may also communicate with one another at different times and at different places (for example through e-mail, voice mail, fax machines, computer conferencing, and shared database systems). They may also interact at the same time but from different places (for example, company meetings or training programs with team members or trainees in different locations linked together at the same time through audio, video, or computer conferencing). In addition, although team members may work in the same place, they may be physically present at different times through shared workstations.

At the juncture of same time and same place

and different time and different place interactions is communication that can be engaged in anytime and anyplace. The key to establishing an anytime and anyplace workplace is mobility, consisting of portability and connectivity wherever one is (O'Hara-Devereaux and Johansen, 1994). Technology that supports portability and connectivity includes lightweight laptop computers, modems, and cellular phones. In their book *Global Work: Bridging Distance, Culture, and Time,* O'Hara-Devereaux and Johansen (1994) suggest that users may need to "prepare to go to work in the anytime/anyplace office with (indeed probably wearing) a wide range of portable, task-specific computer devices capable of performing such on-the-road jobs as calendaring and note-taking, document reading, or voice and text communications" (p. 88).

Social Presence and Information Richness

Available communication tools can also be evaluated according to the degree of social presence and information richness each technology offers. As teams select their communication tools and decide for what purposes each will be used, they will need to consider the degree of information richness and social presence that each communication tool offers. Social presence refers to the degree to which a specific type of technology facilitates warmth, sensitivity, and a personal connection with others. Face-to-face meetings have a high level of social presence, allowing for facial expressions, touch, posture, and other nonverbal cues to be communicated along with the verbal message. E-mail and other forms of written communication have far less social presence. Despite the fact that we can add emotions in our written messages by way of a variety of emoticons (i.e., sad or happy face icons), it is still much harder for a virtual team member to feel a high level of involvement or sense of interpersonal dialogue in this medium. E-mail is more of a one-way communication answered by another one-way communication, rather than a two-way personal dialogue exchange. Whether communications are synchronous or asynchronous also adds to the degree of social presence experienced. Synchronous communication tools, such as face-to-face, audio conferences, and videoconferences, have more social presence than asynchronous communication tools, such as e-mail or voice mail.

The concept of information richness was developed by Daft and Lengel (1984) to explain information processing behavior in organizations. Richness was defined as "the potential information-carrying capacity of data" (p. 196). More specifically, communication channels differ in their ability to handle multiple cues simultaneously, facilitate rapid feedback, and be personal. Rich communication methods are highly interactive and rely on a great deal of information, thereby reducing confusion and misunderstanding. Face-to-face communication is the richest channel because it provides for the maximum amount of information to be transmitted during a communication exchange. Multiple cues (such as words, posture, facial expression, gestures, and intonations) and immediate feedback (both verbal and nonverbal) can be shared. Lean or less rich communication methods are static or one-way and convey much less information. Computer-mediated communication is a lean channel, because no nonverbal cues are present. Moderately rich forms of communication include videoconferencing, audio conferencing, and telephone conversations. Written letters and memos are the leanest forms of communication. Figure 2 categorizes some of the common communication tools available to virtual teams according to whether they are rich or lean and whether they offer high or low social presence.

COMMUNICATION TOOLS FOR COLLABORATION

Although virtual teams may need electronic communication tools more than traditional co-located teams, in reality, team members who live in the same city need the appropriate communication tools just as much as team members who are dispersed across the globe. In this section, some of the more common tools available for communicating virtually are described. The tools are classified in Figure 3 according to whether they support synchronous or asynchronous interaction.

Synchronous Communication Tools

Face-to-Face Meetings

The most obvious and yet least-used method for communicating is the face-to-face meeting or discussion. Virtual teams may need to use these meetings as well. In fact, the majority of the virtual teams have some face-to-face contact, even if only a few times a year. Face-to-face meetings for virtual teams are generally needed early in the team's creation to assist team members in sorting out what their roles will be, what goals the team will pursue, what norms will govern the team's behavior, and to develop the needed trust and personal bond to sustain them in their future of working virtually together. Common uses for face-to-face meetings are listed below.

Face-to-face meetings in virtual teams are commonly used for the following reasons:

Figure 2. Dimensions of information richness and social presence

Tools That Are Rich and Offer High Social Presence	Tools That Are Lean and Offer Low Social Presence
Face-to-face meetings or discussions	Shared database systems
Synchronous computer conferencing (with audio and video links)	Bulletin boards
	Intranet Web pages
Videoconferencing	E-mail
Audioconferencing	Voice mail
	Fax; standard or express mail

- To conduct strategic planning sessions and discuss the overall direction of the business
- To assess the previous year's efforts and establish goals for the upcoming year
- To conduct idea generation or brainstorming sessions
- To make creative decisions on current work
- To assess and review prior and current work projects
- To prepare team members for work assignments by establishing agendas, assigning roles and tasks, and setting goals
- To celebrate team success
- To establish, solidify, and maintain human bonds
- To address sensitive issues such as personnel and performance issues and talk

through potential solutions
- To maintain client relationships
- To communicate when there are technological problems with other methods
- To respond to team members' personal crises

Most people think of face-to-face meetings as having little or relatively simple technology (such as a blackboard, flipchart, or whiteboard). However, technology can and does enter into face-to-face meetings as well. Technology that enhances face-to-face meetings may include overhead projectors, videos, computer display systems, electronic whiteboards that allow team members to save dry-erase marker notes made on the board to a connected computer, and integrated software packages shared through each participant's computer workstation. These types

Figure 3. Synchronous and asynchronous communication tools

Synchronous Communication Tools	Asynchronous Communication Tools
Face-to-face meetings	Asynchronous computer meetings
Synchronous computer meetings	Bulletin boards and Intranet Web pages
Videoconferencing	E-mail
Audioconferencing	Group calendars and schedules
Telephone	Voice mail
	Fax; standard or express mail

of technological products can help virtual teams to plan strategically, brainstorm and generate ideas, and evaluate their ideas. Technology used in these meetings can also assist in documenting and providing an electronic record of the face-to-face meeting for later reference.

Synchronous Computer Meetings

When it is not feasible to hold a meeting face-to-face, holding team meetings via a computer network is a workable option. And if these computer meetings are synchronous and have the capability to include text, audio, and video links, they can come quite close to possessing the levels of information richness and social presence that exist in face-to-face interactions. In these synchronous meetings, team members can transfer and send one another text and data files. A variety of tools may be incorporated into a synchronous computer meeting.

Team members may, for example, share typed conversations in electronic chat rooms. Internet Relay Chat (IRC) technology is basically an online equivalent of a conversation in real time. However, the chat occurs through a keyboard. For creative work, setting up separate, dedicated chat rooms to discuss different ideas, topics, or projects may be useful. On-line chat rooms also give team members the opportunity to find others outside their team who share similar interests or can offer assistance, advice, or relevant information. An added benefit to IRC technology is that it automatically creates a transcript of each chat session, which participants may review.

Instant messaging (IM) is similar to a chat room except it is between two people (not an entire team) and one does not have to enter the chat room to converse. Through an Internet Chat Query (ICQ), a team member can see if another team member is online. The IM chat box pops up on the screen, allowing team members to talk through text in a live, synchronous conversation. Some wireless phones are now also capable of instant messaging so team members can be reached by IM even when they are offline.

Electronic chat rooms may be combined with interactive whiteboards that display shared documents and allow users to sketch thoughts or ideas. Interactive whiteboards are extremely useful for virtual teams doing creative work. They allow team members to generate ideas and to write and sketch designs or diagrams in a shared whiteboard workspace for all team members to see and collaborate on. One example is The SMART Board™ (designed by SMART Technologies Inc.), which turns the computer and projector into a powerful tool for collaborating. (The SMART Board can be used as an electronic or interactive whiteboard, with or without a projector.) With a computer image projected onto the board, individual team members press on the large, touch-sensitive surface to access and control applications. Using a pen from the SMART Pen Tray, team members can draw, record notes, or highlight important information. All notes can be saved to a computer file to be printed, e-mailed, or posted to the Web.

Desktop video systems are useful in allowing team members to transmit and share either still visual images or full motion video. In addition, desktop audio links allow for real time, parallel voice discussion about the shared work. Sometimes referred to as Internet telephony, team members speak to one another via computer microphones and speakers.

Synchronous computer meetings require that all team members have computer, video, and audio capabilities and specialized groupware software. Although the more sophisticated multimedia synchronous conferencing systems can be costly and require all team members to have compatible systems, these systems can be an asset to virtual teams doing creative work. In addition, these systems provide an electronic record of the meeting so that absent members may later attend the meeting or so the team may have a record for future use and learning. Common uses of synchronous computer meetings are listed below.

Synchronous Computer Meetings are Commonly Used to do the Following:

- Brainstorm and generate ideas
- Generate and evaluate alternative solutions
- Sketch or draw ideas, preliminary designs, prototypes, or concepts
- Display relevant data for problem solving
- List and subsequently prioritize ideas, options, or potential solutions
- List, discuss, and share opinions on certain topics
- Gain team input on initial product design
- Gain team consensus and agreement on later stages of product design
- Maintain team member involvement in complex and long-term projects
- Gain input from a variety of stakeholders on complex projects
- Capture information in meetings that would otherwise be captured on a flipchart
- Create an archive of meetings for later review

Videoconferencing

Videoconferencing supports synchronous communication of both audio and video. Dispersed team members get a sense of their colleagues' social context and physical environment. Videoconferencing requires members to use specialized video facilities, which usually requires members to communicate from a specialized room. The effectiveness of a videoconferencing session, however, varies greatly depending on the quality of video picture, which may differ in terms of motion quality (jerkiness) and resolution of the image. When the video quality is high, videoconferencing can be a good alternative to more expensive face-to-face meetings. Video rooms are often superior to desktop video links because they provide higher quality images. Common uses for videoconferencing are listed below.

Videoconferencing sessions are commonly used for the following reasons:

- To conduct strategic planning sessions
- To discuss and define problems
- To list, debate, and prioritize potential solutions
- To make straightforward (not complicated) decisions
- To state and discuss opinions on specific topics
- To provide a forum for large keynote meetings (such as speakers or company state-of-the-union addresses)
- To celebrate team success

Audioconferencing

In an audioconference, all team members are simultaneously connected via a telephone call. Conference calling works well for small groups, while for larger groups a bridge is used to connect different phone lines. Audioconferencing is a relatively inexpensive and yet still effective alternative to face-to-face meetings for remote team members. It is especially useful for meetings that do not require team members to focus on a document or other visual image (unless the document or image can be shared electronically via a desktop). However, the structure and preparation required for an effective audioconference are much greater than for a face-to-face meeting. Common uses of audioconferences are listed below.

Audioconferences are commonly used for the following reasons:

- To generate ideas
- To assess and review current work
- To review previous work
- To raise new issues or concerns

Telephone

In spite of all the sophisticated communication tools available to assist teams in doing collaborative and creative work, the telephone still remains one of the more common forms of communication for those who are working across time and geographic boundaries. And with the advent of cell phones, people are more accessible by phone than they have been in the past. Some organizations are finding it helpful to combine cell phones, pagers, and voice mail so that if someone leaves a message, the voice mail system calls out the pager and relays the message. Then the team member can use his or her cell phone to return the message. Common uses of the telephone are listed below.

Telephone calls are commonly used for the following reasons:

- To get input, feedback, or a second opinion about how to proceed
- To ask project related questions and get answers
- To share ideas or discuss important information
- To touch base, keep in touch, or establish personal contact
- To communicate when there are technological problems with other methods
- To respond to individual team members' personal crises

While the telephone is an effective method, it is difficult to record or document a conversation for future review. Often, outcomes and actions taken after the session depend on individual memory and any notes taken.

Asynchronous Communication Tools

Asynchronous Computer Meetings

There are a variety of groupware software tools that allow virtual team members to work on projects asynchronously through shared database systems or shared files. Shared database systems allow team members to transform textual documents and e-mail messages into databases and create fields that can be searched and indexed. Information is frequently distributed on servers, and individual team members have the ability to search the database and transfer information to their personalized databases and tailor it for their own use. More sophisticated systems have the capability to store a variety of data, including multimedia information. Shared database systems provide virtual teams with the following benefits:

- Access to reference materials and stored knowledge from other teams
- A place to store the work of individual team members
- A way to review and ensure that all work in progress is updated to the latest edition and available to all members
- A place to store the team's experiences, lessons, and products for future use

Team members can access shared files anytime from any web browser. This is an ideal way for remote-located or traveling team members to create and collaborate. For security purposes, access to shared files can be limited to only team members. However, with the use of shared database systems and shared files, document management becomes critical so that files are not accidentally deleted or overwritten. Common uses for asynchronous computer meetings are listed below.

Asynchronous Computer Meetings are Commonly Used for the Following Purposes:

- To brainstorm and generate ideas
- To generate ideas for plans and ideas about products
- To comment on products
- To collaboratively author written

documents
- To collect data and discuss trends

Bulletin Boards and Intranet Web Pages

Bulletin board tools provide shared space for the posting of messages and ideas and for asynchronous discussions about questions or issues that do not require immediate answers. Discussions can be structured as linear or threaded. In a linear discussion, responses are added to the end of a linear chain of messages. In threaded discussions, a response can be attached directly to any message, so a discussion can potentially branch out infinitely. In general, threaded discussions seem better for question and answer applications (for example, technical support), while linear structures are more useful for extended conversation on deeper issues. Bulletin boards allow participants to become involved at their own convenience rather than having to match the schedule of others. One can take as much time as needed to read and digest what others have to say and to compose a response before posting a reply. However, it may take a lot of calendar time to complete a bulletin board discussion, and it can be difficult to reach consensus on a decision because it is hard to tell when everyone has had their say.

Many teams use the power of their company's Intranet to set up team web sites. An Intranet is a network of computers within an organization that is accessible to all team members. Unauthorized access from outsiders to the network is prevented with the use of firewalls. In essence, the Intranet is like a protected neighborhood of computers within a larger city of the Internet. Intranet team web pages provide an ideal medium for teams to publicize their efforts within an organization. If the team desires, it may make the Intranet web pages accessible to relevant stakeholders, such as adjunct team members, vendors, clients, or customers. However, firewalls may also be used to limit the access of specific audiences to certain sections of the team's Web site. For example, a potential customer may be able to access a list of products available, but not access files on work-in-progress products that are not deliverables yet. Common uses of bulletin boards and team Intranet web pages are listed next.

Bulletin boards and Intranet Web pages are useful for the following purposes:

- Providing a quick overview of where a team and its projects are at
- Giving pertinent information to stakeholders, such as customers
- Orienting new members of a team
- Gathering large amounts of information about specific topics from diverse groups of individuals outside of the team
- Allowing team members to brainstorm
- Planning and generating ideas for product development
- Building on and commenting on the ideas of others
- Storing or archiving specialized topic databases to be used by team members in their shared work
- Collecting data and discussing trends

E-Mail

E-mail is a destination address where an individual can be reached virtually, regardless of geographic address. E-mail is the most common and best understood form of information technology used for work from a distance. Most members of virtual team members view e-mail as a necessity. Many e-mail systems also offer access to a variety of mail protocols, mailboxes with a flexible folder structure, and interfaces to instant messaging services. E-mail can also be merged with other collaborative technologies (for example, audio and video links) to provide higher levels of information richness and social presence.

Studies have shown that e-mail is used for two main purposes: task-related use (such as routine information exchange, status updates, broadcasting requests, coordinating project activities, scheduling meetings) and socio-emotional, non-task related use (such as taking a break from work, keeping in touch) (Steinfield, 1986). E-mail is an excellent way to communicate about simple and straightforward issues and to share and pass along information. It is useful for sending quick, short messages that keep conversations, project pieces, and information moving forward. It can also be used to exchange and review documents using file attachments. And it may function as a stress reliever and relationship builder through the exchange of humorous jokes, inspirational stories, and other personal messages.

E-mail is freeing in that it removes the boundaries of location and time. Team members are no longer bound by rigid schedules or traditional modes of communication. Team members may communicate and interact with individuals across the globe, individuals they may never have been able to communicate with before.

E-mail is best suited for one-to-one communication and sometimes group messaging or copying others. It is not the best choice if you are expecting fast turnaround time, unless norms are in place for when team members should respond.

As with any text-only tool, it is easy for misunderstandings and faulty assumptions to develop through e-mail exchanges. Without the richness of the added cues of voice, eye contact, and body language, an e-mail message can be heard much differently from how it was intended. So there are situations in which e-mail is not the preferred way of communicating. E-mail is not considered appropriate for issues that require high levels of interaction, such as performance-related discussions, or communicating about sensitive issues that may lead to conflict. Reaching compromises or resolving conflicts cannot effectively be accomplished through e-mail. In addition, e-mail is insensitive to cultural norms and cannot adequately convey situational con-

text. Nevertheless, e-mail has a diverse range of purposes. Some of the more common uses of e-mail are listed next.

E-mail is commonly used for the following reasons:

- To convey routine correspondence and check status
- To update team members on schedule and calendar changes, client status, and other requests
- To make announcements or provide written status to multiple people at the same time
- To exchange comments or preliminary drafts and development work, revise plans and documents, and send documents to team members for review and feedback
- To continue threads of either project development or client contact
- To give and get project-related advice
- To make and answer requests
- To exchange hard data and information
- To document, save, and store a copy of a communication or information passed along
- To engage in a written dialogue with another individual team member
- To broadcast same ideas or messages to all members of the team (with the use of a distribution list) or quickly send out a message to the entire team
- To develop policy and set rules
- To follow up on specific policies or rules
- To keep in touch with other team members
- To build personal connection by sharing humor and personal stories

Group Calendars and Schedules

These software tools assist team members in creating and manipulating information on their individual calendars and in scheduling and coordinating team meetings and requests for resources or information that are shared among team members. Each team member's calendar and schedule can be accessible anytime from any Web browser, which reduces scheduling conflicts. Administrative staff can notify all team members of important events by posting this information to all employee calendars at once. To prevent critical events from slipping through the cracks, reminders can be sent via e-mail or wireless devices for important events and appointments. Common uses of calendars and schedules are listed below.

Calendars and schedules are useful for coordinating the following:

- Team members' activities and schedules
- Team members' use of shared resources
- Virtual teams with members who work in different time zones
- Virtual teams that are somewhat large in size
- Meetings with vendors, customers, and clients outside of the team's boundaries

Voice Mail and Pagers

Most of us are familiar with the benefits of voice mail. We call a colleague, client, or vendor with a question, request, or complaint. The individual is away from his or her desk, and a voice message answers instead. Voice mail is a convenient way to leave a message requesting a return call, instead of having to continually call until you finally find the individual in his or her office. Voice mail also offers a quick way to communicate information at a time that is most convenient for the caller. Although voice mail has definitely alleviated the frustration of being unable to reach individuals in their offices, it is not a substitute for interactive conversation between team members. Team members, often traveling and on location at a client site, would use voice mail as a way to leave a message to touch base with one another. Common uses of voice mail are listed next.

Voice mail is commonly used for the following purposes:

- To convey an urgent message (if the norm of the team is that members check their voice mail regularly)
- To relay information or make a request that is easy to understand
- To provide project status updates
- To communicate simple and clearly-stated action items

Criteria for Selecting Appropriate Communication Tools

General Rules and Tips

With the array of technologies available to virtual teams, how do virtual team leaders and members decide which tools to use and under what circumstances? The answer is, it depends. Communication tools that offer high levels of information richness and social presence are not always better. Which tool to use depends on the message to be sent and the nature of the task presented to the team. From this perspective, one may either match or mismatch messages and tools, and virtual team members should optimize their selections of communication tools accordingly. When adopting new technologies (or evaluating existing technologies) for use, it is essential to evaluate them critically instead of assuming they are appropriate for the entire range of the team's tasks. A general rule: First, consider what you are intending to communicate and accomplish. Then, select the best communication tool(s) available to fulfill what is intended.

Another rule-of-thumb is to use communication tools high in social presence and information richness to transmit complex, non-routine, and ambiguous messages (such as brainstorming, resolving conflicts, and strategic planning and direction setting). More straightforward, routine, and simple messages (like updating members on project status) may be transmitted with tools lower in social presence and information richness. Communication failure may occur when a rich

Figure 4. Situations for communication tools

Situations in need of tools high in social presence and information richness	Situations in need of tools low in social presence and information richness
when new team members need to be introduced to the team	when the team is dealing with a routine situation
when the team interacts for the first time with new customers	when the team is exchanging information or hard data between members
when the team addresses touchy or interpersonal issues (deals with conflict; needs to express emotion)	when team members are working on developing their parts of a creative effort
for initial brainstorming or idea generation sessions	when team members are sharing the results of their creative efforts for review
when the team solves a new problem	
when the team is faced with an ambiguous or ill-defined situation or problem	
when evaluating creative efforts for future growth and learning	

communication tool that is also high in social presence is used to transmit a simple or unambiguous message. As a result, the receiver of the message may get confused or even attach additional meaning to the message that was not intended by the sender. More typically, communication failure may result from using a lean communication tool that is low in social presence to convey an ambiguous message. In this situation, the communication tool does not provide enough cues to capture the complexity of the intended message. Figure 5 lists some situations that may call for communication tools that are high in richness and social presence and other situations that may call for tools that are lean and lower in social presence.

Situations for Communication Tools

Some situations require tools that are high in social presence and information richness while others require low social presence and information richness. Figure 4 shows a summary of those situations.

What happens when a team requires a rich communication tool that is high in social presence, but finds that tool is unavailable? (Perhaps the team has no funds or limited travel funds to bring dispersed members together.) Another rule-of-thumb is that when communication can't be rich or high in social presence, use multiple methods of communication. Research suggests that in the absence of rich face-to-face interaction, the more methods of communication used, the better (Kayworth and Leidner, 2000).

Creative Work

Virtual teams doing creative work need to integrate a variety of tools into a workable communication plan. In this section, a model is presented to offer suggestions for which communication tools are most appropriate for use during each stage of the creative process (see Figure 5).

The Web 2.0 Trend and its Impact on Enterprises

Since the 'Web 2.0' (W2.0) movement was from the beginning targeted to either individuals or communities of individuals, knowledge experts and knowledge-based companies immediately considered whether it would be any benefits on applying 'Web 2.0' in their organisational architecture. Singel (2006) and others advised that there were some software vendors (SocialText, Zimbra) focusing their W2.0 products to business. But McAfee (2006) was who really pioneered successfully this idea coining a new term in his article "Enterprise 2.0: The Dawn of Emergent Collaboration". The term 'Enterprise 2.0' was immediately adopted by other authors as the application of the 'Web 2.0' paradigm into the organisational environment. 'Web 2.0' features (also 'Enterprise 2.0') included blogs, podcasts, shared news, social networking, wikis and other technology-based capabilities that allowed users -businesses or individuals- to connect with and learn from each other (Connolly, 2007). Connolly talked about connectivity and being able to measure everything that users are doing online.

Regardless the clear advantages that 'Enterprise 2.0' could bring to 'inside the firewall' some authors (Hoover, 2007; McAfee, 2006; Wiens, 2007) also expressed concerns about adoption hurdles that the new web technologies would have to overcome. Some of those ones were security, lack of expertise of the knowledge workers to be familiar with the new tools, integration with legacy technologies and difficulty to provide a measure on Return Of Investment (ROI). It is important to remark finally that cultural aspects flew over all those. The CIO of global services at British Telecom, claimed that if people do not want to share, they will not share (Daniel, 2007). 'Enterprise 2.0' tools have the singularity that they offer high flexibility in their use cases, they are user-friendly with very short learning curve and most of times not requiring training to start

using them. And especially, their performance improves with the users' contributions. So that, within the fact that are unlocking (or web-enabling) the content accumulated in Content Management Systems (CMS) facilitate web-based exploration and categorisation for content detection and re-use for distribution.

A survey carried out in 2007 revealed practices in terms of 'Enterprise 2.0' approach from different large companies' viewpoint (Hoover, 2007). Some of those companies defined two separated strategies classifying the tools into two major parts. The first was web-based information-sharing. A rising number of organisations were discovering successful business uses for blogs, wikis, syndicated feeds, pervasive search, social networking and collaborative content portals (such as Microsoft's SharePoint). Dye (2007) pointed out that the "metadata that each user left behind made the search process more dynamic, and documents became findable the minute they were going online". As users add tags, votes, links over time, the metadata adjacent to each entry transformed to reproduce the file's evolving function in the information base. If a report on one topic became an significant source for another, a new tag was the only requirement to make available that report on the map for fellow searchers. The second area found by Hoover (2007) was enable voice and messaging through the web, where Voice over IP (VoIP), instant messaging, videoconferencing and combined communications could make it promising to link people in real time online. Finally mash-ups, somewhere in the middle between both areas seemed to get easier integration joining two web-based data fonts simultaneously in one place.

Other extended classification of 'Enterprise 2.0' technologies is SLATES, the acronym that McAfee (2006) used to indicate its six components:

- Search. For any information platform to be valuable, its users had to be able to find

Figure 5. Communication tools according to purpose

Purpose	Appropriate Communication Tools
Talking—These tools provide a shared meeting place for virtual team members to interact anytime during the creative process.	Face-to-face meetings Synchronous computer meetings Videoconferencing Teleconferencing Telephone E-mail and instant messaging systems Bulletin boards
Brainstorming and Generating Ideas—These tools allow team members to jointly share and build on ideas.	Face-to-face meetings Synchronous computer meetings Interactive and electronic whiteboards Teleconferencing Chat rooms Bulletin boards
Doing—These tools support development and design work and offer a shared work-space for development work to occur synchronously or asynchronously.	Synchronous computer meetings Interactive and electronic whiteboards Videoconferencing Asynchronous computer meetings (shared database systems, shared files)
Saving—These tools are used to archive and store creative efforts and to allow these efforts to be reviewed over and over. These tools offer the capability of, as one team member put it, "holding on to the creativity." They assist in building a content repository in which past ways of approaching and resolving client needs or problems are stored. These past approaches then may become frameworks, templates, or outlines later applied to similar client situations.	Asynchronous computer meetings (shared database systems, shared files) Chat room records Audio-link transcripts Interactive or electronic whiteboards (where information is stored to the computer) Bulletin boards Company Intranet Web pages
Finalizing and Closing—These tools allow team members to pull all the elements of a project together and to make final adjustments as needed. They also assist in the process of reaching consensus and closure.	Face-to-face meetings Synchronous computer meetings Shared database systems E-mail Teleconferencing
Evaluating—These tools assist team members in reviewing and assessing creative efforts and outcomes and in capturing these assessments for future learning.	Face-to-face meetings Synchronous computer meetings Videoconferencing Shared database systems (to store team's experiences and lessons for future use)

what they were looking for. Hierarchical structures on intranets seemed not to help in finding information for its users.

• Links, the second key concept, helped to rank results as the best pages were the ones that were most frequently linked to. In order for this to change within companies, many people had to be given the ability to build links. The most straightforward way to accomplish this was to let the intranet be built by a large group rather than a small one.

- Authoring. Most people have something to contribute, whether it is knowledge, insight, experience, a comment, a fact, an edit, a link, and so on, and authorship was a way to elicit these contributions.
- Tags. The categorisation system that emerged from tagging called 'folksonomy', in some ways opposite to taxonomy, which was an up-front categorization scheme developed by an expert. Deploying a tool that allowed tagging within an enterprise would allocate more visible patterns and processes in knowledge work.
- Extensions. Some computers used algorithms to say to users "if you liked that, then by extension you'll like this".
- Signals. New content was added so often that it could become a full-time job just to check for updates on all sites of interest. Signals helped to carry out these tasks and they could come as e-mails alerts, but these contribute to overload the inbox. RSS, a novel technology, allowed the aggregation of content from many different around the Web.

Finally some of the points that were taken to consensus about 'Enterprise 2.0' were:

- 'Enterprise 2.0' technologies did not respect horizontal and vertical boundaries within organisations. They promote emergent collaboration (McAfee, 2006).
- The simpler, the better.
- The user is not only content consumer but also content creator.

Future Trends

An individual can be creative, as can a team and an organization (Woodman, Sawyer, and Griffin, 1993). Team creativity involves more than the sum of creative contributions from each team member. Team creativity involves a synergistic potential, in which the individual efforts of team members result in a level of performance that is greater than the sum of those individual inputs.

Virtual teams pursuing creative work in SMEs need a variety of communication tools to bolster and sustain their creative process. For creative work, it is key to incorporate into your communication plan periodic face-to-face encounters or information technologies that simulate real time face-to-face contact, or both. Asynchronous modes of interaction are beneficial, but creative efforts cannot be accomplished without the opportunity for rich, synchronous interactions.

Communication tools and technologies available for virtual teams are evolving. The development of desktop audio and video links, interactive whiteboards, and internet relay chat, for example, and now with social tools such as wikis, has increased opportunities to simulate the richness of face-to-face contact through technology. Incorporating these tools into a team's communication plan will be crucial for high levels of creativity to occur.

Virtual teams doing creative work also need access to techniques and software tools developed to enhance team and individual creativity. Some of these techniques and software tools have been designed especially for virtual teamwork, while others have been adapted from methods used by more traditional, co-located teams. In either case, these techniques and software tools help to further stimulate creativity in the virtual workplace.

The use of 'Web 2.0' technologies has a lot of potential applications to improve knowledge-based business processes and enhance innovation. It also provides a new platform of tools that can be effectively introduced into organisational agents such as intranets and corporate portals. The success of the incorporation of the 'Web 2.0' paradigm to the organisational environment does not only depend on the toolset but also on the cultural change that the use of these technologies brings 'inside the firewall'.

Researchers have covered the presentation of the different segments as innovative collaboration techniques inside organisational boundaries and the challenges that they may find in the future when they are deployed. Nevertheless, success drivers that would lead to a successful implementation have not been studied. Furthermore, the way the knowledge management practitioners must assess their current strategies and approaches to find whether or not it would be worth to move into 'Enterprise 2.0' tools and their potential benefits have not yet been analysed in depth.

CONCLUSION

With the purpose of aiding in the selection of the appropriate tools to accomplish creative tasks within geographically dispersed teams working in SMEs, we have analyzed a selection of communication tools, both synchronous and asynchronous.

At this point, we would like to leave some important issues that should not be overlooked:

- Communication is the vehicle for creating synergy, for keeping a team together and moving it forward. However, virtual teams face special challenges in trying to effectively communicate with one another across the miles.
- Communication tools can be classified as to whether they support synchronous communication or asynchronous communication. Synchronous communication allows team members to interact with one another simultaneously, as they do in a face-to-face conversation, telephone call, videoconferencing session, or chat room discussion. Asynchronous communication allows communication between team members to occur at different times. Common asynchronous forms of communication are e-mail, shared database systems, and bulletin boards.
- Available communication tools can also be evaluated according to the degree of social

presence or information richness. Social presence is a tool's ability to facilitate a personal connection between team members. Information richness is a tool's ability to transmit multiple cues simultaneously and to offer immediate feedback. Face-to-face meetings have a high level of social presence and information richness, while e-mail and other forms of written communication have far less social presence and offer less information richness.

- Virtual teams report using relatively unsophisticated tools such as e-mail and the telephone more frequently than they used more sophisticated tools. However, the trend is changing, as virtual teams are beginning to use newer technologies such as desktop conferencing with video and audio links, interactive whiteboards, and the Intranet.
- As virtual teams work through their creative process, there is a pattern to the communication tools they use. Virtual teams generate ideas in any number of ways, some doing so primarily face-to-face, while others preferring unstructured electronic exchanges. Ideas are developed, finalized, and brought to closure electronically (for the most part). Evaluation, when formally conducted, is done face-to-face.
- A virtual team needs to take the time to develop a workable communication plan which specifies what tools are most appropriate for use during each stage of the creative process. Following three steps will help virtual teams develop these plans: (1) Examine how current communication tools support (or detract from) the team's creative process; (2) Match the intentions of a specific communication message with the appropriate and available communication tools; and (3) Construct the communication plan to support the team's creative process.

- For creative work, it is key to incorporate into the communication plan periodic face-to-face encounters or information technologies that simulate real time face-to-face contact, or both. Asynchronous modes of interaction are beneficial, but creative efforts cannot be accomplished without the opportunity for rich, synchronous interactions.

REFERENCES

Connoly, J.M. (2007). Techs turn to Web 2.0. *B to B*, 92(4), 24.

Daft, R. L., & Lengel, R. H. (1984). Information richness: A new approach to managerial behavior and organization design. In B. M. Staw & L. L. Cummings (Eds.), *Research in Organizational Behavior* (Vol. 6, pp. 191-233). Greenwich, CT: JAI Press.

Daniel, D. (2007). Seven Ways CIOs can introduce Web 2.0 technologies into the enterprise. CIO Business Technology Leadership. Available at: http://www.cio.com.au/index.php/id;1146975385 (Last accessed: September 2008)

Duarte, D., & Snyder, N. (2001). *Mastering virtual teams: Strategies, tools, and techniques that succeed.* San Francisco: Jossey-Bass.

Dye, J. (2007). Collaboration 2.0: Make the web your workspace. *EContent*, 30(1), 32.

Fisher, K., & Fisher, M. (2000). *The distance manager: a hands-on guide to managing off-site employees and virtual teams.* New York: McGraw-Hill.

Hoover, I. (2007). Web 2.0 tools in business: Proceed with caution—'Enterprise 2.0' must overcome concerns about security and ROI to gain a foothold in business. *Bank Systems & Technology*, 44(4), 41.

Kayworth, T., & Leidner, D. (2000). The global virtual manager: A prescription for success. *European Management Journal*, 18(2), 183–193. doi:10.1016/S0263-2373(99)00090-0

Mcaffe, A. P. (2006). Enterprise 2.0: The dawn of emergent collaboration. *MIT Sloan Management Review*, 47(3), 21–28.

O'Hara-Devereaux, M., & Johansen, R. (1994). *Global work: Bridging distance, culture, and time.* San Francisco: Jossey-Bass.

Singel, R. (2006). Are you ready for Web 2.0? Wired News Torkington, N. 2006. Available at: http://radar.oreilly.com/archives/2006/05/more_on_our_web_20_service_mar.html. (Last accessed: September 2008).

Steinfield, C. W. (1986). Computer-mediated communication in an organizational setting: Explaining task-related and socioemotional uses. In M. L. McLaughlin (Ed.), *Communication Yearbook, 9*, 777-804. Newbury Park, CA.: Sage.

Wiens, J. (2007). Is Web 2.0 Inherently Insecure? *Network Computing*, 18(7), 22.

Woodman, R. W., Sawyer, J. E., & Griffin, R. W. (1993). Toward a theory of organizational creativity. *Academy of Management Review, 18*, 293–321. doi:10.2307/258761

Section 3
Managerial and Organizational Issues

Chapter 15
Enterprise Information Systems:
Aligning and Integrating Strategy, Technology, Organization and People

Paul T. Kidd
Cheshire Henbury, UK

ABSTRACT

The implementation of Enterprise Information Systems is a difficult task, even for large companies. It can be even more so for Small and Medium Size Enterprises (SMEs), for most are seriously constrained in terms of time, money and skills. The key to successful implementation lies in achieving an alignment between strategy, technology, organization and people, and also in achieving commitment to the new technologies. An implementation method called HiSTOP, which stands for High Integration of Strategy, Technology, Organization and People, is described. This method provides a means of adjusting all four elements so that each is appropriate and also so that all four elements fit together. Although the method was initially designed with SMEs in mind, the method is also suitable for larger companies, hence the chapter considers both types of enterprises. The method places emphasis on development of internal implementation competencies. The key foundational principles of the method are discussed along with some key findings from early trials.

INTRODUCTION

One of the expected benefits of Enterprise Information Systems is increased responsiveness, flexibility and agility. Yet sometimes these benefits can also be delivered through non-technical means, namely by an appropriate organizational design, based on the right choice of organizational design parameters:

DOI: 10.4018/978-1-60566-892-5.ch015

differentiation, integration, decision structure, and formalization. And people are also crucial as well, for they need the right skills and motivation to deliver the sought after benefits. But the story does not end with these elements, for strategy must also be considered, because different business strategies require, in general, different forms of responsiveness, flexibility and agility. Therefore the key issues are aligning and integrating these four elements, and dealing with the interactions between them, so that, for example, the needs of the organizational design are reflected in the technology design, and vice versa.

Achieving this alignment and integration is a very difficult thing to bring about, even for big companies with large budgets, capable of buying-in external skills and expertise to support the whole process of selection, design, and implementation. For Small and Medium Size Enterprises (SMEs) the challenges are even more daunting, for most are seriously constrained in terms of time, money and skills. Moreover, SMEs can also be micro versions of large enterprises in that they also bring with them a set of internal organizational politics, conflicts, outdated practices, change resistance, etc., that is to say, the features and problems that are so often found in large enterprises.

SMEs therefore provide a challenging environment with respect to the implementation of Enterprise Information Systems in terms of aligning and integrating Strategy, Technology, Organization and People. What therefore can be done to help such businesses? Answering this question is the focus of this chapter.

However, before addressing the above it is necessary to define the theories and concepts upon which the chapter will be built. After providing a brief overview of the main challenges, a *social shaping of technology* approach is presented. This method is rooted in sociotechnical theory. The method, called HITOP (High Integration of Technology, Organization and People) was developed in the United States in the late 1980s, in the context of implementation of advanced manufacturing technologies within traditional hierarchical mass production environments operated by large corporations. The HITOP method provides a means of considering the organization and people requirements of computer-based manufacturing technologies. This method is briefly reviewed, highlighting its underlying philosophy and assumptions, along with its strengths, weaknesses and limitations.

Following this, a new method is discussed, which is an improved, generalized and extended

version of the HITOP method, and which is based on a broader set of needs and issues, including those of SMEs, and also addressing the requirements to align and integrate Strategy, Technology, Organization and People. The improved version of HITOP is however also relevant to large enterprises.

Armed with this new version of HITOP, which is called HiSTOP (High Integration of Strategy, Technology, Organization and People), the chapter will then consider the key components, which constitute several steps that SMEs and large enterprises can take to improve the implementation of Enterprise Information Systems. These considerations will involve addressing the process by which the design and implementation work is undertaken, as well as the analysis of the interrelationships between Strategy, Technology, Organization, and People. Using HiSTOP, it becomes possible to begin to consider design choices in terms of all four dimensions of the problem.

The conclusions provide insights into critical success factors with respect to acceptance of the method. These factors were identified at an early stage in the development work and were therefore used to shape the method to ensure that it would not be seen as being overcomplicated or too difficult to use. Insights from experiences of using the method are also provided. In particular the finding that different modes of use are possible, since it is not necessary to follow the whole method, and different parts can be used as required according to the inclinations of a particular business and its specific interests and constraints.

BACKGROUND

Failures in the implementation of Information and Communications Technologies (ICT) have been documented in the literature for decades (e.g. see Kidd (1994), pp 55-56, for an overview of failures relating to manufacturing ICT). Failure here is used in the sense that outcomes fall short of expectations (Bignall & Fortune, 1984; Kidd, 1994 (p 192)). Some key reasons for failure in relation to implementation are:

- Technology oriented rather than business and market focused investment plans;
- Inappropriate or non-existent business strategy;
- Failure to link business and Information and Communications Technology strategies;
- Inadequate assessment of the costs and benefits of investments in new technologies;
- Neglect of organization and people issues.

These problems were documented in Kidd (1994), primarily in the context of advanced manufacturing technologies and manufacturing related ICT, but there is a pattern as the problems tend to reoccur across time and across different types of ICT. For example, in the world of enterprise-wide systems such as Enterprise Resource Planning (ERP) and Enterprise Information Systems, gaps between corporate expectations and results are commonplace. For such systems there is now a well-documented catalogue of implementation issues and difficulties, along with prescribed critical implementation factors (e.g. see Davenport, 1998; Holland & Light, 1999; Strong & Volkoff, 2004; Santhanam *et. al.* (2006); Guang-hui *et. al.* (2006); Jing & Xun Qiu (2007)).

Whilst there are many dimensions and issues to be considered in the implementation of enterprise-wide software systems, a number of critical points are worth mentioning.

The first critical point is that it is necessary for firms implementing enterprise systems to make the strategic choices needed to configure the systems and processes. This reduces to being very clear about business objectives.

There can be many reasons for change—technical or business or both. Existing ICT systems may be old, costly to maintain, inflexible, and suffering lots of downtime. Or perhaps the need for change stems from a broader business per-

spective, involving factors such as speed of order fulfillment, inventory reduction, improvements in co-ordination and control, and so on. These are but a few of the potential benefits of Enterprise Information Systems, and there are many more (e.g. see Shang & Seddon (2002)). The key point here is that, whatever the motivation for change, there must be a sound business-driven justification for the implementation. Enterprise Information Systems implementation should be concerned with achieving a return on investment, and this implies identifying business objectives.

Defining and prioritizing business objectives is extremely important. There is universal agreement in the literature about this—if business objectives are not clearly stated and prioritized at the very beginning, before embarking upon any sort of software selection, then the implementation runs the risk of encountering serious problems. Without clear and prioritized business objectives it is unlikely any significant benefits will be achieved.

This in effect corresponds to establishing strategic fit, meaning that an enterprise should achieve alignment between its business environment and internal resources, such that these resources support the strategic goals. As Miles & Snow (1984) have noted, truly outstanding performance is achieved by companies that achieve a tight strategic fit, both externally with the business environment and internally among strategy, structure and process. And while achieving strategic fit is crucial to excellence, it is also extremely difficult to bring about.

Establishing and prioritizing business objectives is therefore essential for managing the process of selecting Enterprise Information Systems software and for determining the detailed functionality required. For example, a prioritized business objective might be to share order information electronically across the business. If this is not clearly specified up-front, then it is not possible to evaluate packages correctly to find one that can support this requirement. Moreover, training objectives cannot be specified to ensure that staff can use this system functionality effectively.

However, it is not enough to just specify generic objectives, for example, improved customer service. Such generic statements do not provide sufficient information for decision making and there is a danger that ICT specialists will begin to make decisions about what functionality is required. As a result, Enterprise Information Systems priorities will still be out of line with business objectives. What is needed is to be very specific, for example, improve order processing and fulfillment by accepting customer orders from any location into one system, assigning shipment dates to available products in real time, scheduling future shipment dates for products not in stock, and checking order status at any time.

A second key point is that of control over the implementation process. Implementing an Enterprise Information System can be risky, is potentially expensive, and involves a lot of time and effort. Sought after benefits, no matter how clearly linked to business objectives, will not be achieved if the system is not implemented correctly, and there are plenty of pitfalls and lots of scope for making mistakes. If a company solely relies on vendors or external consultants for success, then they are likely to experience a significant shortfall between expectation and achievement. For example, it is necessary to avoid a circumstance where inadequacies in the Enterprise Information System software are discovered during the implementation. If this does happen, then implementation teams will find themselves working in a reactive, trouble-shooting mode rather than as part of a strategic plan. Consequently costs will increase, schedules will slip and people will become disillusioned. This is often the cause of major Enterprise Information Systems implementations failing to meet business objectives.

However, it can also be a mistake to follow an entirely in-house approach. The problem of getting business objectives and Enterprise Information Systems into full alignment is a significant one,

and will probably require external help. Also, time needs to be spent explaining the business benefits of Enterprise Information Systems to non-ICT managers. Only after this has taken place, can managers appreciate the role that the Enterprise Information System will play in meeting business objectives. The skills required to undertake this bridging exercise between ICT and non-ICT people are rare, and would normally be brought in for specific projects.

Finally, the third key point is the special nature of Enterprise Information Systems. These are not functional or department based systems. They provide access to information right across the enterprise. This has job design and organizational implications. For example, when people elsewhere have to take decisions using information generated in another part of a business, then these people need to understand what the information means (which has training implications). But the business also needs to decide if jobs and organizational structures need to be redesigned to bring people using the data closer together, for example to work in teams, or to be co-located, or to define jobs around the use of particular types of data. Without such considerations, benefits such as speed of response and flexibility may not be fully achieved simply because there is no alignment between the features of the technology and the organizational design.

Moreover, the organizational structure itself may be outdated and unresponsive, and in need of modernization. For example, it may be too hierarchical, too functional, and be based on narrow departmental perspectives that hinder effective team working and cross-functional operations. Such organizations tend to be inappropriate to modern business environments, and often need to be redesigned to make for more responsiveness and flexibility.

Consequently, implementing Enterprise Information Systems cannot be done in isolation from organizational considerations, and some form of organizational alignment, both with the technology and with the business environment should be undertaken if the expected business benefits are to be fully achieved. Yet, even though organizational issues are a critical area, the matter is often missing from implementation methods, whether these methods be directed at SMEs or large enterprises. For example, the implementation method described by Blackwell *et. al.* (2006), though focused on SMEs, does not provide any specific means for SMEs to undertake organizational redesign or alignment of the organization with strategy and technology. Moreover, even academic research on the topic of organizational issues, while strong an analysis of the issues (e.g. see Ward *et. al.* (2005)), generally does not provide a practical implementation methodology aimed at delivering a means of handling organizational design. Furthermore, implementation methods that claim to be integrated (e.g. see Leem & Kim (2002)), are in fact only integrated in the narrow sense of bringing together a subset of the primary elements, mainly business objectives, economic justification, software evaluation and selection, and implementation. Organizational design and the business of aligning all the components (strategy, technology, organization and people) are just left out of the process.

In summary therefore, it can be stated that addressing all three critical areas discussed above is not easy, and requires a process that can: (i) achieve the necessary alignments; (ii) ensure that the correct decisions are taken; (iii) deliver specifications that are appropriate, and; (iv) provide a means of addressing organization and people issues.

MAIN FOCUS OF THE ARTICLE

Existing Theories, Methods and Concepts

Key among the existing body of knowledge relating to implementation approaches that seek to achieve an alignment between technology, orga-

nization and people is *sociotechnical design*.

The Sociotechnical School's central tenant is that surrounding technology, which can be regarded as a sub-system, there is also a social sub-system. These two sub-systems can be designed to be compatible, either by changing the technology to match the social sub-system, or modifying the social sub-system to match the technology, or a mixture of both.

The Sociotechnical School of thought has been articulated in the form of principles, (Cherns, 1976, 1987) that embody the values and key features of sociotechnical design. These principles, of which there are 11, are: *Compatibility*; *Minimum Critical Specification*; *Variance Control*; *The* Multifunctional Principle–Organism vs. Mechanism; *Boundary Location*; *Information Flow*; *Support Congruence*; *Design and Human Values*; *Incompletion*; *Power and Authority*; and *Transitional Organization*.

Among the above there is a sub-set of principles that are primarily organizational in nature. These are: *The Multifunctional Principle–Organism vs. Mechanism*; *Boundary Location*; *Information Flow*; *Support Congruence*; and *Power and Authority*.

The *Multifunctional Principle–Organism vs. Mechanism* refers to traditional organizations which are often based on a high level of specialization and fragmentation of work, which reduces flexibility. When a complex array of responses is required, it becomes easier to achieve this variety if the system elements are capable of undertaking or performing several functions. *Boundary Location* is a principle that relates to a tendency in traditional hierarchical organizations to organize work around fragmented functions. This often leads to barriers that impede the sharing of data, information, knowledge and experience. Boundaries therefore should be designed around a complete flow of information, or knowledge, or materials, to enable the sharing of all relevant data, information, knowledge and experience. The *Information Flow* principle addresses the provision of information at the place where decisions and actions will be taken based on the information. *Support Congruence* relates to the design of reward systems, performance measurement systems, etc., and their alignment with the behaviors that are sought from people. For example, individual reward for individual effort, is not appropriate if team behavior is required. *Power and Authority* is concerned with responsibilities for tasks, and making available the resources that are needed to fulfill these responsibilities, which involves giving people the power and authority to secure these resources.

There is also another sub-set of principles that largely relate to the process by which technology is designed. These are: *The* Compatibility Principle; *The Incompletion Principle*; and *The Transitional Organization Principle*.

The *Compatibility Principle* states that the process by which technology is designed needs to be compatible with the objectives being pursued, implying that technologies designed without the involvement of users, would not be compatible with the aim of developing a participatory form of work organization where employees are involved in internal decision making. *Incompletion* addresses the fact that when workplace systems are designed, the design is in fact never finished. As soon implementation is completed, its consequences become more evident, possibly indicating the need for a redesign. The *Transitional Organization* principle addresses two quite distinct problems when creating new organizations: one is the design and start-up of new (greenfield) workplaces, the other relates to existing (brownfield) workplaces. The second is much more difficult than the first. In both situations the design team, and the processes it uses, are potentially a tool to support the start-up and any required transitions.

What remain from Cherns' set of 11 sociotechnical design principles, is a sub-set that is significantly technology oriented, although the principles also have organizational implications.

The principles in question are: *Minimum Critical Specification*; *Variance Control*; *Design and Human Values*.

The principle of *Minimum Critical Specification* states that only what is absolutely necessary should be specified, and no more than this, and that this applies to all aspects of the system: tasks, jobs, roles, etc. Whilst this is organizational in nature, it impacts technology as well. It implies that what has to be done needs to be defined, but how it should be done should be left open. In terms of features and functions of technology, the technology should not be over determined, but should leave room for different approaches. It implies a degree of flexibility and openness in the technologies. Turning now to Variance Control, this is a principle that, as its name suggests, is focused on handling variances, these being events that are unexpected or unprogrammed. Variances that cannot be eliminated should be controlled as near to the point of origin of the variance as possible. Some of these variances may be critical, in that they have an important affect on results. It is important to control variances at source, because not to do so often introduces time delays. Next on the list of principles is that of *Design and Human Values*. This is concerned with quality of working life. In the context of the working environment it manifests itself in issues such as stress, motivation, personal development, etc. This principle has both a social sub-system dimension and a technology sub-system dimension, in that both can be designed to reduce stress, and to enhance motivation and personal development.

While these principles are extremely useful from the perspective of organizational design and technology redesign, there are a number of limitations with respect to Enterprise Information Systems. Specifically there is no explicit consideration of, or an attempt to consider, business strategy or the alignment between business objectives and specific organizational characteristics. Nor is there any easy way to link specific features of Enterprise Information Systems technology with organizational requirements. To some extent variance analysis can contribute to this, but variance analysis does not specifically address technical features and consider the organizational implications of these. Moreover, the sociotechnical approach is highly specialized, and the competencies to undertaken this approach are not commonly found in businesses, both small and large.

One method, related to the sociotechnical approach, built upon the principles described above, and one that tackles the issues of competencies and technical features, is HITOP, which stands for the High Integration of Technology, Organisation and PeopleHigh Integration of Technology, Organization and People (Majchrzak *et. al.*, 1991). HITOP is a method that was designed to assist with the implementation of advanced manufacturing and information technologies. The HITOP process allows an analysis to be undertaken of organizational and job-design implications of critical features of proposed technologies. It then helps with the identification of key task and skill requirements so that human resources can be properly planned and developed to meet operational needs.

HITOP comes in the form of a workbook (Majchrzak *et. al.*, 1991), that is in effect, an easy to read analysis manual, providing step-by-step guidance, rationales for analysis, blank analysis forms, and worked examples. It covers a wide range of issues and is based on a six-stage methodology.

The first stage of the methodology involves making an assessment of organizational change:readiness forreadiness for change, which is followed, in the second stage, by an assessment of the technology that is proposed, to identify its critical features. The third step is an analysis of the essential task requirements, which leads to an assessment of the skill requirements. The fifth step is concerned with determining how people should be rewarded. The final step deals with designing the organizational changes that need to be achieved given the technology and people

requirements, which leads to the generation of a specific implementation plan. The HITOP design tool therefore provides:

- An assessment of organizational readiness for change;
- A definition of the critical technical features of advanced technologies;
- The determination of essential job requirements, job design options, skills, training and selection requirements;
- The determination of requirements and options for pay, promotion and organizational structure.

The analysis thus provides a direct and ordered consideration of critical technology, organization and people factors, and helps to identify those factors which require in-depth attention. The analysis also provides an expanded insight into the total organizational and people impacts of specific technologies, going well beyond skills and training. Identification of people and organizational cost drivers in technology implementation is also another result of the analysis.

HITOP allows alternative organizational designs and different ways for managing people to be specified, given specific technology plans. HITOP also provides guidance in determining the appropriate time for implementing technology plans, and helps to identify those equipment and system choices that are likely to create the greatest number of people and organizational problems, so that the implementation team is better prepared to deal with these problems.

By performing HITOP analysis, guidance is provided through an iterative, systems based process in which all the critical features of the organization, people and technology environment are systematically assessed and all implementable options are identified. This enables the consequences of major decisions to be understood before those decisions are implemented. As a result, surprises downstream can be reduced and needed changes to the technology, the organization, or the people involved, can be identified.

Typical benefits of using HITOP include reduced implementation time, improved acceptance of technical changes, and better fit between chosen technologies, organizational designs, and people skills. All these lead to lower implementation costs and the faster delivery of benefits sought from the new technologies (flexibility, cost reductions, etc.).

While this approach has many strong features, and is very good at identifying the organizational and people implications of specific features of the technology (called critical technical features), it does have a number of limitations, which primarily reflect the context in which it was developed.

Firstly, like the sociotechnical approach, HITOP does not explicitly address strategy. In effect this is taken as given, along with technical features, and strategy remains invisible during the process. Moreover the focus of the HITOP reference manual tends to be on one person undertaking the analysis necessary to figure out the organizational and people implications of a given technology. This is not to say that the method cannot be used by a multifunctional, multiskilled team, just that this team-based approach to implementation is not emphasized or supported in the manual. The method was also developed in the context of large organizations seeking to implement new technologies in existing, rather hierarchical organizational designs, and as a result the reference manual tends focus on the implementation of technology, and tweaking the organization to make this work, and the language used in the reference manual is rather technical in nature. Consequently, it is not the most SME-friendly method. In fact, many businesses, both large and small, would struggle to understand the HITOP jargon used in the manual.

The HiSTOP Method

Whatever the limitations of HITOP it is nevertheless a power tool and provides a good starting position for further development. Such development of the method has been undertaken with a view to addressing its weaknesses and providing an even more powerful implementation support tool, and one that also deals with the specific needs of SMEs. Specifically the focus has been upon making the method more user-friendly, so that it can be used by people who are not experts in organizational design or technology implementation, thus making it more suitable for use by SMEs. Additionally, the HITOP approach has been strengthened, for example by introducing strategic considerations into the process. Also the method has been generalized so that it is no longer just appropriate to manufacturing technologies.

The revised method that is being developed is based on a number of foundational principles. These reflect the circumstances often found in SMEs, but the foundational principles are also relevant to the needs of larger companies.

The first of these foundational principles relates to the basic approach or underlying philosophy with respect to the balance between the use of external and internal expertise. Any company engaged in technology implementation, whether this be the implementation of Enterprise Information Systems, or other technologies, can adopt one of four basic approaches:

- passive implementation;
- consultancy-centered implementation;
- sub-contracting based implementation;
- company-centered implementation.

A *passive implementation* approach is one where no-one is really taking the implementation seriously. Reliance on external consultancy expertise is small and the development and use of in-house know-how and capabilities is low. A *consultancy-centered implementation* is one where there is a heavy reliance on external consultants and the development and use of in-house know-how and capabilities is minimal or non-existent. This is a traditional approach that relies on the use of external experts. A *sub-contracting based implementation* is one where a lot of external expertise is used, but the process also involves a high level of development and utilization of in-house know-how and capabilities. Consultants are used as sub-contractors to undertake specific tasks and to provide extra manpower. A *company-centered implementation* involved a high degree of development and utilization of in-house know-how and capabilities. Consultants are used in a selective way, for example, to help set-up change processes and to provide facilitation or to provide specialist technical expertise.

Practical experience suggests that firms implementing advanced ICT such as Enterprise Information Systems are much more successful and do things faster if they adopt an approach that involves a significant development and use of internal expertise. In effect this involves companies doing their own Enterprise Information Systems implementations with external experts supporting the process The method entails training and developing teams of employees to analyze the technology, formulate new organizational arrangements, plan the implementation and manage the changes.

A company-centered method has many advantages over the other styles and is particularly effective in terms of:

- enabling culture change;
- involving those affected by change and achieving ownership of the proposed technologies;
- breaking down organizational barriers and improving cross-functional communications and understandings;
- identifying issues that need to be resolved to make effective use of the technologies;
- tapping into local knowledge about existing processes.

The second foundational principle adopted for the development of the HiSTOP method relates to the issue of complexity versus simplicity. It is very easy to create complex and sophisticated implementation methods that are intellectually pleasing, but this is not very helpful in an industrial setting. It is highly probable that few people within a business would be able to understand a complex method, and even fewer would be willing to use it. It would be an expert's tool and as such would be incompatible with the aim of providing support for non-experts. It would be full of terminology that no-one understood, it would exclude just about everybody and few would believe in it or the results that emerge. For these reasons, HiSTOP is being developed to be as simple as possible, but without compromising the validity and the power of the original HITOP method. One of the challenges has therefore been developing a method that involves a lot of conceptual complexity, but at the same time, is one that is easy to use.

The third foundational principle is that the method should be a group-based process. Group processes are considered to be fundamental to successful implementation. The implementation of technologies such as Enterprise Information Systems require cross organizational working and understandings. As such, an approach based upon a small number of experts working in isolation tends to create an elitist atmosphere. Hiding behind questionnaires, audits, process mappings, etc., experts working in this way rarely establish a working dialogue and establish ownership of change. When implementing new technologies it is necessary to understand and value the process used to implement the technology. Enterprise Information Systems implementation is a real opportunity to transform organizations–people, culture, attitudes and so on. Moreover, the implementation process can be used to establish an environment where it becomes the norm to make better use of the creativity and knowledge of all the people in the company. Using a group process it is possible to achieve several things:

- initiate real teaming and cross-functional working;
- tap into knowledge about what is wrong—people already have a good idea about problems;
- open up a vast resource of new ideas;
- start to unfreeze the status quo and to gain emotional commitment to change.

The fourth foundational principle is that the implementation process should be a dynamic one. This means that the implementation team should not spend too much time looking at the existing situation. Instead they should focus on what needs to be achieved and then figure out how to get there and what problems stand in the way. Many consultancy methods begin with a detailed analysis of the *as-is* situation (getting people to fill-in questionnaires, undertaking detailed process mapping etc). This takes a lot of effort, is pretty dull and is often not required in such detail. It leads to a lot of information that makes for good consultancy reports, but its value in helping with the design a new situation is questionable.

Normally it is not necessary to spend a lot of time and money analyzing and diagnosing work processes that are about to abandoned or changed significantly. It is certainly necessary to understand the current situation, but the analysis that goes on in most companies goes way beyond understanding. The aim should be to:

- use the group's collective knowledge to develop an understanding of the work processes that are being used;
- establish what in the existing work processes is broken and what needs to be fixed;
- get everybody to reach a common understanding of the *as is* situation, what is wrong and how the new technology will help improve the work processes.

Without this common understanding people will not agree about what needs to be done to use technologies such as Enterprise Information Systems, effectively.

The fifth and final foundational principle is that the implementation method should be structured, systemic and systematic. This is an important requirement since structure provides a step by step roadmap to follow and activities to undertake. Systemic means that the method should address the design of the whole system—technology, organization, human resource infrastructure and management practices. Systematic means that the method should make formal links between features of the technology and features of the organization, human resource infrastructure and management practices required to support the technology and to make effective use of it.

The HiSTOP method will now be described. It consists of four phases:

- Strategic Visioning and Assessment;
- Analysis of the Technology;
- Organizational Design;
- Implementation Planing and Execution

The first phase, Strategic Visioning and Assessment, is the point where the strategic dimension is considered. At a basic level this involves: establishing and training an implementation group; verifying the project benefits and links with strategy; and informing people in the organization about the project, its business purpose, what is involved and the process of implementation. This phase can also however be used as an opportunity to review and revise strategy. Importantly also, this phase provides an opportunity to consider the existing organization design, and to ask questions about its appropriateness to the strategy and to consider what organizational changes may in themselves be beneficial, apart from those that might be needed to achieve alignment with the Enterprise Information Systems technology.

The second phase, Analysis of the Technology,

involves: establishing a common understanding of the Enterprise Information Systems technology and the work process that are affected by the new technologies; identifying major tasks involved in the work processes; analyzing variances and their impacts; defining the features of the Enterprise Information Systems technology; and establishing organizational needs. This phase leads to a requirement specification in terms of technology, organization and people.

The third phase, Organizational Design, involves: establishing organizational design constraints and evaluation criteria; generating job and organizational design options; and evaluation of options and final selection of new jobs and an organizational design. This stage leads to an organizational design that is aligned with both strategy and the chosen Enterprise Information Systems technologies. The organizational structure is designed based on some identified requirements, taking account of organizational design issues such as differentiation, integration, decision structure, and formalization (Majchrzak, 1992).

The fourth and final phase, Implementation Planing and Execution, involves: establishing what resources are available and who will do what; creating an implementation schedule; and defining post-implementation follow-up actions. Once these elements have been defined the enterprise is ready to move into actual implementation, but will be doing so with the involvement and commitment of the different people and functions affected by the implementation project.

Each of the above phases is broken down into smaller steps, and along the process there are tools that support the steps.

An important part of the four-phase method, specifically designed into the method, is the consideration of information and its use, something that is crucial to Enterprise Information Systems. In many companies technology, organization and human resources have been planned and managed independently of each other. For example, an engineer might prepare detailed plans to acquire new

technology without simultaneously considering human resource factors or organizational issues. A result of this independent, asynchronous planning is failure of the technology to live up to its potential. One objectives of the method is to analyze the technology to establish what should be done to make the technology work as planned by:

- by identifying the requirements and problems of the technology;
- developing an understanding of the organizational and human resource consequence of the technology;
- considering how the information arising from the technology can be exploited throughout the firm.

The implementation of ICTs such as Enterprise Information Systems should aim to identify and deal with technology, organization and human resource characteristics that are mutually interdependent. Technical features such as: information integration; reliability; flexibility; often generate specific needs for communication, or coordination, or problem solving, or decision making, or all four.

It is important to recognize that ICT, and this is especially so for Enterprise Information Systems, has a dual capability to both automate and inform (Zuboff, 1988). The informing aspects of the technology are often overlooked or not given serious attention. Information generated can be useful for several purposes:

- for continuous improvement activities;
- to support activities undertaken by people in other parts of the company;
- to build up information about customers, process usage, etc.

It is necessary when analyzing technologies such as Enterprise Information Systems to ensure that the informing capabilities of the technology are being fully exploited and if necessary to change the technical specifications or planned use of the technology or both to ensure that this is achieved.

A useful approach when analyzing Enterprise Information Systems is to consider issues of place and time. Features of the Enterprise Information System may affect the place where activities can or need to be done, or where people can or need to be located, or where information generated can be exploited, or all three. Moreover, features of the Enterprise Information System may affect the time needed to undertake activities, or the time to transfer generated information, or the time required to respond to events, or all three.

By looking at issues of place and time it is possible to begin to understand the way that Enterprise Information Systems may no longer fit with taken for granted assumptions about who does what, organizational demarcations, the time needed to do activities, the place where tasks can be done, and so on.

Importantly however, features of the Enterprise Information System must also be examined from the perspective of organizational and people requirements, and these should then be linked to the organizational design. This is done by examining critical technical features, for example information integration and then linking these to organizational requirements in the form of the need for communications between people and groups, co-ordination among employees, and decision making, specifically what decisions and where these are best undertaken (for example locally or remotely).

Once the need for communications, co-ordination, and decision making has been established, these specific needs have to be addressed by re-designing jobs and the organization. This can be broken down into five major design issues:

- differentiation—breaking tasks down into jobs and grouping these into organizational units so that work is done efficiently;

- integration—deciding what coordination mechanisms are needed to ensure effective working between jobs and organizational units;
- decision structure—deciding who takes decision about what;
- formalization—deciding what aspects of the work need to be defined through formal procedures;
- management framework—developing a management approach that supports the new jobs and organization.

FUTURE TRENDS

Information and communications technologies are becoming ubiquitous, both in society at large and in business. Future visions of the information society (for example Kidd, 2007) foresee a world where ICTs are even more crucial and central to business operations that they have been hitherto. In addition, not only will the scope of technology applications expand, but rapid technological change will also result in the need to undertake rapid updating and replacement of installed business supporting technologies such as Enterprise Information Systems. The net result of this will be that implementation of ICTs within enterprises will shift from one-off separate projects to an ongoing process of implementation.

Such a change will require enterprises to improve their implementation capabilities and become agile (or adaptable) in the face of continuing structural changes (Kidd, 2008); structural changes that manifesting themselves in the form of technological innovations and developments.

Enterprises will therefore need to improve their systems design and implementation performance. But this performance should be not be judged just against internal criteria (for example, time to implement), but also against their competitors' implementation performance. As long as an enterprise's implementation performance is below that of its competitors, then they should judge their performance as unsatisfactory. Basically, if some other enterprise can do it better, that is to say, for example, implement an Enterprise Information Systems faster, better and with less cost and disruption, then such a competitor will have a capability of deriving a competitive advantage from their technology implementation processes.

It is likely therefore that at some point in the future, faced with a circumstance where an enterprise needs to improve its technology implementation processes, it will need to take steps that will achieve a rapid improvement in performance. Once this has been achieved it will also need to maintain its lead, and the way it should do this is through a process of continuous improvement. Its competitors' implementation performance should not be viewed as a static target but as a moving one.

Such a vision foresees technology implementation performance as a competitive issue. This will place greater reliance on either developing internal competencies through methods such as HiSTOP, or the complete outsourcing of Enterprise Information Systems, their implementation and their management. In effect companies will have to take a strategic decision, either to keep implementation in-house and use this as a competitive tool, or to outsource Enterprise Information Systems, and compete on other terms. For those who adopt the first approach there is a need to undertake research into the means by which technology implementation processes can be used for competitive advantage and also be continually improved and refined to reflect changing circumstances. The work on the development of HiSTOP provides a starting point for such an advanced perspective on the role of technology implementation as a tool for improving competitive performance.

This is an issue that affects both large and small enterprise, thus HiSTOP, while its development was initially motivated by the needs of SMEs, is in fact relevant to both types of enterprises.

CONCLUSION

Far too many firms underestimate the complexities and difficulties of implementing ICTs such as Enterprise Information Systems. Yet mastering technology implementation can bring significant benefits such as:

- a reduction in the time taken to implement, enabling the sought after investment benefits to be achieved more quickly;
- an increased capability to avoid post-implementation problems leading to reduced costs over the life-cycle of the investment;
- improved capability to match ICT with business needs and to make more effective use of the technologies.

Achieving improved Enterprise Information Systems implementation capabilities is a challenging task in any organization, even more so in an SME, which generally has limited time, money and expertise to undertake implementation projects. The development of the HiSTOP method was initiated with the focus on SMEs, taking into account the three basic constraints of time, money and expertise. The implementation method is relatively simple, is based on a group-based approach, enables a dynamic process of communication and consensus building, and provides a structured, systemic and systematic approach. Importantly efforts have been made to make the method easy to use by:

- avoiding abstract language and concepts wherever possible;
- making things visual by using wall charts, diagrams and pictures, making use of shape, patterns, graphs, and colors.

Initially it was thought that a method might be possible whereby no external assistance would be needed. However, discussions with businesses and preliminary trials have indicated this goal to be idealistic, and some form of external support is unavoidable in most circumstances. However, it also emerged from the above that the method does not need to be used in its entirety, and companies can pick from the method steps and tools and incorporate these into their own internal methods. This was something that was not foreseen at the outset of the work, but with hindsight seems sensible.

REFERENCES

Bignall, V., & Fortune, J. (1984). *Understanding system failures*. Manchester: Manchester University Press.

Blackwell, P., Shehab, E. M., & Kay, J. M. (2006). An effective decision-support framework for implementing enterprise information systems within SMEs. *International Journal of Production Research*, *44*(17), 3533–3552. doi:10.1080/00207540500525270

Cherns, A. (1976). Principles of sociotechnical design. *Human Relations*, *29*(8), 783–792. doi:10.1177/001872677602900806

Cherns, A. (1987). Principles of sociotechnical design revisited. *Human Relations*, *40*(3), 153–162. doi:10.1177/001872678704000303

Clegg, C. W. (1984). The derivation of job design. *Journal of Occupational Behaviour*, *5*, 131–146. doi:10.1002/job.4030050205

Davenport, T. H. (1998). Putting the enterprise into the enterprise system. *Harvard Business Review*, (July-August): 121–131.

Guang-hui, C., Chun-qing, L. & Sai Yun-xiu, S. (2006). Critical success factors for ERP life cycle implementation. In A. Tjoa, L. Min Xu, & S. Chaudhry (Eds.), *Research and Practical Issues of Enterprise Information Systems* (pp. 553-562). Boston: Springer.

Holland, C. P., & Light, B. (1999). A critical success factors model for ERP implementation. *IEEE Software*, (May/June): 30–36. doi:10.1109/52.765784

Jing, R., & Xun Qiu, X. (2007, June). *A study on critical success factors in ERP systems implementation*. Paper presented at the International Conference on Service Systems and Service Management, Chengdu, China.

Kidd, P. T. (1994). *Agile manufacturing: Forging new frontiers*. Wokingham: Addison-Wesley.

Kidd, P. T. (Ed.). (2007). *European visions for the knowledge age: A quest for new horizons in the information society*. Macclesfield: Cheshire Henbury Publications.

Kidd, P. T. (2008). Agile holonic network organizations. In G.D. Putnik & M.M. Cunha (Eds.), *Encyclopedia of networked and virtual organizations* (pp. 35-42). Hershey, PA: IGI Global.

Leem, C. S., & Kim, S. (2002). Introduction to an integrated methodology for development and implementation of enterprise information systems. *Journal of Systems and Software*, *60*, 249–261. doi:10.1016/S0164-1212(01)00096-6

Majchrzak, A. (1992). Management of technological and organizational change. In G. Salvendy (Ed.), *Handbook of industrial engineering* (2nd ed., pp. 767-798). New York: John Wiley & Sons Inc.

Majchrzak, A., Fleischer, M., Roithman, D., & Mokray, J. (1991). *Reference manual for performing the HITOP analysis*. Ann Arbour, MI: Industrial Technology Institute.

Miles, R. E., & Snow, C. C. (1984). Fit, failure and the hall of fame. *California Management Review*, (Spring): 10–28.

Santhanam, R., Sasidharan, S., Brass, D., & Sambamurthy, V. (2006). The influence of knowledge transfers on the implementation of enterprise information systems. In A. Tjoa, L. Min Xu, & S. Chaudhry (Eds.), *Research and practical issues of enterprise information systems* (pp. 579-581). Boston: Springer.

Shang, S., & Seddon, P. B. (2002). Assessing and managing the benefits of enterprise systems: The business manager's perspective. *Information Systems Journal, 12*, 271–299. doi:10.1046/j.1365-2575.2002.00132.x

Strong, D. M., & Volkoff, O. (2004). A roadmap for enterprise system implementation. *Computer*, (June): 22–29. doi:10.1109/MC.2004.3

Ward, J., Hemingway, C., & Daniel, E. (2005). A framework for addressing the organisational issues of enterprise systems implementation. *The Journal of Strategic Information Systems, 14*(2), 97–119. doi:10.1016/j.jsis.2005.04.005

Zuboff, S. (1988). *In the age of the smart machine: The future of work and power*. New York: Basic Books.

KEY TERMS AND DEFINITIONS

Alignment: The process of achieving strategic fit between an enterprise and its business environment and arranging resources internally to support that alignment.

Business Objectives for Enterprise Information Systems: The specific business objectives that should be made explicit prior to Enterprise Information Systems selection, and which should be fully supported by the Enterprise Information System.

Critical Technical Features: Features of technology that have implications for organisation design, specifically in terms of communications, co-ordination, and decision-making.

HITOP: High Integration of Technology, Organization and People

HiSTOP: High Integration of Strategy, Technology, Organization and People

Integration: Bringing together enterprise subsystems to create an enterprise system fit for purpose. These subsystems include strategy, technology, organization, and people.

Strategic Fit: Aligning strategy, technology, organization, and people with the needs of the business environment.

Strategically Driven Implementation: An implementation of Enterprise Information Systems driven by strategy, as opposed to a technology driven implementation where the business strategy is not the primary driver for the implementation.

Structured, Systemic and Systematic Implementation Method: An implementation method that provides a step by step implementation roadmap (structured), addressing the design of the whole system–technology, organization, human resource infrastructure and management practices–(systemic), and making formal links between features of the technology and features of the organization, human resource infrastructure and management practices required to support the technology and to make effective use of it (systematic).

Chapter 16
Developing and Customizing Federated ERP Systems

Daniel Lübke
Leibniz Universität Hannover, Germany

Jorge Marx Gómez
University Oldenburg, Germany

ABSTRACT

Small and Medium Enterprises (SMEs) are the most important drivers in many economies. Due to their flexibility and willingness to innovate they can stand up to larger industry players. However, SMEs – as every other company – need to further reduce costs and optimize their business in order to stay competitive. Larger enterprises utilize ERP systems and other IT support for reducing costs and time in their business processes. SMEs lack behind because the introduction and maintenance of ERP systems are too expensive, the return on investment is achieved too late and the associated financial risks are too high. However, SMEs would like to have IT support for their business. The research behind the Federated ERP System (FERP) addresses the problems SMEs face with conventional ERP systems and offers reasonable and scalable IT support. This is done by decomposing the whole business logic of the ERP system into Web services, which are linked at run-time. The service composition is realized by a workflow system that is also responsible for creating and managing the user interfaces and the data-flow. By integrating only the Web services that are needed (possibly from third parties) the cost is reduced and the functionality can be scaled to the actual needs. However, not only a technical solution is needed but also the development process must be tailored towards SMEs. Small companies cannot afford highly-skilled staff and often do not have defined business processes.

INTRODUCTION

The business world is rapidly moving and Small-to-Medium Size Enterprises (SMEs) are competing within this vibrant marketplace with their flexibility and ability to innovate. They are an important part of the economy. For example, according to the IfM Bonn (2008) SMEs in Germany account for 38.3% of the overall turnover and employ 70.6% of all employees nationwide. In order to operate efficiently, SMEs need enterprise software, like ERP systems, for managing their business operations efficiently. However, ERP systems impose high costs due to their expensive purchase, customizing costs and re-customizing costs whenever business processes are changed. Thus, business process changes that are necessary to stay competitive become more costly as before.

This inevitably leads to the question how to make ERP systems better suited to SMEs in order to make them more competitive in the long run. The answer to this question is decomposed into two parts. The first part is a new architecture for such systems that can be introduced, operated, and maintained cheaper. The second part is engaged with the question on how to come to (new) requirements for the ERP system based on the business processes. A system that can be flexibly changed is worthless if no one knows what the desired result is.

Within this chapter we introduce the Federated ERP System as a new architecture for ERP systems that are especially suited to SMEs. We describe the overall architectural ideas as well as our implementation. In the second part we present a technique for deriving and discovering business processes from textual scenarios – so called use cases known from the software engineering domain.

FEDERATED ERP SYSTEMS

Problem Addressed

An ERP system is a standard software system which provides functionality to integrate and automate the business practices associated with the operation or production aspects of a company. The integration is based on a common data model for all system components and extents to more than one enterprise sector (see Robey et al., 2002; Rautenstrauch et al., 2003).

However, there are some disadvantages associated with conventional ERP systems. The main ones are:

- In most cases not all of the installed components are needed,
- high-end computer hardware is required to run the system, and
- customization of ERP systems is very expensive because product specific know-how of experts is necessary.

Due to the expensive process of installation and maintenance only large enterprises can afford complex ERP systems, which provide business logic for all sectors of the functional enterprise organization. Contrary to these aspects, FERP systems allow the separation of local and remote functions whereby no local resources are wasted for unnecessary components. Furthermore, single components are executable on small computers and due to decreasing complexity of the local system installation and maintenance costs subside, too.

Reference Architecture

Figure 1 gives an overview of the reference architecture of a Web Service-based FERP system. The architecture consists of several subsystems, which are interconnected. Because one of the main objective of an FERP system is to integrate

Figure 1. Reference architecture of an FERP system

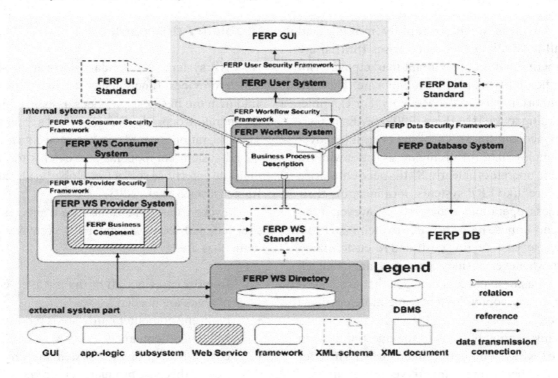

business components of different vendors, all components have to comply with standards. In this approach these standards are described by using XML schema documents. In order to separate the three different layers of a typical layered architecture of conventional ERP systems, each layer is assigned its own standard.

The subsystems of the proposed architecture are the following:

FERP Workflow System (FWfS)

The FWfS coordinates all business processes which have to be described in an appropriate XML-based workflow language. A workflow in this context is a plan of sequentially or parallelly chained functions as working steps. Each step represents an activity which leads to the creation or utilization of business benefits. Workflows implicitly contain the business logic of the overall

system. The function types that can be contained in a workflow in FERP systems are the following:

- Model-based user interface functions, e.g. show, edit, select, control
- Database access functions, e.g. read, update
- Application tasks which are connected to Web Service calls

FERP User System (FUS)

The FUS is the subsystem which implements functions for the visualization of graphical elements and coordinates interactions with end users. This subsystem is able to generate user screens at runtime. Screen descriptions, which have to comply with the FERP UI standard, are transformed to an end device-readable format, e.g. HTML in case of web browsers.

FERP Database System (FDS)

The FDS is the subsystem which implements functions for the communication with the FERP database. This subsystem is able to interpret XML structures which comply with the FERP data standard. The interface differentiates between two kinds of requests. Database update requests contain object oriented representations of business entities as XML trees. Database read requests contain X-Path or X-Query expressions specifying portions of data to be extracted. In both cases the request parameters have to be transformed into different types of request statements that vary depending on the type of database management system (DBMS) that is used. Assuming the use of a relational DBMS (RDBMS), the underlying data model also has to comply with the FERP data standard, which means that the corresponding table structure has to reflect the XML-Schema specifications respectively. The java.net project hyperjaxb2[1] provides a solution to generate SQL statements on the basis of XML schema definitions. Another solution is the application of native XML databases or XML-enabled RDBMS.

FERP Web Service Consumer System (FWCS)

The business logic of FERP systems is encapsulated in so called FERP business components which are wrapped in a Web Service. The FWCS is the subsystem that provides the functionality for the invocation of Web Services. All possible types of FERP Web Services are specified by the FERP WS standard. This standard contains XML schema definitions that describe Web Service operations as well as input and output messages. A Web Service references these types in its WSDL description. Furthermore this subsystem is able to search for Web Services, which are defined by a unique identifier. This way it is possible that different Web Service providers implement the same business component type as Web Service. Beside the implementation of Web Service invocation and search functionality this subsystem is responsible for the interpretation and consideration of non-functional parameters. Examples for those parameters are security policies, payment polices, and Quality of Service (QoS) requirements on the part of Web Service consumers.

FERP Web Service Provider System (FWPS)

The FWPS is the subsystem which implements functions for the provision of Web Services which comply with the FERP WS Standard. The subsystem includes a Web Server which is responsible for the interpretation of incoming and outgoing HTTP requests which in turn encapsulate SOAP requests. The subsystem provides business components of the FERP system as Web Services.

A connection to the FERP Web Service Directory allows the publication of Web Services. Furthermore this subsystem is responsible for the negotiation of common communication policies such as e.g. security protocols or usage fees with the requesting client.

FERP Web Service Directory (FWD)

The FWD provides an interface for the publication and the searching of FERP Web Services based on the UDDI standard. The structure of this registry leans on the FERP WS standard. In this standard Web Services are assigned to categories mirroring the predetermined functional organization of enterprises.

Prototype Development

The following paragraph briefly describes a first implementation of the proposed reference architecture which is based on open source software components. Figure 2 shows the architecture of our prototype. For the implementation of the FWfS we chose the workflow engine of the YAWL

289

Figure 2. Architecture of the prototype

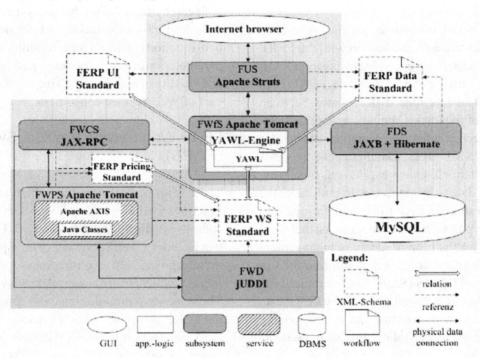

project[2]. The FUS was implemented on the basis of Apache Struts[3]. Our FDS is mainly based on the API of the Hyperjaxb2 project which in turn uses JAXB[4] and Hibernate[5]. jUDDI[6] served as basis for implementation of the FWD. The FWCS uses JAX-RPC[7] (Java API for XML-based RPC) which is provided by the SUN Developer Network (SDN). Our FWPS uses Apache AXIS[8] as basis for the provision of Web Services.

Figure 3 shows an example process model in YAWL

Tasks in our process definitions can be assigned to one of the three function types:

- Database communication (in figure 3 indicated as DB-task)
- End-user communication (in figure 3 indicated as GUI-task)
- Web Service communication (in figure 3 indicated as WS-task)

All other symbols comply with the graphical notation of YAWL. The example process model demonstrates a workflow for the creation of a purchase order[9]. The example includes only one Web Service call which is responsible for the calculation of the total sum of a purchase order which consists of one or more order items. Order items include a price and an amount. The Web Service receives the whole order as XML document without total sum. Having finished the calculation of the total sum the Web Service returns the completed order as XML document. The next workflow task visualizes this XML document. After the user agreed the XML document is transmitted to the FERP database system which transforms it to an SQL-INSERT statement in the next workflow task.

User Interface Generation

Every ERP system needs to be operated by users. In the end, they need to make decisions, retrieve

Figure 3. Process model in YAWL as simplified example for the creation of a purchase order

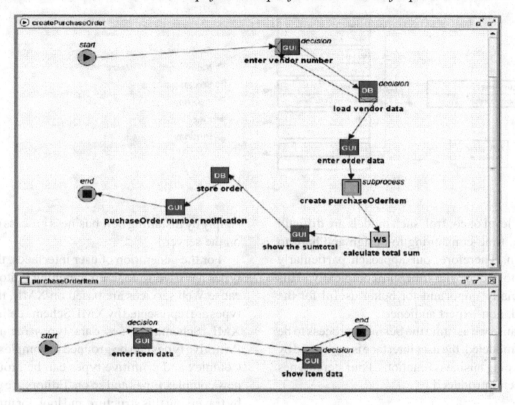

data or enter new records. While classical ERP systems offer clients for personal computers only, now mobile devices, like handhelds and mobile phones are emerging. Because of this situation the Federated ERP system will face many types of clients. Furthermore, these clients need to be easily updatable. For a simple process change it is not feasible to update hundreds of possibly mobile or distributed computers. Thus the user interface must be managed on the server-side and must be platform-neutral.

Our approach for minimizing the effort needed to develop and customize the user interface is to automatically generate the interfaces from the business process descriptions. Much research has been done in the field of model-based user interface (MB-UI), which aims to model user interfaces in the way program logic is modeled in UML. Research in these fields has been going on for more

than a decade. For example, (Paterno, 1999) gives an overview over the field of MB-UI. Numerous design environments have been proposed as result of MB-UI. Each differs in the number and type of models used (for a thorough overview the reader is referred to (da Silva, 2000). However, most approaches share a common element: the task model. Fortunately, this task model is easily related to our approach: The business process model is in fact a task model on a very high abstraction level (see Traetteberg, 1999). Furthermore, the field of MB-UI has matured. Especially insight into reasons for failure of some approaches has been beneficial for our research. Common mistakes and problems concerning practical adoption of MB-UI techniques are listed by (Traetteberg et. al., 2004): The biggest problem has been the complexity of the introduced models. While complex and detailed models give the designer

Figure 4. Generation of a simple user interface for a customer record

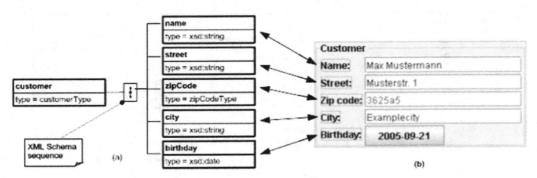

the best level of control, such models are difficult to learn, time-consuming to design and hard to maintain. Therefore, our approach particularly strives to reduce the inherent complexity. This is especially important for being useful for the targeted, non-expert audience.

Because we assume the business process to be already modeled, the user interface is expressed by stereotyping business functions. Four stereotypes have been introduced:

- Selection: The user shall select data from a collection of possible choices. For example: Select product from a catalogue.
- Edit: The user shall edit some information object from the data model. For example, edit order.
- Control: The user wants to explicitly invoke some action. This is used to model navigational decisions. For example, "Accept order".
- User: The user has to do something by himself, e.g. planning, comparing, etc.

These four actions can be attached to a business function and are visualized by small icons on the left-hand side. The annotated business processes are downloaded by the client software, which generates user interfaces from these models and sends the data and user decisions back to the server. This way, the user interface can be edited simply by installing new business process models on the server.

For the generation of user interfaces, the data types are used to look up matching editors. Because Web services are based on XML, the data types are represented by XML Schema definitions. XML Schema defines data types recursively: Primitive types can be grouped to complex types. Complex and primitive types can be grouped to new complex types and so on. Editors are created by traversing this structure and look for matching editors registered in the system. At least for each primitive type, like integers and strings, an editor is provided by the system. Therefore, a (possibly primitive) editor can be generated for each XML Schema. Figure 4 shows a simple generated editor for a customer record.

Figure 5 shows the hierarchical refinement of the example process with user interface stereotypes, and the resulting user interface using a custom editor. The client application shows the processes needing further action by the user, and the processes which are currently executed by someone else. This information is given on the right hand side.

Since the user interface generation is based on the business process description, context information can be given to the user. For example, descriptions of the currently active business function can be displayed. In our prototype these are realized by giving tool-tip information. At this

Figure 5. Refinement of the business process and user interface generation

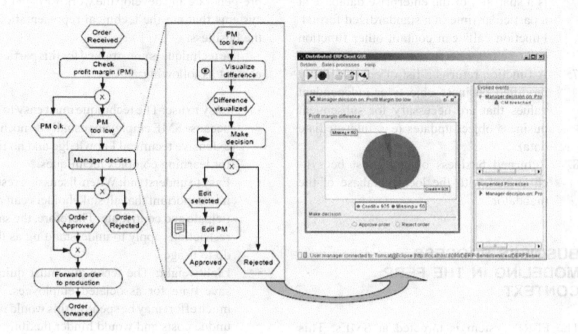

point it is even possible to integrate experience bases to facilitate the communication between developers, process designers and end users.

Since this approach is based on the process description only, it is possible to generate user interfaces for different target platforms. For example, a connector for XForms – an XML standard for describing input forms - is under development and generation of HTML pages is possible as well for integration into intranet and portal applications. For further discussion on the topic of generation of user interfaces from EPC models (see Lüecke, 2005; Lübke et. al., 2006).

FERP as an SOA Instance

Because of FERP system is based on Web Services and their orchestration, we can say that it is a service-oriented architecture solution whereby all functions are available as services and unambiguously addressable. This system works as follows:

1. The network consists of service consuming and service providing network nodes.
2. Each client, which provides an interface to an enterprise is called *mandator* and is connected to the enterprise database.
3. The processing steps of a business process are stored in the local database of a mandator as *workflow*. A workflow in this context is a plan of sequentially or in parallel chained functions as working steps in the meaning of activities which lead to the creation or utilization of business benefits.
4. Finding a function within the P2P-network means that a request which contains the function type must be send to all service providing peers.
5. After receiving the responses to a function type request the mandator must elect a network node to be accessed.
6. A function call contains parameters as business objects and other (primitive) values that are delivered to the service providing net-

work node. A business object in this context is a snapshot of the enterprise database at a particular time in a standardized format. Function calls can contain other function calls.

7. A function returns a list of either directly modified business objects or independent values that are necessary for subsequent business object updates (e.g. intermediate data).

8. Returned business objects must be synchronized with the local database of the mandator.

BUSINESS PROCESS MODELING IN THE FERP CONTEXT

The FERP system is targeted at SMEs. This poses some additional challenges besides the already outlined technical problems. Especially the gathering of requirements - and as their most important part business processes – has to be performed before any implementation of an (F)ERP system can start.

However, in most SMEs the business processes are not defined explicitly, but the organization as a whole has tacit knowledge of the activities that are to be performed and the order in which they have to be performed. But even if SMEs have documented business processes, these descriptions are typically not suited for software development or customization because technical details are missing.

Therefore, the knowledge of process participants needs to be externalized into documented business processes that are suited to be the basis for software development and customization projects because they lack sufficient detail.

Within the FERP context, we propose a lightweight approach to elicitate the business processes and to generate explicit models from there. These explicit business process models can be used to pre-generate and develop the workflows in FERP systems that are the technical representation of the business.

The technique is constrained for this particular context as following:

•   Easy to use: The technique must easy to use because SME employees usually do not have extensive technical knowledge and no time for learning complex techniques.

•   Easy to understand: When discussing results it is important that all stakeholders can participate and contribute. Therefore, the same restrictions apply to understanding as they do to usage.

•   Lightweight: The technique must quickly save time for associated employees. Not much effort may be spend as this would pose undue costs and would hinder flexibility.

•   Offer basis for later development: The results must be usable by the customization team later on. The smoother this transition is the better.

Use Cases as the Basis

We use a use case-based approach for interviewing the users and stakeholders in SMEs and documenting the results.

Use Cases (Cockburn, 2005) are a technique from the Requirements Engineering community. They represent possible scenarios from the point of view of a single main actor. The most common form for documenting use cases are tables as illustrated in table 1:

The table contains additional information like preconditions and success conditions that express goals and constraints from the business and software point of view that are associated with the use case.

For our approach, we assume the use cases to conform to the meta-model as illustrated in figure 6.

The metamodel captures the properties of the tabular template. A use case consists primarily of the main scenario that has a sequence of steps. Each step can be extended for operational sequences that are not default. Each extension consists of a new scenario. Each step within a scenario has an actor, i.e. the role or person that is performing the activity. A use case is written from the perspective of a main actor that is primarily concerned with the goals the use case has. The goals are represented by success guarantees. A use case starts when the trigger applies and may be performed iff all preconditions are met.

Because use cases are nearly freely-written text, they have the advantage that they are easily comprehendible by all kinds of users and stakeholders (Lübke, 2006). Furthermore, the tabular structure imposes a semi-formal format that can be processed by computer programs later on.

Mapping Use Cases to Business Processes

Use Cases are written from the perspective of the main actor only. However, a set of use cases can represent a business process. Therefore, the individual use cases need to be joined together into one large process.

The set of use cases and a use case itself can represent a business process. The steps within the use case can be seen as the activities of the business process. The actors of the step become the actors of the business activities.

Because use cases conforming to the presented metamodel must not contain complex control-flow constructs, they only require a limited set of workflow-patterns (van der Aalst, ter Hofstede, Kiepuszewski, & Barros, 2003). Following workflow-patterns are needed within a use case:

- Sequence: A sequence is used to order the steps within a scenario,
- Exclusive Choice: For attaching extensions to a step, this type of split in the control-flow is needed,
- Simple Merge: When extension jump back, the control-flow is merged with this type of merges.

However, it is necessary to join use cases. This is done by comparing the triggers, preconditions,

Table 1.

Use Case	#3: Thesis Supervisor hands out topic
Primary Actor	Thesis Supervisor
Stakeholders	Thesis Supervisor: wants to hand out topic easily and without much paperwork Student: wants to receive topic quickly Secretary: wants easy to use/read forms for completing registration
Minimal Guarantees	A topic is only handed out once at a time
Successs Guarantees	Student knows topic Supervisor knows all needed adminstrative information of the student
Preconditions	Student has achieved at least 80% of credit points Student has clearance from Academic Examination Office
Triggers	Student wants to sign up for a topic
Main Success Scenario	1. Supervisor checks whether the topic is still available or not 2. Supervisor reserves topic for student 3. System updates list of current thesis 4. Supervisor confirms thesis topic and student's information to the Academic Examination Office 5. System sends confirmation to student, supervisor and Academic Examination Office
Extensions	1a If topic is not available anymore, then EXIT

and success guarantees. The use cases are ordered in a way that success guarantees satisfy triggers and preconditions of the following use cases.

Because a success guarantee can satisfy the preconditions of more than one use case, and the precondition and trigger of a use case can be satisfied by more than one use case, following workflow-patterns are needed:

- Parallel Split: The control-flow of one use case is split to several use cases because more than one precondition can be satisfied,
- Generalized Synchronized Merge: The precondition can be satisfied by one of many use cases.

Because all business process languages support these basic workflow-patterns, the generation can have any language as its target. We demonstrate this by generating EPCs that can be

the basis for composing the Web services of an FERP system.

Generation of Event-Driven Process Chains

For demonstrating our approach we chose Event-Driven Process Chains (EPCs). They are easy to understand and are therefore well-suited for fostering communication between the stakeholders of FERP systems.

The generation of a single use case is done by applying following algorithm:

1. Preconditions and Triggers are converted to events
   ° If there is more than one event, the events will be joined by an AND-join
2. Each Step of the main scenario is converted to a function

Figure 6. Use case metamodel

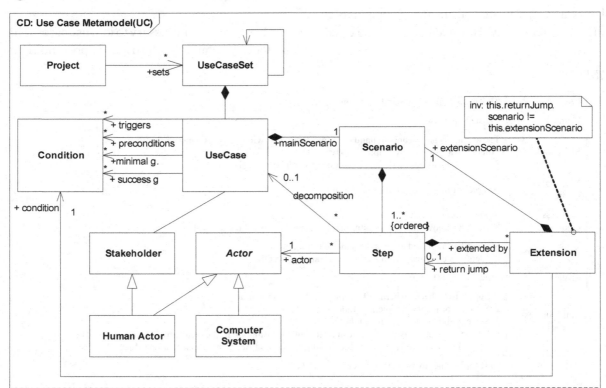

    °   Connected with simple okay-events
3.   Success guarantees are converted to end-events
    °   If there is more than one event, an AND-split is introduced
4.   Extensions are introduced with an XOR-split
    °   The extension condition becomes an event
5.   The extension scenario is converted like the main scenario
    °   Extensions of extensions are handled recursively
6.   Return jumps are realized with an XOR-join
    °   The join is introduced before the function that is the jump target

This algorithm is applied to every use case. In the following step, the use cases have to be joined. Depending on different needs, several join strategies are available:

- Large EPC: Generates a single, large EPC model from all use cases.
- Short EPC: Generates an EPC that has a function for each use case. The details of the use case are discarded and not displayed. This type of model is well-suited for discussing the ordering of use cases and the global control-flow.
- Short EPC with hierarchical refinement: EPCs allow function to be detailed in other EPCs. This approach combines the advantages of the first two approaches by generating a short EPC and placing a more detailed EPC for the use case behind every function.

Common to all three approaches is the strategy for merging the set of use cases to a single model. The events that have been generated by the algorithm above are unified, i.e. all events that have the same name are reduced to a single event. Connectors for the control-flow are introduced accordingly. This is illustrated in figure 7.

Figure 7. Joining multiple use cases in EPC notation to a single EPC model

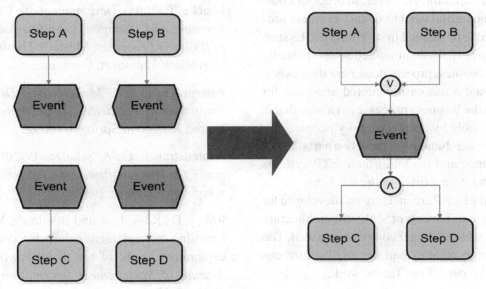

Advantages of the Use Case-Centered Approach

By using textual use cases, it is possible to document and discover business processes. Due to the use of plain, semi-formal text, they can be used by all involved stakeholders. These stakeholders do not need to learn a new notation nor do they have difficulties while interpreting and validating the documented parts of business processes. Use Cases can guide interviews with isolated stakeholders. The generation generates a global view by combining the use cases to a large business process model. The business process model is the foundation for later ongoing development. It can be readily used by developers. Therefore, our approach satisfies the constraints outlined above nicely.

CONCLUSION AND OUTLOOK

Within this chapter we have presented the FERP architecture as an architecture for ERP systems that are well-suited for SMEs; such systems can be flexibly altered, and are comparably cheap to install and maintain. However, in order to know what to change and what to install, business processes need to be defined first. Within SMEs such processes need to be documented because usually no explicit business process documentation exists. We proposed a use case-centered approach for eliciting the business processes in a way that is comprehensibly by non-tech-savvy people.

With the combination of these two parts, SMEs can introduce and maintain their ERP systems and can stay competitive in the market.

While the FERP architecture was developed for addressing requirements of SMEs, the architecture may be suitable for larger companies as well. The assessment to what extend the architecture can scale will be part of our future work.

REFERENCES

Cockburn, A. (2005). *Writing Effective Use Cases.* Amsterdam: Addison-Wesley Longman.

da Silva, P. P. (2002). User Interface Declarative Models and Development Environments: A Survey. In Palanque & Patern`o (Eds.), *DSV-IS, volume 1946 of Lecture Notes in Computer Science* (pp. 207–226). London: Springer.

IfM Bonn (2008). *Schlüsselzahlen Deutschland (Key Indicators Germany).* Retrieved December 28, 2008, from http://www.ifm-bonn.org/index.php?id=99, 2008-12-28.

Lübke, D., Lüecke, T., Schneider, K., & Marx Gómez, J. (2006). Using Event-Driven Process Chains for Model-Driven Development of Business Applications. In Nüttgens & Mendling (Eds.), *Proceedings of the XML4BPM 2006.*

Lübke, D. (2006). Transformation of Use Cases to EPC Models. In M. Nüttgens, F. Rump, & J. Mendling (Eds.), *Proceedings of the EPK 2006. CEUR Proceedings Vol 224.* http://ftp.informatik.rwth-aachen.de/Publications/CEUR-WS/Vol-224/.

Lüecke, T. (2005). *Development of a Concept for Creating and Managing User Interfaces bound to Business Processes.* Master's Thesis, Leibniz Universität Hannover, Germany.

Paterno, F. (1999). *Model-Based Design and Evaluation of Interactive Applications.* London, United Kingdom: Springer-Verlag.

Rautenstrauch, C., & Schulze, T. (2003). *Informatik für Wirtschaftswissenschaftler und Wirtschaftsinformatiker,* Berlin.

Robey, D., Ross, J., & and Boudreau, M. (2002). Learning to implement enterprise systems: An exploratory study of the dialectics of change. *Journal of Management Information Systems, 19*(1), 17-46.

Trætteberg, H. (1999). Modelling Work. Workflow and Task Modelling. In Vanderdonckt, & Puerta (Eds.), *CADUI* (pp. 275-280). Kluwer.

Trætteberg, H., Molina, P. J., & Nunes, N. J. (2004). Making model-based UI design practical: usable and open methods and tools. In Vanderdonckt, Nunes, & Rich (Eds.), *Intelligent User Interfaces* (pp. 376–377). ACM.

van der Aalst, W., ter Hofstede, A.H.M., Kiepuszewski, B., & Barros, A. P. (n.d.). Workflow Patterns. *Journal of Distributed and Parallel Databases, 3*(14), 5-51.

ENDNOTES

[1] Hyperjaxb2 – relational persistence for JAXB objects: https://hyperjaxb2.dev.java.net/ (last visit October 2006)

[2] http://yawlfoundation.org/

[3] http://sturts.apache.org/

[4] http://jaxp.dev.java.net/

[5] http://www.hibernate.org/

[6] http://ws.apache.org/juddi/

[7] http://java.sun.com/webservices/jaxrpc/

[8] http://ws.apache.org/axis/

[9] In order to improve understandability the process was simplified. Changes of entered data and order items are not supported.

This work was previously published in the Journal of Enterprise Information Systems, vol. 5, issue 3, edited by A. Gunasekaran, pp. 45-59, copyright 2009 by IGI Publishing (an imprint of IGI Global).

Chapter 17
EIS Systems and Quality Management

Bart H.M. Gerritsen

TNO Netherlands Organization for Applied Scientific Research, The Netherlands

ABSTRACT

This chapter discusses the support of quality management by Enterprise Information Systems. After a brief introduction in ISO9001, one of the principle and widest-spread quality management frameworks, this chapter discusses the design and implementation of a typical QMS and in particular of key performance indicators, indicating the present state of performance in the organization. While analyzing design and implementation issues, requirements on the supporting EIS system will be derived. Finally, the chapter presents an outlook onto future developments, trends and research. This chapter reveals that key performance indicators can be well integrated in EIS systems, using either relational or object-oriented storage technology.

INTRODUCTION

Quality Management Systems

Over the last decades, enterprises and other organizations from large to small have come to implement quality management systems (QMS). Large Scale Enterprises (LSE's) and Small and Medium Enterprises (SME's) alike, decided to apply QMS to get grip on the product and business process quality level customers nowadays expect. Many

SME's initially did so "because customers ask for it". While customer satisfaction is a pivotal factor indeed, learning to master and apply quality principles correctly also assists in increased employee involvement and productivity, preventing defects from occurring, reducing costs and production times. The key to achieving this is a timely and correct alignment of the delivered quality in business processes at all levels in the organization, board to shop floor. The information needed to know and control quality performance goes hand in hand with other daily operational information within the organization and consequently, quality information

DOI: 10.4018/978-1-60566-892-5.ch017

Figure 1. Global uptake of ISO 9001:1994 (solid bars) and 9001:2000 (hatched bars) up to 2006; China is now the country with the largest number of ISO 9001-based QMS (approx. 200000), comparable to Europe as a whole. Source: (ISO, 2006).

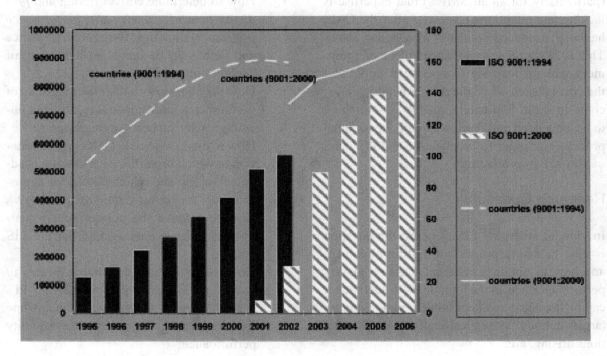

will typically be residing in emerging Enterprise Information Systems (EIS). This is why in this chapter we will discuss quality management within the context of EIS systems, seen from the angle of SME's. A QMS is not the same as an information system; an information system (e.g., an EIS system) supports the implementation of a QMS.

ISO 9001

One of the principle and widest-spread standards to design and implement a QMS is ISO 9001, belonging to the ISO 9000-family of standards. The most recent version of this standard is ISO 9001:2008. Figure 1 based on the 2006 ISO annual survey figures (ISO, 2006) shows the world wide adoption of the standard.

ISO 9001 does not prescribe any quality management system in particular but frames the process of designing, implementing and operating

one, defining guiding principles, requirements and key elements it ought to contain for proper functioning: the *what to*, not the *how to*. Organizations can tailor and scale a QMS framework to their own needs and chose the implementation they see fit, as long as the standardized good quality management practices remain honored. The detailed design and operating of a QMS is critical to its success, however, and ultimately critical to the success of the organization as a whole.

Research Questions and Approach

Designing a fit-for-purpose QMS requires thorough understanding of business strategy and business processes and the readiness to align the QMS with the business processes, vice versa. Generally, alignment and fine tuning is something for the long haul, and of continuous concern. Niven, in (Niven, 2005) estimates that at present at most 10% of the organizations actually achieves their strategic objectives. The problem is often (particularly for small SME's) that expertise is lacking and attention slips away after the QMS has been introduced; compare (Woodhouse, 2004). This is like buying an advanced piece of equipment without learning to operate it optimally: the cost is taken while the deeper benefits never come in sight. Ultimately, quality is something to be embedded and fused with daily operational processes in order to be effective and efficient; *quality drives productivity*.

Research Questions

In view of emerging EIS systems, the question is how to assure proper and lasting alignment and how to obtain a coherent view on quality performance across the organization, such that it can be managed and kept inline with the quality targets defined. More specifically, research questions arising, are:

- How to define a quality performance strategy and measurable quality performance targets; how to store this typically unstructured strategy description in an EIS system?
- How to measure actual quality performance of each of the business processes?
- How to design and implement the quality performance indicators (often referred to as: *key performance indicators*, or KPI's) for each of the business processes in the organization, including strategic control processes?
- How to determine a working definition, a proper format and a fit-for-purpose accuracy for each of the performance indicators; does the EIS systems support storage of this format?
- How to compute and aggregate actual quality performance figures from EIS system residing data?

- How to store recorded quality performance in the EIS system?
- How to determine correct timing and *predictive power* for *lead quality performance indicators*, allowing off-target performance and defects to be remedied before repair becomes impossible?
- How to determine whether the hierarchy of performance indicators coherently and unambiguously supports strategic control?
- How to attain a flexible QMS implementation in which *organizational change* is adopted swiftly and which allows for appropriate *up- and downscaling of activities*?
- How to retrieve the correct actual quality performance data again from the EIS system;
- How to archive and maintain a *history of quality performance* data within the EIS system, allowing reconstruction at any one time in the past of the then present quality performance?
- How to effectively and efficiently build up an *evidence-based track record* of quality performance within the EIS system, for auditing, approval and endorsement purposes?
- How to combine secondary EIS data with quality performance data in *root cause analysis* so as to explore the deeper causes of ill-performance?
- How to combine performance data *across organizational borders*, in case of supply chain, delivery chain or partners delivering bundled products;

Quality in this context is not just product quality; it is also about controlling all processes so that the outcome is under control and about management aspects targeting customer satisfaction. A more accurate definition of quality will be given further down. A (key) performance indicator is a metric expressing the result of a measurement of the performance of a business process. KPI's take the form of business data typically processed and stored in a database on a computer system. Key performance indicators will be explained in detail, in the sections ahead. The term key performance indicator (KPI) has become so common in practice that we also use KPI to refer to quality performance. A lead performance indicator expresses a future performance, for instance expected annual turnover based on current performance. Lead indicators and lag indicators (which record results in the past) will also be discussed in detail in the sections ahead.

In the past two decades, great advancements have been made with respect to the above research questions, see for instance (Adams & Frost, 2008; Ahmad & Dhafr, 2002; Cobbold & Lawrie, 2002b; Hernandez-Matias, Vizan, Perez-Garcia, & Rios, 2008; Hubbard, 2007; Kaplan & Norton, 1996b; Kaplan & Norton, 2001b; Kaplan & Norton, 2001a; Kaplan & Norton, 2001a; Kaplan & Norton, 2006; Kaplan & Norton, 2004a; Niven, 2005; Woodhouse, 2004). None of these contributions discusses the above research questions *in the context of EIS systems*, however. Consequently, it is unclear whether:

- EIS systems are suited to store structured and unstructured pieces of data and information related to a QMS;
- EIS systems adequately support storage of causal and other relationships;
- EIS systems allow lead indicators to quantitatively forecast future scores, trends and performance;
- EIS systems can provide evidence-based quality track records; can it keep track of approvals and results of *plan-do-check-act cycles* for instance; can it reconstruct quality performance at any one moment back in time, for instance in case of a customer claim or complaint? Can it show (evidence of) continuous improvement over a certain period for instance?

- EIS systems do support the access rights and roles to grant all employees proper access to the shared parts of the QMS and quality performance information, and to block improper modifications or manipulations of managed data;
- EIS systems are efficient enough to support recording of performance data and up- and downscaling efficiently;
- EIS systems can combine quality performance data of suppliers, wholesalers, retailers, etc., all having impact on customer perceived quality and satisfaction;
- EIS systems support the kind of transactions needed to operate a QMS;
- EIS systems support reporting of quality performance at all levels in the organization;
- EIS systems require different skills when containing quality performance data;

This chapter addresses these issues.

In order to understand the requirements on the EIS system we need to understand how quality performance is measured, the role of key performance indicators and bad performance alerts therein and finally the role of root cause analysis, in case management intervention is needed.

Research Approach

Approaches to design effective QMS systems covering all relevant aspects in an organization have been primarily developed in the nineties and the beginning of this century (see the early work in (Kaplan & Norton, 1992). Kaplan and Norton take *the constantly transforming organization* and the organization's strategic planning as the starting point, transforming organizational strategy into measurable strategic objectives to which a target can be assigned. A *Strategy Map* (Kaplan & Norton, 2004a; Kaplan & Norton, 2004b; Kaplan & Norton, 2004c; Kaplan & Norton, 2004c) and a *Destination Statement* (Cobbold & Lawrie, 2002a) define the strategic change desired and a time frame for the transition, while a *Balanced Score Card* (BSC) is commonly used to combine different views and aspects of the transition in a single overview (Cobbold et al., 2002b; Kaplan et al., 1992; Kaplan & Norton, 1993; Kaplan & Norton, 1996a; Kaplan et al., 1996b; Kaplan et al., 2001a; Kaplan et al., 2001b). This makes the BSC one of the output forms, to be delivered by the EIS system; more on this later.

Strategic objectives to transform the organization and the products and services it delivers, can only be successfully accomplished if its *critical success factors* (CSF's) are satisfied. Causal relationship analysis reveals how one critical success contributes to the next critical success. Critical success factors can be monitored using KPI's. In fact, this cascade shows how strategic planning is made measurable and manageable down to the operational level; the bottom up cascade of KPI's reports how well the organization's actual performance contributes to realizing the desired transformation at strategic level. This approach leads to very flexible, effective quantitative quality management system implementations and combining them with the efficiency of EIS systems appears very attractive. Flexibility is an important aspect in the context of the growing demand for mass customization and agile manufacturing; more on this later.

For the research approach followed in this chapter, we will adopt the above outlined approach and analyze in every step the requirements and consequences for the implementation in an EIS system. This chapter thus seeks to present answers to the above defined research questions. Not all aspects are equally important: emphasis will be on the design and embedding in an EIS of the KPI's.

Organization of this Chapter

The remainder of this chapter is organized as follows: firstly, a brief overview of ISO 9001 will be presented, among other things discussing its guiding principles and main elements. After this background information, we further focus on the design and characteristics of KPI's needed to learn the requirements for their embedding in an EIS system. The characteristics of properly designed KPI's will be discussed, with special attention to the *dynamics* (the timing, say) of lead indicators. Concluding this chapter, an outlook onto the future of performance-based management will be given.

ISO 9001 OVERVIEW

Brief History of ISO 9001

Quality initiatives go as far back as the fifties and Japan is generally seen as the cradle of industrial quality programming. Deming's early work on statistical process control (SPC) is generally seen as the birth of quality control, one of the main elements of quality management. The idea behind quality management efforts is that by controlling the variability in every process, a greater *consistency in output results* can be obtained. During the seventies and eighties, quality management and QMS systems gained worldwide attention. Starting out with US Army and NATO initiatives, most notably AQAP, the idea of quality management gradually invaded industry at large. Out of various national standardization efforts, the desire grew to come to a standardized worldwide quality management framework. To that extent ISO and more specifically its TC 176/SC2 committee started working on this global standard, beginning of the eighties, resulting in the first version of the ISO 9001 in the late eighties. After its initial 1987 version, ISO 9001 was updated in 1994 (ISO 9001:1994) and 2000 (ISO 9001:2000) and lastly in 2008, formally tagged ISO 9001:2008. Today, over a million organizations worldwide have adopted one of the above management frameworks, with highest penetrations in the realms of engineering and material technologies (International Organization for Standardization ISO, 2008). Some 100 countries participate in and/or follow the ISO 9001 standardization effort nowadays, with over 150 countries being an ISO-member and users spread across nearly 180 countries (Figure 1).

Other Quality Management Standards

With environmental objectives becoming ever more compelling, ISO 9001-based QMS systems are occasionally replaced or complemented by ISO 14001-based systems. The ISO 14000 family of standards deals with *environmental* management. Total Quality Management (TQM) can be regarded as a broader and deepened form of quality management. It lays strong emphasis on quality awareness everywhere in the organization and in its supply and delivery chains. It shares, among others, the quality performance management characteristics with ISO 9001.

Main Principles of ISO 9001

Satisfied customers stand central in the ISO 9001 and all quality management is directed to just that. Keeping customers satisfied is not just a matter of products being free of deficiencies. The customer's explicit and implied needs and expectations should be satisfied by the product and evidently, the product must comply with regulatory and generally implied sustainability demands. All this makes quality a subjective attribute that depends on customer perception. That is why an organization must make quality explicit at beforehand and approve to live up to it so that customers can rely on the design, manufacturing, environmental footprint, servic-

ing, etc. to be inline with their expectations. All businesses processes should be mastered such that process output is guaranteed to be within specified quality bounds, contributing to a customer satisfying product, now and in the future. No organization is static, whether a private enterprise, public agency or non-governmental organization: an organization must constantly strive to a lasting and better satisfaction of its customers (shareholders, partners, the public, the environment ...). The constant transition organizations find themselves in is also approached as a quality controlled business process (the strategic control process) and thus subject to quality management.

Main principles contributing to the above philosophy are:

- A written QMS must be available and accessible to every employee and customer;
- Targeted actions and performance must be verified and validated periodically;
- The QMS must take a quantified approach: it must regularly record quality performance scores (or: KPI scores) and set them off against agreed target values;
- A process-based approach, with plan-do-check-act cycles (PDCA) to drive quality and to repair defects;
- Procedures to report and handle defects;
- Active promotion, commitment and involvement of senior management;
- Central roles and responsibilities shall be formalized and assigned;
- Regular auditing (internally, externally, or by the customer) shall be conducted;
- The QMS must be effective and efficient and support continuous improvement.

There is no room and no need to go into more detail here. In the sections following, the relevant details will be further discussed in relation to their embedding in an EIS system.

Main Elements of a Typical ISO 9001-based QMS

A typical ISO 9001-based QMS consists of the following main elements:

- A handbook describing the QMS in detail, containing mandatory procedures such as a reporting and repairing defects procedure, continuous improvement and auditing procedures, as well as other operational procedures;
- A Strategy map, describing the organization's planned transition;
- Balanced Score Card to consistently report on KPI scores;
- A collection of CSF's and the causal analysis of the hierarchy of CSF's;
- Infrastructure to regularly measure actual performance through KPI scores reporting;
- A data collection of KPI scores and targets;
- Decision making to drive plan-do-check-act cycles and continuous improvement;
- An auditing regime to audit the adherence to the quality management as laid down in the handbook;
- Certificate of compliance to the own ISO 9001-based QMS, to assure customers, shareholders or anyone else of this compliance.

Notice that ISO 9001 does not prescribe all these elements in detail and leaves room for alternatives for some of these elements. This holds for instance for a Strategy Map and for a Balanced Score Card. Most organizations will prefer to integrate these elements in their ISO 9001-based QMS, however, and their use has become common practice. Also note that ISO 9001 does *not* prescribe storing KPI scores *in a computer system*, let alone in an EIS. When preferred so, KPI scores may be paper-based, but in practice virtually all organizations will opt to store them in a database on a computer.

FROM STRATEGY TO KPI'S

Definitions

In this chapter, we will understand quality in a context of producers and consumers of products and services. Quality is not limited to product quality: it extends through all business processes involved in the creation of the product, from component design in the supply chain to the services on a delivered product. *Quality* in this context is defined as the degree to which the inherent characteristics of a product or a service and the way it reaches the consumer fulfill consumer's needs and expectations. A *quality management system* (QMS) is a system supporting a systematic approach to monitor, control and manage an organization's quality performance. A QMS is driven by an underlying information system; an *information system* is a set of cooperating components with a structural organization, with the aim to capture, process, manage and distribute data and information.

A *critical success factor* (CSF) is a core area or a limited number of areas in which satisfactory results will induce successful results in the environment around these area(s). A CSF commonly represents that core action, achievement or performance that if completed successfully, sets forth successful achievement of the rest. A *(key) performance indicator* (KPI) is a metric expressing the result of a measurement of the performance of a business process. Quality management following ISO 9001 takes a quantitative approach, which entails a need for *a-priori known* and *quantified* quality targets. KPI scores are set off against quality targets and should be within an a-priori defined *bandwidth* around the target value. A *Balanced Score Card* (BSC) is a management overview that groups KPI values logically, according to the per-

Table 1. stepwise translation of strategy and strategic change into KPI's and verification that the KPI's as designed contribute to understanding quality performance up to board level.

STEP 1: At board level, strategic objectives are being outlined in the Strategic Planning process and translated into measurable objectives, for instance by collecting them in a destination statement, describing what should be realized within say three years from now. Strategic change (transition) is thus put under Strategic Control. Global CSF's are being identified, a first version of a BSC is being designed
STEP 2: At the management levels below board level (Production Control), these objectives and their CSF's are further worked out in smaller (measurable) goals, linking up the operational processes. A cause-effect analysis is used to identify and verify causal relationships (Causal Analysis) between CSF's at subsequent levels;
STEP 3: Per CSF and for each operational process, one or more KPI's are determined, along with all their characteristics.
STEP 4: Next, bottom up a verification and calibration process is conducted to learn how lower level KPI scores aggregate at the next higher level and how their indication contributes to the performance measurement at the next level. Aspects like interpretation, accuracy, missing values, lead times etc. are verified and validated;
STEP 5: Finally, arriving back at the board level, the final verification is being conducted, which should reveal as to whether the progress towards reaching the destination can be monitored and controlled indeed (Strategic Control), whether ill-performance is timely signaled and risks and opportunities can be monitored and controlled adequately on the basis of BSC and its KPI's.

spective they cover, typically: customer-oriented processes, operational performance, financial performance, and what is commonly denoted as learning (experience, knowledge and growth). The BSC (Kaplan et al., 1992) not only reports on KPI scores, but has been designed such during QMS design, that it also assists in the understanding of collective performances and mutual relationships among individual objectives: *what drives what. Business Activity Monitoring* (BAM) is the acquisition, processing and presentation of real time information (e.g., KPI scores) on activity and performance within an organization.

A Generic Stepwise Approach

Following the research approach as outlined in the Introduction and the above definitions, we can now compile the following generic approach to designing and implementing a QMS, linking KPI's to strategy, and the realization of strategic transition to actual performance. Following the Kaplan and Norton approach top down – bottom up in an iterative process, we arrive at the steps as in Table 1.

In practice, the above stepwise approach is neither fully top-down nor bottom-up, but a middle-out process that iterates until an effective and efficient network of coherent indicators has been established. A scorecard design and the indicators

populating it are in fact strongly intermingled, and simultaneously and iteratively developed in the above marked process. Once the design has been validated, it can be operated.

STEP 1: Starting from Strategy

At board level, a balance has to be found between strategic planning and strategic control. The pressure on organizations to timely adjust their strategy is ever increasing, due to reasons such as globalization, sustainability, exploding energy costs, rapidly changing consumer preferences, mass customization and many others. First step for an organization is to assess its present state of excellence, for instance by means of capability-maturity-modeling (CMM), benchmarking, position auditing or using any other *Business Excellence Model* approach.

A Balanced Scorecard (BSC) captures central KPI's from various strategic perspectives: customer-oriented processes, operational performance, financial performance, and what is commonly denoted as the learning, (experience, knowledge…) and growth perspective. The anatomy of the BSC looks like in Figure 3. The relative weights put on each of the perspectives may vary from organization to organization and is a matter of how organizations see themselves, their *orientation*, and the *maturity*

Figure 2. Generic approach to design and implement a QMS, using an EIS system.

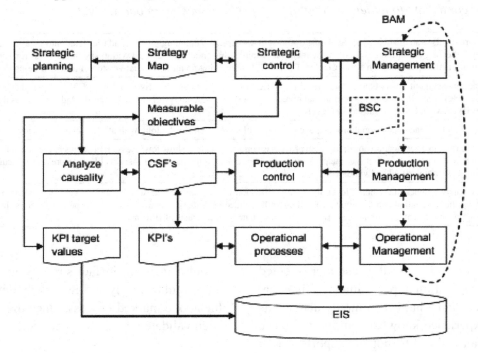

level they position themselves in. A successful transition to a next maturity level can be interpreted as a demonstration of continuous improvement.

A first version of the BSC is typically designed in parallel to the design of Strategy Map and Destination Statement. More detailed scorecards may be designed afterwards and cascading scorecards may be used to aggregate results from various levels of the organization (Bukh & Malmi, 2005). Suppliers performances can be also be linked up (Angerhofer & Angelides, 2006; Bostorff & Rosenbaum, 2003; Brun, Caridi, Salama, & Ravelli, 2006).

What (KPI in a) perspective drives what other (KPI in a) perspective, is among other things depending on the organization's maturity level. Many of today's organizations find themselves in a stage in which operational performance drives financial performance. *Learning* organizations (*knowledge-oriented, human capital-oriented* organizations) go one step further: self-organization and learning

competence drive internal performance which in turn drives financial. Learning organizations will typically work out and weight the Learning & Growth box correspondingly.

Overlooking the above considerations, the following requirements on EIS systems to support the implementation of QMS systems, emerge:

REQUIREMENT 1: Apart from structured information, an EIS system must also be capable of containing, handling and archiving unstructured information like the Strategy Map and Destination Statement

REQUIREMENT 2: An EIS system must be capable of storing and retrieving CMM-scores as input information for the next assessment of the CMM-stage. Factors contained in the EIS system must be labeled as enablers and results; Maturity level assessments must be validated and validation shall be supported by the EIS system

REQUIREMENT 3: The impact of amendments to one of the strategic objectives in terms of CSF's and KPI's affected, can be assessed by the EIS

Figure 3. Anatomy of a BSC. What drives what (arrows) depends (among others) on the organization's maturity level, orientation and ambitions.

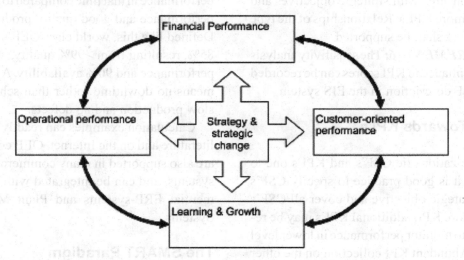

REQUIREMENT 4: The other way around, each KPI and each CSF is linked to (one or more) strategic objectives; these relationships can be described for the purpose of causal analysis

REQUIREMENT 5: Actors can be described on a per-data item or a per-relationship basis, along with access rights, modification and archival roles included

REQUIREMENT 6: Each of the entities and the relationships has an ownership defined

REQUIREMENT 7: Each occurrence of KPI scores (and possibly also CSF qualification) has an explicit validation, by a hierarchy of validators (explicit roles); Each validation shall be assigned a time stamp

REQUIREMENT 8: An EIS system must be capable of reporting quality performance in a form resembling the designed BSC

STEP 2: Towards CSF's

Research on critical success factors (CSF's) is somewhat interwoven with that of KPI's (Forster & Rockart, 1989; Rockart, 1986). Today, there is a substantial body of literature available on critical success factors, performance indicators and measurement as a whole. See for instance (Niven,

2005) and (Hubbard, 2007). For their statistical analysis background, a classic resource is (Dixon & Massey, 1983).

Requirements on EIS systems:

REQUIREMENT 9: An EIS system shall be capable of containing, handling and archiving causal analysis results as unstructured information; Assumptions, conditions and limitations shall be stored along with the causal analysis itself

REQUIREMENT 10: Historic (regular) verification and compliance analysis can be stored as structured information in the EIS system

REQUIREMENT 11: CSF failure analysis can be stored as unstructured information in the EIS system

REQUIREMENT 12: Each occurrence of CSF qualification has an explicit validation, by a hierarchy of validators (explicit roles of type Actor); each validation is assigned a time stamp and can be traced back

REQUIREMENT 13: Once validated, CSF qualifications shall be protected against amendment; they can only be superseded by a revision

REQUIREMENT 14: Release and version management shall apply to all CSF qualifications;

REQUIREMENT 15: Each CSF has one or more relationships with strategic objectives and with one or more KPI's; Relationships of the type many-to-many shall be supported

REQUIREMENT 16: The sensitivity analysis of CSF compliance to KPI scores can be recorded with the CSF description in the EIS system

STEP 3: Towards KPI's

Some organizations tie CSF's and KPI's one to one; whilst it is good practice to specify CSF's for each strategic objective and cover all CSF's by one or more KPI, additional KPI's may be required, e.g. to monitor performance in lower level processes. Abundant KPI collection on the other hand, should be avoided, just like over-accuracy and over-confidence. Accuracy means a low bias of real and measured data. Nowadays, organizations typically have some 10..25 CSF's and KPI's and experience says that in any one decision making process no more than a few (4..8) KPI's should be involved (Woodhouse, 2000).

Pioneering work on KPI's has been done in the early sixties by Daniel (Daniel, 1961). The development of Lean Manufacturing (LM) and Total Productive Maintenance (TPM), mainly in the Japanese automotive industry during the seventies, led to the development of principle *compound* KPI's like Overall Equipment Effectiveness (OEE) and Total Effective Equipment Productivity (TEEP) (Ahmad et al., 2002; Hubbard, 2007; Mather, 2003; Woodhouse, 2000), later supplemented by On Time In Full from Supplier (OTIFS) and On Time In Full to Customer (OTIFC) (Ahmad et al., 2002), covering supply and delivery chain respectively. The OEE is a KPI widely used in industry, to express plant performance, equipment performance, system performance, but also service providing performance, training performance, expert consultancy performance, or anything similar. OEE combines three major factors in a single KPI: *availability, performance* and *quality*, TEEP ads a fourth factor; the *loading*. OEE

seeks to jointly measure planned productive time, performance in that time compared to the nominal performance and good quality production rates. Defined like this, world class OEE's are approx. 85%, resulting from >99% quality, approx. 95% performance and 90% availability. A 100% OEE means no downtime (other than scheduled), no slow production and no defects.

Calculation examples can readily be found in literature and on the Internet. OEE computations are also supported in many commercial software systems, and can be integrated with many commercial ERP-systems and Plant Management Systems.

The SMART Paradigm

In the design of KPI's, the SMART-paradigm is frequently being practiced, e.g. (Ahmad et al., 2002). A SMART KPI has the following properties:

Specific KPI's

Occasionally, sheer competing KPI's can be found. As an example, consider a research organization's ICT-network. The yearly operational cost per seat of the network may be one KPI (target: < 8000 € per seat per year) while yearly productive research hours may be another KPI (target: > 1200 hours per researcher per year) and the quality of research (target: >85% satisfactory to the customer) a third. Perfect corrective and preventive maintenance by the ICT department may easily bring that first target in reach. But at the same time, excessive network down time may obstruct reaching productive research hours (second KPI scores) and jeopardize the quality of work. By combining the three KPI's into a single OEE (Table 2), optimization can be done by lowering the one or raising the other but not at the expense of the others and whilst optimizing the common (global) outcome. Neither availability of the network alone, nor performance in terms of productive hours alone, nor quality alone is specific enough for the overall

Table 2. Left to right: building op compound types of KPI's out of simple types and their evolution into benchmark KPI's like OEE. Left of the solid bar are the structured KPI types, right of the solid bar are the unstructured types. They can either be processed into structured types or stored as unstructured raw data.

	Structured			Unstructured	Assessment type
Simple	Compound	Standard/ best practice/ benchmark		Complex	
- Elapsed time - Lead time - Cost/expenditure - Unit count - Employee count - Customer count - ...	- Rates - Specific cost - ABC cost - Stocks - Fees/wages - Customer profiles ...	- OEE - TEEP - OTIFS - OTIFC - ...		- Data mining - Web log pruning - Questionnaire - Interview - Benchmarking - Reviews - Audit - ...	Self-assessment Mutual assessment Certification

objective; only the OEE, taking all three as input, multiplying them, is specific enough.

Measurable KPI's

A well-known quote in quantified quality management reads (Kaplan et al., 2004c):

You can't manage what you can't measure ...

... and you can't measure what you can't describe

In the context of this discussion, a measurement is defined as follows (Hubbard, 2007): a measurement is a set of observations that reduces uncertainty where the result is expressed as a quantity. Notice that a measurement is never an exact number: there is always some uncertainty associated with each measurement. A clear and concise description is needed of what we want to measure exactly: the object of measurement. Just a name of some phenomenon or variable (indicator) is not enough. The same goes for a measurement method. Apart from the quite measurable phenomena, organizations have a number of less-obviously-measured-but-vital-to-know things, like quality of management and employee motivation. In modern literature, these phenomena are commonly known as intangibles, e.g. (Hubbard, 2007).

Lag and Lead Indicators

KPI's can be subdivided in lag and lead indicators (Nudurupati, Arshad, & Turner, 2007; Woodhouse,

Table 3. SMART KPI characteristics.

S	pecific	The object of measurement must be unambiguously specified
M	easurable	What the KPI is designed to quantify must be measurable and an adequate measurement method must be available
A	chievable	The measurement must be achievable in the time frame given at reasonable cost at the accuracy specified
R	elevant	The KPI must add to an assessment of the performance result and be relevant to the decision making process, in the way designed
T	ime-based	The KPI must be measurable as long and as often as required and at the frequency needed. Discrete measurements must be comparable against the measurements at other moments in time, to monitor its development

2000). A lag indicator reports on a past performance, lead indicators are indicators that flag the advent of an event or state while emerging. Examples are:

- Tooling speed decrease may indicate tool wear, causing productivity to be in peril;
- A rising chisel temperature may indicate wear and breakdown to arrive;
- Decreasing income tax agency website visits may indicate a better understood income tax form and consequently less processing and reviewing capacity needed at the agency next year;
- Employee dissatisfaction may be a lead-in for employee absence due to illness.

Lead indicators require careful (lead) timing, depending on the underlying process dynamics and the intervention model. With process dynamics being such that the targeted value (controlled object) can grow out of control in say 4 days, a monthly KPI is useless as a predictor. An hourly or perhaps a daily KPI would be sufficient, allowing for timely intervention. Critical alert levels and lead time to intervention should also be taken into account. Lead time to intervention (total response time included) should be sufficient to allow for intervention as designed to unroll. Timing is generally not a (big) issue for lagging KPI's, which commonly average or sum up and log past performances over some time interval.

Figure 4 shows an example of timing of a lead variable. The tooling speed indicates tool wear, which must stay above a critical bottom level to obtain proper productivity. According to the measured KPI values (black solid dots), this level is predicted to be reached after 3-4 days; the predicted failure point is indicated in the diagram. The alert level is predicted to be reached slightly after 3.4 days; an alert with the KPI score at day three allows for intervention lead time of 0.8 days. If not sufficient, the alert level can be raised and the alert will be issued earlier. This example is

highly simplified, to illustrate the various aspects discussed inhere. In real practice, correct timing of lead variables is much more complicated.

Furthermore, it is good practice to verify and validate adequate functioning of the KPI, including timing and alert levels (the *dynamics* of the KPI). Scenario play, Monte-Carlo simulation and determining confidence intervals can help to estimate *reliable* alert and intervention levels, so that the *actual* maintenance moment is right to stay on-target. The whole process of alerting, responding and scheduling of the intervention (in total: lead time to intervention) must fit in the time span between alert and failure point, together with the intervention time itself. For further details, refer to (Brun et al., 2006; Dixon et al., 1983; Edgar, 2004; Hernandez-Matias et al., 2008; Hubbard, 2007).

Achievable KPI's

Occasionally, the ideal KPI cannot be measured in the process, while a close-to-ideal KPI is readily available: a matter of what we want to know versus what we can tell you (Figure 5). The trade off is the cost (risk) of not knowing (exactly) what needs to be known, versus using what is readily available. A KPI does not need to be perfect and can never reveal everything about the true state of a process much like a dashboard does not tell every detail about a car, but enough to drive it safely. KPI's must be separated from analysis information to drill down the causes of malfunctioning and off-target performance. Taking a *traffic light* as a metaphor; you do not need to know exactly *why* the traffic light turned to red in order to drive home safely. It may be interesting to know but basically, all you need to know for a safe trip is: green means drive on, red means stop. The same holds for KPI's and the accuracy and uncertainty associated with a KPI. Accuracy is a characteristic of a measurement having low systematic error, whereas precision refers to a low random error (Hubbard, 2007). Simplicity of computation and

Figure 4. Timing example for a tooling speed KPI. After 3 to 4 days, the tooling speed sinks below a critical bottom level and the tool needs replacement and/or readjustment. Measuring the KPI value daily predicts that failure point (here, after approx. 3.8 days) with sufficient accuracy to allow a timely alert for intervention.

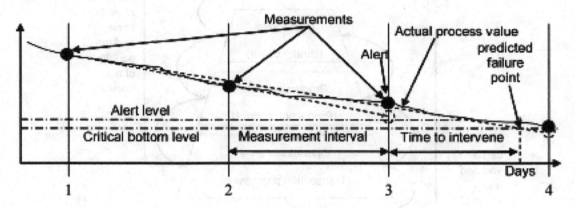

interpretation is to be traded off against chances of a false alert (a false *red*, taking a traffic light metaphor again) or an unjustified performance OK (unjustified *green*). See Figure 6. What false rates to tolerate is a matter of balancing the costs and the risks.

This brings us with the issue of the value of knowing and the cost of not knowing: the more we know, the smaller the uncertainty and the better the decision making, but also: the higher the cost. Where is the tradeoff? What are the chance and the cost of being wrong? Generally, lost opportunities are capitalized and information that can reduce the chances of missing an opportunity is assigned a value (Hubbard, 2007; Woodhouse, 2004). The cost of being wrong is the difference between the wrong chosen alternative (based upon the current information) and the best alternative (should one have had perfect information). Opportunity Loss (OL) is the cost made for an alternative that turns out to be wrong, Expected Opportunity Loss (EOL) is thus the chance times the cost of choosing a wrong alternative. Reducing the uncertainty about the best alternative reduces the chances of making the wrong choice and hence the EOL. The difference in EOL before and after additional measurement is the Expected Value of Information

(EVI) resulting from those measurements. Extra measurements pay off as long as they cost less than the EOL reduction gained (Figure 7).

This theoretical framework may help to determine the "right" quality of measurements and information to support decision making. Computing EVI values at beforehand is complicated, however. Hubbard suggests to compute the EVI to exclude uncertainty altogether, i.e. computing the Expected Value of Perfect Information (EVPI). Since it excludes the entire uncertainty (EOL-after = 0), by definition EVPI is the EOL of the chosen alternative without additional information. Examples can be found in (Hubbard, 2007).

Standardized and Benchmark KPI's

For many applications, lists of useful KPI's have been compiled and disclosed through internet. Branches and professional communities in chemistry, construction, health care, etc. are starting to collect and standardize KPI's, to support self-assessment and benchmarking. For further details and pointers to resources, see (Califf, Gibbons, Brindis, & Smith, 2002; Campbell, Roland, & Buetow, 2000; Dolan, 2001; Drummond, O'Brien,

Figure 5. Finding KPI's means balancing what we need to know and the penalty of not knowing versus what we can tell you and the value of that information.

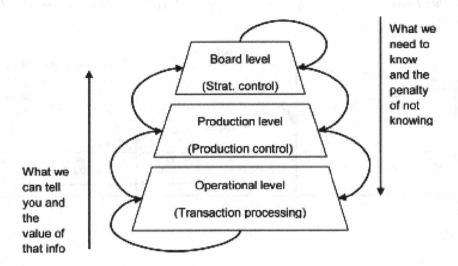

Stoddart, & Torrance, 1997; Gouscos, Kalikakis, Legal, & Papadopoulou, 2007; Holden, 2006; Nudurupati et al., 2007; Puigjaner & Guillen-Gosalbez, 2008; Schultink, 2000; Van den Eynde, Veno, & Hart, 2003).

STEP 4: Bottom up verification

A number of important issues shall be verified once the KPI's have been designed:

- Adequacy of the accuracy of each of the KPI's measured on the measured object with the measurement method identified (Hubbard, 2007);
- Confidence intervals on KPI scores;
- The identification of outliers on the measured KPI's;
- The impact of a *missing value* or a *late arrival*; what if for some reason a KPI cannot be measured (timely)?

Figure 6. KPI scores versus actual state; erroneous missing of bad performance (type-II errors) should be zeroed out. False red alerts (type-I) are costly and slow down performance, but are not immediately catastrophic. The balance is a costs/risk tradeoff.

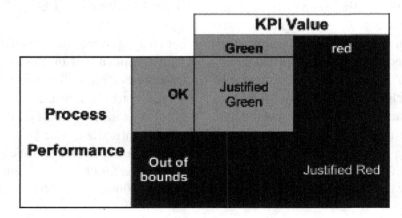

Figure 7. The reduction of EOL (solid curve) versus the additional measurement cost (dashed curve) to achieve that. As long as the loss reduction Δ_{loss} exceeds the cost of additional measurements Δ_{cost}, extra measurements pay off, modified after (Hubbard, 2007).

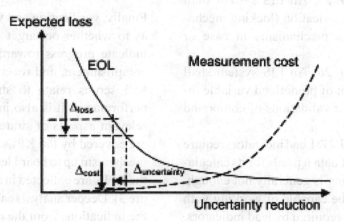

- The adequacy of the lower bound and/or the upper bound (boundary values may be one-sided, yielding a half-open interval) around the target value, and the so obtained equivalence classes of values;
- The association of transaction processing procedures with each of the equivalence classes and boundary values; Underperformance may require transaction processing in the EIS system that differs from the transaction processing in case performance is within limits;
- Reliability and effectiveness of the verification and validation procedure;
- The sensitivity of KPI's and CSF's;
- What to do with prospected results by lead indicators; should a production forecast be corrected as soon as a lead performance indicator predicts the next charge of products to have bad quality?

Important requirements on EIS systems:

REQUIREMENT 17: KPI's are compound values, with a target value, at least one lower or upper bound and possibly a second boundary around the target value; EIS systems shall be capable of storing this compound valued variable. Equivalence classes must be stored

(or computed) by the EIS system, so as to classify the incoming KPI score. Transactions supported by the EIS must be associated with each of the equivalence classes (including the boundary values);

REQUIREMENT 18: For each KPI, the EIS can contain, handle and archive a measured object description, measurement method description and measurement equipment description;

REQUIREMENT 19: The accuracy and confidence interval description (unstructured) of each of the KPI's can be stored in the EIS system;

REQUIREMENT 20: An EIS system must be capable of containing, processing, reproducing and archiving historical time series of KPI scores, along with its validations;

REQUIREMENT 21: An EIS system shall be capable of containing, handling and archiving pointers to root cause analysis objects, to support failure analysis;

REQUIREMENT 22: An EIS system shall allow for readjustment of accuracy of KPI's;

REQUIREMENT 23: An EIS system shall be capable of supporting variable domain-based and state-based transaction processing;

REQUIREMENT 24: An EIS system shall support triggering and transaction processing cascading on predefined variable hierarchies, to allow for compound recomputation of a series of KPI scores;

REQUIREMENT 25: An EIS system shall support exclusive modification (locking mechanisms) and roll-back mechanisms in case or errors;

REQUIREMENT 26: An EIS system shall support the validation of predefined variable hierarchies, to allow for validations of compound KPI values;

REQUIREMENT 27: Lead indicators require timely refreshment of data it needs for its calculations. Version matching is generally not enough. EIS systems should be capable of working with the refreshment rates required by lead indicators. All data must be time stamped;

REQUIREMENT 28: For each lead indicator, an EIS can contain, handle and archive an intervention model. An intervention model in this context is a collection of planned preventive or corrective actions needed to restore proper quality performance. An intervention model is a compound structured object capturing information on actors to intervene, when intervention should take place (lead time), the actions to undertake, the (elapsed) time required and the way in which intervention is to be approved. Apart from a scheduled intervention, the EIS shall support the recording of a realized intervention, registering what action has been conducted. Alternately, an EIS may store a *service level agreement* (SLA), as a model of intervention;

REQUIREMENT 29: An EIS system shall be capable of conducting transaction processing, alerting and reporting synchronously with limited latency; (distributed) system latency and human response time need to be taken into account when verifying and validating lead indicator dynamics, just like time zone differences

STEP 5: Verification Strategic Control

Finally, verification and validation is carried out as to whether on-target KPI scores adequately indicate progress towards strategic change accomplishment, and reversely whether off-target KPI scores relate to strategic control underperformance. It is also important to verify if all relevant aspects of strategic change (transition) are covered by the KPI's. Commonly, the report mechanism up to board level is the BSC on which the KPI's are collected in a coherent scheme (Figure 3). Deeper analysis can help to verify whether the indications from the designed BSC and their mutual relationships provide a valid image of the current state of organizational performance they reflect. Sensitivity analysis, confidence intervals, scenario play can all be helpful instruments to investigate that.

Important for the requirements on EIS systems:

REQUIREMENT 30: An EIS system shall be capable of presenting KPI values organized as in the designed BSC;

REQUIREMENT 31: An EIS system shall allow for a documented validation up to strategic control level;

REQUIREMENT 32: An EIS can present pointers to root cause analysis objects associated to each KPI to allow verification of the indication reflected by the KPI;

QMS AND EIS SYSTEMS

The above listed requirements partly overlap. Furthermore, they have to be evaluated against EIS technological characteristics as we understand them today. This will be done next.

Table 4. QMS-required data types.

Structured data types	Unstructured data types
• Regular types R-DBMS (int, String…), or: • Standard object types in OODB • Date Time type • Actor type • Transaction • Release/Version • Flag data type (validated, archived, …)	• Document type • BLOB data type • Hyperlink data type

Data Types Required

Evaluating the above requirements, the following data types shall be supported by the EIS:

Documents (unstructured data types) may be contained:

- In original format by a Document type;
- In restricted format (e.g., PDF) by a Document type or in a BLOB;
- Scanned, in image format by a Document type or in a BLOB;
- Or in the form of a hyperlink to an external document;

Typical EIS systems are expected to support these types (except Document type), both systems using relational data storage technology (RDBMS) and object-oriented storage technology (OODBMS).

KPI Score Lifecycle

A KPI score lifecycle looks as follows; also refer to (Nudurupati et al., 2007):

- data creation
  - data source management
  - data measurement equipment management
  - measured object collection
  - data measurement and acquisition
  - data collection and structuring/ packaging
  - data registration
  - data transmission or reporting
- data processing
  - data intake
  - data structure validation
  - data completeness and integrity check
  - data access rights validation
  - (singular) data quality control
  - data analysis and validation
  - data equivalence estimation and transaction processing assignment
- data storage
  - data ownership assignment
  - data access rights assignment
  - data release and version assignment
  - data relationships (description etc.) assignment
- data statistical quality control
- data and relationship interpretation
- data distribution
- data release and version management
- data quality control and auditing
- data archiving
- data destruction

There are no stages in the above lifecycle that are not supported in some form by a typical EIS system. The first stage (data creation) may take place outside the scope of an EIS system, but data acquisition may be supported. Statistical analysis is another function that may but not necessarily is supported by an EIS system.

Measured KPI scores are to be evaluated against target values. The ISO principle of continuous improvement entails a regular sharpening of the target value; an organization should evaluate whether the target can be raised to a higher performance level. Target values are coupled one-to-one to the KPI, also have a history and versions, but typically have a lifecycle and refreshment cycle much longer than that of the KPI itself, typically yearly. Also, access rights and credentials needed to modify target values are completely different from those of KPI scores themselves.

Relationships

With respect to relationships: optional and mandatory relationships of the type 0-to-1, 1-to-1, 1-to-n and n-to-m should be supported by the EIS. This includes not only relationships among structured types but also among structured and unstructured types and among unstructured types. EIS systems may be expected to comply with this requirement.

Ownership

All data and all relationships can be assigned an ownership (type Actor) and access rights. Higher

stages of Business Excellence Models, Capability Maturity Models, etc. require that KPI's and all constituent measurements are documented and managed, for instance by a Custodian, or a Data Manager. Change proposals for measurements and change proposals for EIS systems must be merged and become in fact one and the same.

Transaction Processing

Apart from the regular transaction processing, the following specific processing features shall be offered by the EIS system:

- Locked processing, single item or cascading, with roll-back mechanism;
- Constrained insertion and deletion to enforce mandatory data item and relationships;
- Archiving data items with all related data;
- Modify Actors (for instance Ownership) on a group (release, version…) of data;
- Online validation and online auditing, in a work flow manner;
- Manage (contain, handle and archive) unstructured data items;

Figure 8. Flexibility, modularity and extendibility are important aspects of system integration and system architecture. In the embedding of KPI's no unnecessary subsystem dependencies shall be introduced. A proper Objectives-CSF's-Process and KPI's mapping onto subsystems may help to achieve this.

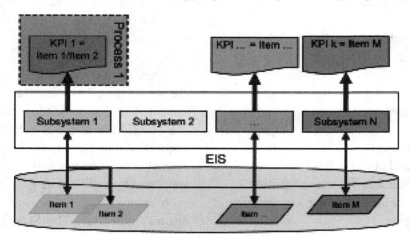

- Verify the validity of an external reference (hyperlinked object);
- Manage externally referenced data objects (documents);

Preferably:

- Apart from sorting and searching structured types (according to their value), searching the content of unstructured types is preferred;

Data Volume

The EIS system must be capable of storing the KPI scores over a longer period of time. Archived data may reside online or moved to some background storage (tape, vault, WORM ...). During the design of the QMS, an estimate can be made with respect to the expected data volume.

Data Distribution

Data distribution is typically through a web interface and is not further discussed here.

EIS Subsystems

Different KPI's may originate from different EIS subsystems. Preferably, KPI's are associated with and also stored in or aggregated from a single EIS subsystem, to maintain optimal system characteristics with respect to:

- Flexibility;
- Modularity;
- Extendibility;

See Figure 8. Flexibility, modularity and extendibility are important aspects of system integration and system architecture. In the embedding of KPI's no *unnecessary subsystem dependencies* are to be introduced. A proper Strategic objectives-CSF's-Process and KPI's

mapping onto subsystems may help to achieve this: Customer-relationship KPI's in the CRM subsystem, resource-related KPI's in the ERP subsystem, etc.

For lead KPI's to function correctly, retrieval, computation, and in fact the availability of the EIS (subsystems) must satisfy the timing requirements as specified. For further details, refer to (Wier, Hunton, & HassabElnaby, 2007).

FUTURE TRENDS

Issues, Controversies, Problems and Potential Solutions

Organizations and their role in society changed and will continue to change. A historical overview of enterprises and their industrial, economic and societal position can be taken from (Mokyr, 2005). Edgar, in (Edgar, 2004) identifies four epochs, with quality movement, the previous epoch, merging with the present 21st –century enterprise view epoch. Traditionally, (for profit) organizations sought to raise business revenues and shareholder values through high outputs while minimizing productions costs. Today, product quality and *operational excellence* are generally no longer sufficient to survive. Firstly, both LSE's and SME's are facing globalization forcing them to reconsider the organization of their activities; outsourcing, supplier chain networks, strategic partner alliances, bundled products, alternate delivery channels like online sales and the like, in a more or less global context. In the US in 2005, less than 5% of the retail activities took place on the Internet, in 2010 this figure is expected to go up to some 13% (Johnson, 2005). There is no room to go further into these developments, see for instance (Gerritsen, 2008), also see (Hoogeweegen, van Liere, Vervest, Hagdorn van der Meijden, & de Lepper, 2006) for further details.

Secondly, customers, having a global overview over available options, prices and conditions, nowadays find themselves in a strongly developed consumers market, and act conformingly. Moreover, customers came to demand personalization, options, connectivity and additional bundled features through appropriate packaging, commonly grouped under the term *mass customization*. A third factor is formed by increasingly compelling regulations and compliance demands. A fourth important factor is the increase of financial and fiscal models organizations (including SME's) can choose from. Organizations develop or reconsider their strategic asset portfolio and changed their views on investments accordingly. Finally, in the twenty first century, organizations cannot operate in splendid isolation: they are (forced to be) aware and confronted with public demands on *sustainability*, setting forth ethical, societal, environmental expectations to comply with.

Organizations are foreseen to transform even more rapidly in the future, to keep up with changing economic and societal demands (Amaravadi Ch, 2003; Ein-Dor, 2003; Fuller, 2003a; Fuller, 2003b; Hassan & McCaffer, 2002; Hoogeweegen et al., 2006; Stevenson, 2000; Tsoukas & Shepherd, 2004; Warhurst, 2005). Contrary to classical economical theory, China managed to show tremendous growth in SME start-ups without having a capitalist regime (Fuller, 2003b). Organizations will further *virtualize* (participate in complex, geographically dispersed, dynamic and constantly changing alliances), become more open and transparent to gain trust and confidence, and much more agile when it comes to opting-in on new opportunities. Organizations will understand and exploit the fact that they are visible 24/7: branding, imaging, reputation and all other *shine factors* (Woodhouse, 2004), become dominant, although it is up to the customer to evaluate and acknowledge these qualities. Company culture will radically change: the distance between managers and workers will diminish and shared company knowledge will become a central asset.

Virtualization will also bring about the need to share formally strictly internal data and infor-

mation with supply and delivery chain and with partners (Puigjaner et al., 2008). The intellectual property concerns will become more important, compared to today. Sharing knowledge (learning organization) empowers virtual companies and partnerships but new management models are needed to render this process successful.

QMS-es tend to integrate with other performance management frameworks, like asset management (see Figure 9). The recent PAS 55, ISO 9001, ISO14001 and other developments are expected to converge into a generic performance-oriented management framework. Lifecycle management will become a leading principle. Product, material and knowledge loops will be closed, which means that for instance car manufacturers take in cars they produced at the end of the lifecycle. Manufacturers will more and more act as an owner, offering the product as an asset to customers.

Branches, collectives, interest groups, etc. will seek to standardize KPI's and large-scale programmes and databases will emerge on internet (www.kpilibrary.com) to support self- and mutual excellence assessment, ultimately levering the global quality of life (e.g. HEDIS, UN Habitat (Holden, 2006). Emerging examples are the Capability Maturity Model modeling (CMM) and EFQM assessment techniques (European Foundation Quality Management), the South African Excellence Model, all developed along the lines of TQM (Ahmad et al., 2002; Cobbold et al., 2002a; Woodhouse, 2000). The construction industry developed the Construction Best Practice Programme (CBPP) that serves similar purposes (Nudurupati et al., 2007).

CONCLUSION

For large as well as medium and small enterprises and other organizations, designing, implementing and using a QMS can naturally and swiftly be integrated in EIS systems using either relational

Figure 9. The embedding of quality management in an asset value-centered asset management framework, after (Woodhouse, 2004). Further development may converge into a generic performance management framework (© 2004, The Woodhouse Partnership Ltd. Used with permission)

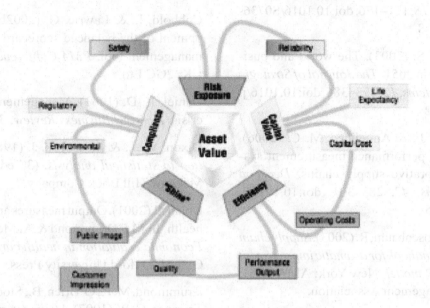

or object-oriented storage technology. A number of requirements must be met, however, as discussed in this chapter. Both structured and unstructured data and information shall be accommodated for, as well as historical data, verification, validation and approval information, version and release and extensive roles and access rights models. The design of adequate KPI's is a key step and interpreting them correctly during operational use, requires thorough cause-effect and accuracy and sensitivity knowledge on the KPI. Reporting of the recorded KPI scores commonly takes place using a balanced scorecard, which groups KPI scores logically, perspective by perspective, so as to express maximum insight and assist maximally in adequate decision making. At various organizational levels up to board level, this evaluation instrument serves to monitor the delivery of performance and quality according to the targets agreed upon. This approach facilitates factual decision making and management control processes. Large, medium and small enterprises

and other organizations may implement systems like this to increase customer satisfaction with zero defects whilst saving resources. Databases of more or less best practice KPI's are starting to appear on internet, realm-by-realm.

In the future, more generic forms of performance management are going to be seen, emerging from the merger of present forms, like quality management and asset management. Although ISO 9001 was considered in the above discussion, all that has been said also applies to other quality approaches, like Total Quality Management (TQM), for ISO 9001 extensions like ISO/TS 16949:2002 for the Automotive industry and largely also for ISO 14001:2004.

REFERENCES

Adams, C. A., & Frost, G. R. (2008). Integrating sustainability reporting into management practices. Accounting Forum.

Ahmad, M. M., & Dhafr, N. (2002). Establishing and improving manufacturing performance measures. *Robotics and Computer-integrated Manufacturing, 18,* 171–176. doi:10.1016/S0736-5845(02)00007-8

Amaravadi Ch, S. (2003). The world and business computing in 2051. *The Journal of Strategic Information Systems, 12,* 373–386. doi:10.1016/j.jsis.2001.11.012

Angerhofer, B. J., & Angelides, M. C. (2006). A model and a performance measurement system for collaborative supply chains. *Decision Support Systems, 42,* 283–301. doi:10.1016/j.dss.2004.12.005

Bostorff, P., & Rosenbaum, R. (2003). *Supply chain excellence; A handbook for dramatic improvement using the SCOR model.* New York: AMACOM; American Management Association.

Brun, A., Caridi, M., Salama, K. F., & Ravelli, I. (2006). Value and risk assessment of supply chain management improvement projects. *International Journal of Production Economics, 99,* 186–201. doi:10.1016/j.ijpe.2004.12.016

Bukh, P. N., & Malmi, T. (2005). Re-examining the cause-and-effect principle of the balanced scorecard. In G.Jonsson & J. Mouritsen (Eds.), *Accounting in Scnadinavia - Northern Lights* (pp. 87-113). Malmo: Liber & Copenhagen Business School Press.

Califf, R. M., Gibbons, R. J., Brindis, R. G., & Smith, S. C. (2002). Integrating Quality into the Cycle of Therapeutic Development. *Journal of the American College of Cardiology, 40*(11), 1895–1901. doi:10.1016/S0735-1097(02)02537-8

Campbell, S. M., Roland, M. O., & Buetow, S. A. (2000). Defining Quality of Care. *Social Science & Medicine, 51,* 1611–1625. doi:10.1016/S0277-9536(00)00057-5

Cobbold, I., & Lawrie, G. (2002a). Classification of balanced scorecards based on their intended use. *PMA Conference.* Berkshire, UK: 2GC Ltd.

Cobbold, I., & Lawrie, G. (2002b). The development of the balanced scorecard as a strategic management tool. *PMA Conference.* Berkshire, UK: 2GC Ltd.

Daniel, R. D. (1961). Management information crisis. *Harvard Business Review, 39*(Sept-Oct).

Dixon, W. J., & Massey, F. J. (1983). *Introduction to statistical analysis.* (3rd ed.) New York: McGraw-Hill Book Company.

Dolan, P. (2001). Output measures and valuation in health. In M.F.Drummond & A. McGuire (Eds.), *Economic evaluation in health care* (pp. 46-67). Oxford: Oxford University Press.

Drummond, M. F., O'Brien, B., Stoddart, G. L., & Torrance, G. W. (1997). *Methods for the economic evaluation of health care programmes* (2nd ed.). Oxford: Oxford University Press.

Edgar, Th. F. (2004). Control and operations: When does controllability equal profitability? *Computers & Chemical Engineering, 29,* 41–49. doi:10.1016/j.compchemeng.2004.07.013

Ein-Dor, Ph. (2003). The world and business computing in 2051: from LEO to RUR? *The Journal of Strategic Information Systems, 12,* 357–371. doi:10.1016/j.jsis.2001.11.011

Forster, N. S., & Rockart, J. F. (1989). *Critical success factors: An annotated bibliography* (Rep. No. CISR WP No. 191, Sloan WP No. 3041-89). Cambridge, MA: Sloan School of Management, MIT.

Fuller, T. (2003a). If you wanted to know the future of small business what questions would you ask? *Futures, 35,* 305–321. doi:10.1016/S0016-3287(02)00083-6

Fuller, T. (2003b). Small bisness futures in society (Introduction). *Futures*, *35*, 297–304. doi:10.1016/S0016-3287(02)00082-4

Gerritsen, B. H. M. (2008). Advances in Mass customization and adaptive manufacturing. In I. Horvath & Z. Rusak (Eds.), *TMCE 2008* (pp. 869-880). Delft, Netherlands: Delft University.

Gouscos, D., Kalikakis, M., Legal, M., & Papado-poulou, S. (2007). A general model of performance and quality for one-stop e-Government service offerings. *Government Information Quarterly*, *24*, 860–885. doi:10.1016/j.giq.2006.07.016

Hassan, T. M., & McCaffer, R. (2002). Vision of the large scale engineering construction industry in Europe. *Automation in Construction*, *11*, 421–437. doi:10.1016/S0926-5805(01)00074-7

Hernandez-Matias, J. C., Vizan, A., Perez-Garcia, J., & Rios, J. (2008). An integrated modelling framework to support manufacturing system diagnosis for continuous improvement. *Robotics and Computer-integrated Manufacturing*, *24*, 187–199. doi:10.1016/j.rcim.2006.10.003

Holden, M. (2006). Urban Indicators and the Integrative Ideals of Cities. *Cities (London, England)*, *23*(3), 170–183. doi:10.1016/j.cities.2006.03.001

Hoogeweegen, M., van Liere, D. W., Vervest, P. H. M., Hagdorn van der Meijden, L., & de Lepper, I. (2006). Strategizing for mass customization by playing the business networking game. *Decision Support Systems*, *42*, 1402–1412. doi:10.1016/j.dss.2005.11.007

Huang, H.-C. (in press). Designing a knowledge-based system for strategic planning: A balanced scorecard perspective. *Expert Systems with Applications*.

Hubbard, D. W. (2007). *How to measure anything; Finding the value of intangibles in business*. John Wiley & Sons, Inc.

Hwang, W. T., Tien, W. T., & Shu, C. M. (2007). Building an executive information system for maintenance efficiency in petrochemical plants -- an evaluation. *Trans IChemE, Part B . Process Safety and Environmental Protection*, *85*, 139–146. doi:10.1205/psep06019

International Organization for Standardization ISO. (2008). *ISO in figures for the year 2007* Geneva: ISO Central Secretariat.

ISO. (2006). [ISO International Organization for Standardization. Retrieved from ttp://www.iso.org]. *Survey (London, England)*, *2006*.

Johnson, C. (2005). *US e-commerce: 2005 to 2010, a five year forecast and analysis of US online retail sales*. Forrester Research.

Kaplan, R. S., & Norton, D. P. (1992). The balance scorecard - measures that drive performance. *Harvard Business Review*, *70*(1), 71–79.

Kaplan, R. S., & Norton, D. P. (1993). Putting the balanced scorecard to work. *Harvard Business Review*, *71*(5), 134–140.

Kaplan, R. S., & Norton, D. P. (1996a). *The balanced scorecard*. Boston, MA: Harvard Business School Press.

Kaplan, R. S., & Norton, D. P. (1996b). Using the balance scorecard as a strategic management system. *Harvard Business Review*, *74*(1), 75–85.

Kaplan, R. S., & Norton, D. P. (2001a). The strategy-focused organization. *Strategy and Leadership*, *29*(3), 41–43.

Kaplan, R. S., & Norton, D. P. (2001a). Transforming the balanced scorecard from performance measurement to strategic management: Part I. *Accounting Horizons*, *15*(1), 87–106. doi:10.2308/acch.2001.15.1.87

Kaplan, R. S., & Norton, D. P. (2001b). Transforming the balanced scorecard from performance measurement to strategic management: Part II. *Accounting Horizons, 15*(2), 147–162. doi:10.2308/acch.2001.15.2.147

Kaplan, R. S., & Norton, D. P. (2004a). How strategy maps frame an organization's objectives. *Financial Executive, 20*(2), 40–45.

Kaplan, R. S., & Norton, D. P. (2004a). Measuring the strategic readiness of intangible assets. *Harvard Business Review, 82*(2), 52–63.

Kaplan, R. S., & Norton, D. P. (2004b). *Strategy maps: Converting intangible assets into outcomes*. Boston, MA: Harvard Business School Press.

Kaplan, R. S., & Norton, D. P. (2004c). *Strategy Maps; Converting Intangible Assets into Tangible Outcomes*. Boston: Harvard Business School Press.

Kaplan, R. S., & Norton, D. P. (2004c). The strategy map: Guide to aligning intangible assets. *Strategy and Leadership, 32*(5), 10–17. doi:10.1108/10878570410699825

Kaplan, R. S., & Norton, D. P. (2006). *Alignment: Using the balanced scorecard to create corporate synergies*. Boston, MA: Harvard Business School Press.

Kim, H.-S., & Kim, Y.-G. (2008). A CRM performance measurement framework: its development process and application. Industrial Marketing Management.

Mather, D. (2003). *CMMS: A timesaving implementation process*. Boca Raton, FL: CRC Press.

Mokyr, J. (2005). *The gifts of Athena; Historical origins of the knowledge economy*. Princeton, NJ: Princeton University Press.

Niven, P. R. (2005). *Balanced scorecard diagnostics; Maintaining maximum performance*. Hoboken, NJ: John Wiley & Sons, Inc.

Nudurupati, S., Arshad, T., & Turner, T. (2007). Performance measurement in the construction industry: An action case investigating manufacturing methodologies. *Computers in Industry, 58*, 667–676. doi:10.1016/j.compind.2007.05.005

Puigjaner, L., & Guillen-Gosalbez, G. (2008). Towards an integrated framework for supply chain management in the batch chemical process industry. *Computers & Chemical Engineering, 32*, 650–670. doi:10.1016/j.compchemeng.2007.02.004

Rockart, J. F. (1986). A primer on critical success factors. In C. V. Bullen (Ed.), *The rise of managerial computing: The best of the center for Information Systems research* (pp. 383-423). Cambridge, MA: Sloan School of Management, MIT.

Schultink, G. (2000). Critical environmental indicators: Performance indices and assessment methods for sustainable rural development planning. *Ecological Modelling, 130*, 47–58. doi:10.1016/S0304-3800(00)00212-X

Stevenson, T. (2000). Will our futures look different, now? *Futures, 32*, 91–102. doi:10.1016/S0016-3287(99)00069-5

Tsoukas, H., & Shepherd, J. (2004). Coping with the future: developing organizational foresightfulness (Introduction). *Futures, 36*, 137–144. doi:10.1016/S0016-3287(03)00146-0

Ugwu, O. O., & Haupt, T. C. (2007). Key performance indicators and assessment methods for infrastructure sustainability -- a South African construction industry perspective. *Building and Environment, 42*, 665–680. doi:10.1016/j.buildenv.2005.10.018

Van den Eynde, J., Veno, A., & Hart, A. (2003). They look good but don't work: a case study of global performance indicators in crime prevention. *Evaluation and Program Planning, 26,* 237–248. doi:10.1016/S0149-7189(03)00028-4

Warhurst, A. (2005). Future roles of business in society: The expanding boundaries of corporate responsibility and a compelling case for partnership. *Futures, 37,* 151–168. doi:10.1016/j.futures.2004.03.033

Wier, B., Hunton, J., & HassabElnaby, H. R. (2007). Enterprise resource planning systems and non-financial performance incentives: The joint impact on corporate performance. *Int.J.of Accounting Information Systems, 8,* 165-190.

Woodhouse, J. (2000). Key performance indicators. Retrieved from http://www.TWPL.com

Woodhouse, J. (2004). Closing the loop: sustainable implementations of improvements. In *ERTC Reliability & Asset Management Conference; Oil, Gas, Petrochem & Power Industries.*

Chapter 18

e–Impresa:
A System Dynamics Strategic Model to Evaluate SME Marketing On Line Investment

Habib Sedehi
Rome University "La Sapienza," Italy

ABSTRACT

Electronic commerce, marketing on line, and network economy are today's keywords of (possible) success. But how many managers effectively know about the cost and benefits of starting to sell their products and services through the Web? How much they should invest at the beginning and how long does it takes to have a break-even point of their investment? In order to give support for better understanding the process of the Web marketing and to have more elements to decide to "dive" or not in this virtual world a **System Dynamics (SD)** *model (Forrester J.W. 1961, 1971, 1980), has been developed. The model has the aim to support* **strategic decisions** *for SME involvement in* **e-Commerce***, pointed out to guarantee sustainable growth and medium-long term success. The project e-Impresa[1] analyses the whole process of the investment in building and maintaining a web site, taking into account the main variables of E-commerce. Through a case study, a SD* **business game** *model has been developed. The model gives the opportunity to users to evaluate different* **what-if analysis** *through the* **simulation** *period time (2 years) at each* **model** *step time (4 weeks). This chapter will explain the overall architecture of the model and will present some results of use of the model in different conditions.*

INTRODUCTION

The decision to start up a web marketing project has to fit well into the general company strategy in order to contribute in achieving the goals of its mission. Indeed web marketing "initiatives" which appear disconnected to the general company strategy both run the risk of the failure and, sometimes, weaken companies' market shares.

The e-Commerce business, beside representing a new market opportunity, also stimulates improvement in the degree of efficiency of the strategic corporate functions (such as the logistic one that's

DOI: 10.4018/978-1-60566-892-5.ch018

going to assume a growing importance in the present economy).

But in order to compete efficiently in the internet market, specific strategies and product systems have to be developed. Indeed, both for network features and for the internet user profile, the traditional commercial strategies don't work over the net. In the virtual market the user plays a very active role; searching for products in which the user is interested and opposes the spammers, i.e. those who disseminate advertisements on web sites and e-mail boxes. This does not allow companies to adopt the traditional commercial formula, often based on mass marketing activities, in order to operate efficiently in the virtual trading. In addition, since the Internet network allows (presently) only bytes, and not atoms, to be sent, the trading of the tangible goods over the net appears too complicated and expensive.

In this contest SME attacking the virtual market have to project strategies aiming:

- to increase the weight of the services in the product system;
- to increase the brand fame in order to induce potential customers to perceive the product as exclusive;
- to reduce the customer's perception of risk throughout the trading process.

In other words e-Companies have to organize their product systems in order to induce customers to appreciate the difference between the perceived benefits and the relative costs, measurable in terms of money, time spent in network purchasing activities (such as browsing, e-mails and so on), and mental effort due to information overload, risks, etc.

Once the general idea of the product system is defined, it's necessary to demonstrate the project's long term economic and financial sustainability and suitability, i.e. the future economic and financial Return On Investments (ROI). In this context

decisions regarding the economic autonomy of the "initiative" or its dependence on the general marketing budget have to be made. In this sense the web marketing initiative can be considered both as a project equipped with independent goals and financial sources and also as part of an investment related to the general marketing budget.

The goal of this work has been to provide the general management of a SME, aiming to attack the virtual market, a tool in order to be supported in a possible web based entrepreneurial idea. Finally it consists in developing a *business game*, based on a System Dynamics **simulation model**, evaluating the effects deriving from alternative e-Commerce strategies and policies.

The paper will be developed through six different paragraphs. Initially an updated excursus on what has been, in the literature, developed both from the theoretical and the experimental point of view, will be described in the background paragraph. In order to best introduce the model structure a case study, on the base of which the whole work has been developed, will be described. After the paper principle paragraph i.e. the model description through System Dynamics methodology, a brief description of the environment and development tool through which the simulation model is developed will be presented. Finally, the results of two possible simulation scenarios dealing with the impact of related what-if analysis will be discussed. The conclusions paragraph will close the paper underlining the operative results which presently are gained.

BACKGROUND

Even though there can be found some case studies results dealing with experiences of companies in adopting web marketing investments and related costs and benefits, the literature is poor of tools to support SME in evaluating in advance such policies. There are not so much work developed in this area also because since the beginning of the new century not so many small businesses used the web(or could use it) to the extent they should, for the marketing of their product (Dilts & Kahai 2004). Looking all over the world the Web is still a new and relatively unfamiliar environment for the marketing of business as well as for the conduct of business research (Barabási 2002). Drew (2002) confirms that however a progressive maturing of the literature in both practitioners oriented and academic publications is more and more growing). Harvard Business Review, Sloan Management Review, California Management Review, Business Horizons, Long Range Planning and the European Management Journal publish articles on the business use of the Web, virtual marketplaces, e-retailing and B2B commerce continuously (Featherstone & Borstorff, 2005).

Since the growth of businesses, in particular for SME that use the Internet as a core infrastructure is a very recent phenomenon, it is hardly surprising that much investigation in the literature to date is of an exploratory nature. Theory approaches has taken place at the intersection of case studies, extrapolation of known characteristics of the technology to business settings and implementation of existing theories of strategy, marketing, psychology, economics and complex systems (Kleindl, 2000).

Much of the literature on business models argue the business model in terms of a customer value proposition, pricing strategy or particular Internet technologies. There is an opportunity for business model analysis from a more holistic perspective. The concept of a business model and its use within strategic management also needs to refined and argued to address the criticisms raised by Porter (2001).

Future evolution of the web site development issues to be used in the business models of the marketing on line context is probably the semantic web. Many articles and books recently are dedicated to this "technology" (Dzbor, 2008; Moradi, 2008; Zhao, 2007).

THE CASE STUDY

This study analyses the start-up of a new web based business idea (Mandelli, 1999). It has been examined a small production company, operating through the traditional distribution chain, in order to overcome economic difficulties, decides to evaluate the web-based trading market.

In particular the case is a company producing electrical scooters, designed for use within factories, airports, nature parks, etc., mainly marketing in the domestic/local area. Having occurred an economic crisis due to the saturation of the national market, the company takes the opportunity to develop a web based business "branch" in order to enlarge its market and hence to compete all over the world.

To this purpose the company's strategic planning pinpointed the following intermediate goals:

- to build a very sound brand image in order to induce potential customers to perceive the company's product system as exclusive;
- to increase the weight of the services offered by the company;
- to create the image of the "company-customer" relationship as a success factor, by opposing the phenomenon of depersonalization peculiar to the "virtual" commerce.

Obviously the achievement of these strategic goals mainly depends on the system of policies and actions developed for this purpose. The aim of *e-Impresa* consists of supporting the company general management in approaching the "best" marketing mix in order to enable the company to be economically competitive in this new market. In other words the simulator has the aim to help the company managers to evaluate the effects produced by the alternative web marketing strategies on all the enterprise sub-systems.

Model Description

The *e-Impresa* analyses the management of a web-based entrepreneurial idea through the following five areas:

1. web visitors management;
2. web site management;
3. Enterprise Information management,
4. production management;
5. economic and financial management.

1. Web Visitors Management

The model distinguishes between two types of visits:

- web new (first time) visits,
- web regular (consolidated) visits.

The first one is carried out by visitors that get to know the web site by means of both the company's marketing traditional actions and of the "word of mouth" factor and browse it for the first time (Bauer, C. and Scharl, A. 2000).

The second one, on the other hand, is carried out by accounting-holding visitors who have already browsed the company's web site (Dwyer, R. 1987).

The figure 1 depicts, using SD influence diagram (Causal Loop Diagram- CLD) (Rooberts, N. et. A. 1983), the main relations determining the dynamics of the "visitors" area. The (+) and (-) signs capture the positive (amplification) and negative (balancing) influence of the starting variable (arrow starting point) in relation to the ending variable (arrow finishing point).

In particular the number of weekly new visits depends on two parameters:

- the amount of start-up investment,
- the amount of investment in advertising and promotion activities.

The start-up investment includes:

- the costs of the web-site first time designing and implementation of its contents, graphics features and interactivity,
- the cost of the web site publishing over the web server of Internet provider,
- the start-up costs of the services necessary to support trading on line such as credit card account, delivery services and so on.

The advertising and promotion investments, on the other hand, include all the initial marketing activity costs such as:

- search engine registrations,
- banner campaigns,
- all the other activities able to promote the "birth" and first step growing of the site.

The higher the investment amount and efficiency the greater will be the size of the new visits.

The transformation of the new visits into regular visits mainly depends on the level of the web site attractiveness. The web site attractiveness is measured by a ratio, ranging between zero and one, determined by the relations between the different investments made in order to maintain or increase the web site attractiveness and the requested investments necessary to realize a very high quality web site.

The dynamic of the new visits is also influenced by the regular visits through the "word of mouth" effect, as with every Internet phenomenon. Indeed the management of the regular visits enables the activation of a positive feedback loop determining an exponential growth or reduction of visits and, therefore, the probability to collect sale orders. This underlines the strategic importance of the

Figure 1. Visitors management influence diagram

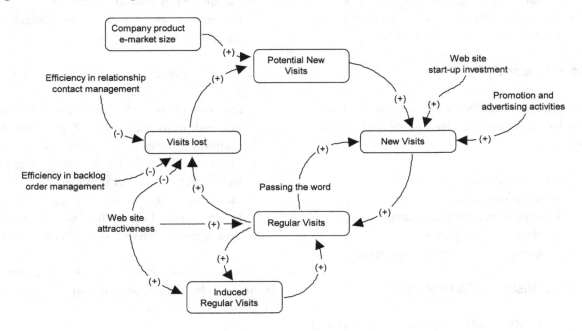

web site management because it is able to activate the phenomenon of the enterprise development or crisis.

Through SD influence diagram (figure 1), it can be observed how strong could be the impact of the attractiveness management on the regular visits dynamics. Indeed the web site attractiveness influences the regular visits in three directions:

- by adjusting the size of the transformation of new visits into regular visits,
- by adjusting the average number of weekly re-visits per regular visitors,
- by adjusting the size of visits lost.

In the first direction it appears clear that visitors are induced to re-visit the company's web pages if their graphic and logical content are appealing and their navigability is satisfactory. Hence the higher the web site attractiveness the greater will be the transformation of the new visits into the regular ones.

The company web site attractiveness also influences the frequency of the site re-visit. In-

deed the higher the web site appeal the greater the average weekly number of the re-visits per regular visitors.

The third type of the impact concerns the loss of regular visits. In particular reduction of the web site appeal produces a decrease in the regular visits because the visitors evaluate this phenomenon as the worsening of the enterprise image.

The visits lost measures the number of the users not satisfied by the enterprise product system. The number of the visits lost, beside the web site attractiveness, depends on the following elements:

- efficiency in the management of the customer relationships,
- efficiency in the managing orders.

The efficiency in the management of customer relationships measures the appropriateness of the company customer service organization to the size of the controlled market. This efficiency is measured by a ratio, ranging between zero and one, representing the company customer service ability to satisfy quickly and fully potential customer information requirements such as the product features, the efficiency of the delivery, the privacy of the transaction data, etc. The higher the efficiency the higher will be the customer satisfaction and the lower will be the number of the visits lost.

The efficiency in the managing orders, on the other hand, represents the relationship between the management of the web business unit and the other functions of the company such as the production, the marketing, the human resources and the finance. A low level of the efficiency means that the web site sales potential is higher than the enterprise production capacity and the company is not able economically to cope with all the orders. Such a situation weakens the enterprise image both in the off-line and in the on-line market, determining the loss in the global market shares.

2. Web Site Management

The area "web site management" analyses the following issues:

- customer contact management,
- web site attractiveness management.

The first issue analyses the management of the contacts between the company and its present and potential customers. In particular the model distinguishes between two types of contacts:

- information contacts;
- relationship contacts.

The information contacts are those contacts activated by the potential customers information requirements regarding the product features, the efficiency in the delivery, the terms of the payment and so on. These contacts are usually created through the e-mails sent by the company customer service.

The relationship contacts are those activated by the enterprise aiming to maintain contact with the people that previously had connections with the company (such as consolidated customers and visitors).

The figure 2 depicts (through CLD) the dynamics of the contact management. In particular the number of the information contacts received per week is mainly influenced by the dynamics of the web site visits. The higher the number of the visits the greater will be the probability to receive e-mails requiring information.

The company weekly capacity to reply to the received e-mails depends on:

- the number of man days assigned to help desk service,
- the average time necessary to reply to each e-mail.

The experience curves concept well explains that the average reply time is a decreasing function of the total number of processed e-mails. Indeed as the number of processed e-mails increases the help desk personnel gains experience in replying more quickly to them, reducing the average reply time. The reduction of the replay time increases the company efficiency in managing contacts or the ability to the efficiently satisfy potential customers information requirements.

For each new received e-mail at least one record of the customers database is updated. The customer database is a very important resource because it allows the company to develop marketing activities aiming to maintain or improve relations with the present and the potential customers.

The main relationship marketing activities examined by this model are the following:

- creation of the mailing list,
- creation of the newsletter,
- sending of the individual promotional e-mails.

The higher the number of the new visits the greater will be the amount of the information about

Figure 2. Customer contacts management influence diagram

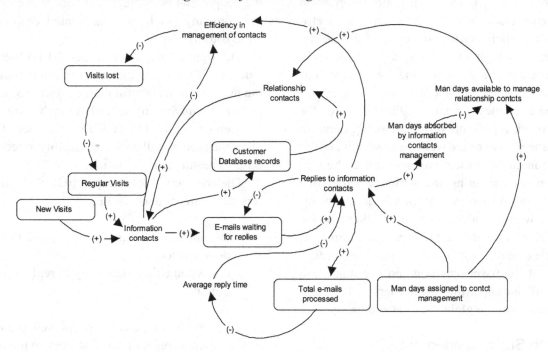

the potential customers and so the more successful could be the relationship marketing activities.

The second issue related to the area of the "web site management" analyzed by the model is the web site attractiveness management which, as previously stated, is measured by a the ratio expressing the general evaluation of the web site in terms of technical features, graphic aspects and content.

The degree of the web site attractiveness mainly depends on:

- the amount and quality of the web site investments in terms of the technical and graphic aspects such as; the navigability rate, the transaction safety, the graphic appeal, etc.,
- the number of the man days dedicated to the web site contents updating,
- the natural ageing process of the web site.

The strategic importance of the web site attractiveness management appears clear in

the figure 3. As it can be seen, it determines the dynamics of the visits, the contacts and the orders.

Hence it is possible to state that the success of a web marketing idea mainly depends on:

- the web site attractiveness;
- the efficiency in management of the relationship contacts and the backlog of the orders.

Indeed as the *attractiveness* aims to create the sales potential, the *efficiency* attempts to transform it into real market shares.

3. Information Management

This area analyses the management of the new economy's principal resource: *information*. It analyses the problem of building and maintaining the customer database in order to utilize the available information:

Figure 3. Web site attractiveness influence diagram

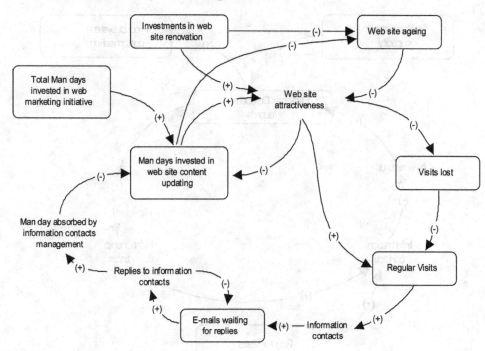

- to develop relationship marketing activities aiming to maintain or improve the relations with present and potential customers;
- to adapt the product system to customer needs.

The customer's database records contain precious information about customer needs and buying practices helpful to provide a product system tailored to customer requirements. The database collects the information deriving from the contacts between the company and its present and potential customers.

Obviously the greater the amount of the information about the customer recorded into the database in terms of the customers e-mail addresses, needs, desires, etc. the more effective will be both the relationship marketing activities and the level of customization of enterprise products (see figure 4).

4. Production Management

This area analyses the biggest problem afflicting the development of e-Commerce, i.e. the interaction between the web product orders and the supply chain capacity.

The figure 5 shows the main relationships existing between on-line and off-line commerce analyzed by this model.

In particular the received e-mails nourish the flow of the new on-line orders according to the average number of received orders per contact. This percentage depends on:

- the degree of the enterprise product system customization,
- the degree of the help desk service efficiency.

The satisfaction of the on-line orders depends on the supply production capacity, i.e. the capacity to produce and timely deliver the products ordered. The enterprise production capacity is a

Figure 4. Information management influence diagramme

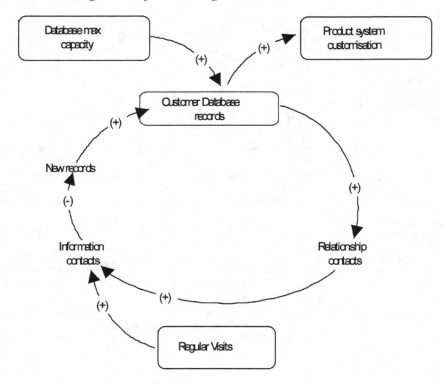

common resource, hence a growing use of it by on-line sales decreases the company capacity to timely satisfy all the off-line orders.

Other relationships between traditional and electronic commerce are represented by the following two effects:

- pulling effect,
- so called "cannibalism" effect.

In the figure 5 the pulling effect is represented by the link between the "Regular visits" and the "New off-line orders". This connection means that the company presence on the web also increase its fame in the traditional market pushing up off-line sales.

The so called "cannibalism" effect, on the other hand, represents the erosion of the off-line sales caused by the increase of the on-line ones. This effect occurs when the web marketing strategies aim to reach the same customer target reached through the traditional marketing policies; indeed in this case customers could be interested to the direct acquisition from the producer, avoiding the mediators. This effect is well showed in the figure 6 through the link between the "New on-line orders" and the "New off-line orders".

Keeping all this in mind it is clear that the economic evaluation of a web-based entrepreneurial idea has to be founded not only on the base of the revenue increase deriving from the web marketing but also considering all the effects that such an idea will produce on the traditional market share.

5. Economic and Financial Management

This area describes both the economic and financial consequences produced by the decisions affecting the other areas (web visitors management, web site management, information management

Figure 5. Production management influence diagram

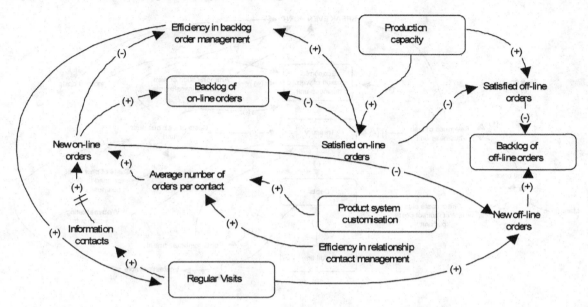

and production management) and the opportunities and constraints that an autonomous economic and financial management offers to the "system of decisions". The figure 6 depicts these relations.

It is first necessary to state that the *e-Impresa* model analyses the web marketing "initiative" as an autonomous business unit with a specific budget, its resources, credit lines and goals. However in order to define correctly the business unit economic results, the share of the general fixed costs, contributing to generate the revenues of the competence, has to be assigned to it. This area analyses the following aspects:

- the financial consequences of the costs and revenues,
- the management of the financial resources,
- the achievement of the break even point.

The following figure 7 describes the main economic and financial dynamics characterizing the web business unit of the company.

The revenues of the web business depend on:

- the number of on-line orders received,
- the selling price determined by summing up to the unit full cost a fair mark-up.

Figure 6. Description of relations between different model's areas

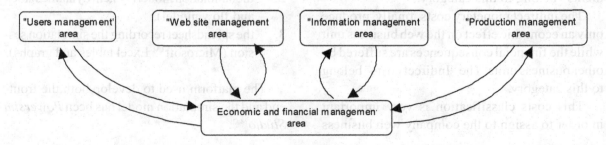

Figure 7. Economic and financial management influence diagram

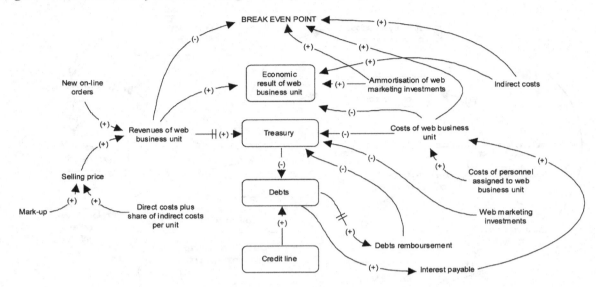

The costs are distinguished by the model into three categories:

- direct monetary costs,
- direct non-monetary costs,
- indirect monetary costs.

The first category of the costs is represented by the direct costs producing the economic impact before or simultaneously to the financial one. The "Costs of personnel assigned to web business unit" and the "Interest payable" belong to this category.

The second type of the costs produces the financial impact before the economic one. For example the long term investments produce an immediate financial outflow and a postponed economic impact. The "Web marketing investments" belong to this category.

The indirect monetary costs, finally, produce only an economic effect on the web business unit while the financial consequences are suffered by other business units. The "Indirect costs" belong to this category.

This costs classification is very important in order to assign to the company web business unit all relative directly and indirectly costs and so correctly evaluate its goals.

In order to cope with the financial requirements, external financial sources are activated within the measure of the accorded credit lines.

One of the main goals and output of the economic and financial area consists in determining the "Break Even Point" i.e. the point where costs even out revenues.

Description of the Environment and Development Tool

The *e-Impresa* simulation model environment includes three layers:

1. the front end (user interface),
2. the simulation model (system dynamics stock and flow model),
3. the spreadsheet recording the simulation session (Microsoft™ Excel tables and graphs).

The platform used to develop both the front-end and the simulation model has been *Powersim Studio*™2.

Figure 8. e-Impresa front end control panel

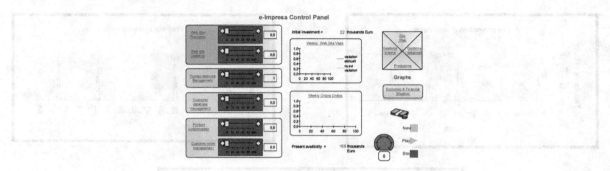

The front end is very simple and intuitive and an exhaustive help on line is available. It contains input levers, essential output graphs and simulation commands. The control panel window of the simulation model is shown in the figure 8.

The System Dynamics model simulates over a period time of 104 weeks (2 years) and the simulation is automatically paused every 4 weeks.

All simulation data (both user's decisions and relative simulation results) are recorded into a spreadsheet in order to allow users to elaborate them with the more common office automation tools.

A What-If Analysis Performed through e-Impresa

A critical resource of the e-commerce is represented by the human resources; hence the size of man days assigned to the web site management assumes a strategic role. Indeed the human [INSERT FIGURE 016] resources management meets a trade off between the corporate image and its production costs: the higher the human resources assigned to the web site management the greater will be the corporate image but the greater also will be the production costs.

Here below two scenarios reproducing two different personnel management approaches are showed.

Scenario 1

The company aims to increase its *virtual market* share through an aggressive strategy based on frequent activities of web site promotion and content updating. But its personnel management policy aims to increase the staff size only when marketing activities begin to produce their effects. In other words the company's personnel management approach is tuned up a short term view. Figure 9 represents the main inputs for this scenario during the simulation time (2 years), i.e:

- the web promotion investments in Euro,
- the web site updating costs in Euro
- the weekly effort assigned to web site management in Man days
- wthe number of weekly web site visits (divided by regular and new visitors),
- the number of weekly e-mails in cue waiting for a reply,
- the weekly and the total (accumulated) economic results.

Scenario 2

In this second scenario the company pursues the same strategy described in scenario 1 with the exception for the human resources management. In fact in this case the company's personnel management is far-seeing oriented i.e. it aims to anticipate the effects of marketing actions, increasing the

Figure 9. Scenario 1 main input variables

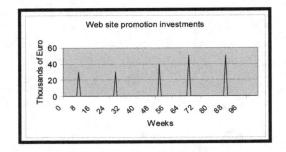

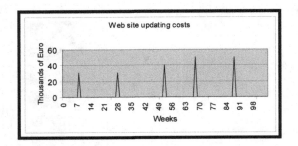

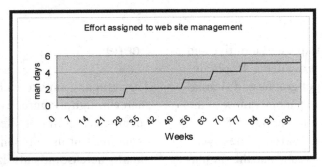

staff size before them begin producing their effects. The figures 11 and 12 represent, with new values, the same input and output variables of the scenario 1.

Comparison between the Two Scenarios

Comparing the two scenarios it can be observed that in the same commercial conditions the results produced in scenario 2 are better than those produced in scenario 1 (see figures 10 and 12). This depends on the different personnel management approach. In fact in scenario 1 the decision to increase the size of personnel staff is not an autonomous decision but it is induced by the increase of visits and contact deriving from marketing actions. (See figures 9 and 10). But the adjustment delay of the size staff to the new potential market determines the accumulation of e-mails waiting for replies and that both reduces the effectiveness of marketing actions and weakens the company's image (see figure 10).

The scenario 2, on the other hand, looks upon the staff size as an important marketing lever. In fact in scenario 2 the staff sizing is decided in advance, almost simultaneously to the web site promotion and updating investments (see figure 11). This action allows company to cope efficiently with visitors and customers needs, preserving its image and increasing the profitability.

Hence even if in the first instance (short time term), scenario 1 seems to reduce corporate costs, it is both quantitatively (company result) and qualitatively (company image) less positive than scenario 2 to sustain company growth over the long time term.

CONCLUSION

Even though the issue of Web Marketing/e-Commerce is very much analyzed and investigated (particularly for the big organizations) in order to best support enterprise enlarging business marketing, there are a huge number of SME, having the

Figure 10. Scenario 1 main output results

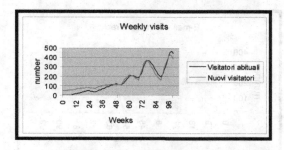

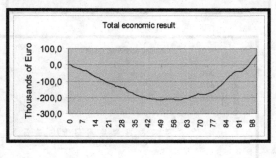

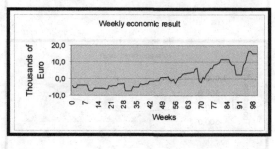

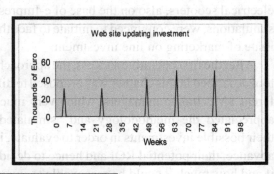

potentiality of exploiting new markets all over the world, that still did not evaluate the cost and benefits of such an opportunity. System Dynamics methodology process analysis, from one side,

and Simulation Modeling, from the other side are two approaches/tools which combined together can very much help "sceptic" entrepreneur first to understand the web marketing process and

Figure 11. Scenario 2 main input variables

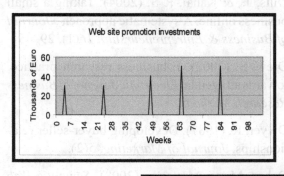

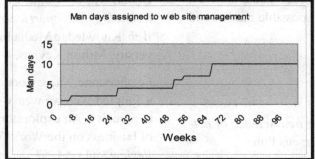

Figure 12. Scenario 2 main output results

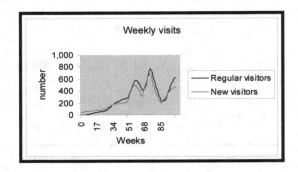

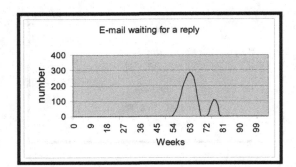

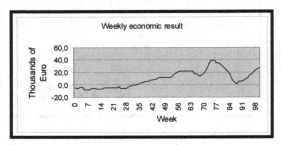

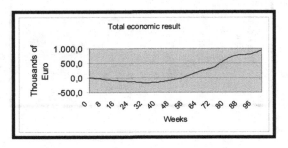

hence to better evaluate possible marketing on line investments.

The model was first implemented and successfully used by the data related to the case study described . The managers of the company producing electrical scooters, also on the base of e-Impresa simulations, were convinced to initiate to face the issue of marketing on line investment.

After the first operative success, the approach/tool described in this chapter was proposed to different SME Italian managers, which very much appreciated the methodology and "simulated" their possible investments in order to evaluate, in advance, their potential ROI and hence to decide if and how much it could be reasonable to invest in this area in order to gain possible market and business.

REFERENCES

Barabási, A. L. (2002). *The new science of networks*. Cambridge, MA: Perseus Pub.

Bauer, C., & Scharl, A. (2000). Quantitative evaluation of Web site content and structure. *Internet Research, 10*(1), 31–43. doi:10.1108/10662240010312138

Dilts, J., & Kahai, P. S. (2004). Taking a small business online: A systematic approach . *Journal of Business & Entrepreneurship, 16*(1), 29–45.

Drew, S. (2002). E-business research practice, towards an agenda. *Electronic Journal of Business Research Methods*.

Dwyer, R. (1987). Developing buyer-seller relationships. *Journal of Marketing, 5*(2).

Dzbor, M., & Motta, E. (2008). *Semantic Web technology to support learning about the semantic Web*. Knowledge Media Institute, The Open University. Milton Keynes, UK: IOS press.

Featherstone, M., & Borstorff, P. (2005). O, What a Tangled Web we weave when first we practice to perceive, An exploratory study of the conduct of business on the World Wide Web. *E-Business Review, 5*(1), 54–57.

Forrester, J. W. (1961). *Industrial dynamics*. Cambridge, MA: MIT Press.

Forrester, J. W. (1971). *Principles of systems*. Cambridge, MA: MIT Press.

Forrester, J. W. (1980). System dynamics - future opportunities. In A. A. Legasto, J. W. Forrester & J. M. Lyneis (Eds.), *TIMS Studies in the management sciences* (Vol. 14, pp. 7-21). Oxford: North-Holland.

Kleindl, B. (2000). Competitive dynamics and new business models for SMEs in the virtual marketplace. *Journal of Developmental Entrepreneurship*, 5(1), 73–85.

Mandelli, A. (1999). *Fare business in Rete*. Milano, Italy: McGraw-Hill.

Moradi, F. (2008). *A framework for component based modelling and simulation using BOMs and semantic Web technology*. Doktorsavhandling, sammanläggning Press.

Porter, M. (2001). Strategy and the Internet. *Harvard Business Review*, 79(3), 63–78.

Roberts, N., Andersen, D., Deal, R., Garet, M., & Shaffer, W. (1983). *Introduction to computer simulation. A system dynamics modelling approach*. Addison Wesley Pub. Company.

Suh, K., Couchman, P. K., Park, J., & Hasan, H. (2003). *The application of activity theory to Web-mediated communication. Information systems and activity theory volume 3; Expanding the horizon*. Wollongong, Australia: University of Wollongong Press.

Zhao, S., & Chang, E. (2007). *From database to semantic web ontology: An overview*. Springer, Heidelberg.

ENDNOTES

[1] *Impresa* in Italian means Enterprise

[2] Powersim Studio™ is a fully-featured simulation model development environment. It can be created user friendly front-end and models and perform simulation runs and analyses.

Chapter 19

Preparedness of Small and Medium–Sized Enterprises to Use Information and Communication Technology as a Strategic Tool

Klara Antlova
Technical University, Czech Republic

ABSTRACT

The objective of this chapter is to emphasize issues connected with adoption of information and communication technology (ICT) as a strategic tool contributing to further organizational growth. This understanding is based on the results of a qualitative analysis of a group of small and medium-sized enterprises (SMEs). Gradual development of a group of 30 organizations has been monitored over the last fifteen years during their co-operation with the Technical University of Liberec. These organizations have hosted one-year student placements where students, as part of their Bachelor's degree course, undertake a long term work experience enabling them to integrate the practical and theoretical aspects of their course. The research focused on SME management's approach to ICT, its utilization for competitive advantage and its relation to and defining of business strategy. Other aspects of the study looked at the effect of ICT on organizational performance, knowledge and skills of the employees, training and organizational culture. The results indicate that successful and growing companies have gradually established business, information and knowledge strategies and make strategic use of ICT.

INTRODUCTION

The current business world is undergoing consistent change. To survive in the current competitive environment companies have to be able to respond to such changes. The ability to react quickly to these changes is itself becoming a competitive advantage for small and medium-sized enterprises compared to those that are unable to be as flexible be they other SMEs or larger companies. These companies also demonstrate their ability to work with large companies with which they create new partnership and strategic

DOI: 10.4018/978-1-60566-892-5.ch019

alliances. These adaptable companies working in global environment with the consistent threat of new competition and changing markets, legislation and suppliers, show it is necessary to possess data, information, knowledge and value the experience of their employees. The need for new knowledge and skills requires that employees improve their skills and knowledge continually; by increasing their intellectual capital employees contribute to consistent improvement in services and product innovation. The transformation of intellectual capital into new products and services, however, requires a new approach to management of the organization, a flexible organizational structure and the use of information and communication technologies.

For many SME owners the business represents their lifestyle fulfilling their personal dreams and visions. The research suggests the approach of the owner, age, personality, experience, managerial skills, education, enthusiasm, etc. are important for growth of SME. The owner's approach may be also influenced by mutual relations with other family members who participate in the ownership or run of the organization. Sometimes quite complicated family relations can be observed to have negative impacts on the running of the business.

The structure of this chapter is as follows; the first part analyses ICT adoption in the group of thirty small and medium - sized companies while the second part looks at the most frequent reasons and problems cited as barriers of ICT adoption. Understanding these barriers can help to find better solutions for ICT adoption and implementation in SMEs and to show how successful, growing companies use ICT as a strategic advantage.

Definition of Small and Middle-Sized Enterprises

SME are considered as a homogenous group of business entities meeting certain criteria, such as turnover, headcount, but the reality is different. In fact it is better considered a heterogeneous group with differing needs and objectives.

The European Union (EU) defines SMEs according to two sets of criteria. First a set qualitative criteria which are characterizes them as: independent leadership connected with ownership of the company, limited division of production and technologies, limited capital owned by one or several owners, focus on local markets, etc. The second a set of quantitative definitions based on comparison of economical factors, i.e. turnover, capital, number of employees.

The definition used for the purpose of this analysis divides the companies according to the following criteria:

- A **medium-sized company** is considered to be an organization with the number of employees between 50 and 250, with an annual turnover not exceeding € 50 million, or its yearly balance sheet not exceeding € 43 million.
- **Small companies** are defined as companies employing less than 50 employees, with an annual turnover or yearly balance sheet not exceeding € 10 million.
- **Micro companies** are defined as businesses employing less than 10 people, with an annual turnover or yearly balance sheet not exceeding € 2 million.

Benefits of SME for Economics

Based on the long term survey of ICT using in European countries (E-business W@tch, 2007) the economic and social benefits of being a small and middle-sized enterprises are:

- Ability to mitigate negative impact of structural changes.
- Ability to work as sub-contractors of large companies.
- Ability to create conditions for development and implementation of new technologies.
- Ability to create work opportunities under low capital investment.

- Ability to quickly adapt to requirements and fluctuation of the market.
- Ability to operate in marginal areas of the market that are not attractive for bigger companies.
- Ability to decentralize business activities.
- Ability to support fast development of regions, small towns and communities.

Negative Factors Affecting Business of SMEs

The development of an SME is also influenced by its surrounding economic environment that impacts the demand for products and services. This either facilitates or limits access of SME to the markets that support its further wealth creation and growth. In addition managers of SMEs have to be able to respond flexibly to changes in their environment and wishes of their customers. To do this they need appropriate tools, not only knowledge of the employees, but also information and communication technologies.

Previous research (Antlova, 2005) showed that potential growth and survival of SMEs is largely dependent on the environment surrounding the companies. Small and middle-sized enterprises are negatively affected by the following factors:

- Low economic power comparing to large companies.
- Difficultly gaining access to capital with a consequent limited ability to finance development activities.
- Worse access to the specialized training and education compared to larger companies.
- Lower access to necessary information and consultancy services.
- Unfair competition from large companies and dumping prices of imported products.
- Limited sale of finished products on the domestic market and increased cost of export.

- Competition of retail organizations managed by financially strong companies.
- Weak position in public tenders.
- Failure to and delay in receiving payments resulting in secondary financial insolvency.
- High administrative demand from the government bodies and agencies.

Literature Review

Existing literature review proposes major differences between SMEs and large organizations (Hekkila, 1991):

- SMEs tend to use computers more as tools and less as a communications medium,
- SMEs have much fewer resources available to implement in ICT solutions.

Planning in a small firm has the following characteristics (Jeffocate, 2002):

- Often done on an ad hoc basis.
- Frequently only a mental activity of the owner or manager.
- Informal, sporadic, and closed.
- Often relying on advice from random acquaintances with less skill and/or less experience than the owner himself.

SMEs have also particular problems in adopting and using ICT. They usually do not have the appropriate skills available in-house and thus have to train existing staff or purchase those skills in the marketplace (Valkokari & Helander, 2007). But ICT must be associated with a systematic approach to management and decision making and its introduction requires careful planning (Kerney & Abul-Nour, 2004). Although the technology is much cheaper than before, it still represents a considerable investment for SMEs, that traditionally lack such funds (Levy, Powell & Yetton, 2002). The introduction of ICT, which may lead to dramatic

Table 1. Organizations grouped by Area of Business and number of employee

Business area (industry)	Total number of org.	Number of org. with 1-9 employees	Number of org. with 10-49 employees	Number of org. with 50-199 employees	Number of org. with 200-250 employees	25% share of a foreign owner
Manufacturing	4		3		1	
Building	4			2	2	4
Services	11	3	8			
Logistic	2	1		1		
ICT	6	1	3	2		
Automotive	3			1	2	3
In total	30	5	14	6	5	7

changes in the business's fundamental activities, requires an awareness and basic knowledge at the management function, but many owners of SMEs appear to be to busy "surviving" to invest time in such projects (Oh & Pinsonneault, 2000; Cocrill & Lewis, 2002). Therefore, there is a significant risk that such efforts to introduce ICT will be unsuccessful, and the cost of such failure may be fatal for the small firm lacking adequate financial and productive cushioning (Craig & Annear, 2003). It is not surprising that, many SMEs have avoided such risks by ignoring ICT (Gemino, Mackay & Reich, 2006).

During the long term qualitative survey the approach to and use of ICT in small and medium companies has been monitored. The aim of the research is to find key factors influencing the preparedness for strategic use of ICT and to be better prepared for further education activities for owners or managers of SMEs.

DATA COLLECTION AND METHODOLOGY

The thirty companies (all from Czech Republic) have been analysed during qualitative research for the 15 years. The data has been collected through the interviews with the managers or the owners and also through the cooperation of

students and their teachers on some real projects. The following Table 1 describes details of business areas of the organizations and their number of employees.

During this long period SMEs developed and passed through the different levels of changes that impact their size and style of management. This development of SMEs is also discussed in the literature (Greiner, 1972). Every stage of development is characterized by several key factors. This research has used the five stages model from Levy and Powell (Levy & Powell, 2005). These five stages of development are:

- **Commencement** (focus on profit, necessity of transparency and acceleration of administration).
- **Survival** (increasing number of customers, higher need for data share inside of the company).
- **Successful position in the market** (competitive pressure, implementation of quality certificates, etc.).
- **Expansion** (financial issues, electronic communication with customers and suppliers).
- **Maturity** (necessity of innovation, change in the management, training and education of employees).

These above mentioned stages are influenced by competitive pressure, changes of the company's environment, necessity of managerial changes and also by a number of other internal and external factors. Therefore the questions for interview with the managers or owners were focused on the development of organizations and the identification of stages such as:

- Market opportunities.
- Managerial experience.
- Surrounding environment of the company.
- New technologies.
- New products of competitors on the market.
- Legal environment etc.
- Cultural internal environment in the company.
- Approach to learning of employees.

The analyzed organizations were divided into five groups according to the level of their development during their business existence. Each group has its specific way of managing of the organization, its organizational structure, presence or absence of the corporate strategy, level of utilization of ICT, internal and external integration ICT supporting processes in the organization and way of utilization of knowledge of the employees. The objective of this division is to emphasize changes of the management information needs and better understanding their approach to ICT, the motivation and the barriers of ICT adoption. For the purpose of division the following parameters have been used, as they significantly contribute to acceptance or not of using ICT:

- Defining corporate strategy – direction of the organization over the long-term (financial situation of the organization, competitive environment and position in the market, parameters of the planning process and assumed development of the organization, way of managing and general culture in the organization).

- Defining of the information strategy: the status and expected development of utilization of ICT (internal communication of employees, using an internal computer network or internet, access from home, support of the management process).
- Knowledge management (focused on knowledge and skills of employees, way of sharing their knowledge).
- Innovation (investment into research and design, searching for new ways and possibilities of services and marketing).
- Communication with customers and suppliers including management of the supply chain and online ordering.

1st Stage of Growth: Commencement

At the beginning of a company's development the owners are able to manage it on their own and are familiar with details. Taking a more detailed look at this initial stage, we can observe very simple organization structure in this first period, employees and the owner have close relations together, strategic decisions are short-term and long-term strategic plan is missing. Investment into ICT is minimal, usually for the purpose of administration. The objective of the organization is mainly to generate profit and to maintain its position on the market. Gradual growth of the company is connected with transmission into the second stage that can be described as "survival".

This lowest level is represented by a group of companies where strategic objectives exist only in the minds of the owners or managers and can be often summed up as an effort to survive. It is common that a corporate strategy is not written and companies in this group run their business mainly in the area of services. Also the development in skills and knowledge of employees is neglected; employees are not motivated to improve their skills and knowledge.

Analyzed organizations have the following characteristics:

- Lack of financial sources for purchase of ICT, training, etc.
- The corporate strategy can be described as "survival" and maintaining its position in the competitive environment of the market.
- Limited number of employees.
- Insufficient knowledge of ICT.
- Communication with the customers and suppliers only by e-mail, phone or in writing.
- Information support is by an office software package.
- Failure of the customers to comply with financial obligations.
- Often little specialization of individual associates with everybody doing what is presently needed.

2nd Stage of Growth: Survival

In this next level the majority of effort is devoted to maintaining stable group of customers with the emphasis on maintaining its position on the market. The strategic plan is still missing and information systems in the organization are usually simple (often a standard office software package). The owner, however, begins to have issues with maintaining his detailed insight into all orders and with the increasing number of employees. Gradually, as the number of orders increases together with the number of customers, employees, suppliers and partners, the owner has to delegate a number of tasks to others employees. Despite this the owner still remains a key person for strategic decision-making. Simultaneously, the need for management changes is emerging. These circumstances lead the company into the third stage when it becomes established in the market.

The survival stage is represented by a group of organizations with slight growth where the increasing number of customers drives the need to speed up administrative processes. Also the need for employees to share growing amount of data and the managers need better overview of customers' orders. The owners in this group are already trying to search for and formulate their corporate strategy. The organization typically tries to establish itself in the areas with lower competition, such as in newly developing areas focused on specialized services requiring for instance environment-related certificates. Information strategy in such organizations is still not defined. Parameters of these organizations can be summed up as follows:

- The organization aims to survive successfully in the competitive environment and possibly improve its position on the market. The corporate strategy is formulated with the objective to decrease cost and increase effectiveness, but some strategies are based on innovated special services responding to e.g. environmental requirements utilizing the benefit of a less competitive environment.
- The owners respond to increasing number of customers by the effort to multiply economic administrative activities striving for maintaining better overview of the financial situation and individual orders.
- Customers of this group are usually small and middle-sized organizations. Some organizations already tried to utilize at some applications of electronic business, e.g. electronic e-shop, or at least start to consider it.
- The organizations typically have software applications for accounting and warehouse management.
- These organizations are very often owned by families and their relationships play key role in decision making, innovation and growth.

3rd Stage of Growth: Successful Position in the Market

In the third stage of growth the company is successfully growing and the manager begins to undertake mid-term planning. In this phase of development, the further growth of the company significantly depends on approach of the manager or owner. The companies are forced to respond to market demands, wishes of the customers and have to be competitive, in order to avoid declining to an earlier stage. Consequently the managers need to have a vision for the organization and to share it with the employees. The need for strategic management is growing and simultaneously the necessity of possessing sufficient information about the company is increasing. This stage is connected with requirements for better utilization of ICT. Typically the companies utilize database of customers, accounting systems and warehouse system. In this group there are organizations trying to increase the number of customers and to respond flexibly to their needs and wishes. In this group of organizations are small manufacturing companies focused on quite special products, e.g. machines for crushing and processing of metal waste, special glass furnaces. These organizations have the following common characteristics:

- Using of ICT is based on applications such as CAD (Computer Aided Design – software design application), in addition to accounting and other administrative applications.
- These organizations are aware of the importance of ICT and often have an information strategy, within which they consider future integration of electronic shopping into their business model.
- The organizations have certain organizational structure, i.e. the owner has got co-workers participating in managing areas of the organization, e.g. commercial, marketing and manufacturing.

4th Stage of Growth: Expansion

This fourth stage of growth or expansion is very hard for the SME, as the company is trying to be an important player in its business area. That is why this stage requires the owner or the manager to have experience of planning and management, as well as sufficient finance to enact these plans. There is also a requirement for increased internal and external communication is.

These organizations are aiming to become important market players. The owners or managers have defined visions they wish to achieve and share them with their employees. With increasing number of employees there is a need for the owner to formalize the organization structure and to delegate responsibility. This is connected with the need to share visions and business strategies of the organization with a greater number of employees, this means taking into account more opinions, experience and knowledge, which is important for success and growth. This group already contains organizations, usually manufacturing facilities that are often a part of supply chain with the following characteristics:

- Standard ERP (Enterprise Resource Planning), systems for communication with their partners, so they utilize electronic exchange of data.
- The organizations have defined corporate and information strategy, they have hierarchic organizational structure and aim to optimize their processes and information support.
- This group differs from the previous groups of organizations by higher utilization of knowledge of the employees.

5th Stage of Growth: Maturity

To achieve further growth the organization has an increasing need for data and information to supporting planning, managing and strategic decision-making. Information is a strategic source determining the business success and providing data about customers, financial results, capabilities and opportunities for evaluating changes to business objectives. That is the only way the organization may ensure its development and growth. Consequently it needs effective tools, i.e. information system enabling the company to maintain, sort, analyze and search for data for the purpose of support of internal processes. The information system may now yield a competitive advantage compared to other companies.

Investment in ICT requires a long-term strategic plan for the organization based on detailed analysis of the current status. The manager or the owner has to have clear vision of the expected outcome and benefit of ICT, this is can demanding on the knowledge of the managers or owners of SME. The purchase of information technologies creates a lasting obligation, as financial sources of SME are limited. Owners of the companies should recognize that information systems may strongly impact on capacity, strength and chance for survival of the company. Speed of technological innovation together with demanding implementation in the company environment support the serious need for planning the use of information technologies. To be successful here implies that each decision regarding information systems will conform to the wider business strategy of the company.

This level of growth is represented by organizations that are significant market players. These organizations typically have higher number of employees (80-250), are managed by a team of managers and have hierarchic structure of leadership. The group differs from the previous groups especially with its focus on management of knowledge within the workforce. These organizations show effort to optimize internal and external processes. Two organizations run their business in the area of ICT and three remaining organizations are manufacturing companies in the building industry. Companies in this last group

with their approach to using ICT and emphases on sharing of employees knowledge can be good role models for others companies. They have the following common characteristics:

- Existence of written corporate and information strategy.
- Matured level of ICT processes is typical.
- They are aware of the importance of knowledge of their employees.
- Access to the information system by employees from home.
- Willingness to support training of employees.
- A culture of innovative in the organization.
- Application of different management methods (Balanced Scorecard, ABC analyses, etc.).
- On-line communication with customers and suppliers.
- Using e-commerce (buying and selling on internet).

Contribution of the above mention categorization is in the identification of different approaches that managers or owners have to ICT adoption and its strategic use. The companies from the forth and fifth groups are successfully developing and growing in the long term horizon. The research into the analyzed companies also investigated the drivers for purchase of ICT. It was typical in these companies that the adoption of ICT was not a given reason to achieve the strategic advantage but the most frequent reasons cited were:

- Pressure from the suppliers, customers and competitors.
- Influence of the specific area of business.
- Size of the organization.
- Implementation of different quality certificates.
- Knowledge of the employees or owners.

Also the majority of the specified factors contributed to decision-making about acceptance of information and communicati on technologies are:

- Technological factors (image of company, relative advantage, need of compatibility).
- Factors arising from the environment of the organization (competitive pressure of customers and suppliers, changes in the market place).
- Organizational factors (management, size of company, specialization of company, costs).
- Individual factors (knowledge of the manager, enthusiasm for ICT, innovation).

It is obvious that the factors mentioned are not all-inclusive and it is recognised that certain simplifications and judgments were applied. These analyzed factors can help to better understand the issues connected with ICT adoption. The next part of the chapter explains these factors in more detail.

Technological Impact

Majority of the bigger companies of the analyzed group that have 25% share of the foreign investment were forced to change their current ICT as a requirement for harmonization of information and communication systems with the parent organization. These organizations had no choice in the selection of an appropriate information system and its supplier; both were nominated by the parent organization. Also management of the information system was carried out by the owning company, usually abroad, with changes to the system, such as enrolling a new user, taking a longer time that might be expected.

Some of the organizations also begin to realize the benefits of electronic business (selling and buying on internet) and trying to keep abreast with competitors. Another reason for implemen-

tation of ICT is gradual aging and insufficient capacity of existing hardware and software in the organization.

The following Table 2 describes how many organizations use ICT for the purpose of communication within the company, with the customers, other options of electronic business, outsourcing, and training in ICT. The comparison brings significant contrast between utilization of electronic mail (used by 100% of all organizations of the analyzed sample) and other ICT applications, such as electronic supplying, acceptance of electronic purchase orders from customers and utilization of an intranet (internal web pages). The least utilized application is electronic supplying and outsourcing. While EDI type of communication with the partners is typically used by all organizations in the automotive industry, all bigger organizations have implemented standard ERP system and devote significant effort to training of the employees in ICT. In case of implementation of any other ICT application a number of companies do not consider further evaluation and monitoring of benefits of the chosen solution.

Impact of the Company's Environment

Very frequent reason for innovation or purchase of ICT is pressure from customers for mutual communication, in order to enable electronic data interchange (EDI). This is a way of electronic exchange of structured data (e.g. orders) on the basis of agreed standards between the information systems of individual business partners. Such pressure from the customers is common in both the automotive industry and between retail businesses. The reason for acceptance of EDI applications by the organizations is to prevent the loss of the current customers and also to attract new ones.

Another reason for innovation of ICT is the frequent need of SME to implement applications for bar code data capture. In these cases the

Table 2. Utilization of Individual Applications in the Analyzed Group of SME

Business area (number of companies)	E- mail	EDI	ERP	El. supply	Intra-net	Online orders	Out- sour-cing	ICT training	CAD
Manufacturing	4								3
Building	4		4					2	
Services	11			1	1				
Logistic	2	1	1						
ICT	6				4			6	
Automotive	3	3	3			3	1		

purchase of applications is typically focused on solving current problems and not on further ICT usage across other areas of the organization, such as in marketing or knowledge management.

Innovation

Innovation, flexibility and the ability to promptly respond to the wishes of customers are one of key advantages of small and middle-sized companies and simultaneously a condition of long-term competitiveness of an organization.

"Innovation represents invention multiplied by business creativeness, management, co-operation, customers, company culture, suppliers, competitors, systemic view, external conditions, natural environment and fortuitous factors."

This definition is based on a long-term research of Prof. Mulej (2007, p. 39) from University of Mariboro in Slovenia, who is intensively involved in the area of SME in the post-communist countries. This definition implies that some factors can not be influenced completely, such as the natural environment, but on the other hand it is necessary to respond to them in time. The following Table 3 specifies percentage share of investment into research in the turnover of the analyzed organizations (as at the end of year 2006). The table shows that especially small organizations do not possess sufficient finance for searching

for new innovative products or services. In this area universities and grant supported by European Union may significantly help.

Organizational Factors

Small companies are characterised by simple organizational structures. This may be considered a positive factor when implementing information systems. Another special advantage of this flat organizational structure is the relative simplicity in the analysis of the organization and the requirements to adjust the information system to the needs of the corporate strategy (if it has been defined) generated by the SME's owners and managers.

Since the Czech Republic has joined the EU there has been an increased need for small and middle-sized enterprises to obtain a variety of certificates (such as those for safety, quality and environmental waste management). As a result small organizations have been looking for ways to keep records of all necessary documents connected with production, customers, safety at work, etc. This demand can be solved by purchasing new ICT applications, but unfortunately they seem not to exploit their further possibilities. Another reason for ICT purchase is an increasing number of customers, growth of the organization and a need to have an overview of all orders. This was found to be especially so within small organizations of the analyzed group, an effort to decrease costs is

Table 3. Share of Investment into Research in the Turnover

Number of Employees in 2007	Share of investment in % 0 (number of companies)	Share of investment in % 0.1-1 (number of companies)	Share of investment in % 1.1-5 (number of companies)	Share of investment in % above 5 (number of companies)
1-9	4			
10-49	9	2		
50-199	3	3	4	
200-250			3	2
In total	16	5	7	2

another frequent reason for implementation or innovation of information and communication technologies.

Management in Small and Middle-Sized Enterprises

Success and competitiveness in SMEs are influenced by a combination of business capabilities of the owner, his visions and strategies, and the ways he chooses to reach his visions. Further important factors are also market impact, flexibility of the employees, ability to innovate, sufficient number of customers and independency in decision-making. Another situation we can see in the case of 7 organizations from the observed group that have 25% share of the foreign capital, is that the decision-making process is strongly driven by the parent organization's company abroad. These organizations, with foreign owners, have access to financial resources to purchase new manufacturing or information technologies or to undertake different marketing activities or training projects.

The way ICT is accepted in the company mainly depends also on previous training and experience of the managers and users. In small companies the training of employees is often insufficient and attitude towards information technologies is more sceptical. Expectations based on increased productivity are in general higher than expectations connected with improved effectiveness, and also higher than real results. However, unlike with large companies, in smaller SMEs the whole information system or its applications are often dependent on a single individual who often has to act in isolation.

Small companies are managed often only by their owner and strategic decisions are made more on intuition than analysis, and often depend on complex family and property-related matters. What makes SME managers invest in information and communication technologies or their innovation? There are numbers of reasons, but the following are the most frequent:

- Respect of the managers or owners to ICT.
- Financial situation.
- Pressure from the customers or suppliers.
- Implementation of certificates standards.
- Enthusiasm of the owner for new technologies.

The above specified reasons are also influenced by the style of management in an SME. As already mentioned in the previous section, the manager of the small or middle-sized company plays a key role in managing the enterprise, and has a much bigger personal influence as could be had in a large organization. This applies both to management and strategic planning. On the other hand, the managers or owners of SME do not prepare long-term strategic plans. The typical features of management in SME are following:

- **Management style**: Autocratic or directive.
- **Decision-making**: insufficient delegation of authority and insufficient purposeful planning, combination of strategic and operational decision-making, ad hoc decisions.
- **Time horizon**: Short-term.
- **Internal environment**: Absence of formal organization structure, management and information systems, high level of uncertainty, insufficiently shared information, absence of standard rules and procedures, usage of subjective criteria (missing formalized system), poor integration activities, poorly defined working procedures, roles and responsibilities.

Despite the above SME owners and managers have to solve problems equal to the problems of bigger companies often without the supporting of knowledge of associates from individual departments (such as ICT, marketing). That is why the managers make decisions in much wider context, i.e. on horizontal and vertical levels. This implies that information needed for decision-making by managers of SME is much more important than information for managers in large companies. As already mentioned, prosperity of SMEs is significantly influenced by experience, knowledge, relations and charisma of the owner or manager. The style of management is very important for success and growth of the company. We can observe several different managerial styles. For example authors Covin & Slevin (1990) describe relation between managing and utilization of ICT. They distinguish business and conservative managerial styles in connection with organic (open) and mechanistic (bureaucratic) structures of the organization. Individual organizations can be divided into the four following groups:

1. Type of organization specified by proactive way of management with respect to ICT and willingness to innovate ICT.

2. Type of organization with conservative style of management and approach to ICT.
3. Type of organization respecting ICT with open, flexible and communicative managerial style.
4. Type of organization with organic structure with respect to ICT.

Results from this research suggest that companies of third type can not be found among small organizations, but only amongst bigger ones. Companies at the edge between "2" and "4" types are typified by transfer to a new managerial style and innovation of information system, often caused by the new incoming management or by young members of the family having graduated university joining the business.

Companies typically demonstrating an enterprise style of management that are making changes in organizational structure are found between "1" and "2" types. Based on the research results these are often companies successfully utilizing information technologies thanks to which they have grown quite quickly (e.g. companies doing their business on the internet) and currently searching for ways to efficiently manage and run a growing company.

It is accepted that differences between management, organizational structure and the approach to ICT of individual companies have been simplified some way. Complexity in individual organizations with all factors and their impacts is much more complicated.

Investment into ICT

SME often tend to utilize information technologies only as a tool for data processing, not as a means of sharing knowledge or strategic advantage. During the implementation of ICT they do not consider their current organizational structure and possibilities of making changes. Furthermore they typically rely on short-term contracts with suppliers. Benefits of ICT for SME can be observed in the following areas:

- Higher productivity and performance of the company.
- Possibility of new organizational forms, e.g. development of business nets, participation in supply chains.
- Increased added value of the product or services.
- Entry to new markets.
- New products or services, changing business processes.
- Utilization of new business channels.
- Responding to new business activities of competitors.

Simultaneously, the advantage of SMEs compared with large companies may be higher flexibility during implementation of information technologies and during promoting of necessary changes arising from the implementation. ICT nowadays largely help small and middle-sized companies in traditional areas, such as warehouse management, payment procedures, administration, sales and improvement of post-sale services. Unfortunately, in real life ICT are not widely used in the areas such as marketing, purchasing and managing relations with customers. This is supported by insufficient knowledge of ICT capabilities and the inability to quantify benefits of ICT for the organization; this is often connected with the absence of corporate and information strategy.

It is necessary to acknowledge that SME usually do not have adequate number of appropriate and experienced employees. Information systems should be connected with a systematic approach to management and planning, while management of SME is based on ad hoc decision-making and short-term planning. Although prices of ICT in certain areas decrease, the costs for SME are still significant. As implementation of ICT often results in dramatic changes, it requires additional support

from management and adequate knowledge. Many owners of the companies are however busy with "the survival of the company" and do not invest time into such projects. They are also afraid of possible risk of failure of the project, do not wish to risk finance and can not see future advantage of ICT. That is why a number of methods were designed that aim to create supporting framework providing the management with guidelines how to proceed during planning of information systems or its innovation.

As financial capabilities of small and middle-sized companies are quite limited, the investment into ICT is often dependent on size of the organization (see following table 4). Despite of current options to utilize loans from European funds, SME are afraid of payback from such projects with managers or owners being risk averse in this context. This situation can be solved by software applications, such as "open source" (software with open source code means both the technical availability of the code and its legal availability or license, that enables users, upon meeting certain conditions, to utilize the source code and to modify it). This software is often freely accessible on the internet. Implementation of such software solutions is, however, demanding in terms of knowledge required by those implementing these systems which is usually absent in SME.

Frequent reason for purchase of ICT applications is to quickly respond to the needs of the customers (e.g. obtaining of bar codes of the goods, requirement for electronic communication, etc). Apart from that, the size of the organization plays an important role in utilization of ICT as development of the organization increases demand for administrative systems if the company is to remain cohesive.

Individual Factors

A frequent reason for innovation of ICT or purchase of new application is the cited dependency of the current system solely on one person who

Table 4. Share of Investment in ICT in Analyzed Organizations Comparing to the Turnover of Individual Organizations in % from the year 2006

Headcount	Number of companies with no investment in ICT	Number of companies with investment 0.1-1%	Number of companies with investment 1.1-5%	Number of companies with investment above 5%
1-9	4			
10-49	6	5		
50-199	4	2	2	1
200-250			4	1

possesses the necessary knowledge and experience. This is usually an employee who developed or implemented the application. Due to shortage of documentation and required compatibility with other applications; the owner recognizes this handicap and searches for alternative solutions and remove the dependency on a single associate.

Another reason for acceptance of ICT may be even enthusiasm and interest in information technologies on the part of the owner or his employees and the need for new and innovative services or products requiring new communication and selling channels utilizing ICT. An example may be also searching for competitive advantages in new areas, e.g. the need to achieve certification in areas such as environmental waste management and related search for new products and services corresponding to these certificates. Gaining certificates requires maintaining very precise documentation that it is not possible without ICT. Another additional reason may be searching for market gaps, the need to be in close contact with customers and to respond to their specific wishes.

Skills and Knowledge in ICT Area

Competitiveness of SME is strongly dependent on availability of company resources. This issue is explained by resource based theory which emphasizes those sources that bring important quality to a business that are hard replicate by its competitors. Such sources encompass especially

long-term process of training and education and the culture of the organization. For example, authors Peppard & Ward define in their article (2004) company sources as *"all assets, abilities, company attributes, organization processes, information and knowledge."*

Skills of the employees in the area of ICT are on higher level especially in bigger organizations, where ICT is commonly used. The following table 5 details results of a questionnaire inquiring about average level of ICT literacy. The questionnaires were distributed to two thirds of employees in each organization. The respondents were to evaluate their ability to recognize and formulate their information needs, their overview of information sources, ability to search for information using ICT, to analyze such information and apply it for solving specific realistic situations or specific tasks. In particular, the questionnaire ascertained the following skills:

- Minimum skills: e.g. sending an e-mail, searching for a file or information on internet.
- Ability to create a folder, search for and copy a file, re-name a file.
- Working skills when using application software.
- Work with office package (spreadsheet, word processor, exporting files).
- Installation of simple application to PC (such as anti-virus program).

Table 5. Average ICT Literacy of Employees in the Analyzed Group of Organization

Headcount in 2007	Average ICT literacy Level 1 (No. of companies)	Average ICT literacy Level 2 (No. of companies)	Average ICT literacy Level 3 (No. of companies)	Average ICT literacy Level 4 (No. of companies)	Average ICT literacy Level 5 (No. of companies)
1-9			1	3	
10-49	5	4	1	1	
50-199	4	6			
200-250	5				

The ability was ranked from 1 to 5 using Lickert's scale, where 1 = the best result and 5 = the worst result.

BARRIERS OF ICT ADOPTION IN SMALL AND MEDIUM-SIZED ENTERPRISES

The most significant barriers of ICT purchase are mainly internal issues of the organizations, such as shortage of associates with appropriate knowledge, financial and often family reasons.

Similarly to the division of individual factors contributing to acceptance of information and communication technologies, in the following section indicates the cited barriers to ICT adoption in SME. They are:

1. Technological barriers (problems of security, insufficient infrastructure).
2. Organizational barriers (management style, shortage of financial sources).
3. Barriers arising from the surrounding environment (insufficient knowledge of the market).
4. Individual barriers (Insufficient knowledge, personal relations in organization).

Technological Barriers

The biggest barrier of utilization of new information and communication technologies is, apart from insufficient infrastructure in the organization, the fear regarding security of internal data. This fear is sometimes a reason for non purchase of ICT from a well-established provider. Some organizations consequently try to design such applications internally although this solution is not always successful. The employees working on this task often lack sufficient knowledge and experience and also unable to document their solution, which can bring some problems in the future. Another barrier may be caused by fear from financial demand but this can be resolved by purchase of application information services using an external supplier.

Decision-Making in SME

One of significant barriers of ICT acceptance in small and middle-sized companies is resistance to organizational changes, especially in connection with older managers or owners. Another barrier may be missing long-term corporate strategy often omitted due to shortage of long-term orders and stable customers. Companies frequently have to respond quickly to individual demands of random customers and do not consider any long-term corporate strategy. That is why planning in such organizations is focused on "sole survival" and on short-term activities. The managers or owners of SME make their decisions on the basis of current need and the current situation. Consequently management processes are very sensitive to market behavior, changing external conditions and market trends.

Time horizon of decision-making in SME is typically short-term, usually in a form of respond to specific event rather than targeted assumptions. Low level of detailed planning often causes issues during implementation and utilization of information systems. Moreover, only a small percentage of leaders of small companies utilize different methods of forecast, financial analysis, and project management. These results are also supported by a study (Ghobadian & Oregon, 2006) analyzing 276 small and middle-sized companies in England. Decision-making process of the managers is rather intuitive, based on instinctive decisions and less dependent on formal models of decision-making. They tend not to pass information and not to delegate decision-making authorities to their inferiors. They are often the only people in the company who have the authority, responsibility and access to the information necessary for identifying business opportunities including utilization of information technologies for strategic and competitive purposes.

Surrounding Environment

Barrier preventing wider acceptance of ICT in small and medium-sized companies is furthermore influenced by an inability to apply ICT in relations with customers and suppliers. The fact that SME do not influence their business-specific surrounding environment, but they are influenced by it and particularly by their customers is an important issue.

Individual Factors

One of the main barriers preventing acceptance of ICT, especially by small organizations is knowledge and skills regarding information technologies. Small companies do not have ICT departments (except for organizations with higher number of employees in the analyzed sample) and rely on either external consultants or friends. A role of such a consultant is not always fully understood which leads to a number of mutual misunderstandings during

specification, purchase and implementation of ICT applications. This problem is connected to a missing information strategy and as previously mentioned an insufficient knowledge of ICT on the part of the owner or manager of the organization. According to this research where the analyzed sample were often using employing less experienced students, owners typically searched for simple and cheap solutions using their own resources, relatives or friends. Based on such solution different problems connected with lack of experience and specific knowledge arise. These solutions do not bring expected benefits. It is often only a "quick fix" and unfortunately a short-term solution of a given issue forgetting about further possibilities of utilization of ICT. This is connected with short-term planning of the organizations. ICT consequently can not contribute to increased competitiveness and becomes only a tool for cost decrease and minimization of administrative burden.

In order to remove this barrier, universities may contribute high-quality knowledge to managers and owners of SME by providing education and training in the area of management and ICT. Other option would be utilization of specific ICT knowledge and skills in a co-operation with other organizations or business networks.

RECOMMENDATIONS AND TRENDS

Technology availability has increased dramatically during the past ten years as a part of the internet phenomenon, mobile applications and the consumer electronics movement. The simplicity of technology solutions has provided users with the ability to make their own choices rather than rely on ICT staff. Now, personal e-mail packages, instant messaging, laptop computers, mobile devices, personal IP (internet protocol) based telephony (Skype) and even personal networking and storage preferences are becoming commonplace.

Software as a service (from external supplier) is becoming a viable option which supports wider ICT adoption in SME. This option removes the need for trained specialists and brings cost-saving. Its benefit is comparably quick implementation, professional technical support and certainty of high-quality backup of the data. Wide implementation of this option now is prevented especially by SME not fully trusting external data storage and low levels of trust in outsource providers and suspicions regarding risk of their bankruptcy.

The growing presence of **open source software** cannot be ignored, so the use of open-source technology will become a common place strategy in more and more organizations. A big advantage of this solution is the minimal level of investment. But on the other hand it requires good ICT knowledge and experience to be had by employees.

Information and communication technology as a **strategic tool** is one of the most significant impacts on enterprise in the near future and it does not matter whether they are big or small. Companies have to think about the using this strategic factor in their corporate strategies if they want to be competitive. These strategies will have to integrate the communication with the customers and their data with product information as a part of an information strategy. Also the communication and sharing of knowledge inside company is more and more important and plays a key role in competitive strategies.

Organizations need to quickly respond to consistently changing conditions, innovation of products and services, which requires employees observing new trends, technologies to be able to improve their knowledge. Such organizations are classified **as learning or intelligent organizations**. These learning organizations (Schwaninger, 2006, p.7):

- Are able to adapt to changing conditions.
- Influence and are able to change their environment.

- Contribute to development of the whole organization.

It does not mean only learning new things, but also to be able to learn from mistakes, in order to prevent re-occurrence of the mistakes. That is why the experience and knowledge needs to be shared across the organization and readily available to all employees. Again appropriate use of ICT is important.

CONCLUSION

SME are exposed to high competitive pressure. When they wish to survive the current business competition, they have to search for new business opportunities. This effort has to be significantly supported by information and communication technologies. But the implementation of ICT can cause a number of issues for SME, such as insufficient financial sources, lack of experience with ICT and insufficient knowledge and skills in the area of computer literacy of employees. That is why the most frequent purpose of implementation of ICT in SME is, as supported by this research, is on survival of the organization in its competitive environment. Apart from that, adoption of ICT in the organizations is strongly influenced by the managerial style of the owner or manager. That is why motivation to purchase and implementation of ICT is also connected to clarification of ownership relations and the authority of individual owners.

Successful performance of SMEs in the business environment and their consequent development is influenced by the ability of the organization to respond flexibly to customers demand and by the ability to innovate in products or services. That is why the owner or manager should from all of the searched groups of companies consistently re-evaluate and search for appropriate corporate strategy, to keep developing himself and his em-

Figure 1. Relation between business and information strategy

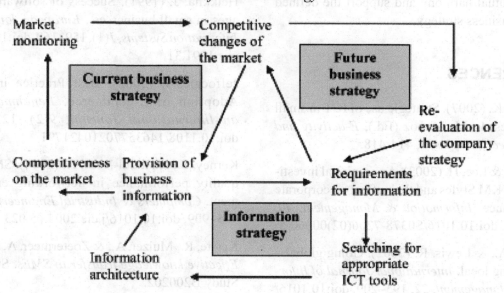

ployees, monitor competitive environment of the market and be familiar with demand and wishes of customers. This consistently repeated process is illustrated by the following Figure 1. All specified activities require the support of adequate tools are currently available within the domain of information and communication technologies.

For ICT to become one of the tools of competitive advantage, organizations will have to have a clear vision of the future and how to reach it. Current information and communication technologies enable a whole range of new business opportunities and are consistently upgraded but especially for the owners of SME it is not easy to keep abreast. Adoption of ICT is connected with higher investment demands that often create barriers to wider acceptance of ICT in small and middle-sized enterprises. Another issue may be also the fact that financial benefit and payback of ICT is not easily quantifiable without specific knowledge.

Current business entities are forced to consistently improve their products and services. They have to utilize information and communication technologies and modern management methods.

This is the only way they can succeed in such competitive environments. Companies have to search for appropriate business strategies using an approach that reflects its own characteristics and to use as many benefits of ICT in the proposed business strategy as possible. Organizations are more and more connected with their suppliers and customers but yet need not loose their legal identity. They have their own culture, managerial style, they search for their own business strategies and should seek to share management decisions with their co-operating partners and customers.

Managers or owners of SME are, however, often afraid of organizational and financial demand of implementation of ICT. This fear can be prevented by adequate strategic planning and preparation. From the successfully growing companies we analyzed we can see the **importance of business, information and knowledge strategy**. Without articulation of these strategies companies will find it difficult to find their way in the current business environment. These strategies have to be followed by other supporting strategies, i.e. marketing, finance and human resources. It is highly important that even those supporting strategies are in mutual harmony and support the defined global business strategy.

REFERENCES

Antlová, K. (2007). Strategic use of ICT in small businesses. In M. Munoz (Ed.), *E-activity and leading technologies*, 3, 414-418.

Choi, B., & Lee, H. (2003). An empirical investigation of KM Styles and their effect on corporate performance. *Information & Management, 40*, 403–417. doi:10.1016/S0378-7206(02)00060-5

Cocrill, A., & Lewis, R. (2002). Going global – Remaining local. *International Journal of Information Management, 22*, 195–209. doi:10.1016/S0268-4012(02)00005-1

Covin, J. G., & Slevin, D. P. (1990). Juggling entrepreneurial style and organizational structure. *Sloan Management Review*, 43–53.

Craig, A., & Annear, J. (2003). A framework for the adoption of ICT and security technologies by SMEs. *16th Conference Small Entrerprise Association of Australia*, Ballarat.

E-Business Indicators. (2007). *A pocket- book.*

Gemino, A., Mackay, N., & Reich, B. H. (2006). Executive decision about ICT adoption in SME. *Journal of Information Technology Management, 17*(1).

Ghobadian, A., & Oregan, N. (2006). The impact of ownership on small firm behavior performance. *International Small Business Journal, 24*(6), 555–586. doi:10.1177/0266242606069267

Greiner, L. E. (1972). Evolution and revolution as organisations grow. *Harvard Business Review*, July/August, 37-46. Chau, S.B., & Turner, P. (2002). A four phase model of EC business transformation amongst SME. In *Proceedings of the 12th Autralasian Conference on Information Systems,* Australia.

Heikkila, J. (1991). Success of software packages in small businesses . *European Journal of Information Systems, 1*(1), 159–169. doi:10.1057/ejis.1991.31

Jeffocate, J. (2002). Best Practice in SME Adoption of E-commerce. *Benchmarking: an International Journal, 9*(2), 122–132. doi:10.1108/14635770210421791

Kerney, S., & Abdul-Nour, G. (2004). SME and quality performance in networking environment. *Computers & Industrial Engineering, 46*, 905–909. doi:10.1016/j.cie.2004.05.023

Kerste, R., Muizer, A., & Zoetermeer, A. (2002). *Effective knowledge transfer to SMEs.* Strategic Study B200202.

Levy, M., & Powell, P. (2000). Information strategy for SME: An organizational perspective. *The Journal of Strategic Information Systems, 9*, 63–84. doi:10.1016/S0963-8687(00)00028-7

Levy, M., & Powell, P. (2005). *Strategies for growth in SMEs.* Oxford: Butterworth Heinemann.

Levy, M., Powell, P., & Yetton, P. (2002). The dynamics of SME information systems. *Small Business Economics, 19*, 341–354. doi:10.1023/A:1019654030019

Martin, L. M., & Matlay, H. (2001). Approaches to promoting ICT in SME. *Internet Research: Electronic Network Applications and Policy, 11*(5), 399–410. doi:10.1108/EUM0000000006118

Mulej, M., & Potocan, V. (2007). *Transition into an innovative enterprise.* University of Maribor, Slovenian.

Nolan, R. L. (1979). Managing the crises in data processing. *Harvard Business Review.*

OH, W., & Pinsonneault, A. (2007). On the assessment of the strategic value of information technologies. *MIS Quarterly, 31*(2), 239–265.

Peppard, J., & Ward, J. (2004). Beyond strategic information systems: Towards an IS capability. *The Journal of Strategic Information Systems, 13*, 167–194. doi:10.1016/j.jsis.2004.02.002

Powell, P., Levy, M., & Duhan, S. (2001). Information system strategies in knowledge-based SMEs. *European Journal of Information Systems, 10*, 25–40. doi:10.1057/palgrave.ejis.3000379

Rivard, S., Raymond, L., & Verreault, D. (2005). Resource-based view and competitive strategy. *The Journal of Strategic Information Systems, 20*, 1–22.

Schwaninger, M. (2006). *Intelligent organizations*. Berlin: Springer.

Tetteh, E., & Burn, J. (2001). Global strategies for SME. *Logistic Information Management, 14*(1), 171–180. doi:10.1108/09576050110363202

Valkokari, K., & Helander, N. (2007). Knowledge management in different types of strategic SME network. [f]. *Management Research News, 30*(7), 597–608. doi:10.1108/01409170710773724

Section 4
Critical Success Factors and Case Studies

Chapter 20
Process Re-Engineering Success in Small and Medium Sized Enterprises

Jeffrey Chang
London South Bank University, UK

Margi Levy
University of Warwick, UK

Philip Powell
University of Bath, UK and University of Groningen, The Netherlands

ABSTRACT

The factors that lead to business process re-engineering (BPR) success in small and medium-sized enterprises (SMEs) are not clearly understood. This article reviews the main contributing factors to BPR success using a framework that considers culture, structure, technology and resource. Eight Taiwanese case studies are used to explore issues contributing to, or impeding, successful process re-engineering in small firms. The analysis shows that BPR success is empowered by innovation, employee empowerment, top management commitment and strategic direction and is dependent upon customer relations, IS involvement and financial resources.

INTRODUCTION

Competition and globalization have led enterprises to restructure to focus on managing change. Business process re-engineering (BPR) is an ap-

proach to business transformation that emphasizes customer-driven, process-oriented management practice, often enabled by information technology (IT). Raymond et al (1998) state that the literature focuses on BPR in large firms and pose the question as to whether BPR success factors are the same for small and medium sized enterprises (SMEs) (firms with fewer than 250 employees SBS, [2003]) as for large enterprises.

This paper investigates BPR to identify the success and failure factors of BPR in small firms. The nature of BPR is briefly outlined. Chang and Powell's (1998) framework which explores BPR in SMEs is adapted to focus in more detail on culture, technology, structure and resources. Using a case approach, the research explores the BPR response of eight Taiwanese firms. This leads to underststanding of the different success and failure factors for BPR in SMEs A revised model for successful BPR in SMEs is then presented and the implications for theory and practice are discussed.

NATURE OF BPR

BPR is 'radical redesign of business processes to achieve dramatic improvements on critical measures of performance' (Hammer, 1990). BPR emphasizes horizontal integration that crosses organizational boundaries - the analysis and design of work-flows and processes within and between organizations (Davenport, 1993). The main elements of BPR are fundamental work process redesign, adding value to final customers, integration of cross-functional specialization, and exploitation of IT. The challenges of BPR initiatives are both technical and socio-cultural. It is technically problematic to develop radical process improvements. The socio-cultural challenge is in dealing with people's reactions to the likely serious organizational changes required (Reijers & Mansar, 2005; Sarker et al., 2006).

Many factors are inherent in successful BPR. First, top management commitment is important to ensure the initiative is maintained and focused. Second, re-engineering focuses on providing customers with greater value (Cameron & Braiden, 2004). Third, re-engineering places a major em-

phasis on employees and their role in resolving problems (Larsen & Myers, 1999). Process improvement involves changes to jobs and the social structure to increase motivation, reduce stress and improve performance by empowerment (Wastell et al., 1994). Fourth, IT is an *enabler* in creating and maintaining flexible business networks (Tinnila, 1995). Finally, a BPR strategy is key, incorporating critical inputs from both corporate and IT planning (Teng et al., 1994; Talwar, 1993). However, as BPR involves changing the firm's competences, it is more likely to be successful if it is emergent, benefiting from organizational learning (Craig & Yetton, 1997).

BPR in SMEs

One of the few BPR studies in SMEs indicates that firms benefit if they respect the underlying principles of BPR. In particular, SMEs need to review business processes around customer requirements using IT more innovatively. Top management commitment and a methodological approach are essential (Ursic et al., 2005). Involvement from employees is also beneficial (Raymond et al., 1998). These principles are evident in Chang and Powell's (1998) SME BPR framework (Figure 1). This framework identifies four key criteria that affect SME BPR success: culture, structure, resources and technology.

Culture: BPR does not work without profound cultural change as it emphasizes leadership, teamwork, empowerment, entrepreneurship and risk-taking (Tersine et al., 1997; Ursic et al., 2005). SMEs are often perceived as more innovative than larger firms (Carrier, 1995) and employees are often given operational responsibility (Brady & Voss, 1995). Decision-making in SMEs is often dominated by the CEO: this may aid or hinder re-engineering.

Structure: Small businesses encourage team and cross-functional orientations (Kinni, 1995). The lack of bureaucracy makes for efficient and informal internal communication networks to manage processes. SMEs are able to respond readily to changing customers' needs. Due to the lack of management layers, small businesses are closer to their customers (Brady & Voss, 1995). Thus, SMEs should be well positioned for re-engineering with their focus on process.

Resources: Two serious problems SMEs face when trying to implement quality management are the owner's lack of business experience and a lack of financial and human resources which may restrict growth (Haksaver, 1996; Witherill & Kolak, 1996). Thus, while survival is the first concern in SMEs, financial constraints may inhibit SMEs undertaking BPR.

Technology: IT infrastructure can be a significant enabler of, or barrier to, the practical options available to planning and changing processes for BPR (Grover et al., 1993). Most re-engineering efforts are technology-driven, with the role of IT changing from producing data to integrating new technologies and assisting people as independent information gatherers (Ribbler, 1996). However, SMEs are unlikely to employ IT staff, (information systems) IS skills are limited and IS investment is often seen as a necessary evil.

This analysis leads to the research question: *what factors enable or inhibit BPR success in SMEs?*

RESEARCH APPROACH

There is little previous research available to investigate BPR success or failure factors. This research is therefore exploratory. Case studies are a powerful method for conducting exploratory research, as it is possible to pose reflective questions. Also, case research is effective when theory is relatively under-developed (Eisenhardt, 1989). Particularly, when the research boundaries are unclear, there is a need to investigate the issue within a real life context, drawing on multiple views (Yin, 1994). Multiple cases ensure that common patterns are identified rather than being

generalized from what might be chance occurrences (Eisenhardt, 1989).

Research Background

In Taiwan, SMEs constitute 95% of all enterprises (Lee & Chen, 1992). Taiwanese SMEs are confronting dramatic environmental changes. Export-oriented SMEs are restricted to labour-intensive and mature-technology industries that constrain technology upgrading, enlarging operations and marketing (Wu & Chou, 1992). Labour shortages and rising wages have led to SMEs losing competitiveness. Financial problems are a major obstacle. Macro-environmental transition has forced SMEs to investigate their internal operations and management. Hence, approaches such as BPR have become popular.

Eight cases are considered (Table 1). In order to mitigate contextual bias, the cases include four SMEs in manufacturing and four in services. Three firms are small and five are medium-sized. Data was gathered through semi-structured interviews with the CEO/management team from each SME. SMEs' perceived BPR satisfaction is a determinant for BPR success. Interview questions were developed based on the themes presented in the BPR framework (Figure 1). SMEs' perceived BPR satisfaction is a surrogate for BPR success or failure. For each sector, two 'successful' and two 'failure' cases are selected to compare success and failure factors.

Most of the case SMEs are seeking to grow by business expansion. For example, Telecoms Supplier is enlarging its sales division to diversify into new markets with new products. Supersonic Machinery is developing technology to manufacture semiconductors. In contrast, Automatic Assembling and Freight Shipping tend to have steady orders and loyal clients. A feature of the SMEs is that their purpose in adopting BPR derives from a desire either to improve efficiency or to enhance capacities, rather than from a 'crisis situation' (Kinni, 1995) (Table 2).

Table 1. Characteristics of BPR case firms

Cases	Employees	BPR Outcome	Industry	Strategy	Market	Sub-contract
Automatic Assembling	10	Success	Manufacturing	Market Segmentation	Steady	Yes
Supersonic Machinery	40	Success	Manufacturing	Diversification	Growing	Yes
Geodetic Surveying	15	Success	Service	Expansion	Steady	No
Freight Shipping	150	Success	Service	Market penetration	Competitive	No
Shoes Trading	100	Failure	Manufacturing	Market penetration	Growing	Yes
Telecoms Supplier	300	Failure	Manufacturing	Expansion	Competitive	No
Financial Institution	200	Failure	Service	Market Development	Steady	No
Retail Grocer	200	Failure	Service	Product develop	Competitive	No

CASE ANALYSIS

Case findings are organized around four criteria: structure, culture, resources, technology (see Figure 1). The analysis investigates success/failure factors that influence BPR performance. Interview data are analysed to determine interviewee perspectives. Table 3 summarizes the findings which are discussed in detail below.

Culture

Owner-led SMEs with ambitious strategies that focus on product innovation and empowering employees are more likely to benefit from BPR than those with limited top management commitment or an autocratic management style with little top-down communication.

Innovation is primarily seen in rapid growth firms. In these firms product innovation takes precedence over process innovation. Since the rapid growth case firms are technology-oriented, use of the latest IT tools and applications to support product innovation is common supporting Wind and West's (1991) observation that innovation is fostered in decentralised, integrated, informal organizations. The cases suggest that innovation

is positively correlated with a team-based orientation. For example, Retail Grocer encouraged 'unconventional ideas' among project members when creating the firm's new image.

Empowering employees is recognized as critical for successful BPR (Janson, 1993; Larsen & Myers, 1999). Higher employee autonomy is more likely in decentralised SMEs, such as Automatic Assembling and Supersonic Machinery. These firms demonstrate that small businesses operate as an empowered team (Kinni, 1995) where knowledge workers are involved in decisions and product discussion.

Top management commitment, coupled with good top-down communication, is considered by all SMEs as the most critical factor in BPR success (Stevenson, 1993; McKeown & Philip, 2003), highlighting the need for direct CEO involvement. Automatic Assembling represents a 'top-down' approach to BPR. The owner-manager oversees several functions - personnel, finance and accounting. His enthusiastic involvement ensured the re-engineering project encountered few difficulties. Such direct involvement tends to occur in smaller firms where structures are less formal and communication lines shorter. In Geodetic Surveying the owner participated in

Table 2. Purpose of BPR in case firms

Purpose of BPR	Case Firms	Number
Process Improvement	All Firms	8
Cost Reduction	Telecoms Supplier, Retail Grocer, Shoe Trading	3
Customer Satisfaction	Supersonic Machinery, Automatic Assembling, Freight Shipping, Financial Institution	4
Quality	Geodetic Survey, Freight Shipping, Financial Institution	3

Figure 1. BPR Framework for SMEs (adapted from Chang & Powell 1998)

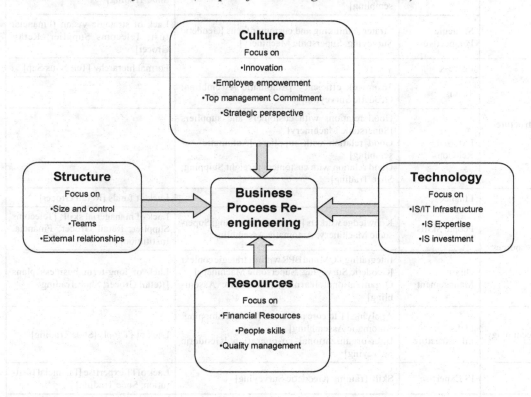

building its client network which was instrumental in BPR success.

The only BPR initiative that was not CEO-led was Telecoms Suppliers, it derived from departmental managers. When the R&D director was asked about the owner's attitude to BPR, he replied: *'We're thinking some good ideas, but the owner's just not interested'*. Limited top management support meant they could not find sufficient financial backup to launch process change.

A *strategic perspective* tends to be lacking in many SMEs. Re-engineering firms' core processes into strategic capabilities increases the chances of BPR success (Wastell et al., 1994; Hale & Cragg, 1996). Five case firms are re-engineering their core processes, which suggests some recognition of the need for strategic thinking. For example, Geodetic Surveying's firm-client interface is largely involved with customer services and product development. Automatic Assembling's integrated IS comprises three major processes: ordering, client/

Table 3. Success and failure factors for BPR

Criterion	Elements	Success factors	Failure factors
Culture	Innovation	Product innovation [Supersonic Mach] Innovative environment [Retail Grocer]	
	Empowering Employees	High employee autonomy [Geodetic Surveying; Supersonic Machinery; Automatic Assembling]	Autocratic management style [Financial Institution; Shoe Trading]
	Top Management Commitment	Top-down approach [all cases expect Telecoms Supplier] Direct involvement [Geodetic Surveying; Supersonic Machinery; Automatic Assembling] Good top-down communication [Automatic Assembling]	Lack of management support [Telecoms Suppliers] Poor top-down communication [Retail Grocer; Financial Institution; Shoe Trading]
	Strategic Perspective	Strategic thinking and customer focus [Geodetic Surveying; Supersonic Machinery]	Lack of strategic vision [Financial Inst; Telecoms Supplier; Retail Grocer]
Structure	Process		Formal hierarchy [Telecoms Sup]
	Teams	Teamwork efficiency [Automatic Assembling; Geodetic Surveying]	
	External Relations	Good relations with customers and suppliers [Supersonic Machinery] Good relation with suppliers [Automatic Assembling] Good relation with customers [Freight Shipping; Shoe Trading]	
Resources	Finance		Lack of funds [Retail Grocer]
	People Skills	Knowledge workers [Geodetic Surveying; Supersonic Machinery; Automatic Assembling]	Lack of managerial skills [Telecoms Supplier; Retail Grocer; Financial Institution]
	Quality Management	Integrating TQM and BPR within strategic context [Geodetic Surveying; Supersonic Machinery] Organizational learning [Automatic Assembling]	Lack of long-term business plans [Retail Grocer; Shoe Trading
Technology	IT/IS infrastructure	Applying IT to core processes [Freight Shipping; Automatic Assembling] Inter-organizational co-operation [Geodetic Surveying]	Lack of IT tools [Shoe Trading]
	IS Expertise	Skill Training [Geodetic Surveying]	Lack of IT expertise [Financial Institution; Shoe Trading]
	IS Investment	High IT spending [Geodetic Surveying]	Lack of funds for IT investment [Retail Grocer]

supplier database and manufacturing. Most of the unsuccessful cases demonstrate a lack of strategic vision. For example, Telecoms Supplier focused on distribution channel expansion and improving sales network efficiency rather than competition issues. Retail Grocer focused on business image, ignoring quality issues. They lost competitive advantage due to a focus on short-term pay-off and failure to implement continuous process change. Shoe Trading's BPR, which focused on process improvement, was also limited. They put this down to their lack of competitive power due to their position as a sub-contractor.

Similarly, Financial Institution launched its Internet banking without considering client resistance about security concerns. The on-line banking system was created by external IT support without careful planning and management backup. The Investment Manager recalls: *'The initial idea was to reduce the workload of operators and to simplify the banking procedures. Clients only need to install the software provided and key in their usernames and passwords. We believed this was the trend of future banking. However, there aren't many people taking advantage of this facility. One reason is that customers are suspicious about this due to security concerns'.* A similar situation is seen at Telecoms Suppliers. The R&D director notes: *'We did not consider the feasibility of the on-line ordering system while creating our web site. Because of the nature of our products, customers are used to buying with sales staff's assistance'.*

Structure

The cases show that the structural factors that influence BPR success are team-working and effective external relations. However, formal hierarchies inhibit success.

Team-based operations bring greater involvement and motivation (Sellers, 1997). These are more likely in smaller businesses, e.g. Automatic Assembling and Geodetic Surveying due to their decentralised structure and shorter lines of communication. In SMEs, a major benefit from team-based operations is to bring greater involvement, increased motivation and communication, and enhanced job performance. The owner of Geodetic Surveying believes: *'All our employees are professionals. They are talented and responsible. There's only about 15 of us and we work as a team. We respect each other and this is the best way to get things done. I never feel superior because I am the boss'.*

The importance of *External relations* is seen with customers and suppliers. Unusually for SMEs, which usually cluster near customers (Brady & Voss, 1995), most of the case firms operate internationally. For example, Supersonic

Machinery sells in SE Asia. Shoe Trading's clients are US and Australian. Thus, using IT as an enabler of re-engineering is likely to be beneficial. Cross-functional integration can be expanded to inter-organizational co-operation (Davidow & Malone, 1992). For example, the focus of Shoe Trading's BPR was improving communication with its 150 contracted manufacturers while building up relationships with foreign clients to secure regular orders.

Geodetic Surveying built an integrated IS with a customer interface to facilitate mutual information sharing, technical support and the latest information about surveying tools. Their clients, mainly civil-engineers, have similar IT infrastructure. Otherwise, costs for establishing such a network would be prohibitive. When asked how they use IT inter-organizationally, the owner replied: *'We are one of the few firms that use computers in geodetic surveying. It's different from traditional manual drawing and the quality is significantly improved. Recently we've built a network system linking to our clients' computers. This on-line network saves time and costs'.*

Automatic Assembling is subcontracted to several major clients while at the same time acting as a subcontractor for about 50 satellite manufacturers. Their re-engineering project is designed to reduce the complexity of business processes by integrating its ordering system, production line and supplier/clients databases. A senior technician describes their current relations with clients/customers/contractors: *'We have been trying to maintain a sound relationship with our clients and down-stream satellite plants. And we're at an advantage of being located in an industrial park where we get support from other SMEs, such as sharing materials and facilities. With different market differentiation/segmentation, we have good relationship with other firms in the industry. There is no malicious competition'.*

The cases reinforce the view that strategic behaviour is the main reason for building relations. Geodetic Surveying's client-oriented interface and Automatic Assembling's integrated ordering system are related to their core processes.

The cases show that *size and control*, particularly in more formal and hierarchical structures may inhibit BPR. This occurs in larger firms, such as Telecoms Supplier, where the main purpose of BPR is to de-emphasize divisions of labour to streamline processes and reduce administrative costs. A reason for this is that processes in SMEs are often lean and owners may not accept the need to change, even within a BPR exercise.

Resources

Success factors in the cases include skilled staff, an emphasis on quality management, and recognition of the value of organizational learning. Failure factors are primarily limited financial resources, limited managerial skills and short term strategic planning.

Limited capital *financial resources* are a major constraint on SMEs' BPR efforts. Financial deficiency restricted Shoe Trading and Retail Grocer from advanced use of IT for functional integration and inter-organisational linkage. Retail Grocer's Planning Manager notes: *'The main reason for adopting BPR was to reduce administrative costs and increase internal efficiency. The owner is not good at financial planning. We had no idea about the return on investment. It's not easy to get the capital we need. So we haven't even gone half-way though our BPR project. Survival is more important'.*

The cases suggest that the amount SMEs spend on IT for BPR depends on the owner-manager's perceived benefits to individuals and the firm (Cragg & King, 1993). For example, the use of IT for BPR at Geodetic Surveying results from the owner's awareness of technological advances enabling better client service.

People skills are important in re-engineering success. This is seen in case firms that are technology-oriented and employ skilled staff (Geodetic Surveying, Supersonic Machinery and Automatic

Assembling). However, limited people skills, particularly poor IT understanding, also restrict success. The Design Manager from Shoe Trading states: *'We built a web site on which the photos of our latest designs are exhibited. However, because of security concerns, on-line ordering has not been feasible. The designers are still drawing manually, which takes much longer, but they seem to be happy with what they are doing.. Although we have installed 3D software that aids design, few people are able to use it'*

SMEs' managerial skills are often limited and may not provide support for radical process change. For example, Shoe Trading had difficulties in retaining its talented designers. The Design Manager describes this it: *'Since the owner started this re-engineering programme, we have felt terribly insecure about everything. You never know... when you'll be sacked. You suspect everybody is seeking new employment. The owner never told us...even though the business condition hasn't been that bad'.*

Quality management is seen by the case firms as important to demonstrate the provision of excellent service to customers. Quality management is only of value when it contributes to organizational learning (Levy et al., 1999). Automatic Assembling is an example of empowering and training employees to create ownership and develop the knowledge base. A senior technician stated: *'We care very much about the process by which new employees learn from the senior technicians. We can't afford lots of time for training. Thanks to IT, we are now able to standardize our products. This is the most efficient way to accumulate our experiences and knowledge. It saves time and simplifies the ordering process'.*

The lack of strategic direction in most case firms limits the benefits from quality initiatives. Retail Grocer had difficulty sustaining their initial benefits from re-engineering and failed to deliver 'core value' to their customers due largely to a lack of strategic vision and long-term business plans. Similarly, the absence of a BPR plan led to Shoe Trading being unable to deal with the consequences of radical process change. A major problem was its inability to retain the firm's main designers since it could not provide sufficient support and establish a proper reward system to deal with workload.

Technology

In growing SMEs, IT is most likely to be applied to product development, usually coupled with R&D. Innovation in SMEs is significantly related to team-based operations and efficiency supported by a good IT infrastructure. Concomitant are sufficient IS skills in the firm. The role of IT in BPR is illustrated by the general manager from Supersonic Machinery: *'BPR to us is not merely process improvement. With our IT professionals, we are trying to broaden our business services, which is consistent with our current policy of differentiation. It allows us to redefine our business direction and customer target'*.

An effective *IS/IT infrastructure* plays an important supportive role as a tool in eliminating time and distance for process integration (Carr & Johansson, 1995). The Internet is extensively used for linking firms with customers, suppliers and others. The case firms use IT widely for process integration and product innovation. Applications, such as spreadsheets, databases, and document imaging for inter-organizational linkage are evident.

Automatic Assembling combined three major functions: ordering system, clients/supplier databases, and production lines. This was achieved by several IT tools such as spreadsheets and workflow software. These tools have increased speed and flexibility in customized production and improved customer satisfaction through efficient communication with customers and satellite manufacturers. A senior technician explains: *'All the contracted down-streamed plants and customers are detailed in a database and connected to the ordering system in which all the firm's products* *are standardised and numbered. This simplifies the ordering process and results in increased flexibility in catering for customers' needs'*.

However, a lack of IT tools, as in Financial Institution and Shoe Trading, inhibits functional integration. Similarly, the use of non-standardized IT platforms between Supersonic Machinery and its 200 contracted satellite firms demonstrates an obstacle to successful implementation.

IS Expertise is often limited in SMEs, with few in-house experts able to undertake new developments (Ferrell, 1996). Financial Institution sought assistance from consultants due to a lack of IT skills, but relying too much on external IT vendors resulted in a loss of control.

IS investment is often constrained by limited finances, as in Retail Grocer. The cases reinforce that IT investment should be aligned with firms' strategic IT planning and business strategy. For example, investment in IT for Internet banking at Financial Institution was suggested by consultants rather than the firm, only to reveal that the time and costs could not be justified.

ISSUES FOR MANAGEMENT

SMEs need to examine whether they are culturally and structurally ready for re-engineering. Specifically, re-engineering requires a strong commitment from owner-managers since they play a decisive role in determining strategic direction. Employee motivation and empowerment is essential to effective internal communication and responsiveness to customers. Indeed, this is supported by Herzog et al. (2007) in a study of Slovenian firms which argues that employee empowerment is vital for BPR success. Training is useful in enhancing managerial knowledge as well as inter-functional work skills. The IS function has to be repositioned to facilitate BPR by investing in IT tools and provide required end-user skills. Change issues, such as resistance and lack of required skills need to be managed strategically at two levels: organizational and technological. This is to ensure that re-engineering efforts are implemented as planned and assessed by new performance standards and targets. Conducting pilots and measuring results regularly may significantly increase efficiency.

Despite much debate on whether IT is a necessity for BPR, this research shows the powerful potential of IT in re-engineering. The role of IT/IS has evolved from automating existing outdated processes to providing firms with an array of opportunities by shortening communication lines and eliminating space and time. This is achieved, in essence, by the innovative use of IT. Alignment of IT strategy and BPR strategy derived from a strategic vision is critical. This is to ensure that IT investment and any required end-user training can be evaluated by internal and external customers, or 'process outputs,' rather than by functional performance or cost savings. Given limited financial and human resources, the knowledge and experiences accumulated from the innovative use of IT and the efforts of R&D provide a valuable basis for continuous process improvement.

ISSUES FOR RESEARCH

Process re-engineering was introduced as requiring top management support, customer focus, IT, employee empowerment and strategic direction. The cases demonstrate that the main issues for success in BPR for SMEs are the strategic direction of the firm, top management commitment and external relations with customers.

The cases suggest that those SMEs with a positive attitude to risk are more likely to benefit from BPR. SMEs tend to engage in more incremental process change methods to cope with reality rather than adopting a radical approach as recommended by many BPR proponents (Johansson et al., 1993). However, strong commitment from top management is essential. In keeping with Tushman et al. (1986), the cases indicate that direct involvement is strongly related to strategic control and project efficiency. Lack of owner support or an autocratic style, as in Financial Institution and Shoe Trading, can hinder re-engineering. However, size and control is possibly less relevant due to SMEs' inherent flexibility. In contrast, greater success is found where top management commitment extends to empowering employees to take greater

Figure 2. Revised Model for BPR in SMEs

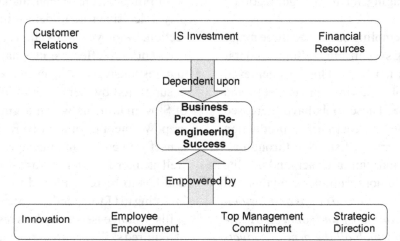

responsibilities and adapt to new performance standards and requirements.

IS investment integrated with strategic direction is necessary for success. The cases indicate that IT has powerful capacities to eliminating time and distance to help firms to achieve functional integration and improve cross-company linkage. Supersonic Machinery and the Telecom Supplier, apply IT to both product innovation and improving client/supplier relations. Geodetic Surveying is expanding IT use to establish a firm-client interface for mutual support and information sharing, success is helped by their clients' similar IT infrastructure. For either functional linkage or inter-organizational co-operation, firms need to have sufficient IT investment and provide training for employees. Apart from the integrated system at the Automatic Assembling that combines ordering system, production, and client/supplier databases, the use of IT for 'process innovation' is relatively rare. IT provides essential support for SMEs' re-engineering. The other technology factors are less important. Financial resources are the main constraint or SMEs. The other resource issues are not as influential on BPR in SMEs. This leads to a revised model to consider BPR in SMEs (Figure 2).

CONCLUSION

The motivations and purposes for SMEs to re-engineer may be different from those for larger firms. In SMEs re-engineering is often a response to positive trends - they tend to re-engineer from a position of strength (Kinni, 1995). First, small firms are short of the time and resources needed to re-engineer and it is unlikely that a small firm that is faltering can muster the required energy. Second, the by-products of success - rapidly increasing volume, straining processes, and increased profits are the impetus for small companies to re-engineer. They need to counter fast growth with processes improvement. Firms pursuing a growth strategy tend to re-engineer in order to enhance their external flexibility, relations with customers and suppliers, and internal efficiency, quality and production.

BPR initiatives are classified by two dimensions: scope and scale (Levene & Braganza, 1996). *Scope* includes the number of functions integrated to form the process (Rockart & Short, 1989). *Scale* is the extent of change in terms of how radical the BPR project (Hagel, 1993). Davenport and Short (1990) identify types of processes as inter-personal, inter-functional, and inter-organizational. Broadbent et al. (1994) contrast approaches to process redesign as simplification and innovation. Based on the strategic nature and radical orientation, Childe et al. (1994) depict a spectrum of process improvement activities, from personal/group improvement, quality improvement teams, process simplification, process re-engineering, business integration, to business re-engineering. While Craig and Yetton (1992) argue that process simplification offers firms the potential to capture some performance advantages and to minimize risk factors, higher levels of BPR, such as business integration, involve organizational and job redesign and new developments in IT. The higher levels of BPR are, in turn, viewed as more strategic and radical with the potential for substantial gains. Therefore, BPR projects in SMEs will involve lower scale and less scope, e.g. individual/group improvement and process simplification, as SMEs' policies are more conservative and owners try to avoid risks.

REFERENCES

Brady, A., & Voss, B. (1995). Small is as small does. *Journal of Business Strategy, 16(2),* 44-52.

Broadbent, M. Butler, C. and Hansell, A. (1994). A Business and Technology Agenda for Information-Systems Executives, *International Journal of Information Management, 14*(6), 411-426.

Cameron, N., & Braiden, P. (2004). Using BPR for development of production efficiency in companies making engineered to order products. *International Journal of Production Economics, 89*, 261-273.

Carr, D., & Johansson, H. (1995). *Best Practices in re-engineering*. NY, USA: McGraw Hill.

Carrier, C. (1995, April-June). Intrapreneurship in large firms and SMEs. *International Small Business Journal* (pp. 54-61).

Chang, L., & Powell, P. (1998). Toward a framework for Business Process Reengineering in SMEs. *Information Systems Journal, 8*(3), 199-216.

Craig, J., & Yetton, P. (1992). Business Process Redesign. *Australian Journal of Management, 17*(2), 285-306.

Craig, J., & Yetton, P. (1997). The Real Event of Re-engineering. In C. Sauer, P. Yetton, & (Eds.), *Steps to the Future*. San Francisco: Jossey-Bass.

Cragg, P., & King, M. (1993, March). Small-firm Computing: Motivators and Inhibitors. *MIS Quarterly* (pp. 47-60).

Davenport, T.H. (1993). Need radical innovation and continuous improvement? *Planning Review, 21*(3), 6-12.

Davenport, T.H., & Short, J.E. (1990). The new industrial engineering. *Sloan Management Review, 31*, 4-16.

Eisenhardt, K. (1989). Building theories from case research. *Academy of Management Review, 14*, 532-550.

Ferrell, J. (1996). Help for the other SMEs, *Manufacturing Engineering, 117*(2), 20.

Grover, V., Jeong, S.R., Kettinger, W., & Teng, J.T.C. (1995). Implementation of business process re-engineering. *J. Management Information Systems, 12*(1), 109-144.

Hagel, J. (1993). Keeping BPR on track. *McKinsey Quarterly, 1*, 59-72.

Hale, A., & Cragg, P. (1996). Business process re-engineering in the small firm. *INFOR, 34*(1), 15-27.

Hammer, M. (1990). Re-engineering work: Don't automate, obliterate. *Harvard Business Review, 68*(4), 104-122.

Herzog, N., Polajnar, A., & Tonchia, S. (2007). Development and Validation of business process reeingineering (BPR) variables: a survey research in Slovenian Companies. *International Journal of Production Research, 45*(24), 5811-5834.

Janson, R. (1993). Technology – Tomorrows Determinate. *Ohio Journal of Science, 93*(4), 78-82.

Johansson, H. et al. (1993). *BPR: breakpoint strategies for market dominance*. Chichester: Wiley.

Kinni, T. (1995). Process Improvement Part 2. *Industry Week, 244*(4), 45-50.

Larsen, M., & Myers, M. (1999). When success turns into failure: a package-driven BPR project in the financial services industry. *Journal of Strategic Information Systems, 8*, 395-417.

Lee, C., & Chen, S. (1992). *The overall environment and the development of Taiwan's SMEs*. Chung-Hua Institution for Economic Research.

Levene, R. J., & Braganza, A. (1996). Controlling the work scope in organisational transformation. *International Journal of Project Management, 14*(6), 331-339.

Levy, M., Galliers, R., & Powell, P. (1999). Assessing information systems strategy development frameworks in SMEs. *Information and Management, 36*, 247-261.

McKeown, I., & Philip, G. (2003). Business Transformation, information technology and competitive strategies: learning to fly, *International Journal of Information Management, 23*(1), 3-24.

Raymond, L., Bergeron, F., & Rivard, S. (1998). Determinants of BPR Success in SMEs. *Journal of Small Business Management, 36*(1), 72-85.

Reijers, H., & Mansor, S. (2005). Best Practices in business process redesign: an overview and qualitative evaluation of successful redesign heuristics. *Omega, 33,* 282-306.

Ribbler, J. (1996). Delivering solutions for the knowledge economy. *On-line, 20*(5), 12-19.

Rockart, J., & Short, J. (1989). IT in the 1990s. *Sloan Management Review, 30,* 7-17.

Sarker, S., Sarker, S., & Sidorova, A. (2006). Understanding Business Process Change Failure: An Actor-Network Perspective. *Journal of Management Information Systems, 23*(1), 51-86.

Sellers, G. (1997, September). Tools for managing your Business Process. *CMA Magazine* (pp. 25-27).

SBS (2003). www.sbs.gov.uk/statistics/smedefs.php

Stevenson, R. (1993). Strategic Business Process Engineering. In K. Spurr, P. Layzell, L. Jennison, & N. Richards (Eds.), *Software Assistance for Business Re-engineering.* Chichester: Wiley.

Talwar, R. (1993). Business re-engineering. *Long Range Planning, 26*(6), 22-40.

Teng, J., Grover, V., & Fiedler, K. (1994). Redesigning business processes using IT. *Long Range Planning, 27*(1), 95-106.

Tersine, R., Harvey, M., & Buckley, M. (1997). Shifting organisational paradigms. *European Management Journal, 15*(1), 45-57.

Ursic, D., Anteric, S., & Mulej, M. (2005). Business Process Re-engineering in Practice - A medium-sized Slovenian Company in Difficulties. *Systemic Practice and Action Research, 18*(1), 89-117.

Wastell, D., White, P., & Kawalek, P. (1994). A methodology for BPR. *Journal of Strategic Information Systems, 3*(1), 23-40.

Wind, J., & West, A. (1991). Reinventing the Corporation. *Chief Executive* (pp. 72-75).

Witherill, J. W., & Kolak, J. (1996). Is corporate re-engineering hurting your employees? *Professional Safety, 41*(5), 28-32.

Wu, H., & Chou, T. (1992). *Obstacles and reactions of Taiwan's SMEs.* Chung-Hua Institution for Economic Research.

Yin, R. (1994). *Case Study Research. Design and Methods* (2nd ed.). California: Sage.

Chapter 21
Challenges and Trends Towards an Effective Application of ERP and SCM Systems in SMEs

Dimitrios Gagalis
Technological Educational Institute of West Macedonia, Greece

Panayiotis Tahinakis
University of Macedonia Economic and Social Sciences, Greece

Nicolaos Protogeros
University of Macedonia Economic and Social Sciences, Greece

Dimitrios Ginoglou
University of Macedonia Economic and Social Sciences, Greece

ABSTRACT

Small and medium-sized enterprises (SMEs) are considered as both the backbone and the main driving force of economic development and innovation. Technology is playing an increasingly significant role in the success or failure of SMEs. The purpose of this chapter is to present international trends and challenges on the field of ERP and SCM systems, thus to: (a) record background information on legacy and current supply chain IT systems for SMEs, (b) discuss the importance of both ERP and SCM systems and the complementarities of ERP and SCM systems, (c) present survey conclusions of ERP and SCM systems adoption in various industries and countries, mainly in Europe and reveal the most prominent trends and barriers, (d) identify the technologies that are used to provide integrated view of information for SMEs, with emphases on both technological and organizational dimensions and recommendations to SMEs and (e) provide future trends, possible future areas of work and conclusions. Contemporary SMEs must carefully examine integration approaches and their technological and organizational issues such as hidden integration costs and management of change considered with human organizational concerns, cultures and business objectives. Application Service Providers, Web Services and Service Oriented Architecture as well as ERP and SCM application's maturity and open source software solutions, especially for SMEs requirements, are amongst the anticipating future trends in the field.

DOI: 10.4018/978-1-60566-892-5.ch021

INTRODUCTION

Business executives, especially in small and medium sized enterprises, experience a period of changes and new trends. Those trends incorporated in the wider context of globalization have led to the search for more effective methods of coordinating materials and information flow in the domestic and external company environment. A key to this coordination is the orientation towards closer relations with all levels of supplies and partners (Meatzer, DeWitt, Keebler, Min, Nix, Smith & Zach, 2001). Today, individual businesses no longer compete as stand-alone entities but rather as supply chains (Christopher, 2000).

A strongly integrated supply chain, combined by cooperation-boosting technologies, constitutes a shared chain of values, which provides increased efficiency, lower costs and more satisfied clients. The appropriate use of information technology (IT) tends to constitute the size of a modern business of minor importance, since major importance is attributed to the level of product and service provision, through a well organized and integrated framework of information systems. SMEs are progressively realizing the importance of analytical IT applications in order to improve their business performance. However, SMEs executives are continuously facing tough decisions in order to incorporate the most suitable software solutions based on their needs and to achieve a greater degree of data integration and incorporate business intelligence capabilities. (Economides & Terzis, 2008).

The primary objective of this article is to present international trends and challenges on the field of ERP and SCM systems, thus to: (a) record background information on legacy and current supply chain IT systems for SMEs, (b) discuss the importance of both ERP and SCM systems and the comlementarity of ERP and SCM systems, (c) present survey conclusions of ERP and SCM systems adoption in various industries and countries and reveal the most prominent trends

and barriers, (d) identify the technologies that are used to provide integrated view of information for SMEs, with emphases on both technological and organizational dimensions and recommendations to SMEs and (e) provide future trends, possible future areas of work and conclusions.

SMEs are mainly characterized by flexibility, as they have only a few managerial levels, they tend towards innovation and differentiation (especially in terms of quality) and more frequent and quick internal communications, decision-making and procedures. On the other hand they are generally more vulnerable than large enterprises because they usually have limited resources in terms of facilities, limited skilled technical capacities, products/services, they have few customers and a weak experience in understanding the expectations and demands of the new knowledge economies.

IT AND SCM CHALLENGES FOR SMEs

The technical definition of SMEs varies from country to country but is usually based on employment, revenue (assets) or a combination of the above two characteristics. More specifically, according to the new European SME definition every SME is a non-subsidiary, independent firm with between 10 and 250 employees (European Commission, Enterprise and Industry Publications, 2005). The number of employees varies across countries. While the most frequent upper limit designating an SME is 250 employees, the United States considers SMEs to include firms with fewer than 500 employees. Small firms are generally those with fewer than 50 employees, while micro-enterprises have at most 10, or in some cases 5, workers.

Furthermore, financial assets are also used to define SMEs. Based again on the new European definition (European Commission, Enterprise and Industry Publications, 2005) the turnover of medium-sized European enterprises (50-249 employees) should not exceed €50 million; that of small enterprises (10-49 employees) should not exceed €10 million while that of micro firms (less than 10 employees) should not exceed €2 million. Alternatively, balance sheets for medium, small and micro enterprises should not exceed €43 million, €10 million and €2 million, respectively. Some countries have different definitions for SMEs in the manufacturing and services sector and may exempt firms from specialized industries. (Glossary of Statistical Terms – OECD, accessed August 2008).

In the last three decades businesses, and especially SMEs, have witnessed a period of massive changes in almost every aspect of the entrepreneur reality. The globalization of markets, the stabilization of political economies and the advances in Information and Communication Technologies (Handfield & Nichols, 2001) created a new and rapidly shifting landscape of business challenges and opportunities.

While the number of world-class competitors in every business sector both domestically and abroad is continually increasing, organizations and leading managers must further utilize Information Technology (IT) solutions and Supply Chain Management (SCM) practices in order to: (a) improve and integrate their internal processes rapidly, (b) streamline their business processes or adopt new business processes with greater flexibility and responsive and minimize operational costs, (c) translate the ever-changing customer needs into product and service specifications and adjust enterprise resources accordingly to fluctuation demands, (d) reduce response time to these customer needs and (e) participate in a supply chain network and develop collaboration synergies with their associates.

Supply chain management (SCM) has increasingly become the key factor for almost every business in order to enhance competitive strength. SCM is defined as the systematic, strategic coordination of the traditional business functions and the tactics across these business functions within a particular company and across business within the supply chain, for the purposes of improving the long-term performance of the individual companies and the supply chain as a whole (Mentzer et al., 2001).

Many academics and experts state that SMEs are the "weaker parts" in a supply chain due to their disadvantages. As Thakkar, Kanda & Deshmukh (2008) summarize from Lewis (2005), John & Riley (1985) and Hvolby & Trienekens (2002) respectively:

Supply chain inefficiency is one of the most prevalent issues facing the small to mid-size enterprise....Supply and process costs represent 30% of an average manufacturing SME's budget and logistics cost incurs about 40% of total supply spending. On the other side, SMEs are now more and more taking part in the global business network participating in many interlinked supply chains. (Thakkar, Kanda & Deshmukh, 2008, p.98)

Professor Simchi-Levi (2000) mentions Information Technology and Decision Support Systems (DSS) as two of the most important issues in SCM. Furthermore, J. Shapiro (2001) highlighted the great significance of Information Technology and SCM by using Michael E. Porter's value chain or value added chain model. He supplemented and extended the above model with the terms IT and SCM, thus demonstrating the ever bigger portion attributed to them during company effort to reinforce the value of business activities.

Today, SMEs are considered as the new well-promising market of information technology applications in SCM. Systems available today can connect all supply chain components (suppliers, manufacturers, distributors, retailers and all clients) regardless of their location. When implemented sensibly, they can strengthen the supply chain, improve communication and minimize lead time and non-value added activities (Handfield & Nichols, 2001).

LEGACY SUPPLY CHAIN IT SOLUTIONS

In the past decades the majority of SME usage of ICT was limited to basic or more advanced technologies such as fixed lines, e-commerce application and information processing systems, and application on operational and administrative tasks, which were "functional silos" or "information islands" isolated from each other. Today, these enterprises are progressively implementing or outsourcing over the Internet (use an Application Service Provider - ASP) much more advanced IT tools, which fall into the category of e-business. Special emphasis is attributing to Enterprise Resource Planning (ERP) software and Supply Chain Management systems (SCMs), such as inventory and warehouse transportation software as well as transportation management software.

Historically, Enterprise Resource Planning (ERP) systems and Supply Chain Management systems (SCMs) are considered as the successors of traditional production management information systems, (Materials Requirement Planning - MRP and Materials Resource Planning - MRP II) systems and traditional distribution systems (Distribution Requirements Planning - DRP I and Distribution Resource Planning - DRP II). All those systems provide material flow management and are frequently characterized as original or conventional supply chain systems (legacy systems) or IT solutions that were designed to support the main functions of a supply chain in its initial stages.

Material Requirements Planning (MRP) constitutes the threshold of all further developments aiming at building an integrated information technology solution for business environments. It emerged as a business need, mainly in typical production environments, and it was very popular during the 60s and 70s. It became a sequential technique for planning and monitoring production, which was particularly used for converting the Master Production Schedule (MPS) for the end products into a detailed schedule for raw material and components. It focused on minimizing stocks while maintaining material adequacy for the production process.

This system substantially limited the level of stock, improved production control and provided timely and accurate information (given the time), thus raising credibility of the company involved. On the other hand MRP had apparent flaws, as it was incapable of optimizing the costs for the acquisition of materials and company supplies and existed mainly as a standardized solution, while it could not meet company special characteristics (Stock & Lambert, 2001). MRP deals only with production scheduling and inventories.

The primary mission of MRP II was to integrate main business functions (production, marketing and finance), as well as additional functions of the planning process (such as human resources, mechanical issues and supplies). Among its great advantages are its abilities to strictly limit stocks and achieve higher stock returns, minimizing overtime work and consequently improving the level of customer service.

But despite all the improvements made to MRP systems, a large number of important weaknesses remained and, in most cases, these weaknesses continue to exist even today in many enterprises that are still using those systems. MRP systems are mainly used for production planning, particularly amongst manufacturing SMEs (Loh & Koh, 2004). But, in general MRP II don't support the appropriate level of today's product differentiation, they can't plan resources based on dynamic organizational constraints and are very difficult and complex to integrate with modern customers and suppliers applications.

On the distribution side, the Distribution Requirements Planning (DRP I) system was able to determine distribution center stock demands and to use demand as data for the aforementioned manufacturing and material supply systems, in order to replenish stocks in multi-level storage systems. Proportionally, Distribution Resource

Planning (DRP II) system expanded DRP I functions in order to incorporate the planning of basic resources in a distribution system, such as storage facilities, available human resources, transport dynamics as well as the necessary component of accurate forecasting. Such a system localized demand forecasts for all product codes (stock keeping units – SKU) on all storage facilities and distribution centers within a particular replenishment time-line. All the above logistics requirements determined the central programming, which in turn affected the Bill of Material (BOM) and consequently MRP I.

In reality, DRP I and II constitute MRP I and II products applied in a company's logistics activities. By using DRP II, production executives obtain advanced knowledge on distribution network needs and are continuously informed of noted changes (Stock & Lambert, 2001). Yet, even DRP systems continue to present major disadvantages, mainly the fact that they are unable to determine which distribution center should supply a particular market and how distribution center functions must be scheduled in order to minimize short-term costs (Shapiro, 2001; Simchi-Levi, Kaminsky & Simchi-Levi, 2000).

Traditional MRP and DRP systems have a variety of insufficiencies which further limit their contribution in the development of an integrated supply chain. As a result, the MRP II system was further expanded during the 90s, leading up to the development of ERP systems, aiming at improving resources planning so that more supply chain levels may be incorporated compared to the MRP II. This is also their main advantage against legacy systems, enabling for better contribution to the process of decision-making, compared to their predecessors (Chopra & Meindl, 2001; Injazz J. Chen, 2001).

ENTERPRISE RESOURCE PLANNING SYSTEMS MAIN CHARACTERISTICS

ERP systems constitute the third generation of software suites. In essence, they synchronize the information flow with the physical flow of goods, facilitate the transfer of data from one function to another and offer central data management. According to Daniel E. O' Leary (2000) Enterprise Resource Planning systems (ERP) are computer-based systems designed to process an organization's transactions and facilitate integrated and real-time planning, production and customer response.

It is evident that today's different ERP packages are characterized by a great deal of variance as to which software modules are included, what applications – features they incorporate and how they are named. These modules usually differentiate depending on the manufacturer of the ERP system and are interconnected in order to ensure satisfactory process monitoring. Each module can be installed on its own or with a combination of other modules. ERP systems modularity allows organizations to implement the appropriate modules that are best feet to their needs. An ERP system offers a common user interface for all program modules.

Norris, Hurley, Hartley, Dunleavy & Balls (2000) state that "ERP is a set of integrated software modules that make up the core engine of internal transaction processing. It transforms transactional data into useful information and collates the data so that it can be analyzed in order to support business decisions" (p.12).

According to Chopra & Meindl, (2001) ERP systems are "operational IT systems but they generally lack the analytical capability to determine what transactions ought to happen" (p.60). Earlier ERP solutions were more suited and available only for large businesses because of their capacity to invest (in terms of time and money). Although ERP vendor's growth rate during the mid and late

90s was 30% - 40%, this percentage has notably dropped in the latest years. This is due not only to ERP market saturation in large companies (Everdingen, Hillegersberg & Waarts, 2000; Gable & Stewart,1999; Olsen & Sætre, 2007), but also to the increasing need for further expansion of ERP analytical capabilities (sophisticated algorithms including linear programming, mixed integer programming etc), thus approaching the Supply Chain Management systems (SCMs) functionality (Chopra & Meindl, 2001).

During the last years many software vendors have offered their "economical ERP version" as an attractive proposal for the SMEs market. In order to implement an ERP system, a SME must make thorough research before choosing the system, dedicate resources in time and money and make the appropriate changes to organizational structure and business processes. SMEs business executives are searching for ERP applications that can quickly embody into their businesses. They are looking for a solution that is scalable and align with the growth of the enterprise, is fast and easy to implement, has a lower total cost of ownership (TCO) and a quick return of investment (ROI). Today, ERP systems are increasingly becoming commonplace in the small and medium enterprise (SME) sectors.

Compared with MPR solutions the first generation of ERP systems, although improved, it was very complex to implement. Furthermore, vendors discovered the lack of analytical capabilities of ERP systems and started to approach the SCM application's functionality, mainly through cooperation and acquisition of specialized SCM software vendors. As a result, in the late 1990s ERP systems extended (ERP II) beyond the enterprise to suppliers and customers with the inclusion of additional software modules such as supply planning, demand planning, plant scheduling, warehouse and transportation management and customer relationship management (CRM). Finally, by 2004 the third generation of ERP systems is further enhanced with new collabora-

tive technologies like Internet. (Turban, Leidner, McLean & Wetherbe, 2006, p. 315).

Nowadays, the capabilities of ERP solutions are even higher. However, they are still having problems trying to optimize over multiple types of constraints, uncertainty issues (internal and external - machine breakdowns, unstable supplies and fluctuating prices of raw materials, or customer changes order, to name a few) and multiple plants. ERP cannot operate well under uncertainty (Koh & Simpson, 2005). Such additional needs are currently covered to a large extent by SCM systems or applications.

SUPPLY CHAIN MANAGEMENT SYSTEMS MAIN CHARACTERISTICS

The necessity of Supply Chain Management systems (SCMs) has been acknowledged by businesses, mainly after the second half of the 90s and following the Y2K issue. However, certain systems in the past (legacy systems) referred to one or more levels of the supply chain (e.g. production, distribution, etc.). Today, SCMs are considered among the most recent software solutions. Developments in the field of these applications have been rapid, resulting in the continuous creation of new and more effective products. There are many different types of these applications that focus on various stages in the supply chain.

Laudon & Laudon (2007), state that supply chain planning systems incorporate high-level mathematical algorithms which generate demand forecasts for a given product and consequently they develop sourcing and manufacturing plans for that product, thus adjust production and distribution plans. The main capabilities of supply chain planning systems are order planning, advanced scheduling and manufacturing planning, demand planning, distribution planning, transportation planning. On the other hand, the authors report that supply chain execution systems aim at effectively managing products from warehouses and distribution centers to the customers. Order commitments, final production, replenishment, distribution management and reverse distribution are some of the most common capabilities of supply chain execution systems.

Chopra and Meindl (2001) distinguish SCM systems as a special category of analytical applications which are focused on planning. They are a combination of many applications (Advanced Planning and Scheduling – APS and Demand Planning as the most popular, Transportation Planning and Content Systems, Revenue Management, etc) and are utilised to connect various stages of the supply chain. They are characterized as "tightly integrated supply chain suites" by their vendors. For instance, a SCM system can include sub applications – modules, such as APS, demand planning, transportation planning and inventory planning. These systems have the necessary analytical capabilities and they are the only systems that provide the highest level of decisions support functionality at the levels of planning and strategy. Other analytical SCM applications are focused on execution tasks, which are designated by planning systems. Such applications are Inventory Management Systems which produce a suggested inventory policy aimed at an optimised balance between maintenance costs and the cost of inventory loss, MES (less analytical than an APS system), Transportation Execution (less analytical than its planning counterpart - transportation planning) and Warehouse Management Systems (WMS).

Stock & Lambert (2001) recognise the harmonious interconnection and coexistence of Transportation Management Systems (TMS), Order Management Systems (OMS) and Warehouse Management Systems (WMS) as a necessity for the successful structure of the supply chain.

Simchi-Levi, Kaminsky & Simchi-Levi (2000) state that supply chain systems are included directly in the planning of the supply chain and combine short- and long-term elements of Decision Support Systems (DSS). According to the authors some of the DSS elements in the supply chain are demanding planning, inventory management, fleet planning, production scheduling, sales and marketing region assignment and workforce scheduling. Other similar DSS in the field of management of the supply chain are delivery management, logistics network planning, supplies planning and lead time quotation.

SCM systems are generally distinguished from Supplier Relationship Management (SRM) systems and Customer Relationship Management (CRM) systems but the close collaboration that should be developed between them, aimed at achieving a value chain, is being recognised.

Today, SCM systems along with an extended range of Web-based technologies (intranets, extranets etc) constitute the new business framework of electronic supply chain management (e-SCM). These types of e-business applications have also been developed for SMEs. "e-SCM is the collaborative use of technology to enhance business to business (B2B) processes and improve speed, agility, real control and customer satisfaction" (Norris et al, 2000, p.82). This strategic approach allows supply chain members to communicate instantly with each other, sharing up-to-date information and considering all supply chain levels (purchasing, manufacturing, packaging, logistics) at the same, thus allowing SMEs to achieve significant benefits as they manage to operate in close interaction with large enterprises.

SMEs do not share the same strategic visions and they don't have the same technological infrastructure or expertise. Different businesses use supply chain IT tools differently and they adopt them at a different pace or approach. Furthermore, it must be noted at the outset that not all SMEs need to adopt supply chain IT tools to the same degree of sophistication. Some SMEs occupy small and clearly defined niche markets, sometimes entirely local, that do not need the global connectivity available through the Internet (Taylor & Murphy, 2004). Other companies require only a few of the ERP's software modules (mainly SCM modules) yet much purchase the entire package (or decide to lease modules from ASPs). For these reasons, even ERP suites or ERP specific modules may not be attractive to everyone (Turban et al, 2006).

SMEs, especially in manufacturing and retail sectors, can truly benefit from more advanced IT solutions such as Enterprise Resource Planning (ERP) and SCM systems. On the other hand, by holding back investment in supply chain IT solutions, SMEs face the risk of permanently falling behind in the developments in supply network management (Stefansson, 2002). Thus, it is extremely important for executives to select the appropriate IT strategy for their enterprise. In discussing this strategy they must closely examine the strong correlation of ERP and SCM systems, always with regard to their specific enterprise requirements.

COMPLEMENTARITY OF ERP AND SCM SYSTEMS

Traditional or conventional ERP systems, thus mainly first generation systems and in many cases early extended ERP versions, which are the widest spread solutions in contemporary enterprises, are characterized by both advantages and disadvantages. More specifically their main advantages are briefly the following:

- they are characterized as the "single point of control" in an enterprise, providing a single and central location for all data and easier data maintenance
- they are broadly considered as homogeneous transactional systems and "internal technological hubs" (Norris et al, 2000, p.25), as they handle day to day business transactions with focus on internal process efficiency and effectiveness and automation (Chopra & Meindl, 2001; Pais, 2004; Shapiro, 2001)

- they enable information sharing and co-operation technologies (such as Internet) and at the same time they adjust faster and better than legacy systems in the use of those technologies, thus allowing for better monitoring of supply chain processes (Chopra & Meindl, 2001; Norris et al, 2000; Shapiro, 2001)
- they provide satisfactory information diffusion in real-time and in an extensive range of supply chain functions (horizontal levels), thus substantially reduce any communication delays among supply chain participants (Chopra & Meindl, 2001; Shapiro, 2001)
- they enable data exchange by describing business operational processes, in order to make them more productive (passive contribution - Shapiro, 2001) and
- they generally require a short and relatively simple training period (Chopra & Meindl, 2001; Simchi-Levi et al, 2000), as users learn only one set of new business practices, with a common look and feel for every module, instead of more.

On the other hand their broadly discussed (Allen E., 1999; Chopra & Meindl, 2001; Injazz J. Chen, 2001; Pais, 2004; Shapiro, 2001; Simchi-Levi et al, 2000; Stock & Lambert, 2001) disadvantages, especially in comparison with SCM analytical applications, are that:

- ERP focus only on the operational level rather than on strategic and tactical levels (myopic business scope at vertical - decision-making levels), and as a result they have relatively weak or "rudimentary" (Turban et al, 2006. p. 313) analytical capabilities (such as continuous planning techniques)
- they contain raw data which are stored with no previous notable processing (static

data), so they are generally week in supplying dynamic data to SCM analytical applications
- their speed of processing requests is relatively slower (due to greater number of tasks) than other SCM solutions
- all the demand, capacity and material constrains in ERPs are considered in isolation of each other
- their return of investment (ROI) is relatively slow and
- their installation project is generally considered as very expensive, time-consuming and difficult (in part due to the big number of users) and it entails strict and inflexible procedures, which do not always comply with enterprise philosophy and are difficult to change. Thus it poses a great element of risk, mainly for SMEs (Cragg & King, 1993; Mabert, Ashok & Venkataramanan, 2000; Thong, 2001).

Today, the new ERP solutions are even more extended with a bigger range of analytical capabilities and more mature and proven. Furthermore, they are continuously becoming less complex to install and train, easily accessible (due to the advent of the open source, web enabled and wireless technologies) and relatively less expensive as they offer need based applications. All the above new trends make ERP solutions specifically tailored to suit the business processes of the SMEs. In the recent years, the leading ERP vendors have steadily penetrated the SMEs market with their mid-range ERP systems. For example, SAP released the "SAP Business One" and "SAP All-In-One" mid-range ERP system, while Oracle has also launched the "Oracle E-Business Suite" for the SMEs sector.

As their counterparts, SCM applications are also characterized by both advantages and disadvantages. Above their main advantages (Allen, 1999; Chopra & Meindl, 2001; Pais, 2004; Shapiro, 2001; Simchi-Levi et al, 2000), especially in comparison with ERP suites are:

- their focus on strategic and tactical -planning levels (high functionality on vertical – decision making levels) as they have extensive and strong analytical capabilities, thus they can be used for both planning and strategic decisions
- their systematic search for features that improve SCM through an operational and modular integration of decisions (active contribution - Shapiro, 2001)
- the simultaneous management and adjustments of all parameters in real-time with regard to all the considered constraints (demand, capacity, material)
- their increased speed in processing specific decision-taking requests
- their less complex functions and the smaller number of specialized users that they are applied to and
- in general their faster implementation and return of investment (ROI).

On the other hand their disadvantages (Allen, 1999; Búrca, Fynes & Marshall (2005), Chopra & Meindl, 2001; Pais, 2004; Shapiro, 2001; Simchi-Levi et al, 2000), compared to ERPs, are:

- that they are less comprehensive than their counterparts as they are characterized by a myopic functionality at horizontal levels of the supply chain spectrum
- their strong dependence to Transactional IT (mainly ERP systems) because they take all available data from them in order to provide forecasts and future scenarios (typical DSS output) as well as, to optimize and support the decision making process,
- their different look and feel per application
- their planning level as well as their integration issues which require quite a large amount of specific and expensive expertise to develop, thus they are costly and

- their necessary training process which is long and relatively complex due to the diversified skill sets that required to support them.

Today, SCM software application providers are steadily working in order to develop new decision-support tools and minimize SCM system's deficiencies, thus extending their functionality in the horizontal level of the supply chain. As their counterparts, the SCM software solution environment has also matured greatly, which is mainly attributed to the ongoing industry consolidation (acquisitions, merges and alliances of leading ERP and SCM systems providers. Beyond these, Gilmore (2008) acknowledges that the latest very positive and interesting trends of supply chain software industry are the emphasis towards proving and substantiating value for customers and building real integration and work flows among suite components; the lower cost implementations; and the growing attraction for more "custom" solutions with less pain, cost and rigidity, through Service Oriented Architecture (SOA). Contemporary SMEs, as well as large enterprises, are starting to exploit these trends.

We must emphasize that to a great extend, the majority of limitations of ERP suites are the strengths of SCM software application and reversely many SCM application's limitations are the strengths of ERP systems. All the aforementioned ERP and SCM system's advantages and disadvantages and current trends clearly outline the strong correlation of those systems and at the same time they justify their increased convergence in an effort to develop a solid SCM IT approach.

COMPLEMENTARITIES OF ERP AND SCM SYSTEMS – SC IT ARCHITECTURE APPROACHES

Thorough use of information in a supply chain presupposes its collection, access and analysis. SMEs, especially in the manufacturing sector, need to make operational, tactical and strategic decisions on the majority of the horizontal levels of the supply chain spectrum, thus they need to have both ERP and SCM system's core functionalities.

More specifically Turban, Leidner, McLean & Wetherbe (2006) clearly state that the: "...use of ERP and SCM software is not necessarily an either-or decision. Rather, the two can be combined and used together...the analytical SCM information systems have emerged as a complement to ERP systems, to provide intelligent decision support or business intelligence..." (p.313)

Furthermore, Chopra and Meindl (2001) suggest that the full value of an ERP system cannot be realized without the problem-solving activity of analytical solutions. Conversely, in order to be productive analytical solutions need accurate data from a variety of functions, mainly through an ERP system. Therefore, managers often combine these two types of applications to produce the best supply chain solution.

In their proposal of the end-stage system architecture for the 21st century company Norris, Hurley, Hartley, Dunleavy & Balls (2000) also acknowledge the complementarity of ERP and SCM systems. They state that the company's ERP system is situated at the centre, as it is the transaction-processing engine and generator of its internal data, which are stored in a data warehouse. Moreover, the authors recognize that these data can be utilized in any number of ways by the company's decision-support software (as SCM application) for business analysis both inside and outside the company, which may be part of the ERP package or may be provided by another (usually

SCM) vendor. "ERP and e-business technologies supercharge each other" (p.1).

The same authors and many others (Allen, 1999; Pais, 2004; Shapiro, 2001; Simchi-Levi et al, 2000) also state that ERP is and will continue to be a transactional back-bone (or core infrastructure) for manufacturing companies through which decision support, data warehousing and other e-business applications connect, get and give information. Thus "installing and maintaining ERP is tactical…Without ERP, neither SCM nor CRM works to its full potential" (Norris et al, 2000, p.169).

The compementarity of ERP and SCM systems is also acknowledged in an effort to recognize the main appropriate supply chain information technology (SCM IT) architecture approaches. By studying an extensive literature review for the purpose of a survey research in Greek SMEs, Protegeros, Tahinakis, Mylonakis and Gagalis (2007) summarized these approaches as follows:

- Standalone SCM applications; for example one or more BoB solutions, such as APS, WMS and TMS (Møller, 2005; Chopra & Meindl, 2001; Murphy & Wood, 2004; Petri & Szekely, 2005; Shapiro, 2001; Simchi-Levi et al, 2000; Stock & Lambert, 2001).

- ERP as a total solution from one vendor with (one or more) SCM modules (extended ERP or ERPII) (Møller, 2005; Chopra & Meindl, 2001; Petri & Szekely, 2005; Búrca et al, 2005; Simchi-Levi et al, 2000).

- Conventional ERP combined with (one or more) standalone SCM best-of-breed (BoB) applications from a different vendor, which constitute the best-fit solution in each category (Chopra & Meindl, 2001; Pais, 2004; Petri & Szekely, 2005; Shapiro, 2001; Simchi-Levi et al, 2000; Verwijmeren, 2004).

- Combination of extended ERP (or ERPII) with standalone SCM application(s) (for example an ERP with an APS module and a standalone-BoB WMS) (Møller, 2005; Chopra & Meindl, 2001; Pais, 2004; Petri & Szekely, 2005;).

- SCM transactions through internet technologies (for example B2B, e-hubs, online portals and ASP) (Chopra & Meindl, 2001; Murphy & Wood, 2004; Búrca et al, 2005).

ERP with SCM applications, either as ERP modules or integrated as a best-of-bread (BoB) SCM provider's solution, constitutes the majority of the most common approaches.

In the above landscape of SCM IT solutions small and medium sized enterprises have more choices than ever before. SMEs can either buy their system directly from a software (ERP or SCM) vendor or indirectly through a value added reseller (VAR). Furthermore, they can choose to rent or outsource (application service providers - ASP) one or many of the above solutions in an effort to drastically reduce initial investment costs and use applications that they otherwise could not afford. All the above options have their advantages and disadvantages too.

We must also emphasize that SMEs' executives should be extremely sceptical of vendors who claim that their products are "one size solutions" or "appropriate for any size of organisation". A big number of ERP vendors still claim that their product substitutes every useful analytical capability, so there is really no need for best of bread (BoB) SCM applications. On the other hand, many SCM vendors claim that their SCM solutions constitute a strong, integrated suite of application which they don't presuppose the installation of a single central ERP system.

The truth lies somewhere between the above views. As Norris, Hurley, Hartley, Dunleavy & Balls (2000) point out "No one path will lead to success" (p.16). Each company must carefully audit its performance and decide its strategy so as to find out the best-fit IT application functionality, in terms of both ERP implementation and e-business.

SURVEY FINDINGS AND TRENDS ON ERP & SCM SYSTEM'S ADOPTION IN SMEs

A variety of surveys from different continents and sectors of the economy reveal different views and perspectives on the scope and range of ERP and SCM systems implementation in SMEs worldwide.

A summary report of the sectoral e-Business Watch Surveys 2007 (European Commission, e-Business W@tch, 2008) - in 7 EU countries, (DE, ES, FR, IT, PL, SE, UK) point out that in some of the manufacturing and service sectors SMEs are widely using e-business software systems like ERP and SCM in order to achieve cost-reduction and optimisation of logistics operations. The use of these systems has notably increased among SMEs in the past 3-4 years. More specifically, companies in the chemical, rubber and plastics (CRP) industry attribute great emphasis in the use of applications which support production, supply chain management and B2B trading processes. Furthermore, in the steal industry 76% of firms have an Order Management software application while 59% have an ERP and 27% a SCM system.

Similar conclusions are also drawn from the Food and Beverages sector report 2006 (European Commission, e-Business W@tch, 2006) – in EU-10 countries, (Czech Republic, Germany, Spain, France, Italy, Hungary, the Netherlands, Poland, Finland and the UK). Cost effective supply chains and traceability along the value chain are the main challenges in Food and Beverages (F&B) industries that require sound investments on e-business applications like ERP and SCM systems.

AMR Research's Supply Chain Management Spending Study for 2007-2008 (Fontanella & Klein, 2008) also reveals the continuous growth of supply chain software market both in North America and Europe. The recent study, which was based on a survey of 336 IT and supply chain professionals of both large and medium-sized enterprises, projects an increase in supply chain software spending (including maintenance, personnel and hardware costs) at an average of almost 12% in 2008, and a 7% overall growth in software spending alone. Almost 25% of SMEs decide to increase spending primarily in order to meet varied service delivery requirements among their customers. More than 50% of midsized companies admit that they will increase supply chain technology investments for 2008, either by replacing legacy applications or by adopting new technologies for greater flexibility, as they acknowledge the positive contribution of supply chain technology to their success. On the replacement side, the most prominent trend is the upgrade of order management applications due to high maintenance costs and difficulties in integration issues. Moreover, 85% of European companies cite WMS integrating issues as the main reasons for replacement.

Another relevant survey on the degree of SCM software application's adoption in Greek SMEs (Protegeros et al, 2007) revealed the following trends and conclusions:

- ERP is the technological backbone for the majority of enterprises (81.1%). The percentage of enterprises that exclusively hold one or more ERP modules is 32.4%, whereas 16.2% have applied one or more best of breed (BoB) solutions. Nearly half of the SMEs sample applied a combination of ERP (with or without ERP SCM modules) with best of breed systems. The most common SCM applications for Greek SMEs are ERP SCM modules and Best of Breed solutions with WMS and OMS
- enterprises were positioned in the SCMs market mainly after 1994, whereas the implementations of those applications have

presented a rapid development since 1998.

- the potential market trends indicate strong application development possibilities such as WMS, ERP SCP modules, MES, and especially APS and TMS which manifest strong upward trends
- the large majority of enterprises reports reduced inventories and order processing time as well as improved level of customer service by 10% to 20%
- compatibility with older applications and the lack of skilled personnel are considered as the main problems, whereas the coordination of in-house project team with software suppliers and the training of human resources are considered amongst the major cost factors in implementing SCMs and
- the majority of enterprises (55.5%) consider ASP an unattractive or slightly attractive solution

On the other hand, today there is also evidence that in many countries or regions SMEs are seriously fallen behind in terms of competitiveness and e-business developing solutions. Kotelnikov (2007) reports that in the Asia-Pacific region (China, Hong Kong, Indonesia, Japan, Malaysia, Philippines, Republic of Korea, Singapore, Taiwan, Thailand), which hosts the fastest-growing ICT markets and industries in the world, SMEs have been slow in most developing countries to adopt ICT. The main reasons are major internal and external inadequacies such as limited ICT literacy, inability to integrate ICT into business processes, week understanding of the knowledge economy's demands as well as poor ICT infrastructure, incomplete government regulations for e-commerce and high costs of ICT equipment. More specifically, 90% of Thai SMEs still uses basic communication technology (fixed phone line and fax) and only 1% uses a more advanced ICT tool like CRM software. Moreover, and despite the great effort of domestic SMEs support organiza-

tions, in the manufacturing sector only almost 10% of Malaysian SMEs have used ERP, 10.1% CRM software, 13% computer-aided manufacturing and 24.8% computer-aided design, while of SMEs as a whole, only 30% have a web presence and use ICT extensively in daily operations.

In the 2006 Annual survey on e-business status from the Korea Institute for Electronic Commerce (KIEC, 2006), which covered all industry types except for public administration, national defence and social security sector, housekeeping service, and international & foreign organizations, among the surveyed companies with e-business related systems, ERP was introduced most by 24.8% of companies, followed by electronic bidding system (11.4%) and SCM (3.6%). The proportion of companies, mainly SMEs, with major e-business systems in place - ERP, Electronic Bidding, SCM, B2BI, MES in particular - increased from 2005, with the use of ERP growing from 23.0% in 2005 to 24.8% in 2006. On the other hand, SCM and MES systems deployment, which is considerably low, grew from 2.9% and 1.3% in 2005 to 3.6% and 2.3% in 2006 respectively. Amongst the main obstacles in introducing and further promoting e-business solutions in Korean SMEs are excessive system deployment cost by 36.8%; lack of confidence in return on investment (ROI) (32.0%); and lack of specialized personnel (21.8%). Furthermore, 64.4% of the surveyed companies reveal that they prefer governmental support for e-business in system deployment, in training and education on e-business (33.9%) and in tax incentives (22.8%).

Different surveys record different views and perspectives on the scope and range of ERP and SCM systems implementation in SMEs worldwide. As some of the survey results showed, many enterprises today are facing problems, in trying to exchange data between internal and external supply chain applications, thus integrate older with new software applications. Due to the dynamic character of the supply chains, SMEs are constantly being challenged to invest in integration technologies in order to improve efficiency and effectiveness of their supply chain services and to stay competitive.

INTEGRATION ISSUES IN SMEs

One of the most difficult, complex and challenging task for every company is the integration of its intra and inter-organisational supply chain information systems. These disparate systems may usually vary between custom - legacy systems, which are mainly autonomous systems, or ideally the major source for internal information, such as ERP systems or even the inter-enterprise, analytical e-business solutions, such as the supply chain management applications.

The achievement of this challenging task requires the use of a great range of traditional and new integration technologies and approaches that are intertwined under the umbrella of the emerging integration software generation called Enterprise Application Integration (EAI). From a technical perspective, Themistocleous, Irani & Sharif (2000) propose that EAI is achieved at the following three (3) integration layers: transportation layer; transformation layer; and process automation layer.

The most common integration technologies are extensively (Kitsiou, Matopoulos, Manthou & Vlachopoulou, 2007; Linthicum, 1999; Ruh, Maginnis & Brown 2000; Themistocleous and Irani, 2003) categorized as:

- Message Oriented Technologies, or Internet Oriented Language / Standards such as:
  - Electronic Data Interchange - EDI (and EDIFACT) facilitates the application-to-application electronic exchange of syntactically structured data-oriented documents, thus it achieves integration at the data level, but not at the process level. Many characterize it as a complex and very expensive technology with high initial capital investment
  - Extensible Markup Language - XML (and electronic business XML - ebX-ML) is an open standard, platform independent, web enabled which describes the contents of a page or file. It allows flexible and easy data binding of different applications and it has a relatively high diffusion in medium and large companies that seek for e-business on the web. However, XML is only a complementary technology of other EAI technologies (middleware etc).
- Object Oriented Technologies or Distributed Object Technologies (DOT), which include:
  - Common Object Request Broker Architecture (CORBA), a middleware technology with interface-generating mechanisms that provide good solutions for portability, scalability and interoperability in heterogeneous environments.
  - the family of Component Object Model Technologies / Distributed Component Object Model Technologies - COM/DCOM, COM+ (for example proprietary Microsoft's COM/DCOM) as a major competitor to CORBA which enables software components distributed across networked computers to communicate.
  - Enterprise JavaBeans (EJB), which is a platform independent Java API (developed by Sun Microsystems) that defines component architecture for multi-tier client/server systems and it can be implemented into existed systems with little recompiling and configuring
- Database Oriented Technologies, for example Open Database Connectivity (ODBC)

as a standard software API method allow developers to easily write applications that can access data stored in various database management systems (DBMS)

- Interface Based Technologies, in general, which include Application Programming Interfaces (APIs), thus sets of routines, protocols and tools for building software application consistent with the operating environment. Open interfaces allow external access to the functionality of systems. All programs that use a common API will have similar interfaces. For example, in many cases of ERP integration, APIs are provided by ERP systems to allow other applications to access ERPs functionality or data (Zahavi, 1999).

Moreover, message broker is an open standards-based messaging middleware or intermediary program that provides secure interoperability between enterprise applications from various sources as it transform documents or XML messages (in cases of e-business applications) from one data format into another, maps the data, shares the data between different systems and operating environments and distributes processing and messaging functions in order to avoid overloads and failures during the data exchange.

Another continually upward and attractive category of integration technologies for SMEs is Web Services and Service-Oriented Architectures (SOA). These mainly refer to software components that use standard internet technologies to interact with one another independently of platform or programming language through the use of agreed protocols and XML based message formats. Amongst the most common XML-based protocols are:

- Simple Object Access Protocol (SOAP), which is characterized as a lightweight XML-based messaging protocol (independent of any operating system) for

communicating with and invoking web services. It is considered as a less complex alternative to CORBA

- Web Services Description Language (WSDL) is a format or mechanism for describing XML-based network services, regardless of the underlying communications protocol and request structure
- Universal Description, Discovery and Integration (UDDI), which provides directories and descriptions (a registry) of online services for electronic business

All the aforementioned technologies have their limitations and thus they must not considered as "one size solution - single correct approach" or a "panacea" to solving all integration problems. On the contrary, there is a general consensus that these technologies must be combined together in order to efficiently and effectively support the functional unification of disparate applications within supply chains.

Themistocleous, Irani & Love (2004) also recommend an extremely useful framework to support the selection of appropriate combinations of integration technologies, when enterprises seek to integrate one or more classifications of disparate system types, such as the SMEs' challenges of integrating their intra and inter-organizational supply chain information systems. More specifically, this classification includes briefly the following:

- Custom to custom integration: custom or legacy systems, which generally have limited points of access-integration, can be integrated in a common infrastructure through their databases and user interfaces, as the possible points of integration. Thus, this type of integration is supported by technologies that extract data from a database or a screen.
- Custom to packaged integration: legacy system can be integrated with packaged applications like ERP systems through

many different approaches, techniques and tools and on various levels including data, objects/components, and at an interfaces level.

- Custom to e-business integration: legacy applications and e-business solutions must integrate in order to support the automation of specific business processes. This type of integration requires technologies that support the incorporation and exchange of data, objects, and interfaces.

- Packaged to packaged integration: disparate packaged systems such as different ERP versions or different ERP modules can be unified into a common integrated infrastructure. This classification of systems usually requires Application Programming Interfaces (APIs) and technologies that support the extraction and transmission of data, messages and objects.

- Packaged to e-business integration: the integration of these types of systems allows packaged ERP systems to work as back-office system, thus support e-business processes like e-supply chain management. This classification of systems requires technologies that unify data, objects, interfaces and messages

- E-business to e-business integration: different e-business applications which are based on more flexible and open architectures can be integrated and support the functionality of each other. This type of integration can be facilitated by message based technologies, distributed object technologies, and database oriented technologies.

- Custom to-packaged to e-business integration: this is a holistic integration approach of processes and applications on departmental, enterprise or cross-enterprise level. Thus it requires integration technologies that support all the types of integration levels, thus data, message, objects, interface and processes.

ORGANIZATIONAL INTEGRATION ISSUES AND CONCERNS

The integration along the supply chain leads to optimum flow and monitoring of information and processes enables trading partners within the value chain to better coordinate and collaborate and it strongly supports executives in decision making.

At the same time, integration project poses many organizational issues and concerns that SMEs must drastically deal with in order to maximize their benefits. Integration technology issues such as functionality, performance and costs need to be simultaneously considered with human organizational concerns, cultures and business objectives.

Small and medium sized enterprise managers must:

- Choose the appropriate integration approach and manage an integration project that requires the alignment of the possibly different accompanied technologies from various IT expert parties. This is not a trivial task for SMEs since they usually have limited skilled technical capacities, experiences and resources as well as different priorities. Thus, they need to further support their in-house IT staff with external technology consultants in order to better predict their future IT needs and requirements and decide based on a well-defined set of selection criteria (such as data scalability, adaptability, performance, security, different types of cost, customer support etc). Business managers need to be very careful in their choice and always keep in mind the interlinked strategic investments in skills and organizational restructuring.

- Have to be aware that managing an integration project usually demands a customised trade-off between central and local project activities. Central project activities (overall project management, standardization determination etc) may cause unnecessary delays, while local project activities (i.e. individual project management) may create conflicts.

- Acknowledge the hidden integration costs that are associated with the solutions supported methods for interfacing with trading partners. Many e-business solutions (ERP SCM modules, BoB or both) need to be further modified in order to address the enterprise's specific needs and processes. This modification adds to the cost of purchasing the software. "Semi-customization expenses can run two or three times the cost of the packaged software" (Rapp, 2002, p.37). Another hidden cost factor of integration project is the SME's inability to handle data quality issues in an organisational holistic view (Lam & Shankararaman, 2004).
- Deal with organisational challenges that are related to change management issues such as people (training and support), culture resistance and, if required, process changes or reengineering. Compared with larger enterprises SMEs have the advantage of been flexible, with a small number of employees, but at the same time they are less experienced in dealing culture changes. Different integration approaches require different management tools. "The degree to which systems force cultural and process changes is a key management decision" (Applegate, Austin & McFarlan, 2007. p.351).
- Primarily seek to achieve internal process integration in order to further implement inter-organizational supply chain integration.
- Realize that supply chain integration challenges SMEs as an entity to drastically overcome their natural resistance in revealing business secrets to their trading partners. The adoption of an integrated supply

chain approach (mainly through internet) requires a trade-off between autonomy and control in each supply partner relationship. Partners need to be willing to allow partners to view their systems and processes in order for the end-to-end process to work correctly (Búrca et al, 2005). Organisations also need to understand the implications of integration across the entire supply chain. At the same time, high priority must be attributed to data security in a system-wide integration among trading partners due to the insecure nature of the Internet and the premature stage of Web services. In considering of all critical security aspects SME's managers must adopt the most appropriate solutions (for example encryption, authentication etc).

All the aforementioned issues and challenges have constantly achieved utmost importance for enterprise's functionality and thus they must be carefully examined.

FUTURE TRENDS

As previously mentioned a number of very important information technology trends in favour of SMEs are already on the way to be put on the map. These anticipating trends are briefly summarized as follows:

- Application Service Provider's (ASP) and Web service's further growth: despite ASP's current problems (e.g. customization) and web service's premature characteristics and risks associated with early adoption issues, it is expected that in the future more and more individual professionals and SMEs will increasingly find it much easier to "lease" software on a per use basis from ASPs, thus avoiding the difficulties and the initial high costs of installing, operating and maintaining ERP and BoB SCM systems. Furthermore, more standardized web services and service-oriented architectures (SOA) for SCM and ERP will be defined and become commodities for the majority of SMEs value chains participants. Through Web services, ASP model is expected to tailor services and efficiently and effectively meet the diverse requirements of SMEs in a variety of business sectors. Major software companies are complementing their products with the usage-based business model characteristics.

- The continuation of the ERP and SCM software vendor's battle, mainly in the midsized market: as previously mentioned ERP systems will further extend their analytical functionalities and be more focused on inter-organizational supply chain integration, while SCM systems will build real integration flows and lower their implementations costs. ERP and SCM systems will continue to be complementary approaches for achieving the same strategic challenges. This battle will provide more mature and proven application solutions to small and midsized enterprises. Some SMEs will be increasingly attracted by ERP SCM modules, mainly due to the integration cost's factor, while others will choose ERP and BoB solutions due to their increased customization needs and greater long-term flexibility. The choice implemented will depend on its company's strategy in terms of both ERP implementation and e-business. This strategy will be mainly driven by the current state (e.g. financial and human resources) of the enterprise, the customer demands and the state and systems of the enterprise's partners.

- The shift of ERP and SCM application's vendors towards vertical market segmentations, with emphasis on the adjustment of possible intra-sector differences: ERP and SCM vendors will increasingly try to adopt vertical marketing segmentation tactics, thus achieving quick, easy and less expensive packaged solutions in customized markets or industry sectors. This shift's magnitude may possibly determine the winner (if any) of the above battle in the midsized market.

- Development and diffusion of enterprise open source software (OSS) and further growth of in-house applications development in SMEs: despite the different views on whether the use of OSS leads to cost reduction for SMEs or that the use of OSS increases by firm size, OSS's public and business awareness steadily grows. Moreover, given the scale, the level of customization and the cost of many ERP and SCM systems today as well as the emergence of modern and advanced OSS business tools, many SMEs especially small (in niche market) may progressively consider the OSS as an alternative approach for implementing ERP and SCM software. This growing awareness of OSS is expected to further increase the in-house applications development in SMEs, which was revealed in many survey results, mainly for European firms. Today, software applications development with the use of modern OSS tools is already considering as less expensive than just a few years ago. Every company must be able to modify and upgrade its system's functionality whenever needed.

- Further increase of government initiatives for the support of SME's information and e-business practices: the leading role of SMEs in the economic growth of every country must further acknowledged by governments. Policies and programs are expected to run in favor of SMEs and strengthen the e-business efforts of those companies. These initiatives must be well addressed by region and targeted at specific company's requirements.

Possible future areas of research could be directed at studying more thoroughly the ERP and SCM system's adoption (regional environment, sector characteristics, selection criteria, best practices) taking into consideration the differences between small and medium-sized enterprises. . Future studies should consider cross-country and cross-continent comparisons with emphasis on the aforementioned trends.

CONCLUSION

Small and medium-sized enterprises are considered as the new well-promising market of information technology applications in SCM. Although traditional or legacy Supply Chain IT solutions had a variety of insufficiencies, which further limited their contribution in the development of an integrated supply chain, many enterprises particularly in the manufacturing sectors are still using those systems for production planning. Transactional-based Enterprise Resource Planning (ERP) systems as well as the more analytical-based Supply Chain Management Systems (SCMs) are the most prominent Enterprise Information Systems (EIS) with even higher capabilities than the previous years. To a great extend, the majority of limitations of ERP suites are the strengths of SCM software application and reversely many SCM application's limitations are the strengths of ERP systems. Thus, they are complementary solution in the SMEs effort to develop a solid supply chain information technology (SCM IT) architecture approaches. ERP with SCM applications, either as ERP modules or integrated as a best-of-bread (BoB) SCM provider's solution, constitutes the majority of the most common approaches.

Due to the dynamic character of the supply chains, SMEs are constantly being challenged to invest in integration technologies in order to improve efficiency and effectiveness of their supply chain services. Today, many enterprises, mainly SMEs, have different approaches towards supply chain integration. Enterprise Application Integration (EAI) efficiently integrates functionality in a supply chain and leads to cheaper and easy managed supply chain IT infrastructures, thus it is considered as a very suitable integration approach for SMEs.

SMEs must carefully examine all the available integration technologies in order to properly combine them together and confront their integration problems. In dealing with technological and organizational issues of integration SMEs managers need to choose the appropriate integration approach, apply customised trade-off between central and local project activities in managing the integration project and at the same time keep in mind interlinked strategic investments in skills and organizational restructuring. Hidden costs that are associated with the solutions supported methods for interfacing with trading partners of integration must also be acknowledged as well as change management issues such as people (training and support), culture resistance and, if required, process changes or reengineering. Integration is generally perceived as the key barrier to BoB solutions and the primary reason companies choose the ERP SCM modules solution.

Finally, amongst the anticipating future trends in the field are the Application Service Provider's (ASP), Web Service's and Service Oriented Architecture's (SOA) further growth; the continuation of the ERP and SCM software vendor's battle, mainly in the midsized market; the shift of ERP and SCM application's vendors towards vertical market segmentations; the development and diffusion of enterprise Open Source software (OSS) and further growth of in-house applications development in SMEs and the further increase of government initiatives for the support of SME's information and e-business practices. These latter initiatives must be well addressed and targeted in an effort to minimize the gap between large and small companies.

REFERENCES

Allen, E. (1999). *ERP vs. SCM- What's the difference*. Retrieved March 27, 2006, from http://supplychain.ittoolbox.com/documents/academic-articles/erp-vs-scm-whats-the-difference-226#

Applegate, L. M., Austin, R. D., & McFarlan, W. F. (2007). *corporate information strategy and management, text and cases*. New York: McGraw-Hill/Irwin.

Chopra, S., & Meindl, P. (2001). *Supply chain management - Strategy, planning and operation*. London: Prentice Hall.

Christopher, M. (2000). The agile supply chain: Competing in volatile markets. *Industrial Marketing Management, 29*(1), 37–44. doi:10.1016/S0019-8501(99)00110-8

Cragg, P. B., & King, M. (1993). Small-firm computing: Motivators and inhibitors. *MIS Quarterly, 17*(1), 47–60. doi:10.2307/249509

Economides, A., & Terzis, V. (2008). Evaluating tax sites: an evaluation framework and its application. *Electronic Government . International Journal (Toronto, Ont.), 5*(3), 321–362.

European Commission. Enterprise and Industry publications (2005). The New SME definition user guide and model declaration. Retrieved from http://europa.eu.int/comm/enterprise/enterprise_policy/sme_definition/index_en.ht

European Commission. Enterprise and Industry Directorate General, e-Business W@tch (2006). *Food and Beverages (F&B) Sector Study, Sector Report No. 1/2006*. Retrieved July 20, 2008 from http://www.ebusiness-watch.org/studies/sectors/food/food.htm

European Commission. Enterprise and Industry Directorate General, e-Business W@tch (2008). *E-Business in Europe – 2008, Industry perspectives on e-business developments and ICT impact*. Retrieved July 20, 2008 http://www.ebusiness-watch.org/key_reports/documents/BRO08.pdf

Everdingen, Y. V., Hillegersberg, J. V., & Waarts, E. (2000). ERP adoption by European mid-size companies. *Communications of the ACM, 43*(4), 27–31. doi:10.1145/332051.332064

Fontanella, J., & Klein, E. (2008). Supply chain technology spending outlook. Supply chain management review. Retrieved September 10, 2008 from http://www.scmr.com/article/CA6549303.html?industryid=48316

Gable, G., & Stewart, G. (1999). SAP R/3 implementation issues for small to medium enterprises. In *Proceedings of the 5th Americas Conference on Information Systems* (pp. 779-81). Milwaukee, WI.

Gilmore, D. (2008). Supply chain software: AMR research remains bullish on supply chain software spend. SCDigest Editorial Staff. Retrieved August 16, 2008, from http://www.scdigest.com/assets/On_Target/08-05-19-2.php?cid=1688

Handfield, R., & Nichols, E., Jr. (2001). *Introduction to SCM*. London: Prentice Hall.

Hvolby, H., & Trienekens, J. H. (2002). Supply chain planning opportunities for small and medium sized companies. *Computers in Industry, 49*(1), 3–8. doi:10.1016/S0166-3615(02)00054-4

Injazz, J. C. (2001). Planning for ERP systems: Analysis and future trend. *Business Process Management Journal, 7*(5), 374–386. doi:10.1108/14637150110406768

Kitsiou, S., Matopoulos, A., Manthou, V., & Vlachopoulou, M. (2007). Evaluation of integration technology approaches in healthcare supply chain. *International Journal of Value Chain Management, 1*(4), 325–343. doi:10.1504/IJVCM.2007.015091

Koh, S. C. L., & Simpson, M. (2005). Change and uncertainty in SME manufacturing environments using ERP. *Journal of Manufacturing Technology Management, 16*(6), 629–653. doi:10.1108/17410380510609483

Korea Institute for Electronic Commerce. (2006). Annual survey on E-business status 2006. Retrieved August 21, 2008, from http://www.oecd.org/dataoecd/59/27/35372094.pdf

Kotelnikov, V. (2007). *Small and medium enterprises and ICT. Asia – Pacific development information programme e-primers for the information economy, society and policy.* UNDP-APDIP and APCICT, 1-27. Retrieved August 12, 2008, from http://www.unapcict.org/ecohub/resources/small-and-medium-enterprises-and-ict

Lam, W., & Shankararaman, V. (2004). An enterprise integration methodology. *IT Professional, 6*(2), 40–48. doi:10.1109/MITP.2004.1278864

Laudon, K. C., & Laudon, J. P. (2007). *Essentials of business information systems.* Upper Saddle River, NJ: Pearson Prentice Hall. Lewis, E. (2005, September). Now is SMEs' time to compete on-demand supply chain solutions are affordable for the small distributor. *Industrial Distribution.*

Linthicum, D. (1999). *Enterprise application integration.* MA: Addison-Wesley.

Loh, T. C., & Koh, S. C. L. (2004). Critical elements for a successful ERP implementation in SMEs. *International Journal of Production Research, 42*(17), 3433–3455. doi:10.1080/00207540410001671679

Mabert, V. A., Ashok, S., & Venkataramanan, M. A. (2000). Enterprise resource planning survey of US manufacturing firms. *Production and Inventory Management Journal, 41*(2), 52–58.

Meatzer, J. T., DeWitt, W., Keebler, J. S., Soonhong, M., Nix, N. W., Carlo, D. S., & Zach, G. Z. (2001). Defining supply chain management. *Journal of Business Logistics, 22*(2), 34–47.

Møller, C. (2005). ERP II: a conceptual framework for next-generation enterprise systems? *Journal of Enterprise Information Management, 18*(4), 483–497. doi:10.1108/17410390510609626

Murphy, R. P., Jr., & Wood, F. D. (2004). *Contemporary Logistics.* London: Prentice Hall.

Norris, G., Hurley, R. J., Hartley, M. K., Dunleavy, R. J., & Balls, D. J. (2000). E-Business and ERP, Transforming the enterprise. New York: John Wiley & Sons, Inc

O'Leary, D. E. (2000). *Enterprise Resource Planning Systems - Systems, Life Cycle, Electronic Commerce, and Risk.* New York, USA: Cambridge University Press.

OECD Glossary of Statistical Terms. (2005). Small and Medium-sized Enterprises (SMES) definition. Retrieved July 12, 2008, from http://stats.oecd.org/glossary/detail.asp?ID=3123

Olsen, K. A., & Sætre, P. (2007). ERP for SMEs – is proprietary software an alternative? *Business Process Management Journal, 13*(3), 379–389. doi:10.1108/14637150710752290

Pais, A. V. (2004). Supply chain management for SMEs – a boon for achieving distinction.1-9. Retrieved August 2, 2008 from http://escc.army.mil/doc/ERP/ERP_white_papers/Supply_Chain_Management_for_SMEs-A_Boon_for_Achieving_Distinction.pdf

Petri, H., & Szekely, B. (2005). Logistics information systems: an analysis of software solutions for supply chain co-ordination. *Industrial Management & Data Systems, 105*(1), 5–18. doi:10.1108/02635570510575153

Protogeros, N., Tahinakis, P., Mylonakis, J., & Gagalis, D. (2007). The entrepreneurship reality in the field of supply chain management (SCM) systems – The Hellenic market paradigm. *International Journal of Technology Marketing, 2*(1), 19–52. doi:10.1504/IJTMKT.2007.011584

Rapp, V. W. (2002). *Information Technology strategies, how leading firms use it to gain an advantage*. New York: Oxford University Press, Inc.

Ruh, W., Maginnis, F., & Brown, W. (2000). *Enterprise application integration*. A Wiley Tech Brief. New York: John Wiley & Sons Inc.

Seán de Búrca, Fynes, B., & Marshall, D. (2005). Strategic technology adoption: Extending ERP across the supply chain. *The Journal of Enterprise Information Management, 18*(4), 427–440. doi:10.1108/17410390510609581

Shapiro, J. F. (2001). *Modeling the supply chain*. MIT, Boston: Duxbury Thomson Learning.

Simchi-Levi, D., Kaminsky, P., & Simhci-Levi, E. (2000). *Designing and managing the supply chain: Concepts, strategies and case studies*. New York: McGraw-Hill.

SMEs: development of constructs and propositions. *Asia Pacific Journal of Marketing and Logistics, 20*(1), 97-131

Stefansson, G. (2002). Business-to-business data sharing: a source for integration of supply chains. *International Journal of Production Economics, 75*(1-2), 135–146. doi:10.1016/S0925-5273(01)00187-6

Stock, J. R., & Lambert, D. M. (2001). *Strategic logistics management*. London: McGraw-Hill International Edition.

Taylor, M., & Murphy, A. (2004). SMEs and E-business. *Journal of Small Business and Enterprise Development, 11*(3), 280–289. doi:10.1108/14626000410551546

Thakkar, J., Kanda, A., & Deshmukh, S.G. (2008). Supply chain management in

Themistocleous, M., & Irani, Z. (2003). Towards a novel framework for the assessment of enterprise application integration packages. In *Proceedings of the 36th Hawaii International Conference on System Sciences*, HICSS, (p.234a).

Themistocleous, M., Irani, Z., & Love, P. (2004). Evaluating the integration of supply chain information systems: A case study. *European Journal of Operational Research, 159*, 393–405. doi:10.1016/j.ejor.2003.08.023

Themistocleous, M., Irani, Z., & Sharif, A. (2000). *Evaluating application integration*. Paper presented in Seventh European Conference on Evaluation of Information Technology (ECITE 2000), Dublin, Ireland, MCIL Reading, UK, 193- 202.

Thong, J. Y. L. (2001). Resource constraints and information systems implementation in Singaporean small business. *Omega, 29*(2), 143–156. doi:10.1016/S0305-0483(00)00035-9

Turban, E., Dorothy, L., McLean, E., & Wetherbe, J. (2006). *Information technology for management, transforming organizations in the digital economy*. Hoboken, NJ: John Wiley & Sons, Inc.

Verwijmeren, M. (2004). Software component architecture in supply chain management. *Computers in Industry, 53*(2), 165–178. doi:10.1016/j.compind.2003.07.004

Zahavi, R. (1999). *Enterprise application integration with CORBA*. New York: Wiley.

KEY TERMS AND DEFINITIONS

Advanced Planning & Scheduling (APS): APS are techniques that deal with analysis and planning of logistics and manufacturing over the short, intermediate, and long-term time periods. APS describes any computer program that uses advanced mathematical algorithms or logic to perform optimization or simulation on finite capacity scheduling, sourcing, capital planning, resource planning, forecasting, demand management, and others. These techniques simultaneously consider a range of constraints and business rules to provide real-time planning and scheduling, decision support, available-to-promise, and capable-to-promise capabilities.

Application Service Providers (ASPs): ASPs are a way for companies to outsource some or almost all aspects of their information technology needs. They may be commercial ventures that cater to customers, or not-for-profit or government organizations, providing service and support to end users. ASPs are broken down into five sub-categories: (a) enterprise ASPs: deliver high-end business applications, (b) local/regional ASPs: supply wide variety of application services for smaller businesses in a local area, (c) specialist ASPs: provide applications for a specific need, such as Web site services or human resources, (d) vertical market ASPs: provide support to a specific industry, such as healthcare, (e) volume business ASPs: supply general small/medium-sized businesses with pre-packaged application services in volume

Warehouse Management Systems (WMS): WMS systems are used in effectively managing warehouse business processes and direct warehouse activities, including receiving, put away, picking, shipping, and inventory cycle counts. Also includes support of radio-frequency communications, allowing real time data transfer between the system and warehouse personnel. They also maximize space and minimize material handling by automating put away processes.

Small and Medium Sized Enterprises (SMEs): SMEs is made up of enterprises which employ fewer than 250 persons and which have an annual turnover not exceeding 50 million euro, and/or an annual balance sheet total not exceeding 43 million euro.

Enterprise Application Integration (EAI): EAI are unrestricted sharing of data and business processes throughout the networked applications or data sources in an organization. There are four major categories of EAI: (a) database linking: databases share information and duplicate information as needed, (b) application linking: the enterprise shares business processes and data between two or more applications, (c) data warehousing: data is extracted from a variety of data sources and channelled into a specific database for analysis, (d) common virtual system: the pinnacle of EAI.

E-Business: The administration of conducting business via the Internet. This would include the buying and selling of goods and services, along with providing technical or customer support through the Internet. e-Business is a term often used in conjunction with e-commerce, but includes services in addition to the sale of goods.

Enterprise Resource Planning Systems (ERPs): ERP is a business management system that integrates all facets of the business, including planning, manufacturing, sales, and marketing. As the ERP methodology has become more popular, software applications have emerged to help business managers implement ERP in business activities such as inventory control, order tracking, customer service, finance and human resources.

Supply Chain Management (SCM): SCM encompasses the planning and management of all activities involved in sourcing and procurement, conversion, and all logistics management activities. Importantly, it also includes coordination and collaboration with channel partners, which can be suppliers, intermediaries, third-party service providers, and customers. In essence, supply chain management integrates supply and demand management within and across companies.

Decision Support Systems (DSS): DSS refers to an interactive computerized system that gathers and presents data from a wide range of sources, typically for business purposes. DSS applications are systems and subsystems that help people make decisions based on data that is culled from a wide range of sources. DSS applications are not single information resources, such as a database or a program that graphically represents sales figures, but the combination of integrated resources working together.

Service Oriented Architecture (SOA): SOA is a computer system term which describes an software architectural concept that defines the use of services to support business requirements. In an SOA, resources are made available to other participants in the network as independent services that are accessed in a standardized way. Most definitions of SOA identify the use of web services (using SOAP and WSDL) in its implementation, however it is possible to implement SOA using any service-based technology.

Chapter 22
Contrasting Approaches to Preparedness:
A Reflection on Two Case Studies

Lorraine Warren
University of Southampton, UK

Ted Fuller
Lincoln University, UK

ABSTRACT

This chapter reflects on ongoing research in SMEs in the manufacturing and service sectors. It contrasts different approaches to the issue of preparedness from an organisational and social perspective, in two cases where new enterprise-wide business processes were implemented and integrated in different settings. In both cases, the emergence of new systems presented a huge challenge to companies hard-pressed to marshal the resources to mount effective change and implementation projects on this scale. The cases presented enable a comparison of different strategies used, one firm responding to organic growth, and the other to rapid industry-driven change. The chapter focuses not on the implementations per se, but instead on the issue of preparedness for change. The chapter concludes by drawing out general lessons concerning how to support and maintain organisational preparedness for enterprise wide change in different industry settings.

INTRODUCTION

A few years ago, I worked with a small manufacturing company in the UK horticultural industry that was experiencing the need for improved communication and control across the enterprise as growth took place (Warren, 2002, 2003, ab). Parts of the business responsible for different product lines wanted to talk to each other, more efficient financial management systems were essential to meet increased orders, and further, there was a need to develop more internet-oriented customer management and marketing systems. This situation resulted in a two-year project with the local university under the (then) Teaching Company Scheme (which has now evolved into the Knowledge Transfer Partnership programme) which employed a graduate under university supervision to analyse and redesign the company's management and information systems in an enterprise-wide endeavour. During the scheme, through an extensive consultancy, development and training programme, we introduced Beer's Viable System Model (VSM) (Beer, 1981, 1985) as a learning vehicle to support the development of a conceptual design for integration that at the time, in itself, met the company's needs. Later on, this turned out to be a stepping stone on the road to a technological implementation of the design. The project was deemed successful, with the organisational learning that took place through using a simplified version of the VSM during the analysis and design phase being seen as essential to success. Through a variety of participative fora, staff across the enterprise developed insight into the need for change and made input into how the new systems would work. Over the period of the project, a sense of 'preparedness' for change emerged among all sections of the workforce.

Based on this experience, presented in the first case below, I went on to develop successfully this *modus operandi* for developing new business systems (in terms of preparedness for implementation) with other small companies, both service and manufacturing, public and private sector (Ragsdell and Warren, 1999; Warren, 2003c). It was only when I encountered a different kind of company that seemed to be operating and growing in a new way, that I realised I was seeing a different kind of preparedness. At this point, my research took a new direction. Thus, the second case I present examines a 'rapid response' to industry change from a service company in the airline industry. In this case, competitive advantage (and indeed survival) is linked to the rapid embedding of new systems in short time frames as new business

models emerge across a whole industry. This chapter therefore examines, in reflective mode, the two projects that proved to be landmarks in my understanding of how small organisations organise for enterprise-wide change.

BACKGROUND

The first cluster of SMEs I worked with, although they were quite different in location and purpose, all had one thing in common: they were all relatively localised firms, experiencing fairly linear growth patterns, in relatively predictable sectors, that were yes, subject to change and competition, but by and large, the basic business models held true for quite long periods of time. What they seemed to be experiencing was growth in line with classical stage model theory, and as predicted by Greiner (1972), at a certain point, they were coming up against a 'crisis of control'. Classical 'stage models' of growth for small firms, whilst they differ in their detail, identify a series of phases through which growing businesses progress, each presenting different managerial challenges. Stage models suggest that an appropriate response from the owner-manager (OM) is required if the firm is to grow effectively, or indeed to survive (Greiner 1972; Churchill & Lewis 1983; Scott & Bruce 1987).

Although stage models have been criticised widely for their owner-centric, deterministic, linear perspective, it is notable that they all predict that problems may arise as existing management and information systems become unable to meet the needs of expanding firms, either in terms of coping with increased throughput, or providing the flexibility to meet the opportunities and challenges in the business environment. Greiner's model, for example, points to a phase of delegation, where OMs appoint others to deal with functional aspects of the business organisation that they once dealt with themselves. This can be followed by a 'crisis of control', if the result of delegation is poor communication between different parts of the organisation. It is suggested by the model that a phase of co-ordination should then follow, where management and information systems are reviewed and developed to improve communication and effect better reporting and monitoring procedures. Notwithstanding the critique of stage models, this does seem to reflect the experience of many small firms in conditions of organic growth. At this point, many OMs consider technological integration across the enterprise (Waring & Wainwright, 2000), the point where I was called in to oversee the project at the firm at the heart of the first case, APCO.

The situation at the second company, FD, was quite different from the above, where the enterprise-wide change appears manageable through quite rational management planning processes (albeit with a strong interpretive dimension as we shall see below). FD was established by two founders in 1984 to provide brokerage services in the air travel industry. This industry has certainly presented far more volatile conditions over the last twenty years than those experienced by the firms identified above. Airline service companies have had to survive an environment completely transformed by successive rounds of deregulation, the reshaping of the travel industry through new patterns of consumer behaviour, and the impact of new technology at every level of operation. The airline industry is distinctive in that it is international and truly global, yet it has a degree of uniformity imposed by safety and security considerations. It is also highly regulated in terms of who can participate and how – through what systems, both technological and regulatory bodies. FD has little power or influence over supra-national events that have the potential to threaten the survival of the firm unless decisive managerial action is taken, typically over relatively short timescales, and at the level of the enterprise. For example, the effects of terrorist action on the demand for travel, the continued opening of trading regulations, direct internet bookings and air-crashes are all features

of the landscape outside the control of the firm. FD is remarkable in that it has survived for 24 years, having employed up to 100 people prior 9/11, in an industry which has been through huge political, economic, social and technical change on a global scale. Growth had occurred through what the OM described as 'enforced agility', where disruptive industry events had led to the rapid-fire development of new business models that operated as distinctive and separate business units within the firm. Nonetheless, there was still a need for the underlying system architecture of the firm to have a degree of interoperability that still allowed for the anticipation of speedily implemented change. The ongoing research carried at FD is being undertaken not to instigate phases of planned integration, but instead to gain better understanding of how such 'anticipatory systems management' contributes to the agility and sustainability of firms operating in volatile environments.

In the next section, the two case studies are presented, followed by a reflective conclusion that draws out contrasts concerning the idea of 'preparedness' for system-wide process change. In the first case, we see that preparedness is something that needs to be worked at and developed as step change approaches. In the second we see that preparedness is quite different, it is a 'way of being' in anticipation of constant and unpredictable change. These differences have consequences for the nature of enterprise design.

Case Studies and Reflection

1. APCO: Developing Preparedness

APCO are a small family company with a £2M turnover, producing and supplying a range of building and garden products to civil engineering contractors, large home improvement/garden centre companies, and directly to the end consumer. Starting out 70 years ago as a concrete products manufacturing company supplying to the building industry, the company had undergone a typical diversification of its customer and product base, into four departments, organised around the key product ranges: flood defence products, aggregates, concrete slabs and decorative garden products, all acting to some extent as separate production units, but drawing on the same operative and support staff pool. That 'mix' was seen as important in coping with seasonal and market fluctuations across the different sectors addressed. The firm was controlled by the Managing Director (OM) with the aid of his father, ex-OM, semi-retired and operating as Chairman. Alongside a four-person management team and a small administrative staff, 22 full-time production operatives were employed by the company, some in a supervisory capacity. Over time, the company had adopted a rather tall (though not inflexible) hierarchical structure, built around 5 levels of operations and management that were not functioning well in terms of information flows and needed a complete redesign, even to support current levels of activity. Further, the company was seeking to expand, while achieving economies of scale through automation of certain sections of the manufacturing operation. This brought further challenges to the management and information systems of the company, as in the need to develop and integrate new inventory control systems and new marketing systems to cope with increased orders and recognise the growing importance of the internet.

It was clear that the time had come to initiate a project to support the planned expansion and deal with an accumulated problem set at root and branch level (Waring & Wainwright, 2000). However, previous change initiatives had had mixed results, not due to a lack of top level support, but a lack of enthusiasm from middle managers as they became side-tracked by pressing production issues. This loss of enthusiasm had soon spread to the shop floor, where momentum rapidly dissolved. This past history of failed initiatives, and also a real fear of redundancy as rumours of the automation project circulated added up not only a lack of preparedness for systems integration, but resistance to change altogether.

This lack of enthusiasm did not come as a surprise. At the time of the project, a literature concerning success factors for enterprise systems integration had begun to emerge (Holland et al., 1999; Chen, 2001; Al-Mudimigh et al., 2001; Nah et al., 2001; Waring & Wainwright, 2000), which highlighted a range of organisational issues in addition to technically dominated concerns. This was in some part a backlash against the enthusiasm of software companies to sell 'off the shelf' integration packages to companies in the 90s, whether they were suitable or not. There was a consensus that the pre-implementation phase was crucial to the success of the eventual endeavour, with the need to:

- Establish the need for the project in line with the strategic objectives of the business
- Understand, simplify and perhaps re-engineer key business processes
- Establish appropriate change management procedures.

Yet achieving the above is not straightforward and raises complex issues, with a number of authors highlighting cases where poor conceptualisation and a lack of meaningful engagement of system users in the early stages had compromised success overall (Waring & Wainwright, 2000; Markus & Tanis, 2000; Van Stijn & Wensley, 2001). These general organisational complexities can take on a particular character in the small firm environment. (Fuller & Lewis, 2003), drawing on a 2-year qualitative study of 38 small firms, note the powerful influence of OMs in 'managing meaning' around technological projects (supporting stakeholder relationships in the supply chain in this study). This influence may be particularly powerful where no dedicated IS/IT professionals are employed, commonly the case in small firms.

Not surprisingly then, in light of the prevailing zeitgeist at the time, we took an interpretive approach to the pre-project phase which encouraged user ownership of solutions and prioritised learning about the organisational situation over a technologically-driven push towards a predetermined and poorly conceptualised notion of integration (or Fuller & Lewis, 2003's 'orderliness'). We also sought throughout to maintain an ethical stance towards the workforce, by trying to follow the tenets of Critical Systems Thinking (Jackson, 1991, 2000) a journey chronicled in (Warren, 2003a). This consisted of full workplace meetings, one-to-one meetings, and the formation of project workgroups, to address issues of data modelling, systems integration, organisational design and user engagement. Of course, this path, which lasted for the full two years of the project, is never smooth and there was some evidence in the early stages of our involvement that the academic input into project design was not welcome in all quarters, with comments such as:

What do those boffins know about a concrete company? Nothing! They're just here to put us out of a job!

You want to put us out of work and you don't have the guts to do it yourself, and you've brought that lot in, and their bits of paper, to do it for you.

If you want to sack me, just do it, I can't be bothered with all this.

I appreciate what you're trying to do, but me gathering all these facts and figures will just put me out of a job. That pretty picture [VSM schema] you're waving around is just a map to the [social welfare office] as far as I'm concerned.

Why do we need boffins from the university to tell you what's wrong, I've been telling you for years!

Yet in spite of this early suspicion and many wobbles along the way, the project was a success: automation of production took place, and notwithstanding an investment in plant of £200K, there was a corresponding increase in profit, without loss of any staff. This expansion is supported by effective management and information systems, which have addressed a range of immediate operational and tactical communication problems, in addition to supporting broader strategic objectives concerning better marketing and better relationships with customers and suppliers. At the time, this was a *conceptual* integration, to build an enterprise-wide system architecture, not a software implementation. Better business process and communication systems could be managed with existing software, and it was seen as more important to get people working effectively in new working patterns in a new organisational design. Of course, over time, as networking and the internet have become increasingly important, new hardware and software have been purchased, but the initial design held fast for many years, a testament to the rigorous values of the project.

One of the key elements in this success was the use of Beer's VSM (1981, 1985) to support the design of the new integrated management systems; this part of the journey is chronicled in (Warren, 2003b). In very simplified terms, Beer sees any organisation as being made up of five systems connected through communication and control channels, in contrast to traditional organisation charts:

System 5: Policy (policy formulation)
System 4: Development (intelligence gathering and reporting)
System 3: Control (day to day running of the organization)
System 2: Coordination (of System 1)
System 1: Implementation (directly concerned with the task of the organization)

Derived from cybernetic principles as a means of 'engineering' organisations with hard-wired communication channels, later applications of the VSM have drawn on more socially oriented thinking; Espejo et al. (1996) characterise the model as a hermeneutic enabler of organisational learning where systems of communication and control can be developed in interactive settings.

Of course the VSM in its 'raw' form is intimidating to new users. Yet without developing shared understanding of the principles of the model by a significant number of the project management team, the analysis and design phases would have been compromised. By building up from general discussions of accessible ideas such as strategic, tactical and operational information, varying depths of understanding concerning the VSM were shared. Many members of the workforce were happy with the general concept of a five-layer information architecture model and began to use the vocabulary of the five layers of the VSM directly in their contributions to design meetings, and further, to different extents, in implementation discussions with colleagues from across the whole workplace. It was clear that the model was being used in the hermeneutic sense (Espejo et al., 1996), not as a 'recipe' or 'cookbook' formula to produce a predetermined 'hardwired' structure. The vocabulary of the model led to explication, clarification and definition of existing procedures, which in many areas were rather vague and ad hoc. It could be argued that a Community of Practice (CoP) had grown up around the VSM, where learning took place and innovative ways of managing information were developed 'on the ground' using a new shared vocabulary. Like Lave and Wenger (1991, p. 56), masters (academic and associate), young masters (OM and team) and apprentices (those who were drawn into the project team from the periphery) could be identified at different times in the project. The 'meaning' of the VSM application was therefore ambiguous, dynamic and reflexively mediated by negotiation in practice. In conclusion, what has taken place

here is that knowledge transfer could be equated with the establishment of a CoP around the VSM within the project context. Through the CoP, a spirit of preparedness for change came about.

2. FD: Gaining Insight into Preparedness

Like APCO, FD had diversified into different business areas over the years. However, unlike APCO, which had experienced largely linear growth, for FD, the pattern of expansion had been far more discontinuous, driven by both opportunities and shocks in the airline industry. In 1984, the business started with three people brokering between airlines and holiday tour operators. By 1992, four separate business units were operating, in various areas of brokerage. However, in 1993, deregulation removed the need for this type of brokerage role and FD downsized to two business divisions concentrating instead on niche brokerage activity between small airlines and large airports in the UK. Over the next few years, FD expanded again, and in 2001, pre 9/11, the company boasted over 100 employees, a brokerage division, a ticketing call centre and a branded charter service with two 737 aircraft. Post 9/11, the charter service was in liquidation and the call centre survived only at the 11th hour. Up to 2007, the business has continued in a highly dynamic and competitive environment, with around one hundred staff providing general sales agency (GSA, a development of the niche brokerage activity) and an overspill ticketing call centre.

During its existence, FD has had to innovate to remain 'fit' within the business environment, by repeatedly restructuring and rapidly establishing new corporate ventures in response to industry change. Each venture has remained under the FD umbrella: all the employees work in the same building and there is flexibility across operations as the workforce respond to different demand at different times. Yet while there is an overarching veneer of systems integration for basic functions such as payroll and marketing, the underlying architectures of the different divisions remain largely distinct, and dependent on dedicated industry systems. Unlike APCO then, there is no desire for consolidation and co-ordination to support expansion, rather the need is for a fast and flexible response that enables new divisions to be bolted on to the FD structure – and at the same time, such structures can be very quickly jettisoned if they become unprofitable.

Both authors have worked with FD for many years, researching into the sustainability of small entrepreneurial businesses in such volatile settings. Our latest study focussed on the emergence of yet another new business model in FD, this time for a 'long-tail' web-based internet onward-flight regional airline booking system, A-A.com, which is intended to cater for a niche market not covered by the large travel companies such as expedia or ebookers. Unlike the APCO case, the development of this potential new business up until almost the implementation point, was driven almost entirely from the top, by two members of the senior management team, P (the Managing Director) and J (the Technical Director and owner of a large shareholding in the firm). The full account of this journey is summarised in Warren et al, (2008).

The pre-launch phase of the development of A-A.com commenced in 2004. The idea was first articulated by P and J during a meeting in a Moscow hotel foyer, while waiting for a client who was late for an appointment. This conversation was part of ongoing discussions regarding the 'fitness' of FD, updating the GSA business' web presence and looking for higher growth opportunities to supplement the overspill call centre, which was being challenged by competition from India. Initially, A-A.com was expected to grow out of, and supplement the newly web-focussed GSA division. J then began to work on the feasibility of the idea with his commitment really crystallising when he attended a Travel Distribution Summit in Philadelphia in May 2005, where he developed a new *"sense of urgency"* about *"missing this*

bandwagon". Early in 2006, J began to seriously discuss online booking with system providers. Meanwhile, the GSA system continued its full migration to the web.

At this point, the idea underwent a major shift in its trajectory. Because both P and J were becoming increasingly convinced over time of the likelihood of A-A.com becoming highly profitable, a strategic decision was taken to fully exploit the idea by moving out of the model based on the GSA business (a relatively small airline base) to a GDS (dedicated travel industry Geographical Distribution System) system. Effectively this made FD a travel agency, for which IATA (International Air Transport Agency) approval would be required. This approval was achieved in July 2006. Going down this route brought with it the capability to fulfil bookings for hundreds of other airlines in IATA, not just the GSA base. The first booking was on 29 September through GSA, prior the launch of A-A.com as a separate entity in January 2007. Since then, A-A.com has operated as a separate arm within FD, with ongoing effort (through the appointment of new staff) being directed into the building of technological infrastructure, web presence, markets, and increasing the participating airline base. The underpinning architecture of the GSA and the GDS are linked, but A-A.com has a separate character.

During our research period with FD, our studies have shown that unlike APCO, senior figures in FD spend their time in constant state of preparedness for organisational change, a form of 'anticipatory systems management', where temporary, ephemeral, unstable organisational structures appear and develop ontological status over time. Some go on to 'become' part of the firm and others are discarded either before, or soon after, implementation. Elsewhere, we have used and developed understandings of emergence rooted in complexity theory to explore this situation in more detail (Fuller et al., 2007 a,b). In FD, preparedness manifests as repeating patterns of behaviour. (Fuller et al., 2004, 2006) and (Fuller et al., 2007 a,b) have characterised these 4 inter-related behaviour patterns, as 'processes of emergence', patterns that lead to the emergence of novelty in entrepreneurial settings: new services, new products, new careers, or in this case, new business models. These processes of emergence, set out in Table 1, have been characterised as the 'EROS' model – Experiments, Reflexivity, Organising, Sensitivity.

The processes in Table 1 should be seen as inter-connected, not separate, and we argue that it is the multi-dimensional concentration on these patterns of behaviour that is at the heart of entrepreneurial competence through effective strategising over time to produce a *sustainable* business. The four EROS processes interact to produce new emergent structures over time. Each process inter-relates with the other through multi-layers of cognition, language, performance and relationships with others, albeit strongly influenced by the entrepreneur. For FD's directors, preparedness is a state of mind, a way of being, not a sit-down session at 2pm on a Tuesday afternoon. In brief:

Experiments

At FD, new things were constantly being tried out, often in very informal ways. There is a sense in which social interactions were used to search for and examine possibilities for new activities which might be formalised as experimental projects if judged to hold promise. If these worked,

they were built upon. If they didn't work they were changed or dropped. The projects or reorganising of activities were relatively small scale and were talked about in terms of seeing what would work. Experiments could be as tenuous as conversations, mental models, thought experiments, or interactions with casual contacts, or, they could involve more significant discussions with suppliers or new partners. The character of the firm is to repeatedly experiment with new initiatives and projects, sometimes in the most tenuous of informal ways. A-A.com is a typical example of FD's tradition of doing things in this way. It began with the casual conversation in Moscow, which P remembers as significant, but J has a much more vague recall of the genesis of the idea. This was the start of a new discourse that might – or might not – persist over time. In this case, it did. Over time, the experiment, in the form of new identities, new products, new services and new stakeholders acquired precedence over the old order through the sensing of a changing business environment. This growing sense of project identity was something that P fostered, an example of this being the production of an internal newsletter, the Altimeter, that focussed on the project alone, not FD in its entirety. A key element of this experimental behaviour is that major resources are not committed till quite late on in the project, when there is a need for rapid embedding of systems. During the 2 years from

Table 1. EROS Processes of emergence

Process	Behaviour
Experimenting	Diverse exploratory behaviours that might (or might not) become part of the firm over time; new things tried out in often very informal ways, small scale; often developed through exploration of social interactions; shared experiential learning across project teams and stakeholders; 'what works'
Reflexivity	Continuous reflection on the identity of the firm and the self-identity of its owner(s) through the discourses within the business and with stakeholders; vision setting through narratives of self and firm; 'who we are'
Organising	Organising around a dominant logic (or project); patterns established through negotiated practice; pattern-making and pattern-breaking; 'what needs to be done now'
Sensitivity	Interpretation of shifts in industry landscape; detection of difference; weak signals; triggers and thresholds for change; 'what we might do'

conception to implementation (around the same period of time as the APCO project), the vision of A-A.com changed significantly on at least two occasions, prior to the rapid implementation stage at the end.

Reflexive Construction of Identity

The significance of identity for self, the firm and the industry, in which were constituted motivations, roles, daily practice and behavioural imperatives, was paramount in FD, particularly for P. Reflexivity describes the process by which the individual constantly assesses the relationship between 'knowledge' and the "ways of doing knowledge" (Calás & Smircich 1992). Reflexivity links the cognitive domain of the individual to their experienced environment which for the entrepreneur, includes the everyday practices of doing business with others. P, as shaper and decision maker influences the emergent structures of the firm and the context (Fuller & Lewis, 2003). A continuous reflection on the identity of the firm and the self-identity of its owner(s) through the discourses within the business and with stakeholders was central to the direction and identity of the firm, as well as the entrepreneur. For Stacey (2003), strategy is the evolving patterns of an organisation's identity. Thus, an inability to reshape organisational identity puts the future at risk for the firm. This does not mean that the FD was in a state of drift. Two constant themes in FD's history have been P's overwhelming self of 'being something' in the airline industry, and the sense of the company having a unique selling point developed from very specialist expertise in the industry. For A-A.com to work for P and FD, it had to have the distinctive qualities as a niche provider linking to the lesser known reaches of the airline industry. This is strongly bound in the ongoing intertwined life narrative of P and FD, the desire to be independent and the deep desire to be embedded in the specialist regions (geographically and conceptually) of the airline industry. It

is also strongly bound in the relationship with J who realises the vision through continuous grasp of an industry that has seen enormous systems development and change since the first joined the firm. P trusts J to enable anticipation and response to change that has enabled the gradual development of a unique core competence around industry knowledge over time. Thus A-A.com becomes a realistic possibility, triggered by a sense of industry change yet rooted in the existing identity of the firm.

Organising Domains

An organising domain is a space where activities are organised around a dominant logic. Lichtenstein links activity domains, which "guide organizational activity and also prescribe limits to the system's capacity to get the work done" with "organizing domains," which in his studies of successful young businesses emerged rapidly in a self-organizing process, e.g. *"Once agreement for a new mission had been reached, a new set of organizing domains rapidly emerged to implement that goal"* (Lichtenstein, 2000). In volatile or high velocity landscapes in particular, the speed at which new regularised practices can be put into place contributes to the sustainability of the enterprise. The tension between innovative (pattern breaking) practices and recurrent practices (maintaining patterns) requires managerial judgement, and for A-A.com, occurs quite late on in the project. Yet the business cannot just 'act' overnight. A-A.com is shaped – both constrained and enabled by the regulatory requirement and the technical infrastructure, i.e. IATA registration and the GDS; these require anticipatory management and system building, a partial commitment of resource, even though at this stage, there is still a sense that the project may not necessarily come to fruition. The most significant resources are only committed at a very late stage, once the first order has been realised through the GSA system.

Sensitivity to Conditions

The evidence from FD suggests that the management were highly aware of changes in the external environment and also of the potential cash-flow and profitability produced by the business model. The main issue for this business seemed to be mainly one of when to enact new patterns, and more particularly when to break existing ones. The key trigger points for A-A.com were firstly, J's trip to the Philadelphia Conference when he realised with a sense of urgency that if FD did not act soon they would be beaten to the market by someone else. The second trigger point was the decision to move out of the GSA-driven model for A-A.com and purchase the GDS/IATA registration and (with reference to the point made earlier) adopt a slightly extended identity for the firm, in terms of the travel agency.

Taken in totality, these four areas of process provide an entrepreneurial mechanism that has proved significant in the sustainability of FD over a prolonged period of time demonstrating the ability to perform and survive in an industry which is increasingly dominated by dedicated travel industry systems that are deeply intertwined with advanced web analytics. This industry context is fast-moving and an excellent example of the need to strategise and anticipate on a contingent and agile basis. The conception and development of alternative-airlines.com is deeply embedded in this intricate context and decisions taken impact across the whole business; it is not a simple stand-alone project that can be picked up or put down on an *ad hoc* basis. There is evidence that the EROS processes are at the heart of FD entrepreneurial culture. Yet EROS is not simply a cultural model, a vague cultural soup which allows good things to somehow happen. It is based on the language and understandings of complexity theory and in part therefore explains how certain essential sets of activities result in the emergence of new systems, though the outcomes are not predetermined.

CONCLUSION

Unlike the APCO project, which was a step change redesign to provide an enterprise-wide platform for the future, A-A.com is another example in FD's long history of a business unit which is nurtured separately in isolation then rapidly embedded in the FD structure on a just-in-time basis, when it is sensed that the industry pressure to do so is becoming critical, if a competitive edge is to be obtained. Resources of money, people and time are only committed at the last moment and shifts in the trajectory of systems projects are to be expected. It cannot be said that the FD exemplified Pathfinding (Turner & Crawford, 1994) competences in its everyday approach to business. It did not routinely or explicitly undertake formal foresight activities, such as scenario planning, it was not able to assess the "total impact of any particular change" that strategic awareness assumes (Gibb & Scott, 1985). Nor was there evidence of the "highly visible vision of the future" that Hamel and Prahalad (1994) associate with Strategic Intent. Instead, the firm exists in a constant state of preparedness that results in the partial construction of new systems against the potential existence of developing projects that may or may not be realised. This means that full enterprise-wide integration to effect communication and control, which was an important need for APCO, is less significant for FD, where integration is not an issue in itself. It may be necessary for two underlying system architectures to be connected (as in the GSA and A-A.com projects), but it may not: in which case, separate development is the order of the day, as any given project may need to be jettisoned at a later stage.

This mindset, developed to cope with the exigencies of a volatile industry environment, is in complete contrast to the situation at APCO, where the need is to establish a robust platform that integrates and supports the needs of the company over the coming years in what is expected to be a relatively stable environment. Reflecting the stability of the past, in a firm that has existed in a rural environment for over 60 years, there is a need to develop a sense of preparedness in the workforce from the bottom-up. This took considerable time, effort and sensitivity, in context carefully informed by the principles of participative intervention.

In summary, the issue of preparedness is one that is often taken for granted in the literature. At one time, the concern was limited to technical matters related to data collection and user/system requirements. In the early 00s, the emphasis shifted to the social concerns of the pre-project phase. What these contrasting case studies show is that for some companies, the whole notion of systems integration is a moveable feast at best and may even be undesirable in certain types of industry/firm, where more flexible or readily disposable arrangements might be needed. The recent world financial crisis certainly tells us how volatile the business environment can be. We will be carrying out further research into the normative implications of our work.

REFERENCES

Al-Mudimigh, A., Zairi, M., & Al-Mashari, M. (2001). ERP software implementation: an integrative framework. *European Journal of Information Systems, 10*(4), 216-226

Beer, S. (1981). *The Brain of the Firm*. Chichester: Wiley

Beer, S. (1985). *Diagnosing the System for Organizations*. Chichester: Wiley

Calás, M., & Smircich, L. (1992). Rewriting gender into organizational theorizing: Directions from feminist perspectives. In M. Reed & M. Hughes (Eds.), *Rethinking organization: New directions in organizational theory and analysis* (pp. 227–253). London: Sage

Chen, I. J. (2001). Planning for ERP systems: analysis and future trends. *Business Process Management Journal, 7*(5), 374–386

Churchill, N., & Lewis, V. (1983, May/June). The five stages of small business growth. *Harvard Business Review* (pp. 30–50).

Espejo, R., Schuhmann, W., Schwaninger, M., & Bilello, U. (1996). *Organisational Transformation and Learning*. Chichester: Wiley

Fuller, T., & Lewis, F. (2003). Relationships mean everything. *British Journal of Management, 13*, 317-336.

Fuller, T., Moran, P., & Argyle, P. (2004). Entrepreneurial foresight; a case in reflexivity, experiments, sensitivity and reorganisation. In H. Tsoukas & J. Shepherd (Eds.), *Managing the Future: Foresight in the Knowledge Economy* (pp. 171-8). Oxford: Blackwell

Fuller, T., & Fewster, R. (2006). *The emergence of Tesco.com: A study of Corporate Entrepreneurship*. Paper presented at the Babson-Kauffman Entrepreneurship Research Conferemce, Kelley Business School, Indiana

Fuller, T., Warren, L., & Argyle, P. (2007a). Sustaining Entrepreneurial Business; a complexity perspective on processes that produce emergent practice. *International Entrepreneurship and Management Journal, 4*(1), 1-17.

Fuller, T., Warren, L., & Welter, F. (2007b, November). *Towards an emergence perspective on entrepreneurship*. Paper presented at RENT XXI, Research in Entrepreneurship and Small Business, Cardiff (pp. 22-23).

Gibb, A. A., & Scott, M. G. (1985). Strategic Awareness, Personal Commitment and the Process of Planning in the Small Business. *Journal of Management Studies, 22*(6), 597-625

Greiner, L. E. (1972, July/August). Evolution and Revolution as Organisations Grow. *Harvard Busi-*

ness Review (pp. 37-46).

Hamel, G., & Prahalad, C. K. (1994). *Competing for the future*. Boston: Harvard Business School Press.

Holland, C. P., Light, B., & Gibson, N. (1999, June 23-25). A critical success factors model for emterprise resource planning implementation. In *Proceedings of the Seventh European Conference on Information Systems*, Copenhagen (pp. 288-301).

Jackson, M. C. (1991). *Systems Methodology for the Management Sciences*. New York: Plenum

Jackson, M. C. (2000). *Systems Approaches to Management*. New York: Kluwer

Lave, J., & Wenger, E. (1991). *Situated Learning: Legitimate Peripheral Participation*. New York: Cambridge University Press.

Lichtenstein, B. M. B. (2000). Self-organized transitions: A pattern amid the chaos of transformative change. *Academy of Management Executive, 14*(4), 128-141.

Markus, M. L., & Tanis, C. (2000). The enterprise systems experience – from adoption to success. In: R. W. Zmud (Ed.), *Framing the Domains of IT Research: Glimpsing the Future through the Past* (pp. 73-207). Cincinnatti, Ohio: Pinnaflex Educational Resources Inc.

Nah, F. F. H., Lau, J. L. S., & Kuang, J. (2001). Critical factors for successful implementation of enterprise systems. *Business Process Management Journal, 7*(3), 285–296.

Ragsdell, G., & warren, L. (1999). Learning from Beer: Using the Viable System Model for Organisational Design. *OR Insight, 12*(4), 16-23.

Scott, M., & Bruce, R. (1987). Five Stages of Growth in Small Business. *Long Range Planning, 20*(3), 45–52.

Stacey, R. D. (2003). *Strategic Management and Organisational Dynamics, the Challenge of Complexity*. London: FT Prentice Hall.

Trunick, P. A. (1999). ERP: promise or pipe dream. *Transportation and Distribution, 40*(1), 23–6.

Turner, D., & Crawford, M. (1994). Managing Current and Future Competitive Performance: The Role of Competence. In G. Hamel & A. Heene (Eds.), *Competence Based Competition* Chichester: Wiley.

Van Stijn, E., & Wensley, A. (2001). Organisational memory and the completeness of process modelling in ERP systems. *Business Process Management Journal, 7*(3), 181–194.

Waring, T., & Wainwright, D. (2000). Interpreting integration with respect to information systems in organizations – image, theory and reality. *Journal of Information Technology, 15*, 131–148

Warren, L. (2002). Towards Critical Practice in a Teaching Company Scheme. *OR Insight, 15*(4), 11-19.

Warren, L. (2003a). Towards Critical Practice in SMEs. *Systemic Practice and Action Research, 16*(3), 197-212

Warren, L. (2003b). The crisis of control: a progressive approach towards information systems integration for small companies. *Information Systems and E-business Management, 1*(4), 353-371.

Warren, L. (2003c). Supporting Knowledge Management through he Viable System Model. *Systemist, 25*, 156-165.

Warren, L., Fuller, T., Argyle, P., & Welter, F. (2008, September). *A complexity perspective on entrepreneurship: a new methodology for research in high velocity environments*. Paper presented at the British Academy of Management conference, Harrogate, UK.

Chapter 23
Critical Success Factors (CSFs) for Enterprise Resource Planning (ERP) Solution Implementation in SMEs:
What Does Matter for Business Integration

Simona Sternad
University of Maribor, Slovenia

Samo Bobek
University of Maribor, Slovenia

Zdenko Dezelak
University of Maribor, Slovenia

Ana Lampret
SRC.SI, Slovenia

ABSTRACT

Enterprise resource planning (ERP) solution implementation is a complex process, that requires substantial resources and efforts, and yet the results are very uncertain. The ERP hype has already reached SMEs, so the authors have examined the strategies, methods and critical success factors from SMEs point of view. The results of our survey in SMEs in Slovenia have shown that SMEs have to pay attention to different critical success factors in different phases of the implementation process. Moreover, there are differences in implementation process as opposed to large companies. Case studies of two SMEs have shown similar results. Recommendations for future SME implementations and comments of our findings can be found in conclusion.

INTRODUCTION

Enterprise resource planning (ERP) solutions support business processes on operative level in organizations. ERP solution typically consist of (Wallace & Kremzar, 2001) an enterprise-wide set of management tools that balance demand and supply; contain the ability to link customers and suppliers into a complete supply chain; employ proven business processes for decision-making; provide high degrees of cross-functional integration among sales, marketing, manufacturing, operations, logistics, purchasing, finance, new product development and human resources; and enable people to run their business with high levels of customer service and productivity, and simultaneously lower costs and inventories; and provide the foundation for effective e-commerce. We can say that ERP systems consist of multi-functional standards, multi-languages, multi-legislative software modules and offer process integration across an entire organisation.

An ERP system can improve business operations flow in organization. ERP solutions are designed by principles of best practices, which means, that ERP vendors search for the best organizational business models in a branch and then incorporate that business model in their package. ERP systems require an organization's core business processes to be reengineered in line with those implicit in the software (Davenport, 1999).

Over the past few years, critical success factors (CSF) of ERP implementation have been well studied (Estaves & Pastor, 2001) in large companies, but very little attention has been paid to CSFs of ERP implementation in SMEs. Although they all have the same goal, that is to improve some aspect of the organization, e.g. strategic, organizational, business, management, operational, or IT-infrastructure (Hedman & Borell, 2002), experience show that different CSFs have to be considered when implementing ERP system in large or in SME organization. To give a contribution to the whole matter, we intend to explore the implementation process of ERP systems in SMEs with intent to compile recommendations.

In the first part of the chapter ERP implementation strategies, methods, and critical success factors from the SME viewpoint will be discussed. In the second part a field research (mainly findings and not scientific details) conducted in Slovenia on the sample of organizations (mainly SMEs) will be presented which have implemented Microsoft Navision solution (Microsoft Dynamics NAV or prior version of Navision solutions) and SAP solutions (My SAP ERP or prior version of solutions). CSFs, their importance, differences between Navision and SAP projects and how CFSs influence each other have been researched. In the third part case studies of two Slovenian SMEs will be analysed which have successfully implemented Navision and which have redesigned and integrated their processes. On the basis of the field research and case studies recommendations for SMEs will be presented.

ERP IMPLEMENTATION (STRATEGIES, METHODS AND CRITICAL SUCCESS FACTORS FROM THE SME VIEWPOINT)

ERP Implementation Strategies and Methods

A review of past research in the area of ERP implementation has revealed that there are different approaches and strategies for ERP implementation. Organizations have to consider different strategies early in the project, because this decision influences all aspects of ERP implementation projects and can ultimately lead to either success or failure.

Shields (2001) for example talks about three stages of ERP project implementation. The first stage consists of pre-project activities including initial commitment. The second stage deals with specific project implementation activities: start, manage, analyze, configure, test, change, support, prepare and go-life. The third stage is focused on post-project activities, which are as important as the first two phases, since we have to perform various activities for further improvement of the adopted system. The fact that each phase includes several activities is a result of aggressive implementation time, set by management.

Bancroft, Seip and Sprengel (2001) grounded a five phases model: Focus, As-Is Phase, To-Be Phase, Construction and Testing Phase, and Implementation Phase. The Focus Phase is essentially a planning phase, which includes activities: setting up of the steering committee, selection and structuring of the project team, development of the projects guiding principles and creation of a project plan. The As-Is Phase includes analysis of current business processes in the light of the ERP functions, installation of the ERP package, mapping of business processes on to the ERP functions and also required training of the project team. The To-Be phase follows and consists of high-level design, detailed design subject and user acceptance, followed by interactive prototyping and constant communication with users. The Construction and Testing Phase activities are development of a comprehensive configuration, test instance with real data, building and testing of interfaces, designing and testing reports, and system and user testing. The Implementation Phase itself consists of building networks, installing desktops and managing user training and providing support.

So far the article considered strategies that different authors have developed. Because of high number of failed ERP implementation projects, ERP vendors have developed their own methodologies that best fit their package. Because of the leading market shares of SAP and Navision ERP packages, we have also examined their respective implementation methodologies.

There are two methodologies used to implement SAP projects: Conventional and ASAP (Ac-celerated SAP). The conventional methodology, better known as the SAP Procedure Model, was widely used to implement SAP solutions (Khan, 2002). This methodology requires a very detailed analysis of the existing systems, current functionality, and business processes to be conducted. As a result, often organizations were driven in mirroring existing systems instead of adopting those of the SAP solution. Today this methodology is still preferred by very large companies. On the basis of this findings SAP introduced the Accelerated SAP (ASAP) implementation methodology in 1996 (Miller, 1998). This methodology promotes project management principles, team members, business process consultants, external consultants and technical areas support. Moreover SAP has provided additional components, tools and accelerators for supporting ASAP implementations. ASAP produces a process-oriented, direct project plan to specifically contributing direction throughout SAP R/3 or mySAP ERP implementation (ibidem). ASAP methodology is composed of roadmap, toolkit, service, and support and training (ibidem). The roadmap is a detailed project plan that describes all activities throughout the implementation. Among other it also includes detailed technical guidelines to support technical project management. The ASAP roadmap consists of five phases: Project Preparation, Business Blueprint, Realization, Final Preparation, and Go-live and support. Phase I - Project Preparation consists of organizational readiness and preparation for the project. Phase II - Business Blueprint deals with the scope which is narrowed to fit the industry-specific processes to reflect the future vision of a business. Phase III – Realization means that the business blueprint becomes reality. During this phase, the system is configured and tested. This is achieved through simulation, validation, unit and integration testing, data conversions and preparation of interfaces, enhancements and reports. In phase IV - Final Preparation in which refining the system, preparing go-life plan, end-user training, knowledge transfer, system administration, data migration and final testing and fine tuning have to be performed (Khan, 2002). In the last phase Go-live and Support, final checks should be done before and after taking-off and also procedures and measurements are developed to review the benefits of an ongoing basis.

Similarly, Microsoft has also developed its own methodology for implementing Microsoft Dynamics ERP packages, called Microsoft Dynamics SureStep (Microsoft, 2007). This methodology provides implementers with implementation guidance combined with project management discipline, tools and template sets that enable Diagnostics, Analysis, Deployment, Migration, Configuration and Upgrade. SureStep methodology helps in reducing risk by making implementation projects simpler, faster and more manageable as it unifies project management terminology, tools, roles and streamlines processes and communication among the project stakeholders. The methodology entails a phased approach, the phases are: Diagnostics, Analysis, Design, Development, Deployment and Operation. The Diagnostics Phase deals with gathering information in order to prepare an adequate proposal for the customer. The basis for such document is detailed requirements and gap/fit analysis. During the Analysis Phase a functional requirements are documented and agreed upon. These details are then incorporated in existing project plan and schedule. The Design Phase includes the design of both the overall solution configuration and the design of specific customizations and integrations needed to cover business requirements identified during the previous phase. Mapping and designing of data migration processes also have to be performed. The Development Phase includes the actual development of customizations, integrations and data migration processes that are set through design specifications. Components are also being tested and verified. This phase is followed by Deployment Phase including all activities related to final system and load testing, training of end users, and the actual cut-over to the new production environment. The main goal of the Operation Phase is the transition into on-going support, final project and software related documentation is also prepared. The methodology emphasises the need for careful project team assembly and definition of members' roles and responsibilities, as well as communication channels.

CRITICAL SUCCESS FACTORS IN ERP PROJECTS

Experience in the past ERP projects has shown, that there is a great need for a better understanding of what exactly makes the crucial difference between success and failure of such projects. Organizations strive to create conditions, in which they can implement chosen solution in expected time, scope and evaluated costs. In order to do so, organizations should be aware of what are critical success factors of ERP implementations (Sternad & Bobek, 2004).

The subject of CSFs in ERP implementations has been widely covered by scientific papers in the past years. A study of previously published papers that are focused on success factors of ERP implementation has been conducted. Twenty four papers have been reviewed, if one author has more than one paper in that area, the latest publication has been chosen. The following list shows major CSFs mentioned by authors. In that list there are only those factors, which are mentioned more than five times, there are fourteen such factors. Number in brackets represents number of authors, who mentioned CSF. These factors are:

- top management support and involvement (21);
- clear goals, objectives and scope (18);
- project team competence and organization (16);
- user training and education (15);
- business process reengineering (BPB) (14);

- change management (13);
- project management (13);
- effective communication (10);
- user involvement (10);
- data analysis and conversion (10);
- consultants (9);
- project champion (9);
- architecture choice (package selection) (9);
- minimal customization (9).

More factors have been found, which were mentioned by less than five authors. Those factors are: legacy system management, methodology of project, effective control, interdepartmental cooperation, management of expectations, dedicated resources, steering committee, package selection, organization culture, vendor partnership, vendor tools, system integration and testing, knowledge transfer, performance measures, organizational characteristics, monitoring, national culture etc.

In the following paragraphs the most cited critical factors which have significant impact on ERP implementation success are explained.

If the number of times factors have been mentioned is considered, it can be said, that the most important success factor is top management support and involvement. Sustained management support, cited as the most relevant factor in implementation projects, is unavoidable throughout the implementation project (Somers & Nelson, 2003; Nah, Lau & Kuang, 2001; Umble, Haft & Umble, 2002; Aduri, Lin & Ma, 2002; Gattiker & CFPIM, 2002; Stratman, 2002). Top management is responsible for making fast and effective decisions, resolve conflicts and promote organisation-wide acceptance of the project. This factor may also be independent across regions and countries (Ngai et al., 2007). Top management role is seen in monitoring the progress of the project, providing directions to the implementation teams and establishing clear priorities (Mabert, Soni & Venkataramanan, 2003). Often top management views the installation of an ERP system as

primarily a technological challenge and assigns its responsibility to the IT department (Jarrar, Al-Mudimigh & Zairi, 2000), which can lead to serious problems due to lack of managerial insight.

Aduri et al. (2002) identified clearly defined business and strategic objectives as the most important factor. And some authors added (Al-Mashari, Al-Mudimigh & Zairi, 2003; Khan, 2002; Umble et al., 2002; Parr & Shanks, 2000; Ngai et al., 2007) that having a clear defined vision/mission and the formulation of the right policies/strategies it can serve as the blueprint for any organization success. Clear goals and objectives, should be specific and operational and indicate the general directions of the project (Somers & Nelson, 2003) and should also provide a clear link between business goals and IS strategy (Finney & Corbett, 2007). Well-defined objectives help to keep focus, and are essential for analyzing and measuring success. Objectives also must be measurable, and the savings must be quantified for each objective (Welti, 1999). Project scope is the initial blueprint of an implementation plan (Gargeya & Brady, 2005). Within the plan, budgetary and resource need to be established. It is also related with concerns of project goals clarification and their congruence with the organisational mission and strategic goals (Estaves et al., 2002). Reif (2001) pointed out that project scope is defined as closely corresponding to the range of outcomes and the extent to which the organization will be affected.

This factor is very broad and includes various aspects of project teams, such as competences, knowledge, organization etc. Mabert et al. (2003) and Wang et al. (2007) mentioned that implementation team spent extra time up front to define in great detail exactly how the implementation would be carried out. Selecting the right employees to participate in implementation process and motivating them is critical for the implementation's success (Khan, 2002; Jarrar et al., 2000). Team must consist of right mix of business analysts, technical experts and users from within the organization and consultants from external companies (Parr & Shanks, 2000; Bancroft et al., 2001; Skok & Legge, 2002; Ngai et al., 2007), who are chosen for their skills, past accomplishments, reputation, flexibility and the ability to be entrusted with critical decision making (Umble et al., 2002).

Lack of user training and understanding ERP system processes are responsible for many ERP implementation failures (Somers & Nelson, 2003). Some authors (Al-Mashari et al., 2003; Umble et al., 2002; Aduri et al., 2002; Bradford & Florin, 2003; Bancroft et al., 2001; Estaves et al., 2002; Akkermans & Helden, 2002; Gargeya & Brady, 2005) added that inadequate training has been one of the significant reasons of many ERP systems failure. If users do not understand how a system works, they tend to invent their own processes using those parts of the system they are able to manipulate (Umble et al., 2002). So, to realize full benefits of ERP, end users have to use it properly. The main reason for education and training is to increase the expertise and knowledge level of the people within the company. To make end user training successful, the training should start early, preferably well before the implementation begins (Umbe et al., 2002). Organizations should also consider that through a managerial consensus, that changes are necessary and possible they can charge them to disseminate this information to their subordinates (Gargeya & Brady, 2005).

ERP systems are essentially developed as instruments for improving business processes such as manufacturing, purchasing or distribution (Al-Mashari et al., 2003) and they are built around best practices in specific industries (O'Leary, 2000). However, the software my not necessarily fit our business processes, because implementing ERP is not a matter of changing software systems, rather it is a matter of repositioning the company and transforming business practices (Jarrar et al., 2000). So we can chose between customization of ERP packages for a better fit and changing our business processes to fit the packages (Bradford & Florin; 2003). If we chose customization of the software it results in higher implementation cost and longer implementation (Davenport, 1999). ERP system implementation is a good opportunity for reengineering existing business processes to the best business standard. In order to be successful organizations should first perform a throughout analysis of current business processes and compare the results to ERP packages and choose the appropriate one based on the mutual fit (Ngai et al., 2007)

The existing organizational structure and processes found in most companies are not compatible with the structure, tolls and types of information provided by ERP systems (Umble et al., 2002), because every ERP system imposes its own logic on an organization's strategy, organization and culture. These changes may significantly affect organizational structures, policies, processes and employees, and can cause resistance, confusion, redundancies, and errors if not managed effectively. Many ERP implementations fail to achieve expected benefits possibly because companies underestimate the efforts involved in change management (Somers & Nelson, 2003; Al-Mashari et al., 2003; Stratman, 2002). Because of that, it is important that an organization carefully plans and supervises the transformation in all phases of implementation process.

The importance of communication across different business functions and departments is well known in the IT implementation literature, because communication has a high impact from initiation phase until system acceptance, as it helps to minimize possible user resistance. Communication has to cover the scope, objectives and tasks of an ERP implementation project (Al-Mashari et al., 2003). Effective communication is needed in project team and within the organization. Khan (2002) explained that good communication in project team can be ensured by weekly team meetings, postings on the company intranet; formal and informal information sessions etc. Al-Sehali (2000) said that the progress of the ERP project should be readily discernible to all of the employees in the organization.

ERP systems cross-functional and departmental boundaries, cooperation and involvement of all people in the organization are essential (Somers & Nelson, 2003). Gattiker and CFPIM (2002) said that system implementation represents a threat to users perceptions of control over their work and a period of transition during which users must cope with differences between old and new work systems. Involving users, in the stage of defining organizational information system needs, can decrease their resistance to the potential ERP systems. This gives users the feeling of involvement in decision making (Wang et al., 2007). User involvement is important during ERP system requirements analysis as is during the implementation process.

The quality of pre-existing data and information systems has been cited as an important factor in the successful implementation of ERP system (Gattiker & CFPIM, 2002; Ngai et al., 2007). If problems with data are not fixed in legacy systems, they will be apparent in the new system as well (Al-Sehali, 2000). Zhang et al. (2002) and Umble et al. (2002) said that ERP modules are intricately linked to one another. Data should definitely be managed properly to ensure their consistency and accuracy. The data residing in the legacy systems, both master data and transaction data, needs to be migrated to ERP system (Khan, 2002). This effort often involves translating existing data to the specifications required by the new ERP system (Reif, 2001).

Because of the great complexity of implementation projects, know-how and experience of consultants is essential. The success of a project depends strongly on the capabilities of the consultants because often the consultant is the only one with in-depth knowledge of the software (Welti, 1999; Al-Sehali, 2000). They provide a very valuable service by filling gaps, providing expertise, and thinking outside the box (Khan, 2002; Wang et al., 2007). Somers and Nelson (2003) added that

organizations frequently use consultants for setup, installation, and customization of their software availing themselves of the consultants' experience, comprehensive knowledge of certain modules, and experience with the software application.

Since the combination of hardware and software and the organizational, human and political issues make many ERP projects huge, complex and risky, effective project management is crucial from initiation to acceptance (Somers & Nelson, 2003; Akkermans & Helden, 2002; Stratman, 2002). Because ERP systems implementation is a set of complex activities, involving all business functions and often requiring between one and two years, thus organizations should have an effective project management strategy to control the implementation process, avoiding overrun of budget and ensuring the implementation within schedule (Zhang et al., 2002).

Project champion is a person who has a good understanding of what is going on and is very influential (Skok & Legge, 2002). The presence of such a person has facilitated many successful IS projects. Since usually this person is a high-level executive, he/she can perform crucial functions of transformational leadership, facilitation and marketing the project to the users. He/she has the authority to make substantial organisational changes happen (Akkermans & Helden; 2002; Ngai et al., 2007; Finney & Corbett, 2007).

All ERP packages have to some extent limited capabilities. Some packages are more suited for larger companies, some more for smaller ones. Akkermans & Helden (2002) added that some packages have become a "de facto" standard of industry; some have a stronger presence in certain parts of the world. To increase the chance of success, management must choose software that most closely fits its requirements such as hardware platforms, databases, and operation systems (Zhang et al., 2002). A gap analysis of organization requirements and ERP features with the involvement of technical staff and key users is a necessary exercise (Ngai et al., 2007). Selection of a package with the best fit will minimize the effort, time and risks for narrowing the gap through business process changes, or customization later (Ngai et al., 2007).

The integrative design of ERP systems increases the complexity involved in source code modification, most companies significantly underestimate the effort required for modifications (Mabet et al., 2003). Al-Sehali (2000) said that the vendor's code should be used as much as possible, even if this means sacrificing functionality, so upgrades from release to release can be done easily. On that base, Parr and Shanks (2000) and also Finney and Corbett (2007) suggest that we use vanilla ERP solution, which means minimal customization. Therefore, every modification request should be carefully evaluated.

Most of above citied research had been conducted in large companies where scope, time and resources of implementation are different as for SMEs. Because of that it is expected that the ranking of importance of CSFs is different depending on the company size. That means that large companies have to dedicate more attention to some CSFs and SMEs to other CSFs. Importance of each CSF also differs depending on the chosen package and implementation methodology used. In the next chapter a survey to examine the importance of CSFs in Slovenian SMEs has been conducted.

ERP IMPLEMENTATIONS IN SMEs IN SLOVENIA

To investigate importance of CSFs of ERP implementation in Slovenian companies an empirical study has been conducted. Therefore a web questionnaire with three parts has been designed. In the first part the purpose was to obtain general picture of responded companies (size, branch and implemented modules), the second part refers to the realization of implementation of an ERP solution and the third part refers to investigation of

CSFs which have a major impact during process of implementation of ERP solutions. Web questionnaire has been mailed to 54 companies with an implemented SAP solution and 117 companies with an implemented Microsoft Navision solution. There have been 45 responses to the survey questionnaire, which represent 26 percent. Of the 45 answers received, 22 (or 49 percent) belong to SAP solution, and 23 (or 51 percent) belong to Navision solution (see Table 1). In table 1 it can also been seen that 13 received answers belong to small companies (29 percent), 13 answers belong to medium companies (29 percent) and 19 answers belong to large companies (42 percent). Because SAP solution is known as ERP solution for large companies and Navision solution in known as ERP solution for SMEs, it has been checked if there is correlation between them in our data. Therefore it has been found that there is weak positive relationship between solutions and size (r = .365, p<0.05). Because observations in this article involve only SMEs, large companies have been excluded from further investigation in this article.

The SMEs under consideration are for the most part from industry (34.6 percent), followed by retail (23.1 percent) and service (23.1 percent). Most SMEs have three or more modules implemented and most of them plan to implement other modules in the future as well.

Second part of web questionnaire focuses on process of choosing and implementation of

Table 1. Distribution of organization size and solution

	SAP	Navision	Total
Small companies	1	12	13
Medium companies	5	8	13
Large companies	16	3	19
Total	22	23	45

* Slovenian classification of organization size has been used

a selected ERP solution. On the question what are the reasons of a company to decide to implement ERP solution the most frequent answers are: integrity of a solution, better access to data, modernization of existing business processes with ERP solution, single data entry, incompatibility of previous information systems, demand of owners, better reports, adaptability and flexibility of ERP solution etc.

There are a lot of ERP solutions that could be considered and evaluated during selection process. In fact there are a lot of ERP solutions for most of the processes and functional areas. Because there is not enough time to look at all these solutions in detail before making a decision, the short list of solutions (2 to 4) should be made on preliminary research. On the question which are ERP solutions on the short list, the most frequent answers are: ERP solutions from local vendors, Navision, SAP and Oracle. It is not surprising that ERP solutions from local vendors is most frequent answer because these solutions are cheaper than Navision or SAP solutions. But a question has been raised why a particular ERP solution has been chosen and the most frequent answers are: integrity of a selected ERP solution, efficiency and stability operation of an ERP solution, support of an ERP vendor, cost and price of an ERP solution, and requirement of an owner or other business partners (customers, vendors etc.).

Furthermore it has been investigated what share of ERP business processes cover business processes of a company. Four answers have been given to choose from: completely, almost completely, partly or badly. 25 answers have been received where 20 percent say completely, 64 percent say almost completely and 16 percent say partly. Nobody says badly. The next question is which of the following approaches SMEs use for implementation: Big Bang Approach, Phased Approach, Parallel Approach, Process Approach or Hybrid Approach (combination of previously mentioned approaches). Of 25 answers received 40 percent SMEs used Big Bang Approach, 16

percent SMEs used Phased Approach, 20 percent SMEs used Parallel Approach, 8 percent SMEs Process Approach and 16 percent SMEs Hybrid Approach. Correlation between approach and size and between approach and solutions is not significant.

Furthermore the companies have been asked how they have implemented their ERP solution. Three answers have been available: methodology of an ERP vendor, their own methodology or other. Of 24 answers 70.8 percent of companies use the implementation methodology recommended by an ERP vendor and 29.2 percent of companies use their own implementation methodology. Nobody has chosen other.

On the question how much your business processes have to be adopted to business processes of an ERP solution SMEs have been able to choose between: entirely, largely, partly or nothing. 28 percent of SMEs say largely and 72 percent say partly. Entirely and nothing has not been chosen. These results have been expected because the fact that if coverage between existing business processes and business processes of ERP solution is under 60 percent, it is not recommend to choose and implement a particular ERP solution. The correlation between adoption of business processes has been examined with solution, size, branch and number of implemented modules. Correlations with solution and with size have not been found. But moderate relationship ($r = .4103$, $p<0.05$) has been found with branch of SMEs. It is thought that the reason for that relationship lies in the fact that business processes of singular ERP solutions are covered better for different kinds of branches. So for SAP solutions it is known that they are more often implemented in industry meanwhile the Navision solutions are more present in service. The hypothesis that there is no relations between business processes and the number of implementation modules has been rejected because the relationship between them ($r = -.578$, $p<0.01$) has been found.

In the following part of the second part of questionnaire it has been researched how well the implementation has gone through. The first question refers to duration of an implementation process. Available answers are: 3 months or less, between 3 and 6 months, between 6 and 9 months, between 9 and 12 month and one year or more. From table 2 it can be seen that most durations of implementation ERP solutions for SMEs are between 3 month and one year (70.8 percent). There is a positive moderate relationship between the time of implementation and the size of a company (r = .518 p<0.01). There is also correlation between the time of implementation and the implementation approach (r = .504, p<0.01). This result is expected because different approaches of implementation have different time scopes of implementation planned. In previous page it has been found out that 40 percent of SMEs use Big Bang approach for which it is known that it is the fastest approach because of the rule which says that all modules of ERP solutions must be implemented at the same time and therefore no interfaces between an ERP solution and legacy information systems have been made.

In addition it has been deeper investigated whether the duration of an implementation process lasts longer than it has been planned. Answers yes or no have been available. 8 implementations (33.3%) last longer than they have been planned and the reasons for that are: changing scope of implementation, weak knowledge about func-

Table 2. Duration of implementation process of ERP solutions

Months	Answer	Percent
Under 3	3	12.5
3 - 6	7	29.2
6 9	5	20.8
9 – 12	5	20.8
More than 12	4	16.7
Total	24	100

tionality of ERP solutions, passive collaboration within project team during the analyze phase, key users have been overloaded with daily tasks and they do not have time to participate in the implementation process etc. The hypothesis has been given that there is no relationship between big problems during an implementation process and degrees of ERP business process covering over business processes SMEs.

On the question wheatear scope of expected functionality changes during an implementation, following answers have been available: big decrease, small decrease, no changes, small increase and big increase. Out of 24 answers 20.8 percent have chosen small decrease, 45.8 percent no changes, 20.8 percent small increase and 12.5 percent big increase. Big decrease has not been chosen. Some of the answers why the scope changed are: "during an implementation we found out new functionalities of the ERP solution for which it would be foolish to release it out of the project"; "after analyzing and defining business processes key users understand importance of the ERP solution better and that was leading to the increase in scope", "bad analysis and defining processes, and bad cooperation with top management".

Beside scope, real costs of implementation changed from expected have been looked into. Further options have been given to choice: smaller than planned, little smaller than planned, same as planned, little bigger than planned and a lot bigger than planned. Nobody has chosen much smaller from planned and a little smaller form planned, 29.2 percent have chosen the same as planned, 41.7 percent have chosen a little bigger than planned and 29.2 percent have chosen a lot bigger than has been planned. These reasons for extent costs have been pointed out: bigger scope of functionality than planned, more consultants' hours, bigger number of interfaces with other information systems as planned, persistence at adaptation of ERP solutions to existent processes and procedures.

At the end of the second part of the survey it has been asked if any big problems have occurred during an implementation process. Yes or no answers have been available. 33.3 percent have chosen answer yes and 66.7 percent have chosen answers no. On the question why there have been problems during the implementation the most frequent answers are: user resistance for change, bad training and bad user manuals, unsuitable consultants, bad computer literacy, poorly included middle management, the solution has not been tested enough by users, bad defining of business processes etc. No correlation with other questions in these part of questionnaire, except with method of implementation ($r = .483$, $p<0.05$), has been found out.

The third part of the survey has been designed to study importance of CSFs in SMEs. Respondents have been asked to rank fifteen of the most important CSFs of ERP implementation listed in previous chapter in accordance to their importance. CSF effective communication has been divided on two CSFs, the first is communication between a project team and an organization and the second is communication within a project team. Number 1 stands for the most important factor to the number 15 which stands for the least important factor. 31 answers have been received, which represent 65 percent of responded SMEs. The results of CSF survey are presented by following arithmetic means ($M_{CSF x}$) where number 1 is the most important factor (has the smallest arithmetic mean):

1. clear goals, objectives and scope ($M_{CSF 1}$= 2.59);
2. project team competence and organization ($M_{CSF 4}$= 5.88)
3. top management support and involvement ($M_{CSF 2}$= 6.35)
4. user involvement ($M_{CSF 9}$= 6.94)
5. communication between project team and organization ($M_{CSF 6}$= 7.18)

6. user training and education ($M_{CSF 10}$= 7.59)
7. communication within project team ($M_{CSF 7}$= 7.71)
8. business process reengineering (BPB) ($M_{CSF 12}$= 8.12)
9. data analysis and conversion ($M_{CSF 15}$= 9.12)
10. project champion ($M_{CSF 3}$= 9.25)
11. minimal customization ($M_{CSF 14}$= 9.44)
12. consultants ($M_{CSF 8}$= 9.56)
13. project management ($M_{CSF 5}$= 10.47)
14. change management ($M_{CSF 11}$= 11.13)
15. architecture choice (package selection) ($M_{CSF 13}$= 11.75)

A comparison of ranking list of CSFs between the list of professional literature and the conducted survey is presented in table 3. From the table 3 it can be seen that those very important CSFs in both areas (professional literature and survey) are: clear goals, objectives, scope and planning; project team competence and organization, and top management support and involvement. On the fourth place the survey puts CSF user involvement, but literature puts it on the eighth place. The biggest difference in ranking of CSFs between them is in factor change management and factor project management. Professional literature put them on sixth place, but our survey put them on the fourteenth place. Almost the same stands for the factor project management which is on the thirteenth place. The factor business process reengineering which literature puts on the fifth place and survey on the eighth place also has to be taken into account. For other CSFs the place of ranking changes for a place up or down in the ranking table between literature and the survey. In the table 3, thick line divides upper and lower part of the table. A correlation between ranking list of survey and ranking list of literature has been explored. High statistical correlation at the 0.01 level ($r = .674$) exists between them.

In the ranking list of the literature at the beginning of the paper (also seen in the second column

Table 3. Comparison of ranking list CSFs between the professional literature and the survey

		Literature	Survey
CSF1	clear goals, objectives and scope (18)	2	1
CSF4	project team competence and organization (16)	3	2
CSF2	top management support and involvement (21)	1	3
CSF9	user involvement (10)	8	4
CSF6	communication within project team* (10)	8	5
CSF10	user training and education (15)	4	6
CSF7	communication between project team and organization*(10)	8	7
CSF12	business process reengineering (14)	5	8
CSF15	data analysis and conversion (10)	8	9
CSF3	project champion (9)	12	10
CSF14	minimal customization (9)	12	11
CSF8	consultants (9)	12	12
CSF5	project management (13)	6	13
CSF11	change management (13)	6	14
CSF13	architecture choice (package selection) 9)	12	15

*If the some number occurs in literature more times, it means that it has been equally important by the authors

of table) there are more CSFs with the same number in brackets which represent number of authors, who mentioned these CSF. It can be presumed that there are more groups of CSFs which have the same importance. Rank of individual CSFs and variation rank between answers of SMEs have been calculated regarding a place of their standard means. 15 CSFs have been put in four groups. Inside each group there are no distinctive differences between CSF ranks. The first group consist of only one factor which is clear goals, objectives and scope (CSF1). In second group there are following factors considered: project team competence and organization (CSF4), top management support and involvement (CSF2), user involvement (CFS9), communication within project team (CFS6), user training and education (CFS10) and communication between project team and organization (CFS7). In the third group of equally important CSFs are: business process reengineering (CSF12), data analysis and conver-

sion (CSF15), project champion (CSF3), minimal customization (CSF14) and consultants (CSF8).

The last and the least important group of equally important CSFs consist of: project management (CSF5), change management (CSF11) and architecture choice (CSF13). Rank of individual CSFs and variation rank between answers of SMEs have been presented in Figure 1.

Correlation between single CSFs in the survey has also been examined and it can be seen that:

- strong positive correlation at 0.01 level is between:
  - clear goals, objectives and scope (CSF_1) and change management (CSF_{11}) (r = .715)
  - project team competence and organization (CSF_4) and effective communication within project team (CSF_6) (r = .654)
  - communication between project team and organization (CSF_7) and architecture

Figure 1. CSFs presented by standard means and variation rank between answers

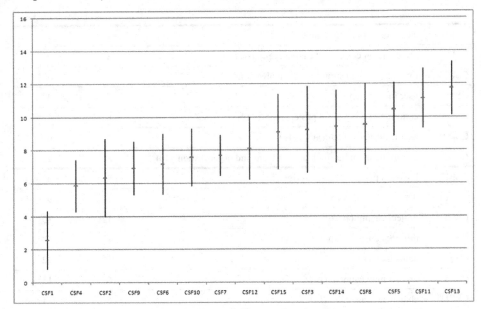

choice (package selection) (CSF_{13}) (r = .596)

- moderate positive correlation at 0.05 level is between:
  - top management support and involvement (CSF_2) and project champion (CSF_3) (r = .479)
  - top management support and involvement (CSF_2) and project team competence and organization (CSF_4) (r = .432)
  - project team competence and organization (CSF_2) and project management (CSF_5) (r = .555)
  - communication within project team (CSF_6) and communication between project team and organization (CSF_7) (r = .496)
  - communication between project team and organization (CSF_7) and data analysis and conversion (CSF_{15}) (r = .437)
  - business process reengineering (BPB) (CSF_{12}) and change management (CSF_{11}) (r = .428)
- moderate negative correlation at 0.05 level is between:

  - clear goals, objectives and scope (CSF_1) and consultants (CSF_8) (r = -.526)
  - clear goals, objectives and scope (CSF_1) and minimal customization (CSF_{14}) (r = -.546)
  - top management support and involvement (CSF_2) and communication between project team and organization (CSF_7) (r = -.413)
  - top management support and involvement (CSF_2) and user training and education (CSF_{10}) (r = -.449)
  - communication within project team (CSF_6) and minimal customization (CSF_{14}) (r = -.482)
  - change management (CSF_{11}) and x minimal customization (CSF_{14}) (r = -.440)

The results of this survey have shown that CSFs have an important role in implementation process of ERP solution implementation in SMEs. On this basis the importance of CSFs through a case study in two different Slovenian companies that implemented ERP solution Microsoft Dynamics NAV in the recent past has been investigated.

ERP IN SMEs – EXPERIENCES FROM SLOVENIA

Managing an ERP Implementation in a Small, but Fast Growing Company

Companies of up to 40 employees with a certain turnover size are considered "small" or in some countries, such as Slovenia, up to "mid-size". While employee number and financial parameters may be an indication of the extent of a company's information technology needs, they certainly do not suffice for segmentation in terms of business software needs. They do not reflect the number, extent and complexity of business lines, business processes and organization model of the company. Unfortunately, many implementers and producers of business software (such as CRM and ERP) tend to limit (or at least base) their market segmentation and consequently business strategies to a handful of indicators – such as employee number or PC number, turnover and other financial figures. This fact makes it harder for SMEs to choose the right solution, both in terms of product and license model and in terms of implementer. This is because implementers, as well as an ERP solution vendor, build their business success on and around repeatable projects with a relatively fixed functionality set (although it may be "wide"). However, in many cases companies may be small in size and even turnover, but their strategy for winning the market and furthering their growth may lay in the diversity and width of services and/or product range they provide.

Let us take the example of company X (at the beginning of the project its annual turnover was 7 million EUR and it had 23 full time employees) is specialized in stainless steel wholesale. The company also engages in manufacturing to the extent of providing services of cutting, curving, welding to customer specification. The company operates primarily in Ljubljana, and has recently opened 2 subsidiaries in Slovenia and a related company in Croatia.

When company X decided to embark on the project of "renovating" its ERP system in 2004, it had in fact already outgrown its current system which effectively consisted of two separate applications – one covered finance, while the other covered the material handling. The two systems were consolidated almost entirely manually and held in line by two key persons. Although processes and records were in place to cover the main business process of stainless steel wholesale and additional services of minor processing of this steel, most of the employees in purchase, sales and manufacturing depended on their islands of manual records and unstructured exchange of information. On top of wholesale and small-scale simple manufacturing, the company also planned to embark on a form of retail sale of stainless steel items, which amounted to over-the-counter sales of small quantities of items. Obviously, it was in the interest of the company, to keep investment value and TCO in check.

The implementer was a local Microsoft Dynamics partner, the holder of the largest market share in MS Dynamics NAV implementations in Slovenia and a Microsoft Gold Certified partner, whose operations include development of independent specialized solutions for financial and telecommunication companies. The implementer tried to limit the range of functionality as well as extent of customization and new development. At the same time, both were aware that the solution needed to provide the customer with a system that would not only cover the company's current needs but also support and fuel its further development and growth. In addition, the project team faced two more challenges.

Firstly, the implementation of a contemporary integrated comprehensive ERP system (Microsoft Dynamics NAV) meant a new concept, record and process model for the company. For example, the creation and posting of a sales order and from it a shipment note and invoice could effectively be done in the sales department directly thus immediately influencing the stock, customer ledger, payables and general ledger records. While the new system would streamline processes and reduce the potential for errors due to multiple data inputs, it would also transfer a lot of the responsibility to other employees.

Secondly, in SMEs, employees tend to cover multiple roles and responsibilities in the organization and processes. Such companies tend not to have free resources for internal projects and/or reorganization as they devote all their effort to the core business. In addition, the IT department does not exist, is outsourced or is represented by a single person with generalist knowledge.

The first compromise company X made was the choice of product – Microsoft Dynamics NAV may have been more expensive than local products and providers in terms of license and implementation services, but it offered a wide range of well tested functionality company X needed (accounting, sales, purchase, inventory, basic manufacturing). The license modularity and licensing by user meant at least the license part of the project investment value could be approached on the pay-as-you-grow basis.

The next step was reaching the right balance between company X adapting to Microsoft Dynamics NAV built-in process model and business logic and vice-versa. In fact, the company and the implementer agreed on adhering to almost completely standard functionality in the domain of finance, accounting and inventory. On the other hand, most of the customization and modification was made in the areas where company X derived its market comparative advantage from – sales (particularly quotes, pricelists, etc.), manufacturing, purchase (rules for replenishing stock, inventory turnover). These areas were also the ones where most changes have been made also after the initial deployment, as the company evolved and grew.

The business process change brought on by the implementation of an integrated system into a company, which had previously consisted of information islands, proved the most difficult challenge to overcome. This was offset by interim organization and process changes – some records were initially double checked and manually posted by key users to avoid errors. With some additional and repeated user trainings provided by internal key users and the implementer, the new concepts and advantages of the system were eventually adopted and even welcomed by the end users.

Project management/ownership challenge proved to be relatively simple to overcome, made possible by strong support and involvement of the sponsor – the owner and manager of the company. The absence of a dedicated business system manager was offset by appointing different heads at different stages of the project – the first stage focused primarily on the sales and purchase and was managed by head of sales. The later stages focused on enhancing the first-implemented standard functionality in inventory and manufacturing. By commencement of that stage, the company X had grown to the point where it needed a dedicated post to manage those areas of operation – this person consequently also managed the respective stage of the implementation. On the other hand, the fact that the financial/accounting area had previously been covered by an almost completely separate but entirely standard system had made it possible to implement it simultaneously in the first stage.

Three years of full operation after go-live with the new system, the company X's turnover has tripled to 22 million EUR, while the number of full time employees has doubled to 49.

ERP IMPLEMENTATION IN HETEROGENEOUS INTERNATIONAL BUSINESS SYSTEMS

An international group with a central domicile in Switzerland planned to introduce a common ERP system. Through its 8 daughter companies, the group is present in as many countries. The group is a distributor of the leading construction mechanization producer for the area of Slovenia,

Croatia, Bosnia and Herzegovina, Serbia, Montenegro, Macedonia and Kosovo. The group also offers its customers other producers' machinery and equipment.

The group's individual members' ERP requirements vary significantly:

- The companies are active in very different countries with different, highly dynamic and changing market conditions, legislature and business cultures;
- The different market and, consequently, company sizes (from a few employees in Kosovo to more than 100 in Croatia);
- Different ranges of business lines or offerings (from the relatively narrow purchase and sales of machinery and financial management in Switzerland to the full range of 6 business lines in Slovenia, Serbia and Croatia).

Despite these differences, the group aimed for a unified basic solution and a centralized business information system. The implementation project goals thus comprised:

- Unification and optimisation of business processes within the group and within the individual members;
- Unification of business records, rules and master data;
- Unification of information systems and replacement of some of the legacy subsystems no longer supported and developed by the providers;
- Improvement of knowledge and best-practice transfer among member companies; and
- Last but not least greater efficiency of the business information system with respect to three key factors: usability, TCO manageability and continued development and growth.

The information technology within the group is managed centrally, by a 4-member team located in Slovenia, while the groups' centralized business information system is set up in Switzerland.

The group chose the Microsoft Dynamics NAV product to be the basis of their new ERP and selected a Slovenian-based IT group to implement the new system. The key criteria for those choices were:

- A standard, proofed product with as wide a geographical coverage as possible;
- Wide range of functionality and the possibility of customization and addition of new functionality;
- A single counterpart, unified management and execution of the project in the relevant west Balkan countries;
- A project team with the right balance of experience, knowledge and creativity and flexibility for the provision of a comprehensive ERP solution for the group.

Following the initial analysis and design phases the group decided on a centralized system set up, which would, upon completion, cover (among others) accounting and finance, sales of new and used machinery, equipment, engines, accessories and spare parts, rental of used machinery and equipment, interfaces integrating Dynamics NAV with the principal's (vendor) information systems.

A typical business system implementation approach based on the commonly used methodology (the IT group selected uses its own tested business solution implementation methodology based on the Microsoft Dynamics© Sure Step© Implementation Methodology).

The challenge of such an approach in international heterogeneous organizations lays in the simultaneous deployment in all the business lines in all the countries. It is difficult to ensure the availability and quality involvement of the relevant resources, particularly the key users on the customer side. These individuals must simultaneously work on the project as well as ensure the business of the company does not suffer. The extent of efforts required and challenges related to resource availability typically result in a later "go-live" date" thus delaying the visibility of the project results and ROI.

"On-time", "on-budget" "in-line with design document" are not the only success criteria for an ERP project – it is essential that the final result is an ERP system that effectively supports the current needs of the company once the system is deployed. With a large-scale big-bang projects (they may last up to a year or longer) run the risk of resulting in a system which no longer reflects the needs of the company once it is finally is deployed, because all the stages preceding the go-live have taken longer, have not been user-tested, etc. An approach which is phased in terms of the coverage of different business lines and/or countries in different stages allows both the customer and the implementer a better overview of the effects of the different sets of functionality deployed on the business as well as an opportunity to amend the system to the ever-changing demands, and last but not least a better control over the costs and risks of the project.

For the group project a phased approach was chosen, which reflects the complexity of the requirements as well as the group's team availability. During the preparation stages, before even choosing the implementer and product, a business process analysis was made by KPMG group. Once the implementer was selected, the project team was defined – a combined team of

the group's internal resources and the IT group's NAV team lead from Slovenia. In the next stage the functional requirements and system design were finalized. The project plan (as shown in Figure 2) was aligned with the complexity of the group's requirements and business priorities. The team managed the implementation from Slovenia, while the first deployments were executed in Switzerland and Serbia.

The stage took only 28 days from the installation of the standard product to the first postings and documents issued (e.g. invoices). The next stage focused on the first company which is active in all of the business lines – the Serbian company. This member company was chosen because it represented the best compromise between company size, operation size, human resources structure and external factors. The implementation in this company provided the group with the final proof of concept of the solution from the point of view of a single, central, but international system. The successful completion of this stage of the project meant that a virtually identical system can now be deployed in other member companies in a fairly short time.

CONCLUSION

Like many new fields in information systems, ERP solutions have many synonyms, such as integrated standard software packages, enterprise systems, enterprise wide systems, integrated vendor systems etc. ERP solutions allow organizations to

Figure 2. The project plan

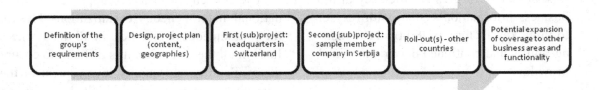

replace their existing information systems, with a single integrated system. They are defined as customizable, standard application software which includes integrated business solutions for the core processes and the main administrative functions. They can be also defined as comprehensive package software solutions seek to integrate the complete range of a business processes and functions in order to present a holistic view of the business from a single information and IT architecture. ERP solutions consist of more modules and they support business processes on operative level in an organization.

ERP solutions are designed by principles of best practices, which means, that ERP vendors search for the best organizational business models in branch and then adopt that business model in their ERP solutions (Sternad & Bobek, 2004). Instead of tailoring the ERP system specifications to meet organization requirements, organizations have to adopt business processes to an ERP system.

According to that, organizations should select the ERP package which: fits organization, provides industry functionality, supports changing business environment, easily integrates with other information systems in organizations, supports vendor by implementation, must be complete, are stable and have good support after implementation, have availability of implementation accelerators such as training materials, user procedures, help text, process models etc. (Shields, 2001).

To be successful with EPR implementation a SME has to take in account the implementation strategy, implementation method (implementation process) and implementation CSFs. A lot of ERP implementations are failures, because companies which bought ERP solutions think that ERP implementation is a technological and not management issue. Failures in ERP implementation showed that management issues are underestimated. Because of that it is very important that organizations have to create overall conditions in which they can implement chosen solution in expected time, scope

and evaluated costs. That means that organizations should be aware of which are most critical success factors (CSFs) of ERP implementations. Prior researches conducted by several researchers report a set of CSFs among which 19 are refereed by more than one researcher. Those CSFs have been researched within Slovenian companies which have conducted ERP implementation processes in near past. The paper points out correlation between CSFs and SMEs our findings to prior published researches.

It s been concluded that the most important factors for authors and also for Slovenian SMEs are: clear goals, objectives, scope and planning; project team competence and organization and top management support and involvement. At the forth place of our survey there is user involvement but literature puts it at the eight place. The biggest difference in ranking of CSFs between them is in factor change management and factor project management. Professional literature puts them on sixth place, but our survey put them on the fourteenth place. Almost the same stands for the factor project management which is on the thirteenth place. Factor business process reengineering which literature puts on the fifth place and survey on the eighth place has also to be taken into account. All other CSFs are on both ranking lists located more or less on similar ranking.

Our findings have also been confirmed through the two case studies that have been conducted in two SMEs in Slovenia. Though every single ERP implementation is different, it has been found that there are some CSFs that are more important than others and these CSFs are the ones that should be given special attention during the implementation process.

REFERENCES

Aduri, R., Lin, W., & Ma, Y. (2003). *The price tag of Enterprise Resource Planning (ERP) system implementation failure: version 2.0.* Retrieved

September 29, 2003, from http://erp.ittoolbox.com/documents/document.asp?i=2374.

Akkermans, H., & Helder, K. (2002). Vicious and virtuous cycles in ERP implementation: a case study of interrelations between CSF. *European Journal of Information Systems, II*, 35-46.

Al-Mashari, M., Al-Mudimigh, A., & Zairi, M. (2003). Enterprise resource planning: taxonomy of critical factors. *European journal of operational research, 146*(2), 352-364.

Al-Sehali, S. (2000). *The factors that affect the implementation of enterprise resource planning (ERP) in the international Arab gulf states and United states organizations with special emphasis on SAP software.* Doctoral dissertation, University of Northern Iowa. Retrieved August 10, 2003 from Proquest.

Bancroft, N., Seip, H., & Sprengel, A. (2001). *Implementing SAP R/3* (2nd ed.). Greenwich, Manning Publications Co.

Bradford, M., & Florin, J. (2003). Examining the role of innovation diffusion factors on the implementation success of enterprise resource planning systems. *International journal of accounting information systems, 4*(3), 205-225.

Davenport, T.H. (1999). Putting the enterprise into the enterprise system. *A Harvard business review: on the business value of IT.* Harvard Business School Publishing: USA.

Estaves, J., Pastor, J.A., & Casanovas, J. (2002). *Using the Partial Least Squares (PLS) method to establish CSF interdependence in ERP implementation projects.* Retrieved Augst 10, 2003, from http://erp.ittoolbox.com/documents/document.asp?i=2321.

Finney, S., & Corbett, M. (2007). ERP implementation: a compilation and analysis of critical success factors. *Business Process Management Journal, 13*(3), 329-347.

Gargeya, V.B., & Brady, C. (2005). Success and failure factors of adopting SAP in ERP system implementation. *Business Process Management Journal, 11*(5), 501-516.

Gattiker, T.F., & CFPIM. (2002). Anatomy of an ERP implementation gone awry. *Production and Inventory Management Journal, 43*, 96-105.

Hedman, J., & Borell, A. (2004). Narratives in ERP system evaluation. *Journal of Enterprise Information Management, 17*(4), 283-290.

Jarrar, Y.F., Al-Mudimigh, A., & Zairi, M. (2000). ERP implementation critical success factors – the role and impact of business process management. *ICMIT, 2*, 122-127.

Khan, A. (2002). *Implementing SAP with an ASAP methodology focus.* San Jose: Writers Club Press.

Mabert V.A., Soni, A., & Venkataramanan, M. A. (2003). Enterprise resource planning: Managing the implementation process. *European Journal of Operational Research, 146*(2), 302-314.

Microsoft (2007). *Using the Microsoft Dynamics Sure Step Methodology for Microsoft Dynamics AX.* Microsoft Dynamics GP, Microsoft Dynamics NAV, Microsoft Dynamics SL. (Internal source; restricted access).

Miller, S. S. (1998). *ASAP - Implementation at the speed of business.* New York: McGraw-Hill.

Nah, F.F., Lau, J.L., & Kuang, J. (2001). Critical factors for successful implementation of enterprise systems. *Business Process Management Journal, 7*(3), 285-296.

Ngai, E.W.T., Law, C.C.H., & Wat, F.K.T. (2007). Examining the critical success factors in the adoption of enterprise resource planning. *Computers in Industry, 59*, 548-564.

O'Leary, D.E. (2000). *Enterprise resource planning system: Systems, life cycle, electronic commerce and risk*. USA: Cambridge university press.

Parr, A., & Shanks, G. (2000). A model of ERP project implementation. *Journal of Information Technology, 15*, 289-303.

Reif, H. (2001). *Complementing traditional information systems implementation methodologies for successful ERP system implementation*s. Doctoral dissertation, Virginia Commonwealth University. Retrieved August 10, 2003 from Proquest.

Shields, M.G. (2001). *E-business and ERP: Rapid implementation and project planning*. New York: John Wiley & Sons Inc.

Skok, W., & Legge, M. (2002). Evaluating enterprise resource planning (ERP) systems using an interpretive approach. *Knowledge and process management, 9*(2), 72-82.

Somers, T.M., & Neslon, K.G. (2003). A taxonomy of players and activities across the ERP project life cycle. *Information & Management, 41*(3), 257-278.

Sternad, S., & Bobek, S. (2004). ERP solution implementation critical success factors: What does matter and what does not. *Acta systemica* (pp. 27-31). International Institute for Advanced Studies in Systems Research and Cybernetics, Windsor, Ontario, Cananda.

Stratman, J.K. (2002). Enterprise resource planning (ERP) competence constructs: Two-stage multi-item scale development and validation. *Decision Sciences, 33*(4), 601-628.

Umble, E.J., Haft, R.R., & Umble, M.M. (2002). Enterprise resource planning: Implementation procedures and CSF. *European journal of operational research, 146*(2), 241-257.

Wallace, T.F., & Kremzar, M.H. (2001). *ERP: making it happen – the implementer's guide to success with enterprise resource planning*. New York: John Wiley & Sons, Inc.

Wang, E.T.G., Shih, S-P., Jiang, J.J., & Klein, G. (2007). The Consistency among facilitating factors and ERP implementation success: A holistic view of fit. *The Journal of Systems and Software, 81*, 1609-1621.

Welti, N. (1999). *Successful SAP R/3 implementation – Practical management of ERP projects*. England, UK: Addison-Wesley.

Zhang, L., Lee, M.K.O., Zhang, Z., & Banerjee, P. (2002). Critical Success Factors of Enterprise Resource Planning Systems Implementation Success in China. *Hawaii International Conference on System Sciences*.

This work was previously published in the Journal of Enterprise Information Systems, vol. 5, issue 3, edited by A. Gunasekaran, pp. 27-46, copyright 2009 by IGI Publishing (an imprint of IGI Global).

Chapter 24
Enterprise Resource Planning (ERP) Embedding:
Building of Software/ Enterprise Integration[1]

Dominique Vinck
Université P. Mendès, France

Igor Rivera-Gonzales
Instituto Politécnico Nacional, México

Bernard Penz
Institut National Polytechnique, France

ABSTRACT

This chapter analyses the mutual processes according to which the tool (ERP) and the organisation adapt to each other. It documents the live experience of technological change during the introduction of ERP in a medium-sized enterprise. Focusing on the election of the new tool and its appropriation by firm members, it does not simply reduce the process to a handful of factors (of success or failure), but analyses the different negotiations between actors leading to the reconstruction of both the tool and the organisation. It thus takes an in-depth look at the role of technology rather than just resorting to a simplistic and deterministic search for causal connections. Tracing the construction and meshing of the performance of both organisation and tools within the company, it reviews a set of dichotomies between technology and society, initial project and "impact," but also action and submission to constraints. Hence, the chapter explores the learning processes and the redefinition of actors, organisation and tools.

INTRODUCTION

The introduction of information systems (IS) is generally regarded from three major points of view. In computer sciences, researchers look at solutions and specifications that make it possible to meet social needs or develop new opportunities for social dynamics. In order to succeed in this, they require information and models pertaining to the organisation and the users. They then integrate these in their concept or design procedures. The role of the social sciences is to supply computer scientists

DOI: 10.4018/978-1-60566-892-5.ch024

with the elements they lack. Social scientists are thus experts, acting on behalf of society and human beings. However, many social scientists are reluctant to be reduced to simple instruments, claiming that they have their own scientific goals with respect to information systems (IS). These goals are either to study the impact of information technologies (IT) and what social actors do with them or to explore the interesting social processes emanating from the new situations created by these tools. A third point of view is that of managerial researchers who are interested in methods and models for introducing and managing IS. They compare experience and build prescriptive models for implementation. Between these three approaches, there is an emerging consensus that argues for better integration and embedding of IT according to the social and organisational context. Computer scientists want to integrate social variables in technical models; social scientists complain about engineers' and computer scientists' lack of ability to understand what is going on in society with IT and promote the idea of taking its social aspects better into account; management scientists suggest participatory design procedures and a methodology for the consultation and progressive integration of users.

The introduction of Enterprise Resource Planning (ERP) in enterprises is a phenomenon that has existed for over ten years now. Most big companies have their own ERP while the dissemination of this kind of IS is being extended to SMEs and non-industrial organisations (public authorities and universities among others). Alongside the dissemination process, the ERP tools themselves evolve as they adapt to new contexts. The original ERP tools were designed for big organisations and were not therefore suitable for SMEs. Thus, what can be observed is a continuous process of innovation and transformation of the tools alongside the simultaneous transformation of SMEs and other organisations. These two processes can be studied as a global phenomenon by looking at the main

trends in terms of the technological, organisational and social aspects.

This chapter explores the integration process from the point of view of one SME. Looking at the process in a more detailed way makes it possible to describe and analyse the mutual processes of adaptation between one new tool (ERP) and one specific organisation. The chapter documents the live experience of technological change as the ERP tool is introduced in a medium-sized enterprise. It focuses on the election of the new tool and its appropriation by firm members. It does not simply reduce the process to a handful of factors (of success or failure), but analyses the negotiations between actors that lead to the reconstruction of both the tool and the organisation. It goes through a set of dichotomies between technology and society, initial project and "impact", but also action and submission to constraints.

The chapter underlines the benefits of such an approach in terms of understanding what is going on. Using the Actor-Network Theory (ANT) and its concept of translation, it focuses on the specific translation process between an ERP tool and an SME. Studying the mediating webbing in the very fabric of the firm and the way in which this ties in with the performance of both its organisation and the tool, the chapter provides some original empirical results. These point to a different analysis from that of the usual approach adopted by both engineers (thinking in terms of optimising functionality) and social scientists (thinking in terms of use and impact). It highlights the potential of ANT when it comes to addressing the challenges of IS research.

BACKGROUND

The dissemination of ERP in industrial organisations is a major contemporaneous industrial phenomenon. It affects the organisation and the practices of many enterprises. It is situated at the border of three major trends: the rationalisation of working organisations, the computerisation of production processes and operations (Computer-Assisted Manufacturing, Material Requirement Planning and Manufacturing Resource Planning), and the computerisation of offices and relations between departments (Computer-Integrated Manufacturing) and organisations (Electronic Data Interchange, Internet). ERP gathers data from various departments and offers new management opportunities in terms of controlling the whole organisation. Furthermore, data in ERP systems are connected via procedures that reflect best industrial practices.

This does not mean the end of industrial history, i.e. with organisations having no choice other than to adopt ERP and adapt to incorporated best practices. On the contrary, alongside the dissemination process, "best practices" can be seen to vary according to the main regions of the world and according to activities. This reflects a specific conception of management and cultural singularity (Brown & He, 2007; Chien, Hu, Reimers & Lin, 2007). Furthermore, the firms having implemented ERP have discovered its limits and now require either complementary tools or an additional computerisation process.

With the idea being to conform to best practices, it might be thought that organisational innovation is accordingly limited, in other words that organisations have to adapt and submit to the new tool (Kallinikos, 2002). On the contrary, this chapter will show that the entire election and implementation process offers many opportunities to rethink the configuration of both the organisation and the tool. In fact, what actually happens is that the innovation process is opened up rather than closed. Simultaneously, both internal and external enterprise actors – including software editors and consultants - enter into a learning process. This process shows them what the organisation could be like and what the ERP could do and mean to them.

ERP has indeed given rise to a plethora of publications. Botta & Millet (2005) identify more than 1,500 publications up until to 2004. Today, over one hundred publications dealing with ERP are produced every year. This ERP literature (Heili & Vinck, 2008) shows that, with respect to many questions, there are many controversies. For instance, the ability of ERP to be an instrument allowing firms to meet the challenges of their environment continues to be subject to debate. Laudatory papers like those of Davenport (Davenport, 1998, Davenport, Harris & Cantrell, 2003) can be contrasted with more critical ones questioning the ability of ERP to be a suitable managerial tool (Kallinikos, 2004; Dillard, Richala & Yuthas, 2005; Lemaire & Valenduc, 2004). Sia, Tang, Soh & Boh (2002) deplore the temptation of company boards to cover the overcosts generated by the installation of ERP by making savings on manufacturing base costs, by concentrating power and standardising. Others (Shang & Seddon, 2000), show that boards use ERP to control departments and affirm their ascendancy over data processing specialists. Depending on the case, the control exerted by the tool is either programmed, hierarchical and routinised, serving the cause of centralism, or, on the contrary, interactive and distributed, hence fostering appropriation and learning.

Literature on ERP also reveals a broad variety of approaches. These reflect different schools of thought and theoretical trends, which often correspond to quite distinct scientific communities (engineers, managerial scientists, sociologists). These approaches can be put into four sets:

- The first set covers work on a deliberate managerial approach, often marked by a certain technical determinism. The analysis of (Shang & Seddon, 2000) is exemplary from this point of view; it endeavours to identify the benefits brought to the enterprise by the introduction of ERP.

Their investigation is based on the analysis of accounts of ERP implementation published on the Web by these enterprises and backed up by interviews.

- A second set focuses more on the "social construction" of ERP; the ERP tool is seen here as the materialisation of a number of social relations (power relations, among others) which, through technical determinism, affect the organisation directly. The work of Kallinikos (2002) is a good example of this insofar as it seeks to explain the impact of ERP on organisations starting with the organisational paradigms inscribed in the ERP system itself.

- A third set of work explores the relations between technology and organisation. The work of Orlikowski (1992) and her followers is a good example of this set. They qualify the transformations initiated by the introduction of ERP using the theory of structuration (Giddens, 1984), but also using categories borrowed from the theory of contingency. The latter explains organisational forms starting with variables such as the type of technology or the size of the company. Contrary to the previous set of works, these researchers believe that the organisation that adopts the new tool will "digest it". This process leads to a new, singular organisational form, which is not produced by the tool or by the former organisation but by a kind of structuring of the two. "Every engagement with a technology is temporally and contextually provisional, and thus there is, in every use, always the possibility of a different structure being enacted" (Orlikowski, 2000, p. 412). Publications with a similar approach also result from the French sociology of work tradition (Segrestin, 2004; Guffond & Leconte, 2004).

- A last set of papers corresponds to a marginal trend in the field of information systems and ERP. Inspired by the actor-network theory (ANT) and by the sociology of action, they are less interested in organisational models and their changes than in action itself. This approach leads to dense and nuanced analyses, which have a limited capacity in terms of producing generic results (Barley, 1990; Emirbayer & Mische, 1998; Jones, 1999; Walsham, 1997). It looks at material agency. Hanseth (Hanseth & Braa, 2000) and Monteiro (2000) refer to ERP as an agency or a powerful actor and an ally in the transformation of the organisation that is engaged. The ERP tool becomes an independent actor and is increasingly resistant to control. In fact, in ANT terms, agency is inherent, not to human beings or technology, but to the network itself.

This chapter will concentrate especially on this last scientific approach. It uses the concept of *translation* (Callon, 1986), i.e. the processes according to which a settlement is temporarily stabilized in which heterogeneous actants – tools, people, texts, etc. – are enrolled. Translation has four moments: problematisation (creation of new hypothetical relations), *interessement* (tentative displacement of entities as they connect up in the new settlement), enrolment (acceptance of the new role definition) and mobilisation of allies. Thus, translation means displacement. It involves a new definition and distribution of roles and the sketching of a new scenario. The resulting translation is always potentially reversible. This chapter will focus on a specific translation occurring between commercial software, the software editors, the consulting companies and an SME (starting with its initial intention, organisation and practices). The objective is to understand how a statement like "firm E uses and benefits from a specific information system" emerges. From an ANT perspective, this can be studied through the ideas of *translation and attachment* and leads to an analysis of the role of technology rather than a simplistic and deterministic search for causal connections. It reveals the mediating webbing in the fabric of the firm in relation to the performance of both its organisation and the tools. ANT helps to go through a set of dichotomies: between technology and society, initial project and "impact", activity and submission, individual actors and the global structure of technological developments, market trends and organisation. ANT allows relevant entities to be grasped irrespective of scale. Unlike the approaches mentioned above, ANT does not presuppose distinctions between IT and society or organisation. This chapter will show how useful it is to move away from such a priori distinctions.

Regarding the election and implementation process, the chosen approach highlights processes that appear to be more interesting to look at than either the critical success factors or the adequacy of the tool and the organisation. This chapter therefore contributes to understanding what goes on during this phase. It underlines that the most interesting point for the enterprise is the learning process that is engaged and the opening up to organisational innovation. The value of ERP implementation lies not so much in the technology, but in the process of implementation itself.

METHOD

According to the ANT theoretical and methodological framework (Latour, 1987), a field inquiry consists in following actors and intermediary objects (Vinck & Jeantet, 1995) and looking at the practices and associations built by actors. Thus, the actor-network theory is used to direct the research methodology: going out into the field, carrying out long-term observation and participating observation work, following actors, writing up narrative accounts and ethnographies (Vinck, 2003), looking at tools, traces and materials, and entering into technical considerations and

practices with actors. Field data collection then makes it possible to document the live experience of technological change, the election of new tools, their appropriation and the negotiations involved in the re-construction of the tools and the firm. In this particular case, studying the real means behind action makes it possible to develop an understanding of the simultaneous building of the IS and the firm.

The field research described in this chapter was carried out in an industrial firm that produces metallurgical powders. The first observation period lasted six months and was in the planning/scheduling department. The objective was to acquire an understanding of their specific practices. In fact, the research team's work increased the firm's consideration of this department. Prior to this, the planning/scheduling activity was not seen to be important. Following the initial observation period, the firm began to think about how to improve the department. The idea of changing the IS used for planning/scheduling emerged. Next, a 2-year participatory observation period in the firm ensued during which the idea of buying and implementing new Computer-Assisted Manufacturing (CAM) software was explored. However, the firm decided to implement Enterprise Resource Planning (ERP) software instead, in other words a set of computer programs dedicated to the integrated management of the firm. The company came to progressively rethink its production management practices, the way it was organised and what the technology could really do and what they really wanted. By meeting and following the firms' actors, we were able to collect detailed data. According to the ANT methodological principles, and whenever it was possible, we followed the actors as they went out to meet software editors and integrators and attend technology exhibitions. However, due to industrial and commercial considerations, our study was limited by the fact that it was often not possible to follow other actors, especially software integrators. Moreover, one of these firms forbade our presence as an observer taking notes.

Figure 1.

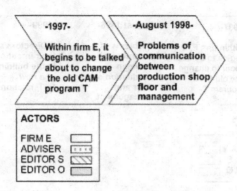

Our participation mainly consisted in watching, observing, collecting data from both inside and outside the company and writing accounts allowing information, opinions and views to be circulated. Intermediary reports and talks became an integral part of the firm's reflexivity. It is also clear that our presence contributed to the collective learning process. By going into the field, following actors and associations, producing accounts and hence moving away from a priori distinctions, as such, it might be considered that the ANT approach helped to embed the IS, even if this was not the initial objective.

TRANSLATION OF A DIGITAL DREAM

Before the implementation of a new IS, various moves to transform both the tools (at least their meaning) and the organisation can already be seen. An organisation does not start from a static situation. It evolves through the interplay and strategies of the actors involved. In the present case, the translation process begins with a rising problematisation in firm E. Working with an old CAM program (called T), the engineer in charge of the production since 1997 begins to talk about changing the production management software and starts to look for a new tool. In August 1998, an

external audit shows a number of problems in terms of communication between the production shop floor and management. These concern production control and continuous progress management. Furthermore, the editor of the CAM program in use suggests replacing it with new software. All of these reasons contribute to the idea of looking for new programs to replace the old one. The logistics and purchasing manager is in favour. The previous and embedded E – T relationship (between firm E and software T) is destined to change into E' – T', with the hypothesis being that the performance of E will be improved and that T' will be a new CAM program. (Figure 1)

Within firm E, the move mainly concerns two directors who are engaged in the building of a new E' – T' relationship. They quickly involve new actors. In 1999, they state their intention before the board of group G to which firm E belongs. However, the board asks them to wait until the changeover to the year 2000. Furthermore, the IS manager of group G proposes the assistance of an adviser and firm E accepts this idea. Thus, the network of the project associating firm E, its software T and group G is associated with new entities: an adviser A and a few potential software tools. The adviser is selected according to his reputation in professional journals and software exhibitions. He is qualified as non-interested in the choice because he is neither a software editor

Figure 2.

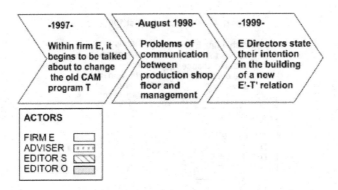

nor an integrator. Thus he appears to be a good potential mediator between firm E and the very complicated and constantly changing software market. The board of group G also proposes the help of one of its software specialists (adviser B), who already has experience introducing new CAM software. (Figure 2)

The network progressively extends, simultaneously supporting and diverging from the initial impulse. An action emerges. Adviser A suggests a methodology in 3 steps: building a list of 6 to 8 programs corresponding to firm E's expectations; pre-selecting 2 after consulting the software editors; and selecting the final program based on an in-depth comparison of the two pre-selected programs. After discussion, and before signing the contract, they decide that the first list should include 7 to 8 programs and the final short list 3. Meanwhile, editor S of program T proposes its new program S, more "client-oriented, easy to use and modern". The production manager of firm E gives adviser A information about program T along with data relating to production. He then invites the independent adviser A and the group G adviser B to assess the suitability of the new program S. The idea is also that adviser A may have a better understanding of the firm's needs. In April 2000, the contract between firm E and adviser A is ready but covers only the first step of the proposed methodology. The firm sets up

an in-house CAM committee made up of quality, planning/scheduling, sales, purchasing, accounts and production managers. The committee is chaired by the production manager. The members have to help design the solution, validate the specifications, disseminate information to employees, check program suitability, take part in the selection process and introduction of the new program and define their respective departmental needs. The production manager then gives a set of data to editor S in order to test the new program. The sociotechnical network now comprises more objects (sets of data, methodology, programs, contracts) and more actors (internal and external to the firm); some of these act as spokespersons for others (departments, experience built up in firm E, complex and changing market). (Figure 3)

Drawing up a precise description of "who and what is related, and how" gives an indication of what is going on, what action occurs and the consistency of the network. No single factor can explain what appears. In the same way, the identity and characteristics of the IT, the organisation and the relationship between IT and organisation, are part of a mutual definition process; they are part of the fabric. For instance, what is firm E? For editor S, firm E is both a current user of its program T and a potential client of the new program S and is represented by both the production manager and a set of data describing "what the

Figure 3.

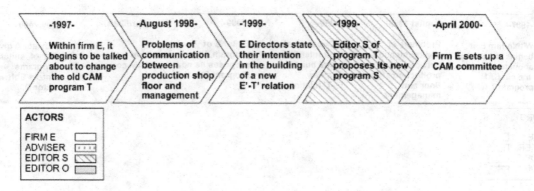

real production activities of the firm are". For adviser A, firm E is a contractual client, having signed only for the first step of the methodology proposed, wanting program S to be included in the comparative work, assisted by another adviser from group G and represented also by both the production manager and a set of data. In this way, ANT helps to describe the various perspectives for each actor but also for each material entity, using the various sets of relations.

ANT also helps to explore the robustness of the sociotechnical arrangement. For example, editor S asks firm E to send a set of data describing its production activities. Once the editor receives this, it tells the firm E CAM committee that its new program S will be suitable given the set of data received. The editor does not however check this suitability as "it is very costly" to do so. The editor proposes to do the verification if firm E signs the licensing agreement for program S. Such a proposal - asking for a set of data and then saying that the new program will be suitable - can be interpreted as an *interessement* device. However, like Callon's scallops and fishermen (Callon, 1986), firm E is able escape from this translation.

In May 2000, adviser A gives a list of 5 potentially suitable programs (and not 7 or 8 as planned). Among these, is program S. Two out of the five are then eliminated by the CAM

committee. One of the programs meets the firm's expectations perfectly, but adviser A thinks it requires high investment, is complicated and only for big companies. This appraisal is linked to the fact that the production manager asks the editor of this big program for an example of its use in medium-sized firms and never receives an answer. Progressively the complex IT world is translated into a small set of 3 relevant programs. The "short list" in the hands of the committee reflects the translation process between the CAM world and firm E. Relative irreversibility is created. The next step of the translation process is the selection of one software program and its implementation, but things are not that simple. None of the 3 programs selected satisfies the expectations of firm E. All three require specific additional development. The translation can only succeed if the IT is transformed. Furthermore, for at least one of these software tools, the board's expectations will only be satisfied if it also buys another program designed for financial management. Consequently, the CAM committee asks another software editor (O) about such a program. A new actor enters into the game and, with them, another program too. This new program is not only able to deal with financial aspects but with the commercial side of the business too. There is no tool for production, but one could be developed. This therefore leads to a new translation of the IT world with

Figure 4.

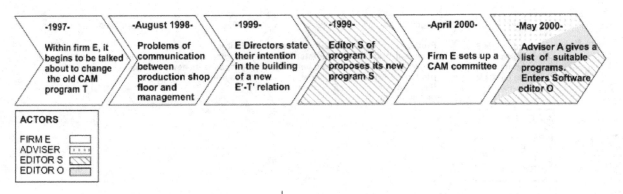

4 potential programs: three resulting from the selection process followed by the independent adviser and the CAM committee, and one added by the newly arrived software editor. According to ANT, these moves have to be identified and understood. Indeed, there are certainly plenty of moves to be explored. (Figure 4)

Meanwhile, in June, during an internal meeting of firm E, the idea of having a serious rethink about the firm's organisation is put on the table. Two years earlier, the production manager thought that introducing a new CAM program would be a good opportunity for improving the company's organisation. There were no major problems, but the idea was to do better. Now, looking at the organisation, they nevertheless conclude that it is no longer adapted to the new commercial and production requirements. They also raise a new argument: the firm would no longer manage "articles" but "lots". The problem is that none of the programs selected are able to do this.

New events occur. For instance, there is talk of firm E buying firm C (a lab working for firm E). Its general manager suggests another methodology for implementing a CAM program. Also, a specific relationship is set up between firm C's general manager and firm E's production manager, who is at the head of the CAM committee. Meanwhile, in order to pursue the selection process internally, the committee disseminates the file written by adviser

A to key people. The 150 key questions in the file are designed to assess the CAM software and refer to commercial aspects, technical aspects (including openness and user-friendliness) and functional aspects. In September 2000, three programs are selected: S (by editor S, the editor of program T already in use), Q, and the newly arrived program O (proposed by the new adviser and editor O). The reason program O is included is that it is adapted to the accounting program in use, which is highly suitable given the specific accounting rules in the country. In November, the committee compares the programs again according to new criteria: possible integration with other software, cost and durability of the firm. In December, only programs S and O are still competing. S is the first program proposed in 1998 by the editor of program T (currently being used) and O is the last program to be added to the list. Editor O is asked to supply additional information based on advisor A's list of 150 key questions. The commercial delegate of editor O responds positively to practically all the questions. Furthermore, in January 2001, he offers to guide the firm through the implementation of the program. Editor O is not only a software editor but an integrator too. In February, he advises the company to adopt another version of the software, which is more suitable for firm E, and then sells it to them. In March 2001, the CAM committee becomes the ERP commit-

Figure 5.

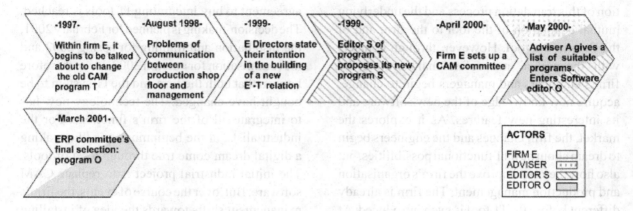

tee and proceeds with the final selection. A vote is applied: 2 people are in favour of program S (among them firm E's production manager) and 4 people vote for program O (among them firm C's general manager). Following all the different moves (the appearance of new actors, software and criteria, the circulation of the list of key questions, the decision-making, etc.), the choice falls on program O. The actors involved are not really responsible for this choice. The material arrangements and practical matters are just as important as the various people involved (Dugdale, 1999). In fact, even before any explicit decision is made, the sociotechnical arrangement points the action in a certain direction. This has much to do with what "action into the organisation" means. All the ingredients of the situation simultaneously constitute the decision-making system. Decision occurs from such a sociotechnical arrangement. It constitutes a means of ordering (Law, 1994) priorities. (Figure 5)

EVERYTHING MOVES

The board of firm E progressively expresses the desire to change the CAM tool and explores the idea of installing a new one. It engages in a software search process. The idea is to select the software, then buy and implement it. Various alternative software possibilities are discovered along the way while, at the same time, a new market trend in industrial software emerges and is gradually disseminated: ERP software. This means that new considerations have to be taken into account regarding what the firm really needs. After meeting commercial IT people and advisers with their key questions, and reading IT and professional production literature, the firm's managers are encouraged to reflect on their own organisation, practices and needs. This leads to a shift in all the initial ingredients.

The translation process appears clearly. The initial problematisation is to select and buy commercial CAM software to replace the old package and improve the firm's performance. If the commercial software can be adapted for installation in firm E and linked to the firm's specific production system, then the relationship between this IT and the firm's production activities will be entrenched. It is also clear for the engineers that a short software translation process is required in order to adapt it to the specific features of the company's production system and organisation. Most commercial software includes characteristics that need to be specified. This is called "parameterisation". Conversely, they anticipate that the operators in the firm will need to be trained to work on the new tools. This is the initial perception of this translation process and the underlying mutual adaptation of the tool to the firm and of the firm to the tool. However, through contacts with "the market" and professional literature, the firm's engineers and managers begin to change, acquire new knowledge of the new software and its interesting new features. As it explores the market, the firm changes and the engineers begin to dream about new IT functional possibilities, but also how they can improve the firm's organisation and production management. The firm is already different before the IT tool is even introduced. At this point the parameters have not yet been set. The story is just beginning and we can already see that simplistic and deterministic causal connections are of no relevance. There is no technical determinism; the firm changes before the IT tool is even introduced. There is no economic determinism, no necessity, just an idea that emerges. There is no social determinism explained by the social or professional interest of a specific group. It is more the result of interactions between actors, ideas, journals, existing tools, etc., in a specific sociotechnical configuration.

When following the building and embedding of a specific IT tool in an industrial firm, it can be seen that the company shifts towards wanting more and more things. From the initial idea of replacing one IT tool with another, the managers begin to think about setting up links with other existing in-house software or new, shop-bought software. Starting from the existing sociotechnical configuration and from current practices, local changes and new relations are expected. With respect to both the in-house discussions and the involvement of the various departments, as well as the current ideas to be found in the professional milieu, the idea of integration emerges in the CAM committee. However, unlike what occurs on the market with top-down software dedicated to integration, firm E engages in a bottom-up integration process following the needs and forces present in the firm. The ERP idea gradually enters the

company and becomes a new demand. Finally, an agreement to buy integrating IT tools is reached. The decision-making is planned for February 2001, the installation and training for spring 2002 and the routinisation for autumn 2002. It can therefore be seen that both the firm and the IT system to be bought have changed. The technology now has to integrate all of the firm's functions. For the industrialists, at the beginning, it is like making a digital dream come true through a set of tools. The initial industrial project is to replace CAM software. But, over the course of events, the firm's management shifts towards the idea of installing ERP software and, what is more, developing functions and links with other software. Translation is certainly the right word.

PARAMETERISATION AS A KEY MOMENT IN THE TRANSLATION PROCESS

Once the software, editor and integrator have been selected, the relationship between the new IT and the organisation can be consolidated. This involves visiting a program O user to confirm the "impressions" of the ERP committee and then negotiating the contract. A new ERP project group is set up in firm E. Its mission is to accompany the implementation. Integrator O proposes the following working programme: collection of the different departmental specifications, analysis and validation, modelling, drafting of the technical files for the software programming, work on adaptations, analysis by the client, manual entry of data by firm E, automatic recovery of data, assistance, testing and training. (Figure 6)

Many people in firm E are involved when the work starts in order to define the specifications. This represents an opportunity to look at practices. During the course of the action, new ideas, problems and solutions emerge. Many firm E members, in fact, start the big job of defining the needs and specifications. Based on this, integrator O starts

Figure 6.

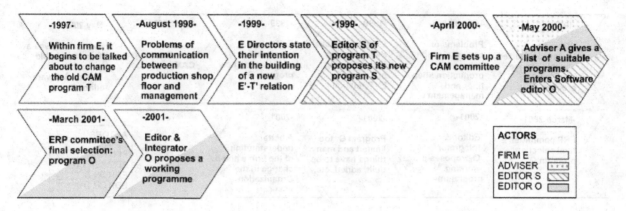

-1997-
Within firm E, it begins to be talked about to change the old CAM program T

-August 1998-
Problems of communication between production shop floor and management

-1999-
E Directors state their intention in the building of a new E'-T' relation

-1999-
Editor S of program T proposes its new program S

-April 2000-
Firm E sets up a CAM committee

-May 2000-
Adviser A gives a list of suitable programs. Enters Software editor O

-March 2001-
ERP committee's final selection: program O

-2001-
Editor & Integrator O proposes a working programme

ACTORS
FIRM E
ADVISER
EDITOR S
EDITOR O

work on developing and integrating the software. Program O is then presented as a standard requiring only a few specific developments. However, it gradually appears to be too limited and many things have to be built, added or transformed. The parameterisation process turns into a transformation process involving some of the fundamental aspects of the software. (Figure 7)

In each department of the firm, people look into their activity in order to identify their needs and define their specifications. This process allows them to explore the activity, share information and knowledge about products, their scope and variability, about the process and its constraints. They

also bring up new questions, for instance: "Why do we need scheduling software?" Indeed, this does not appear to be necessary for the production department, while it does for quality control in the laboratory and for packaging. They observe that the scope of firm E's products and that of the laboratory (firm C) diverges. They also discover that more days are needed to control the quality of a product than to produce it and that quality control is mixed up with strategic Research and Development activities. Given the constraints of the new software, they focus their attention on their specific product coding process. Thus, independently of the introduction of the software, they start

Figure 7.

-1997-
Within firm E, it begins to be talked about to change the old CAM program T

-August 1998-
Problems of communication between production shop floor and management

-1999-
E Directors state their intention in the building of a new E'-T' relation

-1999-
Editor S of program T proposes its new program S

-April 2000-
Firm E sets up a CAM committee

-May 2000-
Adviser A gives a list of suitable programs. Enters Software editor O

-March 2001-
ERP committee's final selection: program O

-2001-
Editor & Integrator O proposes a working programme

-2001-
Program O: too limited and many things have to be built, added, etc.

ACTORS
FIRM E
ADVISER
EDITOR S
EDITOR O

Figure 8.

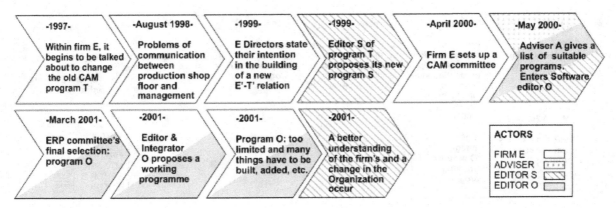

recoding work. The organisation begins to change in relation to the chosen software. They now want to code the products in an "unambiguous" way and this collective work leads to a change in the organisation. They also re-build the division of work between departments. So, in relation to the parameterisation of the new software, both a better understanding of the firm's activity and a change in the organisation occur. Simultaneously, they learn to identify their expectations, which focus more on the interfaces than on the resolution of problems (planning and scheduling). Afterwards, they become aware of what they really need. There is thus co-production of the IT specifications and of the new organisation. Furthermore, it has to be underlined that the new organisation is not the consequence of the constraints imposed on it by the IT tool, but the result of relatively autonomous action within the network. (Figure 8)

While all of this work is going on, some members of the ERP committee begin to have doubts about the solution offered by program O. The ERP project leader visits another user of this program, but does not come up with any relevant answers. In May 2002, during a meeting of the ERP committee, the question "why have we chosen program O?" is raised. The possibility of coming back on the choice is explored. They even consider going back to program T, which is currently in use, and improving it. During the

consolidation of the relationship between the IT tool and the organisation, both the program and the firm change. The actors think back to the past and to the reasons why program T, 4 years earlier, was considered to be no longer satisfactory. Then, each actor separately engages in a new exploration of the market, involving meeting up with users. They thus collect a lot of data, not only concerning the technical characteristics of the programs but also their use and integration in practices and the reliability of editors and integrators. Firm E members clearly enter into an important learning process. The assessment questionnaire for choosing the software is also reconsidered. It only contains technical considerations, but the firm needs information about the robustness of the software editor: financial solidity, number of developers and users of the software, as well as the experience of users other than those recommended by the editor.

The members of the ERP committee gradually realise why there are so many failures with ERP implementation: only 20% of ERP implementation is successful. The reasons given are that company needs and purposes are not clearly expressed to begin with and specifications are incomplete. However, how is it possible for a company to express its needs when it has no previous experience? How can specifications be completed without trial and error, experience and

Figure 9.

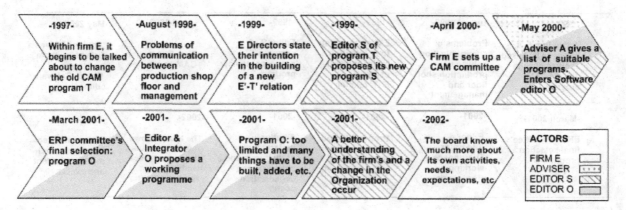

learning? Thanks to the ERP selection process, the specification work and ad hoc development in firm E, the board knows much more about its own activities, needs, expectations and the real possibilities offered by the software. It feels itself empowered to require more (Lee & Myers, 2004). Not only does the firm now ask for clear answers to its specifications, but it also wants to be able to check functions, by looking at how a client uses them or how they are simulated by the developer. If this is not possible, they demand clear answers in terms of the time needed for a given function to be developed, the cost of developing a function specifically for the firm and information about alternatives if there are any. (Figure 9)

The parameterisation phase appears to be a key process during which there is co-production of both the IT solution and the firm. It is neither a question of simply adapting the IT tools to the organisation nor of adapting the organisation to the tools. Something quite different actually unfolds out of which new sociotechnical arrangements emerge.

"HAVE WE FAILED?"

Growing difficulties appear in relations between firm E and integrator O. The integrator does not respect the deadlines when providing answers to specific needs. It does not produce any contractual specifications. This leads to a lack of software integration and a build-up of delays regarding the transmission of new versions. Finally, the integrator goes into receivership and is no longer able to fulfil the contract. The relationship between program O and firm E goes back to its problematic status. Doubts and difficulties about program O emerge. The integrator is no longer able to support its implementation. The ERP committee members have doubts about the usefulness of a scheduling program and engage in a search for other software, geared more towards interfaces.

This situation may be qualified as a failure. However, two months later the ERP committee members feel that it has become much more competent and expert. The failure regarding the introduction of program O corresponds to an important learning process. As it looks into the software issue, the management of the firm discovers its own organisation. They are able to raise new questions, gain knowledge, rethink their own practices and analyse what the company really does. The internal analysis of the firm is linked with the process of expressing needs for specifications. Furthermore, firm E's managers have acquired a much broader knowledge. They know that the robustness of inter-firm relationships

Figure 10.

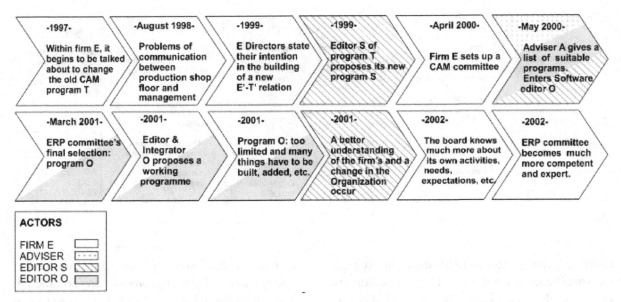

is not only supported by the signing of a contract. They know that it is crucial to meet up with IT users and that the robustness of their partner is just as important as the technical characteristics of its products.

They discover that implementing ERP leads to the start of a rationalisation process, which is relatively independent of the IT issue. At the beginning, they see this as a process for translating IT requirements into the activity and usual practices into the program. Yet, they discover that they can also abandon some common practices, whether this is due to IT requirements or not. New opportunities for action come about thanks to the rationalisation process. Even if no software is chosen and implemented in the end, the firm changes for the better; it shifts through what it learns about its own practices and thanks to the rationalisation of these and its organisation in general.

The firm also discover that asking an adviser for help is no longer necessary once the firm members have their own experience and learning. The learning process is also related to the initial study carried out by a consultant, visits to exhibitions and conferences, articles read in the press,

what various integrators and editors have to tell them (following internal or external visits), visits to users where specific questions can be raised, etc. After each visit, reading or encounter, the firm managers think back to their own situation, practices, issues, purposes, etc. With each event they become more aware of problems, possible solutions and criteria. They produce new knowledge about both their own situation and needs and the real possibilities of existing commercial software. They become experts. Each series of questions they bring up with the integrator is more precise and difficult to answer. Integrators are surprised by the questions asked by the firm members. They say that normally nobody asks such questions. They even encounter difficulties answering them; at times firm members become aware of the fact that integrators sometimes give the wrong answers to questions. Discussions with the editors and integrators become more detailed because the managers are already aware of the considerations and what is officially said about ERP. (Figure 10)

The failure allows the firm to learn that responsibility cannot be limited to a specific actor who is alone in control of the state of affairs, answerable in terms of his actions and charged with their consequences. On the contrary, from a pragmatic point of view, responsibility seems more distributed in a dispersed network, even if for legal reasons there is a process of producing a responsibility and attaching it to a limited number of entities. The firm's lessons for future action are geared more towards building another network, one that is more stable and predictable or in which the firm can maintain its position even if related entities lack consistency. There is no one person or party responsible; the firm as a whole learns to be careful about everything and about its partners. The editor – integrator is not completely controllable just because there is a contract. The board of the firm wants a better guarantee. At the end of the day they learn that the best guarantee is to develop their own competence and ability to adapt and redefine action, benefiting from opportunities and negotiating continuously. There is a progressive refusal to give credit to just a few apparently founding aspects: the contract, the editor's financial stability, the written specifications, the software properties, etc. On the contrary, the firm members get involved in a process of making things more visible and linkable. They complete the list of usual criteria for comparing software: the technical properties of the software are included along with the characteristics of the editors and their practices. They want to see by themselves; they no longer accept what editors and integrators say and write; they contact users in order to have discussions and demonstrations of specific questions. Thus, less and less things are excluded from their investigation. Anything may be relevant in the decision process.

BEYOND DETERMINING OR DETERMINED ACTION

Using ANT it has been possible in this study to switch focus from the firm and the IT tool to a sociotechnical arrangement of agency. Such a shift calls into question both technical determinism and the theory of action, which presuppose an actor. This theory looks only at the active part of things. The idea, on the contrary, is to go beyond the dichotomy between action as something that is determining (supposing a free actor) and action as something that is determined (referring to deterministic and sometimes invisible structures). ANT thus makes it possible to get a simultaneous grasp on action and submission. Thus, "the action in organisation and technology" can no longer be thought of in the following terms: "passive submission to new constraints", "free action", "action limited by a set of constraints" or "action with and on the constraints". We propose instead to think of action in terms of submission and action, dispossession and control, without any dichotomy.

The hypothesis is that it is also productive to discipline actors and objects, the firm and the software. "Constraints" become generous aspects of things, which create the firm and the IT in action. The emerging attachment (Hennion & Gomart, 1999) of the firm to a specific type of software and of the IT to an organisation takes the form of a consensual self-abandonment of previous practices, accepting that external forces (editors, integrators, users, software, market, etc.) take over. Accepting being under somebody else's influence while reigning in their own control opens up new careers for both IT and organisation. It then becomes interesting to look at the sociotechnical arrangements, which make this active dispossession possible. This implies shifting from the idea of the firm as actor and of the IT as a determining element in the mechanisms through which active involvement happens. Thus, designers and users put their autonomy and control at risk in the name of possible evolution, discoveries, experience, learning, etc.

The agent emerges now as it actively submits itself to a collection of constraints. There is action thanks to submission, control thanks to dispossession and conversely. Such emergence, however, is linked to tentative preparation. The firm emerges as an actor that is not alone, but rather entangled in a collection of other firms, events, texts, objects, etc.: a research partner, integrators and software editors, exhibitions, users, professional journals, demonstrations, and internal practices, procedures that gradually become more explicit and coded. The IT tool appears as an agent in the same way. The firm emerges as a structure housing skilled actors as an effect of the process and of the sociotechnical arrangement. Thus, it is no longer relevant to presuppose a priori skilled actors, able to act. The action, on the contrary, evolves as an unanticipated effect of the sociotechnical network.

There is a trend in sociology leading to the idea that a free actor needs to be replaced by something else. ANT proposes networkisation of the actor in which each entity of the network contributes to the sociotechnical action. The capacity to act is an effect of association, which cannot be reduced either to free actors or to a priori structures or systems. ANT suggests forgetting about a priori distinctions between entities in order to account for the shared production of action as the performance of a specific configuration. Furthermore, we can no longer sustain the idea of distributed action between human and non-human entities. On the contrary, the idea is to account for the network, which produces action, intelligence and so on. Action is an emerging effect of the network in which there are no necessarily determined sources of action. What appears cannot be reduced to action. There are also things, which just occur, like the transformation of the firm with the introduction of an IT tool; the firm enters into a certain history and is transformed by its involvement and progressive attachment to a new sociotechnical collective made up of various delegates (human like the adviser or non-human like the list of key questions). These delegates are mediators, which do not just repeat or transfer intentions and actions but transform them in unexpected ways. Thus, something occurs and generates new effects.

However, things do not appear simply. Happenings, which are out of control, require preparation and conditioning. The firm opens itself up and becomes sensitive and receptive to many signals both inside and out. It also becomes more patient; its deadline is extended to 12 months. Activity and passivity are not opposites. The success of the project is no longer attributable to the technology (its intrinsic logic or the application of the right methodology for implementing it) or to the actors (their clear strategy and their reasoning). On the contrary, firm E members are not aware of this opposition. The decision (to implement ERP or to choose a tool) is neither a pure agreement, nor an illusion. It can be described through the different ways actors, objects (Hayles, 1992), texts and practices help to induce what occurs. What happens then is the mutual webbing of the firm and of the software. This can be thought of as a sort of passing from one state to another: from adapting the organisation to modern IT to expressing the firm's personality; from individual problem-solving to benefiting from trends; from making and controlling (technical mastering and application of the right procedures) to feeling what happens to the firm; from properties and performance of software to what happens through them. In the same way, the software passes through several stages: from implementation and adaptation to new potential in action; from an isolated tool with general performance levels to a specific ingredient of a specific and collective sociotechnical action; from data processing to an active part of the global shift.

FUTURE TRENDS

It is difficult to identify trends from a case study. However, the work behind this chapter reveals the importance of the various ongoing moves in the situation described. These moves correspond to the displacement and redefinition of the organisation, actors and technology itself. One of the main results of the study is the identification of the collective endeavour and the way it settles to form a heterogeneous network from which collective awareness, learning and decision emerge. This result depends on the collective move but not so much on the new tool that failed to be introduced. Such a point is probably relevant to any situation and should be taken into account by the actors in order to avoid misunderstanding. What appears important here for the actors is the apprenticeship. What they learn about ERP, the market, but also about their own organisation seems to have a major impact. This is something that could be optimised through future investigation in the field of IS implementation. Thus, rather than asking "how to adapt the organisation to the new tool" and "how to adapt the tool" a more relevant question would be "how to improve learning?"

The chapter also highlights the shift from mastering and controlling to feeling and benefiting from opportunities. Such a move can be surprising and appear to have little rationality but seems an interesting point to study in other cases in an effort to further conceptualise it. The organisational action can no longer be thought of in terms of "passive submission" versus "free action" but needs to be conceptualised as simultaneous submission and action, dispossession and control, without any form of dichotomy. Similarities may be explored through the study of design processes and innovative activities.

These two points can be usefully linked in order to develop a new paradigm to study what goes on when ERP has become part of a routine. Given the case study outlined in this article, we can predict that the learning process will continue as the actors become accustomed to the tool and discover its limits. They will probably develop new practices, meanings and performance with their own ERP, thus opening up once more to a process of innovation.

CONCLUSION: POTENTIAL FOR IS RESEARCH

In this chapter we have shown how the ANT approach can be useful compared with the usual approaches of engineers, social scientists and management scientists. Looking at networks of related entities and the translation process provides access to the multiple moves and reconfigurations that lead to the building and stabilisation of an embedded IT tool. This approach not only offers the advantage of avoiding a priori and sterile distinctions (like technology/organisation, active/passive, free/determined, generic/specific), but opens up major process for understanding IT embedding: the mutual reconfiguration of both IT and organisation.

Studying the mutual reconfiguration of IT and organisation through, for instance, the parameterisation process, differs from both the sociology of design (explaining the origin of IT) and the sociology of use (looking at the people from the point of view of the IT tool, the impact on them, how they adapt to it or the activities they develop). Such a study focuses on a space where many new things emerge from the specific sociotechnical arrangement. Devices (firm or software) are not only constraints, but also opportunities for action in both directions. They create and make way for new capacities within the software and the firm, both of which pass through such devices. Among other things, this prompts the emergence of "software in use", as it becomes embedded, and "an organisation using software". Studying this space helps us to understand organisation building, the learning process of individuals and groups, and IT building. What we have seen is that beyond simply leading to the adaptation of the software, feedback affects integrators, editors and software design alike. This confirms the results of Boersma and Kingma (2005), who argued that the implementation of ERP is more than an adaptation process for both the IS and the organisation. We suggest that ERP, actors and organisation are transformed and engaged in an original trajectory. This leads to a diversity of ERP in use.

ERP performance differs between firms with the same management activities that even use the same supporting systems and technologies because ERP projects are enterprise projects which imply most of the departments of the organization and games of actors. For this reason an ERP project will always be different from another one. It does not matter if two ERP projects have the same software tools, the same technology or the same implementation strategy, there are several elements forbidding projects to be similar. Investigations performed in many companies have shown that: a) the game in power relations between actors and b) the protection of its political standings before of the ERP's introduction are elements of considerable importance causing that a project has a different development than another one.

Another interesting point in IS studies relates to the question of alternatives. Is there alternative software? In fact, rather than alternative software, as it was thought at the beginning and also supposed through software implementation methodologies, the actors discover that they have to face multiple versions of multiple and more or less combinable and adaptable modules. Furthermore, all these things undergo rapid changes. The world moves and is incredibly unstable. Rational methodologies supporting decision-making are inconsistent with what is going on. What can a firm do about this? Where are the options if it is not simply a question of software alternatives? What is at stake and what is required? What do the options and the decisions consist of? How should the actors choose? Making a choice supposes that it is possible to locate a decision instance, the content of decisions and alternatives to help with decision-making. The ERP's are IT tools which helps to solve organizational troubles but there is an infinity of other ITs (CRM, SRM, WMS…). All the troubles about data transference are not solved by the ERP. The selection of an ERP and other software systems must depend on the problematic

to be solved and not on the type of enterprise or financial competitiveness. On the other hand, as shown in this case study, many ERP editors did not count on their own ERP systems for small and medium companies. Nowadays, there is an important diversification of ERP solutions for any type of company. Moreover, many companies, after looking into the negative impact of their ERP implementation, have reconsidered to solve their troubles about SI with system development at home.

In fact, decision emerges through a number of contingencies and forces, and also through a number of places and moments. Furthermore, decision instances are themselves subject to shifts and reconfigurations. When it comes to possible options, these can appear from outside the company or be imported through industrial partners, editors, integrators, exhibitions, journals, researchers or members of the organisation, but they are not structured. A process of clarification of the alternatives is engaged through textual moves and discussion. Argumentative formats and settings become crucial: the procedure used by the consultant, the kind of table and list of criteria and the composition of the meetings where things are discussed. In the case study described, the first software package selection experience seems to render the options explicit. However, the decision is made elsewhere and based on other elements. With the second experience and continuing build-up of further experience, knowledge and expertise, it becomes much more difficult to put things into boxes or base decisions on whole options. Furthermore, during each new discussion, new things and aspects appear, options shift and the impression that options are everywhere emerges. Options are both everywhere and elsewhere and hence require new investigations. One more year is needed, during which the world continues to change. Furthermore, the firm learns to break down the commercial software and its ingredients and start thinking about an ERP tool that might combine the properties of the various software solutions in a specific way. A new dream emerges, but is continuously challenged by the strategies and reliability of the editors, integrators and software modules. In short, building up knowledge by looking in detail at the options leads to a general proliferation of alternatives at all levels. The practical problems involve restricting this proliferation. But the question is how to do this. In fact, two other changes appear through this decision-making process: a learning process and a shift from mastering and controlling to feeling and benefiting from opportunities.

REFERENCES

Barley, S. (1990). The alignment of technology and structure through roles and networks. *Admistrative Science Quaterly,* (35), 61-103.

Botta, V., Millet, P. A., & Grabot, B. (2005). A survey on the recent research literature on ERP systems. *Computers in Industry, 56*(6), 510–522. doi:10.1016/j.compind.2005.02.004

Boursma, K., & Kingma, S. (2005). From means to ends: The transformation of ERP in a manufacturing company. *Strategic Information Systems,* (14), 197-199.

Brown, D., & He, S. (2007). Patterns of ERP adoption and implementation in China and some implications. *Electronic Markets, 17*(2), 132–141. doi:10.1080/10196780701296287

Callon, M. (1986). Some elements for a sociology of translation. Domestication of the scallops and the fishermen of St-Brieuc bay. In J. Law (Ed.), *Power, action and belief. A new sociology of knowledge?* (pp. 196-233). London: Routledge and Kegan Paul.

Chien, S.-W., Hu, C., Reimers, K., & Lin, J.-S. (2007). The influence of centrifugal and centripetal forces on ERP project success in small and medium-sized enterprises in China and Taiwan. *International Journal of Production Economics, 107*(2), 380–396. doi:10.1016/j.ijpe.2006.10.002

Davenport, T. (1998). Putting the enterprise into the enterprise system. *Harvard Business Review,* (July-August): 121–130.

Davenport, T., Harris, J., & Cantrell, S. (2003). *The return of enterprise solutions: The director's cut*: Accenture Institute for Strategic Change.

Dillard, J. F., Richala, L., & Yuthas, K. (2005). Enterprise resource planning systems: A physical manifestation of administrative evil. *International Journal of Accounting Information Systems, 6*(2), 107–127. doi:10.1016/j.accinf.2005.02.001

Dugdale, A. (1999). Materiality: Juggling, sameness and difference. In J. Law & J. Hassard (Eds.), *Actor-network theory and after* (pp. 113-135). Oxford: Blackwell.

Emirbayer, M., & Mische, A. (1998). What is agency? *American Journal of Sociology, 103,* 962–1023. doi:10.1086/231294

Giddens, A. (1984). *The constitution of society: Outline of the theory of structuration*. Berkeley: University of California Press.

Guffond, J.-L., & Leconte, G. (2004). Les ERP, puissants outils d'organisation du changement industriel. *Science and Society,* (61): 33–51.

Hanseth, O., & Braa, K. (2000). Who's in control: Designers, managers or technology? In C. Ciborra (Ed.), *From control to drift* (pp. 125-147). Oxford: Oxford University Press.

Hayles, C. (1992). The materiality of informatics. *Configurations, 1,* 147–170. doi:10.1353/con.1993.0003

Heili, J., & Vinck, D. (2008). Penser les relations entre technique et organisation: Un examen de la littérature. In D. Vinck & B. Penz (Eds.), *L'équipement de l'organisation industrielle. Les ERP à l'usage* (pp. 43-81). Paris: Hermes.

Hennion, A., & Gomart, E. (1999). A sociology of attachement: Music amateurs, drug users. In J. Law & J. Hassard (Eds.), *Actor-network theory and after* (pp. 220-247). Oxford: Blackwell.

Jones, M. (1999). Information systems and the double mangle. In T. Larsen, L. Levine & J. DeGross (Eds.), *Information systems: Current issues and future changes* (pp. 287-302). Madison: OmniPress.

Kallinikos, J. (2002). *Re-opening the black box of technology: Artifacts and human agency.* Paper presented at the 23 ICIS, Barcelona.

Kallinikos, J. (2004). Deconstructing information packages: Organisational and behavioural implications of ERP sytems. *Information Technology & People, 17*(1), 8–20. doi:10.1108/09593840410522152

Latour, B. (1987). *Science in action: How to follow scientists and engineers through society.* Cambridge, MA: Harvard University Press.

Law, J. (1994). *Organizing modernity.* Oxford; Cambridge, MA: Blackwell.

Lee, J.C., & Myers. M.D.. (2004). Dominant actors, political agendas, and strategic shifts over time: a critical ethnography of an enterprise systems implementation. *Strategic Information Systems,* (13), 355-374.

Lemaire, L., & Valenduc, G. (2004). Entre rigidité et maléabilité. Le double visage des ERP. *Science and Society,* (61): 53–69.

Monteiro, E. (2000). Actor-network theory and information infrastructures. In C. Ciborra (Ed.), *From control to drift* (pp. 71-84). Oxford: Oxford University Press.

Orlikowski, W. J. (1992). The duality of technology: Rethinking the concept of technology in organisations. *Organization Science, 3*(3), 398–427. doi:10.1287/orsc.3.3.398

Orlikowski, W. J. (2000). Using technology and constituting structures: A practice lens for studying technology in organisations. *Organization Science, 11*(4), 404–428. doi:10.1287/orsc.11.4.404.14600

Segrestin, D. (2004). Les ERP entre le retour à l'ordre et l'invention du possible. *Science and Society,* (61): 3–15.

Shang, S., & Seddon, P. (2000). *A comprehensive framework for classifying the benefits of ERP systems.* Paper presented at the Americas Conference on Information Systems AMCIS.

Sia, S., Tang, M., Soh, C., & Boh, W. (2002). Enterprise resource planning (ERP) systems as a technology of power: Empowerment or panoptic control? *ACM SIGMIS Database, 33*(1), 23–37. doi:10.1145/504350.504356

Vinck, D. (Ed.). (2003). *Everyday engineering. An ethnography of design and innovation.* Cambridge, MA: MIT Press.

Vinck, D., & Jeantet, A. (1995). Mediating and commissioning objects in the sociotechnical process of product design: A conceptual approach. In D. Maclean, P. Saviotti & D. Vinck (Eds.), *Designs, networks and strategies* (Vol. 2, pp. 111-129). Bruxelles: EC Directorate General Science R&D.

Walsham, G. (1997). Actor-network theory and is research: Current status and future prospects. In A. Lee, J. Liebernau & J. DeGross (Eds.), *Information systems and qualitative research* (pp. 466-480). London: Chapman and Hall.

ENDNOTE

[1] The authors thank the French CNRS Research Programme STIC-SHS (Sciences et Techniques de l'Information et de la Communication – Sciences Humaines et Sociales) for the grant that made this research possible. Thanks too to enterprise E which helped us by opening its doors and providing financial support. Thanks to the referees.

Chapter 25
The Management of CRM Information Systems in Small B2B Service Organisations:
A Comparison between French and British Firms

Călin Gurău
GSCM – Montpellier Business School, France

ABSTRACT

The new communication and information systems have significantly increased the possibilities offered to professional companies for developing and maintaining long-term customer relationships. However, technology alone cannot ensure the success of CRM strategies. The implementation of a customer-centred culture, shared by the entire professional organisation, requires the combination of human resources, expertise and technology in order to identify and satisfy the needs of the existing customers. Considering a sample of French and UK professional SMEs, this chapter investigates the type of CRM strategy implemented by these firms, as well as the usage intensity of various communication channels, both by companies and clients. The satisfaction of client organisations is analysed from a multi-level perspective and a diagnostic procedure is proposed in order to identify the gap between the perceptions service provider firms and clients on various dimensions of the CRM process.

INTRODUCTION

The development of new Information Technology and Telecommunication (ITT) systems, such as the Internet or mobile phones, has opened new possibilities for improving the relationship between service providers and clients (Brechbühl, 2004; Smith, 2000).

DOI: 10.4018/978-1-60566-892-5.ch025

Many studies (Iyer, 2003; Kalakota & Robinson, 2001; Leger, 2000; Zeng, Wen & Yen, 2003) have emphasised that, in a digital economy, the quality of customer-company interactions represents a complex combination between the feasibility and usability of the ITT systems used as interaction channels, and the efficiency of the CRM procedures implemented by the firm.

On the other hand, the interaction between clients and service providers in the Business-to-Business (B2B) market, often takes place through a variety of channels, both digital and non-digital. In these conditions, customer satisfaction will be determined by the capacity of the firm to manage effectively multi-channel customer interactions, integrating CRM procedures with channel management (Johnson, 2002). Significant research has been conducted on consumer's use of various communication channels and the relative satisfaction level of customers. Iyer (2003) presented a comparison between the level of satisfaction associated with the use of various communication channels for accessing customer services. 62% of respondents have associated a high level of satisfaction with online chat, followed by 49% of respondents for in-person communication and 46% for telephone interaction. At the other end of the scale, postal mail and fax communication were associated with a high level of satisfaction only by 24% of respondents.

This chapter presents a study of B2B service interactions, which attempts to identify the main strategies related with the management of CRM information systems, and to measure the preference of both service providers and client firms for various channels of interaction.

The digital communication channels are considered together with the traditional channels in the context of CRM applications implemented by service organisations (web design and consulting firms). The company-customer interaction is treated as a multi-dimensional process, which involves a systemic side – the ITT system implemented by the firm, and a procedural aspect – the CRM procedures applied by the service provider in various stages of its interaction with the customer. Considering this approach, the study has the following research objectives:

1. To study the main strategies for managing the CRM information systems used by small B2B service organisations.

2. To identify the communication channels used by firms and their integration with customer management procedures.
3. To analyse the level of satisfaction determined by the interaction between service organisations and client firms in relation with the use of ITT and ITT-based customer management procedures.

For a better understanding of the overall context of B2B interactions, both digital and non-digital communication channels have been analysed and evaluated, in relation with the CRM procedures implemented by service provider organisations. After a brief discussion of the previous studies published in this area, the chapter presents the research methods applied to collect primary and secondary data. The research data are then analysed and presented in direct connection with the formulated research objectives. The chapter concludes with a synthetic discussion of the main findings, which are used to propose a diagnostic procedure for measuring the level of satisfaction of company-customer interactions, analytically developed on the ITT and CRM dimensions.

BACKGROUND: INFORMATION SYSTEMS AND APPLICATIONS FOR CRM

The development of new CRM technology applications increased the capacity of firms to manage more efficiently their customers. These applications, properly run on the available ITT platforms, can link the customer interface with front office operations – sales, marketing, customer service, etc. and with the back office support - logistics, operations, human resources, etc. (Chen & Popovich, 2003). However, the structure and the functionality of the CRM information system will be different from one company to another, depending on its specific activity profile and strategic objectives.

Some organisations consider the CRM system as a simple technology solution to integrate database and sales automation in order to reduce the cost of transactions and marketing activities. Others define it as a communication tool that permits the customisation of company-customer interaction (Peppers & Rogers, 1999 and 20012001). However, both these descriptions are limitative. The CRM system must be based on the implementation of a customer-centric culture which should permeate the entire organisation, and modify, according to its logic, the strategy, structure and operations of the entire enterprise (Rheault & Sheridan, 2002).

The interface between the organisation and its customers is represented by a number of 'touch points', in which takes place the interaction between customers and organisational systems (Fickel, 1999). These touch points can include fixed and mobile phone, fax, Internet, email, online discussion forums, or face-to-face encounters. Traditionally, these touch points were controlled by separate information systems, and sometimes, by different organisational departments. The revolution introduced by CRM applications is the capacity to collect the data from all these touching points into a centralised database that can be dynamically accessed by any person within the organisation (Eckerson & Watson, 2000).

For an effective implementation and use of the CRM system, these touch points have to function properly. Iyer (2003) has investigated the preference and the level of satisfaction of the customers that have accessed customer service facilities, including in his study both digital and non digital communication channels. The findings indicate a large variability both in the number of clients using various communication channels, as well as in their level of satisfaction. The data collected from these touch points has to be then organised and archived in a centralised database, which should be capable to process large volumes of data coming from multiple, heterogeneous channels (Eckerson & Watson, 2000).

The ITT system and data warehousing technology represent useful tools for implementing a customer-centric CRM system. However, the way in which these are used by company employees to build and maintain satisfactory relationships with the customers represent the central element of the CRM philosophy (Metallo, Cuomo & Festa, 2007). Some researchers have even outlined the danger of alienating the customers by using an excessive technological approach to relationship marketing (Hughes, Foss, Stone & Cheverton, 2007).

Particularly in service organisations, customers expect to be managed in a personalised way by a company representative, who can keep track of their specific needs and problems. Harrison-Walker and Neeley (2004) attempted to develop a typology of customer relationship building on the Internet in B2B marketing, by combining the various stages of the purchase decision process with the levels of relationship marketing proposed by Berry and Parasuraman (1991). Despite the merits of this model, the real-life applications may be somehow different, depending on the specific situation of the market and on the strategic orientation of the firm. For example, the small and medium-sized enterprises might not have the necessary resources to implement and apply all the stage of this model. On the other hand, in some industries the customers themselves might demand a specific type of relationship.

Simon (2005) argues that B2B Professional Services firms should implement a customer service management framework based on key account managers who have professional skills rather that relying on complex technological systems. The specific nature of this sector requires a good knowledge of ethical and professional issues, as well as the capacity to treat every customer as a separate case; this approach is often not compatible with automatic, technological-based systems.

Despite the clear importance of professional advisors, the technology can play a big role in increasing the efficiency of company-customer relationships, especially for effective communication and data collection. This chapter investigates the importance of both technology and personal CRM procedures, for business customers' satisfaction, in B2B Professional Services of business consulting and web design. In order to understand the difference between various national markets, this study analyses data collected about UK and French small and medium-sized professional service firms.

RESEARCH METHODOLOGY

In order to evaluate the CRM strategies applied by professional SMEs, both secondary and primary data have been collected and analysed. The academic literature and professional reports dealing with CRM implementation have been accessed in order to understand better the main issues related with this topic. Following this literature review, primary data has been collected during Spring-Summer 2006, in four distinct stages:

(1) 100 web design firms and 150 consulting firms, randomly selected from the yellow pages national directories of France and the UK, have been contacted through email or telephone and invited to participate to this study. 39 web design firms and 68 consulting firms responded affirmatively to this request in France, while in the UK 44 web design firms and 69 consulting firms agreed to provide information for this study. 12 of these companies (6 French and 6 British, 3 from each of the two sectors of activity) were contacted for a detailed pilot study based on telephone or face-to-face interviews, in order to design and finalise the list of research questions.

(2) Following the pilot study phase, a semi-structured questionnaire was sent to the participating firms by email, and when necessary, a reminder telephone call was applied. The questionnaire was returned by 103 French firms and by 111 British firms. When necessary, additional clarifications of qualitative nature were asked through additional email messages. Each of the respondent firms provided the name and the contact details of three of their most important organisational clients.

(3) After eliminating the double entries (some firms were client to both web design and consulting firms), 131 French client companies and 153 British client firms have been contacted through email or telephone and invited to participate in the study. A pilot study was also conducted with 12 of these companies, in order to design and finalise the list of research question.

(4) A semi-structured questionnaire was then sent to the client companies, supported by a reminder telephone call. 102 questionnaires were returned by French firms and 123 by British firms. Once again, when necessary, additional clarifications of qualitative nature were required through additional email messages.

The questionnaire sent to services companies (web design and consulting) contained questions related to:

- the company profile: number of employees, sector of activity, number of customers;
- the main communication channels used for company-customer interaction and their perceived effectiveness;
- the main CRM strategies designed and implemented by professional services organisations, both from the point of view of managing the touch points with the customers, as well as considering the customer relationship procedures applied by company's personnel.

The questionnaire sent to client companies comprised the following categories of questions:

- the company profile: number of employees, sector of activity, year of incorporation;
- the relation with the service organisation/s: how the relation was initiated, the length and the evolution (stages) of the relation, the general level of satisfaction;
- the level of satisfaction related with various aspects of the service provider-client interaction (the level of interactivity allowed by the information and telecommunication technologies used by the service company, the effectiveness of key account or customer relationship management procedures).

The collected data were analysed both quantitatively and qualitatively. From a qualitative point of view, a content analysis has been applied to the received answers, providing a picture of the main stages of company-customer interaction, of the main factors influencing the quality of these interactions, as well as of the specific application of CRM techniques. The quantitative aspects of the collected data have been analysed using the SPSS software, applying cross-tabulations.

PRESENTATION AND ANALYSIS OF DATA

The interaction between service organisations and client firms can be separated into two distinct stages: (1) the initial contact and (2) the transactional period.

1. The Integration of ITT Applications and Customer Management for the Initial Contact Stage

The quality of ITT applications (web site, email, fax, telephone and mobile phone) is essential for initiating the interaction between the service organisation and the client firm. Both categories of respondents – firms and clients - emphasised that often the service organisation is selected through an Internet search, or using printed professional databases (such as the Yellow Pages). The potential client attempts then to find relevant information about the selected firm, in order to evaluate its capabilities and level of expertise. This information can be often found readily available on the service organisation web site. On the other hand, the prospective client also wants to contact the service organisation in order to complement the online information or even to make sure that the service organisation is easily reachable and readily available to the requests of their clients.

All service organisations that provided primary data emphasised the importance of the initial contact stage for attracting the client and projecting the desired professional image. The communication with the client firm is either co-ordinated by a centralised reception service, or customers can directly contact a professional expert. The type of interaction during the initial contact stage is significantly influenced by the sector of activity, the size, and the number of customers of the service organisation (see Table 1).

In France, both centralised reception and customer managers are used primarily by consulting organisations in comparison with web design firms. On the other hand, for the UK firms, the centralised reception is preferred by consulting firms (57.5% of the investigated firms), while the customer manager contact is implemented by two thirds (66.2%) of the web design companies. The reason for this different approach is the possible complexity of the problem raised by the client firm. Often, the consulting firm needs to collect and analyse preliminary data in order to correctly understand what are the needs of the client firm, and how they can be satisfied. Only after this stage the project is allocated to the appropriate expert or group of experts within the consulting firm.

Company size is strongly influencing the level of available resources, especially in terms of time and personnel. On the other hand, the larger firms may have a more structured customer interaction service, with a centralised reception.

Table 1. The type of initial contact service implemented by the respondent professional service organisations

	Centralised reception		Customer manager	
	France N %	UK N %	France N %	UK N %
Web design	23 46.9	17 42.5	23 42.6	47 66.2
Consulting	26 53.1	23 57.5	31 57.4	24 33.8
Micro firms	13 26.5	10 25	28 51.9	26 36.6
Small firms	17 34.7	23 57.5	12 22.2	25 35.2
Medium-sized firms	19 38.8	7 17.5	14 25.9	20 28.2
Less than 10 clients	7 14.3	3 7.5	22 40.7	21 29.6
10 to 30 clients	22 44.9	18 45	15 27.8	41 57.7
More than 30 clients	20 40.8	19 47.5	17 31.5	9 12.7
Total	49 100	40 100	54 100	71 100

This is certainly true for the French firms – a larger percentage of small-size and medium-size firms prefer to use a centralised reception service for the first contact with clients, while in the UK, the small firms show a large majority in implementing the centralised reception service. The micro-size firms tend to have a more direct and informal contact with clients in comparison with small and medium-sized companies, using a customer manager as the first contact with the client organisations. This can be explained by a strategic approach based on the customisation of company-customer interaction, in order to take advantage of the flexibility offered by the small organisational size.

The organisation of the centralised reception service seems also to represent a choice of the organisations with more clients. In fact, both in France and in the UK, the larger proportion of organisations that implement a centralised customer reception have more than 10 clients. On the other hand, in France, the firms with less than 10 clients are clearly preferring to use a customer manager for the first customer contact; while in

the UK are rather the firms with 10 to 30 clients that adopt this customised approached.

2. The Usage Intensity of Various Communication Channels

The service organisations indicated the intensity of use of various communication channels during their interactions with client organisations (see Table 2).

Email, telephone, mobile phone, and face-to-face communication represent high intensity communication channels for a large majority of professional service organisations (more than 64% of respondents). On the other hand, fax and postal mail, although used in some measure by all the respondent organisations, seem to have a lower intensity of use.

The intensity of use is different between the French and the UK service organisations. The UK firms are characterised by a slightly higher intensity of use of the email, telephone, mobile phone and face-to-face communication, but a lower intensity of use of the fax and postal mail.

Table 2. The intensity of use of various communication channels by client organisations to interact with their service providers

Communica-tion channels / Intensity of use	Email N %	Telephone N %	Mobile phone N %	Fax N %	Face-to-face N %	Postal mail N %
France						
High	88 85.4	67 65	74 71.8	8 7.8	66 64.1	43 41.7
Medium	15 14.6	36 35	24 23.3	83 80.6	35 34	38 36.9
Low	0 0	0 0	5 4.9	12 11.6	2 1.9	22 21.4
Total	103 100	103 100	103 100	103 100	103 100	103 100
UK						
High	106 95.5	111 100	98 88.3	3 2.7	102 91.9	29 26.1
Medium	5 4.5	0 0	7 6.3	84 75.7	7 6.3	75 67.6
Low	0 0	0 0	6 5.4	24 21.6	2 1.8	7 6.3
Total	111 100	111 100	111 100	111 100	111 100	111 100

It can be concluded that in terms of communication, the UK firms adopt a more flexible, and at the same time, a more customised approach in the interaction with their clients. This trend was confirmed by the explanations provided during the interviews, the UK professionals emphasising the need for 'ease of use', 'flexibility', 'mobility', and 'interactivity', in order to better service their clients and to obtain a competitive advantage in a highly fragmented market.

3. The Organisation of the CRM Function

The respondent service organisations use three CRM models:

a. decentralised CRM – each customer is managed by a key account manager;
b. centralised CRM – the information concerning each customer is organised in a centralised archive;
c. integrated CRM system – a digital customer database is integrated with online customer applications.

The implementation of a particular system is influenced by the specific activity of the firm, its size and its number of customers (see Table 3).

The web design firms, probably because of their professional expertise in information systems, implement in a larger proportion an integrated CRM system, in comparison with the consulting firms. On the other hand, the complex nature of consulting projects can represent a reason for the use of a decentralised database, managed by the customer manager in charge of the project. In fact, the majority of consulting firms, both in France and in the UK, use a decentralised database. On the other hand, the centralised CRM is used mainly by consulting firms in France, and by web design firms in the UK. The reasons indicated by the French firms for this choice is the possibility to have more consultants servicing the same clients, while in the UK consulting firms this is happening less often.

The micro organisations have predominantly implemented a decentralised CRM system. At the other side of the scale, the integrated CRM system is preferred by a majority of small and medium-sized firms. This choice is determined partly by the level of available resources and partly by the

Table 3. The main CRM strategies used by the investigated firms

	Decentralised CRM		Centralised CRM		Integrated CRM	
	France N %	UK N %	France N %	UK N %	France N %	UK N %
Web design	3 15.8	4 12.5	18 48.6	27 77.1	25 53.2	33 75
Consulting	16 84.2	28 87.5	19 50.4	8 22.9	22 46.8	11 25
Micro firms	12 63.2	21 65.6	19 51.4	13 37.1	10 21.3	2 4.5
Small firms	5 26.3	9 28.1	10 27	15 42.9	14 29.8	16 36.7
Medium-sized firms	2 10.5	2 6.3	8 22.6	7 20	23 48.9	26 59.1
Less than 10 clients	14 73.7	19 59.3	13 35.1	2 5.7	2 4.3	3 6.8
10 to 30 clients	5 26.3	11 34.4	10 27	4 11.4	22 46.8	14 31.8
More than 30 clients	0 0	2 6.3	14 37.8	29 82.9	23 48.9	27 61.4
Total	19 100	32 100	37 100	35 100	47 100	44 100

strategic approach adopted by service organisations. A decentralised system is less expensive and increases the customisation of the service, based on a long-term relationship between the service specialist and his/her client. On the other hand, the centralised and the integrated CRM systems require more resources for their implementation, but then permit an increased flexibility for managing the customer within the organisation.

The situation is similar regarding the number of clients of the service organisations: the organisations with a small number of clients (less than 10) are predominantly using a decentralised CRM system, which permits a closer relationship between the client and the customer manager. On the other hand, the service organisations that interact with a medium or large number of clients need a centralised or an integrated customer database in order to efficiently co-ordinate customer relationships on a dynamic basis. This strategic choice is clear in the case of UK service organisations, while the French firms show a more balanced distribution in relation to the centralised and the integrated CRM system.

4. The Intensity of Use of the Main Communication Channels from the Client Firms Perspective

The values displayed in Table 4 represent important terms of comparison with the same type of data provided by the personnel of service organisations in Table 2. Any discrepancy between the level of intensity allocated for various communication channels by service organisations and customers indicates a possible source of problems and dissatisfaction. In France, the client organisations indicate a more intensive use of the telephone, mobile phone and face-to-face communication than that of the service firms, but attach a lower importance to email, fax and postal communication. In UK, the differences between professional and service organisations are less important; however, the clients show a clear preference for mobile phone (all client organisations indicate a high intensive use), but less for email and fixed phone.

The importance of interactivity, mobility and customisation is once again emphasised by these results. On the other hand, the findings can also be

Table 4. The intensity of use of various communication channels by client organisations to interact with their service providers

Communication channels / Intensity of use	Email N %	Telephone N %	Mobile phone N %	Fax N %	Face-to-face N %	Postal mail N %
France						
High	78 76.5	93 91.2	85 83.3	0 0	83 81.4	23 22.5
Medium	24 23.5	9 8.8	14 13.7	63 61.8	17 16.7	73 71.6
Low	0 0	0	3 3	39 38.2	2 1.9	6 5.9
Total	102 100	102 100	102 100	102 100	102 100	102 100
UK						
High	98 79.7	111 90.2	123 100	12 9.7	114 92.7	16 13
Medium	17 13.8	12 9.8	0 0	90 73.2	9 7.3	98 79.7
Low	8 6.5	0 0	0 0	21 17.1	0 0	9 7.3
Total	123 100	123 100	123 100	123 100	123 100	123 100

used as an indication of the optimum combination of various communication channels in a complex communication portfolio, properly calibrated to the needs and wants of organisational clients.

5. The Level of Satisfaction of Client Organisations

In France, less then half (44.1%) of the client organisations are highly satisfied by their overall interaction with service organisations; however, on the other hand, only 2% have indicated a low level of satisfaction (see Table 5). The satisfaction related to ITT equipment and connections has the higher levels: 55.9% of the respondent client firms are highly satisfied, and 44.1% medium satisfied. It seems that the low satisfaction of the French client firms is mainly related with the performance of the CRM system. This area has the lowest percentage of highly satisfied client firms (41.2%), and 2 respondents have indicated a low level of satisfaction.

The situation is very similar for the UK organisations, although the percentage of client firms that indicate a high level of satisfaction is slightly higher than that of French firms. However, it is interesting to note that the number of UK client firms that are not satisfied with the services of professional firms is much higher than in France (3.3% of firms indicate a low level of general satisfaction, 8.1% are not satisfied with the ITT connections, and 7.3% consider that their level of satisfaction with CRM services is low).

Many respondents have outlined their perception that a failure of the interaction process is usually determined by a poor organisation of CRM procedures, and not by the functioning of ITT systems. However, even when communication is defective as a result of an ITT malfunction, the situation is interpreted as a defective CRM organisation and co-ordination. This indicates the importance of a good integration between ITT systems and CRM procedures, but also the necessity of approaching the management of the ITT system not only as a technical problem, but rather as a customer relationship issue. This requirement is consistent with the re-design of corporate structures and functions around a customer-centred approach, and confirms the conclusions of Simon (2005) and of Stan et al. (2007).

Table 5. The level of satisfaction of the client organisations in various areas of evaluation

Areas of evaluation / Level of satisfaction	General N %	ITT N %	CRM N %
France			
High	45 44.1	57 55.9	42 41.2
Medium	55 53.9	45 44.1	58 56.8
Low	2 2	0 0	2 2
Total	102 100	102 100	102 100
UK			
High	62 50.4	67 54.5	58 47.2
Medium	57 46.3	46 37.4	56 45.5
Low	4 3.3	10 8.1	9 7.3
Total	123 100	123 100	123 100

6. Dimensions of Client-Service Provider Interactions

In the information provided for this study, the client firms have emphasised the main characteristics defining a highly satisfactory interaction with service providers:

- visibility: the information about the service organisation and its activities, as well as complete contact details, should be easily available;

- reliability: the information provided by the service organisation should be error-free and updated;

- accessibility and mobility: the customer managers should be easily accessible through a variety of communication channels, both digital (email, mobile phone) and non-digital (face-to-face, telephone);

- efficiency: the specific information required by the customer should be quickly provided;

- usefulness and customisation: the information presented to the customer should

Table 6. The specific requirements of each interaction dimension in the ITT and CRM contexts

Dimension	ITT context	CRM context
Visibility	The company is reachable through various communication channels; detail contacts are easily available on various digital and non-digital supports.	The CRM is co-ordinating a multi-channel interaction with customers, insuring a large diffusion of contact details, and their correctness.
Reliability	The communication lines with the company are functioning well.	The information provided by the company is correct and up-to-date.
Accessibility and mobility	ITT lines permit an easy communication with the company, through fixed and mobile devices.	The CRM is co-ordinating the data collection and integration through various fixed and mobile communication devices.
Efficiency	Quick ITT connection.	Waiting times to obtain information reduced to the minimum possible.
Usefulness and customisation	Communication through a customised mix of ITT device.	Personalised information/solutions provided to the customer.

be adapted to its particular needs and profile.

These dimensions are not specifically related with ITT or CRM, but rather represent a synthetic perception of the effective functioning of the communication system of service organisations. For each of these dimensions, specific requirements can be identified for the ITT system and CRM procedures (see Table 6).

The requirements listed in this table outline the importance of an effective integration between ITT systems and CRM procedures, the two elements representing respectively the organisational hardware and software of a well-organised professional firm. Any imbalance between these two sides of company-customer interaction has the potential to determine specific crises situations that can reduce customer satisfaction and trust. Therefore, the service providers should develop simple, but effective diagnostic tools, capable to present the existing situation of these requirements and to indicate areas of possible improvement.

FUTURE TRENDS: A DIAGNOSTIC PROCEDURE FOR EVALUATING THE EFFECTIVENESS OF B2B INTERACTIONS

Based on the information provided by respondents, it is possible to suggest a diagnostic procedure for evaluating the effectiveness of B2B interactions.

The interaction dimensions presented above are difficult to evaluate objectively. The perceptions regarding the level of effectiveness of each dimension will vary from respondent to respondent. However, this one-to-one approach is in line with a customer-centric orientation that has to be projected in all the operations of the service provider.

On the other hand, since the interaction is a bi-dimensional process between the service provider and the client, the perceptions regarding the effectiveness of communication should be measured at both ends of the interaction channel. Therefore, the evaluation of each dimension will be made by both the personnel of the service provider, and by the client organisation.

Finally, since the final perception represents an effect of the complex interaction between ITT systems and CRM procedures, both these aspects should be included in the diagnostic framework.

The proposed diagnostic procedure has three main stages:

1. A clear definition of the five dimensions characterising the B2B interaction, and their interpretation in the context of ITT and CRM systems, should be established by the customer relations department. This definition can be reached through repeated meetings of the service provider organisation with a panel of clients, when the interaction procedures are standardised for most of the customers, or with each individual client when the customer approach is highly personalised.

2. An evaluation of each dimension should be made by the personnel of the service provider and represented on a bi-dimensional graph, comprising both the ITT and the CRM aspects. Each dimension will be measured on a scale from -5 to +5, although the division of scales can be adapted to the needs of the organisations. Using the two measurements given for each dimension a vector can be drawn, as represented in Figure 1.

3. Each client organisation should then evaluate the five interaction dimensions, which are represented as vectors on the bi-dimensional graph used to display the perception of the service provider personnel.

This graphic representation permits an easy identification of the main problems related with

Figure 1. The representation of an interaction dimension as a vector on a bi-dimensional graph

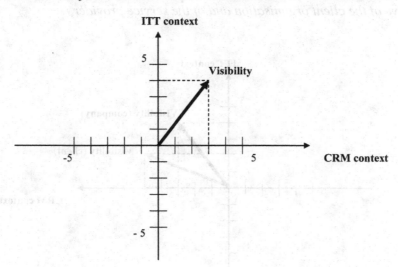

company-customer interactions, as well as the possible differences between the perceptions of the service provider personnel and the client organisation (see Figure 2). The causes of these perceptions should be carefully identified, in order to provide a realistic map of the present situation. This diagnostic can than provide the starting point for the improvement of company-customer interactions, through specific actions designed and applied at ITT and/or CRM level.

CONCLUSION

The quality of company-customer interactions determines the level of satisfaction of client organisations, and, as a consequence, the length and the value return of the B2B relationships. The development of advanced ITT devices offers today multiple possibilities for B2B interactions, but, on the other hand, increases the pressure on service organisations to adopt a multi-channel model, integrated with a customer-focused approach.

This paper attempted to identify the type and the characteristics of B2B interactions between professional service organisations and client firms, and to evaluate the level of satisfaction of the cli-

ent organisations, using a sample of companies from France and the UK. The preference of client organisations regarding various communication channels contradicts in some aspects the intensity of use indicated by professional service firms. This indicates the need for a complex evaluation of the main communication procedures and the integration of all company-customer interactions into a multi-channel system. On the other hand, although the client firms seem quite satisfied by their interaction with professional organisations, in a number of cases the indicated level of satisfaction was low, mainly in relation to the CRM procedures and applications.

Five main interaction dimensions have been identified as the framework used by client organisations to evaluate the quality of B2B interactions. These dimensions are complex constructs that have a double projection in the context of ITT systems and CRM procedures.

After providing a general description of these dimensions, the paper proposed a diagnostic procedure for evaluating the perception gaps between the service provider firm and the client organisation, concerning the quality level of each dimension. This diagnostic can be adapted and used by each service provider organisation to identify possible

Figure 2. The representation of an interaction dimension as a vector on a bi-dimensional graph, both from the perspective of the client organisation and of the service provider

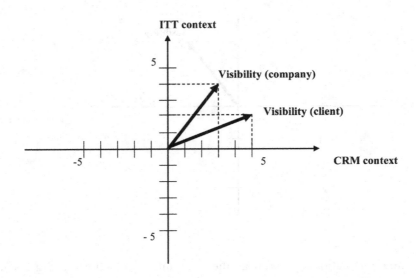

areas of customer dissatisfaction and requirements for future improvements.

This study has a number of limitations determined mainly by its exploratory approach. Although the response rates obtained from both service providers and customer organisations are high, the populations of study were fairly limited in number and activity area. On the other hand, the findings regarding the importance allocated to various channels of communications show only a general trend, and do not permit the design and application of a personalised interaction framework with each client organisation. On the basis of these general results, future research projects can adopt a case study approach, to investigate the particular strategies or models implemented by specific service provider organisations to maximise the value of their customer relationships.

REFERENCES

Berry, L., & Parasuraman, A. (1991). *Marketing services: Competing through quality*. New York: The Free Press.

Brechbühl, H. (2004). Best practices for service organisations. *Business Strategy Review, 14*(1), 68–70. doi:10.1111/j.0955-6419.2004.00302.x

Chen, I. J., & Popovich, K. (2003). Understanding customer relationship management. *Business Process Management Journal, 9*(5), 672–688. doi:10.1108/14637150310496758

Eckerson, W., & Watson, H. (2000). *Harnessing customer information for strategic advantage; Technical challenges and business solutions*. Chatsworth: The Data Warehousing Institute.

Fickel, L. (1999). Know your customer. *CIO Magazine, 12*(21), 62–72.

Harrison-Walker, L. J., & Neeley, S. E. (2004). Customer relationship building on the Internet in B2B marketing: A proposed typology. *Journal of Marketing Theory and Practice, 12*(1), 19–35.

Hughes, T., Foss, B., Stone, M., & Cheverton, P. (2007). Degrees of separation: Technological interactivity and account management. *International Journal of Bank Marketing, 25*(5), 315–335. doi:10.1108/02652320710772989

Iyer, A. (2003). Beyond the phone: Benefits of the integrated contact center. Retrieved September 2008, from http://www.crm2day.com/highlights/EpyEVVAyZFuVTSlcjp.php.

Johnson, L. K. (2002). New views on digital CRM. *MIT Sloan Management Review, 44*(1), 10.

Kalakota, R., & Robinson, M. (2001). m-Business: The race to mobility. *eAI Journal*, December, 44-46. Retrieved October 2007, from http://www.bijonline.com/PDF/mBusinessKalakota.pdf

Leger, P. (2000). Customer interaction in the digital age: Strategies for improving satisfaction and loyalty. The Utilities Project Vol 1. Retrieved September 2008, from http://www.utilitiesproject.com/documents.asp?grID=86&d_ID=150

Metallo, G., Cuomo, M. T., & Festa, G. (2007). Relationship management in the business of quality and communication. *Total Quality Management, 18*(1-2), 119–133.

Olsen, G. (2000). An overview of B2B integration. *eAI Journal*, May, 28-36. Retrieved September 2008, from http://www.bijonline.com/PDF/B2BOverview%20-%20Oslen_1.pdf

Peppers, D., & Rogers, M. (1999). *The one to one manager: Real-world lessons in customer relationship management*. New York: Doubleday.

Peppers, D., & Rogers, M. (2001). *One to one B2B: Customer development strategies for the business-to-business world*. New York: Doubleday.

Rheault, D., & Sheridan, S. (2002). Reconstruct your business around customers. *The Journal of Business Strategy, 23*(2), 38–42. doi:10.1108/eb040236

Simon, G. L. (2005). The case for non-technical client relationship managers in B2B professional services firms. *Service Quality Quarterly, 26*(4), 1–18.

Smith, K. E. (2000). CRM sizzles in the digital economy. *VARBusiness, 16*(25), 104–105.

Stan, S., Evans, K. R., Wood, C. M., & Stinson, J. L. (2007). Segment differences in the asymmetric effects of service quality on business customer relationships. *Journal of Services Marketing, 21*(5), 358–369. doi:10.1108/08876040710773660

Zeng, Y. E., Wen, H. J., & Yen, D. C. (2003). Customer relationship management (CRM) in business-to-business (B2B) e-commerce. [f]. *Information Management & Computer Security, 11*(1), 39–44. doi:10.1108/09685220310463722

Chapter 26
Elements that Can Explain the Degree of Success of ERP Systems Implementation

Carmen de Pablos Heredero
Rey Juan Carlos University, Spain

Mónica de Pablos Heredero
Rey Juan Carlos University, Spain

ABSTRACT

The implementation of an Enterprise Resource Planning System (ERP) is a risky and high cost action, even more when we are dealing with small and medium sized enterprises. Although many studies have shown the importance of paying attention to critical success factors in ERP implementations, there is still a high degree of failures and bad experiences around ERP implementations. Most literature has shown experiences of success and failure coming from large sized firms. But there is a lack of information of what has happened in the area of small and medium size firms, and for some economies, they are essential. In this chapter, we try to show a model containing the main elements that can better explain the degree of success and of failure in ERP implementations by providing examples mainly affecting to the circumstances of small and medium size firms. In our model, we propose 5 main groups of variables affecting final results in ERP implementations.

INTRODUCTION

In the last years, many firms have implemented ERP systems, particularly in the industrial sector.

ERPs, enterprise resource planning systems are software packages that allow a complete management of the different processes in a firm. This way by using a modular system, the ERP systems also support different functional areas such as production, sales, distribution, finance, human resource management, maintenance, and so on. (Rashid, Hossain and Patrick, 2001).

They make easier the planning and controlling of all the resources, material, financial and human ones, by warehousing the whole information for the firm's decision making process in a unique centralised database (Mabert et al., 2003:303).

The main objective that firms usually seek in ERPs systems is to integrate their activities and organise their processes to make the best of informa-

DOI: 10.4018/978-1-60566-892-5.ch026

tion and communication technologies. However, the implementation of an ERP system has some risks, mainly derived from the great quantity of different resources that the process demands (human and material ones) and the uncertainty in the deadlines. Both questions are directly affected by the way in which the process of implementation is taking place. It is then important to analyse the key factors that can offer better possibilities of achieving success when implementing the system.

In this chapter we try to describe the main causes that can affect to the final results in an ERP implementation. For that reason first of all we include a brief explanation on the literature on ERP system benefits, after that we offer a more detailed discussion about the literature appeared on critical success factors for ERP's implementation, finally we propose a model for firms to take into account ERP's Critical success factors.

The main literature reviews on these factors are the research coming from Clausen and Koch (1999), Holland and Light (1999), Koch (2001), Fui-Hon et al. (2003), Umble, Haft y Humble (2003), Al-Mashari, Al-Mudimigh y Zairi (2003),

Finney and Corbett (2007), Kumar et al. (2008), Wang et al. (2008).

The methodologies often used to know about critical success factors are the following ones,

- the studies normally apply surveys and interviews with managers,
- the workers and the external agents implied in the decision making, implementation and use of the system are questioned too.

THE LITERATURE ON ERP SYSTEM BENEFITS

From the nineties, the ERP systems have been one of the greatest investments in IT for the organisations. They are considered one of the best systems that firms can have in order to increase their competitiveness.

ERP systems can provide lots of benefits in firms (Summer, 1999:233). They allow, for example to compete in a global context, to reduce the warehousing material and the costs of production

Figure 1. An ERP schema

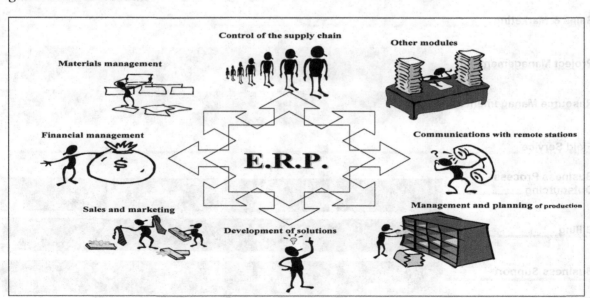

and the increase in the level of service offered to the customer (Ang et al., 2002).

ERP providers use as main marketing arguments the multiple advantages that for a firm arise as a consequence of the integration of their activities and the availability of their information at almost real time. However, in some occasions, these good perspectives are not achieved, and starting to work with the new system may mean big costs for the firms, and can even erode their competitive position.

Akkermans and Van Helden (2002:35) recognise that the ERP implementation demands a great effort and compromise from all the organisational levels. The problems that the firms face when trying a successful implementation have long been explained in the literature review (Holland and Light, 1999, Rosario, 2000, Esteves and Pastor, 2001, Wang et al., 2008).

Trying to find solutions to the problems that the implementation of ERP systems can offer, different academics and consultants have done research on the process of implementation and more specifically, about the determination of the factors that contribute to the success in the implementation, best known as critical success factors (Summer, 1999, Hong and King, 2002, Umble et al, 2003, Fui-Hoon et al., 2003, Finney and Corbett, 2007).

However, most small business owners still today think of ERPs in terms of old communication principles. For them, the ERP is no more than an upgraded version of old systems.

Amongst the common misconceptions regarding integration of ERP we have found (Holland and Light, 1999),

- The transfer of information is unidirectional

Figure 2. The processes of support in the ERP system

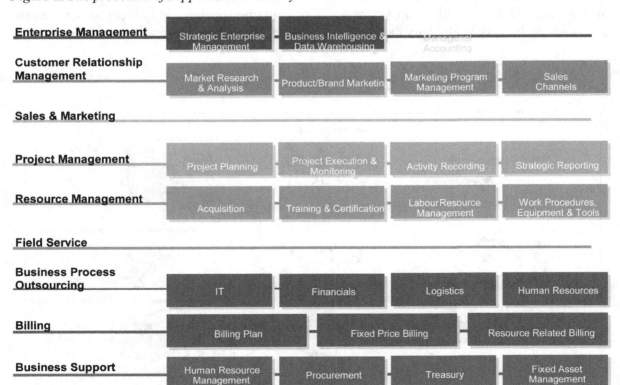

The information can flow in both directions, either from or to the ERP. If the ERP is integrated with the plant, it will demand a bi-directional information flow.

- The ERP integration is all about copying data

Since older methods of integration follow a system of coping a tag and its profile, business owners think that modern ERP system can be integrated the same way.

- The ERP can come up with standardized answers all the time

Many people think that the queries related to a business process follow a set pattern, as do their answers. But they are wrong. Even if the system knows the right question, the right answer may depend on a number of factors.

- One must use only the latest ERP technology

Although the latest ERP integration technologies offer many advantages to small business owners, they have their own share problems. The biggest one is the integration of a new technology to the old systems. Sometimes retaining older applications may be more useful than overhauling them completely.

- ERP to plant integration needs to be total

The ERP system deals with business process, although the plant, system deals with manufacturing and procurement issues. While the plant capacity fluctuates, the ERP capacity remains stable.

- Data security is compromised when you integrate plant to ERP

Many people are concerned about what happens to the data that is not on site. The ERP programmers have spent a lot of time and money on making the system as tool proof as possible, so even data that is not protected by elaborate passwords are not easily accessible by non authorized personnel.

- Installing an ERP system means that you can keep fewer IT staff

The ERP system is not meant to replace your IT staff, it is there to help them with day to day problems related to maintenance and troubleshooting.

ERP BENEFITS

Seddon et al. (1999) argue that is not worth it to talk about the benefits of IT systems without identifying the stakeholder group in whose interest benefits are judged.

Markus and Tannis (1999) explains that no single measure of enterprise system success is sufficient for all the concerns in an organisation's executives might have about the enterprise system experience, and that different measures are needed at different stages in the systems lifecycle.

The five benefits that Markus refers to are the following ones,

- Operational benefits

ERP systems automate business processes and enable processes changes. In this way we can admit according to the operational benefits revised in the literature review (Weill, 1990; Lichtenberg, 1995; Brynjolfsson and Hitt, 1996; Weill and Broadbent, 1998)

- Cost reduction
- Cycle time reduction
- Productivity improvement

- Quality improvement
- Customer services improvement
  - ◦ Managerial benefits

A few consider the most relevant literature centred on the managerial benefits of information systems (Zani, 1970; Keen, 1991, Rockart, 1979). We can consider the following ones emerging from the application of ERP systems,

- Better resource management
- Improved decision making and planning
- Performance improvement
  - ◦ Strategic benefits

ERP systems offer the opportunity for achieving competitive differentiation by customizing products or services for individual users, at a lower cost (Victor and Boynton, 1998), to support a link with customers (Vitale, 1986, Malone and Yates, 1987) or related business parties (Venkatraman, 1994). According to these authors and derived literature review, we can admit that the implementation of ERP systems offers the following strategic benefits in firms,

- Support business growth
- Support business alliance
- Build business innovations
- Build cost leadership
- Generate product differentiation
- Build external linkages
  - ◦ IT infrastructure benefits

Davis (1989), Davenport (2000) and Weill and Broadbent (1998) stress the infrastructure building as one of the fundamental management objectives in IT investment. ERP systems as integrated and standard application architecture provide the following infrastructure benefits,

- Build business flexibility for current and future changes
- IT costs reduction

- Increased IT infrastructure capability
  - ◦ Organizational benefits

Information technology, the accumulated information and the application of knowledge are important factors that facilitate organizational learning behaviour (Garvin, 1993).

ERP systems produce the following organisational benefits,

- Support organisational barriers
- Facilitate business learning
- Promotes empowerment
- And helps to build common visions

CRITICAL SUCCESS FACTORS: REVISION OF THE LITERATURE

Themistocleous et al. (2001:9046) motivated by the high degree of failed ERP implementations, describe that a 96.4% of ERP implementations in the international context fail due to the high costs and the poor planning of deadlines. Most of firms and consultants try to hide the causes of the main problems because they are reluctant to admit these failures. Only a few cases of failures as Hershey Foods, FoxMeyer Drugs and Whirlpool have been reported in the literature review (Pang, 2001: 15).

This is the reason why most studies try to collect information about firms having success in ERP implementations and this way identify the "lessons learned" or determine the factors that can lead to the success in the projects.

The Critical success factors (CSF) are the factors that are critical for the success in an organisation, in the sense that if the objectives that are associated with the factor neither are nor accomplished, then the organisation will fail in the achievement of the final objectives (Rockart, 1979: 240).

The establishment of the critical factors of success has long been spread in the literature in the area of information technology. For example, we

Table 1. Most cited CSF

Support to the management The presence of a project leader
The management of the project
Use of the best prepared personal at complete time
Effective communication
Degree of cooperation and inter-department communication
Management of expectations
Level of technical knowledge and business by users
Degree of participation of final users
Standardisation and discipline in the implementation proceedings
Adequate selection of the ERP provider
User's training
Implementation strategy
Clarity in the reach and objectives of the project
Use of external consultants
To develop a minor quantity of modifications to the system
Level of integration between the provider of the system and the customer
Conformation of a group to follow the project
Business project reengineering
Use of tools of support

can find studies about CSF in systems that allow electronic meetings (Grohowski et. al., 1990), the use of computers in small firms (Lai, 1994), e-business and the maintenance of software (Sneed and Brossl, 2003).

In the area of the projects for the implementation of ERP systems, the CSF means the essential ingredients for having success in the final implementation (Colmenares and Otienzo, 2005:628). The identification of the CSF in the local organisations is a way to increase the possibilities of achieving a proper implementation in the ERP system (Sum et al., 2002:274).

Nah et al (2001:7) mention "there is little and very fragmented research on the critical success factors in the implementation of ERP systems"

Taking into account the papers coming from Falkowski et al., 1998, Bingi et al., 1999, Holland and Light, 1999, Stefanou, 1999, Summer, 1999, Rosario, 2000, Wee, 2000, Esteves and Pastor, 2001, Nah et al., 2001, we can affirm that the twenty CSF more cited are the following ones. (See Table 1).

Finney and Corbett (2007), establishes the following critical success factors for ERP implementations,

- Top management commitment and support. It refers to the need to have committed leadership at the top management level
- Visioning and planning: it requires articulating a business vision to the organisation, identifying clear goals and objectives and providing clear link between business goals and IS strategy

- Build a business case: it involves conducting economic and strategic justifications for implementing and ERP
- Project champion: he or she should possess strong leadership skills, business, technical and personal managerial competencies
- Implementation strategy and timeframe: The need to address the implementation strategy and to, specifically, implement the ERP under a phased approach
- Project management: the ongoing management of the implementation plan. It involves the planning stages and also allocating of responsibilities to various players, the definition of milestones and critical paths, training and human resource planning
- Change management: it refers to the need for the implementation team to formally prepare a change management program and be conscious of the need to consider the implications of such a project
- Managing cultural change: it refers to the identification and usage of strategies that are needed to implement cultural change
- Balanced team: the need for a team to realise the implementation that spans the organization
- Communication plan: the communication between the IT personnel and business actors
- Empowered decision makers: the need for the team to be empowered to make necessary decisions in due time
- Team morale and motivation: the need for the project manager to nurture and maintain a high level of employee morale and motivation during the project
- Project cost planning and management: To know the real costs for the project and dedicate money to it
- BPR and software configuration: it must provide a complete description on how the business will operate after the package is in use

- Legacy system considerations: it is needed to know about the current legacy system and it will be a good indicator of the nature of the scale and potential problems
- IT infrastructure: the organisation must be well prepared in the IT architecture and skills
- Client consultation: the need for communicating and consulting various key stakeholders, in particular de client
- Selection of the ERP: the system must match the business processes
- Consultant selection and relationship: it is important to establish the way of knowledge transfer from the consultant to the company
- Training and job redesign: it refers to the need to plan for training facilities and establish compensation plans
- Troubleshoooting and crises management: the need to be flexible and learn from unforeseen circumstances
- Data conversion and integrity: the ability of the team to ensure data accuracy during the conversion project
- System testing: in the final stages of the implementation process, the project team should consider the inclusion of testing exercises
- Post-implementation evaluation: to use performance measures in order to know results of the implementation

Fui-Hoon et al. (2003) and later on Finney and Corbett (2007) offer a complete revision of the authors offering publications in journals of reference, dealing with CSF affecting ERP implementations in different contexts. Next table summarises the citations they offer in their articles, (Table 2).

In a recent interview with a group of consultants specialised in the ERP implementation in the Spanish market (Realtech, Plaut, Strategys, 2008), we concluded as main elements to consider

Table 2. The academic literature review on CSF's

Critical Success Factor	Authors
Top management commitment and support	Roberts and Barrar (1992), Bingi et al., (1999), Buckhout et al. (1999), Summer (1999), Holland et al. (1999), Wee (2000) Shanks et al. (2000), Murray and Coffin (2001), Motwani et al. (2002), Lee (2003); Yusuf et al., 2004,)
Visioning and planning	Roberts and Barrar (1992), Falkowski et al. (1998), Buckhout et al. (1999), Holland et al. (1999), Rosario (2000), Shanks et al. (2000), Al-Mudimigh et al., (2001), Al-Mashari et al. (2003), Mandal and Gunasekaran (2003) Wee (2000)
Build a business case	Chen (2001), Xu et al. (2002), Roy (2003)
Project champion	Falkowski et al. (1998), Summer (1999), Stefanou (1999), Sumner (1999), Rosario (2000), Shanks et al. (2000), Murray and Coffin (2001), Kraemmergaard and Rose (2002), Mandal and Gunasekaran (2003)
Implementation strategy and timeframe	Roberts and Barrar (1992), Falkowski et al. (1998), Holland et al. (1999), Cliffe (1999), Sumner (1999), Gupta (2000), Murray and Coffin (2001), Rosario (2000), Scott and Vessey (2000), Siriginidi (2000), Motwani et al. (2002), Robey et al. (2002), Mandal and Gunasekaran (2003), Umble et al. (2003)
Project Management	Roberts and Barrar (1992), Falkowski et al. (1998), Holland et al. (1999), Sumner (1999), Shanks et al. (2000), Scheer and Habermann (2000), Wee (2000), Nah et al. (2001), Somers and Nelson (2001, 2004)
Change Management	Roberts and Barrar (1992), Falkowski et al. (1998), Bingi et al. (1999), Holland and Light (1999), Murray and Coffin (2001), Rosario (2000), Shanks and Parr (2000), Siriginidi (2000), Sumner (1999), Ross and Vitale (2000), Wee (2000), Aladwani (2001), Nah et al. (2001), Sommers and Nelson (2001, 2004), Wood and Caldas (2001), Kumar et al. (2002), Skok and Legge, (2002)
Managing cultural change	Aladwani (2001), Nah et al. (2001), Davison (2002), Skok and Legge (2002), Tarafdar and Roy (2003)
Balanced team	Falkowski et al. (1998), Bingi et al., (1999), Buckhout et al. (1999), Holland et al. (1999), Stefanou (1999), Sumner (1999), Gupta (2000), Rosario (2000), Shanks and Parr, (2000), Siriginidi (2000), Soh et al. (2000), Wee (2000), Willcocks and Stykes (2000), Nah et al. (2001), Sommers and Nelson (2001, 2002), Kumar et al. (2002), Mandal and Gunasekaran (2003), Ribbers and Schoo (2002), Kalling (2003), Bajwa et al. (2004)
Communication plan	Falkowski et al. (1998), Holland et al. (1999), Sumner (1999), Rosario (2000), Wee (2000), Kumar et al. (2002), Grant (2003), Mabert et al. (2003), Manda and Gunasekaran (2003), Shanks et al. (2000), Yusuf et al. (2004)
Empowered decision makers	Gupta (2000), Shanks and Parr (2000), Chen (2001)
Team morale and motivation	Bingi et al. (1999), Wilcocks and Stykes (2000), Skok and Legge (2002), Trimmer et al. (2002), Barker and Frolick (2003), Mandal and Gunasekaran (2003)
Project cost planning and management	Bingi et al. (1999), Holland and Light (1999), Al-Mudimigh et al. (2001), Somers and Nelson (2001, 2004), Ribbers and Schoo (2002), Trimmer et al. (2002)

continued on following page

Table 2. continued

Critical Success Factor	Authors
BPR and software configuration	Roberts and Barrar (1992), Bingi et al. (1999), Buckhout et al. (1999), Holland and Light (1999), Sumner (1999), Shanks et al. (2000), Soh et al. (2000), Siriginidi (2000), Wee (2000), Aladwani (2001) Palaniswamy and Frank (2000, 2002), Al-Mudimigh (2001), Murray and Coffin (2001), Nah et al. (2001), Sommers and Nelson (2001, 2004) Gulledge and Sommer (2002), Hong and Kim (2002), Ribbers and Schoo (2002) Kraemmergaard and Rose, (2002), Trimmer et al. (2002), Al-Masari et al. (2003), Grant (2003), Voordijk et al. (2003), Bajwa et al. (2004)
Legacy system considerations	Roberts and Barrar (1992), Holland and Light (1999), Siriginidi (2000), Al-Mudimigh et al. (2001), Nah et al. (2001), Al-Masari et al. (2003)
IT Infrastructure	Bingi et al. (1999), Holland et al. (1999), Rosario (2000), Scheer and Habermann (2000), Siriginidi (2000), Wee (2000), Murray and Coffin (2001) Sommers and Nelson (2001, 2004), Kumar et al. (2002), Palaniswamy and Frank (2002), Tarafdar and Roy (2003), Bajwa et al. (2004)
Client consultation	Holland and Light (1999), Al Mudimigh et al. (2001), Al-Mashari et al. (2003), Mandal and Gunasekaran (2003)
Selection of ERP	Chen (2001), Sommers and Nelson (2001, 2004), Kraemmergaard and Rose (2002), Al-Mashari et al. (2003), Yusuf et al. (2004)
Consultant selection and relationship	Bingi et al. (1999), Willcocks and Stykes (2000), and Al-Mudimigh et al. (2001), Kraemmergaard and Rose (2002), Al-Mashari et al. (2003), Motwani et al. (2002), Skok and Legge (2002), Trimmer et al. (2002), Kalling (2003), Bajwa et al. (2004)
Training and job redesign	Bingi et al. (1999), Cliffe (1999), Siriginidi (2000), Kumar et al. (2002), Motwani et al. (2002), Robey et al. (2002), Trimmer et al. (2002), Stratman and Roth (2002), Mandal and Gunasekaran (2003), Tarafdar and Roy (2003), Voordijk et al. (2003)
Trobleshooting and crises management	Holland and Light (1999), Nah et al. (2001), Al-Mashari et al. (2003), Mandal and Gunasekaran (2003)
Data conversion and integrity	Xu (2002), Umble et al. (2003), Bajwa et al. (2004), Sommers and Nelson (2001, 2004), Yusuf et al (2004)
System testing	Nah et al. (2001), Kumar et al. (2002), Al-Mashari et al. (2003), Yusuf (2004)
Post-implementation evaluation	Holland and Light (1999), Ross and Vitale (2000), Nah et al. (2001), Al-Mashari et al. (2003), Mandal and Gunasekaran (2003), Tarafdar and Roy (2003), Umble et al. (2003)

in order implementing with success an ERP solution in a firm,

- To check before contracting an ERP the state of the art of the data that are going to be further processed in the ERP system
- There must be a high managerial support to install the software

- There must be a responsible for the software installation (preferably one that does not belong to the top management in the firm)
- There must be training programs for the users
- It is very important to check that the software meets the needs of the whole

Figure 3. The need of changing processes

Support to the management
The presence of a project leader
The management of the project
Use of the best prepared personal at complete time
Effective communication
Degree of cooperation and inter-department communication
Management of expectations
Level of technical knowledge and business by users
Degree of participation of final users
Standardisation and discipline in the implementation proceedings
Adequate selection of the ERP provider
User's training
Implementation strategy
Clarity in the reach and objectives of the project
Use of external consultants
To develop a minor quantity of modifications to the system
Level of integration between the provider of the system and the customer
Conformation of a group to follow the project
Business project reengineering
Use of tools of support

company (if the software provides the final reports but it worsens the work for employees, it can lose competitiveness)

THE PROPOSED MODEL

In our model we propose 5 main groups of variables affecting to the final results in ERP implementations,

1. the decision-making policy of the firm in the ERP selection, implementation and use
2. the training characteristics of the people involved in the ERP implementation and final use
3. The organisational inertia in the firm
4. The final internal user satisfaction
5. The final external user satisfaction

1. THE DECISION-MAKING POLICY OF THE FIRM IN THE ERP SELECTION, IMPLEMENTATION AND USE

We include as main variables here the following ones,

• The existence of managerial support,

Finney and Corbett (2007) stresses in their study how this aspect is one of the most cited in the literature review (Roberts and Barrar (1992), Bingi et al., (1999), Buckhout et al. (1999), Summer (1999), Holland et al. (1999), Wee (2000) Shanks et al. (2000), Murray and Coffin (2001), Motwani et al. (2002), Lee (2003); Yusuf et al., 2004). Besides in our recent interview with consultants specialised in ERP implementation in the Spanish market this aspect is highly stressed as one of the most important CSFs.

Top management support in ERP implementations offer two main aspects,

Figure 4. The steps in the process of change

Critical Success Factor	Authors
Top management commitment and support	Roberts and Barrar (1992), Bingi et al., (1999), Buckhout et al. (1999), Summer (1999), Holland et al. (1999), Wee (2000) Shanks et al. (2000), Murray and Coffin (2001), Motwani et al. (2002), Lee (2003); Yusuf et al., 2004,)
Visioning and planning	Roberts and Barrar (1992), Falkowski et al. (1998), Buckhout et al. (1999), Holland et al. (1999), Rosario (2000), Shanks et al. (2000), Al-Mudimigh et al., (2001), Al-Mashari et al. (2003), Mandal and Gunasekaran (2003) Wee (2000)
Build a business case	Chen (2001), Xu et al. (2002), Roy (2003)
Project champion	Falkowski et al. (1998), Summer (1999), Stefanou (1999), Sumner (1999), Rosario (2000), Shanks et al. (2000), Murray and Coffin (2001), Kraemmergaard and Rose (2002), Mandal and Gunasekaran (2003)
Implementation strategy and timeframe	Roberts and Barrar (1992), Falkowski et al. (1998), Holland et al. (1999), Cliffe (1999), Sumner (1999), Gupta (2000), Murray and Coffin (2001), Rosario (2000), Scott and Vessey (2000), Siriginidi (2000), Motwani et al. (2002), Robey et al. (2002), Mandal and Gunasekaran (2003), Umble et al. (2003)
Project Management	Roberts and Barrar (1992), Falkowski et al. (1998), Holland et al. (1999), Sumner (1999), Shanks et al. (2000), Scheer and Habermann (2000), Wee (2000), Nah et al. (2001), Somers and Nelson (2001, 2004)
Change Management	Roberts and Barrar (1992), Falkowski et al. (1998), Bingi et al. (1999), Holland and Light (1999), Murray and Coffin (2001), Rosario (2000), Shanks and Parr (2000), Siriginidi (2000), Sumner (1999), Ross and Vitale (2000), Wee (2000), Aladwani (2001), Nah et al. (2001), Sommers and Nelson (2001, 2004), Wood and Caldas (2001), Kumar et al. (2002), Skok and Legge, (2002)
Managing cultural change	Aladwani (2001), Nah et al. (2001), Davison (2002), Skok and Legge (2002), Tarafdar and Roy (2003)
Balanced team	Falkowski et al. (1998), Bingi et al., (1999), Buckhout et al. (1999), Holland et al. (1999), Stefanou (1999), Sumner (1999), Gupta (2000), Rosario (2000),

- It provides leadership
- It provides de necessary resources
- To successfully implementing an ERP system, firms need spend time with people and provide them with the needed resources. The implementation could fail in case that the critical resources are not available when needed.

For achieving success in a project of ERP implementation it is important to involve the managers in the organisation. Managers must involve to the rest of the people in the organisation in the collaboration and support with the project.

For that reason, periodical committees headed by the main managers in the firm must be cel-

Figure 5. Tools for the management of the change

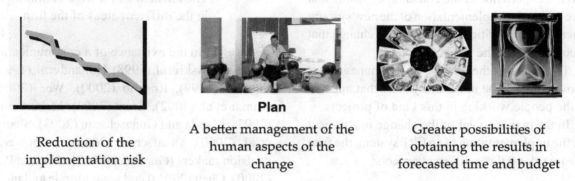

Plan

Reduction of the implementation risk

A better management of the human aspects of the change

Greater possibilities of obtaining the results in forecasted time and budget

ebrated. The organisation must be kept informed about the evolution of the project and about the problems arisen.

• The existence of clear procedures established for the required re-engineering of business processes in the firm

It has mainly to do with managing the cultural change, identified in Finney and Corbery (2007) by the following authors (Aladwani (2001), Nah et al. (2001), Davison (2002), Skok and Legge (2002), Tarafdar and Roy (2003)) and Business Process reengineering Roberts and Barrar (1992), Bingi et al. (1999), Buckhout et al. (1999), Holland and Light (1999), Sumner (1999), Shanks et al. (2000), Soh et al. (2000), Siriginidi (2000), Wee (2000), Aladwani (2001) Palaniswamy and Frank (2000,

2002), Al-Mudimigh (2001), Murray and Coffin (2001), Nah et al. (2001), Sommers and Nelson (2001, 2004) Gulledge and Sommer (2002), Hong and Kim (2002), Ribbers and Schoo (2002) Kraemmergaard and Rose, (2002), Trimmer et al. (2002), Al-Masari et al. (2003), Grant (2003), Voordijk et al. (2003), Bajwa et al. (2004)

Implementing ERP systems requires the redesign of the existent business processes. Many times the ERP implementations fail because some firms underestimate the extent to which they have to change processes. Motwani et al. (2002) suggested that the organisations should be prepared for fundamental change to ensure the success of the business process reengineering.

The companies must profit from the ERP implementation to optimise their business processes by promoting the change in the management system

Figure 6. Schema of the different phases and associated tasks

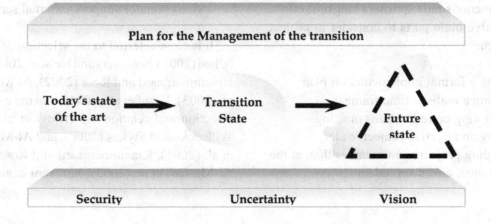

Plan for the Management of the transition

Today's state of the art → Transition State → Future state

Security   Uncertainty   Vision

and the experience in the consultancy teams that take part in the implementation of the new system. Therefore, it is critical the process of change that accompanies to the project.

The focus in the change of the management allows surpass the uncertainty state that appears in the people working in this kind of projects.

In the management of the change in a project for the implementation of an ERP system, the firm must work on three different aspects:

- The effectiveness of the project management

It has to do with the aspects of change management (Roberts and Barrar (1992), Falkowski et al. (1998), Bingi et al. (1999), Holland and Light (1999), Murray and Coffin (2001), Rosario (2000), Shanks and Parr (2000), Siriginidi (2000), Sumner (1999), Ross and Vitale (2000), Wee (2000), Aladwani (2001), Nah et al. (2001), Sommers and Nelson (2001, 2004), Wood and Caldas (2001), Kumar et al. (2002), Skok and Legge, (2002)) and project cost planning and management(Bingi et al. (1999), Holland and Light (1999), Al-Mudimigh et al. (2001), Somers and Nelson (2001, 2004), Ribbers and Schoo (2002), Trimmer et al. (2002)

Project management plans, co-ordinates and controls the complex and diverse activities of modern, industrial and commercial projects.

The implementation of ERP systems implies the working of different activities, all involving business functions and requiring a long time effort. There are five main parts to consider in project management

1. having a formal implementation plan
2. offering a realistic time frame
3. celebrating periodic status meetings
4. having an effective project leader
5. including project team member that, at the same time, are stakeholders

○ The existence of a wide commitment in the different areas of the firm

It refers to the existence of a communication plan (Falkowski et al. (1998), Holland et al. (1999), Sumner (1999), Rosario (2000), Wee (2000), Kumar et al. (2002), Grant (2003), Mabert et al. (2003), Manda and Gunasekaran (2003), Shanks et al. (2000), Yusuf et al. (2004)), empowered decision makers (Gupta (2000), Shanks and Parr (2000), Chen (2001)) and team morale and motivation (Bingi et al. (1999), Wilcocks and Stykes (2000), Skok and Legge (2002), Trimmer et al. (2002), Barker and Frolick (2003), Mandal and Gunasekaran (2003).

Taking into consideration that the ERP systems are enterprise wide information systems that attempt to integrate information across all functional areas in an organisation, it is important to get the needed support from all functional areas from the organisation. Everyone in the organisation must be responsible for the whole system and key users from different departments must have cleared the project implementation phases.

When realising the implementation of an ERP, a previous methodology must be established, where clearly the steps in the project and the involvement of each of the key-users and the consultancy team that takes part in the implementation are specified.

- The existence of a wide commitment in the different stakeholders in the implementations (vendor support, external services)

It is close referred to the selection of the ERP (Chen (2001), Sommers and Nelson (2001, 2004), Kraemmergaard and Rose (2002), Al-Mashari et al. (2003), Yusuf et al. (2004)) and the consultant selection and relationship (Bingi et al. (1999), Willcocks and Stykes (2000), and Al-Mudimigh et al. (2001), Kraemmergaard and Rose (2002), Al-Mashari et al. (2003), Motwani et al. (2002),

Skok and Legge (2002), Trimmer et al. (2002), Kalling (2003), Bajwa et al. (2004).

It is very important for the customer that decides to implement an ERP system in his/her organisation and for the providers, to align the implementation services with the achieving of the objectives fixed for the project.

Those objectives must be clearly defined in the design document elaborated once that the analysis and requirements feeding phases have been finished. The design document must contain the situation of the business processes before the implementation and the future situation, once that the business process reengineering effort to implement the ERP systems, has taken place

2. THE TRAINING CHARACTERISTICS OF THE PEOPLE INVOLVED IN THE ERP IMPLEMENTATION AND FINAL USE.

It is related to the aspects of training and job redesign (Bingi et al. (1999), Cliffe (1999), Siriginidi (2000), Kumar et al. (2002), Motwani et al. (2002), Robey et al. (2002), Trimmer et al. (2002), Stratman and Roth (2002), Mandal and Gunasekaran (2003), Tarafdar and Roy (2003), Voordijk et al. (2003), data conversion and integrity Xu (2002), Umble et al. (2003), Bajwa et al. (2004), Sommers and Nelson (2001, 2004), Yusuf et al (2004)) and system testing (Nah et al. (2001), Kumar et al. (2002), Al-Mashari et al. (2003), Yusuf (2004). The interviews with the consultants offer us a similar criterion when they refer to the need of establishing training programs for the users.

As we know by the nature of an ERP system, it includes all the material and human resources related to the management of the information in the firms. In this sense, a first vision distinguishes between both types of human resources in the information system of a firm: the final users and the personal working on them.

Final users are all those persons that take part

in the information system of a firm to get the final product, as defined by Garcia Bravo (2000). We can consider that all the members in an organisation are potential final users of the system, since all of them are going to use and modify information.

The role of final users has more relevance in the last years due to the decentralization of these systems. This way, a greater proportion of the people in the organisation are involved not only in the processing of information and the obtaining of a result, but in some other activities as can be the development of the systems.

The personal of the information systems include all the workers in charge of the ERP development, management and maintaining. Traditionally it has been considered that this people is specialised in the information system by being named system techniques.

The change in the role of the information systems in the organisations has evolved along time. This way, by considering the ERP strategic role, it has been considered that the responsibilities in the ERP are not just technical ones but they necessarily include some other functions related to the strategic management or the firm's policy. Additionally part of this workers must have specific skills in the management of human resources.

For that, we must also consider widely extended the differentiation between managerial and ethical skills.

It is also traditional the division of people of information systems according to the hierarchical order of responsibility assumed. We can consider this way, that the system always includes a top executive of the company, the Chief Information Officer, CIO, directly reporting to the President or the chief Executive Officer in the firm (CEO); a certain number of intermediate managers, with limited responsibilities, the technical personal, specialised in some tasks if a certain added value in the firm, and therefore with a margin of decision, and the operations personal, in charge of the performance of concrete task of structural character, this means, low autonomy.

Figure 7. People from the IS working on ERP system (McLeod, 2000)

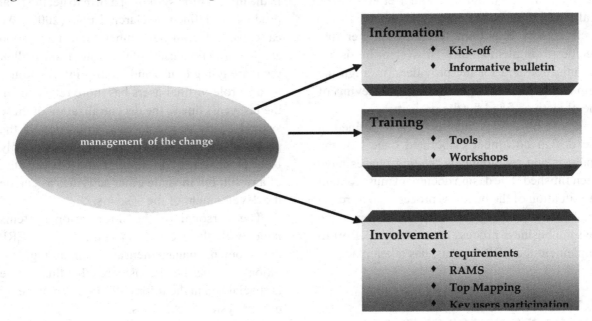

Functions of the Workers in ERP Systems

Monforte Moreno (1995) refers to the organisation of the ERP systems to a series of functions, independent from the firm's dimension, which we can sum up in the following ones,

Development of the systems, programming and operations of exploitation: it includes the tasks related with the analysis, design, development and implementation of the ERP systems in the firm, together with the programming and maintaining of applications.

Security of the ERP systems and installations, It includes the needed operations to avoid the loss of information, the prevention of physical and logical attacks to the system or the insurance of the buildings against human or natural errors.

The administration of the ERP information, related with the management of the use of the resources of information systems and the "internal payment" of these services to the departments requiring them.

Standards and system techniques, it refers to the planning in the acquiring of new technologies and their implementation in the firm. One of the main tasks for this aims it is the constant seeking of the technological environment, to analyse the new availabilities of resources for acquisition.

In a similar way, McLeod (2000) propose a scheme of the organisation adapted to the model of the life cycle, reflected in figure 1. The main character is the CIO with a wide group of responsibilities and functions. In the middle level, the author situates a group of supervisors of the different areas of the system, under his/her control. And reporting to these last ones, we can find the technical people and the operators working in each of the functions.

Mc Leod refers to a functional organisation in the department of information systems in the firm. If we take into account a matrix structure, we must add in the horizontal direction, the existence of different projects, with a person in charge in each case. The authority of the responsible of the various projects can be in charge of a group of firms.

In fact, McLeod, manifest how his drawing it is not necessarily a unique model nor a fundamental referent, by indicating that the drawings of different firms reflect in a more precise way the existent responsibilities. In this sense, the analysis of the more frequent asked positions from the human selection firms can contribute to better define which ones are the human resources profiles that can better contribute to establish the profile of the main specialists related with information systems.

The Annual Report from the Michael Page Consultancy firm (2005), specialised in the search of specific profiles related to the information technologies, considers the existence of four types of functions in the ERP system, by indicating which ones are the profile of responsibility in each of them.

The managerial functions offer the main responsibilities of the information system. The Chief Information Officer (CIO) is the main responsible of them, with a main managerial profile.

The observation of the most demanded profiles to a specialised consultancy firm in human resources offers a vision on the variety of profiles that correspond with human resources in the information system. However, it seems that the key factor for the identification of these responsibilities, and therefore, for the definition of the needed human resources is in the identification of the functions, and the specific responsibilities of each level.

In this group of functions or responsibilities, we can stress the Chief Information Officer, as the main responsible of the system and at the same time, an important part of the executive management of the firm. This situation makes more interesting to plan a study on the functions of the CIO and on the abilities that this person must have to match these functions.

Human Efforts of the ERP Implementation and Rewards

The strategic management in the human resource area refers to a group of policies that define the strategy of human resources in a firm, this means, the main decisions related to this area. They can have a significant influence over the organisation and the results.

Some of the main human resources policies widely studied have been the following ones,

Recruitment policy: it deals with integrating in the organisation people having the required skills for the development of a group of activities and firm's functions in relation with the ERP system. In this sense, one of the decisions more studied is "to do instead of buying", that faces the internal formation of the new personnel with the search in the market of the human resources containing the proper profile in competencies. It also belongs to this ambient the decision about the factors that must be taken into account when searching new human resources.

Training and development policies, they have to do with the increase of stock of individual skills coming from the human resources in the firm, that can besides contribute to the improvement of collective skills. Inside this ambit, we can consider the decisions around the quantity of training to be offered about the ERP system.

Policies on the design of the work profile, they mainly refer to the variety of functions and tasks included inside a work profile around the ERP system. Inside this part, policies for job enrichment and level of specialisation desired are included.

Rewarding policies, related with the rewards that the workers receive from their work. In this sense, we must consider included here all the decisions dealing with rewards, shares offered, holiday programs and any other extra reward.

These policies will be the main part in the strategy with ERP workers.

Ferrat et al (2005) realise an empirical analysis where they consider five different configurations in the human resources policy in a firm:

- Policies oriented to the human capital: the responsible for the people management in the ERP system treats to motivate them to keep them in the firm. This means the use of rewards techniques by including the promotion of different groups taking part in the ERP implementation.
- Policies oriented to the tasks: the work profiles in the ERP systems tend to a high rotation, with high salaries according to technical aptitudes.
- Technical people rewarded: being offered great economic incentives. Their selection is only based on their technical skills. We are often dealing with a high rotation work profile. It is due to a limited offer of professionals containing certain abilities.
- Work assured. This is the main way to maintain workers, to offer them stability at work, further of incentive policies and a feeling of belonging to the group of the organisation.
- Work utility. A greater emphasis is paid for an important level of incentives, the search of non technical knowledge and the work stability, by leaving apart a sense of belonging or work enrichment.

It seems clear that the human resources policies of the information system can be varied, especially by having into account the wide number of available tools in this area.

The Ethics and the ERP System

The CIO must be the highest responsible for the computer ethics in the ERP system, and must then supervise and pay attention to the influence of the ERP over society and consider the policies that can be adopted for a correct use of the technology.

For Moor (1985) there are three main factors that make society be cautious with their use,

- The logical malleability, which makes that an ERP, can be programmed to operate in various ways. This makes society be afraid of the bad use of information systems, as can be the physing practices (trying to capture user keys)
- The transformation factor. ERP have radically changed the way workers interact. This capacity of change makes people ask themselves about the proper use of a resource with such a power of change.
- The invisibility factor that promotes the ERP system to be a true "black box" for some users. They know what it produces but they do not know how and why it produces it.

This preoccupation for the ethics is immediately perceived by people working with the ERP systems, especially for those in charge of the more invisible part of them.

Many countries have developed Acts that punish some non-ethic conducts. We count on with the existence of ethical codes associated to a professional conduct related to information technologies and systems, probably the more extended ones are the ACM and IEEE (Association for Computer Machinery e Institute of electrical and Electronics Engineers) and the DPMA (Data processing managerial association), The ICCP (Institute for certification of computer professionals) the ITAA (Information technology association of America). In Europe the CEPIS (Council of European Professional Informatics Societies) has its own ethical code.

Parker (1988) proposes ten actions to promote the ethical conduct in the employees in the information system of a firm that could be extended to the ERP cases,

Figure 8. The change in the organisation

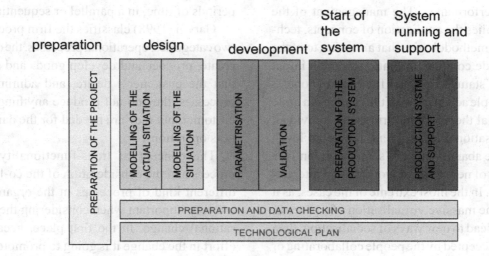

- To formulate a conduct code
- To establish the clear acting rules in situations of ethic conflict
- To clearly specify the sanctions applied in non ethic conducts
- To public recognise the ethical conducts
- To develop programs, meetings and recommend readings
- To inform, promote the knowledge of the Acts implied with the proper use of IS and IT at Organisations
- To delimitate the ethical responsibilities if each worker according to their tasks.
- To promote the use of "restructuring programs" for people avoiding ethical norms.
- To promote the integration of workers in the professional associations
- To offer example with the own acts.

3. THE ORGANIZATIONAL INERTIA IN THE FIRM

It is referred to the following aspects: visioning and planning Roberts and Barrar (1992), Falkowski et al. (1998), Buckhout et al. (1999), Holland et al. (1999), Rosario (2000), Shanks et al. (2000), Al-Mudimigh et al., (2001), Al-Mashari et al. (2003), Mandal and Gunasekaran (2003) Wee (2000), change management Roberts and Barrar (1992), Falkowski et al. (1998), Bingi et al. (1999), Holland and Light (1999), Murray and Coffin (2001), Rosario (2000), Shanks and Parr (2000), Siriginidi (2000), Sumner (1999), Ross and Vitale (2000), Wee (2000), Aladwani (2001), Nah et al. (2001), Sommers and Nelson (2001, 2004), Wood and Caldas (2001), Kumar et al. (2002), Skok and Legge, (2002), balanced team Falkowski et al. (1998), Bingi et al., (1999), Buckhout et al. (1999), Holland et al. (1999), Stefanou (1999), Sumner (1999), Gupta (2000), Rosario (2000), Shanks and Parr, (2000), Siriginidi (2000), Soh et al. (2000), Wee (2000), Willcocks and Stykes (2000), Nah et al. (2001), Sommers and Nelson (2001, 2002), Kumar et al. (2002), Mandal and Gunasekaran (2003), Ribbers and Schoo (2002), Kalling (2003), Bajwa et al. (2004). It is in relation with the need of establishing a responsible for the software installation referred by the consultants in the interviews.

The organisational inertia has to do with aspects in relation to culture, values and ways of group expression in the organization. Organizational change implies the leaving of some structures, procedures and behaviours and the adoption of other ones, with the main objective of improving the final performance. The management of the change implies the application of concepts, techniques and methodologies that are going to make it possible de complex migration from an initial not desired status to another final desired one.

The simple acceptation of the change is a quite controversial theme in the firm, at an individual and organisational level. At an individual level, it means the abandonment of some habits and the acceptance of new ways of working and interacting at work. In the most extreme of the cases, as it would be the massive virtualisation of a process, it can even lead to new ways of socialisation, than can not be accepted by the people collaborating or working at the organisation. At an organizational level, this situation is even more complex, since there are more people implied that have to deal with the imposition of a decision that can dislike others.

The management of change must start with the challenge of determining what is going to be changed. We have to distinguish between people; they must make decisions in relation to what it is going to be changed since they have responsibilities in the organisations, and those who are directly related in the process, people who are asked in an informal way and those others who are not even asked for. Once the change has been implemented, there will be people informed and trained in the process and people who have just been informed. These circumstances logically are going to have an impact in the change, in a positive or negative way.

The Process: The Main Axis for the Change

Organisations develop their objectives through processes. A process is a group of tasks allocated in different firm areas and that develop a group of functionalities or specialisations. In this sense, we can say that a process is trans-functional. A process has a point of start and end and around it many different functions are working in different periods of time, in a parallel or sequential way.

Garvin (1998) classifies the firm processes in two categories: operational processes, the ones that create, produce and develop goods and services that the customer's desire, and administrative processes, they do not produce anything for the customer, but they are needed for the daily business operations.

The concept of trans-functionality in the process and the consideration of the co-living of different kind of processes in the organisations are very important when considering the organisational change. In the first place, because the effort in the change it is going to promote impact in the whole process, because any of the firm's task is part of a whole business process, and, in the second place, because a change in any part of a process, it does not matter its nature, will have an impact in a process connected with the previous one but of different nature (for example a working process has an impact in a decision making one). In this sense, and just as an example, the automatic feeding of a customer's data by using a corporative Intranet (work process) can allow that any point of selling can directly solve a decision that affects the customer, and in case of not counting with that automatic feed, it will be impossible to develop this process (for example the process of offering a bank loan to a customer).

Models of Change Oriented to Processes

The management of change does not only mean a decision in the choice of the new ERP tools for the management of work, it also constitutes a decision on how to maximise the competitive advantages that the technology can offer to the firm. In the nineties the term business process reengineering (BPR), (Hammer, 1991) appears. Champy and Hammer (1994:32) define business process reengineering as the "fundamental thinking and radical redesign of business processes with the main objective of reaching drastic improvements". The objective of the business process reengineering it is not a pure change on any existent process, but the development of a new one that substitutes the previous one by following the criteria of firm's value.

In contrast with the concept of BPR, it appears the concept of organisational development (OD), also known as "planned organisational change". This concept proposes a model of change based in the participation. The main premise in this orientation consists of accepting what attitudes, values and behaviours of a group of members in an organisation are, and what it is important to be changed before promoting any change in the system.

In the organisational development we must to take into account not only the processes, but the quality of life of workers too. For that reason we work with the concept of decrease in the hierarchical distance amongst them and a different distribution of power that helps to develop a culture of mutual trust. While the BPR is developed from up to down (it is an action imposed from the management in the organisation), the organisational development follows a bipolar strategy, it could be up down, or the other way around.

The organisational development (OD) includes a structural approach and personal for the change. The structural aspect relates with the creation of a favourable framework. It means a change in the rules and description of work tasks. The personal aspect is centred on the promotion of the skills and a desire coming from the employees to accept the support in the change process. The effective application of the organisational development is mainly supported in two principles:

- To help people to take care of themselves
- And involve everyone that can be affected by any change initiative

Normally in the management of the change, basic models based in the sequences "unfreeze-build and freeze" are used. The main idea is to change the organisation from an organizational way and a determined cultural model maintained along time and for that, it is needed to unfreeze, for building a model of acting that better fits with the environment and the technological possibilities at the moment, and try to make that model work and be maintained in the organisation "freeze".

This model has to be rapidly moved since the innovation rate that the information technologies offer runs at a fast speed.

Any effort that attempts to managing the change in a clever way must recognise the absolute need to generate a lack of satisfaction with the start point. This way the optimal point of start is guaranteed to sell or convince about different ways of developing the processes.

We offer here some ways of creating an environment of change in the organisations,

- To create a dissatisfaction: by showing lack of skills in the status quo, by communicating relevant variations in the internal profile and the external situation, that show the need of change. For example, the globalisations of the markets have made appeared the need of marketing the products in new geographical areas. For that reason, it is important for the system and the people in the company to be able to work in different languages and currency.
- To reduce the fear for the change: by establishing open discussions, based on the experience of other companies and other parts in the organisation. For example, the resistance to change can be a decisive cause for the failure of a project of ERP implementation. For that reason, most companies apply for the collaboration of external consultancy firms experienced in the same industry, to be informed before starting any project.
- To create energy in the company around the benefits of the change in people from

Figure 9. Organization of teams

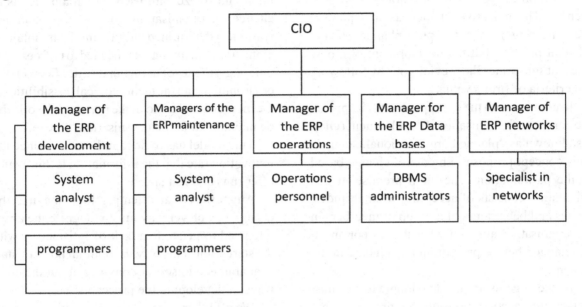

an individual and collective perspective. For this reason the information must be properly managed. It must reach to everyone in the firm and it must help people to be involved and enthusiastic with the new project. The firms can use different channels to offer the information

- Kick-off: a meeting with all the participants. A starting point in the project with an explanation of the main objectives and the methodology used to achieve them.
- The information bulletin
- The periodical information, to publicity the project state of the art
- The development of the Intranet: public information of the generated documents from the project to the firm's intranet.

- To build support for the change: by identifying the persons in charge of the change efforts and work with them. Before starting a project, it is important to define who are responsible of it in the firm that it is implementing the system and in the external collaboration groups too.

- To define specific objectives for the change: in detail and that can be measured in clear deadlines. Work teams are usually established to fix the objectives associated to the different business areas implied in the project and measure the persecution of the objectives and typical deviations.
- To define awards and punishments in the change and their impact in the profiles and work places. In the contracts of collaboration with external providers, it is important to include mechanisms of punishment by both parts (provider and customer). They can be activated in case there are deviations in the final ERP functionality or in the initial agreed deadlines.
- To plan the adequate training and synchronised with change. In the various phases of the project, different training plans are established according to the different users implied on them. As we descend in the organisational levels, the training required is more specific and specialised.
- To communicate the efforts for the change and make participate to the employees in them, etc. Communication matrixes must

be defined where the different people's profiles and the related information with the project are informed in each of the project steps.

However, any effort for the change must also recognise the appearance of a group of situations that are going to promote the desired modifications. Amongst them, we can stress,

- Immobilisation: a feeling of being unable to plan and understand. It can be especially relevant when the transition is negative represented or unexpected. For example, a situation in which someone can lose a work that he or she specially loves.
- Minimisation: a negative for the change that it exists or it is going to take place. It has a positive effect in time, and it is also influenced by psychological mechanisms.
- Depression: to recognise that the change can not be avoided, joined to a feeling of being unable to stop it.

Laisser-faire: an acceptance of the reality

- Tests: in the new situation, one tries to experiment new ways of work, socialisation and so on. Sometimes all mixed with a sense of irritability.
- Search of sense: after the energy consumed in the previous phase, it is the search of understanding why things are different.
- Internalisation: once finished the transition, changes are incorporated in the behaviour. People must be involved in the management of change that accompanies to a project of implementation of a new ERP system, and they must make feel part of the main success. For that reason two types of meetings must be established according to the degree of interrelation of the different hierarchical levels in the structure of the organisation:

- RAMS (Requirement analysis for management systems), group meetings with the users for the requirements. The consultancy team collects the initial information to develop the further work. It is a nice moment to identify some opportunities of improving the functionality of the system or changes at an organisational level produced by the implementation.
- Top Mapping: personal meetings with the main responsible of each area. The main objective of this action it to complete the firm's vision and its future.

Apart from creating the need and desire of change and define results, it is needed to consider the resources for the change plan (money, personal, time, managers, consultancy firms and new work profiles, etc.). it is also needed to decide in which way the progress of the plan it is going to take place.

Amongst the most common failures that are going to be produced in the management of change, we can stress,

- To dedicate less attention to the work places, responsibilities, structures and resources.
- To change the program preview at first glance.
- To wrongly assign responsibilities of change to people that are not prepared.
- A non realistic estimation of the time dedicated to the change.
- The lack of identification of the desired emotions in the employees during the implementation of the change.
- The inadequate consideration on how to be involved in the change.
- Not considering contingency plans for events that are not be taken into account previously.

- To ignore the need of communication the results expected for the change.
- Not to recognise the work of all those that have promoted the change
- A deficient thought in the expectations created about the change
- Not to pay attention in how maintaining the employees motivated and involved.

All of them are typical failures in the projects of ERP implementations, The managerial positions must take into account that we are dealing with strategic projects for the company and therefore, the resources assigned to them must be independent of the typical daily tasks. This is very important to organise the required time to the project.

We can include as main critical factors in the implementation of ERP systems here the following ones,

- To involve the final customer in the project
- To design the needed measures to make final users real participants in the project
- To synthesis the demanded needs and translate them in computer terms
- To create a technological culture
- To discuss and propose improvements in the processes
- To warranty the internal and the external coordination of the project by minimising risks
- To establish roles and responsibilities of the project form the initial phase
- To assign the proper people profiles to the project, with the proper level of authority, experience and capacity
- To use a proper methodology specialised in ERP implementations
- To develop a plan of quality
- To make sure that the personal in the project is trained enough and the management of the change takes place.

And amongst the main characteristics that make possible the change of the management we can stress,

- A wide access of the most complete information possible
- To have the organisational skills for manipulating ambiguity
- To promote organizational innovation
- To open the organization to be ready to take risks.
- To have the kind of information systems required clear.
- To develop the skills to manage the conflict.

Information and communication technologies play an important role in the change. They enable and make it possible the change in the actual business environment.

The organisation is in a constant need of change. When a certain process is clearly inefficient, an effort for the redesign is developed. Afterwards in time, and until again the situation in the new process can be maintained, the firm will periodically develop initiatives for the continuous improvement.

Methodologies for implementing changes coming from ERP implementations in the firm.

The main methodologies explaining change in firm's processes are considering the following principles exposed by Hammer and Champy (1996),

- Organise around results, not tasks
- Make that those that are going to be benefited from the final results be the ones implied in the change
- Include the work of processing information in the real work produced by the information
- Treat geographically dispersed resources as if they were centralised

Table 3. Organisational changes and principles of the redesign of processes (Davenport, 1996)

Change	Result
Working units	From functional departments to processes
Change of work	From simple tasks to multidimensional work
Change in people's role	From training to education
Measure of the results	From measuring activities to measuring results
Organisational structures	From hierarchical to flat structures
Change in business leaders	From seekers to leaders

Table 4. The process of change (Davenport, 1996)

1. Identification of the processes to change
2. Identification of the change enablers
3. Understanding today's processes
4. Development of the vision of the process
5. Design and build of a prototype of a new process

- Link parallel activities instead of integrating tasks
- Position the decision making point where the work that it is going to be performed and provide control in the process
- Reach the information once and in its primary source.

This brief list shows the main keys of change efforts when trying to restructure organisations around processes, further specialised functions. Some way, this principles change the ones traditional coming from the division of work orientation.

The application of this principles has offer a group of organisational changes, extended along firms and collected in the Table 3,

Davenport (1996), by considering these principles, describes five steps for the change of processes that can be applied to help in a successful ERP implementation. (Table 4)

In the identification of the processes to change, the main processes in the organisation must be described. They will be limited by clearly defining

their point of start and end. Lastly, an evaluation about the degree of satisfaction in these processes will be developed.

In the identification of the change enabler's step, the main elements that come from inside and outside the firm and can have an influence in the effort of the change are identified. The ERP information technologies and human resources in the firm can be essential, as we have already previously defined.

In the following phase, it is important to understand the existent processes. It is really difficult to describe where we want to arrive if we do not know about our starting point. Besides, understanding where some failures are being done today can help us preventing them in future occasions. Besides, this phase implies communicating to the implied agents in the processes of today the desire to promote changes or substituting them.

In the vision of the process, it would be convenient try to find a link between that vision and the strategy for promoting a logical congruence in these elements that need to change. Strategy and processes in the organisations must look at

Figure 10. Business change and information technologies

the same direction. For that, it is needed to draw the new process. In this sense, some steps can be of help,

- To evaluate the up to day competitive strategy to determine the direction in the process
- To consult with customers the process on expectations of results in the same
- To compare amongst the improvement expectations and examples of existent innovations
- To fix the objectives of results in the new process
- To develop the specific attributes of the new process. This means establishing the basic characteristics it tries to build.

In the design of the new process, we can use a group of ideas that can help us to generate the process, for example, the brainstorming, or use techniques that can help us analysing viability, success and benefits of new processes; clearly draw a new process and communicate it to all the implied people; to develop a strategy for modifying the process from old to new, and be realistic with the need of converting the organisation with the implementation of a new process.

The Role of Information and Communication Technologies in the Change Efforts

The actions guiding to the change of business processes has made appeared two kind of opin-

ions, those thinking that the ERP possibilities can promote changes in a radical way in the firm processes and those other that think that the need of changing obsolete organisational structures is a great opportunity to incorporate the ERP systems. Davenport and Short (1990) put together these two options by establishing a bi-directional recursive relation between this two arguments, by admitting that the information technology is the essential tool to promote business process reengineering and the other way around.

Davenport and Short (1990) put into relation the business process reengineering and the information technologies in a bidirectional way, supporting the hypotheses that "each of them makes us thinking of the other". These same authors present examples on how information technologies promote business processes. Some authors even consider a BPR effort as an alternative way for implementing information technologies in the information system.

We think that the efforts of change and the implementation of ERP systems in a firm are just tools that allow in the building of more rational and efficient processes. Information technologies must be essential elements for promoting the change.

4. THE FINAL INTERNAL USER SATISFACTION

It is based in the system testing (Nah et al. (2001), Kumar et al. (2002), Al-Mashari et al. (2003), Yusuf (2004) and pos-implementation evaluation (Holland and Light (1999), Ross and Vitale (2000), Nah et al. (2001), Al-Mashari et al. (2003), Mandal and Gunasekaran (2003), Tarafdar and Roy (2003), Umble et al. (2003). It is highly related with the feedback we have obtained from the consulting firms operating in the Spanish market since they stress that it is very important to check that the software meets the needs of the whole company.

It refers to the participation in the system development and implementation by different representatives of the target groups. System implementation means a threat to users perceptions of control over their work and a period of transition during which users must cope with differences between old and new work systems. User involvement is effective because it offers perceived control by taking part in the whole plan.

Users can be involved twice when implementing an ERP system

- User involvement at a stage of definition of the company's ERP system needs,
- User participates in the implementation of the ERP system.

5. THE FINAL EXTERNAL USER SATISFACTION (FIRM'S CUSTOMERS)

It is inspired in the client consultation process Holland and Light (1999), Al Mudimigh et al. (2001), Al-Mashari et al. (2003), Mandal and Gunasekaran (2003). It has to do with the training programs for the users that the consultants surveyed have mentioned us.

A group of variables explaining final customer satisfaction of the ERP deliverables must be taken into account before implementing the ERP system. The ERP system implementation demands of great human and technical efforts to promote a desired situation in which the final external user feels much more satisfied.

Satisfaction and results are considered, variables of the greatest importance when defining different styles of internalising ERP systems in the firms. Maybe the most complete analysis is developed by Ives and Olson (1983) where they reach a complete methodology that allows measuring the user satisfaction in IT use. This approach has been mentioned in various analyses that study the impact of information and communication technologies in firms of different nature. It seems to be a useful tool to be applied to the case or ERP implementations due to the difficulty in measuring such abstract term as satisfaction.

CONCLUSION

ERP systems have a great potential to promote improvements in the competitive position of the firms. However, the obtained results when they start working in firms are not often as positive as some organisations could expect. When analysing the failures in the implementation of ERP systems, we can affirm that the way in which the process is understood and how the implementation takes place highly conditions the results of the mentioned process and its future performance.

The implementation of an ERP system is, above all, a project. This simple preliminary assumption allows extrapolating to the development of the process the main principles of project management, properly adapted to the specific features dealing with the daily operating of a system like this.

In this chapter we have proposed a model containing different critical success factors that can help to make the best of the ERP implementation and exploitation according to the objectives of the firm. The model is composed by five different aspects,

The decision-making policy of the firm in the ERP selection, implementation and use, we have included as main variables here the following ones,

- The existence of managerial support,
- The existence of clear procedures established for the required re-engineering of business processes in the firm
- The effectiveness of the project management
- The existence of a wide commitment in the different areas of the firm
- The existence of a wide commitment in the different stakeholders in the implementations (vendor support, external services)

The training characteristics of the people involved in the ERP implementation and final use. Training and personal education is very important. The training actions must take place in a permanent way, before the implementation and after their conclusion, and they allow people understand that apart of using software, they must have clear the way in which the processes in the system work. We have consider here as the main variables the following ones,

- Education: the information that the employees have received on the ERP system.
- Training: the sessions where the people in the firm learns about how the ERP system operates and how it affects the different firm's processes
- Ethical issues: the position of the people in the firm to make a good use of the system taking into account firm's values and proper codes of conduct

The organizational inertia in the firm. It has to do with aspects in relation to culture, values and ways of group expression in the organization. We have considered a shared group of values in the organisation and how they can promote or avoid a proper implementation and an afterwards degree of use. Unless a previous business process reengineering is developed before the implementation, it is difficult to obtain optimal results. New systems do not work with old rules.

New software demands of a new way of doing things. People and systems must be integrated around the logical and more rational processes required at each moment.

The final internal user satisfaction, this is a key question, the final employee satisfaction of the ERP use promotes the daily usage and the desire of improving it.

The final external user satisfaction, the reason of being of any ERP system in the firm is to provide best options that allow promoting the final customer satisfaction in the firm's deliverables

REFERENCES

Akkermans, H., & Van Helden, K. (2002). Vicious and virtuous cycles in ERP implementation: a case study of interrelations between critical success factors. *European Journal of Information Systems*, *11*(1), 35–46. doi:10.1057/palgrave/ejis/3000418

Al-Mashari, M., Al-Mudimigh, A., & Zairi, M. (2003). Enterprise Resource Planning: A taxonomy of critical factors. *European Journal of Operational Research*, *146*, 352–364. doi:10.1016/S0377-2217(02)00554-4

Ang, J. S. K., Sum, C. C., & Yeo, L. N. (2002). A multiple-case design methodology for studying MRP success and CSFs. *Information & Management*, *39*(4), 271–281. doi:10.1016/S0378-7206(01)00096-9

Brynjolfsson, E., & Hitt, L. (1996). Productivity, business profitability and consumer surplus: Three different measures of Information Technology Value. *MIS Quarterly*, *20*, 121–142. doi:10.2307/249475

Champy, J., & Hammer, M. (1994). *Business process reengineering*. Barcelona: Parramón.

Clausen, C., & Koch, C. (1999). The role of spaces and occasions in the transformation of information technologies – Lessons from the social shaping of IT systems for manufacturing a Danish context. *Technology Analysis and Strategic Management*, *11*(3), 463–481. doi:10.1080/095373299107456

Colmenares, L., & Otieno, J. (2005). Critical Success factors of ERP implementation. In M. Khosrow-Pour (Ed.), *Encyclopedia of Information Science and Technology* (pp. 628-633). Hershey, PA: Idea Group Inc.

Davenport, T. H. (1993). Need radical Innovation and continuous improvement? Integrate process reengineering and TQM. *Strategy and Leadership*, *21*(3), 6–12. doi:10.1108/eb054413

Davenport, T. H. (1996). *Innovation of processes. Redesign of work by using information technologies.* Madrid: Diaz de Santos.

Davenport, T. H. (2000). *Mission critical- Realizing the promise of enterprise systems.* Boston, MA: Harvard Business School Press.

Davenport, T.H., & Short, J.E. (1990). The new industrial engineering: Information technology and business process redesign. *IEEE Engineering Management Review*, 46-60.

Davis, F. F. (1989). Perceived usefulness, perceived ease of use and user acceptance of information technology . *MIS Quarterly*, *13*(3), 319–340. doi:10.2307/249008

De Pablos Heredero, C. (2001). Management of information systems in the firm. Madrid: ESIC.

Esteves, J., & Pastor, J. (2001). Analysis of critical success factors relevance along SAP implementation phases. In *Proceedings of the Seventh Americas Conference on Information Systems* (pp. 1019-1025).

Falkowski, G., Pedigo, P., Smith, B., & Swamson, D. (1998). A recipe for ERP success. Beyond Computing. *International Journal of Human-Computer Interaction*, *16*(1), 5–22.

Finney, S., & Corbett, M. (2007). ERP implementation: a compilation and analysis of critical success factors. *Business Process Management Journal*, *13*(3), 329–347. doi:10.1108/14637150710752272

Fui-Hoon, F., Zuckweiler, K. M., & Lee-Shang, J. (2003). ERP implementation: Chief Information Officers' perceptions on critical success factors. *International Journal of Human-Computer Interaction*, *16*(1), 5–22. doi:10.1207/S15327590I-JHC1601_2

García Bravo, D. (2000). *Sistemas de información en la empresa. Conceptos y aplicaciones*, Madrid: Pirámide.

Garvin, D. A. (1993). Building a learning organization. *Harvard Business Review*, (July-August): 78–91.

Garvin, D.A. (1998). The processes of organization and management. *Sloan Management Review*, summer, 81-98.

Grohowski, R., McGoff, C., Vogel, D., & Martz, J. (1990). Implementing electronic meeting systems at IBM: Lessons learned and success factors. *MIS Quarterly*, *16*(4), 369–384. doi:10.2307/249785

Hammer, M. (1991). Business process reengineering: Do not automate, obliterate. *Harvard- Deusto Business Review*, third semester.

Holland, C. P., & Light, B. (1999). A critical success factors model for ERP implementation. *IEEE Software*, (May/June): 30–36. doi:10.1109/52.765784

Ives, B., & Olson, M. (1983). The measurement of user information satisfaction. *Management of Computing*, *26*(10), 519–529.

Keen, P. G. (1991). *Shaping the future: Business design through information technology.* Cambridge, MA: Harvard Business School Press.

Koch, C. (2001). BRP and ERP: Realising a vision process with IT. *Business Process Management Journal, 7*(3), 258–265. doi:10.1108/14637150110392755

Kumar, V., Movahedi, B., Kumar, U., & Lavassani, K. M. (2008). A comparative study of enterprise system implementations in large North American corporations. *11th International Conference Business Information Systems, Innsbruck, Austria, May 2008* (pp. 390-398).

Lai, V. (1994). A survey of rural small business computer use: Success factors and decision support. *Information & Management, 26*(6), 297–304. doi:10.1016/0378-7206(94)90027-2

Lichtenberg, F. (1995). The output contributions of computer equipment and personnel: A firm level analysis. *Economics of Innovation and New Technology, 3*(3), 201–218. doi:10.1080/10438599500000003

Mabert, V., Soni, A., & Venkatamara, M. (2003). Enterprise Resource Planning: Managing implementation process. *European Journal of Operational Research, 146*(2), 302–314. doi:10.1016/S0377-2217(02)00551-9

Malone, T. B., & Yates, J. (1987). Electronic markets and electronic hierarchies: Effects on information technology on market structure and corporate strategies. *Communications of the ACM, 30,* 37–45.

Markus, L. M., & Tannis, G. (1999). *The Enterprise Systems Experience: From adoption to success.* Peter Drucker Graduate School of Management, Claremont Graduate University, Claremont, CA.

McLeod, R. (2000). *Management information systems.* Mexico, D.F.: Prentice Hall.

Monforte Moreno, M. (1995). *Sistemas de información para la dirección.* Madrid: Pirámide.

Moor, J. H. (1985). What is computer ethics? *Metaphilosophy, 16*(4), 266–275. doi:10.1111/j.1467-9973.1985.tb00173.x

Motwani, J., Mirchandani, M., & Gunasekaran, A. (2002). Successful implementation of ERP Projects: Evidence from two case studies. *International Journal of Production Economics, 75,* 83–96. doi:10.1016/S0925-5273(01)00183-9

Nah, F., Lau, J., & Kuang, J. (2001). Critical factors for successful implementation of enterprise systems. *Business Process Management, 7*(3), 285–296. doi:10.1108/14637150110392782

Pang, L. (2001). Manager's guide to enterprise resource planning (ERP) systems. *Info Tech Talk, 6*(2), 13–16.

Parker, D. (1988). Ethics for information systems personnel. *Journal of Information Systems Management, 5,* 44–48. doi:10.1080/07399018808962925

Rashid, M., Hossain, L., & Patrick, D. (2002). The evolution of ERP Systems: A historical perspective. In F. F.-H. Nah (Ed.), *Enterprise resource planning: Solution and management* (pp. 306-332). Hershey, PA: IRM Press.

Rockart, J. (1979). Chief executives define their own data needs. *Harvard Business Review, 57*(2), 238–241.

Rosario, J.G. (2000). On the leading edge: critical success factors in ERP implementation projects. *Business World,* May, 21-27.

Seddon, P., Staples, S., Patnayakuni, R., & Bowtell, M. (1999). Dimensions of information systems success. *Communications of AIS, 2,* 17–26.

Sneed, H., & Brössler, P. (2003). *Critical success factors in software maintenance- A case study*. In *Proceedings of the International Conference on Software maintenance (ICSM'03)* (pp. 190-198).

Sommers, G., & Nelson, C. (2003). A taxonomy of players and activities across the ERP project life cycle. *Information & Management, 41*(3), 257–278. doi:10.1016/S0378-7206(03)00023-5

Stefanou, C. (1999). Supply chain management (SCM) and organizational key factors for successful implementation of enterprise resource planning (ERP) systems. In *Proceedings of 5th Americas Conference on information Systems* (pp. 800-802).

Sum, C., Ang, J., & Yeo, L. (2002). A multiple-case design methodology for studying MRP success and CSFs. *Information & Management, 39*(4), 271–282. doi:10.1016/S0378-7206(01)00096-9

Summer, M. (1999). Critical success factors in enterprise wide information management systems projects. In *Proceedings of 5th Americas Conference on Information Systems* (pp. 232-234).

Themistocleous, M., Irani, Z., O`Keefe, R., & Paul, R. (2001). ERP problems and application integration issues: An empirical survey. In *Proceedings of the 34th Annual Hawai International conference on System Sciences, 9* (pp. 9045-9053).

Umble, E. J., Haft, R. R., & Umble, M. M. (2003). Enterprise Resource Planning: Implementation procedures and critical success factors. *European Journal of Operational Research, 146*, 241–257. doi:10.1016/S0377-2217(02)00547-7

Victor, B., & Boynton, A. C. (1998). *Invented here*. Boston, MA: Harvard Business School Press.

Vitale, M. R. (1986). American Hospital Supply corp. The ASAP system. *Harvard Business School Case Study*, March, 1-17.

Wang, E., Sheng-Pao, S., Jianj, J. J., & Klein, G. (2008). The consistency among facilitating factors and ERP implementation success: A holistic view of kit. *Journal of Systems and Software, 81*, 1601–1621.

Wee, S. (2002). Juggling toward ERP success: Keep key success factors high. *ERP news*. Retrieved January 22, 2002, from http//.erpnews.com/erpnews/erp904/02get.html-Weill, P. (1990). *Do computers pay off?* Washington, DC: International Center for Information technologies.

Weill, P., & Broadbent, M. (1998). *Leveraging the new infrastructure: How market leaders capitalize on information technology*. Boston, MA: Harvard Business School Press.

Zani, W. (1970). Blueprint in MIS . *Harvard Business Review*, (November-December): 25–37.

KEY TERMS AND DEFINITIONS

Information and Communication Technologies: tools to treat information, they can be composed by telecommunications technologies, as for example telephone, cable, satellite and radio, and digital technologies, as for example computers, information networks and software

ERP System: Enterprise Resource Planning, a business management system that integrates all the facets of the business, including planning, manufacturing, sales, etc.

Critical Success Factors: (CSF's) are the critical factors or activities required for ensuring the success of your business

Processes: A series of operations performed in the making or treatment of a product or service

Change: To give a different form or appearance to; transform

Business Process Reengineering: it is a radical redesign of a process in order to reach great results

Managerial Support: help offered and promoted by the managers in a firm

Team: a group of two or more individuals who interact dynamically to achieve a shared objective

Chapter 27
Change Management Strategies for ERP Implementation in SME and a Case Study in Turkey:
Anadolu Bilişim Hizmetleri (ABH) Success Story

Özalp Vayvay
Marmara University, Istanbul, Turkey

İlhan Derman
ABH, Istanbul, Turkey

Ergin Beceren
ABH, Istanbul, Turkey

ABSTRACT

SMEs differ from large firms in terms of environmental uncertainty, dependency, centralization, specialization, strategy, systems, resources and flexibility. Because of these distinguishing characteristics, the results of research carried out in large firms cannot be transferred directly to small firms. This is particularly true of the critical success factors for change management and technology implementation. Generally, SMEs tend to adopt new technologies after large firms. The case study in Turkey, represents the change management activities on ERP implementation by a consultancy firm (ABH) on an international corporation's Turkey located SME.

ERP OVERVIEW

ERP stands for "Enterprise Resource Planning" and represents the latest stage in the evolution and expansion of production planning and control techniques for manufacturing enterprises from material require-

ments planning (MRP) ERP systems are comprised of a suite of software modules, with each module typically responsible for gathering and processing information for a separate business function, or a group of separate business functions. ERP software modules may include accounting, master scheduling, material planning, inventory, forecasting, finite scheduling, distribution planning and others.

DOI: 10.4018/978-1-60566-892-5.ch027

A typical ERP system integrates all of the company's functions byallowing the modules to share and transfer information freely. In addition, all information is centralized in a single relationaldatabase accessible by all modules, eliminating the need for multiple entries ofthe same data. While large firms usually budget heavily for ERP and mayinstall a substantial number of the available modules, smallerfirms often adopt a piecemeal approach, starting with a few modules or a fewcomponents of each module. Customers and suppliers withnetwork security clearance are allowed to access certain types of information by way of an external communication interface (Muscatello, et al., 2003).

ERP Benefits and Limitations

One of the primary objectives for installing ERP as well as one of its principalbenefits is the ability to integrate business processes. The use of ERP has also been found to be critical inimproving customer satisfaction. ERP has also been found to be effective in reducing inventorycosts, improving efficiency and increasing profitability. In addition, ERP has also been credited with reducing manufacturing lead times.

Other potential benefits of ERP include: drastic declines in inventory; breakthrough reductions in working capital; abundant information about customer wants and needs; and the ability to view and manage the extended enterprise of suppliers, alliances, and customers as an integrated whole. It should be noted, however, that not all enterprises that have implemented ERP are satisfied with the results of their investments.Many businesses consider their implementation attempts to be failures. In addition some firms succeed in their implementation while others fail, it is critical to understand that, although the technical capabilities of ERP systems are relatively well proven, implementing these systems is not a simple matter of purchasing and installing the technology. Many believe that, as with all advanced technol-

ogy systems, managerial issues, from planning to implementation, present major barriers to the effective adoption of ERP systems. (Muscatello, et al., 2003).

Many large organisations have made significant investments of both time and capital to implement ERP systems, however not all implementations go as well as intended Traditional project management challenges are magnified in such environments, making the implementation more difficult, expensive and failure-prone the five key critical success factors are (Kemp & Low, 2008):

- top management support,
- business case,
- change management,
- project management
- and training.

CHANGE MANAGEMENT

Change management is a particularly important factor in the adoption, adaptation and acceptance phases of ERP systems implementation. Moreover many ERP implementations fail to achieve the expected benefits possibly because companies underestimate the effort involved in change management.

ERP system, change management is required to prepare users for the introduction of the new system, reduce resistance towards the system and influence user attitudes towards that system. The ERP adoption model suggests that change management and management support should positively influence system awareness, feelings towards the system and the intention to adopt that system for users to actually adopt the system.

Change management initiatives for a new information system should focus on changes specifically in the areas of technology, business process and organisation, and IS culture. Therefore, change management should focus on creating an environment where the change can be implemented. Suggested activities include: project championship, training, communication of system features and benefits communication of new business processes and organisational structure and rewards and incentives (Kemp & Low, 2008).

A transformational innovation implementation model, does not explicitly consider the impact that change management has on implementation climate. A climate favourable to the implementation of a new system represents favourable user experiences and attitudes towards the implementation. Therefore, in organizational strategies with managing the change that occurs during the implementation at an individual or departmental level, user attitudes towards the system are more likely to be positive and the overall implementation climate is more likely to be favourable. The construct of "change management" has been added to the innovation implementation model to represent the effect that change management can have on implementation climate. The implementation climate for an innovation can be described as the sum of employees' observations and experiences regarding the innovation. By this model we can describe the situation where users' awareness, feelings and intention to adopt an ERP system are affected by change management and management support. User awareness, feelings and intention to adopt an ERP system are equivalent to the experiences and observations of users during an ERP implementation, therefore the an ERP adoption model can be considered as providing a greater level of detail regarding change management and implementation climate.

Through using this model, the impact of change management on implementation climate and innovation effectiveness can be investigated. Specifically, the research questions are:

- Do the identified change management activities affect the implementation climate?
- Does implementation climate (feelings awareness response, favourable feelings

response and favourable adoption intention) impact the effectiveness of the ERP implementation?

Therefore performing change management strategies is going to support the total quality management (TQM) initiatives.

Innovative Change Management Model

As a first step in the longer-term empirical validation of the revised innovation implementation model to describe how the change management activities during an ERP implementation affect the Change management team

Most of the change management activities are targeted at specific groups of users, rather than being intended for all users of the systems (Kemp & Low, 2008).

Strategies include:

- Communicating information on system features, system benefits and changed processes using various options including organisation newsletters, "open days" conference room pilots of the system, and departmental briefings.
- Implementing a project championship program. The change management team, with assistance from the organisation general managers and HR staff.

These change agents, known as "Communicators" are the primary communication channel in support of the system implementation. Education and training the users across the organisation, focusing on the departments where change would be greatest. The change management activities had the required effect on the climate for implementation (Kemp & Low, 2008):

- Adopting a phased implementation to help minimise resistance to the changes.
- Benefits analysis

STRUCTURE OF SME

As an Organizational structure the most small to medium enreprises (SMEs) operate in a highly dynamic world, where both internal and external requirements may change. Changes may come from the need to be more cost-effective, from customers in the form of requirements for new products and product variants, from government agencies in the form of regulations, or by advances in technology. Often the SME structure is the weaker part in a supply chain and thus the ability to adapt to changes imposed by customers or suppliers will be an important competitive factor. Most SMEs have utilized the flexibility that comes from having a lower number of orders, customers, employees, etc. when changing processes and practices. It is therefore important that this flexible IT management is retained when new IT systems are implemented.

Small to medium sized enterprises may not have the resources to do a careful study of available systems, neither to plan nor to perform a low-risk implementation. Further, many small companies, especially niche companies, have more to risk by standardizing core functions, and by conforming to a system that reduce their ability to comply with changing internal and external factors.

When the strategic IT management embodies important business strstegies, i.e., when the IT system has strategic significance, the system has to reflect these changes. The company must therefore be able to modify the software and to add new functionality whenever needed. This is not easy to achieve with a general ERP system as a SME Strategy. Attending user conferences to promote general modifications to the kernel part of an ERP system is at least time-consuming and therefore unacceptable. Add-on modules are a possible solution, but these often only work until the next version of the standard system is installed (Olsen & Sætre, 2007).

One problem with smaller businesses is that they often lack the in house expertise and knowl-

edge to handle the requirement process as well as the implementation of an ERP and also to fully estimate the expected effects and outcomes of such an implementation. Small companies often do not even have their own IT department and if they have one, they are usually not experienced in such large scale system changes. Another important aspect to take into consideration is that an ERP system is not primarily a matter for the IT-department but of the entire company and especially the top management due to the impact on the business processes. Additional implications can of course occur if the company at the same time is undertaking a total reorganization of the company. This reorganisation can sometimes be necessary due to the implementation of the ERP but of course, reorganisations are often caused by other external or internal factors as well.

SMEs do not function as a collection of formal structured departments. Project implementation of ERP systems in SMEs is simpler in some aspects and more complicated at times (Huin, 2005).

Unless these deviations are well understood, managing ERP projects in SMEs will continue to be slow, painful and at times even unfruitful (Buonanno, et al., 2005):

1. Low Levels of Organizational Hierarchy.
2. CEO Involvement in Operational Decisions.
3. "Blurred" Departmental Walls.
4. Production Modes in SMEs.
5. Planned Forecasts vs Real Forecasts.
6. Rate of Changes in Orders.
7. Short Lead-time in Manufacturing.
8. High Staff Turnover.
9. Customers_ Special Demands.

In the light of the identified business factors, it is therefore necessary to verify the association between these factors and the use of ERP systems by testing the following six main hypotheses (Buonanno, et al., 2005):

H1. The company size affects the adoption of ERP systems.

H2. The market area affects the adoption of ERP systems.

H3. The membership of a group affects the adoption of ERP systems.

H4. The presence of branch offices affects the adoption of ERP systems.

H5. The level of diversification affects the adoption of ERP systems.

H6. The degree of functional extension affects the adoption of ERP systems.

Therefore another hypothesis to be tested is focused on the matching between organizational issues and ERP system adoption (Buonanno, et al., 2005):

H7. The extent of planned organizational change is directly related to the use of ERP systems (the greater is the planned organizational change, the greater is the rate of adoption of ERP systems).

ERP Implementation Strategies in SME's

Deep et al (2007) claims that ERPs is getting more common in the SME sector and are viewed as a way to reengineer processes and gain advantages towards their competitors in the trade. Before the ERPs where more or less restricted to larger enterprises due to the economic and technological differences. The situation is changing since the SMEs are more and more appealed by the benefits that can be achieved from ERP systems although an ERP can be devastating for SMEs due to unclear objectives and a confused understanding of what and how an ERP can help gain performance

improvements or competitive advantages. (Deep et al, 2007)

The likelihood of a SME to implement some kind of ERP is increasing according to Nach & Lejeune (2008) although the ERP-projects are especially challenging to carry out in SMEs. The problem with implementing ERPs in SMEs is that they have inadequate human and financial resources compared to the larger companies and the chance of surviving or getting back on track if the implementation fails is far lesser than in the large companies. Another aspect that influences the projects is that during the ERP projects the SME's managers only carry out their role to the extent that they have skill and knowledge about compared to larger enterprises where they have a different level of resources. (Nach & Lejeune &, 2008)

To be successful in selecting an ERP in a SME, Deep et al (2007) has concluded some basic thoughts to be aware of while doing the selection. The first thing is to be aware of that the selection of an ERP system begins and ends with a realistic estimation of what the value adding processes should be. Here it helps to structuring the processes and brings out specific areas of standardization and it would be useful to have the key indicators and variables that would be the outputs from the ERP for decision making and analysis. The actual selection should be a team decision and it imperative to include as many end-users as possible, either directly or indirectly in understanding needs and expectations. Each department is specialized and unique in what they do and therefore it is crucial to involve them all since the ERP will affect the entire organization. Another thing that is important is the uniqueness of the change management scenarios within the SME since there is usually less experience of complex systems and education will thus be necessary and essential.

A quick review of ERP research revealed different strategies for implementing ERP successfully. One can classify these strategies into organizational, technical, and people strategies.

Organizational strategies for promoting ERP implementation success include change strategy development and deployment,change management techniques, project management, organizational structure and resources, managerial style and ideology, communication and coordination, and IS function characteristics (Aladwani, 2001).

Change Management Plan in SME's

Improvement strategies it management, such as ERP implementation, commonly involve change. Hence, responsiveness to internal customers is critical for an organization to avoid the difficulties associated with this change. To assist top management with the complex organizational problem of workers' resistance to ERP implementation, This should address such questions as (Aladwani, 2001):

- Who are the resisting individuals and/or groups?
- What are their needs?
- What beliefs and values do they have?
- What are their interests?

The answers to these fundamental questions may offer a good starting point in determining the sources of employees' resistance to the ERP system. This could well be applied to the context of implementing an ERP system. For example, some users may raise issues about their computer illiteracy, or may say that they have spent many years doing an excellent job without help from an ERP system. Other users may develop beliefs that their jobs will be threatened by the new system, or that they will not know how to do the job within the scope of such a system. Yet another group of users may stress values such as the importance of existing power and authority structures, which may be jeopardized by the new ERP system.

Strategy Implementation Phase in SME's

Management can use the knowledge regarding potential users from the previous stage to set up strategies that can best overcome users' resistance to the ERP system, and to convince as many users as possible to adopt it. If this is the case, it is more appropriate to find an action sheet for implementing the selected strategies. The three-level adoption process (think-feel-do) provides a good framework for describing this phase. In an attempt to change the attitudes of potential users of ERP, management must first try to affect the cognitive component of users' attitudes (Aladwani, 2001).

A major strategy for achieving this goal is communication. One effective communication strategy is to inform potential users of the benefits of ERP. The marketing people usually communicate the benefits of a product, rather than its attributes, to customers, in order to draw their attention and heighten their realization. Top management, in the same way, can create more effective awareness for the ERP system by communicating its benefits to the workers (Aladwani, 2001).

In many cases, ERP implementation failed because of lack of communication. Knowledge about what the system can deliver to the organization and its workers can build anticipation for the system. Nevertheless, one must watch out for unrealistic workers' expectations, which may deepen the resistance problem, thus causing its failure from the outset (Aladwani, 2001).

Moreover, the success of future introduction initiatives depends on building a cumulative base of credibility by management. Another communication strategy is to give a general description of how the implemented ERP system will work. In the marketing context, customers are usually reluctant to buy a product if they do not know, at least in general terms, how it operates (Aladwani, 2001).

Likewise, ERP users are expected to be reluctant to welcome the new system if they do not know how it works. Teaching each of the various user groups how the ERP system works is important in creating awareness. Thus, from the outset, management should explain to potential users how the ERP system is going to work. For example, management should clarify the general inputs and outputs of the system, determine departments that will provide the data, and define the computer knowledge needed to operate the system, etc. In all cases, it is of paramount importance that the support staff responsible for executing these communication strategies possess adequate political skills so that the awareness stage ends up in accordance with the plan (Aladwani, 2001).

The second step in the strategy implementation phase is to influence the affective component of users' attitudes. The first strategy that can be used by management is cost minimization. The low-cost strategy as one that can be used by marketers to help an organization survive in a competitive environment. This strategy has a useful implication for ERP. If management wants the new system to be adopted by the users, then users' adoption costs should be kept to a minimum. Further, if change agents convince ERP users that their net outcome of the adoption process will be positive, then they will develop strong feelings toward accepting and adopting the new system. The cost minimization strategy should be developed in such a way that it affects both individual workers and influential groups (Aladwani, 2001).

On the individual level, the ERP system has to minimize the perceived cost for each employee in order to create a positive adoption attitude. For example, if the worker realizes that the ERP system is an opportunity for enhancing his or her job, thus making it more appealing with minimal additional costs, then (s)he most likely will develop an interest in the ERP system. Moreover, influential groups within the organization are also looking at the cost aspect of the implementation effort. In the ERP context, the users' perceived high quality of the

ERP system would surely have a positive impact on their attitudes toward that system. Some ERP systems have an unwieldy user interface, which can cause problems. Generally, system users do not scientifically measure quality attributes of the system, rather each user constructs his or her convenient perception about the system depending on his or her real (or socially constructed) experience. Additionally, hands-on training is another important driver of ERP implementation success (Aladwani, 2001).

Adoption of ERP Systems in SME's

SMEs differ from large firms in terms of environmental uncertainty, dependency, centralization, specialization, strategy, systems, resources and flexibility. Because of these distinguishing characteristics, the results of research carried out in large firms cannot be transferred directly to small firms. This is particularly true of the critical success factors for information technology development, operation and use. Generally speaking, SMEs tend to adopt new technologies after large firms (Nzaou, et al., 2008).

The results show that highly formalized management is not necessary to minimize risk. The proposed model adds to our understanding of the ERP adoption process in small manufacturing firms, especially as regards the minimization of implementation risk from the adoption stage onwards (Nzaou, et al., 2008).

The 11 factors for the ERP implementation success (Gargeya & Brady, 2005):

(1) ERP teamwork and composition;
(2) change management program and culture;
(3) top management support;
(4) business plan and vision;
(5) business process re-engineering and minimum customization;
(6) effective communication;
(7) project management;

(8) software development, testing, and trouble shooting;

(9) monitoring and evaluation of performance;

(10) project champion; and

(11) appropriate business and information technology legacy systems.

Implementing an ERP system is one of the most challenging projects any company, regardless of size, can undertake. Success does not come easily, and those who implement only for an immediate return on investment are in for a rude and expensive awakening. It is clear that most companies implement ERP systems just to stay competitive. The process has to be part of the business objective, and it has to be clear that a successful "go-live" is not the brass ring. This fateful date, set early on in project planning, cannot be viewed as the end goal or even the end of the project, but rather only a milestone along road to the true goal – realizing the benefits (Gargeya & Brady, 2005).

CASE STUDY IN TURKEY

Industrial manufacturers produce some of the most complex products in the world. The manufacturing industry includes businesses engaged in the mechanical or chemical transformation of materials or substances into new products. These businesses are usually described as plants, factories, or mills and characteristically use power driven machines and material handling equipment. Businesses engaged in assembling component parts of manufactured products are also considered manufacturing if the new product is neither a structure nor other fixed improvement. Also included is the blending of materials, such as lubricating oils, plastics, resins, or liquors.

They also face intense business pressures, including price erosion, growing environmental requirements, and global competition. Increased speed, reduced costs, more accurate fulfillment,

and value-added services (VAS) are everyday requirements. In the context of the economical conditions in Turkey, responsiveness speed to the customer, adapting constantly changing volumes and delivery schedules are the indicators to be able to lead in the manufacturing industry. It is supposed to be considered both cost and lead time constraints by tracing the online data gathered from the distributed department while responding to the customer quotation

Demand can come from several areas. Some of the areas that might create this demands are, quotations, which are taken into account when generating the master plan depending on the success percentage that is assigned to the quote. Sales order have not been satisfied, there may be a Sales Forecast for some items, and some production orders for which are short some of the components.

There are many different possibilities which are tried to cover as many of these throughout the demand fulfillment process. There are two critical points for the companies in manufacturing industry which goes toward seamlessly. Two different manufacturing policies when fulfilling the customer demands are adapted These policies are called as "Make to stock (MTS)" and "Make to Order (MTO)".

The firm's primary production comes from efficient capacity and its resulting MTS production. But since MTS has the disadvantage of not exactly matching demand in the period, the firm restricts its efficient capacity (MTS output) to avoid building excess stock of the standard product. Concurrently, it holds some separate flexible capacity that it uses in MTO fashion only if it realizes demand exceeding MTS capacity. The result is that efficient capacity is fully utilized, while flexible capacity is used only if there is sufficient demand.

The critical point to establish the streamline workflow for supply chain management is to generate master data like items, bill of material, manufacturing operations, work center capacity accurately. It is overwhelmingly crucial to manage master data in order to perform the processes which satisfy the each chain of supply sources.

XYZ company needed smoother operations to sustain the company's growth curve. After much deliberation, the SME implemented an ERP solution in 43 days and was pleasantly surprised by the results.

XYZ, a manufacturer of has been developing and manufacturing components for the household and professional appliances sector since 1963. A co-operative enterprise with a customer-oriented policy since it was set up. They needed to scale up its operational efficiency to support its growth targets. The goal was as ambitious as it was daunting. The company had to manage three operational manufacturing units (fourth is coming up) and was heavily dependent on customer demand cycles.

Defying the traditional myth that ERP is only meant for large enterprises, XYZ chose to implement an ERP solution. It deployed ERP in 43 days, which helped in effective inventory management and allowed the company to cater to seasonal spikes in demand.

At the Company

XYZ is an OEM supplier and has its own brand manufacturing components for the household and professional appliances. The company operates in a highly competitive business environment.

Issues with Old System

Prior to implementing an ERP, the company used another software for financial accounting along with stand-alone software for automating the HR function.

XYZ, the level of automation was not robust enough to take care of the highly dynamic and competitive environment as well as the future growth requirements.

Further, maintaining data security as well as the accuracy of facts, accounts, and inventory

management was just not possible with this system alone. Apart from these issues, the solution resulted in pile-ups of surplus inventory.

Without an effective enterprise-wide system the company was inclined to keep higher levels of goods in inventory, which were often not required, leaving too much scope for revenue loss to the company. Due to the unavailability of even the smallest of components like a sticker, production could get delayed adversely impacting the time-to-market.

On the other hand, maintaining excess inventory levels could be an expensive proposition considering the costs involved in holding the inventory.

Key Requirements

What XYZ required was a solution that would help the company improve operations while remaining competitive by performing the following functions:

- Effective allocation, planning and control of crucial resources of men, machines and materials.
- Well-tuned production environment with good synchronization among the various units to enable adaptation to the fluctuations in demand.
- Effective cost control to be able to deliver better value to its customers.
- Inventory visibility among the various units and inventory reduction across the supply chain.
- Availability of up-to-date and concise information to the top management to allow better decision-making.

These requirements, the company understood, warranted an enterprise-wide automation solution.

Why ERP

While the need for an ERP was imperative, one of the key concerns was the time taken to adopt new information architecture and the disruptions that could arise in the organization's operations. The fact that ERP has been notorious for time and cost overruns was bound to create apprehensions and influence the final decision. Especially so when XYZ had already deferred the decision to implement an ERP system earlier.

Yet, one of the company's biggest compulsions was to plan production for the coming season. It needed a solution that would allow smooth and quick adoption of a new system without any compromise in its functionality.

The solution provided everything XYZ was looking for: robustness, close fit with the business requirements, and cost-effectiveness.

One of the biggest ERP consultancy firm in Turkey (Anadolu Bilişim Hizmetleri A.Ş.) company was chosen for implementing the solution because of its vast experience in ERP implementation and project management skills. Moreover, its 'Speed' framework promised to carry out the implementation in less than two months.

Implementation Process

ABH framework used in-built templates and pre-configured business processes, that helped XYZ deploy the ERP system in 43 working days, including training the users.

XYZ's comprehensive background work in terms of requirement assessment, outlining the needs and objectives, and the kind of solution required further helped speed up the process. With Singh directly involved in day-to-day activities of the implementation, the decision-taking cycle was considerably shortened, as there was no time wasted in accessing the different hierarchies for the decision to be taken.

A Successful Implementation

Besides 'Speed' some of the other reasons for successful implementation were:

- Short turn-around time for resolving issues as regular meetings involving top management of XYZ were held to sort out contentious issues.
- Effective project management and coordination ensured completion of mapping and master data for remote sites.
- Some of the activities were done in parallel like data collection, which began at the initial phase with the involvement of second line users.
- Proper documentation of processes was done for effective knowledge transfer.
- Non-standard practices and procedures were streamlined and changed using ERP procedures, process engineering (PR) and process re-engineering (BPR), and change management techniques.
- Very effective and logical system-testing gave sufficient confidence to the company to completely switch over to ERP rather than following the normal practice of using the legacy system simultaneously. This helped prevent duplication of data entries.

Modules of Solutions

The company implemented the Manufacturing, Finance, and the Distribution modules of ERP.

The Manufacturing module provides functionalities like Master Production Scheduler (MPS), Material Requirement Planning (MRP), Production Planning (PP) and Control, and Capacity Requirements (CCR).

Under the Finance module, the solution delivers functionalities like General Ledger, Accounts Payable and Receivables, Costing, Fixed Assets, and Taxation.

The distribution module includes Purchase Control, Inventory and Sales and Marketing functions.

How ERP Helped

The ERP implementation eliminated the information islands that were scattered across XYZ's business units and replaced disparate systems with a single one.

One of the most prominent benefits of deploying ERP at XYZ has been effective inventory control. The company is now able to maintain the right inventory levels for all its product lines so as to avoid both over and under availability of stock.

Inventory visibility across the various units has also helped make better-informed decisions and commitments to end customers.

Another key realization with ERP has been the inculcation of a disciplined approach leading to more effective and efficient way of working. The company is now able to meet its delivery deadlines well on time in order to be able to take the lead over its competitors. Moreover the Company will manage and Mis system much more effective in the future.

CONCLUSION

Targets of SME companies are focused on strong and robust tools and models for real time planning, decision making, faster and accurate customer response. The bottleneck that they are face to face is to take under control their supply chain flow and measure the system based on the key factors.

In the context of in this study in order to compare the results the metrics are The following list of benefits is preliminary and should be evaluated as such:

- Trust amongst the supply chain partners was increased through information exchange.
- The success of the supply chain co-operation could be continuously monitored.
- The result of actions initiated by the partnership could be evaluated.
- The ERP system provided a focus on critical performance measures.
- By using inter-enterprise performance measures potentials for improvement in the supply chain could be identified and implemented within the ERP system.
- Planning security could be enhanced through better information exchange.
- The ERP system provided an effective framework to discuss joint improvement efforts in a structured way.

The developed reports which retrieve the statistical data in order to trace the performance of process flow in supply chain management are run on the system on daily basis. The strategic goal aimed is "consistently deliver the product, which is manufactured according to the make to stock policy, to the customer on time". In the scope of this study, implied performance measurements are,

- On time delivery performance to requested date (%)
- Fill Rate % by Order
- Order Fulfillment Lead Time in Days

For each of the two period (before ERP and ERP), it is taken the 200 sales order in order to evaluate the delivery performance metrics.

According to the statistical history the critical performance indicators are measured.

11% reduction with ERP practice is handled in terms of on time delivery performance to requested date.

6% reduction with ERP practice is handled in terms of fill rate % by order (for MTS only)

Figure 1. On time delivery performance

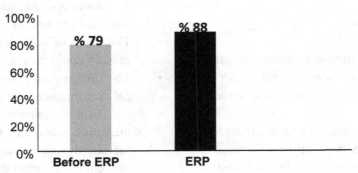

Figure 2. Fill Rate % by Order (MTS only)

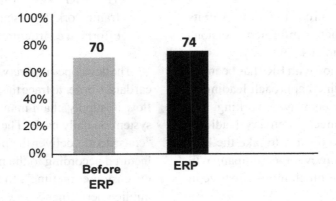

Figure 3. Order Fulfillment Lead Time in Days (MTS only)

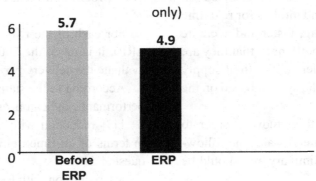

14% reduction with ERP practice is handled in terms of order fulfillment lead time in days (for MTS only)

Performance measurement provides an approach to identifying the success and potential of management strategies, and facilitating the understanding of the situation. It assists in directing management attention, revising company goals, and business reengineering processes. Henceforth, accurate performance measurement is helpful in the improvement of supply chain management.

As the system stabilizes and once the required data is generated, the company hopes to start utilizing the system for generating intelligent analysis reports like understanding demand patterns in the market, and specific patterns of demands from its OEM partners. Moreover Software industries and information industries should have to focus on SME information technology market, to develop new SME specific vertical solutions.

REFERENCES

Aladwani, A. M. (2001)... *Business Process Management Journal*, *7*(3), 266–275. doi:10.1108/14637150110392764

Buonanno, G., Faverio, P., Pigni, F., Ravarini, A., Sciuto, D., & Tagliavini, M. (2005)... *Journal of Enterprise Information Management*, *18*(4), 384–426. doi:10.1108/17410390510609572

Deep, A., Guttridge, P., Dani, S., & Burns, N. (2007). Investigating factors affecting ERP selection in made-to-order SME sector. *Journal of Manufacturing Technology Management*, *19*(4), 430–446. doi:10.1108/17410380810869905

Gargeya, V. B., & Brady, C. (2005)... *Business Process Management Journal*, *11*(5), 501–516. doi:10.1108/14637150510619858

Huin, S. F. (2004)... *International Journal of Project Management*, *22*(6), 511–517. doi:10.1016/j.ijproman.2003.12.005

Kemp, M. J., & Low, G. C. (2008)... *Business Process Management Journal*, *14*(2), 228–242. doi:10.1108/14637150810864952

Muscatello, J. R., Small, M. H., & Chen, I. J. (2003)... *International Journal of Operations & Production Management*, *23*(8), 850–871. doi:10.1108/01443570310486329

Nach, H., & Lejeune, A. (2008). Implementing ERP in SMEs: Towards an ontology supporting managerial decisions. *2008 International MCETECH Conference on e-Technologies (mcetech 2008)* (pp. 223-226).

Nzaou, P. P., Raymond, L., & Fabi, B. (2008)... *Business Process Management Journal*, *14*(4), 530–550. doi:10.1108/14637150810888064

Olsen, K. A., & Sætre, P. (2007). [f]. *Business Process Management Journal*, *13*(3), 379–389. doi:10.1108/14637150710752290

Compilation of References

Abdinnour-Helm S., Lengnick-Hall, M.L., & Lengnick-Hall, C.A. (2003). Pre-implementation attitudes and organizational readiness for implementing an Enterprise Resource Planning system. *European Journal of Operational Research, 146*(2), 258-273.

Aberdeen Group. (2006). *ERP in the mid-market*. Boston: Aberdeen Group, Inc.

Acimovic-Raspopovic, V., & Stojanovic, M. (2008). Pricing quality of service in DiffServ IP networks. In G. Putnik & M. Cuncha (Eds.), *Encyclopedia of Networked and Virtual Organizations*, Vol. II (pp. 1245-1251). Hershey, PA: Information Science Reference.

Adams, C. A., & Frost, G. R. (2008). Integrating sustainability reporting into management practices. Accounting Forum.

Adler, P. S., Mandelbaum, A., Nguyen, V., & Schwerer, E. (1995). From project to process management: An empirically-based framework for analyzing product development time. *Management Science, 41*(3), 458–484. doi:10.1287/mnsc.41.3.458

Adler, P. S., Mandelbaum, A., Nguyen, V., & Schwerer, E. (1996). Getting the most out of your product development process. *Harvard Business Review*, (March-April): 134–152.

Aduri, R., Lin, W., & Ma, Y. (2003). *The price tag of Enterprise Resource Planning (ERP) system implementation failure: version 2.0*. Retrieved September 29, 2003, from http://erp.ittoolbox.com/documents/document.asp?i=2374.

Advanced Knowledge Technologies. (2008). *3 store – Scalable storage solutions for next generation knowledge services*. Retrieved October 15, 2008, from http://www.aktors.org/technologies/3store

Afshar, M., et al. (2004). *Process-centric realization of SOA*. Retrieved October 15, 2008, from http://soa.sys-con.com/node/46870.

Aggarwal, R. (2004). Making BPM work. DM Review, *14*(9), Retrieved October 1, 2008 from http://www.dmreview.com/issues/20040901/1009167-1.html

Ahmad, M. M., & Dhafr, N. (2002). Establishing and improving manufacturing performance measures. *Robotics and Computer-integrated Manufacturing, 18*, 171–176. doi:10.1016/S0736-5845(02)00007-8

Ahmed, T., Asgari, A., Mehaoua, A., Borcoci, E., Berti-Équille, L., & Georgios, K. (2007). End-to-end quality of service provisioning through an integrated management system for multimedia content delivery. *Computer Communications, 30*(3), 638–651. doi:10.1016/j.comcom.2006.10.009

Akkermans, H., & Van Helden, K. (2002). Vicious and virtuous cycles in ERP implementation: a case study of interrelations between critical success factors. *European Journal of Information Systems, 11*(1), 35–46. doi:10.1057/palgrave/ejis/3000418

Aladwani, A. M. (2001). Change management strategies for successful ERP implementation. *Business Process Management Journal, 7*(3), 266–275. doi:10.1108/14637150110392764

Alison, C. (2002, Dec). Works management. *HortonKirby, 55*(12), 30–33.

Allen, E. (1999). *ERP vs. SCM- What's the difference*. Retrieved March 27, 2006, from http://supplychain.ittoolbox.com/documents/academic-articles/erp-vs-scm-whats-the-difference-226#

Al-Mashari, M. (2002). ERP Systems: A research agenda. *Industrial Management & Data Systems*, 165–170. doi:10.1108/02635570210421354

Al-Mashari, M., & Zairi, M. (2000). Information and business process equality: The case of SAP R/3 implementation. *Electronic Journal on Information Systems in Developing Countries, 2.*

Al-Mashari, M., Al-Mudimigh, A., & Zairi, M. (2003). Enterprise resource planning: taxonomy of critical factors. *European journal of operational research, 146*(2), 352-364.

Al-Mudimigh, A., Zairi, M., & Al-Mashari, M. (2001). ERP software implementation: an integrative framework. *European Journal of Information Systems, 10*(4), 216-226

Al-Sehali, S. (2000). *The factors that affect the implementation of enterprise resource planning (ERP) in the international Arab gulf states and United states organizations with special emphasis on SAP software.* Doctoral dissertation, University of Northern Iowa. Retrieved August 10, 2003 from Proquest.

Amami, M., & Beghini, G. (2000). Project management and communication of product development through electronic document management. *Project Management Journal, 31*(2), 6–19.

Amami, M., Beghini, G., & La Manna, M. (1993). Use of project management information system for planning information systems development projects. *International Journal of Project Management, 11*(1), 21–28. doi:10.1016/0263-7863(93)90006-9

Amaravadi Ch, S. (2003). The world and business computing in 2051. *The Journal of Strategic Information Systems, 12,* 373–386. doi:10.1016/j.jsis.2001.11.012

Amoako-Gyampah, K. (2007). Perceived usefulness, user involvement and behavioural intention: an empirical study of ERP implementation. *Computers in Human Behavior, 23,* 1232–1248. doi:10.1016/j.chb.2004.12.002

AMR Research PLM Team. (2004). *The product lifecycle management applications report 2003-2008.* AMR Research Inc.

Anavi-Isakow, S., & Golany, B. (2003). Managing multiproject environments through constant work-in-process. *International Journal of Project Management, 21,* 9–18. doi:10.1016/S0263-7863(01)00058-8

Andrews, T., Curbera, F., Dholakia, H., Goland, Y., Klein, J., Leymann, F., et al. (2003). *Specification: Business process execution language for web services version 1.1.* Retrieved January 2005 from http://www-106.ibm.com/developerworks/library/ws-bpel

Ang, J. S. K., Sum, C. C., & Yeo, L. N. (2002). A multiple-case design methodology for studying MRP success and CSFs. *Information & Management, 39*(4), 271–281. doi:10.1016/S0378-7206(01)00096-9

Angerhofer, B. J., & Angelides, M. C. (2006). A model and a performance measurement system for collaborative supply chains. *Decision Support Systems, 42,* 283–301. doi:10.1016/j.dss.2004.12.005

Annotea Project Website. (2008). Retrieved October 24, 2008, from http://www.w3.org/2001/ Annotea

Antlová, K. (2007). Strategic use of ICT in small businesses. In M. Munoz (Ed.), *E-activity and leading technologies, 3,* 414-418.

APEC Profile of SMEs. (2003). What is an SME? Definitions and statistical issues. *Journal of Enterprising Culture, 11*(3), 173–183. doi:10.1142/S021849580300010X

Applegate, L. M., Austin, R. D., & McFarlan, W. F. (2007). *corporate information strategy and management, text and cases.* New York: McGraw-Hill/Irwin.

Arbor, A. (2005). *Annual PLM market analysis report: Comprehensive information and analysis of the plm market.* Retrieved December 2006, from http://www.cimdata.com/press/PR05-0809.htm

Archer, N., & Ghasemzadeh, F. (1999 b). An integrated framework for project portfolio selection. *International Journal of Project Management, 17*(4), 207–216. doi:10.1016/S0263-7863(98)00032-5

Argyropoulou, M, Ioannou, G., & Prastacos, G.P. (2007). ERP implementation at SMEs: an initial study of the Greek market. *International Journal of Integrated Supply Management, 3*(4) 406-425.

Argyropoulou, M., Ioannou, G., Koufopoulos, D., & Motwani, J. (2008). Performance drivers of ERP systems in small and medium-sized enterprises. *International Journal of Enterprise Network Management, 2*(3), 333-349.

Argyropoulou, M., Ioannou, G., Soderquist, K.E., & Motwani, J. (2008). Managing ERP system evaluation and selection in SMEs using the 'six-imperatives' methodology. *IJPM, 1*(4), 430-452.

Artto, K. A., & Wikström, K. (2005). What is project business? *International Journal of Project Management, 23*, 343–353. doi:10.1016/j.ijproman.2005.03.005

Awduche, D., Berger, L., Gan, D., Li, T., Srinivasan, V., & Swallow, G. (2001). RSVP-TE: extensions to RSVP for LSP tunnels. *IETF RFC 3209 (Standards Track)*. Retrieved October 31, 2006 from http://www.rfc-editor.org/rfcsearch.html

Baker, F., Iturralde, C., Le Faucheur, F., & Davie, B. (2001). Aggregation of RSVP for IPv4 and IPv6 reservations. *IETF RFC 3175 (Standards Track)*. Retrieved October 31, 2006 from http://www.rfc-editor.org/rfcsearch.html

Bancroft, N., Seip, H., & Sprengel, A. (2001). *Implementing SAP R/3* (2nd ed.). Greenwich, Manning Publications Co.

Banuls, V. A., & Salmeron, J. L. (2007). Benchmarking the information society in the long range. *Futures, 39*(1), 83–95. doi:10.1016/j.futures.2006.03.006

Barabási, A. L. (2002). *The new science of networks*. Cambridge, MA: Perseus Pub.

Barad, M., & Gien, D. (2001). Linking improvement models to manufacturing strategies – A methodology for SMEs and other enterprises. *International Journal of Production Research, 39*(12), 2675–2695. doi:10.1080/002075400110051824

Barley, S. (1990). The alignment of technology and structure through roles and networks. *Admistrative Science Quaterly,* (35), 61-103.

Bartholomew, D. (1999). Lean vs. ERP. *Industry Week, 248*, 1–6.

Bartholomew, D. (2003). ERP: Learning to be Lean. *Industry Week*. Retrieved July 19, 2008, from http://www.industryweek.com/ReadArticle.aspx?Article ID=2289.

Bauer, C., & Scharl, A. (2000). Quantitative evaluation of Web site content and structure. *Internet Research, 10*(1), 31–43. doi:10.1108/10662240010312138

Beck, K. (1999). *Extreme programming explained: Embrace change*. Boston: Addison Wesley.

Beck, K., Beedle, M., van Bennekum, A., Cockburn, A., Cunningham, W., Fowler, M., et al. (2001). *Agile programming manifesto*. Retrieved from http://www.agilemanifesto.org

Beer, S. (1981). *The Brain of the Firm*. Chichester: Wiley

Beer, S. (1985). *Diagnosing the System for Organizations*. Chichester: Wiley

Bell, M. (2008) *Service-oriented modeling: Service analysis, design, and architecture*. Hoboken, NJ, USA: John Wiley & Sons.

Belton, V., & Stewart, T. J. (2002). *Multiple criteria decision analysis: An integrated approach*. Boston, Dordrecht, London: Kluwer Academic Publishers.

Berg, R. (2006). Empowerment, productivity and profit: The promise of business process management. *Insurance News Net Magazine*. Retrieved September 25, 2008 from http://insurancenewsnet.com/article.asp?=top_news&id=73920

Berners-Lee, T., Hendler, J., & Lassila, O. (2001)... *Scientific American, 284*(5), 34.

Berry, L., & Parasuraman, A. (1991). *Marketing services: Competing through quality*. New York: The Free Press.

Berry, M. (1998). Strategic planning in small and high tech companies. *Long Range Planning, 32*(3), 455-466.

Bhagwat, R., & Sharma, M.K. (2007). Performance measurement of supply chain management: a balanced scorecard approach. *Computers and Industrial Engineering, 53*, 43-62.

Bignall, V., & Fortune, J. (1984). *Understanding system failures*. Manchester: Manchester University Press.

Binnig, H., & Rohrer, H. (1982). Scanning Tunnelling Microscopy. *Helv. Phys. Acta, 55*, 726–731.

Bircher, B. (1976). *Langfristige Unternehmensplanung*. Bern, Stuttgart: Haupt.

Blackwell, P., Shehab, E. M., & Kay, J. M. (2006). An effective decision-support framework for implementing enterprise information systems within SMEs. *International Journal of Production Research, 44*(17), 3533–3552. doi:10.1080/00207540500525270

Blake, S., Black, D., Carlson, M., Davies, E., Wang, Z., & Weiss, W. (1998). An architecture for Differentiated Services. (1998). *IETF RFC 2475 (Proposed standard)*. Retrieved April 26, 2003 from http://www.rfc-editor.org/rfcsearch.html

Blumberg, M. (2008). *Case study: Web 2.0 runs on Email*. Retrieved December 15, 2008, from http://www.returnpath.net/blog/2008/07/case-study-web-20-runs-on-emai.php

Bonvik, A. M., Couch, C. E., & Gershwin, S. B. (1997). A comparison of production-line control mechanisms. *International Journal of Production Research*, *35*(3), 789–804. doi:10.1080/002075497195713

Bostjancic, S., & Stojanovic, M. (2007). SLAM: an object-oriented application for IP Quality of Service negotiation. In B. Milovanovic (Ed.), *Proceedings of the 8th International Conference on Telecommunications in Modern Satellite Cable and Broadcasting Services – TELSIKS 2007, Vol. 1* (pp. 87-90). Serbia: University of Nis, Faculty of Electronic Engineering.

Bostjancic, S., Timcenko, V., & Stojanovic, M. (2008). A common framework for inter-Provider IP Quality of Service specification. In B. Milovanovic (Ed.), *Proceedings of the XLIII International Scientific Conference on Information, Communication and Energy Systems and Technologies - ICEST 2008, Vol. 2* (pp. 429-432). Serbia: University of Nis, Faculty of Electronic Engineering.

Bostorff, P., & Rosenbaum, R. (2003). *Supply chain excellence; A handbook for dramatic improvement using the SCOR model*. New York: AMACOM; American Management Association.

Botta, V., Millet, P. A., & Grabot, B. (2005). A survey on the recent research literature on ERP systems. *Computers in Industry*, *56*(6), 510–522. doi:10.1016/j.compind.2005.02.004

Boubekri, N. (2001). Technology Enablers for supply chain management. *Integrated Manufacturing Systems*, *12*(6), 394–399. doi:10.1108/EUM0000000006104

Bouras, C., & Sevasti, A. (2005). Service level agreements for DiffServ-based services provisioning. *Journal of Network and Computer Applications*, *28*, 285–302. doi:10.1016/j.jnca.2004.07.001

Boursma, K., & Kingma, S. (2005). From means to ends: The transformation of ERP in a manufacturing company. *Strategic Information Systems*, (14), 197-199.

Boutellier, R., Gassmann, O., & Zedtwitz, M. (2008). *Managing global innovation – Uncovering the secrets of future competitiveness*. Berlin, Heidelberg: Springer.

Brackett, S.W., & Isbell, A-M. (1989). PMIS – an integrated approach for the management and distribution of project information. *Project manage journal*, *20*(3), 5-10.

Braden, R., Clark, D., & Shenker, S. (1994). Integrated services in the Internet architecture: an overview. *IETF RFC 1633 (Informational)*. Retrieved April 26, 2003 from http://www.rfc-editor.org/rfcsearch.html

Braden, R., Zhang, L., Berson, S., Herzog, S., & Jamin, S. (1997). Resource reservation Protocol (RSVP) – version 1 functional specification. *IETF RFC 2205 (Standards Track)*. Retrieved April 26, 2003 from http://www.rfc-editor.org/rfcsearch.html

Bradford, M., & Florin, J. (2003). Examining the role of innovation diffusion factors on the implementation success of enterprise resource planning systems. *International journal of accounting information systems*, *4*(3), 205-225.

Bradford, M., Mayfield, T., & Toney, C. (2001) Does ERP fit in a Lean world? *Strategic Finance, May*, 28-34.

Brady, A., & Voss, B. (1995). Small is as small does. *Journal of Business Strategy*, *16(2)*, 44-52.

Bragg, S. (2004) Software solutions taking Lean manufacturing to the next level. Retrieved July 20, 2008, from http://www.oracle.com/lean/arc_leanmfg.pdf

Brechbühl, H. (2004). Best practices for service organisations. *Business Strategy Review*, *14*(1), 68–70. doi:10.1111/j.0955-6419.2004.00302.x

Broadbent, M. Butler, C. and Hansell, A. (1994). A Business and Technology Agenda for Information-Systems Executives, *International Journal of Information Management*, *14*(6), 411-426.

Brown, D., & He, S. (2007). Patterns of ERP adoption and implementation in China and some implications. *Electronic Markets*, *17*(2), 132–141. doi:10.1080/10196780701296287

Brown, J. (2003). *Product lifecycle management proving value at heinz: A PLM case study from the consumer goods industry - Food and beverage* (Tech-Clarity Research Report).

Browning, T. R. (2002). Process integration using the design structure matrix. *Systems Engineering*, *5*(3), 180–193. doi:10.1002/sys.10023

Brun, A., Caridi, M., Salama, K. F., & Ravelli, I. (2006). Value and risk assessment of supply chain management improvement projects. *International Journal of Production Economics, 99*, 186–201. doi:10.1016/j.ijpe.2004.12.016

BRW. (2002, November). *Fast 100 Issue*. Cited by Business Technologies for SMEs, October 2003, Conference at Sydney.

Brynjolfsson, E., & Hitt, L. (1996). Productivity, business profitability and consumer surplus: Three different measures of Information Technology Value. *MIS Quarterly, 20*, 121–142. doi:10.2307/249475

Bueno, S., & Salmeron, J. (2008). TAM-based success modelling in ERP. *Interacting with Computers, 20*, 515–523. doi:10.1016/j.intcom.2008.08.003

Bukh, P. N., & Malmi, T. (2005). Re-examining the cause-and-effect principle of the balanced scorecard. In G.Jonsson & J. Mouritsen (Eds.), *Accounting in Scnadinavia - Northern Lights* (pp. 87-113). Malmo: Liber & Copenhagen Business School Press.

Buonanno, G., Faverio, P., Pigni, F., Ravarini, A., Sciuto, D., & Tagliavini, M. (2005)... *Journal of Enterprise Information Management, 18*(4), 384–426. doi:10.1108/17410390510609572

Burkett, M., O'Marah, K., & Carrillo, L. (2003). *CAD versus ERP versus PDM: How best to Anchor a PLM strategy* (AMR Research Report). Retrieved September 27, 2008, from http://www.ptc.com/WCMS/files/17636en_file1.pdf

Burkett, M., O'Marah, K., & Karofsky, E. (2007). *MatrixOne acquired by Dassault Systemes – PLM consolidation close to an end*. Retrieved September 27, 2008, from http://www.amrresearch.com/content/View.asp?pmillid=19236

Burkett, M., O'Marah, K., & Kemmeter, J. (2002). *Product lifecycle management: What's real now?* (AMR Research Report). AMR Research Inc.

Burlton, R. T. (2001). *Business process management: Profiting from process*. Indianopolis, Indiana: SAMS.

Burns, P., & Dewhurst, J. (1996). *Small Business and Entrepreneurship* (2nd ed.). London: Macmillan Press.

Burton, T. T., & Boeder, S. M. (2003). *The Lean extended enterprise: Moving beyond the four walls to value stream excellence*. Fort Lauderdale, FL: J. Ross Publishing.

Caillaud, E., & Passemard, C. (2001). CIM and virtual enterprises: A case study in a SME. *International Journal of Computer Integrated Manufacturing, 14*(2), 168–174. doi:10.1080/09511920150216288

Calás, M., & Smircich, L. (1992). Rewriting gender into organizational theorizing: Directions from feminist perspectives. In M. Reed & M. Hughes (Eds.), *Rethinking organization: New directions in organizational theory and analysis* (pp. 227–253). London: Sage

Calhoun, P., Johansson, T., Perkins, C., Hiller, T., & McCann, P. (2005). Diameter mobile IPv4 application. *IETF RFC 4004 (Standards Track)*. Retrieved July 25, 2007 from http://www.rfc-editor.org/rfcsearch.html

Calhoun, P., Zorn, G., Spence, D., & Mitton, D. (2005). Diameter network access server application. *IETF RFC 4005 (Standards Track)*. Retrieved August 30, 2007 from http://www.rfc-editor.org/rfcsearch.html

Califf, R. M., Gibbons, R. J., Brindis, R. G., & Smith, S. C. (2002). Integrating Quality into the Cycle of Therapeutic Development. *Journal of the American College of Cardiology, 40*(11), 1895–1901. doi:10.1016/S0735-1097(02)02537-8

Callon, M. (1986). Some elements for a sociology of translation. Domestication of the scallops and the fishermen of St-Brieuc bay. In J. Law (Ed.), *Power, action and belief. A new sociology of knowledge?* (pp. 196-233). London: Routledge and Kegan Paul.

Camarinha-Matos, L. M., & Afsamarnesh, H. (2007). A comprehensive modelling framework for collaborative networked organisations. *Journal of Intelligent Manufacturing, 18*(5), 529–542. doi:10.1007/s10845-007-0063-3

Camarinha-Matos, L. M., & Afsarmanesh, H. (1999). *Tendencies and general requirements for virtual enterprises*. In L. Camarinha-Matos & H. Afsarmanesh (Eds.), *Proceedings of the IFIP TC5 WG5.3 / PRODNET Working Conference on Infrastructures for Virtual Enterprises: Networking Industrial Enterprises* (pp.15-30). Boston, MA: Kluwer Academic Publishers.

Camarinha-Matos, L., & Afsamarnesh, H. (2008). *Collaborative networks: Reference modelling*. New York: Springer.

Cameron, N., & Braiden, P. (2004). Using BPR for development of production efficiency in companies making engineered to order products. *International Journal of Production Economics, 89*, 261-273.

Campbell, S. M., Roland, M. O., & Buetow, S. A. (2000). Defining Quality of Care. *Social Science & Medicine, 51*, 1611–1625. doi:10.1016/S0277-9536(00)00057-5

Čančer, V. (2003). *Analiza odločanja: izbrana poglavja (Decision Analysis: Selected Chapters, in Slovenian)*. Maribor: Faculty of Economics and Business.

Čančer, V. (2006). Selection of the information systems' development in enterprises by multi-criteria decision-making. *Manažment v teórii a praxi [Online ed.]*, Vol. 2, No. 2, 10-18. Consulted in February 2008. Retreived from http://casopisy.euke.sk/mtp/clanky/2-2006/cancer.pdf

Čančer, V., & Mulej, M. (2008). Informal systems thinking in the form of operations research. Managing the unmanageable – 16th Interdisciplinary Information Management Talks, Linz.

Carr, D., & Johansson, H. (1995). *Best Practices in re-engineering*. NY, USA: McGraw Hill.

Carrier, C. (1995, April-June). Intrapreneurship in large firms and SMEs. *International Small Business Journal* (pp. 54-61).

Carugi, M., & De Clercq, J. (2004). Virtual private network services: Scenarios, requirements and architectural constructs from a standardization perspective. *IEEE Communications Magazine, 42*(6), 116–122. doi:10.1109/MCOM.2004.1304246

CASOS. (2008). *Computational models and social network tools*. Retrieved December 12, 2008, from http://www.casos.cs.cmu.edu/computational_tools/tools.html.

Castro, J., Kolp, M., & Mylopoulos, J. (2002). Towards requirements-driven information systems engineering: Rhe Tropos project. *Information Systems, 6*, 365–389. doi:10.1016/S0306-4379(02)00012-1

Cha-Jan Chang, J., & King, W.R. (2005). Measuring the Performance of Information Systems: A Functional Scorecard. *Journal of Management Information Systems, 22*(1), 85-115.

Champy, J., & Hammer, M. (1994). *Business process reengineering*. Barcelona: Parramón.

Chan, K. C. C., & Chung, L. M. L. (2002). Integrating process and project management for multi-site software development. *Analysis of Software Engineering, 14*(1-4), 115–143. doi:10.1023/A:1020553624256

Chand, D., Hachey, G., Hunton J., Owhoso, V., & Vasudevan, S. (2005). A balanced scorecard besed framework for assessing the strategic impacts of ERP systems. *Computers in Industry, 56*, 558-572

Chang, L., & Powell, P. (1998). Toward a framework for Business Process Reengineering in SMEs. *Information Systems Journal, 8*(3), 199-216.

Chappell, D. A. (2004). *Enterprise service bus*. Cambridge, MA: O'Reilly.

Chassot, C., Auriol, G., & Lozes, A. (2003). QoS management protocol for end-to-end communication architecture implemented over a differentiated IPv6 network. In J. Charzinski, R. Lehnert, & P. Tran-Gia (Eds.), *Proceedings of the 18th International Teletraffic Congress*, Vol. 5b (pp. 1251-1260). Berlin, Germany: Elsevier Science.

Chen, I. J. (2001). Planning for ERP systems: analysis and future trends. *Business Process Management Journal, 7*(5), 374–386

Chen, I. J., & Popovich, K. (2003). Understanding customer relationship management. *Business Process Management Journal, 9*(5), 672–688. doi:10.1108/14637150310496758

Cheng, T. C. E., & Podolsky, S. (1993). *Just-in-time manufacturing: An introduction* (2nd ed.). London: Chapman & Hall.

Cheng, Y., Farha, R., Tizghadam, A., Kim, M. S., Hashemi, M., & Leon-Garcia, A. (2005). Virtual network approach to scalable IP service deployment and efficient resource management. *IEEE Communications Magazine, 43*(10), 76–84. doi:10.1109/MCOM.2005.1522128

Cherns, A. (1976). Principles of sociotechnical design. *Human Relations, 29*(8), 783–792. doi:10.1177/001872677602900806

Cherns, A. (1987). Principles of sociotechnical design revisited. *Human Relations, 40*(3), 153–162. doi:10.1177/001872678704000303

Chien, S.-W., Hu, C., Reimers, K., & Lin, J.-S. (2007). The influence of centrifugal and centripetal forces on ERP project success in small and medium-sized enterprises in China and Taiwan. *International Journal of Production Economics, 107*(2), 380–396. doi:10.1016/j.ijpe.2006.10.002

Choi, B., & Lee, H. (2003). An empirical investigation of KM Styles and their effect on corporate performance. *Information & Management, 40*, 403–417. doi:10.1016/S0378-7206(02)00060-5

Chopra, S., & Meindl, P. (2001). *Supply chain management - Strategy, planning and operation*. London: Prentice Hall.

Chrissis, M., Konrad, M., & Shrum, S. (2003). *CMMI: Guidelines for process integration and product improvement*. Boston: Addison-Wesley.

Christopher, M. (2000). The agile supply chain: Competing in volatile markets. *Industrial Marketing Management, 29*(1), 37–44. doi:10.1016/S0019-8501(99)00110-8

Chung, S. H., & Synder, C. A. (1999). *ERP initiation- A historical perspective*. Americas Conference on Information Systems, August 13-15, Milwaukee, WI, 1999

Churchill, N., & Lewis, V. (1983, May/June). The five stages of small business growth. *Harvard Business Review* (pp. 30–50).

CIMdata. (2002). *Product lifecycle management: Empowering the future of business*. Retrieved September 27, 2008 from http://www.ariondata.es/servicios/documentacion/PLM_Definition_0210.pdf

CIMdata. (2003). *PDM to PLM: Growth of an industry*. CIMdata Research Document. Retrieved January 2005, from http://www.cimdata.com/press/PR03-0325.htm

CIMdata. (2004). *PLM and ERP integration: Business efficiency and value* (CIMdata Research Report). Retrieved January 2005, from http://www.cimdata.com/php/download_reports.php

CIMdata. (2007). *Defining Mid-market PDM* (CIMdata Research Report). Retrieved May 2007, from http://www.cimdata.com/publications/PDM_and_MidMarket_Final.pdf

Cimiano, P., et al. (2005). Gimme' the context: context-driven automatic semantic annotation with cpankow. In *WWW '05*, (pp. 332-341). New York: ACM Press.

Clausen, C., & Koch, C. (1999). The role of spaces and occasions in the transformation of information technologies – Lessons from the social shaping of IT systems for manufacturing a Danish context. *Technology Analysis and Strategic Management, 11*(3), 463–481. doi:10.1080/095373299107456

Clegg, C. W. (1984). The derivation of job design. *Journal of Occupational Behaviour, 5*, 131–146. doi:10.1002/job.4030050205

Cobbold, I., & Lawrie, G. (2002). Classification of balanced scorecards based on their intended use. *PMA Conference*. Berkshire, UK: 2GC Ltd.

Cobbold, I., & Lawrie, G. (2002). The development of the balanced scorecard as a strategic management tool. *PMA Conference*. Berkshire, UK: 2GC Ltd.

Cockburn, A. (2005). *Writing Effective Use Cases*. Amsterdam: Addison-Wesley Longman.

Cocrill, A., & Lewis, R. (2002). Going global – Remaining local. *International Journal of Information Management, 22*, 195–209. doi:10.1016/S0268-4012(02)00005-1

Cohen, F. (2003). *Java testing and design: From unit testing to automated web tests*. Prentice Hall Publishing.

COIN. (2008). *Enterprise collaboration & interoperability*. Retrieved December 12, 2008, from http://www.coin-ip.eu.

Collaborative Open Ontology Development Environment CO-ODE project webpage. (2008). Retrieved October 07, 2008, from http://www.jisc.ac.uk/index.cfm?name=project_coode&src=alpha

Colleman, T., & Jamieson, M. (1994). Beyond return of investment. In L. Willocks (Ed.), *Information Management: The Evaluation of Information Systems Investments* (pp 189-205). Chapman & Hall London.

Colmenares, L., & Otieno, J. (2005). Critical Success factors of ERP implementation. In M. Khosrow-Pour (Ed.), *Encyclopedia of Information Science and Technology* (pp. 628-633). Hershey, PA: Idea Group Inc.

Comstock, G., & Sjolseth, D. (1999). Aligning and prioritizing corporate R&D. *Research Technology Management, 42*(3), 19–25.

Connoly, J.M. (2007). Techs turn to Web 2.0. *B to B, 92*(4), 24.

Cooper, D., Grey, S., Raymond, G., & Walker, P. (2004). *project risk management guidelines.* Chichester: John Wiley & Sons Ltd.

Cooper, R. (2001). Winning at new products—Accelerating the process from idea to launch. Massachusetts: Perseus Publishing.

Cooper, R., & Edgett, S. (2003). Overcoming the crunch in resources for new product development. *Research Technology Management, 46*(3), 48–58.

Cooper, R., Edgett, S., & Kleinschmidt, E. (1997). Portfolio management in new product development: lessons from the leaders I. *Research Technology Management, 40*(5), 16–28.

Correa, C. (1994). cited by Aladwani (2001). Change management strategies for successful ERP implementation. *Business Process Management Journal, 7*(3), 266–275.

Covin, J. G., & Slevin, D. P. (1990). Juggling entrepreneurial style and organizational structure. *Sloan Management Review*, 43–53.

Cox, J., & Blackstone, J. (Eds.). (2008). *APICS dictionary* (12th ed.). Chicago, IL: APICS Educational Society for Resource Manage.

Cragg, P. B., & King, M. (1993). Small-firm computing: Motivators and inhibitors. *MIS Quarterly, 17*(1), 47–60. doi:10.2307/249509

Craig, A., & Annear, J. (2003). A framework for the adoption of ICT and security technologies by SMEs. *16th Conference Small Entrerprise Association of Australia,* Ballarat.

Craig, J., & Yetton, P. (1992). Business Process Redesign. *Australian Journal of Management, 17*(2), 285-306.

Craig, J., & Yetton, P. (1997). The Real Event of Re-engineering. In C. Sauer, P. Yetton, & (Eds.), *Steps to the Future.* San Francisco: Jossey-Bass.

CrossWork Website. (2008). *Cross-Organisational Workflow Formation and Enactment.* Retrieved October 14, 2008, from http://www.crosswork.info/.

CTS. (2008). *Manufacturing software reviews.* Retrieved July 20, 2008 from http://www.ctsguides.com/manufacturing.asp

Cunningham, H., Maynard, D., Bontcheva, K., & Tablan, V. (2002). GATE: A framework and graphical development environment for robust NLP tools and applications. In *Proceedings of the 40th Anniversary Meeting of the Association for Computational Linguistics (ACL'02), Philadelphia.*

Cunningham, J.B. (1995). Strategic considerations in using action research for improving personnel practices. *Public Personnel Management, 24*(2), 515-529.

da Silva, P. P. (2002). User Interface Declarative Models and Development Environments: A Survey. In Palanque & Patern`o (Eds.), *DSV-IS, volume 1946 of Lecture Notes in Computer Science* (pp. 207–226). London: Springer.

Daft, R. L., & Lengel, R. H. (1984). Information richness: A new approach to managerial behavior and organization design. In B. M. Staw & L. L. Cummings (Eds.), *Research in Organizational Behavior* (Vol. 6, pp. 191-233). Greenwich, CT: JAI Press.

Daniel, D. (2007). Seven Ways CIOs can introduce Web 2.0 technologies into the enterprise. CIO Business Technology Leadership. Available at: http://www.cio.com.au/index.php/id;1146975385 (Last accessed: September 2008)

Daniel, R. D. (1961). Management information crisis. *Harvard Business Review, 39*(Sept-Oct).

Davenport, T. H. (1993). Need radical Innovation and continuous improvement? Integrate process reengineering and TQM. *Strategy and Leadership, 21*(3), 6–12. doi:10.1108/eb054413

Davenport, T. H. (1996). *Innovation of processes. Redesign of work by using information technologies.* Madrid: Diaz de Santos.

Davenport, T. H. (1998). Putting the enterprise into the enterprise system. *Harvard Business Review,* (July-August): 121–131.

Davenport, T. H. (2000). *Mission critical- Realizing the promise of enterprise systems.* Boston, MA: Harvard Business School Press.

Davenport, T. H., & Short, J. E. (1990). The new industrial engineering: Information technology and business process redesign. *Sloan Management Review*, 11–27.

Davenport, T., Harris, J., & Cantrell, S. (2003). *The return of enterprise solutions: The director's cut*: Accenture Institute for Strategic Change.

Davenport, T.H., & Short, J.E. (1990). The new industrial engineering. *Sloan Management Review, 31,* 4-16.

Davis, F. F. (1989). Perceived usefulness, perceived ease of use and user acceptance of information technology . *MIS Quarterly, 13*(3), 319–340. doi:10.2307/249008

De Pablos Heredero, C. (2001). Management of information systems in the firm. Madrid: ESIC.

Deep, A., Dani, S., & Burns, N. (2008). Investigating factors affecting ERP selection in made-to-order SME sector. *Journal of Manufacturing Technology Management, 19*(4), 430–446. doi:10.1108/17410380810869905

Deep, A., Guttridge, P., Dani, S., & Burns, N. (2007). Investigating factors affecting ERP selection in made-to-order SME sector. *Journal of Manufacturing Technology Management, 19*(4), 430–446. doi:10.1108/17410380810869905

Deepak, V. (2007). *Simplifying BPM implementations: Business process management.* Executive Insights Gordian Transformation Partners Inc. Retrieved October 1, 2008 from http://www.bptrends.com/resources_publications

DeLone, W.H., & McLean, E.R. (1992). Information systems success: The quest for the dependent variable. *Information Systems Research, 3*(1), 60-95.

DeLone, W.H., & McLean, E.R. (2003). The DeLone and McLean model of information systems success: a ten-year update. *Journal of Management Information Systems, 19*(4), 9–30.

Denny, M. (2002). *Ontology building: A survey of editing tools.* Retrieved October 07, 2008, from http://www.xml.com/2002/11/06/Ontology_Editor_Survey.html

Dietrich, P., & Lehtonen, P. (2005). Successful management of strategic intentions through multiple projects – Reflections from empirical study. *International Journal of Project Management, 23*(5), 386–391. doi:10.1016/j.ijproman.2005.03.002

Dillard, J. F., Richala, L., & Yuthas, K. (2005). Enterprise resource planning systems: A physical manifestation of administrative evil. *International Journal of Accounting Information Systems, 6*(2), 107–127. doi:10.1016/j.accinf.2005.02.001

Dilts, J., & Kahai, P. S. (2004). Taking a small business online: A systematic approach . *Journal of Business & Entrepreneurship, 16*(1), 29–45.

Dixon, W. J., & Massey, F. J. (1983). *Introduction to statistical analysis.* (3rd ed.) New York: McGraw-Hill Book Company.

Dolan, P. (2001). Output measures and valuation in health. In M.F.Drummond & A. McGuire (Eds.), *Economic evaluation in health care* (pp. 46-67). Oxford: Oxford University Press.

Dooley, L. (2000). *Systems innovation management.* PhD thesis, Galway, National University of Ireland.

Dou, D. (2005). Ontology translation on the semantic Web. *Journal on Data Semantics II (. LNCS, 3360,* 35–57.

Drew, S. (2002). E-business research practice, towards an agenda. *Electronic Journal of Business Research Methods.*

Drummond, M. F., O'Brien, B., Stoddart, G. L., & Torrance, G. W. (1997). *Methods for the economic evaluation of health care programmes* (2nd ed.). Oxford: Oxford University Press.

DSL Forum. (2007). Broadband multi-service architecture & framework requirements. *Technical Report TR-144.* Retrieved September 19, 2008 from http://www.broadband-forum.org/technical/trlist.php

Duarte, D., & Snyder, N. (2001). *Mastering virtual teams: Strategies, tools, and techniques that succeed.* San Francisco: Jossey-Bass.

Dugdale, A. (1999). Materiality: Juggling, sameness and difference. In J. Law & J. Hassard (Eds.), *Actor-network theory and after* (pp. 113-135). Oxford: Blackwell.

Duin, H. (1995). Object-oriented scenario management for simulation models. In *Proceedings of IMACS European Simulation Meeting, 28-30 August 1995, Gyor, Hungary* (pp. 38-44).

Duin, H. (2007). Causal cross-impact analysis as a gaming tool for strategic decision making. In K.-D. Thoben, J. Baalsrud Hauge, R. Smeds, & J.O. Riis (Eds.), *Multidisciplinary research on new methods for learning and innovation in enterprise networks* (pp. 79-93). Aachen: Verlag Mainz.

Duin, H. (2007). Causal cross-impact analysis as strategic planning aid for virtual organisation breeding environments. In L.M. Camarinha-Matos, H. Afsarmanesh, P. Novais, & C. Abalide (Eds.), *Establishing the founda-*

tion *of collaborative networks* (pp. 147-154). New York: Springer.

Duin, H., Schnatmeyer, M., Schumacher, J., Thoben, K.-D., & Zhao, X. (2005). Cross-impact analysis of RFID scenarios for logistics. In R. Lasch, & C.G. Janker (Eds.), *Logistik Management 2005* (pp. 363-376). Wiesbaden: Deutscher Universitätsverlag (DUV), Gabler Edition Wissenschaft.

Duperrin, J. C., & Godet, M. (1975). SMIC74 - A method for constructing and ranking scenarios. *Futures*, *7*(4), 302–312. doi:10.1016/0016-3287(75)90048-8

Durakbasa, N. M., & Osanna, P. H. (2002). The role of co-ordinate metrology in the hierarchical structure of metrology and the system for measurement instruments confirmation. In *Proceedings of the 5th International Scientific Conference: Coordinate Measuring Machines, Bielsko-Biala, PL*(pp. 55-62).

Duxbury, L., Decady, Y., & Tse, A. (2002). Adoption and use of computer technology in Canadian small businesses: A comparative study. In *Managing Information Technology in Small Business: Challenges & Solutions* (pp. 22-23). Hershey, PA: Information Science Publishing.

Dwyer, R. (1987). Developing buyer-seller relationships. *Journal of Marketing*, *5*(2).

Dyché, J. (2002). *The CRM handbook: A business guide to customer relationship management*. Boston: Addison Wesley Professional.

Dye, J. (2007). Collaboration 2.0: Make the web your workspace. *EContent*, *30*(1), 32.

Dzbor, M., & Motta, E. (2008). *Semantic Web technology to support learning about the semantic Web*. Knowledge Media Institute, The Open University. Milton Keynes, UK: IOS press.

E-Business Indicators. (2007). *A pocket- book.*

ebXML Website. (2008). Retrieved October 15, 2008, from http://www.ebxml.org/geninfo.htm

Eckerson, W., & Watson, H. (2000). *Harnessing customer information for strategic advantage; Technical challenges and business solutions*. Chatsworth: The Data Warehousing Institute.

Economides, A., & Terzis, V. (2008). Evaluating tax sites: an evaluation framework and its application. *Electronic Government* . *International Journal (Toronto, Ont.)*, *5*(3), 321–362.

Eden, C., & Huxham, C. (1996). Action research for management research. *British Journal of Management*, *71*(1), 75-86.

Edgar, Th. F. (2004). Control and operations: When does controllability equal profitability? *Computers & Chemical Engineering*, *29*, 41–49. doi:10.1016/j.compchemeng.2004.07.013

Edward, W. N., Bernroider, N., & Tang, K. H. (2003). A preliminary empirical study of the diffusion of ERP systems in Austrian and British SMEs. *Working Papers on Information Processing and Information Management*.

Ein-Dor, Ph. (2003). The world and business computing in 2051: from LEO to RUR? *The Journal of Strategic Information Systems*, *12*, 357–371. doi:10.1016/j.jsis.2001.11.011

Eisenhardt, K. (1989). Building theories from case research. *Academy of Management Review*, *14*, 532-550.

Elliott, L. (2006). *PLM - Does one size fit all?* Retrieved September 27, 2008, from http://www.deskeng.com/articles/aaabzm.htm

Ellmann, S. (2007). *Management komplexer internationaler Projekte: Netzstrukturen, Governance und Handlungsempfehlungen*. Dissertation at the Universiy of Bremen.

Elonen, S., & Artto, K. A. (2003). Problems in managing internal development projects in multi-project environments. *International Journal of Project Management*, *21*(6), 395–402. doi:10.1016/S0263-7863(02)00097-2

Emirbayer, M., & Mische, A. (1998). What is agency? *American Journal of Sociology*, *103*, 962–1023. doi:10.1086/231294

Engel, T., Granzer, H., Koch, B. F., Winter, M., Sampatakos, P., & Venieris, I. S. (2003). AQUILA: Adaptive resource control for QoS using an IP-based layered architecture. *IEEE Communications Magazine*, *41*(10), 46–53. doi:10.1109/MCOM.2003.1166653

Engwall, M. (2001). *Multi-project management: Effects, issues and propositions for future Research* (Fenix Working Paper Series). Stockholm: Stockholm School of Economics.

Engwall, M., & Jerbrant, A. (2003). The resource allocation syndrome: the prime challenge of multi-project management. *International Journal of Project Management, 21*(6), 403–409. doi:10.1016/S0263-7863(02)00113-8

Enterprise Resource Planning Portal. (2008). Retrieved October 14, 2008, from http://www.erpgenie.com/mysap/bus_connector.htm.

Eriksson, H. E., & Penkar, M. (2000). *Business Modeling with UML: Business patterns at work.* New York: John Wiley & Sons.

Erl, T. (2004) *SOA – principles of service design.* Upper Saddle River, NJ: Prentice-Hall.

Erl, T. (2008) *Service-oriented architecture – A field guide to integrating XML and Web services.* Upper Saddle River, NJ, USA: Prentice-Hall.

Eschenbächer, J. (2008). *Gestaltung von Innovationsprozessen in Virtuellen Organisation durch kooperationsbasierte Netzwerkanalyse.* Dissertation at the Universiy of Bremen.

Eschenbächer, J., Graser, F., Thoben, K.-D., & Tiefensee, B. (2007). Management of dynamic virtual organisations: Conclusions from a collaborative engineering case. In M. Taisch, K.-D. Thoben, & M. Montorio (Eds.), *Advanced manufacturing: An ICT and systems perspective* (pp. 275-284). London: Taylor & Francis.

Eskerod, P. (1996). Meaning and action in a multi-project environment. Understanding a multiproject environment by means of metaphors and basic assumptions. *International Journal of Project Management, 14*(2), 61–65. doi:10.1016/0263-7863(95)00038-0

Espejo, R., Schuhmann, W., Schwaninger, M., & Bilello, U. (1996). *Organisational Transformation and Learning.* Chichester: Wiley

Estaves, J., Pastor, J.A., & Casanovas, J. (2002). *Using the Partial Least Squares (PLS) method to establish CSF interdependence in ERP implementation projects.* Retrieved Augst 10, 2003, from http://erp.ittoolbox.com/documents/document.asp?i=2321.

Esteves, J., & Pastor, J. (2001). Analysis of critical success factors relevance along SAP implementation phases. In *Proceedings of the Seventh Americas Conference on Information Systems* (pp. 1019-1025).

European Commission. (2006). *Table Report e-Business Survey, Version 2.1.* Retrieved May 20, 2008, from http://www.eBusiness-watch.org

European Commission. (2006/2007). *Enterprise directorate-generals, The European e-Business Report 2006/07 edition.* Retrieved June 26, 2008, from http://www.eBusiness-watch.org.

European Commission. Enterprise and Industry Directorate General, e-Business W@tch (2006). *Food and Beverages (F&B) Sector Study, Sector Report No. 1/2006.* Retrieved July 20, 2008 from http://www.ebusiness-watch.org/studies/sectors/food/food.htm

European Commission. Enterprise and Industry Directorate General, e-Business W@tch (2008). *E-Business in Europe – 2008, Industry perspectives on e-business developments and ICT impact.* Retrieved July 20, 2008 http://www.ebusiness-watch.org/key_reports/documents/BRO08.pdf

European Commission. Enterprise and Industry publications (2005).The New SME definition user guide and model declaration. Retrieved from http://europa.eu.int/comm/enterprise/enterprise_policy/sme_definition/index_en.ht

Everdingen, Y. V., Hillegersberg, J. V., & Waarts, E. (2000). ERP adoption by European mid-size companies. *Communications of the ACM, 43*(4), 27–31. doi:10.1145/332051.332064

FaCT++ Website. (2008). Retrieved October 15, 2008, from http://owl.man.ac.uk/factplusplus/.

Falkowski, G., Pedigo, P., Smith, B., & Swamson, D. (1998). A recipe for ERP success. Beyond Computing. *International Journal of Human-Computer Interaction, 16*(1), 5–22.

Featherstone, M., & Borstorff, P. (2005). O, What a Tangled Web we weave when first we practice to perceive, An exploratory study of the conduct of business on the World Wide Web. *E-Business Review, 5*(1), 54–57.

Ferguson, R.B. (2004). *ERP* targets the midmarket. *eWeek, 21*(6), 41.

Ferrell, J. (1996). Help for the other SMEs, *Manufacturing Engineering, 117*(2), 20.

Fickel, L. (1999). Know your customer. *CIO Magazine, 12*(21), 62–72.

Finney, S., & Corbett, M. (2007). ERP implementation: a compilation and analysis of critical success factors. *Business Process Management Journal, 13*(3), 329–347. doi:10.1108/14637150710752272

Fiscehr, M. A., Waugh, L. M., & Axworthy, A. (1998). IT support of single project, multi-project and industry-wide integration. *Computers in Industry, 35*, 31–45. doi:10.1016/S0166-3615(97)00082-1

Fisher, D., Brush, A. J., Gleave, E., & Smith, M. A. (2006). Revisiting Whittaker & Sidner's "email overload" ten years later. In *CSCW2006*. New York: ACM Press.

Fisher, K., & Fisher, M. (2000). *The distance manager: a hands-on guide to managing off-site employees and virtual teams*. New York: McGraw-Hill.

Flegkas, P., Trimintzios, P., & Pavlou, G. (2002). A policy-based quality of service management system for IP DiffServ networks. *IEEE Network, 16*(2), 50–56. doi:10.1109/65.993223

Fontanella, J., & Klein, E. (2008). Supply chain technology spending outlook. Supply chain management review. Retrieved September 10, 2008 from http://www.scmr.com/article/CA6549303.html?industryid=48316

Forrester, J. W. (1961). *Industrial dynamics*. Cambridge, MA: MIT Press.

Forrester, J. W. (1971). *Principles of systems*. Cambridge, MA: MIT Press.

Forrester, J. W. (1980). System dynamics - future opportunities. In A. A. Legasto, J. W. Forrester & J. M. Lyneis (Eds.), *TIMS Studies in the management sciences* (Vol. 14, pp. 7-21). Oxford: North-Holland.

Forster, N. S., & Rockart, J. F. (1989). *Critical success factors: An annotated bibliography* (Rep. No. CISR WP No. 191, Sloan WP No. 3041-89). Cambridge, MA: Sloan School of Management, MIT.

Franken, H. M., de Weger, M. K., & Jonkers, H. (1997). Structural and quantitative perspectives on business process modelling and analysis. In *Proceedings of the 11th European Simulation Multiconference, Istanbul, June 1-4, 1997* (pp. 595-599). Ghent, Belgium: Society for Computer Simulation International.

Fricke, S. E., & Shenbar, A. J. (2000). Managing multiple engineering projects in a manufacturing support environment. *IIE Transactions on Engineering Management, 47*(2), 258–268. doi:10.1109/17.846792

Fu, S., & Raja, J. (2000). Internet based roundness and cylindricity analysis. In M.N. Durakbasa, P.H. Osanna, & A. Afjehi-Sadat (Eds.), *IMEKO 2000 Proceedings, Vol. VIII* (pp. 83-88).

Fu, X., Schulzrinne, H., Bader, A., Hogrefe, D., Kappler, C., & Karagiannis, G. (2005). NSIS: a new extensible IP signaling protocol suite. *IEEE Communications Magazine, 43*(10), 133–141. doi:10.1109/MCOM.2005.1522137

Fui-Hoon, F., Zuckweiler, K. M., & Lee-Shang, J. (2003). ERP implementation: Chief Information Officers' perceptions on critical success factors. *International Journal of Human-Computer Interaction, 16*(1), 5–22. doi:10.1207/S15327590IJHC1601_2

Fuller, T. (2003). If you wanted to know the future of small business what questions would you ask? *Futures, 35*, 305–321. doi:10.1016/S0016-3287(02)00083-6

Fuller, T. (2003). Small bisness futures in society (Introduction). *Futures, 35*, 297–304. doi:10.1016/S0016-3287(02)00082-4

Fuller, T., & Fewster, R. (2006). *The emergence of Tesco.com: A study of Corporate Entrepreneurship*. Paper presented at the Babson-Kauffman Entrepreneurship Research Conferemce, Kelley Business School, Indiana

Fuller, T., & Lewis, F. (2003). Relationships mean everything. *British Journal of Management, 13*, 317-336.

Fuller, T., Moran, P., & Argyle, P. (2004). Entrepreneurial foresight; a case in reflexivity, experiments, sensitivity and reorganisation. In H. Tsoukas & J. Shepherd (Eds.), *Managing the Future: Foresight in the Knowledge Economy* (pp. 171-8). Oxford:Blackwell

Fuller, T., Warren, L., & Argyle, P. (2007). Sustaining Entrepreneurial Business; a complexity perspective on processes that produce emergent practice. *International Entrepreneurship and Management Journal, 4*(1), 1-17.

Fuller, T., Warren, L., & Welter, F. (2007, November). *Towards an emergence perspective on entrepreneurship*. Paper presented at RENT XXI, Research in Entrepreneurship and Small Business, Cardiff (pp. 22-23).

Gable, G., & Stewart, G. (1999). SAP R/3 implementation issues for small to medium enterprises. In W.D. Haseman & D.L. Nazareth (Eds.), *Proceedings of the*

5th Americas Conference on Information Systems (pp. 779-781), Milwaukee, WI.

García Bravo, D. (2000). *Sistemas de información en la empresa. Conceptos y aplicaciones*, Madrid: Pirámide.

Gargeya, V. B., & Brady, C. (2005)... *Business Process Management Journal*, *11*(5), 501–516. doi:10.1108/14637150510619858

Gargeya, V.B., & Brady, C. (2005). Success and failure factors of adopting SAP in ERP system implementation. *Business Process Management Journal*, *11*(5), 501-516.

Garvin, D. A. (1993). Building a learning organization. *Harvard Business Review*, (July-August): 78–91.

Garvin, D.A. (1998). The processes of organization and management. *Sloan Management Review*, summer, 81-98.

Garwood, D. (2002). ERP or flow manufacturing? Collaboration, not separation. *R.D. Garwood, Inc.* Retrieved July 22, 2008 from http://www.rdgarwood.com/archive/hot56.asp.

Gassmann, O., & Sutter, P. (2008). *Praxiswissen Innovationsmanagement – Von der Idee zum Markterfolg*. München: Hanser Verlag.

Gattiker, T.F., & CFPIM. (2002). Anatomy of an ERP implementation gone awry. *Production and Inventory Management Journal*, *43*, 96-105.

Gausemeier, J., Fink, A., & Schlake, O. (1998). Scenario management: An approach to develop future potentials. *Technological Forecasting and Social Change*, *59*(2), 111–130. doi:10.1016/S0040-1625(97)00166-2

Gefen, D., & Ragowsky, A. (2005). A multi-level approach to measuring the benefits of an ERP system in manufacturing firms. *Information Systems Management Journal*, *22*(1), 18–25. doi:10.1201/1078/44912.22.1.20051201/85735.3

Gemino, A., Mackay, N., & Reich, B. H. (2006). Executive decision about ICT adoption in SME. *Journal of Information Technology Management*, *17*(1).

Geraldi, J. G. (2008). The balance between order and chaos in multi-project firms: A conceptual model. *International Journal of Project Management*, *26*, 348–356. doi:10.1016/j.ijproman.2007.08.013

Gerritsen, B. H. M. (2008). Advances in Mass customization and adaptive manufacturing. In I. Horvath & Z. Rusak (Eds.), *TMCE 2008* (pp. 869-880). Delft, Netherlands: Delft University.

Gerst, M., & Bunduchi, R. (2007). The analysis of standardised technology in the automotive industry. In P. Cunningham & M. Cunningham (Eds.), *Exploiting the knowledge economy: Issues, applications and case studies*. Amsterdam: ISO Press.

Ghobadian, A., & Oregan, N. (2006). The impact of ownership on small firm behavior performance. *International Small Business Journal*, *24*(6), 555–586. doi:10.1177/0266242606069267

Gibb, A. A., & Scott, M. G. (1985). Strategic Awareness, Personal Commitment and the Process of Planning in the Small Business. *Journal of Management Studies*, *22*(6), 597-625

Giddens, A. (1984). *The constitution of society: Outline of the theory of structuration*. Berkeley: University of California Press.

Gilmore, D. (2008). Supply chain software: AMR research remains bullish on supply chain software spend. SCDigest Editorial Staff. Retrieved August 16, 2008, from http://www.scdigest.com/assets/On_Target/08-05-19-2.php?cid=1688

Global Shop Solutions. (2008). Global solutions products. Retrieved August 30, 2008 from http://www.globalshopsolutions.com/erp-software/default.asp.

Gordon, T., & Hayward, H. (1968). initial experiments with the cross impact matrix method of forecasting. *Futures*, *1*(2), 100–116. doi:10.1016/S0016-3287(68)80003-5

Götze, K. (1993). *Szenario-Technik in der strategischen Unternehmensplanung*. Wiesbaden: Deutscher Universitäts-Verlag.

Gouscos, D., Kalikakis, M., Legal, M., & Papadopoulou, S. (2007). A general model of performance and quality for one-stop e-Government service offerings. *Government Information Quarterly*, *24*, 860–885. doi:10.1016/j.giq.2006.07.016

Graves, S., Ringuest, J., & Case, R. (2000). Formulating optimal R&D portfolios. *Research Technology Management*, *43*(3), 47–51.

Gray, C. F., & Larson, E. W. (2003). *Project management: The managerial process.* Irwin: McGraw-Hill.

Greasley, A. (2006). Using process mapping and business process simulation to support a process-based approach to change in a public sector organization. *Technovation, 26*(1), 95–103. doi:10.1016/j.technovation.2004.07.008

Greene, A. (2004). Toyota production systems: Lean goes mainstream. *Managing Automation* (April). Retrieved July 20, 2008, from http://www.managingautomation. com/maonline/magazine/read/view/Toyota_Production_Systems__Lean_Goes_Mainstream_3874.

Greiner, L. E. (1972). Evolution and revolution as organisations grow. *Harvard Business Review,* July/August, 37-46. Chau, S.B., & Turner, P. (2002). A four phase model of EC business transformation amongst SME. In *Proceedings of the 12th Autralasian Conference on Information Systems,* Australia.

Greiner, L. E. (1972, July/August). Evolution and Revolution as Organisations Grow. *Harvard Business Review* (pp. 37-46).

Grohowski, R., McGoff, C., Vogel, D., & Martz, J. (1990). Implementing electronic meeting systems at IBM: Lessons learned and success factors. *MIS Quarterly, 16*(4), 369–384. doi:10.2307/249785

Grossman, D. (2002). New terminology and clarifications for DiffServ. *IETF RFC 3260 (Informational).* Retrieved April 5, 2005 from http://www.rfc-editor.org/rfcsearch.html

Grover, V., Jeong, S.R., Kettinger, W., & Teng, J.T.C. (1995). Implementation of business process re-engineering. *J. Management Information Systems, 12*(1), 109-144.

Gruber, T. R. (1993). Towards principles for the design of ontologies used for knowledge sharing. In N. Guarino (Ed.), *Proceedings of the International Workshop on Formal Ontology, Padova/ Italy.*

Grünig, R., & Kühn, R. (2005). *Successful decision-making: A systematic approach to complex problems.* Berlin, Heidelberg, New York: Springer.

Guang-hui, C., Chun-qing, L. & Sai Yun-xiu, S. (2006). Critical success factors for ERP life cycle implementation. In A. Tjoa, L. Min Xu, & S. Chaudhry (Eds.), *Research and Practical Issues of Enterprise Information Systems* (pp. 553-562). Boston: Springer.

Guffond, J.-L., & Leconte, G. (2004). Les ERP, puissants outils d'organisation du changement industriel. *Science and Society,* (61): 33–51.

Gunasekaran, A., Ngai, E. W. T., & McGaughey, R.E. (2006). Information technology and systems justification: A review for research and applications. *European Journal of Operational Research, 173*(3), 957-983.

Gupta, A., Stahl, D. O., & Whinston, A. B. (2005). Pricing traffic on interconnected networks: issues, approaches and solutions. In S. K. Majumdar, I. Vogelsang & M. E. Cave (Eds.), *Handbook of Telecommunications Economics,* vol. 2 (pp. 413-439). North-Holland.

Hadjiantonis, A. M., Charalambides, M., & Pavlou, G. (2007). An adaptive service management framework for wireless networks. *IEEE Vehicular Technology Magazine, 2*(3), 6–13. doi:10.1109/MVT.2008.915322

Haff, W. T., Bikker, H., & Adriaanse, D. J. (2002). *Fundamentals of business engineering and management: A systems approach to people and organizations.* Retrieved July 24, 2008 from http://vssd.nl/hlf/b001.htm#FBEM

Hagel, J. (1993). Keeping BPR on track. *McKinsey Quarterly, 1,* 59-72.

Hale, A., & Cragg, P. (1996). Business process re-engineering in the small firm. *INFOR, 34*(1), 15-27.

Halgeri, P., Pei, Z. J., Iyer, K. S., Bishop, K., & Shehadeh, A. (2008). *ERP systems supporting Lean manufacturing: A literature review.* 2008 International Manufacturing Science & Engineering Conference (MSEC), Evanston, IL, USA.

Hall, D., & Nauda, A. (1990). An interactive approach for selecting IR&D projects. *IEEE Transactions on Engineering Management, 37*(2), 126–133. doi:10.1109/17.53715

Hamel, G., & Prahalad, C. K. (1994). *Competing for the future.* Boston: Harvard Business School Press.

Hameri, A. P., & Nihtila, J. (1998). Product data management - Exploratory study on state-of-the-art in one-of-a-kind industry. *Computers in Industry, 35,* 195–206. doi:10.1016/S0166-3615(98)00064-5

Hammer, M. (1990). Re-engineering work: Don't automate, obliterate. *Harvard Business Review, 68*(4), 104-122.

Hammer, M. (1991). Business process reengineering: Do not automate, obliterate. *Harvard- Deusto Business Review*, third semester.

Hancock, R., Karagiannis, G., Loughney, J., & Van den Bosch, S. (2005). Next steps in signaling (NSIS): framework. *IETF RFC 4080 (Informational)*. Retrieved March 19, 2007 from http://www.rfc-editor.org/rfcsearch.html

Handfield, R., & Nichols, E., Jr. (2001). *Introduction to SCM*. London: Prentice Hall.

Hansen, K. F., Weiss, M. A., & Kwak, S. (1999). Allocating R&D resources: A quantitative aid to management insight. *Research Technology Management*, 42(4), 44–50.

Hanseth, O., & Braa, K. (2000). Who's in control: Designers, managers or technology? In C. Ciborra (Ed.), *From control to drift* (pp. 125-147). Oxford: Oxford University Press.

Harel, D. (1987). A visual formalism for complex systems. *Science of Computer Programming*, 8(3), 231–274. doi:10.1016/0167-6423(87)90035-9

Harmon, P. (2007). *Business process change: A guide for business managers and BPM and Six Sigma* (2nd ed). San Francisco, CA: Morgan Kaufmann Publishers Inc.

Harold, E. R., & Means, W. S. (2004). *XML in a Nutshell* (3rd ed.). O'Reilly Media, Inc.

Harrison-Walker, L. J., & Neeley, S. E. (2004). Customer relationship building on the Internet in B2B marketing: A proposed typology. *Journal of Marketing Theory and Practice*, 12(1), 19–35.

Hassan, T. M., & McCaffer, R. (2002). Vision of the large scale engineering construction industry in Europe. *Automation in Construction*, 11, 421–437. doi:10.1016/S0926-5805(01)00074-7

Hauc, A. (2007). *Projektni management (Project management)*. Ljubljana, GV Zalozba.

Hauc, A., & Kovac, J. (2000). Project management in strategy implementation - experiences in Slovenia. *International Journal of Project Management*, 18, 61–67. doi:10.1016/S0263-7863(98)00071-4

Hauc, A., & Vrečko, I. (2006). Strategy start-up and strategy implementation through the production of multiple projects. *Value management - how to ensure value for project stakeholders - 1st ICEC and IPMA Global Congress on Project Management and 5th World Congress on Cost Engineering, Project Management & Quantity Surveying, Ljubljana, Slovenia*.

Havnes, P. A., & Senneseth, K. (2001). A panel study of firm growth among SMEs in networks. *Small Business Economics*, 16(4), 293–302. doi:10.1023/A:1011100510643

Hayles, C. (1992). The materiality of informatics. *Configurations*, 1, 147–170. doi:10.1353/con.1993.0003

Hedman, J., & Borell, A. (2004). Narratives in ERP system evaluation. *Journal of Enterprise Information Management*, 17(4), 283-290.

Heikkila, J. (1991). Success of software packages in small businesses . *European Journal of Information Systems*, 1(1), 159–169. doi:10.1057/ejis.1991.31

Heili, J., & Vinck, D. (2008). Penser les relations entre technique et organisation: Un examen de la littérature. In D. Vinck & B. Penz (Eds.), *L'équipement de l'organisation industrielle. Les ERP à l'usage* (pp. 43-81). Paris: Hermes.

Heizer, J., & Render, B. (2003). *Operations management*—International edition (7th ed.). Pearson Education Inc, Upper Saddle River, NJ .

Helmer, O. (1972). Cross-impact gaming. *Futures*, 4(2), 149–167. doi:10.1016/0016-3287(72)90039-0

Helmer, O. (1977). Problems in futures research: Delphi and causal cross-impact analysis. *Futures*, 9(1), 17–31. doi:10.1016/0016-3287(77)90049-0

Helmer, O. (1981). Reassessment of cross-impact analysis. *Futures*, 13(5), 389–400. doi:10.1016/0016-3287(81)90124-5

Helsinki University of Technology. (2008) *Web-HIPRE help*. Consulted in May 2008, available: http://www.hipre.hut.fi.

Hennion, A., & Gomart, E. (1999). A sociology of attachement: Music amateurs, drug users. In J. Law & J. Hassard (Eds.), *Actor-network theory and after* (pp. 220-247). Oxford: Blackwell.

Henriksen, A., & Traynor, A. (1999). A practical R&D project-selection scoring tool. *IEEE Transactions on Engineering Management*, 46(2), 158–170. doi:10.1109/17.759144

Hernandez-Matias, J. C., Vizan, A., Perez-Garcia, J., & Rios, J. (2008). An integrated modelling framework to support manufacturing system diagnosis for continuous improvement. *Robotics and Computer-integrated Manufacturing, 24,* 187–199. doi:10.1016/j.rcim.2006.10.003

Herroelen, W. (2005). Project scheduling – theory and practice. *Production and Operations Management, 14*(4), 413–432.

Herzog, N., Polajnar, A., & Tonchia, S. (2007). Development and Validation of business process reeingineering (BPR) variables: a survey research in Slovenian Companies. *International Journal of Production Research, 45*(24), 5811-5834.

Hess, T., & Brecht, L. (1995). *State of the art des business process redesign.* Wiesbaden, Gabler-Verlag.

Hiatt, J. (2006). *ADKAR: a model for change in business, government and our community.* Loveland, Colo: Prosci.

Highsmith, J. (2004). *Agile project management creating innovative products.* Boston: Pearson Education.

Hojlo, J., Burkett, M., & Verma, K. (2007). *PLM market landscape: Evolving To Enable value chain excellence.* 2007 Technology and Vendor Landscape Series. AMR Research Inc.

Holden, M. (2006). Urban Indicators and the Integrative Ideals of Cities. *Cities (London, England), 23*(3), 170–183. doi:10.1016/j.cities.2006.03.001

Holland, C. P., & Light, B. (1999). A critical success factors model for ERP implementation. *IEEE Software,* (May/June): 30–36. doi:10.1109/52.765784

Hollstein, B. (2006). *Qualitative Netzwerkanalyse: Konzepte, methoden, anwendungen.* Wiesbaden: VS Verlag für Sozialwissenschaften.

Homepage, K. (2008). Retrieved October 14, 2008, from http://kontact.kde.org/kmail/.

Hoogeweegen, M., van Liere, D. W., Vervest, P. H. M., Hagdorn van der Meijden, L., & de Lepper, I. (2006). Strategizing for mass customization by playing the business networking game. *Decision Support Systems, 42,* 1402–1412. doi:10.1016/j.dss.2005.11.007

Hoover, I. (2007). Web 2.0 tools in business: Proceed with caution—'Enterprise 2.0' must overcome concerns about security and ROI to gain a foothold in business. *Bank Systems & Technology, 44*(4), 41.

Huang, H.-C. (in press). Designing a knowledge-based system for strategic planning: A balanced scorecard perspective. *Expert Systems with Applications.*

Hubbard, D. W. (2007). *How to measure anything; Finding the value of intangibles in business.* John Wiley & Sons, Inc.

Huberts, A., & van Petten, A. (2007). *Trends in business process management.* Retrieved September 3, 2008 from http://scribd.com/doc/2335647/Trends-in-Business-Process-Management.

Hughes, T., Foss, B., Stone, M., & Cheverton, P. (2007). Degrees of separation: Technological interactivity and account management. *International Journal of Bank Marketing, 25*(5), 315–335. doi:10.1108/02652320710772989

Huin, S. F. (2004). Managing deployment of ERP systems in SMEs using multi-agents. *International Journal of Project Management, 22*(6), 511–517. doi:10.1016/j.ijproman.2003.12.005

Hunton, J.E., & Bieler, J.D. (1997). Effects of User Participation in Systems Development: A Longitudinal Field Experiment. *MIS Quarterly, 21*(4), 359-388.

Hunton, J.E., Lippincott, B., & Reck, J.L. (2003). Enterprise resource planning systems: comparing firm performance of adopters and nonadopters. *International Journal of Accounting Information Systems, 4*(3), 165–184.

Hvolby, H., & Trienekens, J. H. (2002). Supply chain planning opportunities for small and medium sized companies. *Computers in Industry, 49*(1), 3–8. doi:10.1016/S0166-3615(02)00054-4

Hwang, W. T., Tien, W. T., & Shu, C. M. (2007). Building an executive information system for maintenance efficiency in petrochemical plants -- an evaluation. *Trans IChemE, Part B . Process Safety and Environmental Protection, 85,* 139–146. doi:10.1205/psep06019

IBM (2005). *IBM Systems Journal – Special issue on Service-Oriented Architecture, 44*(4), 651-905.

IBM (2008). *IBM Systems Journal – Special issue on SOA: From Modeling to Implementation, 47*(3), 355-473.

IfM Bonn (2008). *Schlüsselzahlen Deutschland (Key Indicators Germany).* Retrieved December 28, 2008, from http://www.ifm-bonn.org/index.php?id=99, 2008-12-28.

In Shaw, et al. (Eds.), *Handbook on electronic commerce* (pp. 431-444), Berlin/ Germany: Springer.

Injazz, J. C. (2001). Planning for ERP systems: Analysis and future trend. *Business Process Management Journal, 7*(5), 374–386. doi:10.1108/14637150110406768

Institute of Electrical and Electronic Engineers (IEEE). (2004). IEEE standard for local and metropolitan area networks: media access control (MAC) bridges. *IEEE Std 802.1D-2004.*

Institute of Electrical and Electronic Engineers (IEEE). (2005). IEEE standard for local and metropolitan area networks: virtual bridged local area networks. *IEEE Std 802.1Q-2005.*

Institute of Electrical and Electronics Engineers. (1990). *IEEE Standard Computer Dictionary: A Compilation of IEEE Standard Computer Glossaries.* New York, NY.

Institute, S. E. I. (2005). Capability maturity model, home page. A methodology of the SEI institute. Retrieved January 10, 2005 from http://www.sei.cmu.edu/cmm/cmm.html

International Organization for Standardization ISO. (2008). *ISO in figures for the year 2007* Geneva: ISO Central Secretariat.

International Organization for Standardization. (1991). *Quality management and quality system elements – Part 2: Guidelines for services.* (ISO 9004-2:1991). (Date of withdrawal: 2001-04-26). Geneva, Switzerland: International Organization for Standardization.

International Organization for Standardization. (2000). *Quality management systems – Guidelines for performance improvements.* [Geneva, Switzerland: International Organization for Standardization.]. *ISO, 9004,* 2000.

International Organization for Standardization. (2005). *Quality management systems – Fundamentals and vocabulary.* ([]. Geneva, Switzerland: International Organization for Standardization.]. *ISO, 9000,* 2005.

International Organization for Standardization. (2008). *Quality management systems – Requirements.* [Geneva, Switzerland: International Organization for Standardization.]. *ISO, 9001,* 2008.

International Telecommunication Union – Telecommunication Standardization Sector (ITU-T). (2004). An architectural framework for support of quality of service (QoS) in packet networks. *ITU-T recommendation* [Geneva, ITU-T.]. *Y (Dayton, Ohio),* 1291.

International Telecommunication Union – Telecommunication Standardization Sector (ITU-T). (2005). Signaling requirements for IP-QoS. *Supplement 51 to ITU-T Q-series recommendations.* Geneva, ITU-T.

International Telecommunication Union – Telecommunication Standardization Sector (ITU-T). (2006). Converged services framework functional requirements and architecture. *ITU-T recommendation* [Geneva, ITU-T.]. *Y (Dayton, Ohio),* 2013.

Irani, Z. (2002). Information systems evaluation: Navigating through the problem domain. *Information and Management, 40*(1), 199–211.

Irani, Z., Ezingeard, J.N., & Grieve, R.J. (1997). Integrating costs of manufacturing IT/IS infrastructure into the investment decision-making process. *Technovation, 17*(11/12), 695-706.

ISO. (2006). [ISO International Organization for Standardization. Retrieved from ttp://www.iso.org]. *Survey (London, England), 2006.*

Ivanović, G., Pantelić, S., Stefanović, B., & Mojović, P. (2008). Processes and software of maintenance management system for vehicles. In *XIV International Scientific Conference on Industrial Systems – IS'08, Proceedings* (pp. 379-386). Novi Sad, Serbia: University of Novi Sad, Faculty of Technical Sciences, Industrial Engineering Department.

Ives, B., & Olson, M. (1983). The measurement of user information satisfaction. *Management of Computing, 26*(10), 519–529.

Iyer, A. (2003). Beyond the phone: Benefits of the integrated contact center. Retrieved September 2008, from http://www.crm2day.com/highlights/EpyEVVAyZFuVTSlcjp.php.

Jaafari, A. (1996). Time and priority allocation scheduling technique for projects. *International Journal of Project Management, 14*(5), 289–299. doi:10.1016/0263-7863(96)84512-1

Jaafari, A., & Manivong, K. (1998). Toward a smart project management information system. *International Journal of Project Management*, *16*(4), 249–265. doi:10.1016/S0263-7863(97)00037-9

Jackson, M. (2003). *Systems thinking. Creative holism for managers*. Chichester: Wiley.

Jackson, M. C. (1991). *Systems Methodology for the Management Sciences*. New York: Plenum

Jackson, M. C. (2000). *Systems Approaches to Management*. New York: Kluwer

Jacobs, R. (2007). Enterprise resource planning (ERP) - A brief history. *Journal of Operations Management*, *25*(2), 357–363. doi:10.1016/j.jom.2006.11.005

Jacobson, I., Booch, G., & Raumbaugh, J. (1999). *The Unified Software Development Process*. Reading, Massachusetts: Addison-Wesley Longman.

Jagdev, H. S., & Thoben, K.-D. (2001). Anatomy of enterprise collaborations. *Production Planning and Control*, *12*(5), 437–451. doi:10.1080/09537280110042675

Jansen, D. (2006). *Einführung in die Netzwerkanalyse Grundlagen, Methoden, Forschungsbeispiele*. Wiesbaden: VS Verlag für Sozialwissenschaften.

Janson, R. (1993). Technology – Tomorrows Determinate. *Ohio Journal of Science*, *93*(4), 78-82.

Jarimo, T., & Korpiaho, K. (2008) Networked partner selection with robust portfolio modeling. In L.M. Camarinha-Matos, & H. Afsarmanesh (Eds.), *Collaborative networks: Reference modelling* (pp. 215-226), New York: Springer.

Jarrar, Y.F., Al-Mudimigh, A., & Zairi, M. (2000). ERP implementation critical success factors – the role and impact of business process management. *ICMIT*, *2*, 122-127.

Jeffocate, J. (2002). Best Practice in SME Adoption of E-commerce. *Benchmarking: an International Journal*, *9*(2), 122–132. doi:10.1108/14635770210421791

Jena – A Semantic Web Framework for Java. (2008). Retrieved October 14, 2008, from http://jena.sourceforge.net

Jiang, J.J., & Klein, G. (1999). User evaluation of information systems: By system typology. *IEEE Transactions on Systems Man and Cybernetics*, *29*(1), 111-116.

Jing, R., & Xun Qiu, X. (2007, June). *A study on critical success factors in ERP systems implementation*. Paper presented at the International Conference on Service Systems and Service Management, Chengdu, China.

Johansson, H. et al. (1993). *BPR: breakpoint strategies for market dominance*. Chichester: Wiley.

Johnson, C. (2005). *US e-commerce: 2005 to 2010, a five year forecast and analysis of US online retail sales*. Forrester Research.

Johnson, L. K. (2002). New views on digital CRM. *MIT Sloan Management Review*, *44*(1), 10.

Jones, M. (1999). Information systems and the double mangle. In T. Larsen, L. Levine & J. DeGross (Eds.), *Information systems: Current issues and future changes* (pp. 287-302). Madison: OmniPress.

Jonkers, H. (1997). *The application of hybrid modeling techniques for business process* performance *analysis*. In Kaylan & Lehmann (eds.), *Proceedings of the 11th European Simulation Multi-conference, Istanbul, Turkey, 1-4 June* (pp. 779-786).

Joseki - A SPARQL Server for Jena. (2008). Retrieved October 14, 2008, from http://www.joseki.org.

Kalakota, R., & Robinson, M. (2001). m-Business: The race to mobility. *eAI Journal*, December, 44-46. Retrieved October 2007, from http://www.bijonline.com/PDF/mBusinessKalakota.pdf

Kalfolglou, Y., & Schorlemmer, M. (2003). Ontology mapping: The state of the art. *The Knowledge Engineering Review*, *18*(1), 1–31. doi:10.1017/S0269888903000651

Kallinikos, J. (2002). *Re-opening the black box of technology: Artifacts and human agency*. Paper presented at the 23 ICIS, Barcelona.

Kallinikos, J. (2004). Deconstructing information packages: Organisational and behavioural implications of ERP sytems. *Information Technology & People*, *17*(1), 8–20. doi:10.1108/09593840410522152

Kalnins, A., Kalnina, D., & Kalis, A. (1998) Comparison of tools and languages for business process reengineering. In *Proceedings of the Third International Baltic Workshop on Databases and Information Systems, Riga, July, 24-28*.

Kane, J. (1972). A primer for a new cross-impact language - KSIM. *Technological Forecasting and Social Change, 4*(2), 129–142. doi:10.1016/0040-1625(72)90010-8

Kaplan, R. S., & Norton, D. P. (1992). The balanced scorecard - measures that drive performance. *Harvard Business Review, 70*(1), 71–79.

Kaplan, R. S., & Norton, D. P. (1993). Putting the balanced scorecard to work. *Harvard Business Review, 71*(5), 134–140.

Kaplan, R. S., & Norton, D. P. (1996). *The balanced scorecard.* Boston, MA: Harvard Business School Press.

Kaplan, R. S., & Norton, D. P. (1996). Using the balance scorecard as a strategic management system. *Harvard Business Review, 74*(1), 75–85.

Kaplan, R. S., & Norton, D. P. (2001a). The strategy-focused organization. *Strategy and Leadership, 29*(3), 41–43.

Kaplan, R. S., & Norton, D. P. (2001). Transforming the balanced scorecard from performance measurement to strategic management: Part I. *Accounting Horizons, 15*(1), 87–106. doi:10.2308/acch.2001.15.1.87

Kaplan, R. S., & Norton, D. P. (2001). Transforming the balanced scorecard from performance measurement to strategic management: Part II. *Accounting Horizons, 15*(2), 147–162. doi:10.2308/acch.2001.15.2.147

Kaplan, R. S., & Norton, D. P. (2004). How strategy maps frame an organization's objectives. *Financial Executive, 20*(2), 40–45.

Kaplan, R. S., & Norton, D. P. (2004). Measuring the strategic readiness of intangible assets. *Harvard Business Review, 82*(2), 52–63.

Kaplan, R. S., & Norton, D. P. (2004). *Strategy Maps; Converting Intangible Assets into Tangible Outcomes.* Boston: Harvard Business School Press.

Kaplan, R. S., & Norton, D. P. (2004c). The strategy map: Guide to aligning intangible assets. *Strategy and Leadership, 32*(5), 10–17. doi:10.1108/10878570410699825

Kaplan, R. S., & Norton, D. P. (2006). *Alignment: Using the balanced scorecard to create corporate synergies.* Boston, MA: Harvard Business School Press.

Kayworth, T., & Leidner, D. (2000). The global virtual manager: A prescription for success. *European Management Journal, 18*(2), 183–193. doi:10.1016/S0263-2373(99)00090-0

Kazovsky, L. G., Gutierrez, D., Shaw, W.-T., & Wong, G. (2008). *Broadband fiber access.* A tutorial from IEEE Communications Society. Retrieved September 25, 2008 from http://www.comsoc.org/freetutorials

Keen, P. G. (1991). *Shaping the future: Business design through information technology.* Cambridge, MA: Harvard Business School Press.

Keizer, G. (2004). *Linux to ring up $35 billion by 2008.* TechWeb news article. Retrieved September 27, 2008 from http://www.techweb.com/wire/showArticle.jhtml?articleID=55800522.

Keller, G., & Teufel, T. (1998). *SAP R/3, process oriented implementation.* Harlow: Addison-Wesley.

Keller, G., Nüttgens, M., & Scheer, A.-W. (1992). Semantische Prozeßmodellierung auf der Grundlage "Ereignisgesteuerter Prozeßketten (EPK)." In A.-W. Scheer (Ed.), *Veröffentlichungen des Instituts für Wirtschaftsinformatik, Nr. 89.* Saarbrücken: Universität des Saarlandes.

Kemp, M. J., & Low, G. C. (2008)... *Business Process Management Journal, 14*(2), 228–242. doi:10.1108/14637150810864952

Kennerley, M., & Neely, A. (2001). Enterprise resource planning: Analysing the impact. *Integrated Manufacturing Systems, 12*(2), 103–113. doi:10.1108/09576060110384299

Kent, J. F. (2002). *An examination of traditional ERP and Lean manufacturing production control methods with a view of flow manufacturing software as an alternative.* MS thesis, University of Oregon.

Kerney, S., & Abdul-Nour, G. (2004). SME and quality performance in networking environment. *Computers & Industrial Engineering, 46*, 905–909. doi:10.1016/j.cie.2004.05.023

Kerste, R., Muizer, A., & Zoetermeer, A. (2002). *Effective knowledge transfer to SMEs.* Strategic Study B200202.

Kersten, W., Kern, E.-M., & Held, T. (2003). Auf dem Weg zur E-Collaboration – Entwicklungslinien im Electronic Business. In W. Kersten (Ed.), *E-collaboration* (pp. 5-27). Wiesbaden/Germany: Gabler Verlag.

Khan, A. (2002). *Implementing SAP with an ASAP methodology focus*. San Jose: Writers Club Press.

Khazanchi, S., Lewis, M. W., & Boyer, K. K. (2007). Innovation-supportive culture: The impact of organizational values on process innovation . *Journal of Operations Management, 25*(4), 871–884. doi:10.1016/j.jom.2006.08.003

Kidd, P. T. (1994). *Agile manufacturing: Forging new frontiers*. Wokingham: Addison-Wesley.

Kidd, P. T. (2008). Agile holonic network organizations. In G.D. Putnik & M.M. Cunha (Eds.), *Encyclopedia of networked and virtual organizations* (pp. 35-42). Hershey, PA: IGI Global.

Kidd, P. T. (Ed.). (2007). *European visions for the knowledge age: A quest for new horizons in the information society*. Macclesfield: Cheshire Henbury Publications.

Kim, H.-S., & Kim, Y.-G. (2008). A CRM performance measurement framework: its development process and application. Industrial Marketing Management.

Kinni, T. (1995). Process Improvement Part 2. *Industry Week, 244*(4), 45-50.

Kirik, S. (2007). *Ermittlung von strategischen Einflußfaktoren für die strategische Planung in kollaborativen Produktionsnetzwerken*. Diploma Thesis at the University of Bremen.

Kitsiou, S., Matopoulos, A., Manthou, V., & Vlachopoulou, M. (2007). Evaluation of integration technology approaches in healthcare supply chain. *International Journal of Value Chain Management, 1*(4), 325–343. doi:10.1504/IJVCM.2007.015091

Klaus, H., Rosemann, M., & Gable, G. G. (2000). What is ERP? *Information Systems Frontiers, 2*(2), 141–162. doi:10.1023/A:1026543906354

Kleindl, B. (2000). Competitive dynamics and new business models for SMEs in the virtual marketplace. *Journal of Developmental Entrepreneurship, 5*(1), 73–85.

Klincewicz, J. G., Schmitt, J. A., & Wong, R. T. (2002). Incorporating QoS into IP enterprise network design. *Telecommunication Systems, 20*(1-2), 81–106. doi:10.1023/A:1015441400785

Knight, P., & Lewis, K. (2004). Layer 2 and 3 virtual private networks: taxonomy, technology and standardization efforts. *IEEE Communications Magazine, 42*(6), 124–131. doi:10.1109/MCOM.2004.1304248

Knoke, D., & Kuklinski, J.-H. (1982) *Network analysis*. Beverly Hills: Sage University Chapter.

Koch, C. (2001). BRP and ERP: Realising a vision process with IT. *Business Process Management Journal, 7*(3), 258–265. doi:10.1108/14637150110392755

Koch, C. (2008). ABC: An introduction to ERP. *CIO*. Retrieved March 18, 2008, from http://www.cio.com/article/40323/ABC_An_Introduction_to_ERP/1

Koch, C. (2008). The ABC of ERP. *Enterprise Resource Planning Research Center*. Retrieved from http://www.cio.com/research/erp/edit/erpbasics.html

Koh, L., & Simpson, M. (2005). Change and uncertainty in SME manufacturing environments using ERP. *Journal of Manufacturing Technology Management, 16*(6), 629–653. doi:10.1108/17410380510609483

Koh, S. C. L., & Simpson, M. (2005). Change and uncertainty in SME manufacturing environments using ERP. *Journal of Manufacturing Technology Management, 16*(6), 629–653. doi:10.1108/17410380510609483

Korea Institute for Electronic Commerce. (2006). Annual survey on E-business status 2006. Retrieved August 21, 2008, from http://www.oecd.org/dataoecd/59/27/35372094.pdf

Kotelnikov, V. (2007). *Small and medium enterprises and ICT. Asia–Pacific development information programme e-primers for the information economy, society and policy*. UNDP-APDIP and APCICT, 1-27. Retrieved August 12, 2008, from http://www.unapcict.org/ecohub/resources/small-and-medium-enterprises-and-ict

Kotter, J. (1990). *Force for change: How leadership differs from management*. New York, NY: Free Press.

Kováč, M., & Švač, V. (2007). Knowledge sharing in project Equal. In *EQUAL for Automotive* (pp. 10-12). Technical University of Košice.

Kowari Metastore Website. (2008). Retrieved October, 14, 2008, from http://www.kowari.org.

Král, J., & Žemlička, M. (2003). Software confederations – An architecture for global systems and global management. In S. Kamel (Ed.), *Managing globally with information technology* (pp. 57-81). Hershey, PA: Idea Group Publishing.

Král, J., & Žemlička, M. (2003). Software confederations and alliances. In *CAiSE'03 Forum: Information Systems for a Connected Society*. Maribor, Slovenia: University of Maribor Press.

Král, J., & Žemlička, M. (2004). Service orientation and the quality indicators for software services. In R. Trappl (Ed.), *Cybernetics and Systems*, volume 2 (pp. 434-439). Vienna, Austria: Austrian Society for Cybernetic Studies.

Král, J., & Žemlička, M. (2005). Implementation of business processes in service-oriented systems. In *Proceedings of 2005 IEEE International Conference on Services Computing*, volume II (pp. 115-122). Los Alamitos, CA, USA: IEEE Computer Society.

Král, J., & Žemlička, M. (2007). Crucial patterns in service-oriented architecture. In *Proceedings of ICDT 2007 Conference* (pp. 24). Los Alamitos, CA: IEEE CS Press.

Král, J., & Žemlička, M. (2007). The most important service-oriented antipatterns. In *International Conference on Software Engineering Advances (ICSEA'07)* (pp. 29). Los Alamitos, CA: IEEE Computer Society.

Král, J., & Žemlička, M. (2007c). Requirements specification: What strategy under what conditions. In *Proceedings of 5th International Conference on Software Engineering Research, Management and Applications (SERA2007)* (pp. 401-408). Los Alamitos, CA: IEEE CS Press.

Král, J., & Žemlička, M. (2007d). Usability issues in service-oriented architecture. In *ICEIS 2007: Proceedings of the Ninth International Conference on Enterprise Information Systems, Volume DISI* (pp. 482-485). Setúbal, Portugal: EST Setúbal.

Král, J., & Žemlička, M. (2008). Engineering education – a great challenge to software engineering. In R. Lee (Ed.), *7th IEEE/ACIS International Conference on Computer and Information Science* (pp. 488-495). Los Alamitos, CA: IEEE Computer Society.

Král, J., Žemlička, M., & Kopecký, M. (2006). Software confederations – an architecture for agile development in the large. In P. Dini (Ed.), *International Conference on Software Engineering Advances (ICSEA'06)* (pp. 39). Los Alamitos, CA: IEEE Computer Society.

Krauth, J. (1992). Simulation for the evaluation of CIM Investments as Part of an enterprise strategy. In *EURO-SIM '92 Simulation Congress Reprints* (pp. 295-300), North Holland.

Krauth, J., Duin, H., & Schimmel, A. (1998). A comparison of tools for strategic simuation and scenario generation with special emphasis on 'soft factors'. *Simulation Practice and Theory, 6*(1), 23–33. doi:10.1016/S0928-4869(97)00005-0

Krcmar, H., & Klein, A. (2003). Collaborative commerce und CSCW – Zum Nutzen der CSCW-Forschung für das collaborative E-Business. In W. Kersten (Ed.), E-collaboration (pp. 5-27). Wiesbaden/Germany: Gabler Verlag.

Kroenke, D. (1981). *Business Computer Systems*. Santa Cruz, CA: Mitchell Publishing, (and more accessibly in his more recent books; e.g., *Using MIS*, Prentice-Hall, 1st ed., 2007, and 2nd ed., 2009)

Kumar, V., Movahedi, B., Kumar, U., & Lavassani, K. M. (2008). A comparative study of enterprise system implementations in large North American corporations. *11th International Conference Business Information Systems, Innsbruck, Austria, May 2008* (pp. 390-398).

Laclavik, M., et al. (2007). Ontology based text annotation – OnTeA. *Information Modelling and Knowledge Bases XVIII* (Frontiers in Artificial Intelligence and Applications, Vol. 154, pp. 311-315). Amsterdam: IOS Press.

Laclavik, M., Seleng, M., & Hluchy, L. (2007). ACoMA: Network Enterprise Interoperability and Collaboration using E-mail Communication. In P. Cunningham & M. Cunningham (Eds), *Proceedings of eChallenges 2007; Expanding the Knowledge Economy: Issues, Applications, Case Studies* (pp. 1078-1085). Amsterdam: IOS Press.

Lai, V. (1994). A survey of rural small business computer use: Success factors and decision support. *Information & Management, 26*(6), 297–304. doi:10.1016/0378-7206(94)90027-2

Lam, W., & Shankararaman, V. (2004). An enterprise integration methodology. *IT Professional, 6*(2), 40–48. doi:10.1109/MITP.2004.1278864

Larsen, M., & Myers, M. (1999). When success turns into failure: a package-driven BPR project in the financial services industry. *Journal of Strategic Information Systems, 8,* 395-417.

Latour, B. (1987). *Science in action: How to follow scientists and engineers through society.* Cambridge, MA: Harvard University Press.

Laudon, K. C., & Laudon, J. P. (2007). *Essentials of business information systems.* Upper Saddle River, NJ: Pearson Prentice Hall. Lewis, E. (2005, September). Now is SMEs' time to compete on-demand supply chain solutions are affordable for the small distributor. *Industrial Distribution.*

Lave, J., & Wenger, E. (1991). *Situated Learning: Legitimate Peripheral Participation.* New York: Cambridge University Press.

Law, J. (1994). *Organizing modernity.* Oxford; Cambridge, MA: Blackwell.

Lawson, C. P., Longhurst, P. J., & Ivey, P. C. (2006). The application of a new research and development project selection model in SMEs. *Technovation, 26*(2), 242–250. doi:10.1016/j.technovation.2004.07.017

Lee, B., & Miller, J. (2004). Multi-project software engineering analysis using system thinking. *Software Process Improvement and Practice, 9,* 173–214. doi:10.1002/spip.204

Lee, C., & Chen, S. (1992). *The overall environment and the development of Taiwan's SMEs.* Chung-Hua Institution for Economic Research.

Lee, J.C., & Myers. M.D.. (2004). Dominant actors, political agendas, and strategic shifts over time: a critical ethnography of an enterprise systems implementation. *Strategic Information Systems,* (13), 355-374.

Lee, O. (2004, March). A case study of Nevada DMV system. *Journal of the Academy of Business and Economics.*

Lee, T. S., & Adam, E. E. Jr. (1986). Forecasting error evaluation in material requirements planning (MRP) production-inventory systems. *Management Science, 32*(9), 1186–1205. doi:10.1287/mnsc.32.9.1186

Lee, T. T. (2000). Apt ERP alternatives. *New Straits Times-Management Times.*

Leedy, P. D. (1997). *Practical research – Planning and design* (6th ed.). NJ: Prentice-Hall, Inc.

Leem, C. S., & Kim, S. (2002). Introduction to an integrated methodology for development and implementation of enterprise information systems. *Journal of Systems and Software, 60,* 249–261. doi:10.1016/S0164-1212(01)00096-6

Leger, P. (2000). Customer interaction in the digital age: Strategies for improving satisfaction and loyalty. The Utilities Project Vol 1. Retrieved September 2008, from http://www.utilitiesproject.com/documents.asp?grID=86&d_ID=150

Leintz, B. P., & Rea, K. P. (1995). *Project management for the 21st Century.* London: Academic Press.

Lemaire, L., & Valenduc, G. (2004). Entre rigidité et maléabilité. Le double visage des ERP. *Science and Society,* (61): 53–69.

Leopoulos, V. N., Kirytopoulos, K. A., & Malandrakis, C. (2006). Risk management for SMEs: Tools to use and how. *Production Planning and Control, 17*(3), 322–332. doi:10.1080/09537280500285136

Levene, R. J., & Braganza, A. (1996). Controlling the work scope in organisational transformation. *International Journal of Project Management, 14*(6), 331-339.

Leventhal, L., & Barnes, J. (2007) *Usability engineering. Process, products & examples.* Upper Saddle River, NJ: Prentice Hall.

Levitt, T. (1960, July–August). Marketing Myopia. *Harvard Business Review, 82*(7–8), 138.

Levy, M., & Powell, P. (2000). Information strategy for SME: An organizational perspective. *The Journal of Strategic Information Systems, 9,* 63–84. doi:10.1016/S0963-8687(00)00028-7

Levy, M., & Powell, P. (2005). *Strategies for growth in SMEs.* Oxford: Butterworth Heinemann.

Levy, M., Galliers, R., & Powell, P. (1999). Assessing information systems strategy development frameworks in SMEs. *Information and Management, 36,* 247-261.

Levy, M., Powell, P., & Yetton, P. (2002). The dynamics of SME information systems. *Small Business Economics, 19,* 341–354. doi:10.1023/A:1019654030019

Levy, N., & Globerson, S. (1997). Improving multi-project management by using a queuing theory approach. *Industrial Project Management, 28*(4), 40–47.

Lewerenz, J. (1999). On the use of natural language concepts for the conceptual modeling of interaction in information systems. In G. Fliedl, & H.C. Mayr (Eds.), *Proceedings of the 4th International Conference on Applications of Natural Language to Databases, NLDB '99*, (pp. 61-75). Klagenfurt/ Austria: Österreichische Computer Gesellschaft.

Lewin, K. (1947). Frontiers in Group Dynamics. Part II-B: Feedback problems of social diagnosis and action. *Human Relations 1*, 147.

Li, M. (2003). Policy-based IPsec management. *IEEE Network, 17*(6), 36–43. doi:10.1109/MNET.2003.1248659

Li, Y., Liao, X. W., & Lei, H. Z. (2006). A knowledge management system for ERP implementation. *Systems Research and Behavioral Science, 23*(2), 157–168. doi:10.1002/sres.751

Liberatore, M. J., & Pollack-Johnson, B. (2003). Factors influencing the usage and selection of project management software. *IEEE Transactions on Engineering Management, 50*(2), 164–174. doi:10.1109/TEM.2003.810821

Lichtenberg, F. (1995). The output contributions of computer equipment and personnel: A firm level analysis. *Economics of Innovation and New Technology, 3*(3), 201–218. doi:10.1080/10438599500000003

Lichtenstein, B. M. B. (2000). Self-organized transitions: A pattern amid the chaos of transformative change. *Academy of Management Executive, 14*(4), 128-141.

Light, M., Rosser, B., & Hayward, S. (2005). *Realizing the benefits of projects and portfolio management.* Gartner . *Research ID, G00125673*, 1–31.

Lin, C., & Pervan, G. (2003). The practice of IS/IT benefits management in large Australian organisations. *Information and Management, 41*(1) 13-24.

Linthicum, D. (1999). *Enterprise application integration.* MA: Addison-Wesley.

Loch, C. (2000). Tailoring product development to strategy: Case of a European technology manufacturer. *European Management Journal, 18*(3), 246–258. doi:10.1016/S0263-2373(00)00007-4

Loh, T. C., & Koh, S. C. L. (2004). Critical elements for a successful ERP implementation in SMEs. *International Journal of Production Research, 42*(17), 3433–3455. doi:10.1080/00207540410001671679

Lopez, H., Massacci, F., & Zannone, N. (2007). Goal-equivalent secure business process re-engineering for e-health. In J. Sztipanovits, et al. (eds.), *Workshop on model-based trustworthy health information systems.* September 28 - October 3, Toulouse, France.

Love, P. E. D., & Irani, Z. (2003). A project management quality cost information system for the construction industry. *Information & Management, 40*, 649–661. doi:10.1016/S0378-7206(02)00094-0

Lovelock, Ch., & Wright, L. (2002). *Principles of service marketing and management* (2nd ed.). New Jersey: Prentice Hall.

Lowson, B., King, R., & Hunter, A. (1999). *Quick response: Managing the supply chain to meet consumer demand.* New York: John Wiley & Sons.

Lübke, D. (2006). Transformation of Use Cases to EPC Models. In M. Nüttgens, F. Rump, & J. Mendling (Eds.), *Proceedings of the EPK 2006. CEUR Proceedings Vol 224.* http://ftp.informatik.rwth-aachen.de/Publications/CEUR-WS/Vol-224/.

Lübke, D., Lüecke, T., Schneider, K., & Marx Gómez, J. (2006). Using Event-Driven Process Chains for Model-Driven Development of Business Applications. In Nüttgens & Mendling (Eds.), *Proceedings of the XML4BPM 2006.*

Lücke, F., & Webering, J. (2003). Gegenwart und Zukunft von Online-Kooperationen. In M. Büttgen,& L. Fridjof (Eds.), *Online-Kooperationen* (pp. 3-14). Wiesbaden/ Germany: Gabler Verlag.

Lüecke, T. (2005). *Development of a Concept for Creating and Managing User Interfaces bound to Business Processes.* Master's Thesis, Leibniz Universität Hannover, Germany.

Lycett, M., Rassau, A., & Danson, J. (2004). Programme management: A critical review. *International Journal of Project Management, 22*(4), 289–299. doi:10.1016/j.ijproman.2003.06.001

MaBE. (2006), The MaBE Middleware. In *Emerging Solutions for Future Manufacturing Systems* (pp. 53-60). Boston: Springer.

Mabert, V. A., Ashok, S., & Venkataramanan, M. A. (2000). Enterprise resource planning survey of US manufacturing firms. *Production and Inventory Management Journal, 41*(2), 52–58.

Mabert, V., Soni, A., & Venkatamara, M. (2003). Enterprise Resource Planning: Managing implementation process. *European Journal of Operational Research, 146*(2), 302–314. doi:10.1016/S0377-2217(02)00551-9

Macheridis, N., & Nilsson, C. H. (2006). *Management of Multi-projects in a Process Oriented Organization.* Lund Institute of Economic Research, Working Paper Series No. 8.

Majchrzak, A. (1992). Management of technological and organizational change. In G. Salvendy (Ed.), *Handbook of industrial engineering* (2nd ed., pp. 767-798). New York: John Wiley & Sons Inc.

Majchrzak, A., Fleischer, M., Roithman, D., & Mokray, J. (1991). *Reference manual for performing the HITOP analysis.* Ann Arbour, MI: Industrial Technology Institute.

Makridakis, S., & Wheelwright, S. C. (1990). *Forecasting methods for management.* Winchester.

Mallach, E. (2006, April–June). System Conversion: Teaching versus Reality. *International Journal of Information and Communication Technology Education 2*(2), 17.

Malone, T. B., & Yates, J. (1987). Electronic markets and electronic hierarchies: Effects on information technology on market structure and corporate strategies. *Communications of the ACM, 30,* 37–45.

Mandelli, A. (1999). *Fare business in Rete.* Milano, Italy: McGraw-Hill.

Maniatis, S., Nikolouzou, E., & Venieris, I. (2004). End-to-end QoS specification issues in the converged all-IP wired and wireless environment. *IEEE Communications Magazine, 42*(6), 80–86. doi:10.1109/MCOM.2004.1304236

Manner, J., & Fu, X. (2005). Analysis of existing Quality-of-Service signaling protocols. *IETF RFC 4904 (Informational).* Retrieved July 15, 2008 from http://www.rfc-editor.org/rfcsearch.html

MarkMail Website. (2008). Retrieved October 14, 2008, from http://markmail.org

Markus, L. M., & Tannis, G. (1999). *The Enterprise Systems Experience: From adoption to success.* Peter Drucker Graduate School of Management, Claremont Graduate University, Claremont, CA.

Markus, M. L., & Tanis, C. (2000). In R.W. Zmud (Ed.), *The enterprise systems experience – From adoption to success, in framing the domains of IT management: Projecting the future ...... through the past* (pp. 173-207).

Markus, M. L., & Tanis, C. (2000). The enterprise systems experience – from adoption to success. In: R. W. Zmud (Ed.), *Framing the Domains of IT Research: Glimpsing the Future through the Past* (pp. 73-207). Cincinnatti, Ohio: Pinnaflex Educational Resources Inc.

Markus, M. L., Axline, S., Petrie, D., & Tanis, C. (2000). Learning from adopters' experiences with ERP: problems encountered and success achieved. *Journal of Information Technology, 15,* 245–265. doi:10.1080/02683960010008944

Marnewick, C., & Labuschagne, L. (2005). A conceptual model for enterprise resource planning (ERP). *Information Management & Computer Security, 13*(2). doi:10.1108/09685220510589325

Marri, H., Gunasekaran, A., & Grieve, R. (1998). An investigation into the implementation of the computer integrated manufacturing in small and medium sized enterprises. *International Journal of Advanced Manufacturing Technology, 14,* 935-42.

Marsick, V.J., & Watkins, K.E. (1997). Case study research methods' in Swanson, R.A. and Holton, E.F. (eds), *Human Resource Development Research Handbook* (pp 138-157). San Franscisco, CA: Berret-Koehler.

Martin, D., et al. (2004). OWL-S: Semantic markup for Web services. Retrieved October 15, 2008, from http://www.w3.org/Submission/OWL-S/.

Martin, L. M., & Matlay, H. (2001). Approaches to promoting ICT in SME. *Internet Research: Electronic Network Applications and Policy, 11*(5), 399–410. doi:10.1108/EUM0000000006118

Martin, M. (1998). An electronics firm will save big money by replacing six people ...... not every company has been so lucky. *Fortune, 137*(2), 149–151.

Martinsuo, M., & Lehtonen, P. (2007). Role of single-project management in achieving portfolio management efficiency. *International Journal of Project Management, 25,* 56–65. doi:10.1016/j.ijproman.2006.04.002

Mather, D. (2003). *CMMS: A timesaving implementation process.* Boca Raton, FL: CRC Press.

Mcaffe, A. P. (2006). Enterprise 2.0: The dawn of emergent collaboration. *MIT Sloan Management Review, 47*(3), 21–28.

McInerney, F. (2008). *Panasonic the largest corporate restructuring in history.* New York: Truman Talley Books St. Martin Press.

McKeown, I., & Philip, G. (2003). Business Transformation, information technology and competitive strategies: learning to fly, *International Journal of Information Management, 23*(1), 3-24.

McLeod, R. (2000). *Management information systems.* Mexico, D.F.: Prentice Hall.

McManus, H. L., & Richard, L. M. (2002). Value Stream analysis and mapping for product development. In *Proceedings of 23rd ICAS Congress* (pp. 6103.1-6103.10). Toronto, Canada.

Meatzer, J. T., DeWitt, W., Keebler, J. S., Soonhong, M., Nix, N. W., Carlo, D. S., & Zach, G. Z. (2001). Defining supply chain management. *Journal of Business Logistics, 22*(2), 34–47.

Meissner, J. O., Schweikert, S., & Wolf, P. (2007). Making SME know, what they don't know: Archetypes of central Swiss innovation profiles and challenges for innovation support. *ESSHRA-Conference 2007 'Towards a Knowledge Society: Is Knowledge a Public Good? Dynamics of Knowledge Production and Distribution'*, Berne.

Mekong Capital. (2004). Introduction to Lean manufacturing for Vietnam. Retrieved August 30, 2008 from http://www.mekongcapital.com/Introduction%20to%20Lean%20Manufacturing%20-%20English.pdf

Meredith, J. R., & Mantel, S. J., Jr. (1995). *Project management: A managerial approach.* New York: John Wiley & Sons, Inc.

Mertens, P. (1993). *Prognoserechnung.* Heidelberg: Physica-Verlag.

Messmer, E. (2000). Thanksgiving no holiday for EDGAR. *Network World, 17*(42), 18.

META Group, Inc. (2003). *80% of users prefer E-Mail as business communication tool.* Retrieved December 15, 2008, from http://www.mariosalexandrou.com/technology-trends/2003/80-percent-of-users-prefer-email.asp.

Metallo, G., Cuomo, M. T., & Festa, G. (2007). Relationship management in the business of quality and communication. *Total Quality Management, 18*(1-2), 119–133.

Metzger, B. (2008). *Linking Lean and ERP systems together for sustained advantage* [White paper of TriMin Systems, Inc.]. Retrieved August 30, 2008 from http://www.triminmfg.com/images/KnowledgeBase/Metzger.pdf

Michel, R. (2002). Multiple paths to Lean: Detector Electronics, Norlen turn to specialized Lean manufacturing solutions. *Manufacturing Business Technology.* Retrieved July 20, 2008 from http://www.mbtmag.com/article/CA254538.html?q=Lean+ERP+software

Microsoft (2007). *Using the Microsoft Dynamics Sure Step Methodology for Microsoft Dynamics AX.* Microsoft Dynamics GP, Microsoft Dynamics NAV, Microsoft Dynamics SL. (Internal source; restricted access).

Miles, R. E., & Snow, C. C. (1984). Fit, failure and the hall of fame. *California Management Review,* (Spring): 10–28.

Miller, E. (2003). *State of the PLM industry.* CIM Data PLM Conference 2003, MI, USA, July 23, 2003.

Miller, E. (2005). *Ask the Expert Ed Miller: Dec 16 2005 Innovative Forum.* Retrieved August 21, 2008, from http://cimdata.com/newsletter/2005/51/02/51.02.01.htm

Miller, E. (2005). *PLM – State of the PLM industry- October 2005.* Retrieved September 29, 2008, from http://www.perceptionsoftware.com/ama/orig/PLM_State_of_Industry_October_2005.pdf

Miller, G. J. (2002). Lean and ERP: Can they co-exist? Retrieved July 19, 2008 from http://facilitatorgroup.net/pdf/LeanERPCoExist.pdf

Miller, S. S. (1998). *ASAP - Implementation at the speed of business.* New York: McGraw-Hill.

Ming, X. G., Yan, J. Q., Lu, W. F., & Ma, D. Z. (2005). Technology solutions for collaborative product lifecycle management – Status review and future trend. *Concurrent Engineering . Research and Applications, 13*(4), 311–319.

Mintzberg, H. (1994). *The Rise and fall of strategic planning.* Eaglewood Cliffs: Prentice Hall.

Mirani, R., & Lederer, A.L. (1998). An instrument for assessing the organisational benefits of IS projects. *Decision Sciences, 29*(40), 803-838.

Modrák, V. (2005). Business process improvement through optimisation of its structural properties. In L. Fischer, (Ed.) *Workflow handbook 2005* (pp. 75-90). Lighthouse Point, FL: Future Strategies.

Modrák, V. (2007). Bridging organizational structure and information system architecture through process (LNCS 4537, pp. 445-455).

Modrák, V., & Manduľák, J. (2008). LPH Vranovn/T-Case study. In L. Fischer (Ed.), *BPM excellence in practice 2008 – Using BPM for competitive advantage* (pp. 51-62). Lighthouse Point, FL: Future Strategies.

Mohapatra, P., Metz, C., & Cui, Y. (2007). Layer 3 VPN services over IPv6 backbone networks: requirements, technology, and standardization efforts. *IEEE Communications Magazine, 45*(4), 32–37. doi:10.1109/MCOM.2007.343609

Mokyr, J. (2005). *The gifts of Athena; Historical origins of the knowledge economy.* Princeton, NJ: Princeton University Press.

Møller, C. (2005). ERP II: a conceptual framework for next-generation enterprise systems? *Journal of Enterprise Information Management, 18*(4), 483–497. doi:10.1108/17410390510609626

Monforte Moreno, M. (1995). *Sistemas de información para la dirección.* Madrid: Pirámide.

Monnerat, R., Carvalho, R., & Campos, R. (2008). Enterprise systems modeling: The ERP5 development process. [Fortaleza, Ceara, Brazil]. *SAC, 08*(March), 16–20.

Monteiro, E. (2000). Actor-network theory and information infrastructures. In C. Ciborra (Ed.), *From control to drift* (pp. 71-84). Oxford: Oxford University Press.

Moor, J. H. (1985). What is computer ethics? *Metaphilosophy, 16*(4), 266–275. doi:10.1111/j.1467-9973.1985.tb00173.x

Morabito, V., Pace S., & Previtali, P. (2005). ERP marketing and Italian SMEs. *European Management Journal, 23*(5), 590-598.

Moradi, F. (2008). *A framework for component based modelling and simulation using BOMs and semantic Web technology.* Doktorsavhandling, sammanläggning Press.

Mordelet, N., Festraets, E., & Wang, M. (2006). The enterprise: A high-value market for broadband services. *Alcatel Telecommunications Review* (3rd Quarter 2006). Retrieved September 5, 2008 from http://www.alcatel-lucent.com

Morello, D. (2005). The IT professional outlook: Where will we go from here? Nielsen, J. (1993). *Usability engineering.* New York: Academic Press.

Morris, P., & Jamieson, A. (2004). *Translating corporate strategy into project strategy: realizing corporate strategy through project management.* Pennsylvania, USA: Project Management Institute.

Morris, P., & Pinto, J. K. (Eds.). (2004). *The Wiley guide to managing projects.* London: Wiley.

Motwani, J., Mirchandani, M., & Gunasekaran, A. (2002). Successful implementation of ERP Projects: Evidence from two case studies. *International Journal of Production Economics, 75,* 83–96. doi:10.1016/S0925-5273(01)00183-9

Motwani, J., Subramanian, R., & Gopalakrishna, P. (2005). Critical factors for successful ERP implementation: Exploratory findings from four case studies. *Computers in Industry, 56,* 529-544.

Müller, C. (2007). *Sanierungsprogramm Power 8 und die Auswirkungen auf die Marktteilnehmer.* Presented at the Collaborative Business Workshop, Hamburg, Germany.

Mulej, M. (2005). New roles of systems science in a knowledge society: Introductory provocation. In J. Gu & G. Chroust (Eds.), *Proceedings of the first world congress The new roles of systems science for a knowledge-based society.* Kobe: International Federation for Systems Research.

Mulej, M., & Kajzer, S. (1998). Ethics of interdependence and the law of requisite holism. In M. Rebernik & M. Mulej (Eds.), *STIQE '98. Proceedings of the 4th International Conference on Linking Systems Thinking, Innovation, Quality, Entrepreneurship and Environment* (pp. 129-140). Maribor: Institute for Entrepreneurship and Small Business Management, at Faculty of Economics and Business, University of Maribor, and Slovenian Society for Systems Research.

Mulej, M., & Potocan, V. (2007). *Transition into an innovative enterprise*. University of Maribor, Slovenian.

Murphy, A., & Ledwith, A. (2006). Project management tools and techniques in high-tech SMEs in Ireland. *High Technology Small Firms Conference 2006*, Ireland: Department of Manufacturing and Operations Engineering, University of Limerick.

Murphy, R. P., Jr., & Wood, F. D. (2004). *Contemporary Logistics*. London: Prentice Hall.

Muscatello, J. R., Small, M. H., & Chen, I. J. (2003)... *International Journal of Operations & Production Management*, 23(8), 850–871. doi:10.1108/01443570310486329

Nach, H., & Lejeune, A. (2008). Implementing ERP in SMEs: Towards an ontology supporting managerial decisions. *2008 International MCETECH Conference on e-Technologies (mcetech 2008)* (pp. 223-226).

Nagendra, P. B., & Das, S. K. (1999). MRP/SFX: A kanban-oriented shop floor extension to MRP. *Production Planning and Control*, 10(3), 207–218. doi:10.1080/095372899233172

Nah, F. F. H., Lau, J. L. S., & Kuang, J. (2001). Critical factors for successful implementation of enterprise systems. *Business Process Management Journal*, 7(3), 285–296.

Nah, F., Lau, J., & Kuang, J. (2001). Critical factors for successful implementation of enterprise systems. *Business Process Management*, 7(3), 285–296. doi:10.1108/14637150110392782

Nakashima, B. (2000). Lean and ERP: Friend or foe? *Advanced Manufacturing (September)* Retrieved July 20, 2008 from http://www.advancedmanufacturing.com/index.php?option=com_staticxt&staticfile=information tech.htm&Itemid=44

Negus, C. (2005). *Linux Bible* (2nd ed.). John Wiley & Sons.

Ngai, E.W.T., Law, C.C.H., & Wat, F.K.T. (2007). Examining the critical success factors in the adoption of enterprise resource planning. *Computers in Industry*, 59, 548-564.

Nicolaou, A. (2004). Quality of post implementation review for enterprise resource planning systems. *International Journal of Accounting Information Systems*, 5(1), 25-49.

Nielsen, J. (1999). *Designing Web usability*. Berkley, CA: Peach Pit Press.

Nielsen, J., & Loranger, H. (2006). Prioritizing Web usability. Indianapolis, IN: New Riders Publishing.

Niven, P. R. (2005). *Balanced scorecard diagnostics; Maintaining maximum performance*. Hoboken, NJ: John Wiley & Sons, Inc.

Nolan, R. L. (1979). Managing the crises in data processing. *Harvard Business Review*.

Norris, G., Hurley, R. J., Hartley, M. K., Dunleavy, R. J., & Balls, D. J. (2000). E-Business and ERP, Transforming the enterprise. New York: John Wiley & Sons, Inc

Nudurupati, S., Arshad, T., & Turner, T. (2007). Performance measurement in the construction industry: An action case investigating manufacturing methodologies. *Computers in Industry*, 58, 667–676. doi:10.1016/j.compind.2007.05.005

Nzaou, P. P., Raymond, L., & Fabi, B. (2008)... *Business Process Management Journal*, 14(4), 530–550. doi:10.1108/14637150810888064

O' Leary, D. E. (2000). *Enterprise Resource Planning Systems - Systems, Life Cycle, Electronic Commerce, and Risk*. New York, USA: Cambridge University Press.

O'Hara-Devereaux, M., & Johansen, R. (1994). *Global work: Bridging distance, culture, and time*. San Francisco: Jossey-Bass.

O'Leary, D. (2000). Supply chain processes and relationships for electronic commerce.

O'Leary, D.E. (2000). *Enterprise resource planning system: Systems, life cycle, electronic commerce and risk*. USA: Cambridge university press.

OASIS. (2008). OASIS Standards and other approved work. Retrieved from http://www.oasis-open.org/specs

OECD Glossary of Statistical Terms. (2005). Small and Medium-sized Enterprises (SMES) definition. Retrieved July 12, 2008, from http://stats.oecd.org/glossary/detail.asp?ID=3123

OH, W., & Pinsonneault, A. (2007). On the assessment of the strategic value of information technologies. *MIS Quarterly*, 31(2), 239–265.

Olsen, G. (2000). An overview of B2B integration. *eAI Journal*, May, 28-36. Retrieved September 2008, from http://www.bijonline.com/PDF/B2BOverview%20-%20Oslen_1.pdf

Olsen, K. A., & Sætre, P. (2007). [f]. *Business Process Management Journal, 13*(3), 379–389. doi:10.1108/14637150710752290

Olsen, K. A., & Sætre, P. (2007). ERP for SMEs – is proprietary software an alternative? *Business Process Management Journal, 13*(3), 379–389. doi:10.1108/14637150710752290

Ontotext Semantic Technology Lab Website. (2008). Retrieved October 15, 2008, from http://www.ontotext.com/owlim/index.html.

OntoWiki Website. (2008). Retrieved October 15, 2008, from http://aksw.org/Projects/OntoWiki.

Oracle (2006). *Oracle Flow Manufacturing datasheet.* Retrieved July 19, 2008 from ttp://www.oracle.com/applications/manufacturing/flow-manufacturing-datasheet.pdf.

Orlikowski, W. J. (1992). The duality of technology: Rethinking the concept of technology in organisations. *Organization Science, 3*(3), 398–427. doi:10.1287/orsc.3.3.398

Orlikowski, W. J. (2000). Using technology and constituting structures: A practice lens for studying technology in organisations. *Organization Science, 11*(4), 404–428. doi:10.1287/orsc.11.4.404.14600

Osanna, P. H., & Si, L. (2000). Multi-functions integrated factory mfif - a model of the future enterprise. In *Proceedings of "Internet Device Builder Conference", Sta. Clara, May 2000, 1-16.*

Osório, A. L., & Barata, M. M. (2001). Reliable and secure communications infrastructure for virtual enterprises. *Journal of Intelligent Manufacturing, 12,* 171–183. doi:10.1023/A:1011204627577

Paez, O., Dewees, J., Genaidy, A., Tuncel, S., Karwowski, W., & Zurada, J. (2004). The Lean manufacturing enterprise: An emerging socio-technological system integration. *Human Factors and Ergonomics in Manufacturing, 14*(3), 285–306. doi:10.1002/hfm.10067

Pais, A. V. (2004). Supply chain management for SMEs – a boon for achieving distinction.1-9. Retrieved August 2, 2008 from http://escc.army.mil/doc/ERP/ERP_white_papers/Supply_Chain_Management_for_SMEs-A_Boon_for_Achieving_Distinction.pdf

Palvia, S., Mallach, E., & Palvia, P. (1991, October). Strategies for Converting from One IT Environment to Another. *Journal of Systems Management, 42*(10), 23.

Pang, L. (2001). Manager's guide to enterprise resource planning (ERP) systems. *Info Tech Talk, 6*(2), 13–16.

Pantelić, S., Avramović, Z. Ž., Conić, M., & Samardžija, N. (2002). Modern software development for bus station activities, In *Proceedings of Transport Systems Telematics, II International Conference* (pp. 339-343). Katowice – Ustron, Poland: Silesian University of Technology, Faculty of Transport.

Pantelić, S., Zeljković, V., Simeunović, D., Conić, M., & Laćimić, L. (2001). Different types of testing during development phase to achieve software high reliability and quality. In *12th MIRCE International Symposium, Proceedings* [CD-ROM]. Exeter, England: MIRCE Akademy.

Parker, D. (1988). Ethics for information systems personnel. *Journal of Information Systems Management, 5,* 44–48. doi:10.1080/07399018808962925

Parr, A., & Shanks, G. A. (2000). Model of ERP project implementation. *Journal of Information Technology, 15,* 289–303. doi:10.1080/02683960010009051

Paterno, F. (1999). *Model-Based Design and Evaluation of Interactive Applications.* London, United Kingdom: Springer-Verlag.

Payne, J. H. (1995). Management of multiple simultaneous projects: A state-of-the-art review. *International Journal of Project Management, 13*(3), 163–168. doi:10.1016/0263-7863(94)00019-9

Peleg, E. (2007). *Model driven development (MDD) for service oriented architecture (SOA) using UML and Metaphor Builder.* Retrieved September 11, 2008 from http://www-05.ibm.com/il/news/events/ruc/pdf/uml_and_metaphor_builder.pdf.

Pelion Systems. (2008). *Pelion Systems Solutions.* Retrieved July 22, 2008 from http://www.pelionsystems.com/solutions.asp

Pellegrinelli, S. (1997). Programme management: Organizing project-based change. *International Journal of Project Management, 15*(3), 141–149. doi:10.1016/S0263-7863(96)00063-4

Peppard, J., & Ward, J. (2004). Beyond strategic information systems: Towards an IS capability. *The Journal of Strategic Information Systems, 13*, 167–194. doi:10.1016/j.jsis.2004.02.002

Peppers, D., & Rogers, M. (1999). *The one to one manager: Real-world lessons in customer relationship management*. New York: Doubleday.

Peppers, D., & Rogers, M. (2001). *One to one B2B: Customer development strategies for the business-to-business world*. New York: Doubleday.

Perko, I., & Bobek, S. (2008). Supporting Business Intelligence in a Knowledge Intensive Environment: BIMAS, a Multi Agent System. *EMCSR 2008*, Wienna.

Perrin, B. (2002). How to – and how not to – Evaluate innovation. *Evaluation, 8*(1), 13–29. doi:10.1177/1358902002008001514

Petri, H., & Szekely, B. (2005). Logistics information systems: an analysis of software solutions for supply chain co-ordination. *Industrial Management & Data Systems, 105*(1), 5–18. doi:10.1108/02635570510575153

Piszczalski, M. (2000). Lean vs. information systems. *Automotive Manufacturing & Production, 112*(8), 26–28.

Pitt, L.F., Watson, R.T., & Kavan, C.B. (1995). Service quality: A measure of information systems effectiveness. *MIS Quarterly, 19*(2), 173-185.

Platje, A., Harald, S., & Wadman, S. (1994). Project and portfolio planning cycle: project-based management for the multiproject challenge . *International Journal of Project Management, 12*(2), 100–106. doi:10.1016/0263-7863(94)90016-7

Poppendieck, M. (2002) *Principles of Lean thinking* (pp. 1-7). Poppendieck LLC.

Portella, J. (2000). *Collaborative management of the product definition lifecycle for the 21st century*. CD-Rom Proceedings, PDT Europe Conference, Noordwijk, Netherlands, May 2000.

Porter, M. (2001). Strategy and the Internet. *Harvard Business Review, 79*(3), 63–78.

Portny, S. E. (2007). *Project management for dummies* (2nd ed.). Indianapolis: Wiley.

Poston, R., & Grabski, S. (2001). Financial impact of enterprise resource planning implementations. *International Journal of Accounting Information Systems, 2*(4), 271-294.

Powell, P., Levy, M., & Duhan, S. (2001). Information system strategies in knowledge-based SMEs. *European Journal of Information Systems, 10*, 25–40. doi:10.1057/palgrave.ejis.3000379

Pramukti, S. (2003). Establishing synergy between small companies and banks. *JAKARTA POST 06/03/2003*. Accession Number: 2W81194803776, Business Source Premier

Pras, A., Schönwälder, J., Burgess, M., Festor, O., Martínez Pérez, G., Stadler, R., & Stiller, B. (2007). Key research challenges in network management. *IEEE Communications Magazine, 45*(10), 104–110. doi:10.1109/MCOM.2007.4342832

Project Management Institute. (2004). *A guide to the project management body of knowledge* (3rd ed.). Pennsylvania: Project Management Institute.

Protogeros, N., Tahinakis, P., Mylonakis, J., & Gagalis, D. (2007). The entrepreneurship reality in the field of supply chain management (SCM) systems – The Hellenic market paradigm. *International Journal of Technology Marketing, 2*(1), 19–52. doi:10.1504/IJTMKT.2007.011584

Puigjaner, L., & Guillen-Gosalbez, G. (2008). Towards an integrated framework for supply chain management in the batch chemical process industry. *Computers & Chemical Engineering, 32*, 650–670. doi:10.1016/j.compchemeng.2007.02.004

Raghunath, S., & Ramakrishnan, K. K. (2007). Resource management for virtual private networks. *IEEE Communications Magazine, 45*(4), 38–44. doi:10.1109/MCOM.2007.343610

Ragowsky, A., & Gefen, D. (2008). What Makes the Competitive Contribution of ERP Strategic. *The Data Base for Advances in Information Systems, 39*(2).

Ragsdell, G., & warren, L. (1999). Learning from Beer: Using the Viable System Model for Organisational Design. *OR Insight, 12*(4), 16-23.

Rahm, E., & Bernstein, P. A. (2001). A survey of approaches to automatic schema matching. *The International Journal on Very Large Data Bases, 10*, 334–350. doi:10.1007/s007780100057

Raiffa, H. (1994). The prescriptive orientation of decision making: A synthesis of decision analysis, behavioral decision making, and game theory. In S. Rios (Ed.), *Decision theory and decision analysis: Trends and challenges*. Boston: Kluwer Academic Publishers.

Rainer, R. K., & Turban, E. (2009). *Introduction to Information Systems: Supporting and Transforming Business* (2nd ed.). Hoboken, NJ: John Wiley & Sons.

Ramayah, T., Roy, M.H., Arokiasamy, S., Zbib, I., & Ahmed, Z.U. (2007). Critical success factors for successful implementation of enterprise resource planning systems in manufacturing organisations. *International Journal of Business Information Systems*, *2*(3), 276-297.

Rangan, R. M., Rohde, S. M., Peak, R., Chadha, B., & Bliznakov, P. (2005). Streamlining product lifecycle processes: A survey of product lifecycle management implementations, directions, and challenges. *Journal of Computing and Information Science in Engineering*, *5*, 227–237. doi:10.1115/1.2031270

Rank, O. (2003). *Formale und informelle Organisationsstrukturen- Eine Netzwerkanalyse des strategischen Planungs- und Entscheidungsprozesses multinationaler Unternehmen*. Wiesbaden: Gabler Verlag.

Rao, S. S. (2000). Enterprise resource planning: business needs and technologies. *Industrial Management & Data Systems*, *100*(2), 81–88. doi:10.1108/02635570010286078

Raouf, A. (1998). Development of operations management in Pakistan. *International Journal of Operations & Production Management*, *18*(7), 649–650. doi:10.1108/01443579810217602

Rapp, V. W. (2002). *Information Technology strategies, how leading firms use it to gain an advantage*. New York: Oxford University Press, Inc.

Rashid, M. A., Hossain, L., & Patrick, J. D. (2002). *The evolution of ERP systems: A historical perspective*. Hershey, PA: Idea Group.

Rashid, M., Hossain, L., & Patrick, D. (2002). The evolution of ERP Systems: A historical perspective. In F. F.-H. Nah (Ed.), *Enterprise resource planning: Solution and management* (pp. 306-332). Hershey, PA: IRM Press.

Rautenstrauch, C., & Schulze, T. (2003). *Informatik für Wirtschaftswissenschaftler und Wirtschaftsinformatiker*, Berlin.

Raymond, L., & Bergeron, F. (2008). Project management information systems: An empirical study of their impact on project managers and project success. *International Journal of Project Management*, *26*, 213–220. doi:10.1016/j.ijproman.2007.06.002

Raymond, L., Bergeron, F., & Rivard, S. (1998). Determinants of BPR Success in SMEs. *Journal of Small Business Management*, *36*(1), 72-85.

Reif, H. (2001). *Complementing traditional information systems implementation methodologies for successful ERP system implementations*. Doctoral dissertation, Virginia Commonwealth University. Retrieved August 10, 2003 from Proquest.

Reijers, H., & Mansor, S. (2005). Best Practices in business process redesign: an overview and qualitative evaluation of successful redesign heuristics. *Omega*, *33*, 282-306.

Reitzig, R. W., Miller, J. B., West, D., & Kile, R. L. (2003). *Achieving capability maturity model integration maturity level 2 using IBM Rational software's* [White Paper]. Retrieved October 1, 2008 from http://www.cognence.com/pdfs/CMMI_ProcessAndRequirementsManagement_WhitePaper%20v1.0.pdf

Resource Description Framework Website. (2004). Retrieved October 15, 2008, from http://www.w3.org/RDF

Rheault, D., & Sheridan, S. (2002). Reconstruct your business around customers. *The Journal of Business Strategy*, *23*(2), 38–42. doi:10.1108/eb040236

Ribbler, J. (1996). Delivering solutions for the knowledge economy. *On-line*, *20*(5), 12-19.

Ringuest, J., & Graves, S. (1999). Formulating R&D portfolios that account for risk. *Research Technology Management*, *42*(6), 40–43.

Rivard, S., Raymond, L., & Verreault, D. (2005). Resource-based view and competitive strategy. *The Journal of Strategic Information Systems*, *20*, 1–22.

Roberts, N., Andersen, D., Deal, R., Garet, M., & Shaffer, W. (1983). *Introduction to computer simulation. A system dynamics modelling approach*. Addison Wesley Pub. Company.

Robey, D., Ross, J., & and Boudreau, M. (2002). Learning to implement enterprise systems: An exploratory study of the dialectics of change. *Journal of Management Information Systems, 19*(1), 17-46.

Robson, W. (1997). *Strategic management & information systems.* London: Pitman Publishing.

Rockart, J. (1979). Chief executives define their own data needs. *Harvard Business Review, 57*(2), 238–241.

Rockart, J. F. (1986). A primer on critical success factors. In C.V.Bullen (Ed.), *The rise of managerial computing: The best of the center for Information Systems research* (pp. 383-423). Cambridge, MA: Sloan School of Management, MIT.

Rockart, J., & Short, J. (1989). IT in the 1990s. *Sloan Management Review, 30,* 7-17.

Rooney, C., & Bangert, C. (2000). Is an ERP System Right for You? *Adhesives Age, 43*(9), 30–33.

Rosario, J.G. (2000). On the leading edge: critical success factors in ERP implementation projects. *Business World*, May, 21-27.

Rosen, E., Viswanathan, A., & Callon, R. (2001). Multiprotocol label switching architecture. *IETF RFC 3031 (Standards Track).* Retrieved April 26, 2003 from http://www.rfc-editor.org/rfcsearch.html

Roser, S. (2008). *Designing and enacting cross-organisational business process: A model-driven, ontology-based approach.* Retrieved October 14, 2008, from http://www.opus-bayern.de/uni-augsburg/volltexte/2008/805/pdf/Diss_Roser_Business_ Processes.pdf.

RosettaNet Website. (2008). Retrieved October 15, 2008, from http://www.rosettanet.org/ cms/sites/RosettaNet.

Ross, J. W. (1998). *The ERP revolution: Surviving versus thriving.* Centre for Information Systems Research, Sloan School of Management.

Rouse-Talley, N. (2007). *PLM Roundtable, Part 2.* Retrieved November 16, 2008, from http://66.195.41.10/Articles/Feature/PLM-Roundtable%2C-Part-2-200703161743.html

Rovere, L., & Lebre, R. (1996). IT diffusion in small and medium-sized enterprises: Elements for policy definition. *Information Technology for Development, 7*(4), 169–181.

Rowe, J. (2007). *Digital manufacturing's growing PLM role,* Retrieved November 16, 2008, from http://manufac-turing.cadalyst.com/manufacturing/article/articleDetail.jsp?id=477580

Ruh, W., Maginnis, F., & Brown, W. (2000). *Enterprise application integration.* A Wiley Tech Brief. New York: John Wiley & Sons Inc.

Rummler, G., & Brache, A. (1990). *Improving performance: How to manage the white space on the organization chart.* San Francisco: Jossey-Bass.

Rzevski, G., & Prasad, K. (1998). The synergy of learning organizations and flexible information technology. *AI and Society, 12,* (87-96). Retrieved August 20, 2008 from http://www.rzevski.net

Saarinen, T. (1996). An expanded instrument for evaluating information systems success. *Information and Management, 31*(2), 103-118.

Saaty, T. L. (1994). *The fundamentals of decision making and priority theory with the analytic hierarchy process.* Pittsburgh: RWS Publications.

Saccomano, A. (2003). ERP vendors consolidate. *Journal of Commerce, 4*(24), 46.

Sánchez, R., Raptis, L., & Vaxevanakis, K. (2008). Ethernet as a carrier grade technology: developments and innovations. *IEEE Communications Magazine, 46*(9), 88–94. doi:10.1109/MCOM.2008.4623712

Sandoe, K., Corbitt, G., & Boykin, R. (2001). *Enterprise Integration.* New York: Wiley.

Santhanam, R., Sasidharan, S., Brass, D., & Sambamurthy, V. (2006). The influence of knowledge transfers on the implementation of enterprise information systems. In A. Tjoa, L. Min Xu, & S. Chaudhry (Eds.), *Research and practical issues of enterprise information systems* (pp. 579-581). Boston: Springer.

SAP Business Workflow (2008). Retrieved October 14, 2008, from http://help.sap.com/saphelp_46c/ helpdata/en/c5/e4a930453d11d189430000e829fbbd/content.htm

Sarbutts, N. (2003). Can SMEs 'do' CSR? A practitioner's views of the ways small-and medium-sized enterprises are able to manage reputation through corporate social responsibility. *Journal of Communication Management, 7*(4), 340–348. doi:10.1108/13632540310807476

Sarker, S., Sarker, S., & Sidorova, A. (2006). Understanding Business Process Change Failure: An Actor-Network

Perspective. *Journal of Management Information Systems, 23*(1), 51-86.

SBS (2003). www.sbs.gov.uk/statistics/smedefs.php

Schantzl, R. E., Loyall, J. P., Rodrigues, C., Schmidt, D. C., Krishnamurthy, Y., & Pyarali, I. (2003). Flexible and adaptive QoS control for distributed real-time and embedded middleware. In M. Endler & D. Schmidt (Eds.), *Middleware 2003* (LNCS 2672, pp. 374-393). Springer Berlin/Heidelberg.

Scheer, A. W., & Nüttgens, M. (2000). ARIS architecture and reference models for business process management (LNCS 1806, pp. 301-304).

Scheer, A.-W. (1998). *ARIS – Business process frameworks* (2nd ed.). Berlin.

Scheer, A.-W., Grieble, O., & Zang, S. (2003). Collaborative business management. In W. Kersten (Ed.), *E-collaboration* (pp. 29-57). Wiesbaden/Germany: Gabler Verlag.

Schein, E. (1990). Organizational culture. *American Psychologist, 2,* 109.

Schmidt, A., & Kiefer, C. (2005). Kooperationen zwischen mittelständischen Unternehmen. In J. Zentes, B. Swoboda, & D. Morschett (Eds.), *Kooperationen, Allianzen und Netzwerke* (pp. 1357-1381). Wiesbaden/Germany: Gabler Verlag.

Schultink, G. (2000). Critical environmental indicators: Performance indices and assessment methods for sustainable rural development planning. *Ecological Modelling, 130,* 47–58. doi:10.1016/S0304-3800(00)00212-X

Schwaninger, M. (2006). *Intelligent organizations.* Berlin: Springer.

Schwartz, D., & Te'eni, D. (2000). Tying knowledge to action with kMail. In *IEEE Knowledge Management* (pp. 33-39), Bar-Ilan University.

Scott, M., & Bruce, R. (1987). Five Stages of Growth in Small Business. *Long Range Planning, 20*(3), 45–52.

Seán de Búrca, Fynes, B., & Marshall, D. (2005). Strategic technology adoption: Extending ERP across the supply chain. *The Journal of Enterprise Information Management, 18*(4), 427–440. doi:10.1108/17410390510609581

SEC Web page. *SEC Filings and Forms* (EDGAR). Accessed at http://www.sec.gov/edgar.shtml on Jan. 5, 2009, last modified Dec. 15, 2008

Seddon, P., Staples, S., Patnayakuni, R., & Bowtell, M. (1999). Dimensions of information systems success. *Communications of AIS, 2,* 17–26.

Segrestin, D. (2004). Les ERP entre le retour à l'ordre et l'invention du possible. *Science and Society,* (61): 3–15.

Seifert, M. (2007). *Unterstützung der Konsortialbildung in Virtuellen Organisationen durch prospektives Performance Measurement.* Dissertation at the University of Bremen.

Sellers, G. (1997, September). Tools for managing your Business Process. *CMA Magazine* (pp. 25-27).

Seradex. (2007). Lean Manufacturing - Seradex ERP Solutions. Retrieved September 3, 2008 from http://www.seradex.com/ERP/Lean_Manufacturing_ERP.php

Serdült, U. (2005). Anwendung sozialer Netzwerkanalyse. In *Zürcher Politik- & Evaluationsstudien,* No. 3.

Seriosity Website. (2008). Retrieved October 14, 2008, from http://www.seriosity.com/products.html

Shakkottai, S., & Srikant, R. (2006). Economics of network pricing with multiple ISPs. *IEEE Transactions on Networking, 14*(6), 1233–1245. doi:10.1109/TNET.2006.886393

Shang, S., & Seddon, P. (2000). *A comprehensive framework for classifying the benefits of ERP systems.* Paper presented at the Americas Conference on Information Systems AMCIS.

Shang, S., & Seddon, P. B. (2002). Assessing and managing the benefits of enterprise systems: The business manager's perspective. *Information Systems Journal, 12,* 271–299. doi:10.1046/j.1365-2575.2002.00132.x

Shapiro, J. F. (2001). *Modeling the supply chain.* MIT, Boston: Duxbury Thomson Learning.

Sharma, M. K., & Bhagwat, R. (2006). Performance measurements in the implementation of information systems in small and medium-sized enterprises: A framework and empirical analysis. *Measuring Business Excellence, 10*(4), 8-21.

Shaw, M. (2000). Electronic commerce: State of the art. In Shaw, et al. (Eds.), Handbook on electronic commerce (pp. 431-444). Berlin/ Germany: Springer.

Shenhar, A. J., & Dvir, D. (2004). Project management evolution: Past history and future research directions. In D.P. Slevin, D.I. Cleland, & J.K. Pinto (Ed.), *Proceedings of the PMI research conference 2004*, London, UK.

Shenhar, A. J., & Dvir, D. (2005): *Project management research - Challenges and opportunities*. Stevens Institute of Technology, Hoboken. [Electronic version].

Shields, M.G. (2001). *E-business and ERP: Rapid implementation and project planning*. New York: John Wiley & Sons Inc.

Sholler, D. (2008, September). *2008 SOA user survey: Adoption trends and characteristics*. Retrieved from http://www.gartner.com/DisplayDocument?id=765720.

Shtub, A., & Bard, J. F. (1995). *Globerson Shlomo: Project management engineering, technology and implementation*. Prentice Hall International Editions.

Si, L., & Osanna, P. H. (1995). Multi-functions integrated factory. In *Proceedings of 11th ISPE/IEEE/IFAC International Conference on CARS& FOF'95, Colombia* (pp. 578-586).

Sia, S., Tang, M., Soh, C., & Boh, W. (2002). Enterprise resource planning (ERP) systems as a technology of power: Empowerment or panoptic control? *ACM SIGMIS Database, 33*(1), 23–37. doi:10.1145/504350.504356

Simchi-Levi, D., Kaminsky, P., & Simhci-Levi, E. (2000). *Designing and managing the supply chain: Concepts, strategies and case studies*. New York: McGraw-Hill.

Simon, D. (1985). *Die Früherkennung von strategischen Diskontinuitäten durch Erfassung von ☐Weak Signals☐*. Dissertation at the University of Vienna.

Simon, G. L. (2005). The case for non-technical client relationship managers in B2B professional services firms. *Service Quality Quarterly, 26*(4), 1–18.

Singel, R. (2006). Are you ready for Web 2.0? Wired News Torkington, N. 2006. Available at: http://radar.oreilly.com/archives/2006/05/more_on_our_web_20_service_mar.html. (Last accessed: September 2008).

Skok, W., & Legge, M. (2002). Evaluating enterprise resource planning (ERP) systems using an interpretive approach. *Knowledge and process management, 9*(2), 72-82.

SMEs: development of constructs and propositions. *Asia Pacific Journal of Marketing and Logistics, 20*(1), 97-131

Smith, B., & Welty, C. (2001). FOIS introduction: Ontology---towards a new synthesis. In *Proceedings of the international Conference on Formal ontology in information Systems - Volume 2001* (pp. 3-9). Ogunquit, Maine/USA. FOIS '01. New York: ACM.

Smith, K. E. (2000). CRM sizzles in the digital economy. *VARBusiness, 16*(25), 104–105.

Sneed, H., & Brössler, P. (2003). *Critical success factors in software maintenance - A case study*. In *Proceedings of the International Conference on Software maintenance (ICSM'03)* (pp. 190-198).

SofTech Inc. & John Stark Associates (2005). *Top 10 PLM pitfalls to avoid*. Retrieved September 27, 2008, from http://www.softech.com/plm-whitepapers/plm-pitfalls-to-avoid.php

Somers, T.M., & Neslon, K.G. (2003). A taxonomy of players and activities across the ERP project life cycle. *Information & Management, 41*(3), 257-278.

Sommers, G., & Nelson, C. (2003). A taxonomy of players and activities across the ERP project life cycle. *Information & Management, 41*(3), 257–278. doi:10.1016/S0378-7206(03)00023-5

Spearman, M. L., & Zazanis, M. A. (1992). Push and pull production systems: Issues and comparisons. *Operations Research, 40*(3), 521–532. doi:10.1287/opre.40.3.521

Spearman, M. L., Hopp, W. J., & Woodruff, D. L. (1999). A hierarchical control architecture for constant work-in-process (CONWIP). *Journal of Manufacturing and Operations Management, 2*(3), 147–171.

Spradlin, C., & Kutoloski, D. (1999). Action-oriented portfolio management. *Research Technology Management, 42*(2), 26–32.

Stacey, R. D. (2003). *Strategic Management and Organisational Dynamics, the Challenge of Complexity*. London: FT Prentice Hall.

Stalker, D. I., & Mehandjiev, N. (2006). *A devolved ontology model for the pragmaticweb*, Paper presented at the First International Conference on the Pragmatic Web, ICPW.

Stan, S., Evans, K. R., Wood, C. M., & Stinson, J. L. (2007). Segment differences in the asymmetric effects of service quality on business customer relationships. *Journal of Services Marketing, 21*(5), 358–369. doi:10.1108/08876040710773660

Stark, J. (2004). *Product lifecycle management: Paradigm for 21st Century Product Realisation*. Springer.

Stefanou, C. (1999). Supply chain management (SCM) and organizational key factors for successful implementation of enterprise resource planning (ERP) systems. In *Proceedings of 5th Americas Conference on information Systems* (pp. 800-802).

Stefansson, G. (2002). Business-to-business data sharing: a source for integration of supply chains. *International Journal of Production Economics, 75*(1-2), 135–146. doi:10.1016/S0925-5273(01)00187-6

Steger-Jensen, K., & Hvolby, H. (2008). Review of an ERP System Supporting Lean Manufacturing. In T. Koch (Ed.), *International Federation for Information Processing (IFIP)*, Volume 257, *Lean Business Systems and Beyond* (pp. 67-74). Boston, MA: Springer.

Steindl, K. G. (1999). *Development of a Software package for the internet based analysis of roundness data*. Master Thesis, TU-Wien, A, and UNC Charlotte, USA, 32-37.

Steinfield, C. W. (1986). Computer-mediated communication in an organizational setting: Explaining task-related and socioemotional uses. In M. L. McLaughlin (Ed.), *Communication Yearbook, 9*, 777-804. Newbury Park, CA.: Sage.

Sternad, S., & Bobek, S. (2004). ERP solution implementation critical success factors: What does matter and what does not. *Acta systemica* (pp. 27-31). International Institute for Advanced Studies in Systems Research and Cybernetics, Windsor, Ontario, Cananda.

Stevenson, R. (1993). Strategic Business Process Engineering. In K. Spurr, P. Layzell, L. Jennison, & N. Richards (Eds.), *Software Assistance for Business Re-engineering*. Chichester: Wiley.

Stevenson, T. (2000). Will our futures look different, now? *Futures, 32*, 91–102. doi:10.1016/S0016-3287(99)00069-5

Stock, J. R., & Lambert, D. M. (2001). *Strategic logistics management*. London: McGraw-Hill International Edition.

Stojanovic, M., & Acimovic-Raspopovic, V. (2008). QoS provisioning framework in IP-based VPN. In G. Putnik & M. Cunha (Eds.), *Encyclopedia of Networked and Virtual Organizations*, Vol. III (pp. 1317-1324). New York: Information Science Reference.

Strategies, A. R. C. (2007). The when, why and how of ERP support for Lean. *SYSPRO*, 1-22. Retrieved July 18, 2008 from http://www.syspro.com

Strategosinc (2008). *Origins & history Lean Manufacturing*. Retrieved July 18, 2008 from http://www.strategosinc.com/just_in_time.htm

Stratman, J.K. (2002). Enterprise resource planning (ERP) competence constructs: Two-stage multi-item scale development and validation. *Decision Sciences, 33*(4), 601-628.

Strong, D. M., & Volkoff, O. (2004). A roadmap for enterprise system implementation. *Computer*, (June): 22–29. doi:10.1109/MC.2004.3

Sturm, F., Kemp, J., & Wendel de Joode, R. (2004). Towards strategic management in collaborative network structures. In Camarinha-Matos (Ed.), *Collaborative networked organisations* (pp. 131-138). Boston: Kluwer Academic Publishers.

Suh, K., Couchman, P. K., Park, J., & Hasan, H. (2003). *The application of activity theory to Web-mediated communication. Information systems and activity theory volume 3; Expanding the horizon.* Wollongong, Australia: University of Wollongong Press.

Sum, C., Ang, J., & Yeo, L. (2002). A multiple-case design methodology for studying MRP success and CSFs. *Information & Management, 39*(4), 271–282. doi:10.1016/S0378-7206(01)00096-9

Summer, M. (1999). Critical success factors in enterprise wide information management systems projects. In *Proceedings of 5th Americas Conference on Information Systems* (pp. 232-234).

Sun, A. Y. T., Yazdani, A., & Overend, J.D. (2005). Achievement assessment for enterprise resource planning (ERP) system implementations based on critical success factors (CSFs). *International Journal of Production Economics, 98*(2), 189-203.

Sydow, J. (1992). *Strategische netzwerke: Evolution und organisation*. Wiesbaden: Gabler Verlag.

Talwar, R. (1993). Business re-engineering. *Long Range Planning, 26*(6), 22-40.

Taniguchi, N. (1974). On the basic concept of nanotechnology In *Proceedings of the. Int. Conf. Prod. Eng., Tokyo: JSPE, part 2* (pp. 18-23).

Taylor, J. (1999). *Management Accounting.*

Taylor, M., & Murphy, A. (2004). SMEs and E-business. *Journal of Small Business and Enterprise Development, 11*(3), 280–289. doi:10.1108/14626000410551546

Te'eni, D., & Schwartz, D. (1999). Contextualization in computer-mediated communication. In L. Brooks, & C. Kimble (Eds.), *Information systems—The next generation* (pp. 327-338). New York: McGraw-Hill.

Team, Q. S. G. (2006). *Manufacturing can actively manage their value streams with Pelion's next generation EasyVSM tool.* Retrieved July 20, 2008 from http://www.qsoftguide.com/cm/index.php?blog=2&p=254&more=1&c=1&tb=1&pb=1

Teng, J., Grover, V., & Fiedler, K. (1994). Re-designing business processes using IT. *Long Range Planning, 27*(1), 95-106.

Tersine, R., Harvey, M., & Buckley, M. (1997). Shifting organisational paradigms. *European Management Journal, 15*(1), 45-57.

Tetteh, E., & Burn, J. (2001). Global strategies for SME. *Logistic Information Management, 14*(1), 171–180. doi:10.1108/09576050110363202

Thakkar, J., Kanda, A., & Deshmukh, S.G. (2008). Supply chain management in

Themistocleous, M., & Irani, Z. (2003). Towards a novel framework for the assessment of enterprise application integration packages. In *Proceedings of the 36th Hawaii International Conference on System Sciences*, HICSS, (p.234a).

Themistocleous, M., Irani, Z., & Love, P. (2004). Evaluating the integration of supply chain information systems: A case study. *European Journal of Operational Research, 159*, 393–405. doi:10.1016/j.ejor.2003.08.023

Themistocleous, M., Irani, Z., & Sharif, A. (2000). *Evaluating application integration.* Paper presented in Seventh European Conference on Evaluation of Information Technology (ECITE 2000), Dublin, Ireland, MCIL Reading, UK, 193- 202.

Themistocleous, M., Irani, Z., O'Keefe, R., & Paul, R. (2001). ERP problems and application integration issues: An empirical survey. In *Proceedings of the 34th Annual Hawai International conference on System Sciences, 9* (pp. 9045-9053).

Third Generation Partnership Project – 3GPP. (2003). End to end quality of service concept and architecture. *Technical specification 23.207, Release 5.* Retrieved July 7, 2007 from http://www.3gpp.org

Thong, J. Y. L. (2001). Resource constraints and information systems implementation in Singaporean small business. *Omega, 29*(2), 143–156. doi:10.1016/S0305-0483(00)00035-9

Tiefensee, B. (2008, September). *Power8 und die Auswirkungen auf die Luftfahrtzulieferindustrie - Erfolgreiche Kooperationen in der Luftfahrtzulieferindustrie.* Presentation at the BIBA Kolloquium.

Torkzadeh, G., & Doll, W.J. (1999). The development of a tool for measuring the perceived impact of information technology on work. *Omega- The International Journal of Management Science, 27*(3), 327-339.

Trætteberg, H. (1999). Modelling Work. Workflow and Task Modelling. In Vanderdonckt, & Puerta (Eds.), *CADUI* (pp. 275-280). Kluwer.

Trætteberg, H., Molina, P. J., & Nunes, N. J. (2004). Making model-based UI design practical: usable and open methods and tools. In Vanderdonckt, Nunes, & Rich (Eds.), *Intelligent User Interfaces* (pp. 376–377). ACM.

Trunick, P. A. (1999). ERP: promise or pipe dream. *Transportation and Distribution, 40*(1), 23–6.

Tschofenig, H., & Fu, X. (2006). Securing the next steps in signaling (NSIS) protocol suite. *International Journal of Internet Protocol Technology, 1*(4), 271–282.

Tsoukas, H., & Shepherd, J. (2004). Coping with the future: developing organizational foresightfulness (Introduction). *Futures, 36*, 137–144. doi:10.1016/S0016-3287(03)00146-0

Tubbs, A. (2005). *Top ten risks to a configuration project and how to avoid them.* Retrieved September 27, 2008, from http://whitepapers.businessweek.com/detail/RES/1203446022_342.html

Turban, E., Dorothy, L., McLean, E., & Wetherbe, J. (2006). *Information technology for management, transforming organizations in the digital economy.* Hoboken, NJ: John Wiley & Sons, Inc.

Turbide, D. A. (2005). *Five ways ERP can help you implement Lean.* EPICOR Software. Retrieved July 16, 2008 from http://whitepapers.zdnet.com/abstract.aspx?docid=351964.

Turner, D., & Crawford, M. (1994). Managing Current and Future Competitive Performance: The Role of Competence. In G. Hamel & A. Heene (Eds.), *Competence Based Competition* Chichester: Wiley.

Turner, J. R., & Speiser, A. (1992). Programme management and its information system requirements. *International Journal of Project Management, 10*(4), 196–206. doi:10.1016/0263-7863(92)90078-N

Turoff, M. (1972). An alternative approach to cross impact analysis. *Technological Forecasting and Social Change, 3*(3), 330–341.

UDDI Initiative. (2002-2003). *Universal definition, discovery, and integration, version 3. An industrial initiative.* Retrieved from http://www.oasis-open.org/committees/uddi-spec/doc/tcspecs.htm#uddiv3.

Ugwu, O. O., & Haupt, T. C. (2007). Key performance indicators and assessment methods for infrastructure sustainability -- a South African construction industry perspective. *Building and Environment, 42*, 665–680. doi:10.1016/j.buildenv.2005.10.018

Ulrich, C. (2004). *Die Dynamik von Coopetition: Möglichkeiten und Grenzen dauerhafter Kooperation.* Wiesbaden: Deutscher Universitätsverlag.

Ulrich, M. (2001). *Critical success factors in a business process integration initiative* [Tactical Strategy Group White Papers]. Retrieved October 1, 2008 from http://www.ebizq.net/topics/ bpm/features/2602.html.

Umble, E. J., Haft, R. R., & Umble, M. M. (2003). Enterprise Resource Planning: Implementation procedures and critical success factors. *European Journal of Operational Research, 146*, 241–257. doi:10.1016/S0377-2217(02)00547-7

United Nations Centre for Trade Facilitation and Electronic Business. (2008). Retrieved October 14, 2008, from http://www.unece.org/cefact/.

Uren, V. (2005). Semantic annotation for knowledge management: Requirements and a survey of the state of the art. *Journal of Web Semantics: Science . Services and Agents on the WWW, 4*(1), 14–28. doi:10.1016/j.websem.2005.10.002

Urman, S., Hardman, R., & McLaughlin, M. (2004). *Oracle Database 10g PL/SQL Programming.* McGraw-Hill Osborne Media.

Ursic, D., Anteric, S., & Mulej, M. (2005). Business Process Re-engineering in Practice - A medium-sized Slovenian Company in Difficulties. *Systemic Practice and Action Research, 18*(1), 89-117.

Valkokari, K., & Helander, N. (2007). Knowledge management in different types of strategic SME network. [f]. *Management Research News, 30*(7), 597–608. doi:10.1108/01409170710773724

Van den Eynde, J., Veno, A., & Hart, A. (2003). They look good but don't work: a case study of global performance indicators in crime prevention. *Evaluation and Program Planning, 26*, 237–248. doi:10.1016/S0149-7189(03)00028-4

Van der Aalst, W. M. P. (2003). *Business process management: Past, present, future* [BPTrends White Papers]. Retrieved October 1, 2008 from http://www.bptrends.com/resources_publications

van der Aalst, W., ter Hofstede, A.H.M., Kiepuszewski, B., & Barros, A. P. (n.d.). Workflow Patterns. *Journal of Distributed and Parallel Databases, 3*(14), 5-51.

Van Der Merwe, A. P. (1997). Multi-project management- organizational structure and control. *International Journal of Project Management, 15*(4), 223–233. doi:10.1016/S0263-7863(96)00075-0

Van Stijn, E., & Wensley, A. (2001). Organisational memory and the completeness of process modelling in ERP systems. *Business Process Management Journal, 7*(3), 181–194.

Vandaie, R. (2008). The role of organizational knowledge management in successful ERP implementation projects. *Knowledge-Based Systems, 21*, 920–926. doi:10.1016/j.knosys.2008.04.001

Vasconcelos, A., Sousa, P., & Tribolet, J. (2005). *Information system architecture evaluation: from software to enterprise level approaches.* Paper presented at 12th

European Conference on Information Technology Evaluation (ECITE 2005), Turku, Finland.

Verma, D. C. (2002). Simplifying network administration using policy-based management. *IEEE Network, 16*(2), 20–26. doi:10.1109/65.993219

Verwijmeren, M. (2004). Software component architecture in supply chain management. *Computers in Industry, 53*(2), 165–178. doi:10.1016/j.compind.2003.07.004

Victor, B., & Boynton, A. C. (1998). Invented here. Boston, MA: Harvard Business School Press.

Vinck, D. (Ed.). (2003). *Everyday engineering. An ethnography of design and innovation.* Cambridge, MA: MIT Press.

Vinck, D., & Jeantet, A. (1995). Mediating and commissioning objects in the sociotechnical process of product design: A conceptual approach. In D. Maclean, P. Saviotti & D. Vinck (Eds.), *Designs, networks and strategies* (Vol. 2, pp. 111-129). Bruxelles: EC Directorate General Science R&D.

Vitale, M. R. (1986). American Hospital Supply corp. The ASAP system. *Harvard Business School Case Study*, March, 1-17.

Vonortas, N. S. (2000). Multimarket contact and inter-firm cooperation in R&D. *Journal of Evolutionary Economics, 10*(1-2), 243–271. doi:10.1007/s001910050014

Vrečko, I. (2007). Mastering strategic crisis with project management usage as a holistic invention-innovation process. In A.W. Małgorzata, J.S. Erich, & M. Mulej (Eds.). *Entrepreneurship and innovation in Europe, Klagenfurt.* Klagenfurt University, Department of Innovation Management and Entrepreneurship.

W3 Consortium. (2000). *Simple object access protocol. A proposal of W3 Consortium.* Retrieved from http://www.w3.org/TR/SOAP

W3C Semantic Web. (2008). *Web Ontology Language (OWL).* Retrieved October 15, 2008, from http://www.w3.org/2004/OWL

Wald, A. (2003). *Netzwerkstrukturen und -effekte in Organisationen: eine Netzwerkanalyse in internationalen Unternehmen.* Mannheim: Gabler Verlag.

Walford, R. B. (1999). *Business process implementation for IT professionals and managers,* Norwood, MA: Artech House.

Wallace, T.F., & Kremzar, M.H. (2001). *ERP: making it happen – the implementer's guide to success with enterprise resource planning.* New York: John Wiley & Sons, Inc.

Walsham, G. (1995). Interpretive case studies in IS research: Nature and method. *European Journal of Information Systems, 4*, 74-81.

Walsham, G. (1997). Actor-network theory and is research: Current status and future prospects. In A. Lee, J. Liebernau & J. DeGross (Eds.), *Information systems and qualitative research* (pp. 466-480). London: Chapman and Hall.

Walton, J. S. (2008). Scanning beyond the horizon: Exploring the ontological and epistemological basis for scenario planning. *Advances in Developing Human Resources, 10*(2), 147–165. doi:10.1177/1523422307304101

Wang, E., Sheng-Pao, S., Jianj, J. J., & Klein, G. (2008). The consistency among facilitating factors and ERP implementation success: A holistic view of kit. *Journal of Systems and Software, 81*, 1601–1621.

Wang, Q., Yung, K. L., & Ip, W. H. (2004). A hierarchical multi-view modeling for networked joint manufacturing system. *Computers in Industry, 53*(1), 59–73. doi:10.1016/S0166-3615(03)00124-6

Ward, J., Hemingway, C., & Daniel, E. (2005). A framework for addressing the organisational issues of enterprise systems implementation. *The Journal of Strategic Information Systems, 14*(2), 97–119. doi:10.1016/j.jsis.2005.04.005

Warhurst, A. (2005). Future roles of business in society: The expanding boundaries of corporate responsibility and a compelling case for partnership. *Futures, 37*, 151–168. doi:10.1016/j.futures.2004.03.033

Waring, T., & Wainwright, D. (2000). Interpreting integration with respect to information systems in organizations – image, theory and reality. *Journal of Information Technology, 15*, 131–148

Warren, L. (2002). Towards Critical Practice in a Teaching Company Scheme. *OR Insight, 15*(4), 11-19.

Warren, L. (2003). Towards Critical Practice in SMEs. *Systemic Practice and Action Research, 16*(3), 197-212

Warren, L. (2003). The crisis of control: a progressive approach towards information systems integration for small companies. *Information Systems and E-business Management, 1*(4), 353-371.

Warren, L. (2003). Supporting Knowledge Management through he Viable System Model. *Systemist, 25*, 156-165.

Warren, L., Fuller, T., Argyle, P., & Welter, F. (2008, September). *A complexity perspective on entrepreneurship: a new methodology for research in high velocity environments.* Paper presented at the British Academy of Management conference, Harrogate, UK.

Wassermann, S., & Faust, K. (1994). *Social network analysis – methods and applications.* Cambridge University Press.

Wastell, D., White, P., & Kawalek, P. (1994). A methodology for BPR. *Journal of Strategic Information Systems, 3*(1), 23-40.

Web Service Modeling Ontology Website. (2008). Retrieved October 15, 2008, from http://www.wsmo.org/.

Weber, D. (2005). *Strategische Planung im Unternehmensnetzwerk am Beispiel industrieller Dienstleistungen im Industrieanlagenbau.* Aachen: Shaker Verlag.

Wee, S. (2002). Juggling toward ERP success: Keep key success factors high. *ERP news.* Retrieved January 22, 2002, from http//.erpnews.com/erpnews/erp904/02get.html-Weill, P. (1990). *Do computers pay off?* Washington, DC: International Center for Information technologies.

Wei, C. (2008). Evaluating the performance of an ERP system based on the knowledge of ERP implementation objectives. *International Journal of Advanced Manufacturing Technology, 39*, 168–181. doi:10.1007/s00170-007-1189-3

Weill, P., & Broadbent, M. (1998). *Leveraging the new infrastructure: How market leaders capitalize on information technology.* Boston, MA: Harvard Business School Press.

Welge, M. K., & Al-Laham, A. (2008). *Strategisches management – Grundlagen, prozess implementerung.* Wiesbaden: Gabler Verlag.

Welti, N. (1999). *Successful SAP R/3 implementation – Practical management of ERP projects.* England, UK: Addison-Wesley.

Weyer, J. (2000). *Soziale Netzwerke - Konzepte und Methoden der sozialwissenschaftlichen Netzwerkforschung.* München: Oldenbourg Verlag.

Wheatley, M. (2005, November). Processes—not applications—make the company go 'round, *Manufacturing Business Technology.* Retrieved August 9, 2008 from http://www.mbtmag.com/archive/2005/20051101.php.

Wheatley, M. (2007). ERP is needed to sustain the gains of Lean programs. *Manufacturing Business Technology.* Retrieved July 18, 2008 from http://www.mbtmag.com/article/CA6450623.html

White, D., & Fortune, J. (2001). Current practice in project management – an empirical study. *International Journal of Project Management, 20*, 1–11. doi:10.1016/S0263-7863(00)00029-6

White, S. A. (2008). *Introduction to BPMN.* Retrieved October 14, 2008, from http://www.bpmn.org/Documents/Introduction%20to%20BPMN.pdf.

White, S., & Miers, D. (2008). *BPMN Modeling and reference guide.* Lighthouse Pt, FL: Future Strategies Inc.

Whitehouse, D. J. (2002). Surface and Nanometrology, Markov and Fractal Scale of Size Properties. In Y.V. Chugui, S.N. Bagayev, A. Weckenmann, & P.H. Osanna (Eds.), *Proceedings of 7th International Symposium on "Laser Metrology Applied to Science, Industry and Everyday Life - LM-2002", Nowosibirsk, Russia* (pp. 691-707).

Whitehouse, D.J. (1991). Nanotechnology Instrumentation. *Measurement + Control, 24* (2), 37-46.

Whittaker, S., & Sidner, C. (1996). Email overload: Exploring personal information management of Email. In *Proceedings of ACM CHI'96* (pp. 276-283).

Wieder, B., Booth, P., Matolcsy, Z. P., & Ossimitz, M.L. (2006). The impact of ERP systems on firm and business process performance. *Journal of Enterprise Information Management, 19*(1) 13-29.

Wiendahl, H.-P. (1997). *Betriebsorganisation für Ingenieure.* München: Carl Hanser Verlag.

Wiens, J. (2007). Is Web 2.0 Inherently Insecure? *Network Computing, 18*(7), 22.

Wier, B., Hunton, J., & HassabElnaby, H. R. (2007). Enterprise resource planning systems and non-financial performance incentives: The joint impact on corporate performance. *Int. J. of Accounting Information Systems, 8*, 165-190.

Wild, J. (1982). *Grundlagen der Unternehmensplanung.* Wiesbaden: VS Verlag für Sozialwissenschaften.

Wildemann, H. (2008). *Innovationsmanagement □Leitfaden zur Einführung eines effektiven und effizienten Innovationsmanagementsystems.* München: TCW Verlag.

Wilhelm, S., & Habermann, F. (2000). Making ERP a success. *Communications of the ACM, 43*(4), 57–61. doi:10.1145/332051.332073

Willcocks, L. (1994). Introduction of capital importance. In L. Willcocks (1994) (Ed.), *Information Management: The Evaluation of Information Systems Investments* (pp. 1-27). London: Chapman & Hall.

Wind, J., & West, A. (1991). Reinventing the Corporation. *Chief Executive* (pp. 72-75).

WinMan. (2003). *WinMan and Lean systems - A white paper on integrating WinMan with Lean systems.* Retrieved August 20, 2008 from http://www.winmanusa. com/PDF/WinMan_Lean_Systems.pdf

WinMan. (2006). *Athena Controls.* Retrieved August 20, 2008 from http://www.winmanusa.com/success.asp

Wirtz, B., & Vogt, P. (2003). E-Collaboration im B2B-Bereich: Strategien, Strukturen und Erfolgsfaktoren. In M. Büttgen, & L. Fridjof (Eds.), *Online-Kooperationen* (pp. 265-284). Wiesbaden/Germany: Gabler Verlag.

Witherill, J. W., & Kolak, J. (1996). Is corporate re-engineering hurting your employees? *Professional Safety, 41*(5), 28-32.

Womack, J. P., & Jones, D. T. (1996). Beyond Toyota: How to root out waste and pursue perfection. *Harvard Business Review,* (September-October): 140–158.

Woodhouse, J. (2000). Key performance indicators. Retrieved from http://www.TWPL.com

Woodhouse, J. (2004). Closing the loop: sustainable implementations of improvements. In *ERTC Reliability & Asset Management Conference; Oil, Gas, Petrochem & Power Industries.*

Woodman, R. W., Sawyer, J. E., & Griffin, R. W. (1993). Toward a theory of organizational creativity. *Academy of Management Review, 18*, 293–321. doi:10.2307/258761

Workflow Management Coalition Website. (2008). Retrieved October 15, 2008, from http://www.wfmc.org/.

Wu, H., & Chou, T. (1992). *Obstacles and reactions of Taiwan's SMEs.* Chung-Hua Institution for Economic Research.

Würer, G. *(1995).* Internationale Allianz- und Kooperationsfähigkeit österreichischer Unternehmen: Beiträge zum Gestaltansatz als Beschreibungs- und Erklärungskonzept. *Linz: Trauner.*

Wysocki, R. K., & McGary, R. (2003). *Effective project management* (3rd ed.). Indianapolis: Wiley.

Yang, J., Wu, C., & Tsai, C. (2007). Selection of an ERP system for a construction firm in Taiwan: A case study. *Automation in Construction, 16*, 787–796. doi:10.1016/j.autcon.2007.02.001

Yarrow, G. (2006). *BEng Thesis: Product lifecycle management systems (PLM) - state-of-the-art report,* University of Durham, UK.

Yates, I. (2004). 2004 Proved Successful for SAP Latin America. *Caribbean Business, 33*(10).

Yen, R., & Sheu, C. (2004). Aligning ERP implementation with competitive priorities of manufacturing firms: an exploratory study. *International Journal of Production Economics, 92*(3) 207–220.

Yin, R. (1994). *Case Study Research. Design and Methods* (2nd ed.). California: Sage.

Yin, R.K. (1994). *Case Study Research Design and Methods* (2nd ed.). Sage, Thousand Oaks.

Yusuf, Y., Gunasekaran, A., & Abthorpe, M. (2004). Enterprise information systems project implementation: A case study of ERP in Rolls-Royce. *International Journal of Production Economics, 87*, 251.

Yusuf, Y., Gunasekaran, A., & Wu, C. (2005, December). Implementation of enterprise resource planning in China. *Technovation.*

Zahavi, R. (1999). *Enterprise application integration with CORBA.* New York: Wiley.

Zani, W. (1970). Blueprint in MIS . *Harvard Business Review*, (November-December): 25–37.

Zeng, Y. E., Wen, H. J., & Yen, D. C. (2003). Customer relationship management (CRM) in business-to-business (B2B) e-commerce. [f]. *Information Management & Computer Security, 11*(1), 39–44. doi:10.1108/09685220310463722

Zhang, L., Lee, M.K.O., Zhang, Z., & Banerjee, P. (2002). Critical Success Factors of Enterprise Resource Planning Systems Implementation Success in China. *Hawaii International Conference on System Sciences*.

Zhao, S., & Chang, E. (2007). *From database to semantic web ontology: An overview*. Springer, Heidelberg.

Zhuang, Q., Feng, J., & Bao, H. (2007). Measuring semantic gap: An information quantity perspective. *5th IEEE International Conference on Industrial Informatics, 2*, 669-674.

Zuboff, S. (1988). *In the age of the smart machine: The future of work and power*. New York: Basic Books.

About the Contributors

Maria Manuela Cruz-Cunha is currently an Associate Professor in the School of Technology at the Polytechnic Institute of Cavado and Ave, Portugal. She holds a Dipl. Eng. in the field of Systems and Informatics Engineering, an M.Sci. in the field of Information Society and a Dr.Sci in the field of Virtual Enterprises, all from the University of Minho (Portugal). She teaches subjects related with Information Systems, Information Technologies and Organizational Models to undergraduated and post-graduated studies. She supervises several PhD projects in the domain of Virtual Enterprises and Information Systems and Technologies. She regularly publishes in international peer-reviewed journals and participates on international scientific conferences. She serves as a member of Editorial Board and Associate Editor for several International Journals and for several Scientific Committees of International Conferences. She has authored and edited several books and her work appears in more than 70 papers published in journals, book chapters and conference proceedings.

* * *

Vladanka S. Acimovic-Raspopovic received her B.Sc. (1976), M.Sc. (1984) and Ph.D. (1995) degrees in electrical engineering from the University of Belgrade. She is professor at the University of Belgrade, Faculty of Transport and Traffic Engineering – Department for Telecommunication Networks and Tele-traffic Engineering. Dr. Acimovic-Raspopovic managed or participated in 3 international and 28 national research projects and studies concerning radio and optical transmission systems and telecommunication networks design and implementation, and also pricing and economic aspects of networks. Her research interests are in the fields of performance evaluation, efficient usage of network resources, QoS routing and traffic engineering in next generation broadband networks. She published in over 130 papers.

Fahd Alizai is completing his PhD (part time) in the School of Management and Information Systems at Victoria University, Australia. He has previously completed a Master in Information Technology (University of Arid Agriculture, Pakistan) and Master in Business Information Systems (Victoria University, Australia). Fahd has been employed as the Project Manager, Software implementation at the University of Ballarat (Australia) for the last two and half years; extensively engaged in Enterprise application implementations. He has eight years of IS experience in several IT fields, including programming, application testing, business development, application integration and so forth. He is aiming to deliver an ERP implementation strategic workable model for midsize businesses that should help then to achieve greater success rates in ERP implementations.

Klara Antlova is a lecturer at the Department of Informatics, Faculty of Economics Technical University of Liberec, Czech Republic. She has been working as a programmer in Technical university Computing centre. She graduated her PhD study at Faculty of Mechanical Engineering, Technical University of Liberec. Now she is a leader of cooperation programme between the university and small companies supported by European Community funds. She is responsible for university teaching scheme: Computing in Business and industrial trainee of students. She published articles in Czech and foreign journals and in proceedings of international conferences. Her other teaching and research interest is e-commerce, knowledge management and project management.

Maria Argyropoulou is a doctoral candidate at Brunel University/London. She received her BS and MS in Kapodistriako University of Athens/Greece and Athens University of Economics and Business/ Greece respectively. She also holds an MBA from Strathclyde University/Scotland where she works as an associate lecturer. She has worked for Greek and international companies for more than 10 years specialising in operations management and ERP systems implementation. Her work has appeared in journals and conference proceedings. Her research interests focus on corporate governance and IT systems implementation and evaluation.

Silke Balzert is a researcher at the Institute for Information Systems (IWi) at German Research Center for Artificial Intelligence (DFKI). In 2005, she received her diploma in business administration from the Saarland University (Germany). Before her employment at the institute, she worked almost 3 years for a management consultancy. Ms. Balzert participated in the European research project Commius and is currently working within the European research project R4eGov, which aims to enable interoperability between large European public administrations. Her research activities comprise Business Process Management and Process Interoperability.

Jorge M. Bauer is director of the research and educational Laboratory "CIM - Computer Integrated Manufacturing" (Flexible Manufacturing - Robotic) of the Engineering Faculty of U.N.L.Z. Buenos Aires, Argentina. He graduated as Dipl.Ing. in mechanical engineering at Technical University Buenos Aires and graduated as Dr.techn. (PhD) at Vienna University of Technology (TUW) (Austria). Prof. Bauer is Lecturer for Automation in Technical Logostics at Technical University Buenos Aires UTN-FRBA. Additionally he is Lecturer at the Department for Production Metrology and Interchangeable Manufacturing at Institute for Production Engineering) of TUW and Lecturer of University U.A.D.E.R (Entre Rios) for Automation and Robotics. He is responsible for a project INCOMAP Ingeniería y Computación Aplicada (automation, quality, industrial computer systems and mechatronics). Prof. Bauer is member of the Austrian Standards Committee "Geometrical Product Specification - GPS" and of the "Austrian Society for Quality Sciences - FQW."

Ergin Beceren, Msc., is working of Business development Departmant at Anadolu Bilisim Hizmetleri A.S. He is currently project manager at ABH. His current main area include project management, strategic management and ERP implementation models. He has been involved in project management over 10 years.

Samo Bobek is a professor of Information Systems at the School of Economics and Business at University of Maribor. He teaches courses in undergraduate level (Introduction to Information Systems, Information Systems in Finance and Banking), master of science program (Information Systems Management, Management Information Systems, Information Systems in Service Organizations) and MBA program (Information Management). Professor Bobek research areas are Strategic Information Systems Planning, Information management, Banking technology. He has published several books in Slovene language. His bibliography includes more than 200 articles, conference papers, research reports etc. Professor Bobek is head of Information and organization systems department. Professor Bobek also acts as consultant to several corporations, banks and insurance firms in Slovenia.

Stephen Burgess completed his PhD in the School of Information Management and Systems at Monash University. His thesis was in the area of small business interactions with customers via the internet. His research and teaching interests include the use of ICTs in small businesses (particularly in the tourism field), the strategic use of ICTs, and B2C electronic commerce. He has received a number of competitive research grants in these areas. He has completed several studies related to website features in small businesses and how well websites function over time. He has authored or edited three books and special edition of journals in topics related to the use of ICTs in small business and been track chair at the international ISOneWorld, IRMA, Conf-IRM and ACIS conferences in these areas.

Thomas Burkhart is a researcher at Institute for Information Systems (IWi) at the German Research Center for Artificial Intelligence (DFKI). In 2008 he received his degree in business administration at the German University in Saarbruecken. His major research fields are Business interoperability as well as ERP-Systems. He is currently working within the European research Project Commius which aims at developing an email based interoperability solution for SMEs.

Vesna Čančer, 1967, Slovenian, holds a PhD in Economic and Business Sciences, and is an Associate Professor of Quantitative Economic analysis at the University of Maribor's Faculty of Economics and Business. Her research focuses primarily on decision analysis, creative problem solving, business process optimization and process management. She has authored or co-authored a number of recent articles, books and papers, and has given invited lectures at several international scientific conferences in the fields of Systems Thinking, Operations Research and Information Management.

Martin Carpenter received a MMath degree from the University of Warwick followed by Master's Degrees in Mathematical Logic and Information Processing from the Universities of Manchester and York, respectively. Since 2004 he has been working as a Research Associate at the University of Manchester on the MaBE, Crosswork, SUDDEN, Commius and Soa4all European research projects. His major research interest lies in the area of distributed, multi agent systems and he hopes to soon complete a PhD in the area of providing support for distributed formation of virtual organisations.

Jeffrey Chang is Principle Lecturer at London South Bank University where he has been director of the Postgraduate Computing and Information Management Programme for several years. His research and teaching interests are in information systems management, the use of IS/IT in SMEs and organizational change and behaviour. He has had papers published in Information Systems Journal and Knowledge and Process Management and in his South Bank programme has developed and taught modules such as Software Project Management and Strategic Management of Information Systems. Jeffrey received his doctorate from Warwick Business School in 2001. His thesis, entitled Exploring the links between business process re-engineering (BPR) and small and medium-sized enterprises (SMEs)', involved an empirical investigation into organizational change within the small business domain, with a focus on how information technology facilitates business transformation.

Wai M Cheung is a Research Officer at the University of Bath, UK. He obtained his PhD from the University of Durham, UK. His current research interests include Cost Estimation in Product Development, Knowledge Management in Design and Manufacturing, Enterprise Systems Integration and Open Source Solutions in Product Development.

Ilhan Derman, Msc., is working of Business development Departmant at Anadolu Bilisim Hizmetleri A.S.She is currently senior consultant at ABH. Her current main area include ERP implementation, performance measurement in supply change management and process management. She has been working as an ERP consultant over ten years.

Zdenko Dezelak is research and teaching assistant of Information Systems at the School of Economics and business at the University of Maribor where he studies a master of science degree. His research areas e-business solutions and implementation of e-business solutions. His bibliography includes several articles, conference papers, research reports etc. He collaborates in several courses in undergraduate level (E-business, Introduction to Information Systems, E- Finance and E- Banking, Enterprise Resource Planning Solutions, E-Business Information Systems) and several courses in master of science program (Business Information Solutions, Strategic Management Issues in E-business). He also cooperates with some companies in Slovenia as a consultant.

Heiko Duin, born in 1965, received his Master of Science in Computer Science in 1992 at the University of Bremen. He started as a research scientist at BIBA in1992. From 1997 to 2002 he was employed at the engineering company PRODUTEC Ingenieurgesellschaft. From 2000 until now he is one of the two managing directors of PRODUTEC Ingenieurgesellschaft. In 2002 he joined BIBA again. He participated in many European projects within the programmes RACE, ACTS, TEN-TELECON, ESPRIT, IST, ICT and NMP during his professional career. In some of them he performed in management functions, such as overall project manager or technical manager. Currently his main interests involve the development of tools to support strategic planning in enterprise networks, the development of serious gaming applications for educational purposes and the development of mobile applications.

M. Numan Durakbasa, Department for Interchangeable Manufacturing and Industrial Metrology (Abteilung Austauschbau und Messtechnik) of the Institute for Production Engineering and Laser Technology, and Nanotechnology Laboratory and vice head of the Department for Certification of Quality Professional at Vienna University of Technology, with long-standing international practical experience as "Quality System Auditor", Austrian expert in the international technical Committee ISO/TC 213 "Geometrical Product Specifications and Verification", as well as ISO/TC 176 "Quality Management and Quality Assurance" and vice chairman of the Austrian Standard Committees ON-K 129 "Quality Management Systems" and ON-K 031 "Anforderungen und Prüfungen der geometrischen Produktspezifikation; Technische Produktdokumentation".

Jens Eschenbächer, born in 1968 graduated as Economist in the end of 1996. He started his career as a controller at CSC Ploenzke AG in Germany in the corporate management department. Between 1998 and 2000 he was working as a research consultant at PRODUTEC Ingenieurgesellschaft. In the beginning of 2000 he joined a PhD-program at the University of Bremen about global logistics management. In parallel he was employed at BIBA since 2000 until today. He was involved in several ESPRIT, IST and ICT Research projects such as ECOLEAD or COIN. In 2004 he created the department "Collaborative Business in Enterprise Networks" which he was leading until the beginning of 2007. In his PhD thesis he is focusing on innovation management in virtual organizations which he finished in the beginning of 2008. Currently he is working as a senior researcher at BIBA.

Maria João Ferro. With a background in computational linguistics, Maria João Ferro is currently working on her PhD thesis on Terminology Management. She is presently lecturing Business English and Research Methods to undergraduate and graduate students at Lisbon School of Accounting and Administration, where she is Assistant Professor.

Ted Fuller is Head of Lincoln Business School at the University of Lincoln in the United Kingdom. Formerly Professor of Entrepreneurship and Strategic Foresight and Head of the Centre for Entrepreneurship and SME Development at Teesside Business School, University of Teesside. Prior to that he was Director of the Foresight Research Centre at Durham Business School. He researches processes of entrepreneurship and the contribution that entrepreneurship makes to the futures of individuals and society. He is member of many boards of academic journals, leads international research programmes, publishes widely and advises government and corporate organisations.

Dimitrios Gagalis, MSc in IS, is on the Teaching Staff in the Department of Information Technology Applications in Administration and Economy at the Technological Educational Institute (TEI) of West Macedonia in Grevena, Greece. He received an MSc in Information Systems and a Bachelor Degree in Mathematics. He has more than 10 years of working experience as an analyst in the private sector and teaching experience in both private and public sector. He has participated in many research projects and committees as well as in several national and international conferences.

Bart H.M. Gerritsen studied mechanical engineering and obtained an M.Sc. and a Ph.D. from the Delft University of Technology in the Netherlands. He became involved in information technology some twenty five years ago and has been active in that field since. He held various positions at TNO, as an IT Manager, as an Information Manager and as a Quality Manager. Amongst others, he has been responsible for an ISO 9001 certification programme at TNO. He is currently working on asset management strategies and knowledge as a strategic asset. Earlier, he has been with CAP Gemini for more than five years and with a Dutch Ministry, as a project leader and an IT expert.

Dimitrios Ginoglou is an Associate Professor of Accounting, Department of Accounting and Finance at the University of Macedonia, Thessaloniki, Greece. He is also a tutor at the Hellenic Open University. He holds a Ph.D. in Accounting, an MA in Management Science and a Bachelor Degree in Business Administration. He has had 20 years work experience in the public and private sector and 25 years teaching experience. He has published articles in academic journals and he has participated in many international conferences.

Jorge Marx Gómez is working as a full-time professor at the business informatics group at Oldenburg University. His research interests include Very Large Business Applications (VLBA), Federated ERP Systems, and Sustainability Reporting.

Călin Gurău is Associate Professor of Marketing at GSCM - Montpellier Business School, France, since September 2004. He is a Junior Fellow of the World Academy of Art and Science, Minneapolis, USA. He worked as Marketing Manager in two Romanian companies and he has received degrees and distinctions for studies and research from University of Triest, Italy; University of Vienna, Austria; Duke University, USA; University of Angers, France; Oxford University and Southampton Business School and Heriot-Watt University, United Kingdom. His present research interests are focused on Marketing Strategies for High-Technology Firms and Internet Marketing. He has published more than 30 papers in internationally refereed journals, such as International Marketing Review, Journal of Consumer Marketing, Journal of Marketing Communications, etc.

Pritish Halgeri graduated from Visvesvaraya Technological University, India in 2006 with a bachelor's degree in Mechanical Engineering. He completed his Master of Science degree in Industrial and Manufacturing Systems Engineering from Kansas State University in Dec 2008. Currently he is employed by Crustbuster Speed King Inc (CBSK) where he works as a Manufacturing Engineer doing continuous process improvement on all the product lines, introducing and implementing Lean concepts and Kaizen events in the plant. Analyzing and establishing the sequence of operations for fabrication, welding and assembly routings through company's MRP system "MAPICS". His background and interest are related to Lean Manufacturing, ERP systems, Six Sigma, Kaizen, Discrete event simulation.

Anton Hauc, 1939, is a full professor at the University of Maribor - Faculty of Economics and Business. He gives lectures at the undergraduate and postgraduate programmes for Project Management, Multi-project management, Programme management and Project oriented strategic management subjects. He has been the founder and still is the head of the Institute for project management at the faculty. Professor Hauc is known as a "father of project management" in Slovenia. He has published the first books on the project management subjects in Slovenia, first started giving lectures from that field at faculties as well as in different companies and other organizations, gave numerous consultancies and is the author of many scientific and expert papers. He founded Slovenian project management association, managed first IPMA international conference on project management in Slovenia and he is IPMA first assessor for certifying project managers. He is strongly connected with the practice and his main research results have always been directed into applicability for practitioners.

Carmen de Pablos Heredero is a Professor in the Business Administration Area at the Rey Juan Carlos University in Madrid, Spain from 1994. She is responsible for the PhD in Business Administration. She is specialised in the impact of information technologies over organisational systems where she develops main research. She has chaired Doctoral Dissertations and Projects on the impact of information and communication technologies in organisational performance. She has presented communications in different international venues and has published in specialised journals. She has also worked as a consultant in the area of IS management at Primma Consulting.

Mónica de Pablos Heredero is an Associate Professor in the Business Administration Area at the Rey Juan Carlos University in Madrid, Spain from 2001. She is teaching and doing research in the impact of new technologies in Organizations, especially in the area of ERPs and CRMs. She is also the CIO for the InSitu Group in Spain. She has been project leader in the SAP ERP implementations in different industries in the international context. She has published on the impact of ERP over organisational final performance.

George Ioannou is an Associate Professor of Operations and Business Processes Management at the Department of Management Science and Technology at AUEB and head of the Operations Management and ERP Systems Research centre of the Management Sciences Laboratory. He has been Assistant Professor at the Industrial and Systems Engineering Department of Virginia Tech and Head of the Manufacturing Systems Integration Laboratory there. His research focuses on the analysis, design, and optimization of operations systems and business processes, combining advanced network and computational technologies with operational research models and methods. He has graduated from the Mechanical Engineering Faculty at National Technical University of Athens, from the Centre for Robotics and Automated Systems in Imperial College of Science, Technology, and Medicine (scholarship SERC) and from the Computer Integrated Manufacturing Lab of Institute for Systems Research, University of Maryland (scholarship by National Science Foundation).

Paul Kidd is an engineer by training, but has spent the majority of his career working on the application of social sciences to technology design, and the development of interdisciplinary design methods. He has published many papers concerned with theories and concepts, as well as applications. Paul has also been involved with the development of technology implementation methods that integrate strategy, technology and organisational design. He has also participated in many research projects that have involved collaboration between social scientists and technologists. For the past 20 years Paul has worked as an independent researcher, writer and consultant, and has had a long running involvement with European Commission supported research programmes. He has also delivered consulting services to many businesses, both large and small, worldwide. He is regularly involved with government agencies, both national and international, in supporting the development, operation and review of various research programmes.

Dimitrios N. Koufopoulos (B.Sc., MBA, PhD MCMI, FIMC) is Senior Lecturer in the Brunel Business School. His work has appeared in the *European Marketing Academy Conference, British Academy of Management and Strategic Management Society* Proceedings and in various journals like *Long Range Planning* Journal, *Journal of Strategic Change* and *Journal of Financial Services Marketing, Corporate Ownership and Control* and *Corporate Board*. His research interests are on strategic planning systems, top management teams, corporate governance, and corporate strategies.

Jaroslav Král graduated in mathematical statistics in 1959 at Charles University. Since 1960 he worked as a programmer, research worker, analyst, and teacher at Czech Technical University, Czechoslovak Academy of Science, Masaryk University in Brno and Charles University in Prague. He is currently Professor at Charles University Prague and Masaryk University Brno. He is the author and coauthor of three books dealing with problems of software engineering. He has active in the research of formal languages, compiler construction and parsing, random number generators and simulations, education, and on (current main interest) service-oriented and soft real-time systems. He has taken part in several projects including compilers, manufacturing control systems for SME (machine tool floor control, logistic support systems and some issues of manufacturing scheduling), and additive random number generator.

Michal Laclavik is a researcher at Institute of Informatics, Slovak Academy of Sciences. In 1999 he received his MSc degree in Computer Science and Physics. He received his PhD degree in Applied Informatics with focus on Knowledge Oriented Technologies in 2006. He is the author and co-author of several scientific papers, and participates in the Pellucid, K-Wf Grid and Commius European projects and several national projects. He has strong scientific and development expertise in email based systems and semantic annotation. He also gives lectures on Information Retrieval at Slovak University of Technology. Finally, he is one of the initiators of the Commius project focussing on email based interoperability for SMEs. His research interests include email analysis and processing, information management and processing, and semantic annotation.

Ana Lampret has been involved in the IT business solutions since 2003, mostly in ERP, but also CRM. Her professional experience in IT includes Business Solutions Sales Manager at Adacta Software (2003-2007, www.adacta-group.com), Partner Technology Specialist at Microsoft Slovenia (2007-2008, www.microsoft.com/slovenia/dynamics). Currently she manages the ERP sales in all Balkan markets for SRC group (www.src.si). Her responsibilities have included acquiring new projects, key account management, and project implementation methodology design. Prior to that, Ana worked in the financial industry (1999-2000, sales consultant at Poteza Stock Broking, www.poteza.si; 2000-2003, sales consultant at First Pension Company/Prva pokojninska druzba, www.prva.net), when she was involved in the project of the internal CRM system implementation (custom design). Ana got her B.A. in Politics and Economics at the University of York, UK in 1999 (http://www.york.ac.uk/depts/pep/). She obtained her International Baccalaureate degree (A-level equivalent) at the United World College of the Adriatic, Duino, Italy (www.uwcad.it).

Margi Levy is an Associate Professor in the Enterprise Group at Warwick Business School, University of Warwick. Before becoming an academic she worked as an IS consultant with Coopers and Lybrand in W. Australia, for a number of financial and software development organizations in London. She has published in a number of journals: Information and Management, Journal of Strategic Information Systems, European Journal of Information Systems, Information Resource Management Journal, International Journal of Technology Management, Small Business Economics. She is the co-author with Philip Powell of the first book to address the study of information strategies for SMEs: Strategies for Growth in SMEs: the role of information and information systems, Butterworth Heinemann, 2005. She is currently researching into IS adoption of new and innovative technologies in SMEs and also the role of intermediaries in SME IS adoption.

Daniel Lübke is a research assistant at the software group at the Leibniz Universität Hannover. He has worked as software developer and trainer before and is currently researching in the fields Service-Oriented Architecture. Further research interests include Agile Software Development.

Efrem Mallach teaches Information Systems in the Charlton College of Business, University of Massachusetts Dartmouth. He has been at the University of Massachusetts since 1988, previously on its Lowell campus, with a four-year break to work in industry. Dr. Mallach has been involved in system conversion since the 1970s, when he managed the development of software conversion and hardware emulation tools for Honeywell Information Systems. He is often called on to advise firms on the best way to approach conversion projects. He also works and consults in analyst relations: advising computer and communications firms how to improve their relationships with this group of industry experts and advisors.

Hélder Fanha Martins. The author is currently writing his PhD thesis on information systems applied to education and training and has written several articles on the topic of virtual teams. His experience in the fields of technology extends to the project management sector as well. Hélder Fanha Martins is lecturer of business management at the Lisbon School of Accounting and Administration (Lisbon Polytechnic). He is currently teaching a Business Simulation course as well as a Principles of Management course.

Roger McHaney is a University Distinguished Teaching Scholar and professor of management information systems in Kansas State University's College of Business Administration. A K-State faculty member since 1995, McHaney teaches courses in enterprise systems, quality management and business computing. His areas of research include discrete event simulation, educational technology, service sector simulations, and organizational computing. McHaney has bachelors and masters degrees from Lake Superior State University in Northern Michigan and a doctorate in computer information systems and quantitative analysis from the Sam M. Walton College of Business at the University of Arkansas. He has taught and lectured in a variety of countries including New Zealand, Australia, China, the UK, and Italy. McHaney has published in numerous journals, written textbooks, and developed an array of instructional material.

Nikolay Mehandjiev is Senior Lecturer in the Manchester Business School at the University of Manchester, having received his Ph.D. in 1997. He researches the provision of flexible services using software agents. These ideas are applied to support "instant" virtual enterprises and to the design of flexible supply networks. He has co-authored two books in the area, and has guest-edited three special issues of international journals, including the Communications of ACM.

Vladimír Modrák is a head of Manufacturing Management Department at Technical University. He obtained a PhD degree in Mechanical Engineering Technology at the same University in 1989. His research interests include Business Process Management, Logistics and Quality Management. Dr. Modrák is Vice-Editor in Chief of a Slovak journal on Manufacturing Engineering and an editorial board member of more international journals such as International Journal of Information Systems and Supply Chain Management and Journal of Cases in Information Technology. He also served as session chair and chairman at International Conferences in information system discipline.

Jaideep Motwani, Ph.D., is a Professor and the Chair of the Management Department at Grand Valley State University. He received his Ph.D. degree in Operations Management from University of North Texas. His research interests include information technology management, enterprise systems, and quality management. He has published in a variety of journals including IEEE Transactions on Engineering Management, Operations Research, Omega, Journal of Operational Research Society, European Journal of Operational Research, International Journal of Operations and Production Management, International Journal of Production Research, and International Journal of Technology Management. Dr. Motwani also serves as a consultant and trainer for a number of organizations in the areas of information technology implementation, project management, and total quality management

P. Herbert Osanna is head of the Department for Certification of Quality Professional, Department for Interchangeable Manufacturing and Industrial Metrology (Abteilung Austauschbau und Messtechnik) of the Institute of Institute for Production Engineering and Laser Technology at the Vienna University of Technology (TUW) and President of the Platform for Quality Siences (Forum für Qualitätswissenscaften – FQW). He is Treasurer as well as Austrian Representative in the General Council of the International Measurement Confederation IMEKO and Vice President of the "Austrian Society for Measurement and Automation - OGMA". He is head of the Austrian Standard Committee ON-K 031 "Anforderungen und Prüfungen der geometrischen Produktspezifikation; Technische Produktdokumentation".

Snežana Pantelić, *MSc Mech E, BSc Math*, has focused her career on information technologies in Serbia, working for private companies (start-ups), industrial corporation "Lola" and Lola Institute and government R&D institutes - "Vinca" Institute and Mihailo Pupin Institute. She was also engaged as a national expert in European Agency for Reconstruction projects in Serbia. A former researcher in IS and information services, she has moved to IS and business process design and IT project management. She has designed and implemented several IS/IT in transportation and manufacturing SMEs, the most complex being „Integral information system of Belgrade Bus Station". Her academic background comes from the University of Belgrade, Serbia. She is a PHD candidate and has a MS from the Faculty of Mechanical Engineering and a BS from the Faculty of Natural Sciences. Her research includes: IS/IT strategic planning & development, IS/IT management, business process design, software development process and management. She has published more than 60 papers.

Z.J.Pei received a PhD in Mechanical Engineering from University of Illinois at Urbana-Champaign. Currently, he is an Associate Professor in the Department of Industrial and Manufacturing Systems Engineering at Kansas State University. He received three US patents and has published 60 journal papers and 80 conference papers. He teaches manufacturing related courses including lean manufacturing and Six Sigma. His current research activities include analysis and modeling of traditional and non-traditional machining processes as well as manufacturing of biofuels. His research has been support by National Science Foundation, Society of Manufacturing Engineers, and industry.

Bernard Penz is a Professor of Operations Research and Logistics at the Industrial Engineering School of the Grenoble Institute of Technology since 1996 and leads his research activity at G-SCOP laboratory. He holds a PhD in Operations Research from University Joseph Fourier of Grenoble in 1994 on the optimization of jobshop scheduling problems. His research interests include Scheduling Theory and particularly scheduling with availability periods, Lot Sizing Problems with transportation constraints, and Supply Chain Optimization. In the last few years, he has worked on Enterprise Information Systems, ERP, and more precisely on the choice of the tool and its implementation.

Igor Perko received a MSc degree in business informatics in 2002. He is a lecturer at the Faculty of Economics and Business, Maribor, Slovenia. His research interests include management support systems, planning and developing information systems, and information support in financial sector. His latest research efforts are in connecting the use of intelligent agents and knowledge management structures to manage the Business intelligence processes. His activities are focused to the cooperation with the business sector; he is also an author of many scientific articles. He can be reached at Igor.Perko@uni-mb.si.

Philip Powell is Deputy Dean, Professor of Information Management and was Director of the Centre for Information Management in the School of Management at the University of Bath. Formerly, he was Professor of Information Systems, University of London, and Director of the Information Systems Research Unit at Warwick Business School. He is the author of seven books on information systems and financial modeling. His work has been published in over 90 international journals and over 100 conferences. He is Managing Editor of the Information Systems Journal and associate editor and editorial board member of a number of other journals. He is a past President of the UK Academy for Information Systems. His research concerns the role and use of information systems in organisations especially issues of strategy and evaluation in the context of small firms. More recently he has contributed to research on e-business and knowledge management.

Nicolaos Protogeros is a assistant professor of Information Systems, E-Commerce, Department of Accounting and Finance at the University of Macedonia, Thessaloniki, Greece. He holds a Ph.D. in Information Systems, an MSc in Remote Sensing and a Bachelor Degree in Mathematics. He has had 15 years work experience in the public and private sector and 12 years teaching experience. He has published articles in academic journal and he has participated in many international conferences.

Igor Antonio Rivera-González is a Professor and Researcher at UPIICSA – Instituto Politécnico Nacional (IPN) in Mexico. He has a PhD in Industrial Engineering at the Institut National Politechnique de Grenoble (INPG) in France, a Master in Industrial Engineer at the INPG and other at the IPN and he has a Engineer Degree in Industrial Electronic of the Tecnológico de Puebla in Mexico. Mr Rivera has published several scientific articles in journals and books of research and he is a referee in two scientific journals.. In addition, he belongs to scientific associations like ESOCITE in Latin America, PROJECTICS in Europe and the Red Mexicana of Researcher in Organizational Studies in Mexico.

Dirk Schaefer is an Assistant Professor in the George W. Woodruff School of Mechanical Engineering at Georgia Tech Savannah, USA. His research interests are focused on the high-impact interdisciplinary area of Information Engineering for Complex Engineered Systems. Prior to joining Georgia Tech, Dr. Schaefer was a Lecturer in the School of Engineering at Durham University, UK. He has published around 75papers on Computer-Aided Engineering and Design as well as Engineering Education in conference proceedings, journals and books. Dr. Schaefer is a member of several professional affiliations including The American Society of Mechanical Engineers (ASME), The Institute of Electrical & Electronics Engineers (IEEE), The Association for Computing Machinery (ACM), The American Society for Engineering Education (ASEE), The European Society for Engineering Education (SEFI), The Institution of Engineering Designers (IED), and The British Computer Society (BCS). Furthermore, Dr. Schaefer is a registered professional European Engineer (Eur Ing) and a Chartered

Engineer (CEng), a Chartered IT-Professional (CITP) and a Fellow of The Higher Education Academy (FHEA) in the United Kingdom.

Habib Sedehi has born in 1951, in Teheran (Iran) and lives in Italy since 1966. He is also Italian citizen. He has obtained his degree (Laurea) in Electronic Engineering at Rome University in 1976 with specialisation in Computer Sciences and Control Systems. With the position of Contract Full Professor of Computer Sciences (Informatics) at Rome University "La Sapienza" - Communication Sciences Department , he teaches System Dynamics Simulation Modelling and Project Management. As consultant, he works in various area of ICT. He has published two books in the area of Software Engineering and general Computer Sciences and authored more than 30 publications in the field of System Dynamics, Software Engineering and Information Technology. He is founder and elected President of Italian Chapter of System Dynamics Society, founder member of Italian Association for System Science Research and Direction Committee Member of Italian Software Metric Association.

Martin Seleng is a researcher at Institute of Informatics, Slovak Academy of Sciences. In 1999 he obtains his MSc degree in Mathematics and Computer Sciences at the Faculty of Mathematics and Physics. He worked previously at Faculty of Economic and Informatics at the Economic University as a researcher and a teacher in the field of mathematics, statistics and computer science. He has strong expertise with email related system development and information system evaluation. Since 2006 he has been employed at the institute. He is an author and co-author of several scientific papers and participates in the K-Wf Grid and Commius European projects and several national projects. He teaches the information retrieval at the Faculty of Informatics and Information Technologies. His research interests include email communication and large scale information processing.

Iain Duncan Stalker is a Senior Lecturer in Mechanical, Manufacturing and Design Engineering at the University of Teesside. An active researcher, his interdisciplinary approach embraces a diversity of interests which unify in the development of intelligent software systems and flexible knowledge structures to facilitate complex, typically dynamic, problem-solving environments. Current work involves the application of modern computing approaches to engineering design and a synthesis of computational and service-oriented approaches to develop novel simulation systems. With expertise in mathematics, engineering and artificial intelligence, previous work includes consultancy for international and local companies and research positions at a number of universities in the UK and Europe.

Simona Sternad is senior lecturer of Information Systems at the School of Economics and business at the University of Maribor where she received a master of science degree in 2005. Her research areas are Business process reengineering, ERP solutions and e-business solutions, implementation of ERP solutions and maintenance of ERP solutions. Her bibliography includes more than 50 articles, conference papers, research reports etc. She collaborates in several courses in undergraduate level (E-business, Introduction to Information Systems, E- Finance and E- Banking, Enterprise Resource Planning Solutions, E-Business Information Systems) and several courses in master of science program (Business Information Solutions, Strategic Management Issues in E-business). Simona Sternad also cooperates with some companies in Slovenia as a consultant.

Mirjana D. Stojanovic received her B.Sc. (1985) and M.Sc. (1993) degrees in Electrical Engineering and her Ph.D. degree (2005) in Technical Sciences, all from the University of Belgrade. She joined Mihailo Pupin Institute in Belgrade in 1985, where she is currently research fellow in telecommunication networking. She managed or participated in development of a number of communication devices and systems for data and voice transmission and network management, which were successfully applied in major Serbian corporate systems. As author or coauthor, she published more than 80 papers in national and international journals and conferences. She is also assistant professor in networking at the University of Belgrade, Faculty of Transport and Traffic Engineering and School of Electrical Engineering. Her research interests include communication protocols, quality of service and traffic engineering in next generation networks, as well as service and network management.

Panayiotis Tahinakis is an assistant professor of Accounting, Department of Accounting and Finance at the University of Macedonia, Thessaloniki, Greece. He is also a tutor at the Hellenic Open University. He holds a Ph.D. in Accounting, an MSc in Accounting and a Bachelor Degree in Business Administration. He has had 10 years work experience in the public and private sector and 12 years teaching experience in several private Universities in Thessaloniki, Greece. He has published articles in academic journals and he has participated in many international conferences.

Özalp Vayvay, Ph.D., is working of Industrial Engineering Department at Marmara University. He is currently the Chairman of the Engineering Management Department at Marmara University. His current research interests include new product design, technology management, business process reengineering, total quality management, operations management, logistics & supply chain management. Dr. Vayvay has been involved in R&D projects and education programs for a over the past 10 years.

Dominique Vinck is a Professor of Sociology at Pierre Mendès France University and at the Grenoble Institute of Technology. He is specialised in sociology of sciences and of innovation (STS and engineering studies), He leads his research activity at PACTE laboratory (joint CNRS and University of Grenoble laboratory), where he directs the module "Sciences and Society". His investigations focus on socio-technical innovation and industrial organizations. He is currently working on micro- and nanotechnologies. Recent publications are: Everyday engineering. An ethnography of design and innovation (MIT Press, 2003), Pratiques de l'interdisciplinarité (PUG, Grenoble, 2000), Sciences et sociétés. Sociologie du travail scientifique (A.Colin, Paris, 2007) and L'équipement de l'organisation industrielle. Les ERP à l'usage (Hermès, Paris, 2008).

Igor Vrečko, 1975, Slovenian, holds MSc in Economic and Business. He is a Teaching Assistant of Project Management and Organization & Management at the University of Maribor - Faculty of Economics and Business. His research focuses primarily on project management and integration of project management with strategic crisis management as well as innovation management. He has a wide practical experiences gained through consultancy projects in many domestic and foreign companies. He has performed numerous invited lectures and managed workshops in different organizations. He is also director of international project management certification process for Slovenia, vice president of Slovenian Project Management Association, official assessor of national profession qualification *project manager*, assessor of research and developing projects under Public Agency of Republic of Slovenia for entrepreneurship and foreign investments and assessor in national commission for innovations.

Lorraine Warren is Deputy Director of Postgraduate Education, and a Senior Lecturer in Entrepreneurship and Innovation at the School of Management, University of Southampton in the United Kingdom. She researches the processes of high technology/high growth entrepreneurship and innovation in dynamic emergent sectors such as the creative industries in the digital economy. She has presented at international conferences and has published widely in peer reviewed journals. She has worked on a number of funded research projects with universities in the US and Russia, and has advised Russian technology institutes on issues of technology transfer. She is a member of the British Academy of Management and an Associate of the Chartered Management Institute.

Dirk Werth is Head of Project Group Business Integration Technologies at the Institute for Information Systems (IWi) at German Research Center for Artificial Intelligence (DFKI). Prior, he was directing a Competence Center in the same organization. Dr. Werth was project manager and overall coordinator of national and international R&D projects as well as of industrial consulting projects. He started his career as scientific staff member at Saarland University, where he is still holding lessons on Enterprise Resource Planning and Business Integration. Dr. Werth holds diploma in Business Administration and in Computer Sciences as well as a PhD in economics. His PhD thesis got the Special Award for Business Process Management from the Federal Association of German Political and Business Economists. His research activities comprise collaborative business processes, business integration and advanced business information systems.

Mehmet Emin Yurci is Head of Materials Science and Manufacturing Technologies Department of the Faculty of Mechanical Engineering at Yıldız Technical University. In the mean time, he was responsible of administrative posts for twelve years. He was vice-rector of the Yildiz Technical University for the last four years of that period. Professor Yurci's topics cover the main topics of his Department. Particulary, he is interested in Metal Forming and Die Design and Manufacturing Techniques. He has published several scientific papers and three text books. Superplasticity, intelligent design of die components, surface quality in fine blanking of sheet metals, residual stresses in the injection molded plastic parts and the effect of recycling rate were some of the latest research topics of Prof. Yurci. During his academic works, he has given special importance on collaborations with industry and other universities. He has taken the initiative and tasks several times in establishing many foundations and collaborations with industry.

Michal Žemlička graduated in computer science in 1994 at Charles University. He is an assistant professor at Charles University. He is interested in software engineering, service-oriented systems, parsing, education, data compression, and database data structures. He took part in several industrial projects. In some areas is his research oriented towards industrial applications.

Index